FROST: CENTENNIAL ESSAYS

FROST
CENTENNIAL ESSAYS

COMPILED BY
THE COMMITTEE ON THE
FROST CENTENNIAL
OF THE UNIVERSITY
OF SOUTHERN MISSISSIPPI

UNIVERSITY PRESS OF MISSISSIPPI
JACKSON

Copyright © by the
University Press of Mississippi
Library of Congress Card Number 73–93331
ISBN 0–87805–055–8
Manufactured in the United States of America
Printed by Moran Industries, Inc., Baton Rouge, Louisiana
Designed by J. Barney McKee

THIS VOLUME IS AUTHORIZED
AND SPONSORED BY
THE UNIVERSITY OF SOUTHERN MISSISSIPPI

Acknowledgments

Grateful acknowledgment is made to the following:

HOLT, RINEHART AND WINSTON, INC.

for excerpts from *Selected Letters of Robert Frost* edited by Lawrance Lathem, Copyright 1916, 1923, 1928, 1930, 1934, 1939, 1943, 1945, 1947, 1949, (c) 1967, 1969 by Holt, Rinehart and Winston, Inc. Copyright 1936, 1942, 1944, 1945, 1947, 1948, 1950, 1951, 1952, 1953, 1954, (c) 1955, 1956, 1958, 1959, 960, 1961, 1962 by Robert Frost. Copyright (c) 1964, 1967, 1970 by Lesley Frost Ballantine.

for excerpts from *Selected Letters of Robert Frost* edited by Lawrance Thompson. Copyright (c) 1964 by Lawrance Thompson and Holt, Rinehart and Winston, Inc.

for excerpts from *The Letters of Robert Frost to Louis Untermeyer*. Copyright (c) 1963 by Louis Untermeyer and Holt, Rinehart and Winston, Inc.

for excerpts from *Selected Prose of Robert Frost* edited by Hyde Cox and Edward Connery Lathem. Copyright 1939, 1954, (c) 1966, 1967 by Holt, Rinehart and Winston, Inc. Copyright 1946, (c) 1959 by Robert Frost. Copyright (c) 1956 by The Estate of Robert Frost.

for excerpts from *The Dimensions of Robert Frost* by Reginald L. Cook. Copyright (c) 1958 by Reginald L. Cook.

for excerpts from *Robert Frost: The Years of Triumph, 1915–1938* by Lawrance Thompson. Copyright (c) 1970 by Lawrance Thompson. Copyright (c) 1970 by The Estate of Robert Frost.

for excerpts from *Robert Frost: Poetry and Prose* edited by Edward Connery Lathem and Lawrance Thompson. Copyright (c) 1972 by Holt, Rinehart and Winston, Inc.

for excerpts from *Robert Frost: The Early Years, 1874–1915* by Lawrance Thompson. Copyright (c) 1966 by Lawrance Thompson. Copyright (c) 1966 by The Estate of Robert Frost. Reprinted by permission of Holt, Rinehart and Winston, Inc.

for a portion of a letter written by Robert Frost to Elizabeth Shepley Sergeant from *Robert Frost: The Trial by Existence* by Elizabeth Shepley Sergeant. Copyright (c) 1960 by Elizabeth Shepley Sergeant. Reprinted by permission of Holt, Rinehart and Winston, Inc.

Grateful acknowledgment is made to The Estate of Robert Frost, Alfred C. Edwards, Executor, for the unpublished letter to Edward Munce in 1949 and the poem "Doom to Bloom," the original version of "Our Doom to Bloom"; and for the unpublished Frost-Burell material.

Grateful acknowledgment is made to the publishers noted:

for excerpts from *The Poetics of Space* by Gaston Bachelard, translated by Maria Jolas. Translation copyright (c) 1964 by The Orion Press. Reprinted by permission of Grossman Publishers.

for excerpts from Writers at Work: *The Paris Review Interviews*, Second Series. Copyright (c) 1963 by The Viking Press, Inc. Reprinted by permission of The Viking Press, Inc.

for an excerpt from Paul Eluard, *Dignes de vivre*, Paris, 1944, by permission of Editions René Julliard.

for excerpts from Emily Dickinson reprinted by permission of the publishers and the Trustees of Amherst College from Thomas H. Johnson, editor, *The Poems of Emily Dickinson*, Cambridge, Mass.: The Belknap Press of Harvard University Press, Copyright, 1951, 1955, by The President and Fellows of Harvard College and by permission of Little, Brown and Company.

for excerpts from *A Swinger of Birches*, reprinted by permission of New York University Press from *A Swinger of Birches* by Sidney A. Cox. Copyright (c) 1958 by New York University.

for excerpts from *The New York Times Book Review* (c) 1923 by The New York Times Company. Reprinted by permission.

for excerpts from William Dean Howells. Reprinted by special permission of New York University Press from *Criticism and Fiction and Other Essays*, edited by Clara M. and Rudolph Kirk. Copyright (c) 1959 by New York University.

for excerpts from Alvan Ryan, "Frost and Emerson: Voice and Vision," reprinted from *The Massachusetts Review*, (c) 1959, The Massachusetts Review, Inc.

for excerpts from Wallace Stevens. Reprinted by permission of Alfred A. Knopf, Inc. from *The Collected Poems of Wallace Stevens*, copyright (c) 1954.

for an excerpt from *The Only World There Is* by Miller Williams. Copyright (c) 1971, 1970, 1969, 1968 by Miller Williams. Published by E. P. Dutton and Co., Inc. and used with their permission.

Contents

Preface

THIS volume of commemorative essays is one record of the achievement of Robert Frost. It is also a record of the cooperative venture of the numerous contributors, whom the editors wish to thank first. Since John Ciardi and James Dickey do not appear as literal contributors, we should like to thank them for the interviews. Dean Charles Moorman and the Administration of the University of Southern Mississippi have been without exception both prompt and pleasant in giving support. Professor R. C. Cook and the editorial board of the University Press of Mississippi supported the project from the beginning. Barney McKee, Director of the Press, has been exceptionally pleasant and helpful at every stage of the work. Terry Hummer efficiently performed a great many prosaic labors. Mary C. Garmany has, throughout the project, been extravagant in time and conscientious in energy. Professor Joe Thrash kindly gave helpful professional advice. Professor Reginald L. Cook has readily and often given so much courteous help that he deserves very special mention and well deserves the compliment that Rabbi Victor Reichert gives him in the essay herein. Finally, we are grateful to Louise Zoerner and Marguerite Reese of Holt, Rinehart and Winston and to Alfred Edwards, Executor of the Frost Estate, for their aid with permissions.

The notes to many papers will attest to the value of the work of Lawrance Thompson who died on April 15, 1973, before completing the biography.

A perfect organization of papers so diverse requires more ingenuity than the editors can manage. Some contributors may wonder at the placement of their essays. But the difficulty has been pleasant at least in that it does indicate the wide diversity of both Robert Frost and those who study his work. Papers have been collected under headings that appeared to show the general topic of the content.

The volume has gradually become somewhat more scholarly in appearance than was originally intended, when the plan was to collect a readable group of essays about Robert Frost and his poetry, with the hope of avoiding that aura of the academic that might well have made Frost wince. Despite the gradual accumulation of scholarly paraphernalia, with some consequent lack of uniformity, for which the editor alone must take the blame, we have attempted to reduce clutter and have intentionally simplified typography. We have, for example, avoided using double quotation marks in some of the papers that dealt with the Frost dialogue poems and have avoided italics in the text itself. We have intentionally removed page references to Frost's poetry as one way of reducing the notes. All references to Frost's poetry are to *The Poetry of Robert Frost*, ed. Edward Connery Lathem (New York: Holt, Rinehart and Winston, 1969), except that occasionally an essay requires the use of earlier versions of Frost poems. Frost's erratic spelling is generally retained without comment.

The index is an afterthought to a volume never intended as a source for research studies. But since certain poems and other subjects consistently appear in the text, a somewhat sketchy index was prepared at the last moment for the benefit of students other than experts in Robert Frost's work. If used in connection with the table of contents, the index will provide even the undergraduate with a helpful guide through the contents of the volume.

The Committee on the Frost Centennial

Jac L. Tharpe, editor
Peggy W. Prenshaw, co-editor
Gordon Weaver, chairman of the Symposium
David C. Berry, co-chairman of the Symposium
Marice C. Brown, chairman of the Committee

FROST: CENTENNIAL ESSAYS

The Quest for "all creatures great and small"

MARICE C. BROWN

Afterer publication of *North of Boston* with its Vermont and New Hampshire settings for narratives of dour, unhappy folk suffering from physical deprivations and cramped spiritual creeds, critics began to insist that Robert Frost's poetic locale was too narrow. Yet, Lloyd Dendinger points out that Frost's paradoxical popularity with the folk as well as with serious readers of poetry lies in the response to the poet's typically American metaphor of discovering a mythical new Eden.[1] Dendinger's perceptive observation stops short, perhaps, in framing the break with the traditions of the past in regional terms of American wilderness. Frost's metaphor embraces, but supersedes, regionalism, especially as it applies to New England. His poetic statement extends beyond the political and social adjustments of his own day to the moral and ethical heritage which had been sorely complicated by unparalleled scientific advances. New spaces as small as atoms and as expansive as spiraling universes had for many thoughtful people necessitated a search for the nature of Nature, an inquiry that was part of a metaphysical probing.

Frost appears to have felt a sense of mystery about both place and space, and one of the most significant relationships in his poetry is the subtle linking of geography and a search for the eternal verities. *Nonplace* is one of his most important settings. In a letter to Susan Hayes Ward, he said the past summer was unreal to him as he wrote the letter and adds: "The feeling of time and space is perennially strange to me. I used to lie awake at night imagining the places I had traversed in the day and doubting in simple wonderment that I who was here could possibly have been there and there.... There is a pang there that makes poetry. I rather like to gloat over it." To Sidney Cox, he said, "Places are more to me in thought than in reality," [2] and indeed one finds that however confined his poetic settings appear to be, the simple locales often assume a range beyond literal boundaries. Frost's journeys, real and metaphorical, became a source

3

of knowledge; and his travels, like Whitman's, were over territory that could not be stepped off, surveyed, or otherwise measured. His observation to Cox implies both recollection in tranquillity and simple wonderment about both the known and the unknown. "The Road Not Taken," for example, may refer to a specific location in England, but the heart of the poem refers to a metaphorical road that remained unexplored and therefore eternally beckoning.

C. Day Lewis says that a poet has "two conscious motives: To create an object in words, and to explore reality and make sense of his own experience." [3] Frost has dealt overtly and repeatedly with the first motive in what he termed sound and sense, but making sense of his experience has been accomplished, as critics often point out, without commitment to a given philosophical system. Indeed, one critic rather harshly termed Frost a "spiritual drifter," [4] for no amount of critical analysis can identify him with a labeled religious creed or ethical canon. On the other hand, I should prefer to call him a spiritual *explorer*, tramping the cumulus meadows of the sky in search of God—any God whose reasoning he can understand. Frost insists that while man cannot expect to understand, he can explore beyond geographical boundaries or any others. Job reminds God, "Because I let You off/From telling me Your reason, don't assume/I thought You had none" ("Masque of Reason"). Yet it is Frost's inability to act emotionally (that is, by faith) in spite of his intellectual uncertainty that prevents his acceptance of Judeo-Christian orthodoxy. The problem is that, though he cannot accept it, he is equally powerless to reject it. The result is that he continues to explore.

Whitman, whose poetic influence on Frost must have been great, had been similarly impelled to search for a satisfactory solution to paradoxes inherent in a weltanschauung that sets man and nature in opposition. In "Passage to India" Whitman finds a harmonizing design in which modern scientific advances are forerunners of a cosmic purpose. Man's soul, which Whitman portrays as expanding amorphously so as to occupy all space, ranges back through time to a paradisiacal beginning, where the godhead receives it in perfect love as a younger brother. In a seeming contradiction, the soul goes back to a mythical and primal source from which it moves to a future at the end of its ranging. To Whitman, the Frostian "design" is a "vast similitude" ("On the Beach at Night Alone") which engulfs all the varied forms in the cosmos, both animate and inanimate.

Frost, like Whitman, searches for a universal harmony, but whereas Whitman's poetic rangings are excursions of single-minded, if jubilant, affirmations, Frost's express doubt as to his destinations and deep concern for what he will find when he arrives. His one expression of apparent assurance, "Into My Own," must be brought into question when it is set against the disproportionate number of poems that agonize over Judeo-Christian theological matters. Frost's insistence that when he enters the metaphysical terrain of "the edge of doom" he will be "only more sure of all I thought was true" cannot be taken at face value. Poems, as well as dreams, may be wishfulfilling.

Whitman, unlike Frost, is able to celebrate a supreme unity of man in nature. His omniscient god is no more than a matrix (a not inappropriate designation for Whitman's ratiocination) from which all diversities emanate and reunite. Frost, too, seeks unity; but God—a great, three-headed gargoyle of Puritan imagination—resists understanding. In "A Masque of Mercy," Frost struggles to work out the mercy/justice contradiction through Keeper, who sees that fear comes from knowing that one's very best may still be short of God's expectations and that he (Keeper) would therefore receive his just deserts of damnation. Consequently, courage, which Jesse Bel declares "the best thing in life," is required for the admittance of mercy into one's heart.

Frost was not only driven to understand the *how* of God's ways, but he was also deeply concerned with the *why*. In "A Masque of Reason," Frost rather neatly secularizes what is basically a theological argument by characters drawn from both Old and New Testaments in a genial commixture with such figures as Karl Marx and Edmund Waller. Important, too, in the de-emphasis of a religious tone is the setting which is reminiscent of the experimental theater of the period: "A fair oasis in the purest desert," where a stylized tree is both a burning bush and a Christmas tree, double symbols of Hebraism and Christianity.

The argument is developed mainly by Job, who longs to discover the reason for his suffering if there is, indeed, a reason. The theme is a pun on Job 13:3—"I desire to reason with God." The antagonist is Thyatira, Job's wife. Appropriately enough, her name is taken from Revelations, Thyatira being the fourth of the seven churches exhorted to repent their evil ways. Specifically, the Church of Thyatira was condemned for following the teachings of the prophetess Jezebel (compare Frost's Jesse Bel in the other masque). Much as Shakespeare used Lear's fool, Frost designs Thyatira's apparent frivolity to clarify and sharpen the argument. God himself belongs to the imagination, she says ("I'd know you by Blake's picture anywhere"). Omnipotent but unknowable as God is, she does not deny His existence—as fabricated by man; what she denies is rational order ("Of course, in the abstract high singular/There isn't any universal reason").

On the other hand, Job longs for comprehension of a rationality which he accepts but cannot discover ("The artist in me calls out for design"). The "design," as finally revealed, is an enigma: "not confusion, but the form of forms,/The serpent's tail stuck down the serpent's throat," a symbol of eternity much more terrifying than Whitman's envelopment in a perfect love that transcends beginnings and endings. Frost calls his play the forty-third chapter of Job, a quip implying that he is no nearer the answer to the problem of God and the universe than he ever was.

Both the masques were written in the forties when Frost was a septuagenarian. The two works overtly bring his spiritual quest into sharp focus, but the theological probing is obvious in an oblique form as early as the publication of *North of Boston* (1914). "The Death of the Hired Man" illustrates the point well, though many analyses and frequent anthologizings make fresh treatment difficult.

Warren expresses his indignation to his wife Mary that Silas, the "hired man," should come, now that he is valueless as a laborer, and throw himself upon their mercy. Rather than returning as a penitent —an elderly prodigal son—he is filled with self-aggrandizing fantasies. Though Warren declares that Silas deserves nothing from him, a sense of human decency evokes the much-quoted definition of home as a last resort: " 'Home is the place where, when you have to go there,/They have to take you in.' " In justice, Silas deserves nothing. Grudgingly, Warren will grant him more than nothing, though less than Mary suggests when she says, " 'I should have called it/Something you somehow haven't to deserve.' " The "haven't to deserve" is, of course, an expression about mercy in its deepest religious sense of undeserved grace.

Within the narrative structure of the poem, Frost examines with rich detail the nuances of being one's brother's keeper. The poem has to do with man's relation to man, but it plumbs the spirit in which the choice is made. Although the death of Silas borders on the sentimental, it skillfully removes from the poet the necessity of ending on a didactic note. All options remain open and reasonable.

Frost's search for man's place in the universe is manifest in few of his poems, but an oblique statement is found in a surprising number of them. In a great many, an abstract locale becomes a metaphor for the pursuit of truth itself. Furthermore, in exploring reality Frost often juxtaposed microcosm and macrocosm. He liked to dwell on the diminutive in the physical world. In so doing he employed a technique that characterizes his poetry, that of approaching a subject from its farthest points rather than from the center. The diminutive, then, becomes a foil for the "yonder." Somewhere between outer space and the microscope stands the poet, towering like a giant over an ant and, at the same time, diminished by stars. In his view of nature, Frost concluded, like Tennyson, "but *if* I could understand .../I should know what God and man is" (italics added).

The paradox of preexistence is explored in a somewhat similar view in "A Never Naught Song," where the poet dwells on spatial disparity. He denies the primordial existence of nothingness, but affirms instead "thought" as primigenial. Thought, however, takes form in a "cunningly minute ... gist," an "atomic One," that contains the physical universe.

In "The Vantage Point," the poet removes himself from his fellow man and goes apart to meditate on the large questions of life and death. Lying on his back, he views a landscape as serene and passive as a painting. The homes of the living and the graves of the dead meld, life and death thus becoming two aspects of the same reality. But tired of such enormity of physical view and intellectual probing, he turns on his side and views the same metaphysical question from another perspective: his breath becomes a wind that shakes the lilliputian bluet (the poem is enriched if one knows that the common name for the flower is *innocence*), and he looks into the crater of an ant hill.

Somewhat akin to the poem above is "For Once, Then, Something." The search for universal truth, rarely perceived and then only dimly, is like looking deep into a well. The persona's own reflection —the physical and apprehensible reality transferred against the summer sky to a godlike figure—sharpens the irony of his ungodlike spiritual blindness. Just as he thought that he discerned "something," or a semblance of something ("Truth? A pebble of quartz?"), a drop of water fell, rippling the surface and blurring the vision, but leaving the impression that there was "then, something," though its blurred features were indiscernible.

Moreover, while a well and its curb are strong foci for empirical knowledge, it is typical of Frost's thought processes that he makes a direct transference from the preciseness of a substantive object—in this case a piece of quartz—to its farthest remove, the unknown and unknowable perceived through his own transfiguration to a god-self. The apparent simplicity of the poem conceals exquisite subtleties which illuminate somewhat Frost's agonizing to *know*.

The cosmos is a common locale for Frost's search for meaning. In the lyrical "Stars," the persona observes that stars express only the inscrutability of the universe. The stars are likened to "Minerva's snow-white marble eyes"; but with a nice turn of irony, Frost points out that the eyes of Minerva, goddess of wisdom, are blind. The stars give the appearance of concern over man's destiny ("As if with keenness for our fate"), but they reveal "neither love nor hate." Where the persona seeks meaning in space, he finds only evidence of a mechanistic universe.

One of Frost's most delicate poems is "An Old Man's Winter Night," presented with images so familiar as to be commonplace. A careful reading reveals the poet's deep concern with the enigma of time. An old man grows old and forgetful. He is "concerned with he knew what," but in a flash, of course, he has forgotten. The flickering *lamp* (human life) is set against the *stars* (nature). Human sounds disturb the sounds of nature. The old man *knows* what he is concerned with: light; but also death ("A quiet *light*, and then not even that"). He is a light "to no one but himself," he says, and concludes that the pale and frigid moon is better than the sun for "such a charge." The charge is to keep *his* snow on the roof and *his* icicles along the wall.

The genitive form is strangely obtrusive. It is ambiguous in relation to the masculine sun as opposed to the feminine moon, but the syntax points strongly to the old man as the pronominal referent. Ice and snow are a common folk symbol for old age, however, and the line is enriched by the ambiguity.

The essence of the poem defies a paraphrase. The last lines return to the old man who is inadequate to the task of housekeeping alone on a winter's night. This observation, however, is an aside. The old man's real concern is the struggle to endure in an indifferent, if not a malevolent, world. He strives to know his human worth, but the cold and "broken moon" has the secret. The old man fears he is of worth only to himself. The fleeting human life span is set against the timelessness of the moon, more appropriate for its charge than the sun (again the Frostian "fire and ice" symbol).

In "The Lesson for Today" the poet presents a dispute between the persona and a Renaissance scholar over which era was more spiritually enlightened. The modern scholar claims equality up to a point, but moderns face a new difficulty: space. The scholar states that a Ptolemaic universe that reduced man on Earth to "vilest worms" whom "God hardly tolerated with his feet" is preferable to the further reduction of man in modern concepts of universes to "a brief epidemic of microbes." However, in either case, man is left in a situation where salvation is difficult. "But," he concludes, "these are universals, not confined to any one time, place, or human kind." The poet implies that the problem of finding God has not abated but that the locale has shifted.

The pervading theme of Frost's poetry is not, as has all too often been pointed out, any consistent attitude toward life or poetic stance. The thread that runs through it all is the quest itself. The questions Frost asks are couched in situations involving human relationships or the larger problems of man's place in the cosmos, the enigma of human existence itself. The poems are often set in recognizable times and geographic areas, but they also often range over the terrain of the imagination occupied by stars, clouds, angels, and other mystic paraphernalia. Not uncommonly, an apparently simple setting grows by extension into the second type.

For example, in "Birches," the persona, more sure of this world than the next, sometimes yearns for surcease from life's travails. He would like to *get away from earth* awhile." Uncertain of what he would find, he needs the assurance of a round trip. "That would be good both *going* [to heaven] and *coming* back," he concludes (italics added here and following).

The collocation of time-space-quest becomes impressive. "Look me *in the stars*/And *tell me truly*" whether the suffering of mankind is not too great a price to pay for life itself ("A Question"). "We dance round *in a ring* and suppose,/But the *Secret* sits *in the middle* and *knows*" ("The Secret Sits"). Back into a time of innocence, in "the *children's house* of *make-believe*," the poet finds his *"watering place."* He enjoins the reader: *"Drink* and be whole again beyond confusion," that is, in perfect knowledge ("Directive"). The immediacy of his own physical weakness keeps an old man from *"giving back the gaze"* (understanding) to the *stars* that shine in empty rooms. He has momentary universal insights: he is "concerned with he *knew what*,/. . . and then *not even that*" ("An Old Man's Winter Night"). A bird in mid-wood (the planet Earth) measures in song the passage of time in succession of seasons. He *"frames"* a *"question"*: *"what to make of"* the fall of man ("that other fall we name the fall"), who has become (by his fall) a "diminished thing" ("The Oven Bird"). Newborn infants are *riders*, "mounted bareback on the *earth*," which the poet describes as a "headless horse." In spite of apparent lack of control, however, mankind has unasserted power, *"ideas* yet that we haven't tried" ("Riders"). Thought and form blend in Frost's quests, but never more exquisitely than in the poem "Reluctance": "The heart is still aching *to seek,*/But the *feet question 'Whither?'* "

The above collocations, far from exhaustive, are sufficient evidence that Frost's obsession with knowing bears a subtle link with time and place. The metaphysical unknown occupies nebulous geographical terrain. Together, these unknowns provide a reason and a place for a quest. They have no beginning and no ending; or, at best, the beginning eludes the memory ("The Trial by Existence") or does not exist at all, and the ending is equally inscrutable. What is left is the *middle* ("In the Home Stretch"); and now, ten years after his death, Frost's simple wonderment must be that "I who was *there* could possibly be *here*."

It is thus that Frost's many readers, also in the middle, structure from his framework of quest a wealth of critical perspectives and find endless variety. The plethora of critical approaches makes possible a book such as this one, offered in commemoration of Robert Frost on the occasion of the one-hundredth anniversary of his birth.

Notes to *The Quest for "all creatures great and small"* by M ARICE C. BROWN

1. Lloyd N. Dendinger, "Robert Frost: The Popular and the Central Poetic Images," *American Quarterly*, XXI (Winter 1969), 804.

2. *Selected Letters of Robert Frost*, ed. Lawrance Thompson (New York: Holt, Rinehart and Winston, 1964), 41–2, 122.

3. C. Day Lewis, "The Making of a Poem," in *From Source to Statement*, ed. James McCrimmon (Boston: Houghton Mifflin Co., 1968).

4. Yvor Winters, "Robert Frost: or, the Spiritual Drifter as Poet," in *Robert Frost: A Collection of Essays*, ed. James M. Cox (Englewood Cliffs: Prentice Hall, 1962), 58–82.

ACHIEVEMENT

Robert Frost had to wait for recognition as a poet; and, ironically, the discussion of his achievement has been prolonged. While estimates of Frost's work, sometimes prompted by the poet himself, began fifty years ago, reactions were often either prejudiced or emotional; and they were based in great part on the perception of Frost as a popular regionalist who had no more than pretensions to artistry. As Lionel Trilling, Randall Jarrell, and other critics began to see the breadth of Frost's work, the question of his place in the American literary canon became a topic for wide discussion and considerable disagreement.

Reginald Cook, who has always been one of Frost's most competent and most appreciative critics, surveys here the criticism of Frost's work and then replies to the sterner critics. Among these is George Nitchie, who continues to feel a deficiency in Frost while perhaps being also fascinated with the enigma that Frost's amazing popularity with all kinds of readers continues to present.

Philip Gerber, with somewhat divided mind, also takes up the question of Frost's eventual placement in the annals of the literary tradition and points out some of the reservations that critics have had as well as some of their prognostications. The essay by Rexford Stamper is a deliberate consideration of many of the major critical documents on Frost's themes. Concentrating on the work rather than the man, he finds that Frost's realistic views place him among the "modern" poets. But perhaps the most complimentary statement about a poet's achievement comes from another poet whose own reputation obviates all interests except that of appreciation. James Dickey's thoughtful praise of Frost's work is generally like John Ciardi's (in "Biography and Reminiscence")—a willing tribute.

J. T.

13

The Critics and Robert Frost

REGINALD L. COOK

1.

"WHEN a man dies," Thoreau said wittily, "he kicks the dust." The dust to which Thoreau makes reference in his witticism rises from the belongings a dead man leaves to be ransacked by and divided among heirs and assigns. That Thoreau's wit might be applied to a *species*, poet, rather than *genus*, man, is obvious. The specific poet to whom the Thoreauvian witticism is to be applied is, of course, Robert Frost, but the application does not, in Thoreau's special sense, concern the disposal of either unpublished memorabilia or household goods. Nor does it concern the dust which rises in the contest between conflicting proprietary interests that Frost belongs, on one hand, to a region whose focal point is San Francisco, his birthplace in 1874, or, on the other hand, to Boston, where he died in 1963. Least of all does it concern the dust cloud, a spin-off of the intenser rivalries among educational institutions which cherish the memory of the poet's inveterate "barding around."

If, as Poe contends, in literature as in law and empire, "an established name is an estate in tenure, or a throne in possession," it might be expected that Robert Frost, in our contemporary locution, "has it made" in the native pantheon. But, on the evidence, do we so readily agree? A cogent minority of critics thinks otherwise. Luckily for the wound-prone Frost, no longer does he have to confront vis-à-vis the adverse critics who challenge all previous high assessments of both poet and *Complete Poems*. "Fame," as Emily Dickinson reminds us, "is the one that does not stay. . . ." Moreover, the "throne in possession" may well be expropriated by another—by Robert Lowell, Theodore Roethke, John Berryman.

Several months of rigorous research confirmed what one learns early in reading literature—that, as Wallace Stevens suggests, there are at least thirteen ways of looking at a blackbird, or, as the members of Captain Ahab's crew on the Pequod make clear in the chapter on

15

the doubloon in *Moby Dick*, each of us reads only according to his own light. How difficult it is, for instance, to find a vantage point from which to examine the position of the modern critic who may be looking hard to see Frost plain. What is seen not only depends upon what is looked for when the critic is a recorder. When the critic is a discoverer, susceptible to the surprises attendant on the differences, angles, and depths in human nature, then, like Picasso, he may say firmly, "I do not seek, I find."

Moreover, there is the formidable problem of expression. The point will be well taken, I think, when Edmund Goncourt tells Arthur Symons, all depends upon the ways of seeing and that out of twenty-four men who will describe what they have all seen, it is only the twenty-fourth who will find the right way of expressing it. The decisive point of a critic's penetration is behind the poet's mask or persona. And we shall see how many critics stop with the projection of an associative image by which they attempt to make a proprietary identifying claim. Behind the mask or persona is that point where the poet and his poetry are inextricably centered. "How can we know the dancer from the dance?" is Yeats's superbly direct way of centering the enigma of identification every critic has to face sooner or later if he is worth his critical salt.

Despite our indifferent American world, where, if poets do not receive a general reading of their poems, certainly critics are accorded an even more diminished response, it is a challenging matter to make one's pitch in a scholarly quarterly or a quality magazine as a critical interpreter of poets and/or poetry. The stimulation is surely not money because there is no money to speak of in writing criticism. The vulnerability of the critic is his local literary reputation, personal pride, perceptiveness, taste, conscience. What the critic really holds at the end of his pen or on his typewriter keyboard is the poet. An informed and sharp-sighted critic can validate the currency of a poet's particular coin. A critic can make a poet look awfully good; he can with a devastating critique just as readily tumble him from the gold standard. The Scottish reviewers once attempted to devalue Keats, and Browning has hardly recovered from George Santayana's "The Poetry of Barbarism." And think of those poets still on the floor where Dr. Johnson left them after *Lives of the Poets*.

Before examining Robert Frost and his critics, we must first ask: Has the critic understood the poet? Does understanding include or exclude the poet's relationship to the great tradition in poetry; to his particular time and place; to the great commercial world of publishing houses and potential reading public; to the critic's own temperament, intellection, sensibility, adequacies, and inadequacies? What if the poet is the Robert Frost who threw a few handfuls of dust in the eyes of his readers from his ambiguous position, always seeming to share confidence and disclose secrets? What of Frost who is now the target of critical interpreters who found him either implacably reserved on important personal matters or fantastically sly, disingenuous, envious, vacillating, self-pitying, egoistical, arrogant, and vindictive? The critic's position is a human one. The more one thinks of a critic's responsibility, the greater one respects the effort of critical interpreters, time out of mind. Occasionally they make a decisive shot —is it luck?—like De Quincey "On the Knocking at the Gate in *Macbeth*," or the consistently penetrating insights of Erich Auerbach in *Mimesis*, whether discussing Odysseus' Scar, the world of Pantagruel's mouth, or the Enchanted Dulcinea. Yet it must be emphasized: human vision is by definition limited. A man cannot see everything, even when it is possible for him to see more than others in areas of interest and special competence. "The angle of vision," says Karl Mannheim tellingly in *Ideology and Utopia*, "is guided by the observer's interests." In approaching the critics of Frost, this is well worth bearing in mind.

2.

Frost's long life of nearly eighty-nine years was less outwardly dramatic than inwardly intense. Beginning with a prolonged struggle for recognition and leading to a tardy breakthrough, his career as a poet culminated with a consolidation of his lyric and narrative gifts, and leveled off in deserving acclaim, at home and abroad. In the early Derry and Franconia years he was on the outer fringe; after four Pulitzer awards he closed in on the center. In spite of his self-defensiveness—"I have written to keep the over-curious out of the secret places of my mind both in verse and letters"—he has not forestalled an identification of the reticence of the poems with the privacy of his life. The record of the life, as it takes shape in the authorized biography by Lawrance Thompson, has not been presented without challenge to tact, accuracy, and sympathetic discernment.

In view of the complexity of Frost's temperament and his poetry's deceptive simplicity, there will be numerous interpretive evaluations. Some of the problems relating to the complexity reflect tensions and paradoxes in Frost's impulses, attitudes, and behavior: for example, the dominance of his personal thrust, the influence of Pound, Amy Lowell, Louis Untermeyer, and others in getting his poetry before the general public; the identification of and differences between "the public" Frost (the poet everyone thinks he knows) and "the other Frost" (Randall Jarrell's private poet); the content and applicability of the theory of "sound posture"; the equivalence of song and speech in his work; the relative merits of the early and later poetry; the examination of the charge of anti-intellectualism (as Yvor Winters and George Nitchie define it); the scrutiny of the poet's assumed insularity; an unequivocal "dating" of the poems; the relative emphases on regionalism and cosmopolitanism, nature and humanity; and estimates of his stature as a poet. These are among the continuing problems that confront the critic.

It is axiomatic that when a poet or poetry is under discussion a plethora of views will prevail. In 1926 Gorham Munson, Frost's first biographer, labeled Frost a classical poet, and over thirty years later reiterated his position. Mark Van Doren called him a symbolist (but not in Arthur Symons' sense). John Lynen interpreted his poetry in the pastoral tradition. Reuben Brower thought this view an overemphasis. Localist (Amy Lowell), revisionist (Louis Untermeyer), ordinary man (Sidney Cox), Emersonian Romantic (Yvor Winters), glorified neighbor (G. R. Elliott), bard (John Ciardi), diversionist (R. L. Cook), each interpreted the poet differently, and Frost, a willing player of this game, has called himself a sensibilitist, an environmentalist, a realmist, a synecdochist, a lone striker, one acquainted with the night, a watcher of the void, a lover who has quarreled with the world, and even an Old Slow Coach!

On neither the higher nor the lower levels of Frost criticism has everything been quiet. Each age not only reads its own books, as Emerson reminds us, it writes its own criticism of them. This has happened to Frost and his poetry. Malcolm Cowley's unlikely image of Frost as "a Calvin Coolidge of poetry" was indignantly repudiated by George Whicher and by Charles H. Foster in sharp rebuttals. Bernard De Voto's raucous attack on Richard Blackmur's opinionated review of *A Further Range* has its contradictory side in view of the latter's oblique but honest avowal of Frost's art before Japanese audiences. J. Donald Adams' reaction to Lionel Trilling's well-intentioned remarks at Frost's eighty-fifth birthday party prompted the poet's ready tongue-in-cheek rejoinder: "No sweeter music can come to my ears than the clash of arms over my dead body when I am down." Robert Lowell refers with waspish asperity to those who write pleasantly of Frost as "a whole dunciad of babbling innocence," and Randall Jarrell's yeasty Frostian euphoria rises in heady remonstrance to all anti-Frost Laodiceans.

One reason for the shades and colorations in critical opinion is the complexity of Frost's temperament, aspects of which we find turned to light in his long struggle for recognition. This is discernible in the many masks and contradictions ascribed to him. The contradictions in the personae ascribed to Frost are so typical they are *sui generis*. A basic contradiction arises from a play of variously reflected moods which underscores Frost's stubbornly adhered to integrity. Such integrity has whetted the modern critic's imagination to see Frost "plain." But is the "plainness" that of William Van O'Connor's "profane optimist," or Lionel Trilling's "terrifying" poet, or James M. Cox's militant nationalist, or Mark Van Doren's "New England poet" who is "in the same breath a part of and for the world"?

A review of the most important criticism of Frost and his poetry during the last fifty years has left a few indelible impressions. First, the critical approaches to Frost are sharply defined. Critics like Amy Lowell, Louis Untermeyer, and Sidney Cox approach the poetry through the man; others, like Cleanth Brooks, Lawrance Thompson, Yvor Winters, George Nitchie, John Lynen, Reuben Brower, Denis Donoghue, and Radcliffe Squires, come to the man through the poetry. In the earlier criticism, which is directed at the personality of the poet, Frost fares well. He fares less well in later criticism. Clearly some earlier critics were entrapped by what Frost seemed to be—Jarrell's engaging public figure. The later view appears in Randall

Jarrell's *Poetry and the Age* (1953). If Jarrell refused to be distracted by the gestures, are we so sure his penetrations are more discerning, say, than Amy Lowell's? Nevertheless, the penetrations are informed, eloquent, forthright, and brilliantly imaginative.

The battle lines are drawn in James Dickey's "Robert Frost, Man and Myth" (1966), an essay in which Jarrell's two Frosts are juxtaposed. There is the public Frost. "Frost is unassailable, a national treasure, a remnant of the frontier and the Thoreauistic virtues of shrewd Yankeedom, the hero of the dozing American daydream of self-reliance and experience-won wisdom we feel guilty about betraying every time we eat a TV dinner or push a computer." And there is the "other" Frost who is supposedly "the man" to be contrasted with this myth. "We watch him live through the decline and death of his alcoholic, ambitious father, follow him as he is shunted around New England as a poor relation, supported by his gentle, mystical mother's pathetically inept attempts as a teacher. We see him develop, as compensation, a fanatical and paranoiac self-esteem with its attendant devils of humiliation, jealousy, and frustration. He considers suicide, tries poultry farming, loses a child, settles on poetry as a way of salvation—something at last that he *can* do, at least to some extent—borrows money and fails to pay it back, perseveres with a great deal of tenacity and courage but also with a sullen self-righteousness with which one can have but very little sympathy." You will hear much of these two contrasting images whenever Frost's name comes up.

Secondly, the dominant impression in reading criticism of Frost is the tentativeness and reserve of the early critics. A critic like Ezra Pound will risk part of his reputation, but only a part—not the chief part—in promoting Frost. Pound did not embrace Frost and kiss both cheeks. Even if an Indian giver, at least Pound, in 1914, stood up and accorded a fellow poet deserving recognition.

Thirdly, the early Frost critics like Untermeyer, Sidney Cox, and Gorham Munson tend to palaver a bit and gild the obvious. Except that Cox's *Robert Frost: Original "Ordinary Man"* (1929) is one of those rare little true-toned encomiums, like Francis Thompson's "Shelley" or Emerson's "Thoreau" which, once read, are always remembered, not for profundity or scholarship, but for genuineness in sympathetic understanding.

Concomitant with the appearance of the approbative critics are the fighters on opposite sides. During the 1930's Frost had achieved recognition; now he was the subject of critical controversy. Estimable poet-critics, like Richard Blackmur, Louise Bogan, and Muriel Rukeyser, tried to cut Frost down to size, and other sharpminded critics like Edmund Wilson, Malcolm Cowley, and Yvor Winters attacked Frost vigorously. "Robert Frost," said Edmund Wilson disparagingly, "has a thin but authentic vein of sensibility; but I find him exceedingly dull, and he certainly writes very poor verse." Malcolm Cowley was critical of the poet's narrow nationalism, failure to sustain the philosophical radicalism of the great New England tradition of the nineteenth century, and lack of interest in universal brotherhood and human charity. Yvor Winters tagged Frost pejoratively as an "Emersonian Romantic," and "a spiritual drifter" who is in no sense a great poet but "at times a distinguished and valuable poet." Perverse and arbitrary, what probably disturbed Yvor Winters' rationalist bent is the inability to separate Frost's mood from his beliefs. "Frost's skepticism and uncertainty," noted Winters, "do not appear to have been so much the result of thought as the result of the impact upon his sensibility of conflicting notions of his own ear—they appear to be the result of his having taken the easy way and having drifted with the various currents of his time." A rebuttal was made by Bernard De Voto, the lively historian of the early frontier, and George Whicher of Amherst, the latter an informed scholar noted for commonsense. Exuberantly, De Voto summed up Frost and his poetry as "the work of an independent and integrated poet, a poet who is like no one else, a major poet not only in regard to this age but in regard to our whole literature, a great American poet." The friendly Whicher found "Frost's distinction is precisely that he has maintained during a time of general disillusionment his instinctive belief in the tradition that lies at the core of our national being, the tradition of liberal democracy."

Scholarly quarterlies and elite magazines joined in a controversy which has persisted through the fifties and sixties. Currently the line-up would show George Nitchie, Denis Donoghue, Isadore Traschen, and Roy Harvey Pearce as formidable critics of Frost as *both* poet and man. The other side includes two English poets, Cecil Day Lewis and W. H. Auden, and American professors like John Lynen, Radcliffe Squires, and Reuben Brower. But as in any vehement argument or quarrel, the views most usually recalled are those of the opposition.

We all like a good fight. The brouhaha over Frost's reputation as a poet shows Blackmur clouting the poet; De Voto, Blackmur; and Gorham Munson, Nitchie; and so on round and round the bent birches. When Blackmur's celebrated review of *A Further Range*, in the *Nation* in 1936, asserted Frost had not learned "his trade," De Voto truculently took him to task in a lead article in the *Saturday Review of Literature* (January 1, 1938). "His [Blackmur's] piece in the *Nation*," wrote De Voto, "may not be quite the most idiotic review our generation has produced, but in twenty years of reading criticism—oh, the hell with scholarly reservations, Mr. Blackmur's *is* the most idiotic of all times. It is one of the most idiotic reviews since the invention of movable type. The monkeys would have to tap typewriters throughout eternity to surpass it, and Mr. Blackmur may regard his immortality as achieved." Withering? Of course. But what De Voto's intemperate language has to do with higher criticism is like Robert Frost's America, a little hard to see. Undeniably this gives us an idea of the virulence of the controversy. Disapprobative critics like Blackmur, Cowley, and Winters were fearless and as convinced of their positions as the gentler more approbative ones had been in *Recognition of Robert Frost* (1937), having also stated their case for the opposition well before Frost died in January 1963.

Fourthly, poetry is assessed as often as it is reread. Enthusiastic appreciations appear as generally as acerbic critiques or scholarly appraisals. After a writer dies, the stones and brickbats really begin to fly. Is the flurry motivated by a sense of rough justice to correct an exaggerated estimate of a previous one? Or, more simply, does a later generation in a fresh perspective see things differently? Whatever the truth may be, recent articles in scholarly publications remind me of young Joe's depressed reflection to his friend George after his father's fall from grace in Hemingway's "My Old Man." "Seems like," says

Joe, "when they get started they don't leave a guy nothing."

Let us consider a scholarly essay, perceptive and provocative, written by Isadore Traschen, entitled "Robert Frost: Some Divisions in a Whole Man," which appeared in the *Yale Review* in the Autumn of 1965. Traschen's thesis is not untypical. "My principal argument," he says, "is that Frost never risked his life, his whole being; he was never wholly lost, like the Eliot of *The Waste Land*. He remained in control, in possession of himself. He did this by keeping himself from the deepest experiences, the kind you stake your life on." However, we shall get nowhere by contending Frost had no compelling inner need to be lost to some cause obviously political or social. Or that it is unnecessary to "get lost" in ways other than the way annoyed friends dismiss the boring companion by telling him to go and "get lost." Frost was in command or, as Traschen admits, "in possession of himself." Of course this is what Frost meant to imply in the often quoted reassuring lines from "Into My Own"—"They would not find me changed from him they knew—/Only more sure of all I thought was true"—lines that echo Emerson's injunction, "Obey the voice at eve obeyed at prime." And Frost's lines have a variant in the startling sentences in a letter to Elizabeth Shepley Sergeant: "Anything I ever thought I still think." And "I take nothing back. I don't even grow."

I expect the point at issue is not whether Frost was in possession of himself—whatever this might mean specifically—it is really whether he refused "the *deepest* experiences." What, exactly constitutes "deepest experiences"? I would assume these to be involved with expressions of love and courage, grief and despair, and notably, a total commitment to one's vocation. Being a poet is in itself a gift and a justification, but it is also a deep compulsion. Frost's dedication to poetry as a vocation is a voice, a locus, a language, an art, a tone, and it has an important context in history. This vocation *is* something to get lost to. But, it is true, it is not as Traschen would prefer it, like kneeling behind the barricades. It is, in Thoreau's phrase, "going up attic at once," which Frost promptly did at Derry, Franconia, Little Iddens, South Shaftsbury, and Ripton. Frost literally risked *everything*. The cost to the poet and his family was *terrific* in ways not quite circumscribed in Trilling's piquant "terrifying." He not only staked his life, he staked that of others—his family's—at a cost Lawrance Thompson in the official biography shows us was very considerable.

Traschen goes on to say that Frost is not one of "the great howlers (like Job) who risked everything." Isn't there an element of the ludicrous in Traschen's point that Frost didn't howl and should have howled? Howled!—How? Like Allen Ginsberg, like Job, or like Isaiah? ("Howl ye, Howl ye; for the day of the Lord is at hand; it shall come as a destruction from the Almighty.") When a man meets adversity or denial, pain or suffering, rebuke or neglect, he may or may not howl. As though it were necessary to make him cringe with humiliation, bow in shame, tremble in terror, hide in guilt. If Frost had to raise his voice, it would never, in his case, be a howl of anguish, nor a scream of rage, but a cry of terror—*can such things be*? It would be to laugh the worst laugh. It would be how to take the curse, tragic or comic.

Each of us, of course, reacts differently to his fate. While tears and shouts are appropriate for those at the Wailing Wall, they are not de rigueur for the warrior at the battle of Maldon. "Purpose shall be the sterner, heart the bolder, courage the more, as our strength littleth." Granted heroic stoicism is at one extreme and the desperate Job is at the other. Scared and goaded, how do we suppose Job's voice sounded when he cried out: "Why died I not from the womb? Why did I not give up the ghost when I came out of the belly?" Or, when he says, despairingly, "My days are swifter than a weaver's shuttle, and are spent without hope?" The point in Frost's "The Oven Bird—"What to make of a diminished thing"—and in "Nothing Gold Can Stay"—"Leaf subsides to leaf"—or in "The Strong Are Saying Nothing"—"There may be little or much beyond the grave,/But the strong are saying nothing until they see"—*under*states. The approach is canny and cautious. This is the Frost tone; not Hebraic fervor but Roman *gravitas*. As W. H. Auden says in *The Dyer's Hand*, "It would be impossible for Frost, even if he wished, to produce an unabashed roar of despair, as Shakespeare's tragic heroes so often can, but the man . . . has certainly been . . . 'one acquainted with the night.' "

I do not think the question is adequately phrased when we ask:

Did Frost have any adversities? We know he faced rejection and neglect, family illness and loss through death, the stern fact of a sister's madness, a daughter's disorder, a son's suicide, his wife's death. The question is more properly asked: How did he take them? Not like Job. Job was the victim of undeserved punishment. Frost's adversities came in part from a choice and an acceptance of a way of life; in part from fate. Some people fall like Mitri Karamazov headlong with their heels up. When they fall in a degrading position they pride themselves on it. And in the very depths of the degradation they begin a hymn of praise—or, Traschen's view, violent protestation. Frost's crises were met differently. His reticences are clear, articulate, firm, and perhaps even more dignified, say, than the ebullience of Dylan Thomas, the rage of Yeats, or the frantic anguish of Job. They cost him his dear life quite as much as their utterances cost Thomas and Yeats and Job their dear lives. Surely we do not fail to recognize what it takes to accomplish something important in literature. What Frost found on his pulses he had power to sustain in rhythmic shocks, long (as in the narratives and dramatic dialogues), or short (as in the lyrics), and the sound is as different as any tune in the head is likely to be. How it can be considered after reading *Complete Poems* that Frost did not feel on his pulses fear, anger, grief, doubt, suffering, and loss *without* cynicism, apathy or despair, is beyond me.

But after admitting this much, it is a false gesture to mistake Frost for a culture hero, like Crockett or Lincoln. Neither was he a victim, as Traschen seems to think he should have been. He made his "strategic retreat," which is thought to imply only evasiveness, and is never seen, as Frost saw it, or as Thoreau practiced it, as a holding action preparatory to the big effort. Derry, Beaconsfield, Amherst, and South Shaftsbury were "strategic retreats," back of each of which was a great effort to lodge some poems "where they will be hard to get rid of."

The case against Frost as a poet has been most comprehensively stated in George Nitchie's *Human Values in the Poetry of Robert Frost* (1960). Nitchie's book is a compendium of most of the adverse critical positions on Frost. He thinks the poet's convictions reflect incoherence, incompleteness, evasiveness, and wrongheadedness, and a prominent anti-intellectual bias. Nitchie believes Frost shies away exasperatingly from major areas of broadly social values and remains uncommitted to explicit statements of theory. Nitchie also thinks Frost never resolves a divided allegiance to prudential and anthropocentric man, fails to create a myth, and that his later poetry thins out alarmingly. In brief, enthusiastic approval of Frost's poetry is excessive and unwarranted. His best poetry is very good but his bad verse, which, in Nitchie's view, predominates, is "very nearly unforgiveable."

Confutation of Nitchie's pejorative opinions are variously encountered, and yet nowhere more formidably than in Reuben Brower's searching analyses in *The Poetry of Robert Frost: Constellations of Intention* (1963). Brower is less uncertain than Nitchie in catching the nuances in the poet's voice. "There is no poet of whose voice we are surer than Frost's," he declares, "no poet whom we hear more distinctly as we read." Historically, Brower thinks Frost breaks from the Romantic tradition and stands with Yeats, Pound, and Eliot in the renewal of the speaking voice in modern poetry. He ranks highly Frost's achievements in the invention of a new blank verse rhythm, in a gift for drama, and in the wise insights into the human condition. Elizabeth Jennings in *Frost* (1964) acutely confutes the charge of anti-intellectualism. As she contends—correctly, I think—Frost wanted as much knowledge as he could acquire, but he did not want "a fixed attitude of mind." He did not want the kind of mind "which has become fixed because it has settled things finally and coldly by reason alone before it has tested them on the senses, the nerves, and the emotions." As for the image of Frost as a farmer, there is the poet's own corrective statement in Richard Poirier's interview, published in *Writers at Work: Second Series* (1965). "I am not a farmer," said Frost, "that's no pose of mine. But I have farmed some, and I putter around."

3.

In the first part of this essay the responsibility and validity of the critic were discussed, and in the second part, the case, according to Frost's contemporary critics, for and against his poetry. I shall close by asking what it is Frost thought he was trying to do and what constitutes his achievement.

In a letter to John Bartlett early in his career (July 4, 1913), Frost claimed, "I alone of English writers have consciously set myself to make music out of what I may call the sound of sense." To bring to book the sound of sense is his avowed aim. But is there not also an unconscious motivation reinforcing this conscious one? I don't think Frost consciously projected an imaginary idea of himself. I do think, however, there is an unconsciously projected image, a persona, a mask. But this does not imply he is a poseur; a mask is not ipso facto a pose. Nor is the wearer necessarily attitudinizing. The creation of an image—public or private—may, as we know, simply be self-induced, the product of the over-stimulated imagination of critic and/or reader. I fail to find in Frost's longer poems any appearance of a dramatized ego as in Ezra Pound's assumed personae of Sigismund Malatesta, Odysseus, Confucius, or John Adams which dominate the *Cantos*, of Byron's Harold in *Childe Harold*, of Marcel in Proust's *Remembrance of Things Past*, of Joyce's Stephen Dedalus in *Ulysses*.

Yet Frost does share with his interpreters an awareness of unconscious objectives in the individual poem as well as in the collected poetry. "The poet," he remarks dryly, "is entitled to anything the reader can find in his poem." If the poem were first thought out and written to certain specifications, there would be little possibility of unconscious motivations. It would be completely contrived. Few good poems seem to have been so written. The suggestibility, so important a part of poetry, leaves not a vacuum, not a hiatus, but the possibility of unconscious as well as conscious motivation, and especially when a poem, as Frost so often said of his poetry, is "a composite."

Does the Frostian view of unconscious motivation also extend to *Complete Poems*? Frost has vividly used the metaphor of constellations to suggest design—that is, unconscious fulfillment of design. As in the early evening we first see the appearance of separate stars, so gradually as the dark gathers separate stars assume ordered positions in constellations—Cassiopeia's Chair; the Cygnus; the Great Bear. Is it not we human beings here below who detect the surprising patterns revealing objects terrestrially recognizable? Or did some Over-Mind suspend the constellations in careful designs for human recognition? Surely Frost's metaphor suggests unconscious intent and fortuitous combination of variant themes in the writing of his poetry. He did not resemble Zola who, at an early age, sat down and wrote the history of the Rougon-Macquart families with great thoroughness and exactitude of detail. On the contrary, from the beginning there was an *unconscious* even if vague, ambiguous, and tentative thrust toward something of which the poet was *not* completely aware. It is possible to identify this unconscious, subtle, and reticent motivation with what the poet later referred to as "a passionate preference" for his subject matter—those atomistic facts of human experience which are the solid substance of his poetic vigil. What we as readers and Frost as creator recognize is, in Emerson's words, "the ravishment of the intellect by coming nearer to the fact." It is the loneliness and love, the envies and denials, the anxieties and terrors, the laughter and sadnesses, the hopes and fears—all the painful and shattering experiences as well as the comic counterpoint which Frost contained—that make these poems, among whose constellated designs are trees, flowers, webs, walls, and stars, of such meaning to so many in our time.

If it can be agreed there must be an *unconscious* motivation, like Emerson's Michaelangelo whose hand in rounding St. Peter's at Rome "builded better than he knew," accompanying the conscious motivation, there is yet another piece of unfinished business. What was it he achieved? Will the poems survive? Some poet-critics like Randall Jarrell would convince his contemporaries by anticipating the tastes and judgments of later generations. These, he says, are the poems which will survive. He names "The Witch of Coös," "Neither Out Far nor In Deep," "Directive," "Design," "A Servant to Servants," "Provide, Provide," "Home Burial," "Acquainted with the Night," "After Apple-Picking," "Desert Places," "The Fear." It is one thing to contend that later generations will winnow wheat from chaff, the solid from the inessential in Frost, but quite another to try to outguess the future. Presumptuous critics fall head-over-heels into an anachronistic fallacy. If a later generation will not be deflected from the poetry by the poet's public image, neither will it be able as we were to associate a living image with the poetry's familiar expression. Moreover, the acceleration of history will conclusively "date" the topical and contemporaneous. Will it be the preurbanized historical fact, or the universal emotion of stubborn independent pride, or the sound of sense alone which will interest readers of another generation in "The Code"? There is really no way of knowing whether later generations will find "Neither Out Far nor In Deep," in Lionel Trilling's judgment, "the most perfect poem of our time." Will a later generation agree with Nim's "younger poet" that Frost's line from "Never Again Would Birds' Song Be the Same," which reads: "And to do that to birds was why she came," is "perhaps the most beautiful single line in American literature?"

I can hear a murmur: "Does it really matter?" I expect it is idle to worry about what a later generation will think or feel. The important question is: What is truly thought and felt about the poet in our time? I think it is important to separate the bonhomie of Frost as a man from the genius exhibited in the poems. A wise saying of D. H. Lawrence's goes, "Never trust the artist, trust the tale." That is not to say, of course, that Frost as artist was a man of duplicity. The poems simply are appraised from an angle different from the poet's. I do not think that Frost was a divided man. But I do think that when one kind of reader opens *Complete Poems* he enters into a private dialogue while another kind of reader enters into a public dialogue. To the latter, "Birches" and "The Tuft of Flowers" are touchstones; to the former, "Acquainted with the Night" and "Design." The unsettling thing to the unsophisticated reader is not the dark poems, the really unsettling thing—what Lionel Trilling meant by "terrifying" —is the darkness in *this* poet.

To explain why the latter is so is beyond my present purpose. It is not necessary to juxtapose man *or* poet; I prefer to join them. Only gross impercipience fails to recognize the stresses and strains of an inner tension which experience imposes on "that queer beast the artist," as James describes the writer. That Frost had trouble keeping his parcels balanced, as he says in the reticent parable "The Armful," is now public knowledge. Thompson's official biography makes our charismatic image of Frost retinal. Who doubts this after having followed his career from the age of sixteen until he was thirty-eight, and watched him creep and stumble and fall and get up again as he followed along the ragged edge of recognition with what repressed rage at being ignored and with what barely suppressed jealousy of his putative rivals, like Masters or Robinson, Sandburg or Wallace

Stevens? Although it is not an unqualified success story, there is a moving quality in disclosing one's wounds with reticence and learning stoically what to make of diminished things. In the beginning the view enforced self-belief by courage; in the end it substituted magnanimity for praise. During the latter years we saw Frost chiefly as one who had survived a conspiring silence to pick his way through the pressing crowd of approbative *and* detractive critics in a personal triumphal march.

If he wore a mask the secret must be behind that mask. Behind it he could quip in mocking seriousness what is earnestly meant, or say gravely what is lightly intended. "Humor saves a few steps; it saves years," says Marianne Moore. Although it is illogical to believe humor is a salvable necessity for a man who had his fourscore and eight years, still it is the greatest of boons. Frost might have thought, as Baudelaire did, "a man must have fallen very low to believe himself happy," but he would not have thought it solemnly.

In one of the earliest remarks I heard attributed to Frost, he had asserted that "a man must not only be known, but felt." True, "We love the things we love for what they are," and we remember them for precisely the same reason. In Frost we always felt a presence of genius, and in the poetry it is such a humanized presence we have come to know. Consequently, we shall best pay our respects to a poet of his stature by coming to terms with the implications of his poetry. And this is what I should think the criticism of poetry was all about. Insofar as critical interpreters of his poetry enable us to see how his intensely personal experience is focused on a single-minded exploration of the common realities in experience *uncommonly* realized, and how, as an emancipated traditionalist, he effectively renewed through "tones of voice" a language really used by man, they have freshened our approach and excited our wonder in poetry. For Frost was a poet whose passionate devotion to the profession of poetry and consummate knowledge of art, whose tangy wit and ability to play provocatively with ideas, whose delight in and understanding of nature, and whose searing personal awareness of the tragic "tears in things" enabled him to evoke a searching vision of the simple but profound truths in human experience.

Robert Frost—2074 A.D.

PHILIP L. GERBER

... and there is the fear of Man: the fear that men won't understand us and we shall be cut off from them. R. F., 1935 [1]

> Poets are likely to be belovèd for only a few of the right reasons, and for almost all of the wrong ones: for saying things we want to hear, for furnishing us with an image of ourselves that we enjoy believing in.
>
> James Dickey, 1966 [2]

REVIEWING Robert Frost's career a decade ago, I posed the long-range query: would Frost be remembered for focusing light on dark verities or for distributing placebos to an anxious age? The question remains pertinent. No cloud is cast over durability. If outward signs mean anything, the Frost boom rolls along its unparalleled course. Check any bookseller's catalog for first-edition prices. He remains the anthologists' darling, the titleholder, his rank as Poet of the Century our most sacrosanct cliché.

Even so, can we credit the sanguinity of George Whicher's conclusion on the poet's seventieth anniversary that coming years could only increase Frost's commanding lead over his contemporaries? Threats to the Frost mystique, bolder now than some decades past, prompt speculation. What boundaries limit his survival? What is the climate of his endurance?

> Mr. Frost is ... an end, not a beginning.
>
> Allen Tate, 1939 [3]

Is there a case against Robert Frost as we now know him? Symptoms of critical disinterest are felt. We have had the letters, the massive biography, de rigueur performances both, invaluable, but finite. Is the barrel scraped clean? While books on Pound, Eliot, Cummings, Stevens, Williams monopolize the announcement pages, major considerations of Frost are in conspicuous absence. Not so frightening a prospect, perhaps, if one argues the man's longevity permitted major assessments in his own lifetime. Might one respond that little remains to be said? That critical attention (distinguished from appreciation) has been on the wane? That Frost has ceased to speak (if speak he did) for our age?

Presupposing Frost's endurance, a safe wager as wagers go, in what capacity might he interest the century to come? His earliest critics (might they be his finest, uncoerced by public reputation?) heralded him as elegist to a fading era.

> [Frost's] is the New England which most of us know only from the verandas of summer hotels, a land of great natural loveliness, with a sprinkling of uncomfortably quaint natives, the Bretons or Basques of America, strange fragments of forgotten people, somehow more remote from us than the Poles and other immigrants who are settling the abandoned farms.   T. K. Whipple, 1928 [4]

1915: A native New-Englander, Amy Lowell, reads *North of Boston*, finds it laboring under the weight of lives twisted, tortured; decrees its watchwords to be *grim, sardonic*; hails its diagnosis of disease consuming a remnant populace, leftovers of the great day, phantom-ridden, morbid, sinking toward insanity. Frost is sad, sad, sad. Bruce Weirick judges Frost the poet of a back-water civilization, no intimation of any great national or spiritual hope-sustaining poems dominated by such tired futility. Clement Wood finds in Frost's work the doddering senility, the decadence of a people living and dying pointlessly, Frost their unwreathed laureate.

> Mr. Frost's work is undoubtedly more finished in its kind than the work of any other living poet, but this very finish precludes growth.   Amy Lowell, 1915 [5]

1924: Percy Boynton summarizes. Frost's people are the final products of duress and adversity, they fall into senescence, their traditions go arid. Mirth, song, play are strangers to them. Far from main-traveled roads, they exist with few human contacts, little allevi-ates their hard and futile existence, all sense of Pauline charity is lost. Their faces crease with hard pride, grim endurance; their backs bow with labor; their futures collapse, done in by pernicious inbreeding.

It is the last possible moment for such agreement. The guns of August 1914 had propelled the Frosts back to America, but of the War itself, no trace in the poems; of the wave of nihilism in its wake, no evidence. *Mountain Interval* appears, then *New Hampshire*, and Frost demands to know how the Russian Novel can possibly be writ-ten on these shores when life proceeds so unterribly. *The Dial* prints something called "The Waste Land." William Carlos Williams dubs it "the great catastrophe to our letters" and gropes for an equivalent image, which history, after long delay, provides—an atom bomb; "it wiped out our world." Things can never be quite the same again. Seeking an antidote to the Eliot poison, men rediscover Frost, sift his poems, and finding what is needed, reshape him in a kindlier image. Those old words, *grim, futile, mordant*, what do they mean, anyway? Beside Eliot's nightmare, Frost is a rising sun. He offers a gallery of family photographs filtered through gauze, so kind to ravaged ancestral faces. Poetry, broken in two, amoebic, spreads in opposite directions, hot in pursuit of Eliot and his parched rock or of Frost and his running brook. The beatification of Robert Frost is underway; canonization will take a little longer.

> Frost? A standard New England poet...
> Whittier without the whiskers.
> H. L. Mecken, 1927 [6]

A gentler landscape is planted, not perhaps what Frost initiated, nor hoped necessarily might predominate; a vision imposed by de-votees upon his two hundred poems. Busy with a career, he offers little resistance, at times seems perversely compelled to propagate the flattery. This cozy universe, to be snared only in nostalgia, never existed at all in the world of stone and wave. But being to modern minds indispensable, it called forth its own invention; a Frost world above all, the poet sole proprietor; a lost world in any event; a pri-vate Utopia USA:

Frost's world—limited as a park and as in-
violate, green, lush with midsummer's wild
blossoms undecapitated among new mown
hay; abounding in trees, birches primarily,
white of bark. Nature unhostile, unpolluted,
unsubdued. Above manageable settlements,
sixty votes to a township, mountains loom,
unsliced for ease of flivver passage. Hills have
no fear of bulldozer. What tract would dare
spew its crescents across these green slopes?

1935: Wall Street, coming down, spills gloom like ink from Atlantic to Pacific. Factories are closing. Cops battle strikers in Cadillac
Square. A man watches the last of his topsoil disappear in a dust
cloud, packs up, heads for the setting sun, finds he has enlisted in an
army of the dispossessed. Granville Hicks is discontent: why does
nothing of this intrude on Frost's universe? Where are those decaying factory towns one used to see north of Boston, those cities hud-
dling with landsmen, those railroads holding New Hampshire in
thrall? Has Frost's state seceded from the forty-eight?

In Frost's World water careens through
troughs of mountain rock, pauses in valley
pools, crystal. One may stoop here, scoop,
and quench a thirst. *No Microbes Allowed.*
A well-curb kneeler spies a pebble down below, far down, luminous. Blueberry thickets
offer plump fruit, ebony skin misted to the
color of sky, shouting *"Pick Me!"*

1945: That Hicks and his gang! Drowned out by the need for
Frost As He Is. Armies gather, brown shirts, black shirts, khaki,
suntan, and one by one the cities go under. And then The Bomb
itself, and from Frost a faint whisper. He is essential now, has the
priority, vurry Amur'k'n, a pure ingot. The flying machine, becoming something called a B-29, is evolving into a jet transport, will
express its mature wish for the moon; for Frost it lodges forever in
the sands of Kitty Hawk. So be it.

> He is being praised too often and with too
> great vehemence by people who don't like
> poetry.   Malcolm Cowley, 1944 [7]

1959: Frost turns eighty-five and Lionel Trilling takes advantage of a birthday feast to attempt the rescue, hacks through layers of tough paint to get at the image below, cuts back to the day when Frost had power to frighten, pronounces him terrifying, his universe a scary place—and finds he has committed sacrilege. Holy mackerel! Why doesn't Trilling crawl out of his Freudian woods and see Frost plain? A reader writes the *Times*: he hopes Frost got a healthy chuckle out of the spat, while downing a plate of buckwheat cakes swimming in good old Vermont maple syrup.

> In Frost's World a season of snow predomi-
> nates, quiet, drowsing as the world dozes;
> woodchucks reel toward earthen burrows;
> white blankets over hill and valley. No be-
> smirch of soot, no spatter of gray salt slush.
> With cosmic indifference the drifts await
> their thaw. Sleighs whisk Edenites from vil-
> lage to woods. Sympathetic steeds toss har-
> ness bells if lingering persists.

1960: Saint Frost is headed for higher things. The politician, sneaking a peek at his watch, declares his miles to go, his promises to keep, and to the rousing cheer of recognition slips expertly out the side door of the hall and heads for Pocatello. The Ascension is scheduled to occur in January, from a podium in Washington. The ceremony is public, held appropriately in outdoor weather, a snowstorm conjured up specially for the occasion.

> Frost leads us away from rather than to the
> center of the preoccupations of the time.
>   Robert Langbaum, 1959 [8]

What is the case against Robert Frost? Not that he became lodged in the world of 1890, but that he was so content in doing so. That his years spanned the phenomena of militarism, mechanization, urbanization, yet these are the x-quantities of his universe. That in his lifetime wheels replaced feet and computers brains; that his rocky acres emptied while megalopolis bloomed; but nothing is allowed to discolor the pastoral dream readers might make of his verses. It is argued that today's headline makes tomorrow's footnote, and said—no doubt apocryphally—that the presence of his indispensable, infinitely comforting snow troubled him once he learned of readers deeply Southern not relating. But the story makes its point, that, attempting universality, Frost strands himself in the final evening of a dying era, premodern; that in point of time his work never advances beyond *North of Boston*; that to a world in future shock, he offers a luminous backward glance at never-neverland.

> In Frost's World who needs a book or daily newspaper? The telephone—in case of need. Men root to the land, venture forth in spring to repair stone fences demarking my plot from yours—*our* plots above all. Home is there when you have to go. Routines endure. Simple folk, supremely self-sufficient, leaning on their own silvered veracity. Change is glacial, ZPG long since achieved. No radio and surely no (color) TV lugs the bribe or the blood into the parlor, and in any case Frost's people are occupied out behind the front fence, chopping thick blocks of maple, for recreation.

Consider the perspective, Frost with his contemporaries. Dreiser, three years earlier coming into the world, after a young manhood on the streets of Chicago, was tossed into the maelstrom known as Pittsburgh. Thousands of workers pouring into that river-constricted triangle helped steel barons pile up millions, then multimillions. Into a sky rosy at night with flame of blast furnaces, skyscrapers reached, marble walls blackening as they rose. The city, one end a warren of workmen's grimy tenements, the other a spacious park meticulously appointed for stone mansions, was an anvil for the forging of new America; the industrial complex its symbol, high-flying Capitalism its method, bitter social strife its result. From that day the city became Dreiser's theme. Restless Americans caught up in the pattern of the future. From this vision came *Sister Carrie*, *The Financier*, *An American Tragedy*.

> The praise heaped upon Frost in recent years is somehow connected in one's mind with a search for ancestors and authentic old furniture.   Malcolm Cowley, 1944 [9]

Consider another. Willa Cather, Frost's senior by a single year, exposed also the horror that was Pittsburgh in the mid-nineties, arriving with great reluctance at the same vision of America-to-come. She saw the wave of industrialism sweep down upon green valleys till beauty fled. She saw her own West chopped into profitable chunks, a bitter sunset for the pioneers. She saw the War (first of the mass disasters), its pyrrhic victory wiping out tradition, all houses becoming like hotels, nothing left to cherish. Like Frost, she preferred the old, the rural, the ordered, idealized in the epic struggle of homesteader against prairie. For her the world broke in two in 1922 or thereabouts, a candid admission, herself stranded on the far side with the old, a living fossil. Yet the present haunts her books, even those far removed in time, in seventeenth-century Quebec, nineteenth-century New Mexico, a dark and malignant cloud despoiling Eden, a seduction of men with the thing-craze, a population balking at any adventure beyond the range of its motor cars. The Cather who wrote *O Pioneer!* also wrote *The Professor's House*.

> Much of Frost's poetry hardly rises above the level of the vignette of rural New England.   Cleanth Brooks, 1939 [10]

These are novelists and not comparable? Consider the poets, embracing their times according to Whitman's counsel. For Lindsay Booth dies blind, and Springfield's sidewalk crowds shout *Bryan, Bryan, Bryan, Bryan!*; for Sandburg the skyscraper cleaves heaven, Hunkies drain a keg along the Desplaines; for Masters the little town makes its final confession. Consider Dr. Williams, between deliveries packing for his journey into Paterson. Consider Pound, his "Make

It New" nudging the century into uncharted regions; Eliot locating the past in a bucket of dust. Consider Cassandra Jeffers sadly smiling as America sinks into the mould of its vulgarity, as men breed on nature inward-turning blades, as megatown snares the hordes like sardines in a seine. Consider Cummings as he dynamites the English tongue and pieces it back together in sunbursts of his own devising.

> We may go to his poetry for diversion and relief from our time, but not for illumination.
> Isadore Schneider, 1931 [11]

Or consider Stephen Crane, in the nineties turning his back on the old century to project a nightmare of the modern, his world-ship rudderless—God's error—cutting silly circles on the surface of time. Set beside Crane, is it possible that Frost, with all his commitment to convention, assumes his rightful place as the last (perhaps the greatest?) of the nineteenth-century bards: Oliver Wadsworth Frost, that household word? Had Frost marketed lithographs rather than verses, would his prints today hang in every 3-ply-veneered family room, strategically flanking the used-brick fireplace to give Currier & Ives a run for their money?

> The new image of Frost as official bard of the administrative establishment and fireside poet to the American people has certain comic overtones... his characteristic vision could scarcely be described as optimistic.
> Stanley Kunitz, 1962 [12]

Is it overdemanding to ask what men a century hence might think of a Frost world even now recycled in terms of sanctuary? His New England is a lonely place, yet in a market where isolation=privilege and a country address=prestige, loneliness commands a rich price. The man whose house and two-car attached garage swarm with tyrant mechanisms sees a land stripped of them as idyllic. And these people of Frost's, in their bright, laconic bubbles of integrity; no matter how lovely, dark and deep the woods, keeping the pledge! What Christmas cards he etches!

> . . . a sort of Olympian Will Rogers out of
> *Tanglewood Tales.*   Randall Jarrell, 1947 [13]

When Frost the synechdochist confronts the synechdochistic future what poems will be winnowed? Is this not the nub of the matter,
that final, pragmatic wish to lodge those few pebbles where they
can't be gotten rid of? The Frost canon of 2074 A.D.—what will it
be when the Untermeyer of that age chooses what goes and what
stays? If Gresham's law, already threatening, prevails, may the poet
be locked into his little postage-stamp of territory mapped out at
the very last possible instant for a pastoral vision, even hypothetical,
to exist or survive; gatekeeper to a forgotten land of the simple, the
innocent, the individual? Will it matter then what the poet's preferences may have been, whether in his plan he balanced theme
against theme? He will be remembered, as all are remembered, according to the world's wish.

> Creatively, there are at least three Frosts—
> the actual artist, the legendary public char-
> acter, posed and professed, and the intent,
> potential poet that might have been.
> Rolfe Humphries, 1949 [14]

The guessing game goes on, every man his own prophet. Make
your own list to seal away for time's reversal. The dramatic poems—
there are two possibilities. "The Death of the Hired Man" and
"Home Burial" hold up equally well, but if tendencies persist, the
latter may be consigned to obscurity. Amy Lowell thought the
"Hired Man" simple and somewhat slight compared with the ghastly
indictment made by "Home Burial," yet the simple and the slight
may be precisely what posterity has in mind; for whose trauma today
is the laying out, the digging, the burial? Who could bear a grave
in a garden, viewed from the picture window? And already the appeal of "Hired Man" lies not in the pathetic waste of Silas' life but
in our hunger for *home*. Did it ever really exist, that deep-rooted
haven defiant of mutability, by kindly folk kept shingled and painted,
ready to take you in, your place set at the table?

> . . . at his worst, a Calvin Coolidge of poetry.
> Malcolm Cowley, 1944 [15]

"The Road Not Taken," simplistic in surface, gilded with a tone of mild regret, seems certain to overwhelm the big scare of "Design." It disheartens to contemplate the loss of "After Apple-Picking," perhaps Frost's all-around best lyric, successful on every level, a perfect thing of its kind. But its intimations of mortality are already resisted in favor of its surface (Frost's nemesis all along, too satisfying, too readily accessible). "Birches," not so different in theme, yet more casually approached, its surface equally accessible, and more universal (every boy climbs a tree, if he can find one, but who picks apples anymore?) may fill nostalgic dreams more comfortably. "Desert Places," that non-identical twin to "Stopping by Woods," must go, its bogeyman writ too large. And the fate of "Stopping by Woods" itself seems sealed. Doomed to endure, the poem is handy even now for newspaper Christmas illustration, so fine for filling out a page of photographs someone has raced miles to collect: snowy fields, unpopulated woods, the relic of a wagon located in some decaying barn, horses from a riding stable hitched to an antique stand. That mouth-watering desire (uncapitulated to) for a silent pause in the dizzying holiday spin was what the public expected. In the classroom the import of the poem is resented. But if not concerning death, then what? A postcard verse with a clever rhyme, little more. To connect this inoffensive genre snapshot with intimations of the grave is taken as an affront.

Is the drift misleading, or may the future agree with Lowell that Robert Frost, "as New England as Burns is Scotch," equals Burns as a poet and is to be ranked accordingly?

But didn't Amy intend that as a compliment?

Notes to *Robert Frost—2074 A.D.* by PHILIP L. GERBER

1. *The Letters of Robert Frost to Louis Untermeyer*, ed. Louis Untermeyer (New York: Holt, Rinehart and Winston, 1963), 262.

2. James Dickey, "Robert Frost, Man and Myth," in *Babel to Byzantium* (New York: Farrar, Straus & Giroux, Inc., 1968), 200.

3. Allen Tate, quoted in Jay B. Hubbell, *Who are the Major American Writers?* (Durham, N.C.: Duke University Press, 1972), 191.

4. T. K. Whipple, *Spokesmen* (New York: D. Appleton & Co., 1928), 95.

5. Amy Lowell, *Tendencies in Modern American Poetry* (New York: The Macmillan Company, 1917), 135.

6. H. L. Mencken, quoted in Hubbell, 171.

7. Malcolm Cowley, "Frost: A Dissenting Opinion," I, *New Republic*, CXI (September 11, 1944), 312.

8. Robert Langbaum, "The New Nature Poetry," *American Scholar*, XXVIII (Summer 1959), 331.

9. Malcolm Cowley, "Frost: A Dissenting Opinion," II, *New Republic*, CXI (September 18, 1944), 347.

10. Cleanth Brooks, *Modern Poetry and the Tradition* (Chapel Hill: University of North Carolina Press, 1939), 111.

11. Isadore Schneider, "Robert Frost," *Nation*, CXXXII (January 28, 1931), 101.

12. Stanley Kunitz, "Frost, Williams, & Company," *Harper's*, CCXXV (October 1962), 100.

13. Randall Jarrell, "The Other Frost," *Poetry and the Age* (New York: Vintage, 1955), 26.

14. Rolfe Humphries, "Verse Chronicle," *Nation*, CLIX (July 23, 1949), 92.

15. Cowley, I, 313.

Robert Frost: The Imperfect Guru

GEORGE W. NITCHIE

A few years ago, with the particular combination of wistful-ness and hubris regularly attending such operations, I made the oc-casion to send some unsolicited poems to an editor and publisher of considerable distinction in my generation. And for special reasons, I cherish the note accompanying the manuscript on its return. The note reads as follows:

> Are you the George Nitchie who wrote that incredibly academic and pompous sentence: "Frost never gives one the clear sense of having mastered, even wrongly, any large-scale aggregation of human phenom-ena"? That is a badly written sentence, with computer language of ex-actly the sort that maddened George Orwell (see his Politics and the English Language) but is also in my opinion arrogant and stupid besides.
> Now reading your own poetry, I find it still more stupid. Your poetry is academic and utterly mindless.

At the risk of debating the undebatable, I wrote back, acknowledg-ing the soft impeachment, and in the brief correspondence that en-sued, two things became clear: first, that it was really my matter rather than my manner that was at fault, since, as X declared, "believ-ing Robert Frost is a great poet, I dislike such jejune criticism of his stature"; second, that he had not read my book on Frost, only a re-view of it. The exemplary part of this anecdote stops here, but *amour propre* urges me to add that, when I had sent him a copy and he had in fact read it, he described it to me as "a fine, fine book."

It does some good, I think, to get this on paper, because it indi-cates that a tendency toward hair-trigger nerves on the part of Frost's defenders, toward a kind of critical overkill, did not perish with Frost's death and was not confined to his generation or that of his immediate juniors—the Sidney Coxes, the Bernard DeVotos, the Robert P. Tristram Coffins, the J. Donald Adamses. The king can still do very little wrong, whether because we are dealing with the

42

Hobbesian state or because we are dealing with theology. I suspect the latter, and I suspect that if we are really to see Frost without the blindness of either love or contempt, we have to consider the guru in him, the man of at least quasi-prophetic wisdom, and the nature of the wisdom he offered. And the traps it led him into.

All right. What did the man of wisdom have to say to and about his fellow men?

Two things stand out. First, he told us that our efforts at working out social and political means of dealing with human problems were really delusions, were undesirable or unnecessary or ineffective. To be sure, he told us so ordinarily in the mode of satire, of jocular needling; but he told us. He told us that life would be what it always was except that "they" are messing it up with dangerous, costly, and unworkable innovations, except that "they" are trying to change things that can't be changed. I grew up in Vermont in the 1930s (Frost, of course, grew up in California in the 1880s) and can claim some expertise in recognizing the type. And I can put in evidence "Build Soil," "A Roadside Stand," "A Case for Jefferson," "The Egg and the Machine," "To a Thinker," and the preface Frost wrote for Edwin Arlington Robinson's posthumously published *King Jasper*, in which, stating his preference for griefs over grievances, Frost aired his grievances. It's all there; so, to be sure, is the splendidly realized tragic vision of the poems in *North of Boston*, antedating the public success, the canonization, the *noli me tangere* of the later years. But then canonization did take place, and we got the rest of it.

We can regard all this as simply amused and amusing partisanship in the peculiarities of American life in the thirties and forties—anybody's privilege, and why not? But I think there's more to it than that. That is, I think that it wasn't just something Frost could turn on for the sake of being sly and amusing, but rather a built-in part of his sense of things in general, partly defensive in nature, something that he had to believe in in order to believe in himself. It corresponds to a deep and devious hostility to ideas of an elaborately social world, because such a world constituted a threat to the image of individually achieved salvation that Frost had developed for himself and identified—or that people identified for him—as New England.

That was the second thing he told us. In New England, it had been different; just possibly, it was still different, if you believed hard enough. And anyway, as he had put it earlier in "The Black Cottage," "why abandon a belief/Merely because it ceases to be true?" Frost, we know, was the New England poet par excellence, in spite of the California birth, the copperhead father, the move to old England as soon as he could afford it. It may still be fair to ask *what* New England was Frost the poet of?

And it's a tricky question. For one thing, it's a nonindustrial New England; I can recall only two factories in it, that in "A Lone Striker" and that in "The Self-Seeker." It's a nonurban New England; I can think of only three poems with urban settings: "A Brook in the City," "Acquainted with the Night," and "A Masque of Mercy." It's a nonmechanical New England; there are perhaps half-a-dozen poems in which railroads appear, two or three with cars, two or three with telephones, no tractors (though there is a buzz saw), and one sawmill (but it's powered by water). And when one remembers how many of these poems are not simply personal lyrics but poems with locales, *place* poems, such omissions are striking. Frost's New England is really a nineteenth-century phenomenon, the New England of subsistence farming, in which social organisms are minimal (the family farm) and in which consequently the individual effort counts for everything, as in "Storm Fear," for instance, or "Stopping by Woods on a Snowy Evening." It's a world without collective social institutions or necessities of any very elaborate sort, and that may be the key to it all.

Now, there's nothing wrong with opting to write of such a world, even though it may be a vanishing world; there's nothing wrong with finding things of value in it, with finding its ideas serviceable. But I think that Frost does two things with that vanishing world that do modify more or less seriously the ideas of value that he finds in it. First, he suggests that the old New England of the family farm, before "they" arrived and took over, is the real New England, that the social world it embodied is the norm from which other social worlds are more or less undesirable departures; second, he suggests that the values of that older, preurban, preindustrial, premechanized world can and should be the values of other worlds as well.

The first of these suggestions—that old New England is the norm, other things accidental deviations—is not true, but that doesn't matter much. A norm that has ceased to exist and that is not coming back is no more a norm, however attractive it may have been. Wordsworth thought much the same thing about the England of the vanishing yeoman farmers and cottagers of his time and place. That means that Frost, like Wordsworth, asks us to look back rather than forward or merely *here* when we are in quest for things of value; and that in turn means that Frost, again like Wordsworth, is of limited service in enabling us to understand where we are or where we are going, our present selves, though they may both be intensely valuable in enabling us to endure the process of going there, like Wordsworth's leech-gatherer in "Resolution and Independence" or the speaker of Frost's "Directive." Again, the sense of the old New England as a norm is not quite true, but it's all right; one may prefer lost causes.

But the second suggestion, that the values of subsistence farming are equally relevant to other social orders, can be positively disabling to Frost as thinker, as wise man, perhaps not so much because it leads Frost to falsify as because it leads him to omit. It may lead to falsification, too. I am not sure, for example, that "A Lone Striker" may not be a case in point. A mill-worker, locked out for half an hour for lateness, simply walks off, declaring that when they want him they can come and get him; it's as simple as that. And it's pretty clear that we are meant to take the mill-worker's behavior as exemplary. Frost, we now know, had done exactly that in 1894. And in 1933, in the depths of the depression, he published "A Lone Striker" in a Borzoi chapbook and reprinted it in *A Further Range* in 1936. And my perhaps tedious point is that in the world of subsistence farming, you can do that; somebody probably will come and get you (they damn well do need you, whatever you assume), and even if they don't, the cornfield will still be there to be plowed when you get over your mad. But in 1933 and 1936 in milltowns that wasn't quite the case; situationally speaking, the likelihood of anybody's coming to get you when you walked out was pretty slim, and the job might not be there when you came back for it; in a world of mass unemployment, there were others who weren't going to wait to be come after. This is real falsification, in its way, though I repeat, this isn't what really matters. Frost is being so much the self-conscious crank about the rugged individualism he recommends in "A Lone Striker" that we recognize it's almost half a joke.

Almost.

Because the things that Frost omits in his devotion to the values of that old New England are something else again, partly I suspect because he knows that he is omitting, and yet that it has for him the force of real gut conviction, something beyond a joke—that old New England was a place where things were real, more real than they can be anywhere else. The result may be a distressing split between Frost's ideas and Frost's experience, and I want to try to illustrate what I mean out of what I regard as a very fine and very moving—but, at least as a "wisdom" document, very incomplete—poem, "Directive," a poem much concerned with ideas of value.

In "Directive" we are invited to make a symbolic journey to an abandoned house on an abandoned farm in an abandoned New England hill town, into a different and simpler order of time, beyond that in which ledge, woods, and silence have come back into their own. In making that journey, we are to experience a kind of ordeal of initiation by responding emotionally to the life that was once there and that has vanished, to the children's games of housekeeping and to the real house, reduced now to an almost vanished cellar hole, its human function over and done with. But we are to go beyond the emotional appeal of this lost world to find both destination and destiny in the mountain brook that supplied the house with water, to drink and be "whole again beyond confusion," sacramentally given back to ourselves.

As with most poems, we can respond to this one in either of two ways, with our nerve ends or with our whole attention. Regarded with the nerve ends, we may find in it a fairly simple and consoling affirmation to the effect that life goes on in spite of loss and change— "Build ye more stately mansions, oh my soul," and all that—but not stuffy; it's an affirmation one has to respect. Only I'm not sure it's exactly what this poem is doing. Regarded with full attention, two things particularly strike me about it. First, the withdrawal into and through the simpler past is a withdrawal into and through a fiction, a falsification. That past is made simple, is made to appear simple, by the loss of detail that really was there when it really was a house, a farm, a town. The world that we are asked to go back to and through is a sentimental falsification of what was once really there—an earthly Paradise, which, as Auden reminds us, "is a beautiful place, but nothing of serious importance can occur in it." [1] It is unreal, and Frost knows it; he tells us so. We are not to stop at that sentimental falsification, but to go through it to something else.

And the second thing that strikes me is that what we are to get through to is not simply the reality that has been falsified by our sentimental awareness of it, that lies behind the earthly Paradise. That is, we don't get through to the old New England of subsistence farming as it really was for the people who lived it, but to a brook. And the brook is what it always was, neither more nor less. We go through sentimental sorrow over the past, through the lost world, in order to become something like the brook, whole beyond confusion. If I consider the poem in the context provided by the body of Frost's work, then I can read it as a disavowal by Frost of his own attachment to that old New England. And this is important because, whether literally or symbolically, that New England was once more the matrix for those ideas of value that he chose to—or had to—identify with. Considered this way, the poem is a kind of recantation of his "belief" in that older world with its minimal social structures and its purely individual measures of worth and meaning. The poem may say, "I have come through even this."

All right. To what?

And the poem doesn't really answer. Perhaps simply to a freedom from sentimentality and nostalgia. Perhaps to some reformulation of human values and ideas. And perhaps into a great emptiness. We go through the human, the abandoned farm and the life it embodied, to the inhuman, the inorganic and indifferent brook, that was there before the people came and is still there after they have gone and that doesn't have the least concern for any of them. The poem's pilgrim has his revelation; the last human thing, that old New England, has lost its hold on him in favor of emptiness, the sense of the abyss, in which there are no social structures, no meanings, and no values to preserve anyway. If the old New England's social values are sentimental fictions, or if they resist transplantation to another context, then rather than accept values of a different sort, we can annihilate the reality of social values altogether, and I suspect Frost is doing this in "Directive."

Roughly speaking, that's what I mean when I say that Frost's devotion to the old New England of subsistence farming leads him to omit things. And of course it's also what I mean when I say that, as thinker or as guru, Frost must be taken with a great deal of caution. There's a real romantic nihilist in him, and romantic nihilists may be exciting, but they make dangerous intellectual and moral guides, especially when they seem to present themselves in the guise of Burkean conservatives. There's an odd and suggestive resemblance that can be adumbrated here. The wholeness beyond confusion gained in "Directive," a wholeness that may be a matter of getting through to the real emptiness of things, has something in common with the critical moment in Jean-Paul Sartre's *The Flies*, when, as Orestes describes it, "Freedom has crashed down on me like a thunderbolt," [2] and he realizes that there is nothing outside himself that can compel him, that the world is empty and valueless, and that he is whole beyond confusion. Like Frost's pilgrim, Orestes has come through. But in the Sartre play, what finally matters is that Orestes goes beyond that moment of breakthrough to reconstruct a world of values in whose terms, and by his own choice, he becomes the scapegoat and hence the savior of Argos. The idea may be ridiculous, but it is *there*; Frost takes us to the edge of something and leaves us, less in the world of *The Flies* than in that of *No Exit*. It's a tremendous experience; but as idea, which may be something other than experience, it has as its clearest element an invitation to a kind of moral suicide, not without dignity, but with a defeat of the human. And is this wisdom? Or is it one of the varieties of Hell?

Hell, as Auden defines it in part three of "New Year Letter,"

> is the being of the lie
> That we become if we deny

> The laws of consciousness and claim
> Becoming and Being are the same.

The entire passage seems to me an apt commentary on Frost, with its surprising moment of unmediated joy, in which one discovers

> The field of Being where he may,
> Unconscious of Becoming, play
> With the eternal innocence
> In unimpeded utterance.

(Just before Randal Jarrell collapsed into nervous breakdown, Mary Jarrell tells us, he "was granted a few magic weeks of Lisztian virtuosity when nothing in his lectures or readings was veiled to him any longer." [3] But nightmare followed.) The kicker is that man must not stay playing with the eternal innocence, must instead

> depart
> At once with gay and grateful heart,
> Obedient, reborn, reaware, [4]

because if he does not, if he tries to take up permanent residence, transient joy becomes lasting horror, the paradisal moment an infernal forever. And it seems to me that Frost wanted—wanted terribly—Becoming and Being to be the same, and that he could never quite forgive Becoming for being Becoming. He knew better, of course, but in some way he had to believe that it wasn't true, that whenever he wanted to he could turn his back and everything would be different, could take one step backward into a world where "they" could not come, where the wrong ones couldn't be saved, as he put it in "Directive." What Yvor Winters once said of Hart Crane—a troubled and magnificent spirit who had chiefly showed us a new mode of damnation—may not be altogether off the mark for Frost as well.

Or then again, it may. What happens to people who go into the wilderness—Conrad's Kurtz, Mann's Aschenbach, Eliot's Celia Coplestone—is not necessarily the responsibility of the authority issuing the summons, and "Directive" remains richly ambiguous. Those who find in it, not a denial of any humanity except Frost's own, but rather an unarguable assertion that man's confrontations with the numinous always take place in solitude, will understandably go on responding to this other approach in the manner of my correspondent, with outrage and anathema. And yet there was in Frost a curious combination of honesty and self-deception that makes him, I suppose, not unlike most of the rest of us. I think that one of the things he could never stop deceiving himself about was his devotion, real or made-up, to that version of New England in which most of his poems seem to be set and of which he liked to think of himself as a spokesman and a specimen. The sense in which man is a social creature, a political animal in Aristotle's sense, gets little acknowledgment in Frost; human efforts to act politically, socially, collectively rather than individually turn into objects of mockery more often than not, mockery from the point of view of the idealized New England yeoman farmer. But Frost's New England yeoman farmer, like Housman's Shropshire lad, another quasi-prophetic figure (whose creator, incidentally, was not a Shropshireman, as Frost was not a New Englander), sees his world clearly because he sees only what he is willing to see. What Frost was willing to see did not include labor unions, welfare agencies, social legislation, braintrusting, city planning, mass movements, the literature of protest, or the New Deal—briefly, it did not include alternatives to that myth of rugged individualism that he had equipped himself with, for reasons he perhaps could not have confronted directly. It was not belief; it was Gospel and it was armor, and it had to be true.

Notes to *Robert Frost: The Imperfect Guru* by GEORGE W. NITCHIE

1. W. H. Auden, "Robert Frost," in *The Dyer's Hand* (New York: Random House, 1962), 340.

2. Jean-Paul Sartre, *No Exit and Three Other Plays*, trans. Lionel Abel (New York: Vintage Books, 1949), 121.

3. Mary Jarrell, in Robert Lowell, Peter Taylor, Robert Penn Warren, eds., *Randall Jarrell 1914–1965* (New York: Farrar, Straus & Giroux, 1967), 297.

4. W. H. Auden, *Collected Longer Poems* (New York: Random House, 1969), 106–107.

"That Plain-Speaking Guy": A Conversation with James Dickey on Robert Frost

DONALD J. GREINER

THE following conversation took place December 15, 1972, in Columbia, South Carolina. Very much aware of the occasion of Robert Frost's upcoming centennial, James Dickey was eager to talk about an artist whose work, he said, has meant very much to him. The conversation was punctuated with readings and witty asides, the most important of which are included below. Neither Mr. Dickey nor I was concerned with interpretations of individual poems. The entire conversation focused upon the more general questions about what makes Robert Frost a great poet and why his poems continue to invite serious reading.

GREINER: We're talking about a poet who was born a hundred years ago; I'm wondering how you would evaluate his status now that he's been dead for more than a decade. In other words, today, are these poems dated; is his poetry the kind that younger poets are going to repudiate the way he rejected the rhythms of a Tennyson or Swinburne?

DICKEY: No, I don't think so. Frost is a poet that the younger fellows may reject and turn their backs on, and so on, but he is a poet whom people are going to come back to. Which is to say that he is a real poet; he's arrived to stay.

GREINER: Your comment suggests that his poems appeal to readers and not particularly to beginning writers. Do his poems have anything to show beginning writers today? I mean, you're teaching students who hope to be poets. . . .

DICKEY: Oh, a very great deal to show them. The plainness and the colloquialism of the language is a very great plus. And for a certain kind of poet, a poet who's learning to write, this may be the way for him.

GREINER: Do you think his poems still speak to the American reader today the way they did maybe twenty or even fifty years ago? Frost was worshipped.

DICKEY: Well, you'll have to dissociate . . . you have to distinguish in the first place between the actual poem and the public personality of the man. And it's hard to make any kind of reasonable assessment of that because the majority of people who revered Robert Frost had read very little of his work.

GREINER: Right, they read only the anthology pieces.

DICKEY: Well, and not even that. No, they only knew him as a public figure, you know, a consultant at the Library of Congress, someone who gave forth with "frosty," if I may be forgiven a pun, saws and cracker-barrel wisdom and things of that nature. But they, mostly the people who I would say—and God knows I don't know what the percentage would be—but ninety, I would say ninety percent of the people who knew who Robert Frost was would never have read any poems of his.

GREINER: Do you think we ought to reread his poems, or should his poems . . . put it this way . . . should his poems be reevaluated now in the light of what we know about Frost the man?

DICKEY: Oh, I don't think so. I'm fascinated by Frost the man, and he certainly must have been one of the worst sons-of-bitches that ever lived. But what really matters is what ends up on the page— what he did as an artist.

GREINER: In your essay in *Babel to Byzantium* you've mentioned the "Frost story."

DICKEY: (laughter) Yeah.

GREINER: I'm wondering, will it ever be possible for us to read "The Gift Outright," say, without thinking of the context of President Kennedy's inauguration; or could we ever read "Birches" or "Mending Wall" or any other of what you call his "beloved" poems without remembering Frost on the grandstand before the worshipful audience, cracking up those in the front row with his little asides? Is it possible that there . . . ?

DICKEY: That's an awful hard question to answer. This is getting exactly back to my point. There's a dissociation between the man and his public image and what he actually did put down on the page. He's a remarkable poet. But he became a personality. And I don't think—I mean, I agree with you—I don't think there really will, at least in our generation, be the possibility of dividing Frost the raconteur and the public personality from the man who wrote some *very marvelous* poems.

GREINER: You know, I think in a perverse sort of way that the negative information which we now know about Frost may eventually help his reputation as a poet. I know students who have been turned off by this image of the white-haired old bard of the nation, who now say, well, this guy really was. . . .

DICKEY: He was human after all.

GREINER: Right. He was not "preachy." He had problems.

DICKEY: And he created most of them himself. (laughter) But he's . . . those Lawrance Thompson biographies—those books are fascinating because you get the dichotomy between the poems as they have come to exist in innumerable anthologies and so on and what went into the poems. I'm very high on literary biographies myself. I was fascinated by those books.

GREINER: They're excellent books. I hope he lives to finish the third volume.

DICKEY: Well, I think it will be finished from what I've learned—the information that I have. But maybe not by him.

GREINER: One more question in this line of thought. Do you think, maybe, in his, in Frost's last years—now this is speculation obviously—do you think he was pursuing finally the reputation more than the art?

DICKEY: Yes, I do. I definitely do.

GREINER: To turn to another idea. In your essay on Frost in *Babel to Byzantium*, you mention "Design," "After Apple-Picking," "Provide, Provide," and "To Earthward" as "a few powerful and utterly original poems." A marvelous way to describe them. Would you revise that list today?

DICKEY: I might put in a few more, but I wouldn't take out any of those.

GREINER: Okay, that's fair enough. In the same essay you mention Frost's, what you call his technical triumph, a triumph of the highest kind. You define it as "the creation of a particular kind of poetry-speaking voice." Yet I note in your list of those four poems that you neither discuss nor name one of the longer dialogue poems in which he literally does have a person speaking. Do these poems seem—a poem like "Home Burial"—do these poems seem startling still, today?

DICKEY: "Home Burial" is a mighty good poem. But when I talk about a special kind of poetry-speaking voice, I don't mean that someone... that someone speaking the poem (whatever the word is), a persona is—necessarily has to be—involved. That's not what I mean. If I didn't get that point across....

GREINER: No, you got it across. My point is that these poems—"Home Burial," "Hired Man"—my point is that when Frost hit it big in England and the United States in 1913, 1914, 1915, he was making it with the so-called dialogue poems which were misread as free verse. I'm wondering if today these poems are no longer—obviously they're not as revolutionary—if they're no longer as interesting, or if they no longer seem as technically innovative? I'm thinking of a poem like "Death of the Hired Man," or "The Fear," or "Home Burial."

DICKEY: Well, I don't know. I really wouldn't be able to pronounce on that because I'm pretty close to the poems, and they've meant a lot to me over the years. What they mean to this generation or that generation or for this reason or that is really not of any particular concern to me. To me personally.

GREINER: You say that Frost—and I agree—you say that Frost is at his best when he's "most rhythmical and cryptic." Are you referring to his well-known love of hinting, of metaphor? He was obsessed with metaphor.

DICKEY: Yes. Yes, he was. But the thing about Frost that makes him so good is that he's able to say the most amazing things without seeming to raise his voice.

GREINER: That's very well put. A poem like "The Most of It" would then.... I remember that Yvor Winters didn't like Frost's poetry but thought highly of "The Most of It."

DICKEY: Well, he didn't think *very* highly of it. But he didn't think very highly of Frost. Yet he liked that poem except that he then proceeded to pick it apart in the most pretentious terms. Let me read this because I don't think that this is a very well-known quote, and it's very quotable. Tom Priestley, J. B. Priestley's son, was the cutter on my movie, the film editor. And he sent me this [*Literature and Western Man*]. I've read it—I've just about read it to pieces, but it's a very good assessment, I think, of Frost. Let's see. Priestley says Frost "is widely recognised as a major poet and is altogether an odd, original, unexpected figure. His poetry is, in his own phrase, 'versed in country matters'; it is not even national but local, New England in scene and manner; it is as frugal with imagery and metaphor as a farmer with his money [laughter]; much of it appears to have the rhythm and tone of cautious conversation, spoken out of the side of the mouth by a man not looking at you—" [laughter]

GREINER: That's good.

DICKEY: "yet through this stealthy rusticity comes almost everything, short of the depths of personal dissolution and the blazing heights of ecstasy, that the modern poet is trying to express—bewilderment and horror, wonder and compassion, a tragic sense of life, which he, however, suggests without bitterness or whining. This is a poet, using his poker-faced rural *persona*, who likes to pretend he is being simple and obvious when he is not, just as many other poets, going with the movement, like to pretend they are being profound when they are not."

GREINER: That's nicely expressed. The idea about the modern strikes me. To continue from what Priestley says, Frost, as you know, for years was criticized as a leftover nineteenth-century poet, as a watered-down Emerson. . . .

DICKEY: Or Wordsworth (laughter).

GREINER: Right. As a man who should be back in the 1850's. Do you think it's Frost's dark vision that makes him modern, one of the qualities that makes him modern since his verse form may not be?

DICKEY: I don't know about that. But I do think that the speech which Lionel Trilling made about him, which I quoted in my article —Frost as a poet of darkness and terror, fear—the motivating emotion in him was fear—is the correct Frost.

GREINER: I would agree. You know, that speech wasn't made until 1959; and while I'm sure isolated readers here and there recognized the element of fear, as you call it, or terror in Frost, for years he was considered a benign nature poet, a goody goody, the kind of poet read to the Camellia Garden Club.

DICKEY: Yeah, those readers might have his face put up on Mount Rushmore (laughter).

GREINER: Exactly, with his hair fluffed up (laughter). I'm wondering, have we only recently discovered these dark poems? Is it because the critic is always lagging behind the poet, or is it because in our age of continuing crisis these poems are now speaking to us more and more—"Neither Out Far nor In Deep," for example?

DICKEY: Yes, I think that's very well said. The best critic, the critic who has understood Frost most deeply was Randall Jarrell.

GREINER: Yes, his work is wonderfully perceptive.

DICKEY: Because Jarrell was something of the same type of man. And he understood the depths under the still pools, you know.

GREINER: He's the one who wrote the long discussion of "Home Burial." What about Frost's wit? his humor? Do you think poems like—I'm just throwing out some—like "October" or "One Step Backward Taken" or "Fire and Ice"—I'm not thinking of his less-successful attempts to be funny in those awful "editorials"—do you think those poems have a place in the final assessment of Frost?

DICKEY: Well, that is the Frost who has a kind of an elephantine local New England humor. The ponderous attempt to be funny and witty is the Frost that I can most easily dispense with, you know.

GREINER: Most readers dismiss the "cute" Frost of the "editorials."

DICKEY: The Frost I like is the plain-speaking guy who can in the most conversational possible way say things that you wouldn't have thought of in a million years.

GREINER: You know, talking tbout the common way of saying something, I find so many students today relishing, understandably, Stevens, or Eliot. . . . I'm thinking of the more famous modern poets . . . or Pound, and dismissing Frost, until they come upon a poem like "All Revelation" or "Directive." And I'm wondering if the so-called easier poems like "Stopping by Woods" or "Birches" have been so over-anthologized, so over-taught that students no longer respond to them and therefore end up with a warped view of Frost's achievement.

DICKEY: As a university professor, as you are, Don, I have become—I couldn't speak for you, but I can certainly speak for myself—I have become very wary and mistrustful of this insistent, universal "talking it" to death. Talking things to death. We are paid to do it, but as far as the art of poetry is concerned I have very serious reservations as to whether or not this is desirable.

GREINER: This is what's happened, I think, to a poem like "Birches" or "Mending Wall" or "Stopping by Woods."

DICKEY: Well, that's what you have when you say you "get" a poet like Frost who's well known, who's taught, as they say, "in classes."

GREINER: And who has an easy literal level.

DICKEY: You get lots of people who get to competing in interpreting him.

GREINER: You remember that Frost's famous comment about "Stopping by Woods" was "All I meant was to get the hell out of there."

DICKEY: Yeah? Well, he was right. Certainly. You read the commentaries on those things and they're so over-read and over-ingenious and so on that the poem just gets mangled and destroyed in the process.

GREINER: Someone in the late '50's or early '60's, I understand, actually counted and decided that "Stopping by Woods" is the most explicated poem in American literature, that it's been "done" so many more times....

DICKEY: Well, but of course it's got to contain a homosexual Freudian overtone, undertone, all that kind of business, you know, ... uh! (laughter) It's just a hideous business. But the poetry, the fun of it, the delight of it, dies when you indulge this over-intellectualizing about it.

GREINER: I like the way Frost hits me with an unexpected word. For example, to pull one out of the hat, in "Fire and Ice," when ice "is also great/And would suffice"—the word "suffice," for example, surprises me, that kind of thing.

DICKEY: Yes, I agree, that's good.

GREINER: Some critics have argued persuasively that Frost is a good poet but not one to be read finally with Yeats or Stevens or Eliot. Now, get the reason: because he did not develop what they call a coherent vision or myth, and because he oversimplifies human experience by writing about modern crises from the vantage point of the rural world. Are those criticisms justified in your opinion?

DICKEY: Not in my opinion, no. I think that he has one virtue that overrides all of those things, and that is that he speaks to people on a very deep level. He speaks to them in a language they can understand, but the meanings of the lines in his poems go very deeply down. He's not a recherché kind of writer like Stevens who is always dealing in riddles and conundrums and that sort of thing. Frost has a great, great, wide spread on the popular world. He shows us here in America that a poet does not have to talk down to his audience, but that he can talk to his audience without condescending.

GREINER: The literal level in my opinion does not hurt Frost at all.

DICKEY: No, I think that's one of the best things he's got going for him.

GREINER: I have so many sophisticated graduate students, though, who feel that he is less than great because of the literal level.

DICKEY: That's one of the finest things about him. I mean you take Wallace Stevens and you keep going round and round in circles, trying to follow his thought and so on, and it's the poetry of a very sophisticated esthete. Frost, whether or not you accept him, is a plain-speaking man, and you are interested in what he says because you can relate to it, whereas you cannot relate to "sixteen ways of putting a pineapple together" (laughter).

GREINER: This would also account, of course, for Frost's very, very broad audience.

DICKEY: Right! He furnishes the figure of the poet in American life who can speak plainly and deeply at the same time.

GREINER: In your reading of Frost—I'm thinking of all of Frost—do you detect any development, change . . . trying out of new things, or would you agree with those who argue that he develops, shows his all in *North of Boston*, which was published in 1914, and from there on out his poems go in generally a straight line?

DICKEY: Yes, I do agree with the latter.

GREINER: That's his serious drawback?

DICKEY: In a way, yes. He never learned the great lesson of Picasso, which was never to be trapped in a single style. He found a single style, and he used it and explored it for the rest of his life. But he was not a man who operated on the frontiers of consciousness, who was trying new things and doing new, such as Picasso, who was continually trying to push out the boundaries of human consciousness. He found one thing that he could do. He didn't try to go out; he tried to go in, to go deeper into what he had already found. And that's another type of writer from somebody like Ezra Pound or Auden who do try to do these new things.

GREINER: How would you define that one thing? Is that a fair question? He found "one thing."

DICKEY: Well, it's a—to come back to what I said earlier—a plain-speaking style which could say profound things.

GREINER: He tried in later years, you know, to move into satire, political commentaries. . . .

DICKEY: Didn't work! No, and there he engaged the worst side of himself which was this elephantine levity and this cracker-barrel philosophizing which is not only unpleasant but painful.

GREINER: One poem of Frost's—I would hesitate to say he was "done" in his early life—but "Directive" which was published in, what, 1947? saves his later poetry for me.

DICKEY: Yes, that's a good poem, and "Provide, Provide" is a wonderful poem. It's a wonderful poem! Boy, I'll tell you . . . when you read Frost, when you read that poem and you read some of the others of about that time, you know the full horror of being a human being, you know, and the real practicality and the practical solutions of how you provide for yourself.

GREINER: A better "proletarian" poem than those by some of the proletarian writers?

DICKEY: Oh, yes, far, far better.

GREINER: Let me ask you one final question which is strictly personal opinion. If—one of these "if" questions—if you had room to include one or two of Frost's poems in a world anthology, right off the top of your head, which ones would you pick?

DICKEY: Of Frost?

GREINER: Yes.

DICKEY: Oh, I'd say "Acquainted with the Night" and "After Apple-Picking."

Robert Frost: An Assessment
of Criticism, Realism, and Modernity

REXFORD STAMPER

W HEN a reader approaches a well known poet, especially one whose first significant poems were completed almost half a century ago, he can expect a fairly unified canon of critical commentary to guide his reading and to direct his attention to important poems or to unravel difficult areas in the poetry. The current dialogue associated with the poetry of either Eliot, Yeats, Stevens, or Pound provides an excellent example of how criticism functions to enrich poetry after the main aesthetic problems have been solved and many readers have reached an accepted, if unspoken, agreement on the poet's status. As yet, however, the critics of Robert Frost's poetry have not agreed upon certain key critical questions which should have been answered long ago—his point of view, his concept of reality, his affinities with the modernists, and the significance of place or the role of imagery in his poetry. Even the basic question, whether Robert Frost is a major twentieth-century poet, remains undecided.

A survey of Frost criticism indicates that this indecision results from the overt political reactions that tainted earlier evaluations of both the man and his poetry. After an interval of praise during which Ezra Pound used Frost as a club to drive home his recurrent observation that Americans were too provincial to appreciate a significant new poet, or in Frost's case a significant older poet, Frost's hard-won status as a major American poet began to suffer. A reappraisal was initiated in the 1930's by critics who used political ideals, quite different from Pound's, as a yard stick for measuring and evaluating all literature.

The most damaging of these attacks came from Granville Hicks who said that Frost had nothing to contribute to the "unification, in imaginative terms, of our culture. He cannot give us the sense of belonging in the industrial, scientific, Freudian world in which we find ourselves." [1] Hicks concluded that Frost is not a major twentieth-century poet. Other critics, following this lead, found a lack of depth and significance in Frost's poetry. William Rose Benét held Frost to be little more than a "wise old woodchuck," [2] and R. P. Blackmur said that Frost was "an easygoing versifier of all that comes to hand, and hence never lacks either a subject or the sense of its mastery." [3] Both Benét and Blackmur decided that Frost's poetry was "too easy" to have significance for a serious twentieth-century audience.

These observations, in a less overtly political context, laid the foundation for more recent assessments of Frost's poetry made by Lionel Trilling and J. Donald Adams. Trilling, in his famous birthday speech, said that Frost was a "terrifying poet" because the vision of the world which informs his poetry is predicated upon an ontological view devoid of certainty or comfort.[4] Trilling's argument basically holds that Frost is a poet of ideas who, finding nothing of ideal certainty in the world, presents through his poetry a bleak vision to his readers. Trilling's assessment counters Hicks's earlier condemnation of Frost's poetic value for a twentieth-century audience. Trilling, giving high praise to Frost's work, says that Frost fulfills the sacred trust of the artist by embodying in his poetry an accurate imaginative presentation of the major concerns of twentieth-century America. Trilling argues that since many intelligent readers see the world as fragmented, an observation that fills them with an unarticulated dread, Frost's poetry appeals to them because of its honest reflection of the artist's struggle to overcome fragmentation and because of its attempt to rise above the horror and terror that result from this view.

J. Donald Adams offers a less sophisticated evaluation of Frost's poetry. Adams reads Frost as a rather uncomplicated poet of Whittieresque Americana whose rural virtues and wholesomeness are lost on such sophisticated twentieth-century New York critics as Lionel Trilling, no matter where they might live. The fundamental difference between these two critics illustrates another vein of Frost criticism. Adams reads Frost as a spokesman for a benevolent force that orchestrates both man and nature in harmonious interaction. This function, seen within a more classical but still romantic tradition, is essentially the same as Trilling's assessment of Frost's poetry. The difference between Trilling's and Adams' position is that Adams reads Frost as responding positively to nature; Trilling, on the other hand, sees Frost as a darker poet who follows in the tradition of Melville and Hawthorne in his treatment of the ambivalent aspects of nature. The two critics, though looking from different vantage points, reach the same conclusion—Robert Frost is a significant modern poet.[5]

George W. Nitchie has made a more recent negative assessment of Frost. Nitchie sees Frost as a minor poet whose work does not embody social consciousness; his central argument against Frost resembles the political criticism of the 1930's: that social thinking has evolved during the past one hundred years from an emphasis on the romantic, self-centered "I" to a collective, group-centered "we," and that Frost, by failing to emphasize this shift, wrote poetry that is outdated and of little social significance. Nitchie's argument, in part, "is based on the proposition that, as poet, Frost seldom exhibits any very vital or immediate sense of collective aims, of broadly social values." [6]

The reader's uneasiness with critics who emphasize Frost's apparent lack of social responsibility comes from a nagging suspicion that their criticism has been directed from afar by F. R. Leavis and the moral imperialists of *Scrutiny*. Although the earlier critics obviously could not have undergone this influence, the impulse to evaluate and to rank on the basis of extra-literary merit remains the same. Nitchie condemns Frost for failing to contribute to the great tradition of writers who have shown their audiences how to adjust socially and morally to the pressures of their age. Nitchie praises Eliot and Yeats, among others, for adopting systems that allow them to adjust to the modern shift in social awareness and condemns Frost for failing to adopt the "Mythotherapy" (to use John Barth's phrase) of choosing a lie with which to infuse his poetry.

This same impulse, to criticize not what Frost has written but what he has not, lies behind Yvor Winters' "Robert Frost: or, The Spiritual Drifter as Poet." Frost's lack of "high seriousness" bothers Winters. Although he recognizes that Frost's poetry is valuable and interesting, Winters concludes that Frost is a dangerous poet because his poetry reveals a lack of sincerity when dealing with ethical, moral, or religious topics. Winters says, for example, that "The Road Not Taken," "The Sound of Trees," and "The Bearer of Evil Tidings" all have a single theme: "the whimsical, accidental, and incomprehensible nature of the formative decision."[7] By reading the poetry as a continuation of Emersonian and Thoreauvian Romanticism, both Nitchie and Winters condemn Frost for what they consider the perverse lack of responsibility in his use of this tradition in his poetry. Nitchie criticizes Frost on social grounds; Winters criticizes him on moral grounds; they both criticize his lack of a governing significance.

The central question behind all of these assessments of Frost's poetry is the Logos of his aesthetic. Recent studies of Frost's poetry only indirectly pursue these earlier criticisms of his politics, his ethics, and his social alliances. Although these questions have yet to receive a definite answer, they are now eliciting less attention while certain other questions concerning his art are being considered. The issues now receiving the most serious investigation are the nature of Frost's view of reality and its corollary, the effects this view has on his poetry.[8]

The chief difficulty in attempting to formulate a coherent statement of Frost's artistic vision is that Frost himself failed to make such a statement. Although he did speak frequently about "the sound of sense," and "the figure a poem makes," [9] and although he did at one time discuss the formation of an "artistic doctrine" based upon Puritanism,[10] the fact remains, as Nitchie points out, that Frost did not subscribe to a unified organization of reality. He did not follow traditional beliefs as did Eliot; he did not subscribe to a recognizable literary philosophy as did Hardy; he did not construct a personal mythology as did Yeats; he did not utilize his poetry for social statement as did Auden; nor did he imply that reality is in the mind of the beholder, thus a flexible material for the poet to mold at will, as did Stevens. Frost opposed subscribing to a rigid ontological world view, as he makes clear in a letter to Mary E. Cooley: "I'm less and less for systems and system-building in my old age. I'm afraid of too much structure. Some violence is always done to the wisdom you build a philosophy out of. Give us pieces of wisdom like pieces of eight in a buckskin bag." [11]

An approach to the problem of whether Frost is a major poet can be made through a consideration of his artistic vision. Although it is obvious that ideas dominate his poems, Robert Frost is not a poet of ideas, for he had a deep distrust of the systematizing logical process. His doubts in ratiocination never reached the point of positive or complete skepticism, but his letters and poems repeatedly reveal his doubt in the validity of any rigid system based upon reason or upon intuition: "We [Frost and E. A. Robinson] doubted any poem could persist for any theory upon which it might have been written" (*Triumph*, 421). This basic distrust explains his refusal to construct his poems according to a preconceived pattern, whether philosophical, mythical, or political, and warns the reader against the search for an internal organizational system to use in assessing his poetry.

Frost also recognized this distrust of systems in others; writing to Bernard DeVoto, he observes, "What I suspect we hate is canons: which are no better than my guidances insisted on as your guidances" (*Letters*, 444). This same rejection of systematized process is seen in his predilection for any thinker who challenged accepted theories. Frost wrote to Louis Untermeyer, "I . . . [am very] fond of seeing our theories knocked into cocked hats. What I like about [Henri] Bergson and [J. Henri] Fabre is that they have bothered our evolutionism so much with the cases of instinct they have brought up" (*Triumph*, 300). But, as he was to write later in "The White-Tailed Hornet," even instinct as a system should not be trusted entirely to explain behavior:

> Won't this whole instinct matter bear revision?
> Won't almost any theory bear revision?

The best way to approach Frost's poetry is without a preconception or system that attempts to explain in advance his vision of reality.

Frost's methodology is much more informative than his ideas. In 1915, Frost remarked on the attitude readers were taking toward his methodology and the importance of method over ideas in his poetry. He wrote Edward Garnett: "They get some fun out of calling me a realist, and a realist I may be if by that they mean one who before all else wants the story to sound as if it were told the way it is because it happened that way. Of course the story must release an idea, but that is a matter of touch and emphasis, the almost incredible freedom of the soul enslaved to the hard facts of experience. I hate the story that takes its rise idea-end foremost, as it were in a formula" (*Letters*, 179). The key to Frost's methodology is found in the phrase "hard facts of experience," which indicates his tacit agreement with those readers who labeled his work realistic; however, the phrase "touch and emphasis" also reveals his distrust of the commonly accepted idea of what constitutes the realistic method.

A fundamental premise in the quotation above is Frost's rejection of experimentation in poetic structure. The aim of a Frost poem is ultimately the same as the aim of an Imagist or Symbolist poem, to release an imbedded idea. Such Imagists as Amy Lowell and such Symbolists as Pound and Eliot developed fragmented patterns in order to juxtapose character, image, and perspective so that the reader could have a nonchronological exposure to the idea in their poetry. But Frost uses a narrative, sequential ordering of events, a structure based on a chronological time pattern, to release the idea in his poems. This difference in technique can explain why many intelligent readers praised the experimenters for opening new imaginative perspectives on reality while they dismissed Frost for anachronistically writing nineteenth-century poetry in the twentieth century.

A reaction against the obvious limitations of the realistic method was well under way by the beginning of the twentieth century and seriously affected most of the intelligent criticism of Frost's poetry. The chief objection artists and critics had to realism was that the idea can easily be lost in the full reporting of detail upon which the method depends. The realistic writer is always in danger of losing the "touch and emphasis" that keep the poem or novel from becoming a catalogue of detail, and without this "touch and emphasis" a work, such as Dorothy Richardson's *Pilgrimage*, is nothing more than an exercise in observation. Yet, in order to present a true account of reality the author must resist the urge to choose a pattern that will infuse his work with a governing significance. The failure to resist such a temptation removes the work of Yeats and Hardy and much of the later work of E. A. Robinson from the realistic canon.

By choosing a governing significance around which to organize his work, the writer negates the realistic principle, which requires the accurate reporting of detail; and he admits, however tacitly, that the significance of that detail can be found ultimately in the writer's consciousness and not in the detail itself, a position taken by Wallace Stevens in his theory of the "Supreme Fiction." Frost never indicates in his poetry, letters, or talks that such an approach to reality could be of any benefit to a man confronting a world that is at best indifferent to his presence.

But Frost's vision of reality dominates his art. He questions not if reality conforms to his vision but if he views it accurately, a point he makes in a letter to Kimball Flaccus: "I wouldn't give a cent to see the world, the United States or even New York made better. I want them left just as they are for me to make poetical on paper. I don't ask anything done to them that I don't do to them myself. I'm a mere selfish artist most of the time. I have no quarrel with the material. The grief will be simply if I can't transmute it into poems. I don't want the world made safer for poetry or easier. To hell with it. That is its own outlook. Let it stew in its own materialism. No, not to Hell with it. Let it hold its position while I do it in art" (*Letters*, 369). Frost considered his method a more honest way of presenting reality than the methods used by his contemporaries. The violent structural juxtapositions, the frantic and sometimes ludicrous groping after organizing principles practiced by many modern poets were, in Frost's opinion, false approaches to reality and to art. "Art," he said, "should follow lines in nature, like the grain of an axe-handle. False art puts curves on things that haven't any curves" (*Triumph*, 77). In Frost's poetry both human and physical nature appear continuous, altering over time. To him, any art that attempted to present the truth of either without following this natural curve was false art, having its reality only in the mind of its creator.

Frost seems to have thought that art should reveal the truth of both objective and subjective reality; and the "false curves" or governing patterns, while they present a view of reality, leave no way for the observer to verify the observation. Actually, art organized from a single point of view is dangerous since it is the product of the individual reasoning and structuring faculty, which interferes with an accurate understanding of physical and human nature.

In the last section of "New Hampshire," which in part consti-tutes his "Essay on Criticism," Frost discusses the limiting stric-tures that hamper the artist if he starts with the assumption that literature must satisfy either the "prude" or the "puke." Once the author chooses either bias, the poem must conform to the "false curve" of the dialectic, leaving no room for spontaneous creativity. Given this choice the poet can respond only by rejecting both tacks, or, as Frost says, "Me for the hills where I don't have to choose." This line gives some insight into the nature of Frost's aesthetic problem. As a realist he was forced to accept some prin-ciple for choosing the details which he would include in his poems, even if his choice was to reject the false curves used by the prudes and the pukes. No doubt Frost was tempted, as are many writers, to see reality as a flux or as chaos; but he, like Yeats, Milton, Keats, or Shakespeare, did not abdicate, as certain critics have charged, the artist's function of ordering and attempting to resolve meaning from this chaos. The prudes and the pukes, as well as writers who deliberately choose a governing significance, seek in art what they want from life, a sense of order and unification; however, if the poet cannot find this sense of order and unification, his art should at least become the record of his search for it.

Frost's poetry always presents a confrontation with a chaotic, ununified world. The world presented in the collected poems is a deceitful, cruel place, and the greatest significance of the poems is their record of Frost's search for a possible practical order that might exist in that world. His poems record his lifelong explora-tion for significance.

In order to clarify the record of his search, Frost did what artists such as Conrad have advised; he began by "creating for himself a world . . . in which he [could] honestly believe." [12] Frost's crea-tion of this world and the use he made of it were noted in 1934 by Cornelius Weygandt, who wrote, "What he does with stories that others than himself may know, that may even be common property, is to isolate them from the chaos of life and recreate for them a little world all their own" (*Triumph*, 247). But the world he chose to create, the limited, rural world of a preindustrial New England, has led to some confusion in understanding his poetry.

The emphasis on physical nature in this world has tempted several readers to suggest Frost chose a transcendental philosophy to infuse his poetry with a governing significance. They see this philosophy as adding to the importance of the mowing, fence mending, apple picking, and star gazing activities that seem to reflect a harmonious interaction between physical and human nature and reveal Frost to be a latter-day prophet of Emersonian idealism.

This transcendental approach to Frost's poetry is founded upon two biases which cannot be substantiated by a close reading of the poetry. The first bias is that a perceivable truth that is in accord with the human spirit and its aspirations can be found in the world of physical nature. The second, and in many ways the most dangerous, bias is that man can perceive that truth. Although Frost did write much about nature and natural objects, the nearest he ever came to accepting either bias was to occasionally wish that it were true. Ultimately, his attitude about the continuity that exists between man and nature is similar to but not so emphatic as E. M. Forster's observation, "Both assumptions are false." [13] In his search for what was true, Frost presents a view of reality that is local and organized, yet which is not confined by the limiting strictures of a governing principle. Frost's poems always emphasize the corporeal aspects of reality; he does not suppress these in favor of an idealistic organization of life.

Robert Frost did not have a single, all encompassing, view of reality. His orientation, as reflected in his collected poems, was to separate reality into three distinct zones, each of which co-exists with, but is basically independent of, other existing zones. Although the exact relationship among these zones is never fully defined in his poetry, Frost wrote enough to allow for generalizations concerning their organization. These three zones cover the basic areas of human awareness: physical nature, human nature, and the supernatural. These zones are separate entities; yet in his poetry he gives some indication that he thought the characteristics and processes that distinguish one zone could possibly extend their influence into another zone.[14]

Although much of Frost's poetry deals either directly or indirectly with the reality of physical nature, he never makes an explicit statement concerning a theory of nature, or more than a general comment on how physical nature influences or is influenced by other existing realities. Physical nature, because it is understandable only in terms of those objects man can perceive through his senses, remains an ambiguous entity, hinting that it contains the key to certitude, but denying any attempt to discover what this key might be.

Frost had a similar understanding of human nature; it is the product of several separable units. He clarifies this view of human nature in a letter to Hamlin Garland: "We are just one more rough abstraction on some principle we needn't go into here from the mass that other abstractions have been made from before and others still will go on to be made from. Principles are always harder to talk about than men. Our best way to define to ourselves what we are is in terms of men. We are eight or ten men already and one of them is Howells" (*Letters*, 266). The phrase "some principle of which we are an abstraction" suggests the transcendental idea that each man has an inexplicable character which he must explore and assert to the fullest. Emerson had popularized this idea decades before when he made his plea for individual self-assertion and self-reliance, but the concept of personality defined in Frost's poetry is obviously not Emerson's. Frost never accepted Emerson's conception of human nature, the idea that as the effect of some divine cause human nature reacted in harmony with physical nature, so that each "eye was placed where one ray should fall, that it might testify of that particular ray." [15] He never demonstrates his belief in such obvious continuity among the realities. For Frost all values, both external and internal, are ultimately defined as personal interaction with another individual or as a man's interaction with his immediate natural environment. Although he does recognize the supernatural as a definite influence on human and natural relationships, he finds its role so vague that he rarely makes an attempt to explain or to understand its significance.

In Frost's poetry the various zones of reality are never entirely revealed to one another. This stance separates Frost's poetry from the romantic acceptance of continuity, and it is the most obvious characteristic of his modernity. His poetry is filled with images dealing with gaps, barriers, and voids which tend to separate and to isolate each reality in its own zone, denying rather than illustrating the continuity of all creation. Frost knew the Emersonian premise that apparent discontinuities should prove to be nonexistent if one could just investigate the problem of reality more thoroughly, and his poetry records his investigations; but the poetry nowhere supports the contention that Frost ever found the continuity that earlier writers found in the universe. The most he allows is a suggestion, as in these lines from "Two Look at Two:"

> As if the earth in one unlooked-for favor
> Had made them certain earth returned their love.

His search leads him to a close investigation of the gaps, barriers, or voids that suggest the possibility of continuity, and the record of this search is one of the most important themes in his poetry. Although each of the separate zones is apparently autonomous, the reader is aware that Frost was uncomfortable with this isolation, for he repeatedly introduces vantage points which might offer a hint of a continuous universe.

No doubt much of Frost's skepticism came from his reading in the scientific literature of the late nineteenth and early twentieth centuries. He had a lifelong interest in science, and he stated that he read many of the leading British scientists while still a young man.[16] Frost was aware that the belief in continuity that had dominated the nineteenth century was disintegrating before the scientific speculations that mushroomed at the close of the century.[17] Each of these speculations, experiments, and observations called into question the certainty of Haeckelian science and probed the established theories of time, space, matter, and the predictability of scientific laws. Repeatedly the older ideas were dismissed as incapable of explaining physical reality. In *The Education of Henry Adams*, Adams exemplifies the extent to which scientific advances had called into doubt former ideas of certitude. He discusses the influence made by Karl Pearson's *Grammar of Science*: "Pearson shut out of science everything which the nineteenth century had brought into it. He told his scholars that they must put up with a fraction of the universe, and a very small fraction at that—the circle reached by the senses, where sequence could be taken for granted— much as the deep sea fish takes for granted the circle of light which he generates." [18] For a poet concerned with understanding the truth of reality, the doubt that scientific method could adequately explain physical nature had aesthetically limiting implications. Marion Montgomery points out how this attitude narrowed the range of Frost's poetry: "Whenever Frost talks directly to or directly of natural objects or creatures, we feel that he is really looking at man out of the corner of his eye and speaking to him out of the corner of his mouth. In all these poems Frost is describing the animal and vegetable natures in man, not reading man's nature into the animal and vegetable worlds, as Wordsworth was inclined to do." [19]

The focus in Robert Frost's poetry is usually at the point where one of the three zones of reality seems to impinge upon another. The resulting action is veiled, leaving the person who observes and judges the facts of his observation unsure whether he understands the significance of what he has seen. Man, like Pearson's deep-sea fish, can know only the limited area he can perceive through his senses, and whatever happens or whatever he observes in the other zones he can interpret only in human terms. Man's limited powers to judge the significance of the interaction which occurs between co-existing zones of reality is the focal point in one of Frost's greatest poems, "Mending Wall."

In this poem, as Clark Griffith points out, "the actions of Nature— the toppling of the rocks or the swelling of the ground after a thaw—seem to protest all barriers which separate man from man." But, Griffith says, this observation is inconsistent with what happens in the poem. Without the wall between them, the speaker and his neighbor would have no opportunity for human interaction. The two are brought together by the natural object which functions to separate them. [20] The important image in the poem is not the wall but the point of contact—the void or gap—which allows each neighbor the opportunity to see into the reality of the other. The presence of this void or gap is not explained. It was caused by "something," although the exact identity of this something is never defined. The reader learns that the void is not the result of recognizable physical or human activities but is caused by the imposition of "something" natural, yet supernatural:

> I could say "Elves" to him,
> But it's not elves exactly....

The void provides the impetus which allows the speaker to see at least partially into the reality of his neighbor; and although he understands neither his neighbor nor nature better as a result of this encounter, he does make this partial insight the basis of his pronouncements on both physical and human nature.

"Mending Wall" does not illustrate the continuity that exists between nature and man or between man and the supernatural, but it does illustrate a recurring theme in Frost's poetry—that vantage points can be found which will allow the observer to question whether continuity exists between separate realities. The poem dramatizes the isolation each zone forces upon the other, but it also illustrates the possibility of symbolic encounters that allow the observer an imaginative view into the reality of other persons and areas of existence. He may not understand this reality, but after his view of it he is partially convinced of its existence.

The interactions and relationships that can exist among the various zones of reality establish the basic concern in Frost's poetry. Over and over again the reader encounters the same themes—the recognition of boundaries in life, the inexplicable nature of the irrational, the difficulty of communication between individuals, the contrary pulls on the individual exerted by his personal isolation and his awareness of his duty to fulfill social obligations, the fear which comes from the realization of aloneness, the presence of natural and metaphysical barriers that diminish personal actions and aspirations, and the saving quality of mind that makes existence possible by its ability to reconcile the contraries which the individual must recognize as an essential quality of existence.[21]

Frost's insights usually are about the fundamental differences between various realities. Physical nature is in flux, and it is controlled by physical laws, the chief of which is the Second Law of Thermodynamics.[22] Human nature, while influenced by its physical being, is dominated by emotion, will, and a desire for order and pattern. Thus human nature cannot be rationally explained. The supernatural is guided by laws known only to itself, laws which both man and nature must accept. Although Frost concentrates on human nature and physical nature in his poetry, he frequently makes references and allusions to the inscrutable nature of God. Thompson reports that Frost "could and did believe in God, even know God, and yet not know (or at least not understand, even while accepting) the inscrutable benevolence implicit in God's causing-designing-ordering" (*Triumph*, 600). Frost's religious belief was not based on rational grounds; rather it resembles the Jamesian will to believe described by Unamuno: "Faith is in its essence simply a matter of will, not of reason; . . . to believe is to wish to believe, and to believe in God is, before all and above all, to wish that there may be a God." [23] This faith is most clearly illustrated in *A Masque of Reason* where not only faith but all human understanding of the realities of nature, man and God depend upon the ability of the mind to grasp imaginatively realities which it cannot understand rationally.

Frost's poetry is also the record of his search for a principle that would unify divergent zones of reality, and even though he usually looks to physical and human nature for a vantage point, the views they provide are enigmatic because he never fully accepts the surface meaning of either. Physical nature is as mysterious in Frost's poetry as it is in Schopenhauer's *The World as Idea and Representation*: its presence dominates the poems, but it is never completely recognizable or accessible to the observer or speaker; Frost sees its objective surface, but he repeatedly suggests that what he sees is a mask concealing some inexplicable force. The poetry indicates his agreement with Schopenhauer's statement, "About *himself* everyone knows directly, about everything else only very indirectly. This is the fact and the problem." [24]

This question of what lies behind the mask of nature is recurrent in Frost's poetry. Although Frost rejects the idea of a transcendental doctrine of correspondences, he frequently implies that such a correspondence might exist if one could see behind the mask. This sense of possibility comes through most strongly in "For Once, Then, Something," in which the speaker, looking into a well, says,

> I discerned, as I thought, beyond the picture,
> Through the picture, a something white, uncertain,
> Something more of the depths—and then I lost it.

Yet the presence suggests more than just a flash of white, and as the poem ends he asks,

>   What was that whiteness?
>   Truth? A pebble of quartz? For once, then, something.

This question, of course, is never answered. As Frost writes in "A Passing Glimpse,"

> Heaven gives its glimpses only to those
> Not in position to look too close.

But there is always the fear that the answer, the governing significance, might be just beyond his line of vision, so always is the search and the maddening suspicion that is voiced in "The Secret Sits:"

> We dance round in a ring and suppose,
> But the Secret sits in the middle and knows.

Frost continues the search for a governing pattern because he recognizes differences between the realities of physical and human nature.

Although Frost does not conclude that order exists in physical nature, he is sure that order could exist in human nature, if only in the individual mind. He wrote in a letter to *The Amherst Student*, "the background is hugeness and confusion shading away from where we stand into black and utter chaos. . . . To me any little form I assert upon it is velvet, as the saying is, and to be considered for how much more it is than nothing" (*Letters*, 419).

The movement in Frost's poetry often leads to the discovery of some semblance of order evolving from an observation of co-existing realities; the reader is made aware of a perspective from which he can see both the chaos and the order, and this moment distinguishes physical from human nature. Frost says of poetry, "Every poem is an epitome of the great predicament; a figure of the will braving alien entanglements." [25] A poem is not external, a picture of the physical world, but internal, the result of a personality's interaction with the chaos of physical reality. Although the "other" exists as a separate reality, it is meaningless until the individual gains an insight into how he might interact with it. His actions reflect the human sense of order and will, and they are not directed by a higher power which coordinates a harmonious balance between the human and the nonhuman.

Frost's discoveries are of new perspectives on reality, and as these reflect the quality of his artistic vision, they are not consistent. Frost constantly shifts, never choosing one view as having primacy over any other; to do so would indicate either that he understands what is behind the mask of physical nature or that he understands God's will. The consistency of his vision comes from the flexibility of his mind as he attempts to make order out of the facts he sees but does not fully understand. The speaker in his poems is usually placed in a position where he can, if he desires, make a choice; but since the exact nature of reality is always unknown, he usually refuses. Frost repeatedly makes the point that choices should never be rigidly made nor rigidly conformed to. His poems demonstrate the way different perspectives can alter the circumstances determining the choices available in any situation, an idea central to "The Strong Are Saying Nothing:"

> Wind goes from farm to farm in wave on wave,
> But carries no cry of what is hoped to be.
> There may be little or much beyond the grave,
> But the strong are saying nothing until they see.

The facts of physical nature influence decisions, especially in how the viewer reacts to these facts. In the poem "Leaves Compared with Flowers," Frost says,

> I bade men tell me which in brief,
> Which is fairer, flower or leaf.

> They did not have the wit to say,
> Leaves by night and flowers by day.

Throughout Frost's poems, this indecision, the inability accurately to grasp reality, is the dilemma of existence. Man is trapped by the range of his senses and the intensity of his passions, yet he must act as if he knew the exact breadth and depth of each. Frost comments upon this dilemma in "The Bear:"

> Man acts more like the poor bear in a cage,
> That all day fights a nervous inward rage,
> His mood rejecting all his mind suggests.
> He paces back and forth and never rests
> The toenail click and shuffle of his feet,
> The telescope at one end of his beat,
> And at the other end the microscope,
> Two instruments of nearly equal hope,
> And in conjunction giving quite a spread.
> Or if he rests from scientific tread,
> 'Tis only to sit back and sway his head
> Through ninety-odd degrees of arc, it seems,
> Between two metaphysical extremes.

This condition, as uncertain as it is, remains the only one by which human nature can assert its separateness from the chaos of physical nature.

In several of his best poems Frost presents characters who are unable to establish a balanced point of view, and these characters, as we might expect, are doomed. In "A Servant to Servants" the speaker is frozen to one vision of reality that is slowly driving her mad; she realizes that this madness results from her rigidity, but she also realizes that she lacks the will to break the frozen pattern that is destroying her sanity. Her opposite, the Hill Wife, is unable to find any object upon which she can focus. Since she lacks the will to force a particular view on reality, her life becomes more and more disorderly and chaotic until she gives herself over completely to the natural process of decay. At the death of the child on whom they have too narrowly concentrated, the couple in "Home Burial" lose whatever unity they had. There is more than the child's death in this poem; the parents too die when their romantic and spiritual love dies as each fails to consider the other's view of the event. In his numerous revisions and treatments of this theme of limited viewpoints, Frost always seems to indicate both that the only safe position is one balanced between rigidity and chaos and that survival depends upon choice. To choose wisely man must be aware of the reality of his situation from as many different points of view as possible, and from his awareness he gains a measure of control over his decisions and actions. This Promethean knowledge lies at the heart of the constant revision and juxtaposition that is fundamental to Frost's art.

Frost's chief aesthetic problem was how to order the expression of subjective experience without forcing a pattern on a world which would not conform to a pattern. Although he was aware of the chasm between subject and object and the problem of ordering experience to reveal coherence, Frost never gives any indication that he doubted the separate reality of external objects and events. He could never agree with Stevens' subjective position that reality is totally in the mind of the observer. Frost's poetry concentrates upon the role of the observer and the observer's reaction. As William Mulder has pointed out, two principles are always at work in a Frost poem, "pressure from within and ... pressure from without." [26] It is this pressure which gives form to Frost's poetry.

Because he did not hold to a single governing principle, Frost has been accused of not taking his art seriously. Nitchie, for instance, writes that "Frost is not really serious about his poetry and the convictions it embodies, and that unseriousness is not simply a matter of habitual irony and whimsical jocularity; rather it is a matter of refusing to recognize certain kinds of difficulty—the difficulty of sticking to things deliberately rather than collecting them like burrs, the difficulty of making 'stylistic arrangements of experience' out of one's perceptions of order, the difficulty of holding reality and justice in a single thought" (Values, 211). This is not exactly the case; it is precisely because he took existence seriously that Frost refused to cheapen it by accepting a principle which would shape his vision stylistically or make it easier for him to write poetry; for Frost's view of man is axiomatically that the rigid life is not worth living and that therefore the poem written by formula is not worth writing.

In one sense, however, Nitchie's comment is correct: Frost did not write from a preconceived pattern or design, nor did such a design evolve as he worked at his art. His whole concern is with vision—to broaden his scope of external and internal reality to include as many different points of view as possible. This concern helps to explain the numerous poems dealing with revised points of view. Frost, much like Henry James, another writer concerned with a just presentation of external and internal reality, frequently uses a revision of his own or another writer's point of view as the main idea in a poem. "I take it," he said, "that everybody has the prejudice and spends some time feeling for it to speak and write from. But most people end as they begin by acting out the prejudices of other people" (*Triumph*, 358). Frost's awareness of the necessity of understanding one's own and another's view of reality in order to write was shared by another poet of this period, William Butler Yeats, who writes, "In our time we are agreed that we make our souls out of some one of the great poets of ancient times, or out of Shelley or Wordsworth, or Goethe or Balzac, or Flaubert, or Count Tolstoy . . . or out of Whistler's pictures. . . . So created, the poet moves on 'to make and unmake reality and to make the truth.' " [27]

The "making and unmaking of reality" is a problem of perspective and revision. Frost is, as Reginald Cook points out, "a poet of perspective. Viewing things in perspective is thematically developed from *A Boy's Will* through *Steeple Bush*, each successive volume containing poems that reflect the new twist he gives his theme." [28] Frost often speaks of the necessity of gaining a perspective, and at one point he hints that this is the central problem of existence: "Our lives are an attempt to find out where we are standing between extremes of viewpoint" (*Triumph*, 418). The balanced view away from the flux of life was a preoccupation Frost shared with James, Woolf, Lawrence, and Joyce, other writers of his generation.[29] The quiet center that allows a perspective and a sense of unification and wholeness is one of the most widespread themes of early twentieth-century literature; and throughout Frost's poems this theme is re-flected in the focal points which allow for a partial view into an-other zone of reality, as illustrated by the gap in "Mending Wall." Frost does not have a given center or a governing significance; rath-er he establishes a juxtaposition between points of view that are contained within the perspective the searcher finds at this still point. He said, ". . . we are given this speed swifter than any stream of light time or water for the sole purpose of standing still like a water beetle in any stream of light time or water off any shore we please" (*Tri-umph*, 304).

Frost uses the principle of juxtaposition to demonstrate the exis-tence of these quiet centers. The basic idea behind this principle is that no object by itself has either definable location or movement.[30] Two objects are required before either can be seen in a proper per-spective. As the Gestalt psychologists have pointed out, whenever one sees, psychologically, physiologically or metaphysically, the object observed is in a context with, or beside, or against other ob-jects. Objects are seen in clusters, framed by other objects which define the zone of the observed object's reality. Poetry for Frost releases its meaning by the juxtaposition of these realities. "Life," he said, "sways perilously at the confluence of opposing forces. Poetry in general plays perilously in the same wild place. In partic-ular it plays perilously between truth and make-believe" (*Letters*, 467). This sway is between the pressure of the objective fact and the pressure of the subjective view one takes of that fact.

Perhaps the most obvious observation about a Frost poem is that it rarely resolves a conflict or reveals a general truth; what the poem will do, however, is clearly define both an objective and a subjective view of reality contained within one dramatic situation. Frost does not offer a new structure for organizing reality, but he does offer the possibility for a view of the physical, emotional, and intellectual facts and associations that compose a single heightened view of real-ity. "The meaning in Frost's poetry," according to Reginald Cook, "derives less from juxtaposing a modern complex world with a simple primitive one than it does from a pursuit of a particular fact until it suggests a general truth." [31] The limited suggestion of a gen-eral truth is all one can find in a Frost poem. He said about his view of poetry and reality, "If I must be classified as a poet, I might be called a Synedochist, for I prefer the synecdoche in poetry—that figure of speech in which we use a part for the whole" (*Triumph*, 485). Yet, this part is meaningless unless it can be associated with another view that will place it in a larger context. "The essential . . . is only reached by striking a balance" (*Triumph*, 433).

It is the balanced view resulting from a juxtaposition of realities that establishes the dominant tone in Frost's poetry. Frost maintained that "Having ideas that are neither pro nor con is the happy thing. Get up there high enough and the differences that make controversy become only the two legs of a body the weight of which is on one in one period, on the other in the next. . . . It is not so much anti-conflict as it is something beyond conflict . . ." (*Letters*, 324–25).

How Frost embodies "something beyond conflict" in his poetry is illustrated in "The Black Cottage" where the minister's monologue on the truth holds both the objective and the subjective attitudes in balance, implying that neither view is the proper one:

> For, dear me, why abandon a belief
> Merely because it ceases to be true.
> Cling to it long enough, and not a doubt
> It will turn true again, for so it goes.
> Most of the change we think we see in life
> Is due to truths being in and out of favor.

This quotation contains two possible ways of looking at the truth: first, truth is permanent, and one can always find it by looking beyond immediate desires; also, truth is bipartite—a combination of objective and subjective—which would mean that the truth cannot be known. Neither view is rejected or accepted; the views are juxtaposed. Even though one can be sure only of the truth of feelings, these feelings might be the reflection of the truth in the situation.

The only way an individual has to judge between these two approaches is to gain a vantage point from which he can see them in perspective. Frost's letters contain many references to his need for distance before he could appraise a situation: "I practically had to wait till I had grown into another person so I could see the problem presented with the eyes of an outsider" (*Letters*, 350–51); "I never saw *New* England as clearly as when I was in Old England" (*Letters*, 160). For the most part, Frost's poems are metaphors which suggest a dual meaning, the truth of the emotion they arouse and the objective fact of the situation they present; both inner and outer realities combine in a single heightened reality that contains both positions. For a Frost poem these two elements always exist. The truth lies somewhere between these two positions, never to be fully contained in the poem itself, but to be localized by the juxtaposition of the points of view.

Frost has several distinct ways of using this principle in his poetry. The most usual method is through the juxtaposition of co-existing realities, as in "Mending Wall" where the presence of the supernatural "Elves" heightens the juxtaposition of physical nature and human nature. Frost juxtaposes attitudes or beliefs, as in the various political, social, and intellectual attitudes which make up such poems as "New Hampshire" and "Build Soil," in order to reveal that each position contains only a portion of a truth and that this portion can be grasped fully only by recognizing the validity of all opposing opinions. A single heightened reality can exert a pull on an individual to make a choice, as in "Stopping by Woods on a Snowy Evening," in which the vague last stanza refuses to clarify whether the speaker's refusal to enter the woods is caused by his acceptance of social obligations, by the negative reaction he has to the presence of physical nature or by his refusal to accept the temptation to return to the flux of physical nature.

Frost's poems fit into thematic groups in only the most superficial way. Reading his collected works is like going on a tour with a stereoscope. Each poem is a still that gives a brief glimpse of the difficulty of discerning the truth in co-existing realities, and each contains the tension between these two positions. Frost believes that all truth contains contraries; the truth cannot be known, but it can be localized in a perspective that contains rather than synthesizes the separateness of opposing points of view.

Such containment has received praise as Frost's chief poetic strength. James M. Cox says, "This cautious refusal to declaim too far or too soon, while it may leave too much unsaid or enclose the issue in a blurred dual vision which accepts both sides, is often one of Frost's most effective modes of self awareness." [32] This dual vision may be Frost's controlling poetic device: Herbert R. Coursen, Jr. contends that "Frost's poetry neither accepts nor rejects the antithesis of involvement and withdrawal; it does *both*, thus indicating that the blending of opposing views is for Frost a key to life." [33] Finally, Reginald L. Cook sees this containment as Frost's most distinctively American trait because when "he speculates on the realities of the world, he doesn't try to reform the world." [34]

The principle of juxtaposition helps to explain the manner in which Frost uses these opposed points of view to heighten his presentation of reality and to achieve his distinct artistic vision. He forces the reader's imagination to work in a fashion similar to the way his eyes function. To juxtapose something is meaningless unless the juxtaposed object is combined with another object offering the original in perspective. The mind, like the eyes, grasps concepts framed by one another. The realities of the situations presented in the poems converge in the reader's mind and produce a new, heightened reality that contains but does not obliterate those contraries which compose it.

This heightening of reality through imaginative perspective appears in such poems as "Tree at My Window" with its emphasis on "inner and outer weather" and in the pair of poems "Birches" and "Wild Grapes," which reverse similar situations. It is the juxtaposed interpretations of facts that reveal Frost's modernity. He did not write in the fragmented forms of other modernist poets, even though he recognized as well as they that the realities of existence are not continuous. Rather, his coherent sequential structure suggests that art's greatest worth is in its demonstration that one can create an understandable order even if one cannot completely understand the informing principles of this order.

Frost's letters and poems continually probe the disparity between a universal knowledge and a knowledge perceivable through the senses. The poems especially reveal a preoccupation with the idea of a Faustian search for the key that will reveal the importance of life and also the flexibility necessary if one is to see the revelatory sign when it might be given. Realizing the necessity for this flexibility distinguishes Frost from other modern and postmodern writers who did not conceive that such a sign is, or ever was, coming. Frost never completely rejects the possibility of a connection between the outer and the inner life. Unlike Pound, Yeats, and finally Eliot, writers of a single vision, Frost's position seems to have been that if one could change his point of view often enough one could finally acquire the knowledge that would obviate change. For this reason Frost demonstrates a great capacity, perhaps greater than any other modern poet's, to reveal to his readers how various perspectives, frequently contradictory, are viable as points of view even if they do not provide an absolute method for understanding existence.

Numerous critics have pointed out that American literature is informed with the metaphors of a "lost Eden," or the "American Adam," or "the American Dream." Nitchie says, "Frost has grafted the healthy Eden myth upon the sometimes dull and jaded life of grey New England" (*Values*, 107–108). Such assertions have been made of so many writers in so many contexts that one hesitates to ask if they are equally true of all American literature, especially of modern literature. Although these themes are found in Frost's poetry, it is not obvious that any one or all three are helpful in discussing the significance of his poetry.

Frost belongs to his time, and a clearer understanding of his achievement results if he is looked upon as a participant in the major transformation taking place in the imaginative orientation to the world during the last few years of the nineteenth century and the early years of the twentieth century. Along with many other writers and artists of this time, he was searching for a way to overcome uncertainty and to create art without relying on fixity and absolutes. Frost's poetic value is that he points out how to contain uncertainty, how to live with it, and finally how to use it as a basis for art.

Frost is a modern poet concerned with the same problems of self, identity, the regenerating power of art, and the need for a basis for action that concern Eliot or Yeats. Frost wrote as a result of his individual reaction to the world around him, not because he was inspired by the memory of a lost Eden, not because he expected to create a new Utopia, but because he lived in a world which forced him to create his own verities. These nineteenth-century metaphors have little value in helping a reader make an assessment of Frost's art. However, the tenuous connection between the various zones that compose his view of reality and the vantage points he presents so that the creative imagination can grasp the reality of these zones do have significance. Frost, as much as any other twentieth-century writer, realized that a loss of certitude led to fragmentation; but he, unlike many of his contemporaries, points out how a juxtaposition of the various views the artist takes of reality might provide a basis for significant human action. Ultimately, one must conclude that Robert Frost is a major twentieth-century artist.

Notes to *Robert Frost: An Assessment of Criticism, Realism, and Modernity* by REXFORD STAMPER

1. Granville Hicks, "The World of Robert Frost," *New Republic*, December 3, 1930, p. 78.

2. William Rose Benét, "Wise Old Woodchuck," *Saturday Review of Literature*, May 30, 1936, p. 6.

3. R. P. Blackmur, "The Instincts of a Bard," *Nation*, June 24, 1936, p. 818.

4. Lionel Trilling, "A Speech on Robert Frost: A Cultural Episode," *Partisan Review*, XXVI (1959), 445–52.

5. For a summary of the positions taken by Adams, Trilling, or both see M. L. Rosenthal, "The Robert Frost Controversy," *Nation*, June 20, 1959, pp. 559–61; Lloyd N. Dendinger, "Robert Frost: The Popular and the Central Poetic Images," *American Quarterly*, XXI (1969), 800.

6. George W. Nitchie, *Human Values in the Poetry of Robert Frost: A Study of a Poet's Convictions* (Durham: Duke University Press, 1960), 12. Future references appear in the text as *Values*.

7. Yvor Winters, "Robert Frost: or, The Spiritual Drifter as Poet," *Sewanee Review*, LVI (1948), 568.

8. I have accepted, except where noted, the observations concerning Frost's artistry made by the following readers of his poetry: Randall Jarrell, "To the Laodiceans," in *Robert Frost: A Collection of Critical Essays*, ed. James M. Cox (Englewood Cliffs, New Jersey: Prentice-Hall, 1962), 83–104; James M. Cox, "Robert Frost and the Edge of the Clearing," *Virginia Quarterly Review*, XXXV (1959), 78–83; Nina Baym, "An Approach to Robert Frost's Nature Poetry," *American Quarterly*, XVII (1965), 713–23; Robert H. Swennes, "Man and Wife: The Dialogue of Contraries in Robert Frost's Poetry," *American Literature*, XLII (1970), 363–72; Reginald L. Cook, "Robert Frost's Constellated Sky," *Western Humanities Review*, XXII (1968), 189–98; Roy Harvey Pearce, "Frost's Momentary Stay," *Kenyon Review*, XXIII (1961), 258–73; Harry Berger, Jr., "Poetry as Revision: Interpreting Robert Frost," *Criticism*, X (1968), 1–23; and John F. Lynen, *The Pastoral Art of Robert Frost* (New Haven: Yale University Press, 1960).

9. For a good example of how these two ideas can be used for the analysis of Frost's poetry see Lewis W. Barnes, "Robert Frost: Reconciliation through Expectancy, Surprise, and Congruency," *Xavier University Studies*, I (1962), 223–37.

10. Lawrance Thompson, *Robert Frost: The Years of Triumph: 1915–1938* (New York: Holt, Rinehart and Winston, 1970), 77. Future references appear in the text as *Triumph*.

11. *Selected Letters of Robert Frost*, ed. Lawrance Thompson (New York: Holt, Rinehart and Winston, 1964), 343. Future references appear in the text as *Letters*.

12. Joseph Conrad, "Novel as World," in *The Theory of the Novel*, ed. Philip Stevick (New York: Collier-Macmillan, 1967), 29.

13. E. M. Forster, "What I Believe," in *Two Cheers for Democracy* (New York: Harcourt, Brace and World, 1951), 71.

14. Studies which consider the theme of separate zones in Frost's poetry are Marion Montgomery, "Robert Frost and His Use of Barriers: Man *vs* Nature Toward God," *South Atlantic Quarterly*, LVII (1958), 339–53; Nina Baym, "An Approach to Robert Frost's Nature Poetry," *American Quarterly*, XVII (1965), 713–23; Swennes, "Man and Wife: The Dialogue of Contraries in Robert Frost's Poetry"; and George W. Nitchie, *Human Values in the Poetry of Robert Frost: A Study of a Poet's Convictions* (Durham: Duke University Press, 1960), 49 ff. and *passim*.

15. Ralph Waldo Emerson, "Self-Reliance," in *Selected Writings of Ralph Waldo Emerson*, ed. William H. Gilman (New York: The New American Library, 1965), 258.

16. Lawrance Thompson, *Robert Frost: The Early Years, 1874–1915* (New York: Holt, Rinehart and Winston, 1966), 90–92; and *Triumph*, 528–32.

17. See John A. Lester, Jr., *Journey Through Despair: 1880–1914* (Princeton: Princeton University Press, 1968) for an excellent account of changes in intellectual attitudes current during Frost's formative years.

18. Henry Adams, *The Education of Henry Adams: An Autobiography* (Boston: Houghton Mifflin, 1961), 450.

19. Montgomery, "Robert Frost and His Use of Barriers," 342.

20. Clark Griffith, "Frost and the American View of Nature," *American Quarterly*, XX (1968), 22.

21. Good studies treating themes in Frost's poetry are John T. Ogilvie, "From Woods to Stars: A Pattern of Imagery in Robert Frost's Poetry," *South Atlantic Quarterly*, LVIII (1959), 64–76; Carlos Baker, "Frost on the Pumpkin," *Georgia Review*, II (1957), 117–31; Swennes, "Man and Wife: The Dialogue of Contraries in Robert Frost's Poetry"; and Radcliffe Squires, *The Major Themes of Robert Frost* (Ann Arbor: The University of Michigan Press, 1963).

22. Baym, "An Approach to Robert Frost's Nature Poetry"; and Berger, "Poetry as Revision: Interpreting Robert Frost," consider in detail the application of the Second Law of Thermodynamics in Frost's poetry.

23. Miguel de Unamuno, *Tragic Sense of Life*, trans. J. E. Crawford Flitch (New York: Dover, 1954), 114.

24. Arthur Schopenhauer, *The World as Will and Representation*, trans. E. F. J. Payne (New York: Dover, 1958), II, 192.

25. Robert Frost, "The Constant Symbol," *Atlantic Monthly*, October, 1946, p. 50.

26. William Mulder, "Freedom and Form: Robert Frost's Double Discipline," *South Atlantic Quarterly*, LIV (1955), 387.

27. William Butler Yeats, "William Blake and the Imagination," in *Essays and Introductions* (New York: Macmillan, 1961), 111.

28. Reginald L. Cook, "The Stand of Robert Frost, Early and Late," *The English Journal*, XLVIII (1959), 237.

29. An excellent study of the pervasiveness of this theme in modern literature is Ethel F. Cornwell's *The "Still Point," Theme and Variations in the Writings of T. S. Eliot, Coleridge, Yeats, Henry James, Virginia Woolf, and D. H. Lawrence* (New Brunswick, N.J.: Rutgers University Press, 1962), especially pp. 3–14.

30. Roger Shattuck, *Proust's Binoculars: A Study of Memory, Time, and Recognition in A la Recherche du Temps perdu* (New York: Random House, 1963) gives a good account of how the principle of juxtaposition applies to the study of literature and the workings of the creative imagination.

31. Cook, "Robert Frost's Constellated Sky," 190.

32. Cox, "Robert Frost and the Edge of the Clearing," 76.

33. Herbert R. Coursen, Jr., "A Dramatic Necessity: The Poetry of Robert Frost," *Bucknell Review*, X (1961–62), 138.

34. Cook, "Robert Frost's Constellated Sky," 191.

NATURE

One theory might claim that Frost's main themes are the trinity of
Nature, Man and Deity and that physical nature appears to be the
dominant theme among the three. Frost might ultimately have used
"Nature" to include all creation. Frost was a remarkable observer
of all aspects of Nature, from flowers to stars. A remark that he was
"wise" in Nature's ways he might have considered a compliment. His
knowledge consisted in great part of an awareness of the diversity
and complexity of Nature, however, with the result that his views
are realistically ambiguous rather than consistent. And he appears
to have felt the ultimate mystery that lay beneath whatever knowledge men might have. Such a respect for ignorance was perhaps as
devout a definition of Deity as Man could devise.

Samuel Coale discusses Frost's concepts of Nature, to conclude
that only in "Stopping by Woods ..." was Frost's approach that
of the Romantic who found himself in some kind of metaphysical
unity with Nature. Professor Coale's observations may lead to the
inference that Frost viewed natural objects as signs of the miracle
and mystery in the creative process of Nature, somewhat as the
Puritans, following Plato, developed a concept of "typology," by
means of which natural objects signified the existence of the supra-
natural.

Margaret Edwards discusses Frost's various approaches to Nature
and suggests that if the poet ever asked what might yet be said of
Pan's wild domain, after the exhaustive efforts of the Romantic poets
and the investigations of modern science, he found the subject still
poetic. If Nature appeared to be the "diminished thing," or if Man
and Nature often appeared to be in conflict, the conflict itself was
resolved in a general harmony that somehow obtains above the apparent contradictions.

Albert von Frank concentrates on "Desert Places" to conclude that the poem deals with a "form of the romantic concept of the analogy between man and nature." Comparisons may be made with other essays herein that interpret the poem and with the observations of Professors Coale and Edwards on the poet's relationship to Nature.

Robert Rechnitz also analyzes Frost's diverse views of the relationship between Man and Nature, to conclude that while Man may be a "diminished thing," he must be manly and spermatic in his performance. Professor Rechnitz finds that Frost's sense of the relationship is such as to be called a sense of the tragic.

The numerous points of view in both Frost and his critics is, rather than evidence of contradiction or confusion, a clear indication that the subject still offers a great deal of poetic material. While Frost may have been very wise in Nature's ways, as both an intelligent observer and an investigator, he found that a richly poetic mystery underlay all one's attempts to explain what Nature was. It was this sense of mystery perhaps that made poetry possible.

The question of Frost's relationship to the poetry of Romanticism links Charles Carmichael's paper with the others in this section, though a glance at the contents of the paper will indicate that it concentrates on the man and poet rather than on the themes. Professor Carmichael writes of Frost within the framework of Morse Peckham's theories of the Romantic poet and the course of lyric poetry since the Romantics. The accumulation of biographical materials has raised the question of Frost's poses and his concepts of himself, and Professor Carmichael's paper provides a theory for those interested in the biography of the poet.

D. B.

The Emblematic Encounter of Robert Frost

SAMUEL COALE

As a poet and as a man Robert Frost has always been too easily associated with the New England landscape. Such an obvious and public association has long obscured the poet's true relationship with nature's landscape, all too easily confusing what we shall call his "emblematic encounter" with nature with Wordsworth's themes of nostalgic loss and recollection in tranquility. Frost's encounter with the landscape is both more realistic and less tragic than Wordsworth's, more a true mutual confrontation of separate "selves" in a moment of equilibrium than a picturesque union of childhood, memory and age. Frost's own theory of emblemism, which we shall separate as he does from the more humanistic aspects of symbolism, carefully and systematically reveals the nature of his poetic stance.

From Wordsworth to Emerson

R. L. Cook quotes Frost as saying "literature begins with geography," and "the land is always in my bones," [1] but Frost's relationship to that geography and land has often been obscured. Wylie Sypher, in his provocative *Rococo to Cubism in Art and Literature*, clearly establishes that, from the Wordsworthian point of view, landscape reflected, or was the symbol of, the state of the poet's soul. Each natural object became an image of the poet's own consciousness, a reflection of his mood. This view became the "psychological picturesque" [2] in romantic art, a way of seeing nature as the sympathetic mirror of the poet's emotions. Aligned with this view was the Wordsworthian notion of time's passing, that as man grew older the natural objects reminded him most vividly of his early relationship with them in the keen "unconscious" state of youth where object and man seemed divinely unified in a state of grace. Each natural object, therefore, became for Wordsworth an acknowledgment of this past union, a comment upon the inadequacy of the present moment. Landscape conspired with time to create that overwhelming sense of romantic loss which could be overcome only momentarily in carefully restored memories. That solace of memory may have urged John Ruskin to exclaim that "true picturesqueness appears in ruins only," suggesting to Sypher that the picturesque may finally be defined as "a reminiscent imagining."

"Birches" is perhaps Frost's most Wordsworthian poem, in which he chooses to think "some boy's been swinging them" in the face of natural evidence to the contrary, and then identifies himself clearly with that lost youthful exercise—"So was I once myself a swinger of birches./And so I dream of going back to be." Yet, the poet, realizing the consequences, thoroughly dissociates himself from notions of escape—"May no fate willfully misunderstand me." He recognizes the reality of nature's ice storm and settles for a halfhearted attempt at Wordsworthian wishful thinking—"One could do worse than be a swinger of birches." In "Nothing Gold Can Stay" he laments the fall of both man and nature and the consequent loss that both suffer, but these poems seem to be exceptions to the general Frostian notion of emblematic encounter.

Frost's poetry does not usually create the picturesque landscape that Wordsworth sought. Frost is far more interested in the present encounter with nature than in recreating a sense of reverie to elude the emptiness of that present. Frost's emphasis on a "stay against confusion" suggests not reverie nor the recollection of past "spots of time" to be illuminated by present emotions and thoughts, but momentary encounter with a natural world at the present moment on the verge of threatening chaos.

In contrast to Emerson's transcendentalism, which has much in common with Wordsworth's romantic theories, Frost does not view nature with or through the Adamic innocent eye of the child. He shares neither Emerson's delight in "the fresh sensation of the child ... as the norm for a valid relation to the universe," nor Emerson's ecstatic faith in such an innocent eye—"Infancy is the perpetual Messiah." Frost has no overwhelming moment of intoxicated revelation.[3] His is a guarded moment, a stay *against* confusion, for he identifies not with the onrush of transcendental vision, not with the process of on-going prophecy, but with the steadfastness of the star. In "Take Something Like a Star" he writes:

It asks of us a certain height,
So when at times the mob is swayed
To carry praise or blame too far,
We may take something like a star
To stay our minds on and be staid.

To "be staid" suggests a position far from Emerson's intoxicating union of the slayer and the slain where process and poet are divinely one and the same. If Emerson struggles to see with a child's eye newly to prophesy a new world reborn, Frost offers to gaze with a seasoned eye firmly fixed on the natural object, respecting its boundaries and limitations, sensing its affinities with some eternal vision or struggle, but himself prophesying nothing.

Emerson identifies with the transcendent and on-going process of vision, most clearly seen in Whitman's poetry in which the poet and the natural world he beholds become divinely inseparable, but Frost rejects the idea. In Frost's poetry the speaker goes forth, reminiscent at first of the manner of the more transcendental poets, but he goes forth in order to return to his starting point: "They would not find me changed from him they knew—/Only more sure of all I thought was true." To steal away "into my own" is in reality to test the outer limits of his vision and to return to a state of equilibrium which exists within those limits set by the objective reality, the unpersonified reality, of the natural world. Thus motion in Frost's poetry is used not to suggest the ultimate union of poet and nature but to define and circumscribe that point of equilibrium at which the poet remains steadfast. Frost mends the wall to keep things as they are, to restore the equilibrium, however fragile, between man and nature. Nature, spared man's self-consciousness and self-awareness, appears to man as both movement and permanence, as the infinite and the finite in a moment in time: nature can be eternally momentary. Man, however, in Frost's view, can hope to be only momentarily eternal, can hope only to "catch up" and meet nature at that precious point of equilibrium, that momentary stay against confusion, which in fact is the poem itself. Instead of reflecting Emerson's symbol of the spirit, Nature embodies Frost's realization of that spirit's limitations and remains forever beyond man's attempts to comprehend it, except in the momentary instances of poetry-making itself. Only in

"Stopping by Woods on a Snowy Evening" (see below) does Frost achieve a complete moment of suspended reverie, somewhat analogous to Wordsworth's and Emerson's, a point at which the motion of stopping is completed and where Frost stops completely.

Reginald Cook states the case most clearly in observing what these ideas of nature do in fact for Emerson and Frost in their respective approaches to the actual writing of poetry: "While Emerson succeeds in vitalizing, and, in turn being vitalized by an abstraction like the Over-Soul, Frost responds to and vitalizes the fact in human experience." [4] Here, Frost's poetic theory recalls Thoreau for whom "a true account of the actual is the purest poetry." Though temperamentally Frost came in *In The Clearing* to agree more or less with Emerson, his poetic stance of the earlier and best poetry is far from the positive public posturing of the worldly-wise, crackerbarrel New England philosopher-poet that Frost chose to be on the stump. The "public Frost" assuredly helped the man himself to ease his grim but never pessimistic vision and helped in many ways to eradicate that vision in the later and more explicit poetry, but that persona cannot overshadow the significant encounter with nature that is not so much diminished Emerson as it is vintage and "true" Frost. Frost would agree with Emerson, as Lawrance Thompson has pointed out, that "God himself does not speak prose, but communicates with us by hints, omens, inferences and dark resemblances in objects lying all around us." [5] But for Frost these remain significant hints embodied in the concrete presence of the objects themselves and man's encounter with them. Such revelations do not comprise a fully developed metaphysical and symbolic system.

Frost's Approach to Nature

Frost is popularly known as a New England poet because of the images in his poetry—snow scenes, stone walls, country roads, woods, farmhouses—those images most easily associated with the calendar art of Currier and Ives, sentimental scenes of the poor delighting in their romantically nostalgic rusticity. The "public Frost" has long traded on such images. Like Mark Twain with his boyhood Mississippi, Frost publicly has associated himself with the simpler New England, his public image blurring the bleaker truths that

North of Boston displayed. Yet Frost did not use such "sentimental" images sentimentally. Beneath the positively assertive "thrust" of his poetry—"The Vantage Point," "The Road Not Taken," "Revelation," "The Tuft of Flowers"—and the popular nostalgia-tinged images of that poetry, Frost expressed a reality less certain and assuredly less popular. The "ulteriority" of his poetry discloses a more bleakly realistic encounter with his world. Often in his remarks, he dissociated himself from the very images he was using in his poetry, avowing that his method was far different from his popularly conceived form. Thompson quotes: "... there is nothing but me. And I have all the dead New England things held back by one hand ... where, many as they are, though, they do not flow together by their own weight.... I hold them easily—too easily for assurance that they will go with a rush when I let them go" (p. 114).

Given his own boyhood experiences, his dislike for the urban experience, and his emphasis upon human survival and renewal, Frost has always associated the best poetry with the rural scene. Thompson quotes further:

> Poetry is more often of the country than of the city. Poetry is very, very rural—rustic. It stands as a reminder of rural life—as a resource—as a recourse. It might be taken as a symbol of a man, taking its rise from individuality and seclusion.... We are now at a moment when we are getting too far out into the social-industrial, and are at the point of drawing back—drawing in to renew ourselves.... (p. 431)

Such a belief finds its natural expression in the New England scene as Frost came to know it and is very much a product of that scene. The "distilled" quality of Frost's verse, his emphasis stylistically on order and restraint in both thought and expression, and his emphasis upon the struggle of the human soul against a bleak, dark background (very much an ethical or "religious" stance) link Frost to the New England mind in American poetry—the ordered stanzas of Emily Dickinson, the natural landscape of Edwin Arlington Robinson, the "iron metres" of Robert Lowell. A distinct rage for order, as Wallace Stevens called it, characterizes the best of Frost's poetry, aware as he was of the dialectical, Manichaean quality of the New England mind, the struggle between order and chaos, light and darkness. He celebrated "any small man-made figure of order and concentration" when viewed against "the background in hugeness and confusion shading away from where we stand into black and utter chaos" as he would celebrate the star "since dark is what brings out your light." The background exists for him unequivocally:

... we were born to it, born used to it and have practical reasons for wanting it there. To me any little form I assert upon it is velvet, as the saying is, and to be considered for how much more it is than nothing.[6]

Frost accepts nature in his poetry as a confirmed objective reality. He does not favor Hopkins' idea of "inscape" in which natural objects are infused with man's own meaning and feelings but favors a landscape whose stubborn reality remains intact and permanent, uninfluenced finally by man, unbounded by his pettier concerns. Thompson quotes him as saying, "Anything you do to the facts falsifies them, but anything the facts do to you—yes, even against your will; yes, resist them with all your strength—transforms them into poetry" (78). Man and nature exist to confront one another, to encounter each other from each other's own "territorial imperative." In Frost's affirmation of separateness exists the vague outline of man's "equality" with nature, though man must finally submit to nature's superior power displayed eventually at his death. Nature remains a permanent "other," impersonally unified beyond man's ability to comprehend it. Man and Nature share some undeclared element of divine force, but each embodies the force independently with as much mutual antagonism as respect. The outcome of such an encounter, though never in doubt since man knows he will die, is never as important as the actual confrontation, the direct action of the encounter itself. Frost's celebration of action—"Mow*ing*," "Mend*ing* Wall," "Stopp*ing* by Woods on a Snowy Evening"—reveals the importance to him of the actual encounter with nature at the point of contact: "The most exciting movement in nature is not progress, advance, but expansion and contraction, the opening and shutting of the eye, the hand, the heart, the mind." [7]

Frost explains that "every poem is an epitome of the great predicament; a figure of the will braving alien entanglements" (SP, 25). He thereby promulgates a survivalist "ethic" similar to those of Hemingway and Stephen Crane who also braved the alien entanglements of nature with a direct action that was somehow akin to a state of grace. In affirming the separateness of man and nature, Frost celebrates that moment of touch which brings each in contact with the other, as in "To Earthward" he suggests: "I long for weight and strength/To feel the earth as rough/To all my length." That immediacy of touch, of action directly taken, reveals both nature's stubborn solidity and man's permanent fascination with that solidity. That moment of touch seems charged, alive to the imagination as if there were some ghost in the stone. "Truth? A pebble of quartz?" Frost asks in "For Once, Then, Something," suggesting that they may be one and the same thing! Since "there are roughly zones whose laws must be obeyed," man's encounter with nature is "the most of it," and Frost celebrates not the natural object's rapid transcendence under the sway and impact of man's own symbolic designs but that object's own stubborn reality that cannot be translated or traduced but that is somehow significant.

Men define their essential existence, their separate identities from nature, in that moment of action, of encounter. Frost seeks no reverie to avoid the present moment, for as he suggests in "Mowing," "The fact is the sweetest dream that labor knows." The whispering of the scythe suggests no more than the sound the scythe makes in laying "the swale in rows." The attempt to discover what more it whispers, what more it may mean, leads only to Frost's idea that anything more than the truth of the present action of mowing "would have seemed too weak," too superficial to match "the earnest love" and the celebration of the act itself. To add too much meaning to the action of the scythe is to take away the meaning, the ultimate mystery of the actual action; transcending the natural fact betrays the totality of that fact. "There is such a thing as getting too transcended. There are limits" (SP, 115), Frost has written. He illuminates the action of the encounter between man and nature and celebrates its sacredness to him.

Similarly in "Mending Wall" the narrator slights the superstitious neighbor for building the wall out of habit and tradition, for not going behind "his father's saying," while the speaker himself never really explains why he is so interested in getting that wall mended: "I have come . . . and made repair"—"I let my neighbor know beyond the hill"—"I could say 'Elves' to him,/But it's not elves exactly." The poem suggests that Frost is aware of nature's power, of that other "frost" that doesn't love the wall, of the power of natural force embodied in the "old-stone savage armed." As a result he pits his own "mending" powers against nature's disruptive powers. He mends the wall not from any love for it but because to mend it is to combat, to counter nature's force. The very mending itself exemplifies that encounter between man and nature, that momentary stay against confusion, cleverly pitting Frost against frost.

Frost's Theory of Emblemism

Frost's poetic theory, which he calls emblemism, reveals how this attitude toward nature has been translated or transmuted into a viable poetic practice: "Symbolism is all too likely to clog up and kill a poem—symbolism can be as bad as an embolism. If my poetry has to have a name, I'd pefer to call it Emblemism—it's the viable emblem of things I'm after." [8] The close relationship between the natural object observed and the viable emblem expressed in his poetry should be obvious. Such a viable emblem he sees in his favorite lines from Poe:

> And the mist upon the hill
> Shadowy—shadowy—yet unbroken,
> Is a symbol and a token—
> How it hangs upon the trees,
> A mystery of mysteries.[9]

The mist in Poe's lines is the token of a deeper mystery, the mystery of the nature of existence itself. Poe has recreated the natural object here in its natural manifestations; no attempt is made to force the object to reflect a mood of the poet, no attempt to humanize and incorporate it into some allegorical mirror of the human soul. It remains a token, an emblem of supreme mystery, and becomes the "something" Frost continually celebrates, a thing unto itself, mysterious in its very presence and "there-ness."

For Frost symbolism suggests human interference with nature, the pathetic fallacy which imposes human definitions and designs upon natural phenomena. The symbolists are too busy personifying nature, casting it in their own shadows, mentally penetrating it to subdue and redesign it. Frost explores the absurd conclusion of such symbolic actions in "Design" where the arrangement of the spider, the moth and the white heal-all seems to suggest the strong possibility of a dark pattern underlying nature's design. Although the terrifying understatement of the final line complements the cosmic chill in the rest of the poem, it also suggests that Frost is clearly dissociating himself from sentimental posturing by undermining the notion of design itself—"If design govern in a thing so small." Design he clearly attributes to symbolist tamperings, Ahab's ego-engulfing illusions, not to nature's own more mysterious presence, though he delights in creating these "assorted characters of death and blight" for "the ingredients of [his] witches' broth."

In "Desert Places" he acknowledges the bleak, snow-white landscape around him but affirms that the real "empty spaces" are within himself. He can scare himself more terribly than any landscape can; thus he breaks away from the notion of Wordsworthian symbolic landscape as represented in "Birches." No landscape can ever reflect the gravity of the mood that is within the speaker, not in nature. His designs are closer to home.

For Frost emblemism boasts no human interference; significance, yes, since nature and man though separate are part of some greater cosmic encounter, but nature's own permanence outlasts any man-made symbolic design upon it. An emblem is like a natural object; in the poetry it represents that natural object and is significant without "symbolic" definition; it is a visible token like Poe's mist whose very existence posits a greater mystery than any symbolist can hope to fathom. To paraphrase M. H. Abrams, the illuminated phenomenal object, or emblem, in Frost's poetry is as opaque as the image of the Imagists and yet as significant of something beyond itself, although not transparently so, as the symbol of the Symbolists. Abrams says, "in both cases, however, the Romantic object is usually cut off from its context in the ordinary world and in common experience and assigned an isolated existence in the self-limited and self-sufficing work of art." That "isolated existence" suggests the emblematic quality of nature in Frost's poetry.

Nature in most of Frost's work is like the mountain in the poem of the same name; it holds man in its shadow as it "stood there to be pointed at." To point, to observe, is to encounter. The man with the cart can elaborate upon old legends of hidden springs and the changing temperature of the water (as the "public Frost" can do so well)—". . . all the fun's in how you say a thing"—but the mountain's sheer presence remains unassailable. In "The Most of It" man's symbolic longing for "counter-love, original response" turns out to be "the embodiment" of a great buck, "and that was all." Frost celebrates the buck's power in its movements: he does not personify it or "symbolize it" into some humanized embodiment of natural benevolence. In "The Wood-Pile" he condemns the bird as "one who takes/Everything said as personal to himself"; then, he considers not the waste of the wood that has been left behind but its natural use "to warm the frozen swamp as best it could/With the slow smokeless burning of decay." The woodpile signifies man's encounter with nature; it becomes the emblem of that encounter and though abandoned becomes for Frost the final emblem of nature's usefulness (however humanly unfulfilling in this instance) and completeness. He suggests not that decay is good but that waste is not utterly bad from a natural point of view.

Perhaps the best example of Frost's theory of emblemism can be seen in the early "Stars." The stars in the poem "congregate" above "our tumultuous snow" as if they were symbols of some more permanent meaning, as if they symbolized a "keenness for our fate." Frost, however, rejects such personification of natural objects, rejects the "symbolism" he describes, and prefers to take the stars *as they are* "with neither love nor hate." They are significant by virtue of their permanence as natural objects, by their very existence and distance from us, but they cannot be symbolically defined or personified; they remain not allegoric or symbolic but in Frost's terms emblematic of man's encounter with the very presence of existence itself, approaching its confusion "with an instrument or tackle it to reduce it. It is partly because we are afraid it might prove too much for us. . . . But it is more because we like it, we were born to it, born used to it . . . " (SP, 107). The stars "congregate," and that action of existence remains itself the mystery of mysteries.

In "An Encounter" Frost presents an ironic example of the emblematic encounter with nature. He comes upon "a resurrected tree . . . a barkless specter" while he is out walking in "a swamp of cedar." He and the tree confront one another as if regarding one another: "He had halted too,/As if for fear of treading upon me." The irony appears when one realizes that Frost is describing a telephone pole "dragging yellow strands/Of wire." The "tree" represents both man and nature as the woodpile did. The speaker has wandered into nature to find only further evidence of man's presence, an ironic encounter but one paralleling the basic pattern of his art.

Frost maintains, "If I must be classified as a poet, I might be called a Synecdochist, for I prefer the synecdoche in poetry—that figure of speech in which we use a part for the whole" (Thompson, 485). He thinks it significant that, "a little thing touches a larger thing" (Thompson, 693), but the significance remains less symbolically defined, far less humanistically oriented, than Emerson or Thoreau would have it, not because Frost is hiding ultimate secrets but because those secrets are implicit in and not separate from the landscape itself. As Cook suggests in his comparison of Frost and Emerson, "Certainly Frost is not smitten with the transcendental ethic that assumes as an axiom a divine sufficiency of man, nor in the application of this ethic to the world of affairs and human institutions."

Frost realizes that nature can overpower man and "win" the encounter hands down; nature will conquer in any case. Such darker explorations of the encounter can easily be seen in "The Fear," "The Draft Horse," "Once By the Pacific," and "An Old Man's Winter Night." Here the alien power of nature is recognized more grimly than before, but in "An Old Man's Winter Night" the tone remains elegiac and skeptical not hysterical or desperate: "It's thus he does it of a winter night." Evil can and does burst forth from "a pitch-dark limitless grove," but finally that very darkness is precious and needed, a part of existence, that background that exists to renew man's lifelong encounter, until death completes the pattern. In "The Literate Farmer and the Planet Venus," he says, " 'We need the interruption of the night/To ease attention off when overtight,/To break our logic in too long a flight,/And ask us if our premises are right.' "

The emblematic encounter between Frost and nature accounts for Frost's insistence that language be "stripped down" to describe that encounter as clearly and as honestly as possible. To Untermeyer, he says, "To me, the thing that art does for life is to clean it, to strip it to form." As Frost encounters nature, so "art should follow lines in nature, like the grain of an axe-handle. False art puts curves on things that haven't any curves" (Thompson, 77). Those curves Frost would associate with his feeling that symbolism interferes with the primary and primal encounter and perhaps makes "frolic architecture" where only snow should be. It follows, as evidenced in *North of Boston*, that Frost would admire the "poetic lifeblood in customary speech" (Untermeyer, 9)—"The common speech is always giving off . . . the special vocabulary of poetry" (Untermeyer, 17)—and that his poetic theories about the "sound of sense" would follow accordingly. In all things Frost meant to "purify" the language by carving it close to the bone, dropping "to an everyday level of diction that even Wordsworth kept above." [10] He insisted that his diction, like the natural objects themselves, should maintain "a stubborn clinging to meaning—to purify words until they meant again what they should mean. Puritanism had that meaning entirely: a purifying of words and a renewal of words and a renewal of meaning. That's what brought the Puritans to America . . ." (Thompson, 483). And we might add that this interest in purity was what brought Frost spiritually to New England and why he remained there always.

For this reason Frost's poetry, like much of Wordsworth's, is extremely free from actual metaphors. The emblematic encounter of man and nature constituted Frost's basic metaphor; it existed *in fact*, in the direct action of the man as poet, not in the creation of symbolic language, those "curves" of "false art." Metaphor existed for Frost not so much in actual figures of speech as in the actual "cutting across" between man and nature and "making a connection in the mind" (Cook, 60). That momentary stay remained itself the perfect metaphor in action. "My motto is that something has to be left to God" (Thompson, 693), Frost said, and perhaps his use of the synecdoche assured just that, a sort of "buried" metaphor in which the concrete object remains visible, an emblem, and the more abstract idea or emotion remains hidden. Such an approach, a kind of "self-restricted actualism" (Cook, 101), focuses the reader's attentions not on the abstract idea but on the actual encounter with the concrete object. To encounter the emblems of nature constituted the primary realm and being of Frost's art.

In emphasizing Frost's realm of encounter I have purposely not concentrated on his humor. That humor aided him constantly in his strategic retreats to "soften" the stark outlines of his art, and his need to do so, to define humor as balance and sanity—"[it is] the good temper of a man in balance. . . . His humor is the inner man surfacing and its origin is in the sanity of the senses" (Cook, 31)—becomes all too clear in Thompson's outstanding biography. The public Frost like the public Twain did indeed soften the harsher aspects of his art by his humor, and perhaps the growth of the "public Frost" in later years served to separate the man psychologically from the darker outlines of those aspects, but it is those aspects which emerge again and again and seem to be the truest focus of his best poetry. It is ironic that Lionel Trilling in 1959 argued for Frost as a dark and "terrifying" poet, and Louis Untermeyer in the 1920's tried to emphasize the light in his poetry, not the publicly perceived dark. The public image of Robert Frost had succeeded all too well; like Whitman he emerged as the "good gray poet" (or perhaps "snowy" is more accurate) in his later years, and the real essence of his art was obscured. He realized what had happened: "the fun only begins with the spirited when you treat the word as a point of many departures. There is risk in the play" (SP, 78). He took the risk willingly and perhaps paid the price.

The Emblem Surpassed: Reverie "By Woods"

Frost admitted that "my best bid for remembrance" (Thompson, 598) would be "Stopping by Woods on a Snowy Evening," and it is ironic that of all the Frost poems we have examined, this is the least "Frost-y." It contains all the "proper" Frost images—snow, woods, darkness, a sleigh—but it is extremely unlike the usual stance of mutual confrontation. Frost advised, "Set yourself against the moon. Resist the moon" (Thompson, 77), but here he has not resisted and has for once slipped into a state of what we may call romantic reverie, a kind of self-hypnosis. Always before, he has resisted the spellbinding, seductive quality of the encounter with nature, placing himself firmly on the far side of his emblems as observer and visitor. In "Into My Own" he wishes that "those dark trees" would stretch away "unto the edge of doom," so that he might enter beyond that boundary line of nature's "territorial imperative" and be unafraid of the possibility of never finding open land, but he guards his impulses carefully with double negatives and the use of the conditional tense. Besides, this is only "one of my wishes." In "The Sound of Trees" he is lured on again "till we lose all measure of pace,/And fixity in our joys,/And acquire a listening air," but he leaves quickly. In "Come In" he resists the luring sound of the thrush "far in the pillared dark" and withdraws into the forest in "A Dream Pang" only to be sought after and pursued: "But 'tis not true that thus I dwelt aloof,/For the wood wakes, and you are here for proof." In "Away!" the longing is identified specifically with "having died."

In "After Apple-Picking," one of the finest poems to explore what might happen *after* the act of encounter, Frost falls asleep, having picked enough apples even if more always remain. The "sleep" mirrors the act of apple-picking and repeats it though in a "magnified" way. Clearly the fact and the dream have merged, and the laborer has trouble trying to tell them apart. Time is suspended as if Frost has become mesmerized by his own actions, and in the poem he tries to understand exactly what this "mesmerization" can be.[11] Is it somewhat like a woodchuck's hibernation, a drift into an "animal sleep" and so part of a natural cycle that assures waking? Is it a prelude to death itself? Or is it "just some human sleep" that has occurred because he's just "overtired"? In either case he has slipped beyond the distinct boundaries of the emblematic encounter with nature into a realm where "magnified apples appear and disappear" and go "surely to the cider-apple heap/As of no worth."

The strangeness of the experience arouses Frost's curiosity, for "essence of winter sleep is on the night," and "I cannot rub the strangeness from my sight." His desire to discover "whatever sleep it is" cannot be fulfilled, and the very form of the poem in its irregular lines is as uncertain as the state of suspension itself. In any event the poem recounts the mysterious state; it does not create or initiate that state itself. Frost is observing what *has* occurred, not what *is* occurring. In the poem itself, he is not involved in or undergoing the entrance to that suspended state.

In "Stopping by Woods on a Snowy Evening" Frost does enter the state of suspended animation within the rhythmic and hypnotic framework of the poem itself; the very rhythmic progression of the poem completely undermines the forward movement implicit in the "promises" in the final stanza, as if the last lines—"And miles to go before I sleep"—in their repetition are a sleepy, final attempt to deny what in fact is already happening. The speaker is stopping, coming to an hypnotic halt; the repetition of the final lines suggests that the poem has come to a full spellbound stop. Frost here has succumbed to that very poetic reverie the emblematic encounter purports to deny, and he does not escape this time. His desire to stop and the scene around him blend inextricably in a form of enchantment or self-hypnosis that often occurs in Coleridge's poems, but unlike Coleridge Frost fails to return to his starting place, however transformed by the thoughts and images expressed in the poem. He is led on into a reverie that is as complete a spell as any in the most romantic of poetry; poetry has become incantation; the art of synecdoche (the stabilizer of the emblematic encounter) has broken down, and we are left immobile and hypnotized by language.

Frost does not wish to be seen in the first stanza, as if he knows that his stopping is somehow the wrong thing to do; he is perhaps feeling some guilt, some sense of foreboding as to the true nature of his giving in to the spell of the woods. "To watch his woods fill up with snow" initiates his reverie. Twice the horse interferes with the gathering spell, first in the poet's thoughts—"My little horse must think it queer"—and secondly in its actions—"He gives his harness bells a shake." The bells awaken the speaker momentarily from the drift of his mood; he acknowledges the interruption as if attempting to rescue himself from the relentless and inevitable direction of the poem itself but acknowledges the interruption only to turn from it—"The only other sound's the sweep/Of easy wind and downy flake." The woods which are filling up in the first stanza are "deep" in the fourth. Once more he attempts to rouse himself to get going —"But I have promises to keep"—but the last two lines assure the victory of reverie, and he has slipped away into some "frozen lake" of some self-hypnotic realm beyond the strict boundaries of his earlier encounters.

Whenever Frost has talked about the poem, he has always emphasized its craft. No one can deny the supreme artistry of the "self-perpetuating" rhyme scheme, what Frost called "my heavy duty poem to be experienced for the rime pairs." We know that despite the legend he did not complete the poem at one stroke, as the early versions of the fourth stanza clearly indicate, but the fact remains that the poem is *experienced* in one full stroke *as a poem*. In celebrating the pure form of the poem, Frost begins to sound like Poe, a self-hypnotic chanter of verses if there ever was one, and Frost suggests that the poem was the product of what he calls "autointoxication."

The idea of enchantment or hypnosis is unusual in Frost's poetry, but he has indicated that he may have been more concerned with such ideas and intuitions than we have previously acknowledged. Frost speaks of the poet as one who "must be entranced to the exact premonition," [12] and for whom "there should be some way to tell ... the excitement of the morning from the autointoxication of midnight" (SP, 51) as if at times he were himself unable to tell the difference. Too, a poem's "most precious quality will remain its having run itself and carried away the poet with it" (SP, 20).

The fact remains that this is the only poem in which Frost is completely carried away with the vision, in which the encounter becomes not a mutual confrontation but a merger of man and nature into a suspended state of complete stasis. Frost was indeed carried away here, for he recognized "the recklessness of the unnecessary commitment I made when I came to the first line in the second stanza. . . . I was riding too high to care what trouble I incurred. And it was all right so long as I didn't suffer deflection" (SP, 26). It is ironic finally that the most un-Frostian poem in the broadest sense has become the star of his collection. "The thing is to get among the poems where they hold each other apart in their places as the stars do" (SP, 97), Frost wrote, but in his most famous poem he celebrates not the ritualistic "holding apart" of the emblematic encounter but a full-bodied, Poesque rite of passage into what appears to be a supreme poetic trance.

The Emblematic Encounter

Frost's emblematic encounter with nature reveals the basic "strategy" of his poetry. He celebrates the physical presence of natural facts and the integrity of action in man's relation to them—"The fact is the sweetest dream that labor knows"—believing that to add too much meaning to them is finally to betray their own elusive and ultimately mysterious solidity, to take away the meaning of the actual encounter. "The Most of It" and "that was all" are one and the same thing. Within the context of a Frost poem each natural fact embodies all potential meaning;[13] it is emblematic of a possible greater meaning, the existence of which we can know only in the thing itself. For Frost Emerson transcended actuality all too easily and finally betrayed its integrity, seeing in it only the narcissistic reflections of his own innocent spirit. Such innocence misleads and betrays; Frost will not abide it. He acknowledges the yearning for transcendence, the desire as expressed in "Directive" to "Drink and be whole again beyond confusion," but he feels that in nature we can only hope to have intimations of a "something" which can be embodied finally only within the natural universe itself.

To embody the emblematic encounter in his poetry, Frost insisted upon "stripping down" language. The closer language approaches the clean lines of this encounter, the better the metaphorical dimensions can be felt: the encounter itself becomes man's metaphorical relationship with the natural world. Since nature cannot maintain this ordered encounter indefinitely, as we can see in "Spring Pools" and "Nothing Gold Can Stay," art must satisfy such longings. Thus the action of the poem, the movement both into nature and into language, sustains the momentary stay against confusion and suggests the possibility of some ultimate reconciliation.

Frost wanted "words that do deeds" (Untermeyer, 38), and in "Stopping By Woods on a Snowy Evening" the deed of stopping is fully realized. In fact the poem in its celebration of a final action, the action of stopping, may be his ultimate achievement as a poet. Looked at in this light the poem illuminates Frost's ultimate encounter with nature where distinct "sides" are no longer distinct, where the final state of grace is a kind of aesthetic completion or death beyond which no encounter is possible. We have reached perhaps that final recognition of truth in nature, a fulfilled interrelationship that can exist only at the moment of the greatest poetic achievement when form becomes all and action stops completely. For Frost this pure celebration of his craft may have been his final intuition of God, although as an orthodox Christian he would always separate God finally from His works whether natural or poetic. Here perhaps he has become his own god.

The final poem from *In The Clearing* best describes that emblematic encounter with nature which Frost, with the remarkable exception of "Stopping By Woods on a Snowy Evening," took to be the raison d'être of his art. As usual he goes "against the trees," his force pitted against nature's own, not in a cosmic struggle for supremacy but in a momentary action that outlines both man and nature against that point of active encounter. As he leaves with his maple cut low, "I link a line of shadowy tracks/Across the tinted snow." He moves across and through nature, his existence "shadowy" yet somehow a "link" with it, a link to some wider, ultimate encounter. Nature has not been defeated "in one tree's overthrow"; nor has man been defeated in his retreat "for yet another blow." Both exist to encounter each other anew, and all that Frost would ask of us is "You come too."

Notes to *The Emblematic Encounter of Robert Frost* by SAMUEL COALE

1. Reginald L. Cook, *The Dimensions of Robert Frost* (New York: Rinehart, 1958), 7, 135. In text as Cook.

2. Wylie Sypher, *Rococo to Cubism in Art and Literature* (New York: Vintage Books, 1960), 91, 108, 96.

3. M. H. Abrams, *Natural Supernaturalism* (New York: W. W. Norton, 1971), 411, 412, 418. Page numbers cite later quotations in order of appearance.

4. Reginald L. Cook, "Emerson and Frost: A Parallel of Seers," *New England Quarterly*, XXXI (June 1958), 216–17. The later quotation is from p. 216.

5. Lawrance Thompson, *Robert Frost: The Years of Triumph, 1915–1938* (New York: Holt, Rinehart and Winston, 1970), 694. In text as Thompson.

6. *Selected Prose of Robert Frost*, ed. Hyde Cox and Edward Connery Lathem (New York: Holt, Rinehart and Winston, 1966), 107. In text as SP.

7. Sidney Cox, *Robert Frost: Original "Ordinary Man"* (New York: Henry Holt, 1929), 25.

8. Louis Untermeyer, *Robert Frost: A Backward Look* (Washington: Library of Congress, 1964), 23. In text as Untermeyer.

9. Daniel Smythe, *Robert Frost Speaks* (New York: Twayne, 1964), 38.

10. Lawrance Thompson, *Robert Frost: The Early Years, 1874–1915* (New York: Holt, Rinehart and Winston, 1966), 434.

11. Emma Gray Emory, "Hypnotism in Nature Poems by Robert Frost," unpublished paper, Wheaton College, May 12, 1972.

12. Philip L. Gerber, *Robert Frost* (New York: Twayne, 1966), 108, 114.

13. My thanks to conversations with Leo Marx, professor of English and American Studies at Amherst College, who helped to clarify some of my ideas.

Pan's Song, Revised:
Robert Frost as the Articulate Backwoodsman

MARGARET EDWARDS

EMERSON sought to inspire an indigenous American poetry derivative of the European tradition yet fully autonomous. He tried to
prod American poets into a self-reliance similar to that which the
colonial settlers had already demonstrated in the Revolution. Robert
Frost seems to have followed Emerson's prescription for poetic insight. Frost found in the natural world his primary metaphors, yet
never shared Emerson's Romantic love for nature. Although Frost
was inclined to flirt with an academic career and had a rural life
first thrust upon him by a firm and generous grandfather, his subsequent adoption of a pastoral life style and his cultivation of the
image of himself as a wise backwoodsman might mark him as a militant Romantic Transcendentalist. But he was not. Both his relationship to nature and his concept of the world of nature were complicated. Frost did not worship the woods or give any respect to those
who would return to "the days when Ahaz sinned/By worship under green trees in the open." Ahaz is a Biblical figure who supposedly offended Jehovah by his devotion to nature instead of the true
god. Frost completely rejects the idea of nature as the reflection of
any deity: "Even to say the groves were God's first temples/Comes
too near to Ahaz' sin for safety" ("New Hampshire").

Frost ultimately rejects Emerson's view of nature. Emerson used
the world of nature as a Bible, whereas Frost used it as a sort of
psychic almanac. Emerson wished to infuse a sensual perception of
nature with the power of "reason" in order to perceive "nature
aloof," to see through natural things the "more earnest vision" of a
greater, abiding spiritual reality. Frost combined his observations of
the world of nature with philosophical abstractions in order to construct a more meaningful human psychology. Over and over again
Frost doubts the idea of a world beyond this world: "However it
is in some other world/I know that this is the way in ours," he says

in "Hardwood Groves." The tone of this rejection is usually light-hearted, even ironical, but firm.

Despite this modern agnosticism, Frost seems to fulfill the Emersonian image of American poet. He lived in and wrote of the isolating farmland of New England. Even though his long life allowed him to witness the thorough, unremitting destruction of such a way of life, Frost continued to use rural metaphor as if everyone had the responsibility of a cow to milk. Most readers of Frost's work tend to justify what harsh critics cite as anachronistic imagery. And their justification of Frost's imagery usually hinges on a conviction that, whatever the metaphor, the psychological truths it embodies are the same, that the subjects the poetry illuminates are universally human and common to all times, even though the source of the analogy is vanishing. The decision as to which path to take in a "yellow wood" can elucidate the drama of personal choice and identity even to those whose feet rarely stray from concrete and gravel walkways, for the simple reason that this drama is so common to us all.

A more negative view might hold that it is dishonest to revive dying images. The poet achieves his effects through nostalgia, not through a present-day recognition, and he thereby cheats future generations whose nostalgic grip will be less firm, their identification therefore incomplete. Better to have the choice between two subway exits than two forest roads! Yet if a poet sees the world of nature as an abiding circumstance in men's lives, then he would do well to be conservative, to follow Emerson's advice and return to the images of nature as he writes. The images of any sophisticated technological society change rapidly and profoundly, and a poet cannot wager that this man-made landscape will not change too. There used to be many folk songs about the railroads; and the locomotive and its whistle came to represent for several generations a call to the "wilderness" of constant travel and foreign places. The train was the most powerful and exotic "animal" a town could know. It was the symbol of all that lay beyond, as well as the physical means to get there. Train wrecks became as legendary as natural disasters. But who would write of the train in this way today? It is not unlike a beast or bird facing extinction; its symbolic power is lost as its plight is recognized. So it is that this perspective vindicates

Frost. If he saw technology as an even poorer source of imagery than unspoiled nature (and his criticism of scientific advances indicates he did), then his return to a more rural way of life and to natural imagery was very prudent.

Frost's view of nature "in the common sense" (to use Emerson's phrase) seems at times contradictory. In one sense Frost is alien to the world of technology and cannot include man's "victory" by annihilation. On the other hand, he quietly predicts what will happen, what is happening. Frost sometimes fails to give the modern reader anything more than a nostalgic revelation when he depicts nature as terrifying and sinister. The hill wife, in the poem by that name, gives herself over to horror:

> She had no saying dark enough
> For the dark pine that kept
> Forever trying the window latch
> Of the room where they slept.

But we can somewhat disregard her revelation and even think it a piece of black humor that a woman should fear a tree's sexual assault, for she is mad. The husband sleeps peacefully for he knows, as we do, that a tree is nothing to fear. The effect of rural loneliness has addled the wife and made her interpret a benign object, a tree by her window, as a frightful intruder. This is not a representation of nature as sinister; it is a portrait of a human misrepresentation. However, the theme of the forest as a potent and enduring force, much like a landlocked ocean, which can engulf and swallow the works of men, is the dominant view of nature in poems such as "The Wood-Pile" and "The Black Cottage." A cottage and a woodpile are, in these poems, both in the process of reverting to original forms by the natural process of decay. The poet rescues both images, retrieves them from the encroaching obscurity, by describing them. In both poems, the forest has the power to wear man and the memory of him away. We hear echoes of Emerson: "Here we find Nature to be the circumstance which dwarfs every other circumstance." [1] Nature is powerful in Frost's poetry. What is more, she is antagonistic to man's survival. Man must do battle against her, persevering even in the face of the assured obliteration of his efforts. "The Birth-place" is a humorous and gentle expression of this grim fact:

> Here further up the mountain slope
> Than there was ever any hope,
> My father built, enclosed a spring,
> Strung chains of wall round everything,
> Subdued the growth of earth to grass,
> And brought our various lives to pass.

The mother earth weans man from her solicitude. He fights to impose his will; he "chains" her, like some beast, with artificial order. A man can be heroic in this struggle, particularly when he builds "further up the mountain slope/Than there was ever any hope." And nature may reward him momentarily with the illusion of his success, seeming "to like the stir," and sometimes aid in his conspiracy to master her. In this vision, however, "nature" is not so much the earth and forest as that fundamental process of change affecting all forms of life. Nature, in this sense, has no mercy on the beautiful forms of the forest either. "Spring Pools" records how they too are locked within the cycle of change, just as man is:

> These pools that, though in forests, still reflect
> The total sky almost without defect,
> And like the flowers beside them, chill and shiver,
> Will like the flowers beside them soon be gone,
> And yet not out by any brook or river,
> But up by roots to bring dark foliage on.

This view of nature as a cycle is much like Eliot's affirmative view in that it sees that the purpose of destruction—in this case the absorption of the pools—is creation. The water will "bring dark foliage on." The pools make summer possible. And yet there is that note of regret for what the inevitable process will "blot out and drink up and sweep away." It is Eliot's vision of the dance viewed less optimistically. Anything "almost without defect," or any outright perfection and whatever embodies it, will "soon be gone." The ideal is momentary. Man must be at war with nature, securing for himself a place in the process, wresting from her with extreme effort a continuity and meaning for his life. Frost writes of this constant and bitter conflict, choosing for a metaphor the image of a man (usually a farmer) who pits himself against the forest, carves out an impermanent space, and establishes a life "in the clearing."

If this struggle were the only theme in Frost's work, without the contradiction of other poems with opposite visions, Frost's understanding of nature would be too limited, for he would seem to recognize only nature's power to change and obliterate man, and not man's power to alter nature. He would have trusted too much the metaphor of the mountain whose clearing fills with trees, covering human effort. But Frost did not let it rest so simply. He was a man of his times, cosmopolitan no matter how leathery his hands or how much he mussed his hair. As he traveled all over the country giving lectures and readings, surely he did not miss seeing the cancer of metropolises. But quietly he rejects the Romantic idea of man's productive subservience to nature's rule. He does not paint grand or terrible portraits of man's power; but he does acknowledge that power. "On the Heart's Beginning to Cloud the Mind" offers an interesting illustration. In the first twelve lines of the poem, Frost constructs that Emersonian image of nature dwarfing man. The sky dominates with its starlight and moonlight. The human light is "flickering" and "pathetic" against the huge night. But suddenly the poet reins in the thought and turns in the opposite direction. The "tale of a better kind" is a tale more truthful. It tells what the "mind" knows, though the "heart" rejects the idea. It acknowledges the power of the human light, which looks small and weak but is a product of human will and ingenuity and subject to human control.

> That far light flickers because of trees.
> The people can burn it as long as they please;
> And when their interests in it end,
> They can leave it to someone else to tend.
> Come back that way a summer hence,
> I should find it no more no less intense.

The reversal is total. Nature, the huge night, and the trees are tamed by that light. And man dominates.

> One looks out last from the darkened room
> At the shiny desert with spots of gloom
> That might be people and are but cedar,
> Have no purpose, have no leader,
> Have never made the first move to assemble,
> And so are nothing to make her tremble.

Frost even strips away any anthropomorphic associations ("that might be people and are but cedar") which might render this landscape as sinister as the hill wife's tree.

Emerson's "Reason" speaking to Frost taught him that the times had changed. Emerson might have written the first twelve lines of this poem and considered it finished. But to write such a poem in an industrial society like ours now would be to give in to "the heart's beginning to cloud the mind," to let nostalgic emotions rule. In "Pan with Us," Frost treats this modern predicament humorously; Pan finds that his powers have lessened, for his

> were pipes of pagan mirth,
> And the world had found new terms of worth.
> He laid him down on the sunburned earth
> And raveled a flower and looked away.
> Play? Play?—What should he play?

Pan's dilemma is the modern poet's: "What should he play?" What should a man write in a world dedicated to "new terms of worth"? The old modes of taking a "pagan" inspiration from nature are no longer sufficient. Emerson's "Pan" provides an effectively ironic contrast:

> O what are heroes, prophets, men,
> But pipes through which the breath of Pan doth blow
> A momentary music. Being's tide
> Swells hitherward, and myriads of forms
> Live, robed with beauty, painted by the sun;
> Their dust, pervaded by the nerves of God,
> Throbs with an overmastering energy
> Knowing and doing. Ebbs the tide, they lie
> White hollow shells upon the desert shore,
> But not the less the eternal wave rolls on
> To animate new millions, and exhale
> Races and planets, its enchanted foam.[2]

And to cross the Atlantic for a moment let's recall that Wordsworth, like Frost, also acknowledged that "times were changed from what they were." Instead of expounding nature's "overmastering energy," he lamented that "little we see in Nature that is ours."

> for everything, we are out of tune:
> It moves us not.—Great God! I'd rather be
> A pagan suckled in a creed outworn;
> So might I, standing on this pleasant lea,
> Have glimpses that would make me less forlorn;
> Have sight of Proteus rising from the sea;
> Or hear old Triton blow his wreathed horn.[3]

Wordsworth could still have faith in a return to the "creed outworn"; but Frost dispels even that hope. Frost lets the "glimpse" materialize. Pan returns to us—as Proteus or Triton might—a sad buffoon, a worker laid off his job. The sight can hardly make one "less forlorn."

What should a poet write? The entire body of Frost's work in his long and prolific life is his truest answer to this question. It is hard to find one definitive statement of purpose. Frost does not give us the dramatic moment of his Muse's arrival. Perhaps the poem entitled "The Oven Bird" is the nearest to a coda, to a manifesto of what this New England/American bard sought to create. The singing bird is a traditional symbol for the poet, the symbol Walt Whitman uses to such great effect in "Out of the Cradle Endlessly Rocking." Walt Whitman hears the voice of his muse come "out of the mocking-bird's throat, the musical shuttle." The bird

> call'd on his mate,
> He pour'd forth the meanings which I
> of all men know.

And the poet:

> Listen'd to keep, to sing, now translating the notes,
> Following you my brother.[4]

If the oven bird becomes Frost's emblem, he is an appropriate one. He is a "mid-wood" or forest bird, not inclined to live near the city. He "makes the solid tree trunks sound again," even as Frost returns to a vanishing rural landscape and makes it reverberate with the poet's vision. The oven bird sings in a world that has decayed from the height of its summer glory: "the early petal-fall is past .../And comes that other fall we name the fall." Likewise Frost writes in a world past its natural and spiritual prime. "And comes that other fall we name the fall" is surely a pun on the Fall of mankind from the bliss of the garden of Eden. The oven bird "says the highway dust is over all," meaning, perhaps, that in Frost's landscape, remote farmland though it may be, the shadow of man's progress is hanging heavy in the air and settling over nature. At the end of the poem, the poet's question to himself is reiterated, not really answered: "what to make of a diminished thing?" A common interpretation of this poem reads mankind or poetry as the "diminished thing." However, the oven bird's question is the same that Pan asks: "What should he play?" Thus the "diminished thing" might be nature herself.

Popular anthologies make it easy to see Frost as a poet who celebrated the bucolic and little else. He touches so lightly on the threat man poses to nature that one might overlook it. Often one feels that the contest is an equal one. A man builds a wall, and the forest tears it down; a man's child dies, yet the grieving man eventually stops grieving; a man makes a clearing, and the seedling trees encroach; men build a town, and a mountain blocks its growth; someone imports a peach tree, but the winter finally withers it; the snow covers everything, but a man can build a fire. In fact, in many of Frost's poems, man's identification with nature can become so complete that the two seem to work in perfect harmony as two halves of some single entity. In "Tree at My Window," Frost might even be instructing the hill wife how she should have interpreted nature:

> Tree at my window, window tree,
> My sash is lowered when night comes on;
> But let there never be curtain drawn
> Between you and me.

Man's mind can see itself mirrored in nature. The imagination can discover itself and the laws of its operation through her. In this poem, the poet's imagination and the tree are allied; the tree is a "vague dream-head lifted out of the ground" tossed by the "outer" as opposed to "inner" weather. Man reflects nature and nature, man. The relationship is static and profound. Nature is not a "diminished thing," but man's enveloping coequal.

Ecological tracts usually emphasize a view of man quite alien to Frost's work. It is now popular to describe man as a member of a marauding, well-equipped species, not as an individual animal, barely equal by himself to the task of survival. Frost is determined that we see man struggling with nature—sometimes as her equal, often as a heroic yet certain victim. The last poem in Frost's last published volume would suggest the importance of this vision of man in conflict with nature by the emphasis of its position in Frost's work as a whole. It is a final statement, and untitled:

> In winter in the woods alone
> Against the trees I go.
> I mark a maple for my own
> And lay the maple low.

This is man in his primary state; man "alone" goes "against the trees," against nature. His relationship to nature is a form of contest which actually admits no winner or loser if one contemplates the infinite dimensions of the cycle. "I see for Nature no defeat/ In one tree's overthrow . . ." says the poet in the final verse. He also asserts, "I see . . . no defeat/ . . . for myself." In this poem, man's destruction, the cutting of the maple, is a part of the cycle. "One tree's overthrow" is not truly against nature, nor is it wasteful. Frost endows with metaphor that perfect balance between man and nature: the lone man chops a lone maple tree. Man locks with nature in a vital struggle; yet even so he is a partner and not a foe. In a balanced relationship with the earth, the changes man undertakes are comfortably absorbed into the larger process, and neither nature nor mankind is diminished. It is what Eliot may have meant when he wrote:

> In my beginning is my end. In succession
> Houses rise and fall, crumble, are extended,

Are removed, destroyed, restored, or in their place
Is an open field, or a factory, or a by-pass.
Old stone to new building, old timber to new fires,
Old fires to ashes, and ashes to the earth
Which is already flesh, fur and faeces,
Bone of man and beast, cornstalk and leaf.[5]

Both Eliot and Frost share Whitman's faith in nature's power to reassert her cycle as certainly as the earth itself revolves. Whitman writes:

To her children the words of the eloquent dumb great mother
never fail,
The true words do not fail, for motion does not fail and
reflection does not fail,
Also the day and night do not fail, and the voyage we
pursue does not fail.[6]

In his final, cryptic poem, Frost strips down Walt Whitman's colossal and arrogant image of the singing foresters felling the redwood, the central image of Whitman's poem, "Song of the Redwood Tree." The heroism is scaled to the individual, and the cut tree is proportionate to an individual's need. The solitary man works for what he must have, takes only that, and leaves.

In the world Frost creates in his poetry, man can play several interchangeable roles as he confronts the natural phenomena surrounding him. He can fear the natural world as alien to himself, as actively working against him to obliterate what he is and has made. He can challenge nature and conquer her, destroy her, and see himself destroyed with her. He can work within nature as an equal partner, the checks and balances as perfect as the inner workings of a fine mechanism. Finally, he can protect and revere her, hoping that by such protection and such reverence he may benefit "a diminished thing."

Such a relationship of respect and protection between man and nature pervades the body of the poetry. "Rose Pogonias," published in Frost's first book of verse, is a very early statement of this relationship. Here "nature" certainly denotes field and forest, Emerson's "Nature in the common sense." The poet tells us of his walk through a meadow in which he discovers a place strewn with flowers, "a temple of the heat." And in this "temple," the poet comes as near as he ever does to Ahaz' sin:

> There we bowed us in the burning,
>   As the sun's right worship is,
> To pick where none could miss them
>   A thousand orchises. . . .

The poet hopes that the very beauty of the spot will save it from the practical mower, who may relent and pass on, "confused with flowers."

Two later expressions of man's compassionate protection of natural things occur in the *Mountain Interval* collection. "The Exposed Nest" relates the story of a child finding a bird's nest full of fledglings. The nest has fallen prey to the mowing machine, and the young birds are left exposed and helpless. The child rebuilds the cover, aware that perhaps the mother bird will not come back to a nest that has been disturbed by humans even of sterling intentions.

> We saw the risk we took in doing good,
> But dared not spare to do the best we could
> Though harm should come of it; so built the screen
> You had begun, and gave them back their shade.
> All this to prove we cared.

And yet this positive, "caring" gesture is lost in a subsequent lack of concern:

> Why is there then
> No more to tell? We turned to other things.
> I haven't any memory—have you?—
> Of ever coming to the place again
> To see if the birds lived the first night through,
> And so at last to learn to use their wings.

This urge to protect is difficult to sustain. The farmer in "Christmas Trees" does a more thorough job of protecting his firs. A city man comes to ask him to sell a thousand of his trees. The farmer is at first astonished for he "hadn't thought of them as Christmas trees," which is what the city man wants. The farmer has thought of them more poetically: "My woods—the young fir balsams like a place/Where houses all are churches and have spires." The city man does not quote a fair price—but even if he had, the farmer would not have been moved to take his trees to "the trial by market everything must come to." Instead the farmer is left the richer for his revelation: "A thousand Christmas trees I didn't know I had!"

And yet nature reciprocates. Her beauty may be the plea she raises to save herself. Her beauty is also man's salvation. "A Servant to Servants" is about a woman who has almost given herself over to the madness inherited from her family. The only fact that keeps her in this world and momentarily relieves the hard drudgery of her everyday life is the glimpse she has through her kitchen window of a small lake. She says to herself:

> It took my mind off doughnuts and soda biscuit
> To step outdoors and take the water dazzle
> A sunny morning, or take the rising wind
> About my face and body and through my wrapper,
> When a storm threatened from the Dragon's Den,
> And a cold chill shivered across the lake.

Her participation in the natural beauty around her, her determined recognition of it and fervent appreciation, are all that keep any meaning in this woman's life. When she despairs of this help, as she does by the end of the poem, she faces the asylum.

The poet includes himself among those who are refreshed and revitalized by nature. If man spares nature's beauty, she will spare his spirit. "A Young Birch" teaches this lesson; the poet tells how he spared a birch while cutting back brush. The birch has grown from the size of a cane into a handsome tree that "dares to lean,/ Relying on its beauty, to the air," an "ornament" in the life of the man who spared it.

Instead of condemning Frost for his "backward" glance into rural life and thinking that he flew in the face of the problems of industrial rapacity, this study vindicates his work, in part, for its insights undoubtedly still addressed to the modern world. Frost's regard for natural things suggests that at times a tree should be allowed to survive on the strength of its beauty alone, so that "the zeal would not be thanked that cut it down." On the other hand, his unsentimental view of the human urge to survive faces the fact of man's unavoidable conflict with the wilderness. Frost encompasses this grim reality in his aesthetic and moral vision, and his poems collectively illustrate the possibility of a life in which man's struggle with nature fits within nature's larger harmonies.

Notes to *Pan's Song, Revised* by MARGARET EDWARDS

1. Ralph Waldo Emerson, "Nature," *The Complete Works of Ralph Waldo Emerson*, Vol. III: *Essays: Second Series*, ed. Edward Waldo Emerson (Boston: Houghton Mifflin Company, 1903), 170.

2. Emerson, "Pan," *Complete Works*, Vol. IX: *Poems*, 360.

3. William Wordsworth, *The Poetical Works of William Wordsworth*, ed. William Knight (Edinburgh: William Paterson, 1883), IV, 32–33.

4. Walt Whitman, "Out of the Cradle Endlessly Rocking," *The Collected Writings of Walt Whitman: Leaves of Grass*, ed. Harold W. Blodgett and Sculley Bradley (New York: New York University Press, 1965), 246–53.

5. Thomas Stearns Eliot, "East Coker," *The Complete Poems and Plays: 1909–1950* (New York: Harcourt, Brace and World, Inc., 1952), I, 123.

6. Whitman, "A Song of the Rolling Earth," *Collected Writings*, I, 221.

"Nothing That Is":
A Study of Frost's "Desert Places"

ALBERT J. VON FRANK

JAMES ELLIS has located the germ for Robert Frost's "Desert Places" in a passage at the beginning of Chapter XVIII of *The Scarlet Letter*.[1] As a result of Hester Prynne's having been "not merely estranged, but outlawed, from society," she "had wandered, without rule or guidance, in a moral wilderness; as vast, as intricate and shadowy, as the untamed forest, amid the gloom of which [she and Dimmesdale] were now holding a colloquy that was to decide their fate. Her intellect and heart had their home, as it were, in *desert places*, where she roamed as freely as the wild Indian in his woods." [2]

The full context of this passage demonstrates Hawthorne's characteristic ambivalence toward Hester's situation: the desert places which constitute her home are figured as a "moral wilderness," but living there has made her free. It has "made her strong," Hawthorne tells us, "but taught her much amiss." The reading of Frost's poem which Ellis constructs on the basis of this germ does generous service to the "moral wilderness" aspect of the "desert places" but slights the positive qualities inherent in the freedom of the experience. Ellis summarizes his interpretation of the poem when he says that what scares the poet "is his recognition of his own *desert places*, the moral wilderness that he feels within himself and that he knows exists in all men. The final stanza [expresses] his somber recognition and confrontation of a world which is barren." This confrontation, made "in the face of the supernatural," is, Ellis suggests, marked by "anguish." [3]

I cite Ellis's reading of the poem for two reasons: first because it reflects the prevailing opinion that "Desert Places" is a deeply despairing poem and, second, because Ellis is alone in recognizing the poem's source in Hawthorne.[4] In my reading of the poem I hope to show—by discovering some of its ideological and philosophical foundations—that it is neither fundamentally a picture of despair nor an essentially confident expression as Brooks and Warren, in *Understanding Poetry*, have claimed.[5] Rather it retains a large measure of the ambivalence of the germ in Hawthorne.

I

> Snow falling and night falling fast, oh, fast
> In a field I looked into going past,
> And the ground almost covered smooth in snow,
> But a few weeds and stubble showing last.

The poet sees the snow and the night descending together, black and white, working together to muffle sensation and obliterate perception; yet they work against each other, paradoxically, to heighten perception. The snow works against the night, giving ghastly light whereby to see the darkness, while the fast falling darkness gives urgency to the need to see, for the opportunity will not last long. What the poet sees is truly "for once, then, something." In the moments before obliteration he sees something with a positive existence, something he can put a name to—a field. He knows it is a field because, for the moment, positive signs of its identity remain: the "few weeds and stubble showing last." It is important to understand, then, that this is a cultivated field and not a natural clearing in the forest; it is nature given purpose and identity by man. Like the snow and the night, the weeds and stubble set up crosscurrents of meaning. The stubble is more clearly the hint of man's presence, the aftermath, quite literally, of man's contact with the land, while the weeds—which can exist only in (and therefore define) a cultivated area—remind us of nature's persistent reclamation of the artificial. What the snow smothers, in addition to everything else, is the vital conflict which the juxtaposition of "weeds and stubble" suggests.

II

> The woods around it have it—it is theirs.
> All animals are smothered in their lairs.
> I am too absent-spirited to count;
> The loneliness includes me unawares.

As the snow piles on, obliterating all distinction, the field becomes
—as the first line three times tells us—an inanimate, dead thing,
unmarked by, and unreflective of, the care of man, the very thing
which gave it its positive identity as a field. Remove the signs of
man's involvement, and it straightway ceases to be "for once, then,
something" and can only be identified negatively: it is the nothingness at the center of the encircling trees; it is the nothingness which
can only be known by the positiveness which surrounds it and
which can only be named in the indefiniteness of a pronoun. This
annihilation is figured as death, the ultimate weight of which in
cosmic fashion smothers *all* life, leaving the poet alone in a dead
universe, touched, himself, by the death that smothers.

Confronted with the deadness, the spiritlessness, of the external
world, the poet notes that he, too, is "absent-spirited"; he, too, is
"included" in the loneliness, which is to say the separateness, of the
universe of material objects. The paradox here is to be included in
separateness, and one arrives at a perception of that paradox by
recognizing the plurality of material existence and understanding
one's own place in the universal array of physical facts—that is, in
nature. This sense is akin to if not identical with Emerson's discovery, made "too late to be helped . . . , that we exist." [6] For Emerson, however, we exist in positive relation to higher values; the
essence of our meaning consists not in separateness but in unity. For
Frost (thus far in the poem) the persona exists negatively, just as the
field may be said to exist negatively. More specifically, the field
(no longer a field, properly speaking) is *known as* the emptiness
which disturbs the continuity of the woods; similarly, the poet-
observer is defined by his absent-spiritedness and thus by his isolation. The analogy between the condition of nature and the condition of personal psychology is a romantic concept and one perfectly
in accord with the ideas of Emerson or Wordsworth. In "Desert
Places," however, the implications of the analogy are necessarily
and entirely reversed since what is analogous in the persona and
the field is the quality of discontinuity. For Wordsworth, and for
many subsequent romantic writers including Emerson, the analogy
between states of mind or dispositions of the spirit and the sympathetic universe was uplifting because it implied, or rather pre-

supposed, an active positive alliance, a radical *continuity*, through God, between man and nature. Nature lives and spiritually supports us, even though it is composed in large measure of inanimate objects, because *we* live and God has allowed us to invest it with our lives. Wordsworth expressed this reciprocal relation when he said, "That from thyself it comes, that thou must give/Else never canst receive" (*The Prelude*, XII, 276–77). Frost appears, in the first three stanzas, to have reversed these implications. The analogy between man and nature appears operative, but the reciprocal relation is negative rather than positive; pluralistic rather than monistic; fragmented in its stress on aloneness rather than unified; deadly rather than life-supporting.

III

And lonely as it is, that loneliness
Will be more lonely ere it will be less—
A blanker whiteness of benighted snow
With no expression, nothing to express.

The third stanza appears at first the weakest on several counts. The purpose it serves seems primarily mechanical. It is necessary to shift the focus from the poet himself back to the scene before him in preparation for the final statement in the last stanza. The first two lines, as Reuben Brower has pointed out, achieve a "Poe-like melancholy," [7] though perhaps by equally Poe-like mechanisms—the use of the archaic "ere" and the mournful reiteration of the word "lonely." A further weakness of these lines might consist in the inadequacy of the physical phenomenon which prompts them. Presumably the quondam field will become lonelier or less expressive than earlier because the snow is now deep enough to hide not only the "weeds and stubble showing last," but also the very contours of the land. Since the annihilation of the identity of the field was earlier accomplished when all signs of its *use*, its pragmatic definition, were covered, this added touch may strike the reader as gratuitous or insignificant by comparison.

The stanza does, of course, accomplish an intensification of mood, though again almost in spite of itself. The gentle hint of "ere it will be less" must be rejected if these lines are to be read as a genuine concentration of despair. The implied rebirth in the necessary melting of the snow and the reemergence of the field as a real thing is an unassimilated lump of hope, working for the moment in stubborn defiance of the tone and meaning of the poem as it stands at this point.

More subtly in defiance of the tone and meaning is the paradoxical assertion that the "blanker whiteness" has "nothing to express"—a proposition which the very existence of the poem appears to jeopardize. "Nothing" actually becomes "for once, then, something" in a context which is consistently negative. The intensity of nothingness—that is, the intensity which is insisted on in the third stanza—begins to lend to that nothingness an almost palpable reality. It is, after all, that quantity which had defined the field and defined the poet; and because nothingness is thus the landmark by which realities are known, it becomes a real, and in a sense a positive, quality. It is truly a case of nothing having escaped Frost's observation; he is like the listener in Wallace Stevens' "The Snow Man" "who listens in the snow,/And, nothing himself, beholds/Nothing that is not there and the nothing that is." Frost evokes a similar awareness in "Neither Out Far nor In Deep" by what Trilling has called "the energy with which emptiness is perceived." [8] That Frost could work such a paradox on us is only to say that he makes emptiness real for us as readers of the poem.

IV

> They cannot scare me with their empty spaces
> Between stars—on stars where no human race is.
> I have it in me so much nearer home
> To scare myself with my own desert places.

The protestation of the first line appears to Reuben Brower "a bit flamboyant." "The scary place," Brower writes, "is thrust off 'there' by the emerging man of wit, by the mind that won't give way to 'absent-spiritedness.' But the gesture . . . opens a worse form of terror by bringing fear where the poet lives most alone." [9] This reading depends on the assumption that the last stanza is essentially disjointed; that something has occurred between lines two and three that leads the poet to reconsider the confident defiance he has just, perhaps too heroically, expressed. In other words, in explaining the sense of the last stanza Brower finds an implicit "but" before the third line. To be sure, the poem has proceeded by crosscurrents to such an extent that it would be easy to see another one here, but in this instance the relationship between ideas seems to be causal rather than antagonistic—a transition which is perhaps better expressed by "because": They cannot scare me with their empty spaces *because* I have it in me to scare myself with my own desert places.

The other assumption implicit in Brower's reading is that the recognition of private deserts in one's own mind involves "a worse form of terror" than the vision of a dead universe. This assumption also needs to be examined, but first it is necessary to determine who "they" are in the opening line of the stanza and why they cannot scare the poet.

Brooks and Warren have suggested that "they" are astronomers, and, insofar as astronomers adopt an inorganic, physical, and scientific viewpoint and speak for a standard, accepted view of the universe, the suggestion is not amiss. But if the intrusion into the poem of prosaic astronomers seems unduly reductive of Frost's intended ambiguity, it might be more appropriate to take "they" to mean nature itself, pluralistically figured, since nature has been felt throughout the poem as a collection of material objects. This reading also seems preferable in light of Frost's earlier use of the third-person pronoun in reference to the woods ("The woods around it have it—it is theirs"). The potential of nature to scare when it is seen, not as an organically active and sympathetic entity, but pluralistically as an accumulation of objects, is a potential which Wordsworth and Coleridge fully recognized. In Chapter XIII of the *Biographia*, Coleridge observed that "all objects (*as* objects) are essentially fixed and dead." For the romantic writer this realization prompts another —that "in our life alone does nature live." The alternative to the pluralistic, scientific assertion that the universe is essentially fixed and dead, subject to no generalizations but those of physics, is the contrary assertion, repeatedly voiced by romantic writers, "That from thyself it comes, that thou must give,/Else never canst receive." In "Desert Places," then, Frost is commenting on one of the most basic romantic assumptions about the universe—that it is essentially responsive to man, that *we* are its vital force, its reason for being. Emily Dickinson expressed this idea when she wrote:

> The Fashion of the Ear
> Attireth that it hear
> In Dun, or fair—
>
> So whether it be Rune,
> Or whether it be none
> Is of within.
>
> The "Tune is in the Tree—"
> The Skeptic—showeth me—
> "No Sir! In Thee!"

Dickinson's retort in her short dialogue with the Skeptic is essentially contained in the dramatic monologue of "Desert Places." What Frost realizes at the beginning of the last stanza is that nature's empty spaces are *truly empty*—not only of matter, but of meaning and that it is only meaning that can scare. The tune is not in the tree, and the lesson of emptiness is not between stars.

Here, in the last stanza, the major paradox of the poem is resolved. The third stanza asserts that the "blanker whiteness" had "nothing to express," though the deadly heavy pall of nothingness was itself a very considerable thing for the "blanker whiteness" to have expressed; and were it not for that very effective expression, the poem would have had no subject. Realizing now, in the fourth stanza, that the idea of nothingness, of emptiness or aloneness, is generated from within the mind outward and not placed in the mind from exterior nature, obviously the "blanker whiteness" truly does not and can not express, but is a mere canvas on which the observer builds out his own inherent conceptions. The tune is not in the tree; the tune of nothingness is not in the snow. Thus what seemed paradoxical in the third stanza is, when seen from the vantage of the fourth, a simple statement of fact. The "blanker whiteness" has "nothing to express"; it has, literally, no meaning.

If meaning does not inhere in nature, it exists only in the mind, just as Emily Dickinson affirmed. Frost agrees with entire explicitness: "I have it *in me*," he says, contrasting the substantiveness of the "it" with the "nothing" that the snow has to express. "I am," in other words, "the repository of meaning." This implied assertion, in turn, gives final development to a major theme of the poem—that of location. The field has been transformed from a positively defined entity into a thing which exists only in relation to exterior fixities, by the agency of the snow. The snow, in addition to symbolizing death, symbolizes an allied concept—doubt, that quality which undermines self-knowledge and self-containment and makes us look outside ourselves for points of reference. The poet is located by a quantity which appears to be exterior, the pervasive nullity of a dead universe. But when the poet-observer comes to understand that he is himself the repository of meaning, he is relocated—or, more properly, he locates himself as definer, namer, potentially as poet—and puts himself positively at the center of the universe. The experience he observes in the field—or rather the romantic misunderstanding he has of it—literally pulls him out of himself and makes him so vulnerable to the apparent deadness that he is nearly smothered in the rarified atmosphere of aloneness and homelessness. The poem restores him to himself, equips him with a sense of who and where he is, defined positively this time, in relation to nature and to the objects to which he will give meaning poetically. He is brought home: "I have it in me so much nearer *home*," he says. Here again we are dealing with two concepts which are related as cause and effect. He can locate "home" because, for the first time in the poem, he can see that there is something *in him* which does not exist elsewhere, and that "something" is the potential to create meaning.

Perhaps the modernity of "Desert Places" is most clearly seen in its acceptance of a universe without inherent prior meaning. There is, in the last stanza, a note almost of relief at the realization that one is not tied to a dead universe; that is, to a universe whose overarching principle is death and separateness. Rather he finds a universe without overarching principles, without prior meaning—a universe which he, as a poet, can fill up and fill out with meaning from his own life. For Frost this insight and the prospect it affords represent a tremendous freedom. "They cannot scare me," seen in this light, is simply another way of saying "the universe cannot impose upon me." Yet this very modern defiance of a priori limitations has a tradition of its own. We hear it in Henry James's remark that Besant's a priori assumptions are valid only in the meanings we attach to them; on another level we hear this tradition in the freedom of Hester Prynne's "moral wilderness," and we hear it, too, in Emily Dickinson's assertion that the "Tune" has no existence prior to the mind which experiences it. To believe otherwise —to believe that the tune is in the tree—is to be a skeptic because it is also to doubt the radical significance of mind, which, in turn, is to be antipoetical and antihumanist. If there is any such thing as a dogma in modern literature, it is that the universe is meaningless and that whatever order one may find in it has been established by the force of man's shaping imagination.

What separates this dogma as it is held by Frost from the same dogma as held by Wordsworth or Coleridge is that the latter two believed implicitly that God so arranged the world as to provide a natural analogy between nature and mind; for Wordsworth and Coleridge man and nature existed in reciprocal interaction because there was essentially no distinction to be made between them, all of reality existing by virtue of "the eternal act of creation in the infinite I AM." We do not find this sort of relationship in "Desert Places." For Frost, meaning is a thing people use to bridge separateness and to bring order out of real, not apparent, chaos; for Wordsworth and Coleridge, meaning flows spontaneously back and forth from man to nature along lines of communication established in the nature of the universe by God.

Wordsworth and Coleridge depend on certain monistical a priori assumptions about God and what He has or has not done to make the universe livable; Wordsworth and Coleridge, that is, were philosophical monists: everything, for them, was a manifestation of the divine spirit, the on-going act of creation. In "Desert Places" Frost clearly repudiates monism as well as a priori assumptions. The analogy which exists between man and nature was not, for Frost, established by God, but is continually being created by man's own imagination: each time one draws an analogy between man and nature, one does so by an act of the will, not in accordance with

the scheme of the universe but in defiance of its essential schemeless-
ness. In other words, for Frost, the analogy itself does not exist a
priori, but must be created every time we wish to give order and
significance to an inherently meaningless universe, just as the field
itself must, every spring, be reclaimed from the insistent chaos of nature. What led the poet-observer into despair at the beginning of
the poem was his Wordsworthian assumption that the analogy does
exist a priori; by the end of the poem the mistake is discovered.[10]

What "Desert Places" expresses, then, is a form of the romantic
concept of the analogy between man and nature. The original concept, of course, was formulated in a philosophically monistic context; Frost gives it to us in a pluralistic context and shows us that
it retains its power to reconcile us with a universe that has changed
with the times, a universe figured pluralistically.

The hopefulness of "Desert Places" becomes appparent only
when the pluralistic foundation on which the poem rests—or rather
shifts about—is understood. For Frost, the advantage of pluralism
lies in the allowance it makes for "the possible other case"—hope in
despair, despair in hope—it allows, that is, for the play with opposites
which constitutes irony. From the pluralistic viewpoint, now, the
"unassimilated lump of hope" in the third stanza appears more fully
integrated; in fact it is the crux of the poem:

> And lonely as it is, that loneliness
> Will be more lonely ere it will be less—

That "ere it will be less" is a part of a stanza which, in its totality,
insists strenuously on an intensification of winter. But the poet's
consciousness is drawn against the grain of immediate experience
to image out "the possible other case"—that time when the field will
return as a real thing. But the truly pluralistic thing about that "ere
it will be less" is that it utterly destroys the symbolic effect of the
snow in a way no simple assertion of its opposite could do. Against
the sentimental attempt to establish the snow once and for all time
as a symbol for the deadness of the universe, Frost places the simple
truth of experience. Spring *will* return and in its return will destroy
attempts to unify nature, monistically, under single symbolic ru-

brics. "I believe in symbols," Frost said. "I believe in change and changing symbols." [11]

That, then, is how Frost uses pluralism to combat the deleterious effects of monism. The positive value of a pluralistic approach can be seen in the last line, in which the poet speaks of "my own desert places." In making "desert places" plural, he implies "the possible other case"—those places which are *not* desert. Had the poet succumbed to his absent-spiritedness—had he accepted the dogma that meaning is exterior to the human mind—he would, quite simply, have had to speak of his own mind as "my desert place."

The beginning of Chapter XVIII of *The Scarlet Letter* tells us that, having made her home in "desert places," Hester is "set free." Like the figure in Frost's poem, she wanders "without rule or guidance . . . criticizing all" from her "estranged point of view." [12] In "Desert Places" Frost has drawn upon the advantages which Hester's outcast existence affords. Her freedom—like that finally expressed in "Desert Places"—consists in not being encumbered by a priori assumptions or limiting, prescriptive ideologies. But Hester's despair is very different from the despair that Frost depicts. Hers is the despair of one who is uncomforted and unenlightened by coherent moral values. She lives in an atmosphere of moral possibilities, though she refuses to take anything more than a highly eclectic advantage of them. It is appropriate, in other words, for Hawthorne to have described Hester's world as a "moral wilderness" and to have located in it the source of both her freedom and her despair. On the other hand, it is not appropriate to transfer that designation to Frost's "Desert Places," a poem which does not present a moral wilderness, nor, finally, any moral questions at all. What is true or appropriate in the source may not always be true of the poem that germinates from it. Frost has very explictly commented on the nature of his debt to sources when he said in "The Figure a Poem Makes" that "The artist must value himself as he snatches a thing from some previous order in time and space into a new order with not so much as a ligature clinging to it of the old place where it was organic." This is necessarily so for a mind such as Frost's that conceived of a work of art as an "order." His own sense of artistic freedom, furthermore, would have nothing to do with a too literal use of sources. The despair of "Desert Places," then, consists most simply in the recognition of the limits of the mind. The freedom which it expresses is the paradoxical counterpoint to the despair and consists in the recognition that the mind is essentially *un*limited.

Notes to *"Nothing That Is"*: *A Study of Frost's "Desert Places"* by ALBERT J. VON FRANK

1. James Ellis, "Frost's 'Desert Places' and Hawthorne," *The English Record*, XV (April 1965), 15–17.
2. Nathaniel Hawthorne, *The Scarlet Letter*, in William Charvat, et al., eds., *The Centenary Edition of the Works of Nathaniel Hawthorne* (Columbus, Ohio: Ohio State University Press, 1962), I, 199. I quote the passage according to the Centenary Edition, but retain Ellis's italics. Ellis ends his quotation at the phrase "desert places," thereby omitting the important evaluative clause that follows. There are several similarities between the poem and the passage from *The Scarlet Letter* other than those which Ellis points out: in both works the scene is a gloomy wood, reference is made to one's psychic "home," and there is an implied analogy in both instances between the physical and psychic settings.
3. Ellis, "Frost's 'Desert Places' and Hawthorne," 17.
4. See, however, other essays in this volume and appropriate notes. [ed.]
5. Cleanth Brooks and Robert Penn Warren, *Understanding Poetry* (New York: Henry Holt, 1938), 193–94.
6. Ralph Waldo Emerson, "Experience," in *Essays . . . Second Series* (Boston and New York: Houghton Mifflin, 1876), 75.
7. Reuben Brower, *The Poetry of Robert Frost: Constellations of Intention* (New York: Oxford University Press, 1963), 109.
8. Quoted by John Lynen, "Frost as Modern Poet," in James M. Cox, ed., *Robert Frost: A Collection of Critical Essays* (Englewood Cliffs, N.J.: Prentice-Hall, 1962), 190.
9. Brower, *The Poetry of Robert Frost*, 109.
10. "The difference, as I see it, is that Wordsworth quite explicitly does, and Frost does not, perceive an organic relationship, a vital continuity, between man and nature." George W. Nitchie, *Human Values in the Poetry of Robert Frost* (Durham, N.C.: Duke University Press, 1960), 28.
11. "What's my philosophy? That's hard to say. I was brought up a Swedenborgian. I am not a Swedenborgian now [1923]. But there's a good deal of it that's left with me. I am a mystic. I believe in symbols. I believe in change and changing symbols. Yet that doesn't take me away from the kindly contact of human beings. No, it brings me closer to them." Quoted in Lawrance Thompson, *Robert Frost: The Early Years, 1874–1915* (New York: Holt, Rinehart and Winston, 1966), 550.
12. Hawthorne, *The Scarlet Letter*, 199.

The Tragic Vision of Robert Frost

ROBERT M. RECHNITZ

I

IN what is perhaps the most jubilant of essays ever written about Robert Frost, Randall Jarrell speaks of the regrettable and inescapable dilemma attendant upon the creation of art in the present century. Man's expanding awareness of himself and his universe has resulted in a discontinuity of the poetic imagination. Thus, of Frost's achievements Jarrell remarks: "If we compare this wisdom with, say, that of ... Goethe, we are saddened and frightened at how much the poet's scope has narrowed, at how difficult and partial and idiosyncratic the application of his intelligence has become, at what terrible sacrifices he has had to make in order to avoid making others still more terrible." [1]

Coming at once to Frost's greatest sacrifice, we note the absence in his dramatic family of an Antony, a Hamlet, a Macbeth. In their stead we find a Hill Wife, a Servant to Servants, an Old Man. History is responsible for this diminution; Frost's genius is responsible for the discovery of value in such lives.

Though there are no tragic heroes in his work, Frost does maintain a tragic vision of the universe, a tragic vision resistant to concise definition, since it exists as an attitude rather than as a concept. The universe remains vast and incomprehensible except for those vague promptings of the sensibility which defy articulation, but which imply

That though there is no fixed line between wrong and right,
There are roughly zones whose laws must be obeyed.

Nature's laws are seen but darkly. "Something there is that doesn't love a wall," but the something is never defined. One misreads the poem, however, if he misses Frost's imputation of a moral regard in nature's fretful anarchy. If morality within anarchy is dismissed

133

as a meaningless paradox, the richness of a tragic universe will not be perceived. A. C. Bradley treats this problem in his *Shakespearean Tragedy*: "... the ultimate power in the tragic world is not adequately described as a law or order which we can see to be just and benevolent. .., nor is this ultimate power adequately described as a fate, whether malicious and cruel, or blind and indifferent to human happiness and goodness.... A view which would be true to the fact and to the whole of our imaginative experience must in some way combine these aspects." [2] Dangerous though it may be to attribute to Frost the Bradlean version of Shakespeare's quickening world, certain analogues contribute to a fuller understanding of all Frost's poetry.

Bradley's idea of the ultimate power as a kind of fate receives the greater part of Robert Frost's attention. Any progression of thought on this subject must be ours, for it is almost certain that Frost holds these various attitudes simultaneously. Yet in one poem the poet reveals himself in the act of revising his thoughts. "The Stars" are regarded first as being a sympathetic audience attending us "As if with keenness for our fate," but in the last stanza Frost shifts his ground:

> And yet with neither love nor hate,
>   Those stars like some snow-white
> Minerva's snow-white marble eyes
>   Without the gift of sight.

It is this latter attitude toward nature that is on the one hand so representative of our time and on the other so unsympathetic to the artistic imagination that Frost seldom adopts it; perhaps this is one occasion Mr. Jarrell has in mind when he speaks of the modern poet's partial and idiosyncratic application of his intellect. Perhaps such a view of nature appeals most to Frost's intellect, but it must soon be abandoned because of its sterility.

Besides, nature is *not* so aloof. If we turn our backs, nature steals a pace forward. The trees, seeing the opening left after the last mowing of "Faraway Meadow," "march into a shadowy claim." With "The Wood-Pile," Frost amplifies the idea of nature's unremitting warfare upon mankind. The poem achieves its end by contrasting the puniness and specificity of man with the featureless ambience of nature. As the poem opens, the narrator is absorbed in his playful exchange with the little bird; both man and bird are individuals—that is the important thing—and they are communicating with each other in a pleasant, ordinary way, the very normalcy of which sustains them both. It is the presence of the bird that makes the wilderness bearable, that holds it back and gives it form. With the discovery of the woodpile, a sudden change occurs. The bird departs, and nature closes in. The woodpile is grey; the world itself turns grey as if enshrouded in fog. The poet confronts chaos, utter formlessness—void. And this void is busily reclaiming that to which man has given shape.

The poem amounts to a synthesis of the remote unconcern of nature and of nature's hostility. Like the pan of dough which fills in the dimples we poke in it, nature slowly sloughs off our efforts to mold it. It is nature's inertia which balks us; its entropy defies man, the champion of progress. It is the poet in Frost that sees this inertia as hostility; it is the twentieth century in him which sees it as mere indifference.

The poet's problem remains: he must search for means to dramatize the hostility or indifference. In "The Most of It," nature answers man's cry of loneliness and desire for "counter-love, original response," by sending him a wild beast.

> As a great buck it powerfully appeared,
> Pushing the crumpled water up ahead,
> And landed pouring like a waterfall,
> And stumbled through the rocks with horny tread,
> And forced the underbrush—and that was all.

The repeated use, four times in three lines, of "and" establishes the lack of causality, the absence of meaning. Man constitutes his world in part by a constant attempt to discover cause and effect, and he is brought up short when he cannot do so. Nature at odd moments—this poem visualizes one of them—is easily capable of working not from causality but from mere sequence.

Still, we cannot infer that nature is evil or that an ultimate power working behind and through nature is evil. We have discovered inertia and simple sequence, but nothing more than that; and neither of these can be termed evil except insofar as they subvert man's will to order. The universe may be enigmatic, but that is not to say it is malign.

In a deceptive little poem, "Spring Pools," Frost records another sequence, this time one in which man is little concerned. The poem can easily be dismissed as a simple pastoral. The tone is tranquil throughout, even the last stanza of admonition. But though the poem deals with spring pools and flowers, with trees and summer foliage, the implication is sinister: the process of life is predatory. Birth is achieved at the expense of life. The trees draw their life-blood vampire-like from the pools, the pools from the winter snow, and so on, each element in nature drawing from each to an extent guaranteed to elate the most fervent Darwinian.

Of course, only the cheapest sort of sentimentality would label natural rapacity as evil; but carried a step further, this implication takes on all the metaphysical horror of a poem like "Design." It would be pretentious to attempt to add anything to Randall Jarrell's commentary on the poem, but Reginald L. Cook offers a remark which contributes to my thesis: Frost's "conjectural inquiry in 'Design' not only implies a subtle but a malefic force at work. And if design operates on the lower level in nature—if it is in the ruck of little things—then, by extension, it must also operate generally in the human sphere of activity since man cannot be separated from the complex, interrelated destiny of the natural universe." [3] Man cannot be separated from the universe around him, and this is, of course, the justification for any poet's concern with nature. There is a correspondence, however tenuous, which the poet senses when his heart vibrates in sympathy with a windhover or lark. Furthermore, we sympathize with the fat, dimpled spider, and with all the other carnivores which inhabit the earth and whose habits we recognize in our own. But before examining Frost's treatment of this correspondence of nature's evil in man, we must return to a discussion of the other half of the tragic universe described by A. C. Bradley.

Nature exhibits a benevolence which, though seldom revealed so explicitly as the malefic, can be traced in poem after poem. Often the good coexists with the evil, and Frost recognized this coexistence early in his career. In "Into My Own" the poet, wishing that the trees "stretched away unto the edge of doom," yearns to enter the woods where he believes he would fully realize his identity. Just how this would happen Frost does not say, but the poem is simple enough because it is squarely in the traditional view of nature as benign teacher. Nature is just, serene, and noble, a demanding teacher yet willing to reward decent human endeavor. She may wear a "mask of gloom," yet she is solid, dependable, and aligned with life.

Further evidence of the coexistence of nature's evil and benign attitudes can be found in a poem already mentioned. That nature is found anarchic in "Mending Wall" is readily apparent—"Something there is that doesn't love a wall,/That wants it down"—and man is right to define his humanity by repairing what nature exerts herself to destroy. But at the same time it is difficult to disregard the lesson she teaches, that walls if thoughtlessly erected may often prove to be insurmountable, and that with each one he builds, man hastens his total isolation.

Throughout the poetry runs the theme of nature's dualism: an order in her anarchy, the order of the passing years, the order of the seasons, the order of life and death. This pattern is pervasive and is evidence that, hidden in multiplicity, perhaps containing it in a way we cannot fathom, unity exists, affording man a sense of meaning, justice, and permanence. In "The Outset," a spring snow appears to be blotting out all renascent life, but the poet realizes after his momentary despair that life will not be denied so easily: "I know that winter death has never tried/The earth but it has failed." Nature will not submit to death; life will continue to renew itself. It will "make the settled snowbank steam," it will "burst into the poet's narrow stall," "give us pleasure in the orchard white," "and make us happy in the happy bees," lade "The fruited bough of the juniper," bring forth the "Steel-bright June-grass, and blackening heads of clover," and thaw "Ten million silver lizards out of snow!"

A twentieth-century poet has only these observations with which to stay the chaos; he sees no overt promise in the skies, no special providence in the fall of a sparrow, no covenant in the rainbow. All that remains is the steady unfolding of sequence, the ordered progression of events. The ultimate power behind the phenomena of this world remains unknowable, try as we may to force it to speak. "We dance around in a ring and suppose,/But the Secret sits in the middle and knows." Some Secret is there. All lines of communication with it may be down, but Frost does not thereby consign man to an unaccommodating, purposeless world. Moving with the wary caution of the sceptic, utilizing only the observable, Frost manages to construct a universe at once tenable to our modern eyes and satisfying to our thirst for justice and meaning. In "Our Hold on the Planet," he reminds us that

> We may doubt the just proportion of good to ill.
> There is much in nature against us. But we forget:
> Take nature altogether since time began,
> Including human nature, in peace and war,
> And it must be a little more in favor of man,
> Say a fraction of one percent at the very least. . . .

Frost's universe, then, contains an almost equal mixture of good and ill. The ultimate power, as Bradley suggests, can be accurately described only as both a law—a just and benevolent order—and a fate—malicious or indifferent.

II

But now we come to another of the great sacrifices imposed upon the contemporary artist. Though he may possess a tragic vision, he seems unable to go further. He writes of no catastrophes; and without catastrophe there can be no tragedy. Death is not necessary, but a point must be reached where the cosmos, wildly engaged in intestine warfare, rips itself asunder in an attempt to cast out the evil which has polluted it.[4] For some reason, perhaps pessimism, perhaps realism, perhaps cowardice, there are no more catastrophes. The good and evil in the world are held in solution; and if we have tragedy at all, we have only a tragedy of inertia.

Certainly the ingredients for struggle are present in Frost. Man, like nature, contains both good and evil. Frost is quick to state that the rapacity in nature is of no importance after one recognizes it as little more than a reflection of what exists within man himself. The deserted, snow-filled field and the empty expanse of space described in "Desert Places" are not frightening, for "I have it in me so much nearer home/To scare myself with my own desert places." Cloistered deep within us resides something more terrifying than anything to be found in nature, and in "A Leaf-Treader" Frost explores it.

> I have safely trodden underfoot the leaves of another year.
>
> All summer long they were overhead, more lifted up than I.
> To come to their final place in earth they had to pass me by.
> All summer long I thought I heard them threatening under their
>   breath.
> And when they came it seemed with a will to carry me with them
>   to death.
>
> They spoke to the fugitive in my heart as if it were leaf to leaf.
> They tapped at my eyelids and touched my lips with an
>   invitation to grief.
> But it was no reason I had to go because they had to go.
> Now up, my knee, to keep on top of another year of snow.

The fugitive in the heart is the yearning for death, the impulse toward destruction of self and of others. It is this fugitive which attributes to the falling leaves the desire to call man after them. If man is not to submit to the call, he can avoid it only through a supreme effort of will, and, as Frost suggests in the poem, the effort is apt to result in violence. But the urge to brutality need not be thus provoked; it is only too capable of rising at its own accord.

Although not companion pieces, two of Frost's sonnets, "Once by the Pacific" and "The Flood," underscore the similarities in the violence of nature and man. Neither will be contained, both bring on the night. But most important of all, Frost demonstrates how *easily* the savage brutality in both nature and man may burst forth. "We choose to say it is let loose by the devil;/But power of blood itself releases blood." Man, through the long, painful struggle which has marked his journey up from the mud, has by trial and error succeeded in enclosing the brute part of himself in the thinnest

membrane of decency. But the membrane is fragile, and his blood—
a symbol of brutality—will, if he is not vigilant, burst through the
membrane and drown him.

The problem is even more difficult, for, as Frost has said, "Keep
the wildness down; we have to; but if we keep it too completely
down we shall discover it breaking out in us, ourselves." [5] The brute
is so much a part of us that it cannot be totally denied. Somehow
the wildness must be given outlet yet at the same time be controlled.
This problem may best be examined in relation to the larger one,
Frost's exploration of a manner of existence.

III

Joseph Conrad once advised Galsworthy that " 'the fact is you
want more scepticism at the very fountain of your work. Scepticism, the tonic of minds, the tonic of life, the agent of truth—the
way of art and salvation.' " [6] Frost begins with a scepticism, and it
is this which restrains him from wholeheartedly embracing any
single school of thought. He rejects the absolute claims of both
instinct and intellect. To label such scepticism spiritual drifting, as
does Yvor Winters, is to miss the point completely. But in an age
which distrusts the "negative capability," Winters' error is common.

To doubt the perpetual efficacy of reason is only to accept an
important, self-evident tendency in human nature. Man is easily
made a victim of whim, of irrational impulse, and of perversity.
On the other hand, Frost nowhere advocates a complete surrender
to such impulses—he has often written of the pain such surrender
can bring. He is well aware that for the most part we live within
the probable, within a paradigm of set behavior which may preclude
greatness but which is necessary if man is to continue to live within
societies. When we falter, the societal pattern is in danger of collapse. "The Impulse" section of "The Hill Wife" describes this
danger:

> And once she went to break a bough
>   Of black alder.
> She strayed so far she scarcely heard
>   When he called her—

And didn't answer—didn't speak—
　Or return.
She stood, and then she ran and hid
　In the fern.

He never found her. . . .

Frost explains nothing, the lines are as abrupt as the action. Improbability cannot be touched upon discursively. We are left to wonder and despair. For no one can escape contingency. And though we walk through the darkened room with our arms before us, an open door may still rap us on the chin, as in "The Door in the Dark." With a keen awareness of such uncomfortable facts, Frost takes up his position of scepticism. And in poem after poem he reminds us that no formulas guarantee success; that the intellect, though valuable, is not infallible and its products not always worthy of the esteem we grant them; and that instinct, or impulse, is far from being trustworthy. In these lines from "To a Thinker,"

> Suppose you've no direction in you,
> I don't see but you must continue
> To use the gift you do possess,
> And sway with reason more or less.
> . . . .
> So if you find you must repent
> From side to side in argument,
> At least don't use your mind too hard,
> But trust my instinct—I'm a bard.

Frost is not being anti-intellectual but is recognizing that even the most exact of intellectual endeavors must be somewhat colored by the observer's temperament. The poem smiles at our scientific pretensions, yet the last two lines, which seem to defend instinct, are more than a little tinged with irony.

With "The White-Tailed Hornet," Frost opens fire in earnest on the other half of the intellect-instinct dualism. Not only does he deride the notion of the infallibility of instinct—"The missed fly made me dangerously skeptic"—he deplores the behavioral psychologies which would reduce man to the level of the insects by insisting that except for greater complexity in reception and response we differ not at all. In opposition to behavioralism Frost reminds us that we have intelligence and once used it to direct our comparisons upward: "With gods and angels, we were men at least,/But little lower than the gods and angels."

Frost recognizes the essential limitations of man. Man has no resource, either intellectual or instinctual, upon which he can blindly depend. Yet with no guarantees, no detailed course of action, no promise of punishment or reward, no external sanctions to bind him, Frost's man still finds sufficient cause to live.

We live, Frost reminds us, we live *decently*, out of a sense of responsibility. Our responsibility reaches out to embrace not only those nearest us, but all mankind, past, present, and future. With one poem, Frost states the theme out of which his life and poetry grow—"Willful Homing."

> The snow blows on him and off him, exerting force
> Downward to make him sit astride a drift,
> Imprint a saddle, and calmly consider a course.
> He peers out shrewdly into the thick and swift.
>
> Since he means to come to a door he will come to a door,
> Although so compromised of aim and rate
> He may fumble wide of the knob a yard or more
> And to those concerned he may seem a little late.

When we first read this poem, we are vexed that Frost ends it with the response of those who have been waiting. But of course that is just the point. We exert ourselves; we fight down the brutality within us, or we direct it against a storm or our work; we stifle the impulse to surrender and drift, so that the people waiting for us at home can have the joy of being angry that we have made supper late.

If man combats the storm out of a sense of responsibility for both others and himself, he is able to do so because he recognizes that he has a chance of succeeding. Nature leaves man some fighting room; the Frostian man learns to recognize and accept the boundaries, but only as guidelines, not as barriers. During "Brown's Descent," Brown acquiesces to the conditions of ice and gravity after once or twice trying to stop his momentum. He "Bows with grace to natural law" and afterwards, with proper New England tenacity, takes the long way home. He is in no way defeated; he simply yields to those forces which are irresistible.

It is a matter of accepting the human condition. Man cannot realize his potentialities until he accepts their limitations. Throughout Frost's poetry there is an implied movement toward this acceptance: the poet ranges within the field of probability, extraordinary experience is curtailed, life is seen as a daily repetition of minor acts of courage deemed heroic by the very nature of their finitude, and death is accepted as inevitable. There is no comprehending this inevitability; it is simply the way things are. The mysteries will never reveal themselves; man can look "Neither out far, nor in deep," and it is this limitation, finally, that he must accept.

Nature willingly prompts man in this lesson. "When the spent sun throws up its rays on cloud/And goes down burning into the gulf below," nature's creatures accept the night, and so, too, must man learn to " 'Let what will be, be.' " The first step toward wisdom is the acceptance of the inevitable. Once he accomplishes this, man's sense of alienation will be mitigated, and he will be able to exist in a closer communion with nature. He will rest more comfortably.

In the comfort lies the danger. Robert Penn Warren's essay admirably elucidates this basic attitude of Frost. Speaking of "Stopping by Woods" he says:

The fact of the capacity to stop by the roadside and contemplate the woods sets man off from the beast, but in so far as such contemplation involves a repudiation of the world of action and obligation it cancels the definition of man which it had seemed to establish. So the poem leaves us with that paradox, and that problem. We can accept neither term of the original contrast...; we must find a dialectic which will accommodate both terms. We must find a definition of our humanity which will transcend both terms.[7]

Man must learn both to accept and to resist the pull of nature. He must be capable of both building and refusing to build walls. He must retain the ability to contemplate while exercising the ability to act.

Frost's solution to the problem is summed up in the familiar line from "Mowing"—"The fact is the sweetest dream that labor knows." Stated again and again, the solution is phrased only a little differently in "Two Tramps in Mud Time."

> But yield who will to their separation,
> My object in living is to unite
> My avocation and my vocation
> As my two eyes make one in sight.

It is only in this manner that man can live within the dialectic mentioned in Warren's essay. Man must control his dreaming—this warning seems to be implied—must somehow contain it within the limits of possibility so that his dialectic will afford him a certain degree of peace. And he will contain it if he can accept Frost's belief that "anything more than the truth would seem too weak." This recognition of the necessity of controlling the dream is crucial to Frost's thinking; and though its utility cannot be denied, one must recognize the extraordinary amount of mental discipline one must exercise to maintain it. To discover the limits for his dreaming, man must first discover his capacity for action. Frost, no less demanding than Socrates, asks man to know himself.

Man must then learn to accept the inevitable and to resist where he can. Even here Frost does not isolate man. Nature itself seems to have discovered the same tactic. The young couple in "West-Running Brook" discover the stream's resistance and thereby recognize a kinship between man and nature.

> "It is this backward motion toward the source,
> Against the stream, that most we see ourselves in,
> The tribute of the current to the source.
> It is from this in nature we are from.
> It is most us."

Life is recalcitrant, and though swept irresistibly toward the "cataract of death," it will not go willingly. It will hearken back to life as long as it has breath.

Man will resist in countless ways. Like "A Drumlin Woodchuck," he will be "instinctively thorough/About . . . crevice and burrow." He will resort to the primitive expedient of exorcising his fear through ritual as in "The Bonfire." He will cultivate his mind with the help of "The Star-Splitter," develop his muscles and coordination by chopping wood, and his sensibilities by reading and writing poetry. He will build a house and live in it, as in "The Cocoon."

> I want to tell them that with all this smoke
> They prudently are spinning their cocoon
> And anchoring it to an earth and moon
> From which no winter gale can hope to blow it—
> Spinning their own cocoon did they but know it.

His home, the fire he builds, his simple day-to-day living, more than anything else, constitute man's resistance to the mutability of nature. But he must couple his daily tasks with a certain activity of will. Like the elderly couple of "In the Home Stretch," he must refuse to succumb to his sense of isolation and must recognize the need to master his imagination.[8]

Man's position is at best precarious. And the preservation of his best qualities seems to depend upon the perpetuation of this very precariousness. If he seeks to suspend the tension between himself and nature, he can only revert to rapaciousness or sink into a lethargic indifference. Rejecting these alternatives, man has no choice but continually to exert himself. Such exertion remains, for the most part for Frost, an individual matter. Each individual must fight his way through the snowstorm alone. But he makes the effort from a feeling of responsibility, exerting himself out of love, a love of self that becomes a love of others. Such a love pervades every poem, and to cite examples would only be a limitation. It is a love which expands until it embraces all men everywhere, but it is never abstract. As Frost points out in "Build Soil," love is rooted in this world and is meaningless until it is involved in action:

> There is no love.
> There's only love of men and women, love
> Of children, love of friends, of men, of God:
> Divine love, human love, parental love,
> Roughly discriminated for the rough.

Frost possesses a tragic vision, but, as we have seen, he writes of no tragic catastrophes. There is no destruction of the old order out of which is born a new. It is tempting to say, therefore, that somehow man's potentiality has diminished. No heroes are left, no one to make a meaningful sacrifice. Yet behind almost all of Frost's poems we sense a belief in the magnitude of man, and we detect in Frost's thought a sense of heroism of which every man partakes by the simple process of living out his life. And though there will be no sudden creation of a better world, perhaps a new world will slowly develop as each man realizes the heroic value he shares with his neighbor.

Notes to *The Tragic Vision of Robert Frost* by ROBERT M. RECHNITZ

1. Randall Jarrell, "To the Laodiceans," *Poetry and the Age* (New York: Vintage Books, 1955), 62.

2. A. C. Bradley, *Shakespearean Tragedy* (New York: St. Martin's Press, 1955), 31.

3. Reginald L. Cook, *The Dimensions of Robert Frost* (New York: Rinehart & Co., 1958), 107.

4. Bradley, 34–40.

5. Frost quoted in Sidney Cox, *A Swinger of Birches* (New York: New York University Press, 1958), 24.

6. Joseph Conrad, quoted by Robert Penn Warren in "Introduction," *Nostromo* (New York: Modern Library, 1951), xix.

7. Robert Penn Warren, "The Themes of Robert Frost," in *The Writer and His Craft*, ed. Roy W. Cowden (Ann Arbor: University of Michigan Press, 1954), quoted in Robert Penn Warren, *Selected Essays* (New York: Random House, 1958), 124.

8. See Alvan S. Ryan, "Frost and Emerson: Voice and Vision," *Massachusetts Review*, I, No. 1 (October 1959), 22.

Robert Frost as a Romantic

CHARLES CARMICHAEL

VIEWING Robert Frost as a Romantic involves an interpretation of his life as well as his work and helps to explain the differences between the widely accepted Robert Frost myth and Lawrance Thompson's biographical portrait. The discovery of periods of isolation, alienation, and terror in Frost's life casts doubt on the validity of the image of a gregarious folk-hero. This basic dichotomy bears marked resemblance to the Romantic's attempt to create a social role distinct from the self. And many instances of ambiguity in Frost's poetry are actually brilliant maneuvers to maintain tension between the traditional philosophical categories of subject and object, between observer and observed. To achieve a constant state of subject-object tension, the Romantics opted for fact, for the hurly-burly of the phenomenal world where striving for perfect adaptation always fails. Similarly, Frost desired raw experience to fashion into poetry, to build castles on the desolate sandlots of fact. The weaker poems of Frost's later years stem, at least in part, from a reduction of tension between subject and object and from an overt acceptance of his social role, the Robert Frost he had created through the years.[1]

Morse Peckham's theories provide an excellent heuristic framework for a study of the structures of Romantic thought. Although similar theories exist, Peckham avoids the pitfalls of literary definitions by stressing, first, the Romantic situation and, second, the several stages of Romanticism. Peckham feels that the Romantic situation involves both a historical and a personal disorientation. With the failure of the Enlightenment—a failure acted out for most people by the French Revolution—the sources of cultural value at the most advanced cultural levels disintegrated. The intellectual structure—the belief in the perfectibility of man and the meaningfulness of the universe—collapsed, taking with it the sense of relatedness to the phenomenal world. The result for the most advanced artists and thinkers was that former social roles were no longer valid. At this point, the Romantic entered a state described by Peckham as Negative Romanticism, experiencing despair and possibly even insanity on the personal level and, on the social level, finding no reason for or means of acting. In *Beyond the Tragic Vision*, Peckham shows that Goethe, Byron, Stendhal, Wordsworth, Carlyle, Balzac, Pushkin, Baudelaire, Browning, Tennyson, Swinburne, Wilde, Mallarmé, and Nietzsche—just to name the writers—experienced the disorientation which accompanies a breakdown of the assumptions underlying a social or a personal explanatory system. This experience is what is called "alienation." A similar experience—resembling, in extreme cases, a severe neurosis or even psychosis—seems to precede any great intellectual breakthrough. To recreate the sense of value, to reorient, to find meaning after experiencing breakdown, the Romantic artist must discriminate between the socially sanctioned role and the self. Rather than accepting invalid roles as sufficient or seeing the existence of value in the world, the Romantics find value in perception of the world. As Peckham says, "Value enters the world through the self, which is not supported by any perceptible social or cosmic order, and the self projects upon the world an order which serves to symbolize that self-generated value."

Isolating the self from the role means the deliberate creation of a social role or, more precisely, an antirole which does not integrate smoothly into society. Such roles include the Byronic Hero, the Poet-Visionary, the Bohemian, the Virtuoso, the Dandy, and the Historian. All these roles enable the role player to maintain a sense of identity from situation to situation, to transcend the values and assumptions of his culture; and these roles, as will be seen, apply to a greater or lesser extent to Robert Frost.

Peckham sees four stages of Romanticism in the nineteenth century. The first stage is Analogism—nature worship as a projection of value from the self; the second is Transcendentalism—the heroic, world-redemptive stage. In the third, the Objectist stage, both the self and the phenomenal world are denied ultimate reality; and in the fourth, Stylism, individually created patterns of behavior symbolize value from situation to situation. This development culminates in Nietzsche, who saw that the fault of Romanticism lay in trying to seek a final answer to the problems of human existence. Realizing that any value system is a projection, not a discovery, Nietzsche preached the transvaluation of values and their continuous transvaluation—in traditional terms, the maintenance of tension between subject and object. Man must redeem the world, and the primary redeemer is the artist, the poet. As Peckham interprets Nietzsche, "The profoundest satisfaction of the human mind is the creation of the world—out of nothingness.... only the experience of reality has value, an experience to be achieved by creating illusions so that we may live and by destroying them so that we may recover our freedom. Value is process, a perpetual weaving and unweaving of our own identities." [2]

Frost's situation was the Romantic's: he experienced profound despair, alienation, and isolation early in his life, and his work in the widest sense was the continuous creation and destruction of a sense of value. His biography, his letters, his prose, as well as his poetry, are evidence that Frost's personal and intellectual position was, in the sense that it represents the furthest advance of Romantic thought, terrifyingly sophisticated. The facts of his life—his early contemplation of suicide, his antiliberal attitudes, his refusal to play the role demanded of highly regarded poets during the Depression—point to a rejection of the explanatory systems of his day. We know that in early manhood Frost rejected the traditional college curriculum; that he felt betrayed at the same time by his future wife, Elinor; that he spent years on a remote New England farm; and that, indeed, he received almost no public recognition for his poetry until age forty—a period of isolation almost without precedent in cultural history. Frost began this long period of isolation only two months after the death of his first child. His mood ranging from discouragement to despondency during the first year or so, he appears to have experienced virtual breakdown. The pressure of trying to account for the death of his son and his own lack of recognition as a poet posed a grave dilemma. The following passage—although from a letter of 1917 shortly after the death of Frost's friend, Edward Thomas—conveys the depth of Frost's despair and apparently refers to the Derry farm years: "I have heard laughter by daylight when I thought it was my own because at that moment when it broke I had parted my lips to take food. . . . No man can tell you the sound or the way of my laughter. I have neighed at night in the woods behind a house like vampires. But there are no vampires, there are no ghouls, there are no demons, there is nothing but me."

Yet, paradoxically, Lawrance Thompson asserts that the period Frost spent on the Derry farm in New Hampshire was the most significant single period of his life. Moreover, Frost himself thought so: "I might say the core of all my writing was probably the five free years I had there on the farm down the road a mile or two from Derry Village toward Lawrence. The only thing we had plenty of was time and seclusion. I couldnt have figured on it in advance. I hadnt that kind of foresight. But it turned out as right as a doctor's prescription." Frost realized that he needed time alone—more than one would allow as sheer writing time—to draw out his creative faculties. He repeatedly sought out isolation, and the cost to himself and his family is a matter of record. Robert Frost's isolation was at times complete, at times more painful than he expected:

> Word I was in the house alone
> Somehow must have gotten abroad,
> Word I was in my life alone,
> Word I had no one left but God.

Besides a poem like "Bereft," evidence of Frost's alienation and personal isolation exists in numerous letters and in his reflections on traditional Christianity. Despite Thompson's assertions of Frost's strong but unconventional faith in God, at times of great emotional trial and great honesty, Frost makes statements that reflect his doubts: "I suppose love must always deceive. I'm afraid I deceived her [his wife Elinor] a little in pretending for the sake of argument that I didn't think the world as bad a place as she did. My excuse was that I wanted to keep her a little happy for my own selfish pleasure. It is as if for the sake of argument she had sacrificed her life to give me this terrible answer and really bring me down in sorrow. She needn't have. I knew I never had a leg to stand on, and I should think I had said so in print." Frost does say in the very next sentence that he believes some "mitigating things." These "things" issue from self-created value.[3]

Frost accomplished the first step in the Romantic quest for value, for "mitigating things," with brutal success. Stripping away the old personality, he fell into that soulless state which Peckham calls Negative Romanticism and which Carlyle in *Sartor Resartus* terms the "Center of Indifference." But moving out of that condition requires some sort of commitment beyond merely providing animal necessities. Frost perceived, although perhaps not consciously, that poetry provides a commitment, a means of creating value. Thus he first reenacted the Romantic creation of a self through his poetry, poetry of great originality. However, in the strictest sense there is no such thing as a self, only selves; and the creation of a consciously assumed social role or, more properly, antirole, provides the only visible social evidence for the creation of value. The Romantic's great problem revolves around the introduction of value into society. Frost, seeing that to reenter society he would have to create a social role, began to adopt certain habits of his laconic New England neighbors to his own purposes. Gradually, he outwardly reduced the isolation of his life and moved back into a relationship with his community as a teacher. Teaching provided an excellent opportunity for donning a role and, as a performing art, offered many of the metaphors for the word "role" that the stage affords. Frost grasped the possibilities. As a high school teacher, he developed the image of an unconventional, innovative educator. To this image he added, primarily while in England from 1912 to 1915, the figure of country wit.[4] Throughout his life—in lectures, in public readings, in college classrooms—Frost extended and refined the role he had created for himself, finally all but abandoning poetry for the role of Poet.

Those critics who see in Frost's so-called retreat to the country a nostalgic longing for the past are correct only so far. The role Frost assumed certainly is an old one, but it was never played as Frost played it. He dusted off the old farmer-philosopher hat and put it on, adding his own creases. For Frost, this role was a means of Romantic negation, a means of rejecting the prevailing cultural values. In our urban society, Frost's role as crackerbarrel philosopher became an antirole, and, for complex sociological and psychological reasons, a nationally treasured one. Seeming to promote social stability and to assert older values, Frost's public image was that of a good, wise old man who made witty remarks to Khrushchev and wrote poetry. Yet his personal life and opinions were more unconventional than his public realized. Even if recent accounts of his personal life err on the negative side, the division between role and self in Robert Frost is abundantly clear.

Just as the self-role dichotomy in Frost resembles that of the typical Romantic, Frost's conception of the creation of value corresponds to the Romantic's. As Peckham says, by the end of the nineteenth century it was apparent that value lay in neither nature nor man, neither subject nor object, but in the maintenance of tension between the two. For the Romantics, a "concept of moments of vision into the heart of things from which neither moral nor metaphysical nor empirical propositions could be derived was not too far away from Darwin's conception of scientific knowledge as not final." [5] Similarly, Frost's theory of poetry—no doubt strongly influenced by William James—exhibits a very conscious awareness of the necessity to maintain the tension between subject and object, to avoid asserting the final meaning of an experience. In "Education by Poetry," Frost demonstrates an awareness that, to humanists grabbing at explanations, the ambiguities in certain scientific theories justify philosophical skepticism. In this connection he describes, though he does not name, the Heisenberg uncertainty principle; mentions with delight that space is curved; and cites Niels Bohr on the quantum theory, that light is both wave and particle. Frost extends this line of thought to poetry: "All metaphor breaks down somewhere. That is the beauty of it. It is touch and go with metaphor, and until you have lived with it long enough you don't know when it is going." Any metaphor, any "stay," any creation of value is temporary.

Frost realized that all intellectual endeavors involve constructs, projections of value from the self onto the world. But he went even further: He realized the necessity to transcend such constructs. In "The Figure a Poem Makes," which includes one of his most famous epigrams, Frost states: "No one can really hold that the ecstasy should be static and stand still in one place. It begins in delight, it inclines to the impulse, it assumes direction with the first line laid down, it runs a course of lucky events, and ends in a clarification of life—not necessarily a great clarification, such as sects and cults are founded on, but in a momentary stay against confusion." Thus Frost's ideas about "stay" and "form" are best seen in the Romantic sense as creations of value which provide explanations not provided by existing cultural values. As Frost puts it, "There is at least so much good in the world that it admits of form and the making of form." Frost, then, agrees with Nietzsche that the human mind must create its own sense of value, its own meaning. And like Nietzsche, Frost rejoices that such is the case: "The background in hugeness and confusion shading away from where we stand into black and utter chaos; and against the background any small man-made figure of order and concentration. What pleasanter than that this should be so?"[6]

In his isolation and alienation, his separation of self and role, his ideas about "stay" and "form," Frost shows himself to be at the forefront of Romantic thought in his day. Even in his interviews Frost maintains the Romantic viewpoint: " 'The most creative thing in us is to believe a thing in, in love, in all else. You believe yourself into existence. You believe your marriage into existence, you believe in each other, you believe that it's worthwhile going on, or you'd commit suicide, wouldn't you?' "[7] These same Romantic ideas—grouped here for convenience under three categories—occur in Frost's poetry. First, his poems illustrate what is usually termed the irresolvable tension between subject and object. Second, Frost returns again and again to the necessity for man to create some value or "stay" or "form" in his life. And, third, certain poems comment on the difference between self and social role.

The problems of discussing subject-object tension in Frost's poetry diminish if one views the idea in a historical context. In Peckham's Analogical stage of Romanticism, the first stage, the poet or artist finds nature to be an emblem for the self. As in Wordsworth's "Tintern Abbey," nature manifests some motion or spirit or some link between man and the world which is really there.

Once the poet discovers such value, it is there forever. However, as we have seen, Frost stands at the end of nineteenth-century Romanticism and the beginning of the "modern" movements in the arts. By this time, the artist at the highest cultural levels had realized the necessity for the continuous introduction and reintroduction of value into the world. Frost's severest critics attack him for indecisiveness,[8] the inability to declare a truth or decide whether an experience is meaningful. But Frost was more intellectually sophisticated than his critics. He realized that, in order to remain free of the mental prisons our minds erect, the artist must maintain his existence in the middle of a process[9]—an idea resembling Keats's "negative capability."

In several poems, Frost explicitly questions the experience which his persona or poet-figure presents. And usually the questioning, the puncturing of an illusion, occurs in the same poem. Perhaps the most striking example of this tension between subject and object is in "A Boundless Moment." The poem shows Frost's penetrating awareness of our huge potential for self-deception. A couple, apparently lovers, are dumbfounded and delighted by finding a flower, the Paradise-in-Bloom, in March, two months before its time. As long as they are under the spell of this illusion, the world has value, "makes sense" for a moment:

> And truly it was fair enough for flowers
> Had we but in us to assume in March
> Such white luxuriance of May for ours.

Thus they have undergone what Kant and the Romantics believe to be the only experience of meaning in the world: "It is the pure experience of value which arises from so intense an observation of the natural world that all roles, all mental categories, disappear." [10] However, in "A Boundless Moment" the poet is of course writing after the experience, and the reader is aware of an irony casting doubt on the surface presentation. The poet-figure was "too ready to believe" or "to assume." The last quatrain presents a statement of the continuing tension between subject and object:

> We stood a moment so, in a strange world,
> Myself as one his own pretense deceives;

And then I said the truth (and we moved on).
A young beech clinging to its last year's leaves.

The poet-figure realizes his mistake; the Paradise-in-Bloom is really a young beech, and the experience of pure value is only an illusion. One should also add, necessarily an illusion. The persona speaks the "truth" and moves on. But notice that here the truth is only heuristic, something to move beyond. Even the last line of the poem questions implicitly the finality of the poet-figure's "truth": the last line is a sentence fragment, the grammatical equivalent of a hesitation or lingering uncertainty.

A similar questioning of a value experience provides the basis for the sonnet "Time Out." In the original format of *A Witness Tree* (1942), "Time Out" introduces a group of poems which present several approaches to the question of meaning in the face of meaninglessness or apocalypse. The title "Time Out" signals a pause the poet takes for a metaphysical inventory, as it were, on a cosmic holiday. The man described in "Time Out" is best conceived as a naturalist and not necessarily a poet. His knowledge of flowers is precise—he knows their common and scientific names—and he seems to be examining the flora of the mountain he is climbing. Absorbed in his study, this man appears to undergo a Wordsworthian exchange of consciousness between the mountain and himself. By forgetting himself in the study of flowers, he experiences a mental transformation. His head assumes the same slope as the mountain. The "slant" given his thought is different from the slant or attitude which he takes in the human world of "enemies defied and battles fought." Yet the poem contains so many grammatical ambiguities —unclear usages of "thing" and "it"—that the reader cannot really sort out what has happened. In addition, the "gentle air" of the poem's setting is obstinate and resists the various interpretations given to it by "cause and sect." Here the air or nature—the object in the subject-object relationship—"will have its moment to reflect."

In "A Boundless Moment" tension between subject and object is maintained by an implied continuous transcendence of experience; in "Time Out," by grammatical ambiguity and a consideration of the object's viewpoint. In "For Once, Then, Something" the experience of value to the poet-figure is pure self-delusion. The poet-figure looks at his image reflected in a well-pool; and, surrounded by a halo of natural objects, he discerns something "white, uncertain," and then loses it. Once he realizes that the well he looks into does not reflect his own sense of value, the meaning of his experience becomes ambiguous, its ambiguity symbolized by whiteness. He loses his sense of value, of orientation. The "whiteness" he perceives does not fit the mental picture he has drawn for himself, and the persona is left wondering about the significance of what he has seen. Was it "Truth? A pebble of quartz?" The answer is not forthcoming. Another example of subject-object tension is in "The Onset." While seemingly a restatement of Shelley's "If Winter comes, can Spring be far behind," "The Onset" actually throws in doubt such a belief. In the first part of the poem, the poet-figure is almost overcome by "winter death." In the second part he reminds himself of the optimistic "precedent" that the earth is always renewed in spring. However, the language and imagery reintroduce doubt and winter death in the description of spring.

> And I shall see the snow all go downhill
> In water of a slender April rill
> That flashes tail through last year's withered brake
> And dead weeds, like a disappearing snake.

Winter and spring imply each other. The tension is never resolved.

In "Circles," Emerson makes a statement reminiscent of Kant and highly relevant to the problem under discussion: the maintenance of tension between subject and object in poems exploring value experiences. Emerson says: "The one thing which we seek with insatiable desire is to forget ourselves, to be surprised out of our propriety, to lose our sempiternal memory and to do something without knowing how or why; in short to draw a new circle." The lovers in Frost's "Two Look at Two" draw a new circle while hiking up a mountain when they encounter a doe and a buck in a rare, almost visionary moment. Preoccupied by "love and forgetting," they pause to turn back but suddenly observe and are observed by a doe and a buck. The encounter is especially remarkable because they expect nothing and keep saying "This is all" when it is not "all." After the deer have left

> Still they stood,
> A great wave from it going over them,
> As if the earth in one unlooked-for favor
> Had made them certain earth returned their love.

Here the encounter between humans and animals seems to imply some response from Nature, but Frost is careful to qualify the meaning of this experience with an "as if." The tension between subject and object in this poem cannot be resolved; indeed there is even some question about who is the subject and who the object, who the observer and who the observed. A similar poem involving only one person, "The Most of It" displays such tension that reading the poem is exasperating, shocking, disorienting—and that is precisely the point. The poet-figure (in reality, Wade Van Dore),[11] set apart from the world, alienated, isolated, turns to nature, here the universe, nonhuman otherness, for a true experience of value. To his surprise, he does experience value of a sort—that is, he gets a response, but

> Instead of proving human when it neared
> And someone else additional to him,
> As a great buck it powerfully appeared,
> Pushing the crumpled water up ahead. . . .

The intellectual sophistication here is astounding and frightening: from this experience the persona can formulate no morals or metaphysic—in other words, nothing follows, either literally or metaphysically. The experience must be held continually in mind and continually transcended. That most human beings cannot endure such tension is evident from the responses of many highly intelligent critics who find fault with "The Most of It" even while admitting its greatness.

Since the Romantic was continually trying to maintain the tension between subject and object, he sought out encounters with "reality," with the phenomenal world. The record of close observation of nature in Frost's poetry is sufficient evidence that he was passionately interested in the phenomenal world. As Thompson points out, the importance of facts for Emerson and Thoreau probably influenced Frost's view of the world—for Thoreau, seeking "facts" was a form of worship; for Emerson, a fact of any kind was a sign of the whole of nature.[12] Frost, at a later stage of Romanticism, also values fact, but for a different reason. In Frost, the emphasis on fact is a ploy for maintaining subject-object tension. It prevents the delusion that the world of fact has no influence at all on the world of mind; it prevents the object from lapsing into the subject. The desire for fact, the longing for, in Richard Wilbur's phrase, the "Things of This World," finds its most exquisite statement in Frost's "To Earthward." Here the poet-figure, no longer able to live "on air ... From hidden grapevine springs/Downhill at dusk," wants to feel the harshness and "otherness" of the physical world.

> When stiff and sore and scarred
> I take away my hand
> From leaning on it hard
> In grass and sand,
>
> The hurt is not enough:
> I long for weight and strength
> To feel the earth as rough
> To all my length.

A continual receptivity to the phenomenal world is necessary to the Romantic artist. As Frost says in "Mowing," "The fact is the sweetest dream that labor knows."

Into the phenomenal world man thrusts his mind and creates his own sense of value. This is the Romantic position embodied many times in Frost's poetry. He shows that it is man's mind which creates value, that none of man's truths is immanent in the natural world. In "Happiness Makes Up in Height for What It Lacks in Length," the poet-figure questions the source of his sense of value:

> I can but wonder whence
> I get the lasting sense
> Of so much warmth and light.

Rather than asserting, as some would, that the sense of value proceeds from a perfect day

> When starting clear at dawn
> The day swept clearly on
> To finish clear at eve

he qualifies by saying "If my mistrust is right. . . ." In other words, his "fair impression" of happiness may be a delusion in the sense that a "perfect day" is not immanent in nature but a creation of the mind. In "Sand Dunes" the poet-figure asserts the power of the mind to create value, or "form," in the midst of a hostile universe. Threatened by inundation from the ocean or extinction from the desert, the mind is yet not cut off from its source of value because that source is the mind itself, not the endangered "cove and cape." As the poet-figure says, the sand dunes can only strip away the hindrances to thought:

> Men left her a ship to sink:
> They can leave her a hut as well;
> And be but more free to think
> For the one more cast-off shell.

"Never Again Would Birds' Song Be the Same" focuses on a slightly different aspect of man's ability to create meaning. The opening line, "He would declare and could himself believe," indicates the effort which one expends on convincing oneself that man does affect the natural world; in this case, that the voice of Eve "added . . . an oversound,/Her tone of meaning but without the words" to the birds' song. The man in the poem has heard the woman's voice intertwined with the birds' for so long that "probably it never would be lost"—in other words, the man will never be able to separate the two. Remarkably similar in theme to Wallace Stevens' "The Idea of Order at Key West," Frost's sonnet celebrates the power of song, of art, to make an experience memorable, to transfix and translate an ordinary experience. In Stevens' poem, it was the singer's "voice that made/The sky acutest at its vanishing." In Frost's poem, the woman came with her voice to add eloquence to birds. In both instances, the "real" world alters to accommodate a woman's voice.

The most subtle and complex statement of this idea, that order and value are a mental construct, appears in the poem "All Revelation." Here Frost realizes that indeed "All revelation has been ours" because our revelation—our sense of value—is something we create. In the third stanza of this poem Frost uses a metaphor from science to illustrate what he means:

> But the impervious geode
> Was entered, and its inner crust
> Of crystals with a ray cathode
> At every point and facet glowed
> In answer to the mental thrust.

The geode is the world, nature, the universe, anything man seeks to make sense of, including himself as an observable phenomenon. Like the birds' song in "Never Again Would Birds' Song Be the Same," the geode changes to accommodate the human drive to order. Everything in the phenomenal world is "impervious"—that is, value is not immanent in it but is created by the mind "In answer to the mental thrust." But Frost made it clear in the preceding stanza that any mental construct is only a temporary "stay" to be continually revised and transcended:

> These things the mind has pondered on
> A moment and still asking gone.
> Strange apparition of the mind!

Man is always unsatisfied with his answers, and he dies seeking new ones. Any final answer being impossible, truly "All revelation has been ours." In his best poems Frost keeps in front of the reader the strange ability of the mind to create a world which makes sense.

In addition to Romantic concepts of subject-object tension and creation of value, Frost's poetry illustrates an awareness of the self-role split. We have noted the social role which Frost created for himself; and, although his own personality embodied the Romantic problem more clearly, his poetry does make some comment on the difficulties of maintaining a social role. "Into My Own," the first poem of his first book, *A Boy's Will*, finds the poet-figure announcing his own quest for meaning. Ignoring social convention, rejecting the "highway where the slow wheel pours the sand," the youth, "having forsworn the world," assures himself that his retreat from the social world and his role will prove his worth:

> They would not find me changed from him they knew—
> Only more sure of all I thought was true.

In "The Vantage Point," the youth achieves a kind of transcendence. From his isolated and alienated position, he observes with equanimity both the social world of man and the world of nature. From *A Boy's Will* to the last poem of *In The Clearing*, Frost announces his refusal to submit either to the structured social world or to the chaos of nature. Frost's "[In Winter in the Woods ...]" serves as a kind of concluding statement to his work. As a Romantic document, the poem has force by its succinct statement of the themes of alienation and isolation. In the woods *alone*, the poet-figure goes against the trees, which are the most imposing natural objects in his surroundings. Determined to work out his own temporary sense of value, he forces the woods to conform, if only for an instant and in a small way, to his vision of order and necessity: "I mark a maple for my own/And lay the maple low." The background of chaos and confusion, a world of nonimmanent value, is symbolized by the woods and by the snow which is about to inundate and negate his achievement: "I link a line of shadowy tracks/Across the tinted snow." The only order in this world is that made by one single personality in the face of a darkening landscape. The Romantic individual cannot depend on social conventions for his sense of value. His retreat does not mean that he is giving up, for the last lines of the poem:

> I see for Nature no defeat
> In one tree's overthrow
> Or for myself in my retreat
> For yet another blow

may be interpreted two ways: the poet-figure is preparing either to receive or to give a blow. His retreat does not necessarily mean that he accepts his failure to subdue the world: it is just as easy to see his retreat as a device for renewal and redirection. The Romantic retreats from the world to achieve transcendence, a sense of the self. In this poem Frost has given his version of the Romantic necessity for retreat and isolation. A similar poetic presentation of the self-role split, the familiar "Stopping by Woods on a Snowy Evening," presents the persona of the poem as an isolated individual. He is highly aware of the differences between a self which seeks to confirm his own particular sense of value and a social role which requires sacrificing a certain amount of selfhood. He has "promises to keep," but he wants to experience some final confirmation of his self. Such a final confirmation is, as numerous commentators have pointed out, death. "Stopping by Woods" shows that the self-role split depends on the maintenance of tension between the subject and object. If the persona yields to the enticements of the woods—and in the repetition of the well-known line "And miles to go before I sleep," Frost suggests the persona might yield—if he lapses completely into the object and finds all value in the woods, he will die.

One of the most difficult tasks of the Romantic artist is to show the social consequences of a Romantic attitude. It is as if the writer says, "What would happen if an ordinary person—ordinary in the sense of having no self-conscious knowledge of Romanticism—were to undergo the sort of disorientation common to the Romantic artist?" The best example of Frost's use of this theme is "Home Burial." In that disturbing poem, Amy, the woman whose husband dug their child's grave as she watched, represents the attempt to assert the self in opposition to the socially validated role. When her husband accuses her of *self*-ishness, she does not consider it a fault. She wants grief to be something outside the sanctions given by the social role of the "grieving mother." By showing the weakness of Amy's position, Frost astounds us with his insight into the problem of ignoring social convention. In this poem one sees what Lionel Trilling meant by the "disintegration and sloughing off of the old consciousness!" [13] Trilling may have realized too that Frost was stating in concrete, New England terms the very problem with which the Romantic poet has always struggled, the validation of a self in conflict with society.

As long as he could suspend himself in the middle of a process; as long as he maintained the tension between self and role, subject and object; as long as he flung himself earthward, Robert Frost wrote some great poetry. However, in later years, as his version of his life became accepted and mythologized by friends, critics, and the mass media, Frost fell more and more easily into the ready-made role: he no longer had to struggle to maintain that identity, that persona. This Robert Frost Myth—the self-created role—included, under the veneer of sage poet, aspects of nearly every antirole mentioned earlier as Romantic poses.

Thus the Robert Frost persona encompasses a Byronic Hero—a conception which provides Thompson one of his major biographical themes. Frost wanted to be a hero in his mother's eyes; and although Thompson perhaps exaggerates this side of Frost's personality, it does seem significant, since the idea is expressed in both the early "The Trial by Existence" with its heroic spirits and in the late "Directive" with its Grail motif.

Although undermined by irony and wit, the Poet-Visionary Frost creates numerous poems—some, like "Two Look at Two," with the revelation qualified and others, such as "The Freedom of the Moon" and "Iris by Night," that do not qualify the revelation.

Like the Poet-Visionary, the Romantic Historian also seeks answers not provided by his culture. In poems like "The Black Cottage" and "The Gift Outright," Frost played his own variations on the role of the Historian who sees beyond his own society's assumptions. His version of this role enabled him in his poetry to pronounce on many public issues. In his lectures and classroom discussions Frost loved to appear—with emphasis on appearance—as a Virtuoso. The Virtuoso must not only be great; he must also seem to be far better than the mere mortals surrounding him. In many poems—"The Silken Tent," a sonnet in one sentence, comes immediately to mind—Frost displays the sheer technical mastery of his craft expected of a Virtuoso. This attitude toward one's art carries over into social situations. For example, at a banquet honoring T. S. Eliot, Frost read a poem which he pretended to improvise but which he had memorized months earlier. For the Virtuoso, the façade of mastery often rivals true accomplishment in the artist's scale of values. Frost capitulated to the social role.

By the time *Steeple Bush* (1947) and especially *In The Clearing* (1962) were published, Frost was by far the most honored poet in American history. The Robert Frost Myth had gained widespread acceptance and apparently was tacitly accepted by the poet himself. Thus he lost a major source of tension in his life; he accepted his public role as the model of his self. His alienation from the predominating culture was reduced to a level as low as possible for a man with Frost's genius. He preferred the Robert Frost who went to Russia and who read at President Kennedy's inaugural to the man who was "acquainted with the night." As a result of accepting the honored role, Frost could not charge his later poems with the tension between subject and object which, we have seen, underlies many of his finest poems. In his later poetry Frost and persona are one; his self and public roles merge. In "Skeptic," there is no real encounter with the phenomenal world:

> Far star that tickles for me my sensitive plate
> And fries a couple of ebon atoms white,
> I don't believe I believe a thing you state.

Here the poet-figure has no intention of revising his model of the universe. The world is to be used as a sort of secular Sunday School text, not experienced as a momentary stay or source of value. He pretends to skepticism, but he actually is completely negative about the value of the phenomenal world.

Although it is impossible to account for the mannerisms of Frost's later poetry, it is simple enough to show that Mannerism threatens any artist who creates a unique style, whether in his life or in his art. As Peckham points out in his work on Romanticism, Stylism, the last stage of nineteenth-century Romanticism, degenerates into Mannerism. All behavior has "style," but the Stylist seizes upon style self-consciously "to symbolize the continuity of identity from situation to situation . . . , the perfect way of symbolizing the sense of order and value and meaning without tempting him to impose that pattern upon reality." [14] The great Stylists, including in Peckham's scheme numerous artists from Swinburne to Hemingway, turned into Mannerists. The example of Hemingway, who was concerned with the Hemingway style in everything he did, provides a fruitful comparison with Frost. Hemingway always played the role of Hemingway. Just so, Frost played the role of Frost and finally played the role in his poetry, too, to its detriment.

Notes to *Robert Frost as a Romantic* by CHARLES CARMICHAEL

1. Harold Bloom calls Frost a Romantic in "Emerson: The Glory and the Sorrows of American Romanticism," *Virginia Quarterly Review*, XLVII (1971), 546–63.

George W. Nitchie presents ideas similar to mine in "Frost as Underground Man," *Southern Review*, n. s., II (1966), 817–21.

2. The discussion of Romanticism is summarized from Morse Peckham's *Beyond the Tragic Vision* (New York: Braziller, 1962); *Man's Rage for Chaos* (1965; rpt. New York: Schocken Books, 1967); and *The Triumph of Romanticism* (Columbia, S.C.: University of South Carolina Press, 1970). The quotations are from *The Triumph of Romanticism*, p. 32 and p. 56. Similar theories appear in Albert Gerard, "On the Logic of Romanticism," *Essays in Criticism*, VII (1957), 262–73; Geoffrey H. Hartman, "Romanticism and 'Anti-Self-Consciousness,'" *Centennial Review*, VI (1962), 553–65; George Boas, "The Romantic Self: An Historical Sketch," *Studies in Romanticism*, IV (1964), 1–16; Earl R. Wasserman, "The English Romantics: The Grounds of Knowledge," *Studies in Romanticism*, IV (1964), 17–34.

3. *Selected Letters of Robert Frost*, ed. Lawrance Thompson (New York: Holt, Rinehart and Winston, 1964), 221, 31, 552, 470–71.

4. Lawrance Thompson, *Robert Frost: The Early Years, 1874–1915* (New York: Holt, Rinehart and Winston, 1966) is the source for biographical material.

5. Peckham, *The Triumph of Romanticism*, 196.

6. *Selected Prose of Robert Frost*, ed. Hyde Cox and Edward Connery Lathem (New York: Holt, Rinehart and Winston, 1966), 18, 41, 106, 107.

7. *Interviews with Robert Frost*, ed. Edward Connery Lathem (New York: Holt, Rinehart and Winston, 1966), 271.

8. For example, see Isadore Traschen, "Robert Frost: Some Divisions in a Whole Man," *Yale Review*, LV (1965), 57–70.

9. See Lawrance Thompson's note about Frost's ability to remain in the middle of a process: *Robert Frost: The Years of Triumph, 1915–1938* (New York: Holt, Rinehart and Winston, 1970), 600.

10. Peckham, *The Triumph of Romanticism*, 41–42.

11. Wade Van Dore, "Robert Frost: A Memoir and a Remonstrance," *Journal of Modern Literature*, II (1972), 554–60.

12. Thompson, *The Early Years*, 273.

13. Lionel Trilling, "A Speech on Robert Frost: A Cultural Episode," *Partisan Review*, XXVI (1959), rpt. in James M. Cox, ed., *Robert Frost: A Collection of Critical Essays* (Englewood Cliffs, N.J.: Prentice-Hall, 1962), 157. Trilling is echoing D. H. Lawrence.

14. Peckham, *The Triumph of Romanticism*, 53.

THEMES

The following seven papers represent a broad range of approaches to the various and subtle themes of Robert Frost. John Conder begins his essay on "After Apple-Picking" by discussing the interpretational difficulties that face the Frost critic, difficulties that ensue chiefly from efforts to show how far the poems extend beyond surface realism. He notes that "After Apple-Picking" exemplifies the richness and thereby the complexity of both surface and associational levels. At the outset of his explication, he isolates two words in the final lines, "trouble" and "sleep," which he considers keys to understanding the theme. The sleep that is about to overtake the speaker may be of several kinds: simply a night's rest or a long seasonal sleep like that of winter, which introduces a tentative parallel. If the sleep is analogous to that of seasonal hibernation, then it holds out assurance that the speaker's desire for and ability to achieve "new harvests" will be renewed. But the speaker finally denies the analogy; human beings do not sleep like the woodchuck in hibernation. And Conder cites other details in the poem which deny the parallel between man and nature. Nonetheless, there is a limited sense in which the speaker resembles the woodchuck: his creative powers are subject to cyclical changes like those brought on by the seasons. Thus it is possible that his sleep will be a renewing rest and will return him to earlier assurances of purpose and value. But the recovery is deliberately left uncertain. Conder concludes that the poem ultimately poses, unresolved, the speaker's hope for and doubt of psychic renewal. The resulting irony is structural as well as thematic, for the poem ends just as the speaker is falling asleep.

The next two papers consider the various themes embodied in Frost's "home" metaphor. Vivian Hopkins explores the lifelong interest in houses that furnished a key image for many of Frost's poems. She traces the sequences of moves that he made from the time of his marriage, showing that he frequently drew on personal experiences and particular houses to create various images of

167

"home." She points out the ambiguities involved in the "home" metaphor: home is a comforting shelter in "There Are Roughly Zones" and a frightening enclosure in "The Hill Wife" and "The Witch of Coös." Briefly she discusses the recurring motif of the abandoned or ruined house, particularly as it operates in "Directive," and concludes by observing that the houses of Frost's poetry frequently symbolize the kinds of contraries which occupied the poet throughout his life. They provide shelter and exact labor; they represent refuge and danger.

Roger Ekins also considers the "home" metaphor. Like Professor Hopkins, he says that "home" serves a variety of thematic functions, but particularly it expresses ambiguous needs and attitudes toward experience. On one level, home is a "house of refuge and a source of protection." Drawing on Mircea Eliade's *The Sacred and the Profane: the Nature of Religion*, Ekins identifies another level of the metaphor: building a home is basically a religious experience, a creation of sacred space, thus justifiably serious business. (One is reminded of Hopkins' account of Frost's continual shopping for houses.) Ironically, home can too successfully insulate one from the world, to the extent that it becomes a personal prison. Hence another aspect of the metaphor is the negative one of the caged prison, such as one finds in "The Subverted Flower." To one who realizes that "home" cannot finally protect from the world, there is the effort to transform "home" from a narrowly physical, protecting house into the broader realm of nature. "Home" thus becomes the woods. This image of home, which would seem to resolve the dilemma of man's need to be housed but not imprisoned, occurs, for example, in "In the Long Night." Ekins shows that Frost extends the metaphor to the furthermost point possible in the two poems "New Hampshire" and "The Star-Splitter." In these, the home space is stretched to include the stars. Ekins reasons that "home" is a key metaphor in many of Frost's poems because it reconciles and embodies contradictory directions pursued by man. And it reminds the reader simultaneously of both the victory and the failure of man's efforts to be "at home" with life.

Nancy Vogel draws on Martin Joos's classification of levels of language to show the manner in which Frost maintains his dialogue in a colloquial style at the same time that he writes in the "frozen" style of poetry. Specifically, Professor Vogel analyzes the role of grammatical structure in the heightened and pleasing effect of the famous lines: " 'Home is the place where, when you have to go there,/They have to take you in,' " and " 'I should have called it/Something you somehow haven't to deserve.' " The emphasis achieved by means of the structure gives an important clue to one of the central issues of the poem, the nature of "home." Like Hopkins and Ekins, Vogel interprets home as a representation of ironies, the epitomizing symbol of any goal which one achieves either by justly deserving it or by receiving it as a merciful gift. Her conclusion is that "The Death of the Hired Man" is admirable stylistically in its achieved form of the debate and in its exploration of the contraries of justice and mercy.

In a comparison of Frost's "The Gold Hesperidee" and Tennyson's "The Hesperides," Robert Fleissner explores the significance of numerological motifs in both poems. Specifically, he traces the parallel structural and thematic uses of the numbers "five" and "three." Although other elements connect the poems (Romantic and anti-Romantic elements and aspects of the Edenic myth), the number patterns provide the most striking correlation. Fleissner considers the question of how much knowledge Frost had of such motifs and of Tennyson's poem. He gives some evidence to show knowledge on the part of both poets, noting especially Frost's interest in Tennyson's poem. But he also makes his case for the correlative use of number patterns on the basis of a shared archetypal affinity for "the Golden Section Proportion, and for the pentagonal symmetry intimately allied with it." Indeed, the latter part of the essay presents a detailed discussion of data drawn from experimental psychology which indicate man's unconscious preference for "golden proportionality." In the case of Frost, Fleissner shows that the poet was doubtless familiar with classical allusions to the Golden Mean, but that he also probably intuited many of the functions which the Mean serves in his poetry. Fleissner urges the point that "Frost, the good Greek" is Greek principally in the mathematical and aesthetic sense, rather than in an ethical one.

The last two papers offer some clear insights into the social and political themes of two poems by Frost. In her discussion of "The Black Cottage," Margaret Allen shows that Frost employs a familiar form, the dramatic dialectic, to probe opposing views of Jefferson's ideal of equality. She traces the subtlety of Frost's double view of the characters in the poem, pointing out that on the surface the old woman seems simply to represent an earlier era and a simplistic acceptance of Jeffersonian doctrine, and the practical, modern minister, a desirable skepticism about easy doctrines of equality. But characteristic contraries operate in the poem. The old woman is also imbued with "resilient vitality" by her trusting belief in the old American ideal, and the minister is "tormented by epistemological uncertainties." As in many of Frost's dialogues, no final resolution of conflict is achieved. Professor Allen shows that Frost's main distrust of the doctrine of equality was his distrust of the "liberal mentality," which he saw as dedicated to enforcing freedom and equality through state control and at the expense of individualism. The poem suggests that Frost was fascinated with the old dilemma of how a nation sustains individualism in an egalitarian society.

In the final paper of this section, Laurence Perrine discusses this same theme, the socialism-individualism debate, insofar as it is central to Frost's "Build Soil." After briefly paraphrasing the poem's argument, which emphasizes the need for "self-cultivation" and "rich individuality," Perrine turns to correcting what he considers misinterpretations of various passages in the poem. Perhaps the most misunderstood passage, he contends, is that on ingenuity in lines 92–125. Clearly Tityrus's attack on ingenuity is meant ironically, Perrine argues, citing evidence in the poem as well as Frost's lifelong admiration for feats of ingenuity. Similarly Tityrus's assertion about what he would do if he were dictator has been taken literally and solemnly, rather than as the playful overstatement that it is. Finally, the conclusion of the poem has been misread. Perrine maintains that Tityrus's last speech indicates not intellectual narrowness, as Yvor Winters would have it, but intellectual responsibility. He concludes his essay with a discussion of the central metaphor, "to build soil." With this figure, he says, Frost enjoins his reader to develop richly the individuality of the self, the nation and the mind as the necessary beginning to significant human achievement.

P. W. P.

"After Apple-Picking": Frost's Troubled Sleep

JOHN J. CONDER

"WHAT do I want to communicate but what a *hell* of a good time I had writing it?" Frost once asked. He hastened to explain what he meant by the "good time" he had when writing a poem. "The whole thing is performance and prowess and feats of association. Why don't critics talk about those things—what a feat it was to turn that that way, and what a feat it was to remember that, to be reminded of that by this? Why don't they talk about that?" [1] Frost's mild impatience with critics clearly implies that his poems are ordered, even though the world of nature appearing in them may resist man's attempts to order it. The problem is that critics, having recognized the depth of the actual in Frost's poetry, have had difficulty unravelling all the strands of the associative pattern operating in certain poems. And in the very attempt to show that the literal meaning of such poems is far from the full meaning, they have limited the poems in other ways.

"After Apple-Picking" is such a poem. A work which one critic describes as "absorbed with 'states-between'" [2] necessarily attracts the same kind of attention given to an evocative poem like Coleridge's "Kubla Khan." And the commentaries clearly illustrate the problem of tracking down Frost's associations. The poem contains a dream, and dreams easily evoke associations with the ideal. This is the association made by the most familiar reading, according to which the poem shows that the ideal "is to be understood as a projection, a development, of the literal experience." [3] The poem also contains apples, and an apple is easily associated with the religious doctrine of the Fall. A more recent interpretation explores this possibility, calling "After Apple-Picking" "a witty, blasphemous poem" which rejects Christian doctrine. [4] The first reading tries to be flexible, allowing for many applications of the theme; the second does not. Together the two interpretations raise the question which is crucial for so many of Frost's poems: What framework should be applied to guide the critic in determining the associations which are operative?

Clearly each element of the poem must be examined in its complex relationship to all the others; but to minimize the danger of subjective interpretations unintended by the poet, these relationships must be modified by an understanding of Frost's world. Frost, of course, has not left us his *Vision*, but other poems of his can illuminate his intention, and critical analyses of his world provide some help. So do scattered comments made by Frost himself, one of the most important of which states that he has a habit of "talking contraries" and hence in any given poem "could unsay everything ... [he] said, nearly." [5]

Approaching "After Apple-Picking" with an eye for contraries unravels many of the puzzles in the poem and reveals its richness. The central problems of the poem are posed in the opening lines of its conclusion with the introduction of the ambiguous word "trouble" and the provocative image of "sleep": "One can see what will trouble/This sleep of mine, whatever sleep it is." Although the trouble and the "sleep" are intimately connected in the lines, for purposes of analysis it is best to keep them separate. The speaker himself does so, since he apparently knows what will trouble his sleep but is uncertain about the kind of sleep overtaking him. Arranged in the order most convenient for answering them, two questions emerge in "After Apple-Picking": What is the nature of the sleep? What is the nature of the trouble?

A complex of familiar references points to death as one possible form of sleep. The very situation of the poem, a surcease from picking apples, recalls the Garden of Eden from which, after the apple was picked (and eaten), man was expelled into a world of sin and death. The speaker affirms that he was "well" on his way to sleep even before his morning venture with the sheet of ice. Since life is a process ending in death, the speaker's comment, juxtaposed against the reference to "heaven," promotes the possibility that the speaker may be journeying to an immortal sleep. The season of the year emphasizes nature's death, while the woodchuck's hibernation suggests a pattern of death and resurrection.

Intriguing though these references are, a reader familiar with

Frost's playful ways ("I like to fool," he said)[6] knows better than to take them hastily at face value. The most popular reading rejects the possibility of death. Since the speaker's dream, according to this account, represents an ideal rooted in the real world, his ability to dream about a job well done represents his heaven on earth. His capacity for contemplation sets him apart from the inferior woodchuck, though he does not affirm that man has an immortal soul.[7]

Insofar as this reading rejects death and immortality as one possible form of sleep in "After Apple-Picking," the commentary is consistent with a general opinion that Frost is nonteleological in his thought. Since he neither affirms nor denies that the emergence of mind suggests ultimate meaning in the universe,[8] Frost would necessarily remain neutral in his attitude toward immortality. But if the speaker's dream and sleep exist in life, then to assert that, after his labors, the speaker "is now looking not into the world of effort but the world of dream, of the renewal," [9] is to oversimplify the poem. This view identifies the dream (interpreted as pleasurable) with the sleep (seen as a time for contemplation as well as renewal) and in the process limits both. Such a reading qualifies the word "trouble" into insignificance (to be troubled by a lovely dream is to be superior to the woodchuck, who cannot dream) and oversimplifies the speaker's attitude toward his experience. Given the feats of association that he makes, given the fact that he speaks in contraries, the speaker's attitude toward his sleep is far more complicated than at first seems clear, and his trouble far more real than might be supposed.

The speaker's attitude toward his sleep is complicated because of the possible kinds of sleep overtaking him. To be sure, this may be a night's sleep from which the speaker will awake, refreshed, ready to turn to those "fresh tasks" mentioned by the puzzled speaker of "The Wood-Pile." This possibility is supported by the reference to "night"; it is at "night" that he is "drowsing off"; the speaker, having completed the last of his labors as best he could, may be about to go to bed.

But the association of night with "essence of winter sleep" gives "night" a metaphoric context and so expands its meaning. Indeed, a simple night's sleep seems an improbable meaning, since the speaker was "well" upon his way to sleep before he dropped the "pane of glass" in the morning. Perhaps, then, his drowsy state may be part of the "essence of winter sleep"; that is, perhaps it is a sleep similar to nature's. Enough correspondences between the human and natural worlds exist to dictate this as one possible kind of sleep. The speaker's apple-picking ceases as the year nears conclusion, and his "drowsing off" is associated with "essence of winter sleep":

> Essence of winter sleep is on the night,
> The scent of apples: I am drowsing off.

If his sleep is to be like nature's, what then is the point of the reference to the woodchuck? Since the woodchuck surely could *not* ". . . say whether it's like his/Long sleep, as I describe its coming on,/Or just some human sleep," the speaker's avowal to the contrary apparently reduces the conclusion to mere whimsy. Presumably woodchucks do not dream and do not desire great harvests. Men do. Presumably men do not go into physical hibernation for months. Woodchucks do. But the point of the reference to the woodchuck is not simply to create a contrast between a human and an animal sleep but also to introduce an implied comparison—an inexact analogy between the speaker's sleep and the sleep of nature.[10] If only man has the potential to desire great harvests, his desires may follow a cycle similar to nature's. They may wax and wane like (or with) the seasons; they may emerge, as the woodchuck does in the spring, or lie dormant for months, as the woodchuck does in winter.

For the man who is ". . . overtired/Of the great harvest I myself desired," such an analogy carries with it its own measure of reassurance. Assuming that the desire for harvests and the act of harvesting together are an emblem of man's creative spirit working its will on the world, a reader can see that implicit in this situation is the question: Will my desire, my will, my talents be resurrected, directed toward reaping new harvests? Although he would find it more comforting to think that "just some human sleep" is a single night's sleep which will restore his powers so that he can turn to "fresh tasks," he can be reassured by the analogy between man and the seasons nonetheless. His desires will lie dormant longer, but they will surely be revived, as nature is. In this case, the speaker will be in the happy position of his counterpart in an earlier work, "To the Thawing Wind," a poem employing many of the same images as "After Apple-Picking." Concerned only with drawing a direct parallel between himself and nature, the speaker of the earlier poem implores the wind: "Give the buried flower a dream." Entreating it further ("Bathe my window, make it flow,/Melt it as the ice will go"), he concludes:

> Scatter poems on the floor;
> Turn the poet out of door.

But "After Apple-Picking" has considerably more depth than "To the Thawing Wind," and the analogy between man and nature, which reassures that man's creative life has wellsprings much like nature's or is as automatic in its processes as those of nature, does not quite hold. The speaker himself is uncertain of the analogy, speculating whether his sleep is like the woodchuck's, "...*as I describe its coming on*,/Or just some human sleep" (italics mine). As he has described that sleep coming on, indeed, the speaker clearly has been speaking contraries. The analogy with nature which his associations establish are, in the process of his speaking, undermined by suggestions that the sleep will be different from nature's.

Those suggestions become explicit in the contrast between the sleep of the woodchuck and "just some human sleep." Precisely because the implied comparison between the speaker's sleep and the woodchuck's is undone by the power of the contrast (men *can* only have a human sleep), the assurance offered by the comparison with nature is also retracted. The contrast between the two kinds of sleep, furthermore, has been anticipated from the beginning of the poem, thus providing the fullest impact to the concluding line, "Or just some human sleep."

From the outset, nature seems to have become alien to the speaker. The first section concludes with the speaker's commenting that he is no longer interested in picking apples, in appropriating nature to his own uses: "But I am done with apple-picking now." The parallel between his drowsiness and the "essence of winter sleep" is, at best, tenuous, held together by an uncommitted colon in the last line of the statement, "Essence of winter sleep is on the night,/ The scent of apples: I am drowsing off." The "essence," in short, is more directly associated with "the scent of apples" than with the speaker's sleep. The parallel tenuously established by the colon breaks down in the next section, which describes the strange sight of the winter world through a sheet of ice. Perhaps he does see through this "glass" "the world of hoary grass," but even that is not certain, and no other object in the external world he views is mentioned. Before he describes the "form" of his dreaming, he significantly lets the pane of ice fall and break, an action in stark contrast to his behavior during the harvest, when he took special pains to keep the apples from falling. Of course, since the ice is melting, the gesture is perfectly normal. Deliberate mention of the detail, nonetheless, suggests his alienation from nature. Once he could handle it (in the literal and metaphoric senses of that term); now he cannot.

If the speaker is divorced from nature, then what would "just some human sleep" be? One can concede that the speaker is physically and mentally fatigued, his desire for a "great harvest" satiated. In that case it is *possible* that he is entering the world of renewal, that his sleep will be composed of pleasant dreams, a contemplation of the ideal based on the real; and it is *possible* that his trouble will be minimal, composed of the physical aftereffects of too much apple-picking: the "ache" and the "pressure" retained by his "instep arch"; the feel of the swaying ladder; the "rumbling sound" of apples. But it is not at all *certain* that his is the sleep of renewal. Indeed, to argue with certainty that this is the sleep of renewal, a reader would have to rest his case on the analogy between man's cycle and nature's, an analogy that seems to fail in the poem. Such an analogy, furthermore, would not be consistent with Frost's point of view, one which sharply differentiates man from nature. A previous critic has argued persuasively that Frost believes, with Emerson, "that nature can be used to uncover and illustrate the underlying laws of the universe, because it operates by such laws. . . . Frost does not take Emerson's next step, to insist that the laws of outer nature correspond to the laws of inner mind." [11] Both Frost's habit of speaking contraries and his point of view toward nature militate against a simplistic view of sleep and argue for a darker side of "just some human sleep."

That darker side can be discerned by recalling what is lost by the failure of the analogy between man and nature. If nature can renew itself automatically, man, viewed as distinct from nature, cannot be assured of such renewal. Nature has her unknown source of creative revival. What is man's? The source of his creativity is the assumption that his harvest has value, that the activity is worthwhile. If the speaker questions the purpose of his activity, doubts the value of his harvest, then indeed his may be a sleep of the creative powers, one which will last until the doubts are removed.

The speaker makes it eminently clear that he once highly valued his harvest. Simply put, he "desired" a "great harvest," and the desire was sufficiently strong to justify extraordinary discipline and control: "There were ten thousand thousand fruit to touch,/Cherish in hand, lift down, and not let fall." The sense of value which he associated with manual contact ("cherish in hand") is confirmed in the lines immediately following:

> For all
> That struck the earth,
> No matter if not bruised or spiked with stubble,
> Went surely to the cider-apple heap
> As of no worth.

The crucial phrase, "As of no worth," is ambiguous and reflects the speaker's habit of "talking contraries," of retracting "everything ... [he] said, nearly." For to describe the fallen apples *as* "of no worth" is to imply their worth. It is not possible to tell whether the speaker, now commenting with the advantage of hindsight, would have characterized these apples in the same way during his actual apple-picking. What is clear is that this description of his past activities implies a sense of relative values (fallen apples are inferior to harvested ones), but a highly ambiguous one. Since the speaker has declared that "... I am overtired/Of the great harvest I myself desired," he is in a mood to apply the same logic of talking contraries to the harvest itself. If the fallen apples are *as* "of no worth," then, he hints, the harvest itself is *as* of great worth, a description which implies its opposite. The exhausted speaker, in short, is in doubt about his values.

Doubts related to questions of value are in his mind as he recounts his apple-picking, so it is not surprising that the dream induced by his venture reflects his confusion. It is by no means certain, of course, whether the "dreaming" is confined to the visual description of the apples or whether it includes all the aftereffects of picking apples. Since this is probably more than a simple night's sleep, it is likely that the dream is much like one experienced when awake, as when a person still feels the rocking of the boat even after he has set foot on firm land. Assuming that the dream embraces the full range of sensations, the reader can observe a striking contrast between the visual and the other sensory elements. Only the apples are "magnified"; there is no suggestion that the "ache," the "pressure," the swaying of the ladder and the rumbling of the apples are felt and heard more intensely than during the actual pursuit of the harvest. Not only are the apples larger than life; they are also autonomous, independent of the speaker's control as they appear in the mind's eye: "Magnified apples appear and disappear."

The erratic movement of the apples, certainly, may be quite consistent with the nature of this dream, one experienced when awake. Stare at an object long enough and its impression is retained after the eyes are closed. The eyelids blink shut, and the speaker sees apples. They flick open, and the apples vanish. Quite possibly the image so retained is magnified. But for readers concerned with the depth of the actual in Frost's poetry, such an explanation is hardly sufficient. Frost no doubt wants to show that the form of the speaker's dreaming is a consequence of the activity which inspired it, since the speaker concludes the dream with the statement, "*For I have had too much/Of apple-picking: I am overtired*" (italics mine), and then describes the apple-picking itself. To settle for a purely naturalistic explanation of the relationship between the two, however, is to limit the poem.

A comparison between the dream and the activity is revealing for what the dream leaves out, and such a comparison must be based on the visual element in the dream, since all the other elements are ascribable to purely natural aftereffects and bear no symbolic relationship to the whole point of picking as many apples as possible: to reap a great harvest. That sense of discipline associated with value during the apple-picking is not present in the dream. The apples are unrelated to the speaker, moving of their own accord, without his direction, his sense of purpose. Furthermore, they are all magnified; the distinction between those harvested and those lost does not exist. Gone is the speaker's sense of relative values. Associated with the statement "... I am overtired/Of the great harvest I myself desired," their magnification and autonomy bring into bold relief the very doubts surfacing toward the end of his description of the actual venture of picking apples. He has literally lost sight of all the values of the harvest. If this *is* a happy sleep of contemplation, the happiness is highly qualified.

Concerned about his values, the speaker is also concerned about the nature of his sleep, a concern imaged in the contrast between himself and the woodchuck. As part of nature, the woodchuck will automatically be renewed. But the speaker may need, for renewal, not simply rest, some period of dormancy, but also some certain knowledge of human values. And where is such knowledge to come from? Recall, this is a poem about what happens *after* apple-picking. Hardly an allegory either supporting or denouncing Christian doctrine, the work nonetheless relies on overtones of the Fall to enrich its complex meaning. When man first picked the apple, he was expelled from Eden to labor by the sweat of his brow, a consequence of his newly found knowledge of good and evil. The speaker lives in a fallen world where he has labored and sweated. But he gains no sure knowledge as Adam did. His ladder is pointed *toward* heaven only, and he has had to descend from it. Man can climb the ladder toward heaven, toward certainty, but when he returns, he discovers how little he has learned with certainty. He cannot even know the nature of his sleep, although the possibilities seem clear.

Perhaps his will be like the woodchuck's sleep, the sleep of nature, in the limited sense that his creative powers are subject to the same kind of cyclical movement observed in the seasons. At worst, this sleep would be like nature's in its duration, though not in its character (unlike nature, man can dream). Such a sleep, induced by physical and mental fatigue, is not a function of man's uncertain values. His values are certain; his ability to act on them, limited. This is the sleep of renewal.

This meaning of "sleep," though possible in the poem, seems obviated by the apparent failure of the analogy between man and nature. Although Frost allows for its possibility in the reference to the woodchuck, such a sleep seems inconsistent with his larger view of man and nature. A second possible sleep, not far removed from the first, is also ascribable to a straining of the physical and mental powers, a strain just severe enough to confuse the speaker's sense of values and to blur his sense of purpose. But if he originally possessed a firmly grounded sense of value and purpose, he can be reasonably certain he will awaken from this sleep, from this confusion about values. A good rest, a night's or a month's, will settle the matter. Thereafter, he can turn to "fresh tasks" with no need to investigate his values. Given Frost's larger poetic world, this meaning is the most likely. The will to live and to create provides the ground for man's values.

But in the world of "After Apple-Picking," recovery is not certain. Frost's "feats of association" are so complicated, his performance in hinting so masterful, that the poem suggests the possibility of a third kind of sleep. If the speaker's encounter with the apples has led him to question not just the nature, but the *source* of his values, then his sleep may be longer, even permanent. It is one matter to recover values lost because of fatigue. It is another to be forced to return to their source, particularly if that source is only the "I myself" who "desired." For when desire fails and values falter, what source outside the self can restore desire? In "After Apple-Picking," the ladder only points *toward* heaven.

What *will* trouble the speaker's sleep, whatever sleep it is? He is only falling asleep in this poem, and he does not yet know which sleep his will be. Its duration will determine its nature. It is his uncertainty as to when (or whether) he will awaken which will be carried into his sleep, troubling it. Ironically enough, only when he awakens will he know what sleep it is—or, rather, was.

Notes to *"After Apple-Picking"*: *Frost's Troubled Sleep* by JOHN J. CONDER

1. Tape-recorded interview with Robert Frost. From *Writers at Work: The Paris Review Interviews*, Second Series, (New York: Viking Press, 1963), 32.

2. Reuben A. Brower, *The Poetry of Robert Frost: Constellations of Intention* (New York: Oxford University Press, 1963), 26.

3. Cleanth Brooks and Robert Penn Warren, *Understanding Poetry* (Rev. ed.; New York: Henry Holt and Co., 1950), 393.

4. William Bysshe Stein, " 'After Apple-Picking': Echoic Parody," *University Review* (Kansas City, Mo.), XXXV, 301.

5. *Writers at Work*, 28.

6. *Ibid.*, 27.

7. See Brooks and Warren, 394.

8. On this point, see Nina Baym, "An Approach to Robert Frost's Nature Poetry," *Atlantic Quarterly*, XVII (1965), 720. Marion Montgomery, pointing out that Frost is not agnostic, does show that Frost is very much aware of man's limitations and therefore hesitates to speak out "on the subject of the supernatural": "Robert Frost and his Use of Barriers," *South Atlantic Quarterly*, LVII (1958), 343. A. M. Sampley, observing that "Frost does not believe in a directionless universe," nonetheless observes that Frost's men are the sort "who can survive in an uncertain universe": "The Myth and The Quest: The Stature of Robert Frost," *South Atlantic Quarterly*, LXX (1971), 289, 294.

9. Robert Penn Warren, "The Themes of Robert Frost," in *Selected Essays* (New York: Vintage Books, 1951), 130. This essay is a somewhat different form of the analysis appearing in Brooks and Warren.

10. Among others who have discussed the analogy between man and nature, see Philip L. Gerber, *Robert Frost* (New York: Twayne Publishers, 1966), 133–37.

11. Baym, "An Approach to Robert Frost's Nature Poetry," 716.

The Houses of Robert Frost

VIVIAN C. HOPKINS

In my Father's house are many mansions.
John 14:1

Home is the place where, when you have to go there,
They have to take you in.
"The Death of the Hired Man"

ROM the time of his marriage to Elinor White in 1895, until his death in 1963, Robert Frost occupied some forty houses. As with other New England writers from Hawthorne to Henry James, the house had a mystique for Frost that was sometimes associated with ownership alone and at times with various themes in his poetry. Ironically, while house and home had diverse meanings for Frost, he was, for much of his life, frequently on the open road living in a succession of rented apartments and furnished rooms.

The house which the family occupied for the longest time was the farm at Derry, "the Magoon place," which Robert's grandfather, William Prescott Frost, bought for him in 1900. The gable roof, ample window space, four bedrooms, barn, shed, and privy all pleased the Frosts. The surroundings of pasture, woodlot, fruit trees, berry bushes, and the beloved "Hyla Brook" were attractive. In October, 1900, when Robert, Elinor, and baby Lesley moved in, the parents were still grieving for the loss of four-year-old Elliott, of *cholera infantum*, in July. Robert's low spirits that fall were reflected in "Despair." [1] But, as the little family was expanded by the births of Carol, Irma, and Marjorie, they found more satisfaction in this home. The children enjoyed sliding and skating in winter, berrying, botanizing, and picnicking in summer. The Derry house was their schoolroom, also, where the parents taught the children. Robert learned farm skills from his helper, Carl Burell. And, probably, the Derry place yielded the longest yardage in poetry of

182

any Frost home—not only for *A Boy's Will* and *North of Boston* but also for many poems in later volumes. When leaving for Plymouth, New Hampshire, in November, 1911, Frost wrote that he was relinquishing title to this farm—but "Only let it be understood/ It shall be no trespassing/If I come again some spring/In the gray disguise of years,/Seeking ache of memory here." The sad aftermath of this poem was Frost's visit to the Derry farm in the spring of 1938, to carry out Elinor's request that her ashes be scattered over Hyla Brook. Shaken by the owner's hostility, and by the many deteriorating changes in the place, Frost departed with the ashes still in the urn.

The Frosts' desire for an English sojourn was expressed in architectural terms—Robert and Elinor wanted to "live under thatch." Actually, "The Bungalow" (Frost nicknamed it "The Bung Hole"), which they rented in Beaconsfield from 1912 to 1914, was not thatch, but stucco, a small five-room house. They were more pleased with the timber and brick cottage, Little Iddens, which they occupied from April to September, 1914. Beautiful country surrounded the cottage; there were picnics with the Gibsons and Abercrombies, and frequent visitors—sometimes too many for Mrs. Frost's strength. For the last few months of their stay in England, the Frosts "camped out" in one of the two cottages (The Gallows) which the Abercrombies rented from Lord Beauchamp. The older cottage (The Study) did indeed have the thatch which the Frosts had dreamed of before leaving home.

The poem "Thatch" reflects the persona's pondering on a difference between himself and his wife. He will not come in until her light goes out; she wants him to come in while the light is still on. As the speaker flushes birds out of the eaves, his sympathy for these harmless creatures softens his own grief. The personal reference to Robert and Elinor comes at the end: looking back at this experience later, the speaker learns that the ancient cottage where they lived is now going to pieces. In September, 1928, Robert wrote to his daughter Lesley, concerning their visit to former English haunts, that the people at the Gallows were unfriendly—perhaps because they had let the place run down and the thatch rot to pieces. By contrast, the Frosts were warmly welcomed at Little Iddens, whose condition was improved.[2] The sad, perplexed mood of "Thatch" is complemented by the exhilarating poem "Happiness Makes Up in Height for What It Lacks in Length," based on the recollection of one perfect day, and apparently inspired by an experience in one of these English houses. The poet writes: "No shadow crossed but ours/As through its blazing flowers/We went from house to wood/For change of solitude."

On their return from England, the Frosts rented rooms in the home of the Lynches, near Franconia, where they had previously camped out. In the spring of 1915 Frost bought William Herbert's farm, a mile from the village, with a small house and barn, hayfield and pasture, and a view of the mountains. The house had no bathroom or furnace, and during the winters they had trouble with the water supply. By 1919 a furnace and bathroom had been added. Elinor wrote to Lesley that Carol was shoveling snow off the roof, which sprang leaks, and that they could not use the bathroom because the water supply had failed. Yet, she wrote, "The house seems awfully cozy and homelike after existence at Caroline Marsh's," (*F.L.*, 50–51). In March she wrote to Lesley again: "It's snowing and blowing a gale from the northeast today, and to have this house thoroughly warm all over in the midst of the white whirling wilderness seems too wonderful" (*F.L.* 59–60). Frost portrayed this kind of situation in "There Are Roughly Zones": "We sit indoors and talk of the cold outside./And every gust that gathers strength and heaves/Is a threat to the house. But the house has long been tried." A house could be a comforting shelter, as in this poem; but it could also inspire trepidation. "House Fear" in "The Hill Wife" dramatizes a woman's terror in coming back into the unlighted house at night. The horror in "The Witch of Coös" is the more intense for its involvement of the whole house. Dispassionately, Mrs. Lajeway tells of the bones that escaped from the cellar, climbed the stairs to the attic, and still keep trying to get through the nailed door behind the headboard of her bed.

Frost began his career of "Poet in Residence" at Amherst College in January, 1917. For a time the Frosts rented houses in Amherst, then in 1919 they bought the Peleg Cole place in South Shaftsbury. In 1921 this "Resident Poet" switched from Amherst to the University of Michigan. That year the family rented a spacious house owned by the widow of Martin D'Ooge, former head of the Classics department, at 1523 Washtenaw Avenue. They moved the next year to a smaller house at 1432 Washtenaw, almost across the street from the D'Ooge house. Elinor described it as "more cheerful and homelike, and more easily taken care of than the other." Of their various Ann Arbor residences, Frost's favorite was the small colonial house at 1223 Pontiac Road, somewhat farther from the campus, and across the Huron River. The family moved there in the fall of 1925, this time taking their own furniture. In Ann Arbor as in Amherst, Frost and his wife came to know many of the promising students and congenial faculty members; they were entertained more than they entertained in return. The artist Jean Paul Slusser lived across the road. He and Frost became good friends, and shared many nocturnal rambles. Subsequently, the Frost residence was moved to Greenfield Village at Dearborn; and, on the site of this Greek Revival house, Slusser built a modern one. The whole episode is a fine instance of the Frostian theme related to "removal—renewal." [3]

In 1926 Frost left Ann Arbor to return to Amherst. That summer he acted as director of the Bread Loaf Writers' Conference and remained associated with this group for the rest of his life. During the twenties and thirties Frost became increasingly a nomad, extending his lecture engagements in order to supply his family's needs. Mrs. Frost went with him to Florida, California, or Texas for the winter months, where they visited their children and sought to preserve their own health.

Looking at farms to buy became a favorite outdoor pastime. Frost enlisted the help of various friends and real estate agents. In the fall of 1928 Charles Monroe showed him a 150-acre farm in a gully near Buck's Cobble. The owner, Charles Hawkins, Monroe's brother-in-law, was willing to sell. There was a fine stand of birches, barns, sheds, and a house of five rooms, with two ordinary fireplaces and one large kitchen fireplace. Frost often purchased a house because of its chimneys and fireplaces. He wrote to Louis Untermeyer: "The kitchen chimney is the best part of it—that and the woods." [4]

The Frosts had just returned from inspection of a house they planned to buy in Florida when Elinor Frost suffered the heart attack which led to her death. Sorrow for his loss was deep and lasting with Robert. He did return to Florida, but sought a location away from Gainesville, where his wife had died. In the winter of 1941 he bought five acres of land in Coconut Grove, near his friend Hervey Allen's estate, and erected two small prefabricated houses on it, one for Carol and Lillian, one for himself. He informed Lesley that one was three-room, with an open fireplace, the other, two-room, with a wood stove (*F.L.*, 229–31). While prefabricated housing may seem out of character for Frost, it does reflect the ideal of economy which he had admired in Thoreau's *Walden*—an ideal contradicted by his recent compulsive buying.

The year 1941 was notable for a purchase of more far-reaching significance in Frost's life than the Florida dwellings—the buying of the Homer Noble farm at Ripton, near Middlebury. During the summer sojourns at Bread Loaf, the Frosts had previously rented quarters. The Noble farm, with its pasture, orchard, barn, and view of Bread Loaf Mountain was satisfying to Frost's tastes. While repairs were being made, he stayed in a cottage in Middlebury—but would sometimes walk out to spend the night alone at the farm (Untermeyer, 328–29). On these occasions he might be conceived as acting out the persona of "An Old Man's Winter Night." Thomson Littlefield, a young friend who had a deep interest in Frost the man and poet—and also in architecture—writes of the Noble farm:

At the time I knew Frost, in the late forties and early fifties, his architectural surroundings were just about as remote from either Wallace Nutting's New England or J. J. Lankes's as if he had lived in the neighborhood of Davenport, Iowa.

That was one of the first things to strike me. For somebody who cared enough about houses to own several,[5] Frost seemed remarkably to take them as conveniences for eating and sleeping and working and keeping books and papers in. And talking in, with the unending succession of visitors come to listen to the greatest flow of talk of the age, or to tell him something he wanted to hear about, or to ask for help or money, or to work at making a lion of him. His houses were the places of a great poet's business. He evidently enjoyed the sorts of security that the business-likeness afforded him, but even as he relaxed in that, he seemed to be bracing his back against their turning him into an item of business—publisher's, scholar's, exploiter's business.

You could see why he wouldn't want the quaint New England bit.

He was willing enough, on occasion, to let people take him for the quaint Yankee sage, but that doesn't mean he would have been willing to live the part. He, 'druther live in neutral houses. He didn't care, nor, certainly, did I. Any place Frost hung his hat was a Pierian springhouse.

The Ripton house is right on the main road from Middlebury to Bread Loaf. My memory isn't going to serve to say whether it is brown shingles or brown clapboards or brown shiplap, but brown it at least was twenty and more years ago. A porch, more for arriving than sitting, looks out on the macadam road, and the rooms beyond cluster in the awkward, space-saving way of houses put up in the era when stoves saved the builder from having to think about any unifying requirements beyond a roof.

Kay and Ted Morrison lived in that house. It was called the Morrisons' house, and while some of the furniture if not most was presumably Frost's, some seemed to reflect Kay's good sense of fitness. Most of what was there was plain, country furniture, not what would have been even then thought of as antique, though nowadays that's exactly what the dealers call it. Just a shade junky. With here and there a really nice wood chair, and just a suggestion, whether from pieces of furniture or stuff that had been left around on the furniture, that somebody had been to Europe.

That was the house where Kay entertained for Frost, and where she sorted out the visitors on their way up to Frost's cottage, and the correspondence going both ways. The barn was there in back, holding (at least when Jamie and I were there in '53) a black mare. And past the barn ran the lane, uphill a quarter of a mile to the cottage. I imagine Frost had built it not too many decades before. It was a bedroom and a bathroom and a living room with some books and a good fireplace. The whole building wouldn't have been more than sixteen or seventeen feet square. Comfortable chairs and a place to write. That was all. And a small porch up maybe two steps from the ground. No plaster to it; just a summer cottage.[6]

My impression of the Cambridge house at 35 Brewster Street, where I interviewed Frost in November, 1956, was similar to that which Tom Littlefield expressed concerning the Ripton houses. The Cambridge living room was somewhat shabby, under- rather than over-furnished, but warm and comfortable. A new puppy was being broken in, and Mrs. Morrison had to clean the rug shortly after my arrival. Both Mrs. Morrison and Frost were most hospitable. When Frost learned that I was a friend of Roy Cowden, he became especially cordial. He autographed my copies of his books and persuaded Mrs. Morrison to give me some of his Christmas-card poems. As he was handwriting "Choose Something Like a Star" in my copy of *Collected Poems*, he looked up at a water color above the dining room table. The painting showed a red barn with a hired man resting against it. "There he is," Frost chuckled, "trying to get out of doing any work."

In Frost's poetry, the close relation of the house to surrounding trees, fields, flowers, water, and mountains has great significance—for example, "A Brook in the City" "held the house as in an elbow-crook." This ambience has perhaps been sufficiently emphasized in Frost criticism. What has received less development is the importance of certain architectural features in the poems.

A window, for instance, often encloses a scene. The upstairs window in "Home Burial" is so placed that it frames the family burying ground, and the wife is tormented when she looks out that window at the child's fresh grave. The counterpart of Mrs. Lynch, in "A Servant to Servants," looks at Lake Willoughby through the kitchen window, as she washes the dishes. And the middle-aged woman of "In the Home Stretch," just moved to the country, looks out her kitchen window at the mowing field and woods, seeking confirmation that this move has been the right one. Frost's terror in hearing the branches of a birch tree scrape against his bedroom window, tormenting his sleep, is transmuted into the harmony of the tree's "outer" and his "inner" weather, in the poem "Tree at My Window." Compare "The Sound of Trees," where the poet watches trees sway, from a door or a window.

Chimneys were especially important to Frost, because he liked fireplaces and because the chimney was a symbol of hearth and home. To Carol he wrote from South Shaftsbury on November 1, 1931: "I'm having a furnace chimney built from the cellar up on the north side of the big chimney and leading into the big chimney between the first and second floors" (*F.L.* 138–40.) In the poem "The Kitchen Chimney," he begs the builder not to set the chimney on a shelf, for the practical reasons of fire hazard and stains on the wall paper; and for the theoretical reason that it would remind the poet of castles he used to build in air. "A Record Stride" describes the Vermont bedroom closet, with a door made of two wide boards, "and for back wall a crumbling old chimney."

A chimney appears as the sole survivor in a country house, in "The Need of Being Versed in Country Things," while the birds nest in the barn across the road. Frost's regret for the ruined house appears in his comment: "One had to be versed in country things/ Not to believe the phoebes wept." Perhaps even more pathetic is "The Old Barn at the Bottom of the Fogs": "Where's this barn's house? It never had a house,/Or joined with sheds in ring-around a dooryard."

The abandoned or ruined house is a favorite Frost motif. In the early "Ghost House" Frost creates an imaginary ruined house to symbolize his mood of apartness. Only the cellar walls are left, and the poet finds his companions in the grave stones under a tree. "The Census-Taker," portraying an abandoned house, covered with melancholy black paper, causes the poet to reflect on the ruined houses of the past, all over the world. The conclusion is understated: "It must be I want life to go on living." The theme of continuity appears also in "A Serious Step Lightly Taken," wherein the persona and his family buy a house impulsively, at first sight, and live there a long time. And in "The Generations of Men," an old charred timber is taken out of the cellar and made the doorsill for the new cottage.

"Directive" is the most eloquent of Frost's poems on deserted or ruined houses. "There is a house that is no more a house," he writes, "Upon a farm that is no more a farm." The poet describes the cellar hole, grown up with lilacs, a tiny field, and a children's playhouse. The listener is advised to pick up the broken drinking glass and "Drink and be whole again beyond confusion." Through the image of the communion, Frost suggests that out of ruin and desolation, personal salvation can be won.

In his theory of poetry, Frost emphasizes again and again the significance of metaphor. "The Figure a Poem Makes" is his most eloquent statement about metaphor, but it is only one of many on this subject. Clearly, in his life and in his poetry, the house is an outstanding symbol. On the level of actuality, the house provides shelter, warmth, hospitality—but in return it exacts repairs, maintenance, bills for painting, plumbing, and heating. By turns it can be a refuge or a threat. On the level of spirit, it becomes a double symbol of removal-renewal, destruction-regeneration. Perhaps "A Steeple on the House" best expresses this earth-spirit simile: although the dweller does not visit the steeple, that structure represents the spirit, emerging from the fleshly house.

Notes to *The Houses of Robert Frost* by VIVIAN C. HOPKINS

1. Lawrance Thompson, *Robert Frost: The Early Years, 1874–1915* (New York: Holt, Rinehart and Winston, 1966), 263–68. The quotation that follows in the text is from Thompson, 368. The following account of Robert Frost's houses depends on Thompson, 393–94, 447–48, 457–58, 278–79 (on Frost's fears), 309 (on "Tree at My Window"); and on Lawrance Thompson, *Robert Frost: The Years of Triumph, 1915–1938* (New York: Holt, Rinehart and Winston, 1970), 507–10, 27–29, 148, 174–75, 215, 367–68, 487–94.

2. Arnold Grade, ed., *Family Letters of Robert and Elinor Frost* (Albany: State University of New York, 1972), 123–25; cited hereafter in text as *F.L.*

3. For this information I am indebted to Dorothy Tyler. Dorothy, Sue Bonner, and Mary Cooley were among Frost's first students at Ann Arbor. He was impressed by their editing *The Outlander* (Thompson, *Robert Frost: The Years of Triumph*, 294, 619–20). Miss Tyler has in progress a book on Frost in Michigan.

4. *The Letters of Robert Frost to Louis Untermeyer*, ed. Louis Untermeyer (New York: Holt, Rinehart and Winston, 1963), January 6, 1929, p. 194.

5. In November 1956, Frost admitted to me that he owned three farms, besides the Florida property and the Cambridge house.

6. Thomson Littlefield to Vivian C. Hopkins, Albany, February 18, 1973.

"At Home" with Robert Frost

ROGER EKINS

"THEN make yourself at home," Frost urges in "Directive." Though the poem deals with a "house that is no more a house,/ But only a belilaced cellar hole,/Now slowly closing like a dent in dough," we are still, ironically, urged to feel at home. In "The Death of the Hired Man," Mary informs her husband, Warren, that Silas " 'has come home to die.' " " 'Home,' he mocked gently./ 'Yes, what else but home?' " she replies. Of course " 'it all depends on what you mean by home,' " and Warren has his own definition: " 'Home is the place where, when you have to go there,/They have to take you in.' " But Mary can't agree: " 'I should have called it/ Something you somehow haven't to deserve.' " It seems clear that Frost doesn't side with the notion that home is merely a place where people are begrudgingly taken care of when, for some reason, they are forced to return. For Mary and for Frost, the question of "responsibility" is irrelevant to the meaning of home.

But in spite of the frequent criticism over Frost's concrete, philosophical statements, there is no clear definition in his poetry of his conception of home. In her essay "Reserve in the Art of Robert Frost," Dorothy Judd makes the important observation that Frost refuses to make a personal commitment "to any philosophical system, poetic myth, or religious belief." [1] He is equally hesitant to make definitive statements about his favorite metaphors, and he should not be expected to, especially with the fascinating metaphor of home. It is simply too complex.

But even if a neat, specific definition of home cannot be found in the poetry of Robert Frost, much insight can be gained by analyzing Frost's use of the metaphor. Of course it is important to keep in mind, as did Frost, that "all metaphor breaks down somewhere"; but, as Frost so metaphorically put it, "unless you are *at home* in the metaphor, unless you have had your proper poetical education in the metaphor, you are not safe anywhere" [2] (italics mine).

191

In an attempt to understand the attraction of home to Frost the obvious is significant. Home is a house of refuge and a source of protection. In one of his earlier poems, "Storm Fear," Frost confronts us with a man who seems immured in his own isolation. But that is the deeper interpretation; on the surface is a picture of a man, his wife, and child, protected from the harsh onslaught of a New England winter. The house, then, serves as a comfortable insulation of man against an unkind Nature. Perhaps this role of the house is best explained by the phenomenologist Gaston Bachelard in his book *The Poetics of Space*. In chapter 2, "House and Universe," he refers to pertinent comments that Baudelaire makes about a painting by Lavieille of a thatched cottage on the edge of a wood in winter and remarks that "A reminder of winter strengthens the happiness of inhabiting. In the reign of the imagination alone, a reminder of winter increases the house's value as a place to live in." [3] But of course the man in "Storm Fear" does not rejoice in "the happiness of inhabiting." He feels threatened by more than the storm.

Perhaps a better example of the sense of security that comes from a good house appears in "There Are Roughly Zones":

> We sit indoors and talk of the cold outside.
> And every gust that gathers strength and heaves
> Is a threat to the house. But the house has long been tried.

Again, Bachelard provides illumination. After relating a passage from Henri Bosco's *Malicroix*, a work which deals with a sturdy dream house called *La Redousse* (corruption of *redoute*: retreat), Bachelard makes the following observation: "Such a house as this invites mankind to heroism of cosmic proportions. It is an instrument with which to confront the cosmos. And the metaphysical systems according to which man is 'cast into the world' might meditate concretely upon the house that is cast into the hurricane, defying the anger of heaven itself. Come what may the house helps us to say: I will be an inhabitant of the world, in spite of the world." [4]

Frost persistently uses the metaphor of home as protector. "A Drumlin Woodchuck" presents a different point of view, but the tension between the home space and the outside world is still very real:

> My own strategic retreat
> Is where two rocks almost meet,
> And still more secure and snug,
> A two-door burrow I dug.

> With those in mind at my back
> I can sit forth exposed to attack,
> As one who shrewdly pretends
> That he and the world are friends.

Certainly the woodchuck and the natural world are not friends. We expect that. But we like to think that things are different for man. We like to believe that man has somehow evolved a little farther than the lower life forms in his struggle against Nature; but just as we watch the woodchuck scamper into its safe burrow, we read "Willful Homing" and watch man fight his way home against the blizzard.

Things don't seem to have changed much, and Frost dramatically reinforces man's estrangement from the natural world in his poem "Triple Bronze" as he attempts to "make limited man snug in a limitless universe." Here the speaker is very much aware of the depth and width of the Infinite and is grateful that the "Powers" have provided him with a thick hide for "inner defense." But beyond that, he is on his own and must construct, of lime, wood, or granite, "A wall too hard for crime/Either to breach or climb." But even that is not enough, and the third layer of bronze, "a national boundary," is needed as a barricade "Between too much and me." Here Frost seems to be creating a personal order out of limitless chaos. Given the "too muchness" of the world outside himself, man has to find some way of creating his own sacred space, his personal cosmological orientation. After all, is not the impulse behind any kind of creative process the need to transform chaos into cosmos?

In his brilliant book *The Sacred and the Profane: the Nature of Religion*, Mircea Eliade devotes a lengthy chapter to "Sacred Space and Making the World Sacred" and concludes: "But since to settle somewhere, to inhabit a space, is equivalent to repeating the cosmogony and hence to imitating the work of the gods, it follows that, for religious man, every existential decision to situate himself in space in fact constitutes a religious decision. By assuming the responsibility of creating the world that he has chosen to inhabit, he not only cosmicizes chaos but also sanctifies his little cosmos by making it like the world of the gods." [5]

Though Frost may infrequently seem "religious," Eliade would insist that Frost's desire to construct walls "of wood or granite or lime" has a deeper motivation than the need merely to keep "crime" out. Suddenly the metaphor of home takes on a significance far beyond that of serving in the simple role of shelter from the elements. When one looks at home as a basically religious experience, one discovers in "A Steeple on the House" a rich meaning in these lines:

> What if it should turn out eternity
> Was but the steeple on our house of life
> That made our house of life a house of worship?

Two other poems refer to the correlation between the construction of a home and the creation of sacred space. "The Census-Taker" presents a very sensitive person who finds a house in the middle of nowhere and experiences a tremendous sense of loss to learn that it is no longer inhabited. His attitude toward this house borders on reverence:

> This house in one year fallen to decay
> Filled me with no less sorrow than the houses
> Fallen to ruin in ten thousand years
> Where Asia wedges Africa from Europe.

In this poem the forces of chaos are triumphant. Eliade's personal cosmogony has failed not only on an individual level, but it has failed symbolically for all of mankind, since the beginning of creation.

Perhaps the clearest treatment of man's struggle to create his sacred space in a profane world appears in "The Birthplace," which deals not merely with the birthplace of several children, but *incipit vita nova*. Here, religious man is trying desperately to increase "our hold on the planet:"

> Here further up the mountain slope
> Than there was ever any hope,

> My father built, enclosed a spring,
> Strung chains of wall round everything,
> Subdued the growth of earth to grass,
> And brought our various lives to pass.

Such words as *built, enclosed,* and *subdued* refer to more than a casual homesteader. A genuine battle is taking place, a battle which is emphasized in the disquieting final lines: "The mountain pushed us off her knees./And now her lap is full of trees." As Eliade puts it, "settling somewhere—building a village or merely a house—represents a serious decision, for the very existence of man is involved; he must, in short, create his own world and assume the responsibility of maintaining and renewing it. Habitations are not lightly changed, for it is not easy to abandon one's world." [6]

Nevertheless, habitations are indeed changed. Frost's poetry is full of abandoned houses. In her article entitled "Robert Frost: Out Far and In Deep," Vivian C. Hopkins says that "throughout Frost's poetry the deserted house has been a symbol of lost culture. . . ." [7] While Hopkins' statement is accurate, it must be extended; for frequently in Frost's poetry, dwelling places are abandoned willfully, even joyfully. These abandoned houses are symbols of expanded, rather than lost, culture. They are left behind by people who find that a four-walled insulation from the world only increases their alienation, creating a kind of personal prison. In "Mending Wall," Frost is certainly speaking of the effects of winter frost and hunters after rabbits, but perhaps he is also referring to these people who have abandoned their homes when he says "Something there is that doesn't love a wall."

There are those, then, who are not at home with a simple dwelling. In "Bereft," for example, the line "Word I was in the house alone" is paralleled with the line "Word I was in my life alone." A sturdy house, in spite of all the comfort and protection it can offer, is not enough for a feeling of well-being and security. Man needs more than simple isolation from "too much." Perhaps that is the problem of the girl in "The Subverted Flower." Rather than being allowed to deal with life directly, she is retrieved by her mother, who "drew her backward home." The wording may suggest that she goes home reluctantly. Perhaps for her, home is more of a prison than a protective shield. For some, there is little difference between prison and protection.

The image of home as a kind of caged prison is extended in "The Lockless Door." Here, the speaker has spent many years in only tentative safety behind a door "With no lock to lock." But the inevitable knock finally comes and the window provides an escape:

> Back over the sill
> I bade a "Come in"
> To whatever the knock
> At the door may have been.

It is suggested that the enclosure no longer offers protection. In reality, it never did. But something else is suggested in the final stanza:

> So at a knock
> I emptied my cage
> To hide in the world
> And alter with age.

There is no effective way of locking the world outside; and having realized this, the speaker elects to quit hiding from the world. Instead, he hides in it. He has no further use of the "cage," or prison, he once called home.

Of course the woman in "The Hill Wife" is afraid of houses, but she is equally afraid of the outside world. For her, no sacred spaces exist; as a result, the ties with reality finally give. But some do find sacred space outside the conventional "home." There are those who do not need to cling to that artificial shelter from the outside world. This attitude is expressed in the poem "Sand Dunes":

> Men left her a ship to sink:
> They can leave her a hut as well;
> And be but more free to think
> For the one more cast-off shell.

Man can extend his concept of home beyond the simple house. There are those who can extend home into Nature; for in spite of the poems we have already looked at, Frost does not always find her unkind. While Frost avoids the transcendentalism of Emerson, he nevertheless "establishes an original relationship" with the outside world. He extends the metaphor of home to include both "inner" and "outer" weather.

This attitude appears early in Frost's work. In the poem "Into My Own," the young speaker wishes to "steal away" into the vastness of "those dark trees" where he could be "Fearless of ever finding open land/Or highway where the slow wheel pours the sand." The result of such an experience? "They would not find me changed from him they knew—/Only more sure of all I thought was true." Here young Robert recognizes the need to venture into the outer world. Just as building a house is a method of creating a sacred space out of chaos, so is "stealing away" into the woods—that is, as long as one is "at home" in the woods.

Another poem which illustrates the desire to extend the limits of the home space is "Tree at My Window":

> Tree at my window, window tree,
> My sash is lowered when night comes on;
> But let there never be curtain drawn
> Between you and me.

Here, Frost seems to be inviting the tree to enter his home. What a contrast with the hill wife in "The Oft-Repeated Dream"! Instead of using the window to close out Nature, Frost finds its transparent qualities useful for combining home and Nature into one. He carries this impulse even further in the poem "In the Long Night" where he says, "I would build my house of crystal. . . ." Here the very walls take on that transparent quality, and the limits of "home" are expanded. While Frost is still housed, he is in no way shut in.

The metaphor of home has grown as the home space grows. Once a mere shelter for man, it now encompasses Nature as well. But Frost takes the metaphor even further. In a short, untitled poem, he presents the following image:

> Four-room shack aspiring high
> With an arm of scrawny mast
> For the visions in the sky
> That go blindly pouring past.

Certainly the irony of the television antenna cannot be ignored, but this is a mere shack attempting to transcend itself. Not content to simply reach out for Nature, the very universe now seems to be its goal.

And this brings us to what for me are some of the most exciting lines to be found in the poetry of Robert Frost. It seems that he was also very fond of them, for he used the same idea in two of his poems. "New Hampshire" as well as "The Star-Splitter" tells of a man who "Burned down his farmhouse for the fire insurance,/And spent the proceeds on a telescope." Of course his reason for committing such a rash act was "To satisfy a life-long curiosity/About our place among the infinities." How tremendous! Here is a man who is not content with a home among the woods. Instead, he is interested in his home among the stars. He extends the metaphor of home to the furthest point possible; and even though Frost seems to laugh at his foolishness, he nevertheless admits that he spent a profitable night with Brad McLaughlin peering through his telescope:

> We spread our two legs as we spread its three,
> Pointed our thoughts the way we pointed it,
> And standing at our leisure till the day broke,
> Said some of the best things we ever said.

It seems that Robert Frost would like to have the best of both worlds. While he points out the foolishness of burning down one's house, he is drawn to the problem of finding one's home in the universe. Surely he would appreciate Georges Spyridaki's concept of home as related by Gaston Bachelard: " 'My house,' writes Georges Spyridaki, 'is diaphanous, but it is not of glass. It is more of the nature of vapor. Its walls contract and expand as I desire. At times, I draw them close about me like protective armor .... But at others, I let the walls of my house blossom out in their own space, which is infinitely extensible.' " [8]

Such a home seems to be one of the things Frost was looking for in his poetry. He created a great deal of good poetry out of "the vast chaos of all [he] lived through," but to imply that he ever really came "home," that he was able to find more than that "momentary stay against confusion," would be dishonest.[9] Frost's failure ever to feel perfectly at home with the Universe is reflected in the concluding lines of "The Star-Splitter:"

We've looked and looked, but after all where are we?
Do we know any better where we are,
And how it stands between the night tonight
And a man with a smoky lantern chimney?
How different from the way it ever stood?

While the poem "Lost in Heaven" seems to rejoice at least a little in man's ultimate homelessness—"Let's let my heavenly lostness overwhelm me"—Frost still suffers from his inability to establish a complete and lasting sense of home.

In "Desert Places" the poet admits that "I have it in me so much nearer home/To scare myself with my own desert places." In both "The Census-Taker" and "The Birthplace" the attempt to establish a home fails. And in spite of the many times when Frost successfully creates a feeling of home in his poetry, we cannot ignore his ultimate comment on homelessness in "Acquainted with the Night:"

I have been one acquainted with the night.
I have walked out in rain—and back in rain.
I have outwalked the furthest city light.

I have looked down the saddest city lane.
I have passed by the watchman on his beat
And dropped my eyes, unwilling to explain.

I have stood still and stopped the sound of feet
When far away an interrupted cry
Came over houses from another street,

But not to call me back or say good-by;
And further still at an unearthly height,
One luminary clock against the sky

Proclaimed the time was neither wrong nor right.
I have been one acquainted with the night.

That Robert Frost was interested in being at home with as much of life as possible is obvious. He has used "home" as shelter, as a means of creating cosmos out of chaos, and he has attempted to extend the dimensions of home to include Nature and even the Universe. He has also dealt with "home" as something which perhaps is not quite attainable, at least in the fullest sense. He has relied on the metaphor again and again in his poetry, but has refused to make a final statement about it. But if he were to make some kind of definitive statement, I think it would be very much like these lines from Paul Eluard:

> *Quand les cimes de notre ciel se rejoindront*
> *Ma maison aura un toit.*[10]
> (When the peaks of our heaven come together
> My home will have a roof.)

Notes to *"At Home" with Robert Frost* by ROGER EKINS

1. Dorothy Judd, "Reserve in the Art of Robert Frost," *Texas Quarterly*, VI, (Summer 1963), 61.

2. *Selected Prose of Robert Frost*, eds. Hyde Cox and Edward Connery Lathem (New York: Holt, Rinehart and Winston, 1966), 39.

3. Gaston Bachelard, *The Poetics of Space* (Beacon Press: Boston, 1969), 40.

4. *Ibid.*, 46–47.

5. Mircea Eliade, *The Sacred and the Profane: the Nature of Religion* (Harcourt, Brace and World, 1959), 65.

6. *Ibid.*, 56.

7. Vivian C. Hopkins, "Robert Frost: Out Far and In Deep," *Western Humanities Review*, XIV (Summer 1960), 262–63.

8. Bachelard, 51.

9. *Complete Poems of Robert Frost* (New York: Henry Holt and Company, 1949), vi–vii.

10. Paul Eluard, *Dignes de vivre* (Paris: Julliard, 1944), 115.

A Post Mortem on "The Death of the Hired Man"

NANCY VOGEL

ROBERT FROST once said that in writing the poems of *North of Boston* he had "dropped to an everyday level of diction that even Wordsworth kept above." [1] How low Wordsworth dropped is a matter for another time and place, but a matter for this time and place is whether Frost "dropped to an everyday level of diction" in "The Death of the Hired Man," one of the poems of *North of Boston*.

In this pastoral poem a New England couple, Mary and Warren, converse chiefly about Silas, a hired man with a talent for walking off the farm during haying time. As man and wife, Warren and Mary might be expected to communicate on what Martin Joos has called the intimate level. No doubt they do communicate on the intimate level in private life, but they cannot do so in public life, that is to say in the poem, because "Intimate speech excludes public information." Frost, consequently, has had to move up to the casual and consultative levels of language, stopping before arriving at the formal level because there, as Joos has noted, "participation drops out." If participation between the speakers had dropped out completely, the poem would have become a collection of monologues; Frost has kept it a dialogue. [2]

In "The Death of the Hired Man" Mary supplies background information: Silas is back. He's in the house, and he wants Warren to get that Wilson boy back when the pasture is put up again. Warren supplies information too, the information that Silas is an undependable hired man who can be depended on to be back when money runs out and no one else needs his help. Like another Silas, he is fond of coin. This supplying of information is one characteristic of the consultative style. A second feature of this style is also found in the poem, namely the continual participation of the person addressed.

Although Mary and Warren are two educated adults, even a

Yankee couple is hardly to be expected to communicate entirely on the consultative level. Ellipsis, a feature of the casual style, helps take some of the starch out of the conversation. For instance, contractions are often used: Mary's line, "Harold's associated in his mind with Latin" and Warren's, "I know, that's Silas' one accomplishment." In addition, ellipsis frequently comes about through the omission of *that*, resulting in a certain informality: Warren's "Mary, confess/He said he'd come to ditch the meadow for me" and Mary's "You wouldn't think they would." Slang, another feature of the casual style, is missing from this poem, and it is missing for a good reason: slang would date the art.

By and large, the conversation between the couple proceeds colloquially (i.e., orally), somewhat on the casual level, true, but more on the consultative level. Sometimes the repartee even seems like that of a debate. As a matter of fact, no less an authority than Professor Reuben Brower of Harvard (the Amherst student Frost gave an "A for life")[3] has called the dramatic classic a "debate."[4] At the same time, the conversation takes place within a poem which, by virtue of its being printed and copyrighted, can be said to be frozen. Because the poem has been iced, analysis is possible: "frozen style lacks two things, participation and intonation. It gains two things of which this is one: the reader can reread." Why reread? One answer goes as follows: "So many labors of love on a single sentence, that many rewards for the rereader."[5] Rereader Joos, in a way, has rewritten a part of "The Figure a Poem Makes": "No tears in the writer, no tears in the reader. No surprise for the writer, no surprise for the reader."[6] Are there sentences in "The Death of the Hired Man" that show evidence of "labors of love"? The question is worth asking; the answer can be inferred from Joos's statement that "The Gettysburg Address is deep enough; and Robert Frost will do. And he'll do and he'll do."[7]

Somehow at key places in "The Death of the Hired Man" Robert Frost chose to use tightly parallel constuctions. Consider, for instance, the middle lines in this passage spoken by Mary:

> Poor Silas, so concerned for other folk,
> And nothing to look backward to with pride,

And nothing to look forward to with hope,
So now and never any different.

Mary's two lines, lines exactly parallel even down to the pattern of stress, center on Silas' utter desolation and heighten his hopelessness as he arrives "home."

Indeed, it is Silas' unexpected arrival home that touches off the exchange between Mary and Warren about the nature of home. The contention begins when Mary announces, "Warren, he has come home to die." His very name suggestive of battle, Warren resents the injustice of being expected to take care of a hired man who doesn't care to be loyal, and there is a stage direction included with his reply: " 'Home,' he mocked gently." Doing a slow burn, Warren shortly gives Mary one definition of home: "Home is the place where, when you *have to* go there,/They *have to* take you in." Her answer soft and her calm madonna-like, Mary replies, "I should have called it/Something you somehow *have*n't *to deserve*" (italics added). Grammatically, the prominent feature in these two definitions of home is the catenative verb structure indicated by the italics.[8] Frost's striking construction makes possible a most important kind of poetic development. The parallel catenative construction links; it links the two definitions structurally, but semantically the definitions are driven worlds apart by the negator in Mary's reply, the *n't* which splits the two definitions and sends them off to opposite spheres. The power in Frost's definitions of home comes from the combination of parallelism in construction and antithesis in meaning. To recapitulate, there are sentences in "The Death of the Hired Man" that manifest "labors of love," and the definitions of home, so precisely structured, hint at important consequences.

The poem is about death; the title gives that much away. But it is about home too. *Home* has more than one meaning, and it means more than house. Silas isn't just coming to the farmhouse with "harplike morning-glory strings,/Taut with the dew from garden bed to eaves...." He's coming home, or to the only place he can claim as a temporal home, on his way to his home eternal. The place in the country offers him temporary sanctuary. All along, Mary has known what home is, or what it ought to be. So has Warren, although he has to be coaxed into admitting it. His definition of home resembles a recalcitrant's ("have to go" and "have to take"): the person going doesn't want to go, and the person welcoming doesn't want to welcome. To Mary, however, home is a place for a homecoming; home is something "you . . . haven't to deserve." And with her statement, the implications begin to widen as *home* comes to mean the eternal home, although nothing is said outright in the poem about heaven or hell. The eternal home that Mary brings to mind is one that, in the Christian tradition, is something which man, after Adam, hasn't to deserve. After Adam came Cain and Abel, and it was Cain who protested, "Am I my brother's keeper?" This same question haunts Warren, particularly since he knows that Silas' banker brother lives thirteen miles down the road. Warren thinks about Silas, gets up off the porch step, picks up a stick and breaks it, thereby signifying the breaking of his hardheartedness: Warren chooses to be his brother's keeper, only to discover that he no longer has a brother.

"Definition: Literature is that text which the community insists on having repeated from time to time intact." As literature, Genesis is a text that the community insists on having available for repetition; from time to time it even insists on the repetition of some of the verses, especially this question from the ninth verse of the fourth chapter: "Am I my brother's keeper?" Literature, it can be concluded, is both original and not original: "In unwritten literatures, as the culture evolves through the generations and the catastrophes, feelings evolve. . . . When the feelings drift right along with the culture, the text keeps in step by modernizing itself continuously; example: any medieval ballad of Scottish border tragedy and its modern versions referring to feuds in our eastern mountains." [9] Another example comes to mind: the story of two brothers in the first book of the Bible and a modern version in Robert Frost's "The Death of the Hired Man."

It is significant that Brower, when he called "The Death of the Hired Man" a debate, added that this poem is a debate between justice and mercy. Always on the side of justice Robert Frost, a self-proclaimed " 'Old Testament Christian,' " [10] continued to explore the contraries of justice and mercy after *North of Boston*, notably in "Directive," *A Masque of Reason*, and *A Masque of Mercy*. Like Warren, Frost came to acknowledge the ultimate superiority of mercy, but not ungrudgingly. Frost once lectured a friend,

Don't pretend you don't know what Milton meant when he said mercy was always first [*Paradise Lost*, Book III]. You know your Milton and your Puritanism. He used it in the sense of first aid to what? To the deserving? No, to the totally depraved and undeserving. That's what we are and have been since the day Eve ate the rotten apple. . . . "In Adam's fall We sinned all." Mercy ensued. . . . It is too easy to understand Milton. He faced and liked the harshness of our trial. He was no mere New Testament saphead. . . . He had a human weakness for success; he wanted the right to prevail and was fairly sure he knew what right was. Within certain limits he believed in the rewards of merit. But after all was said for the best of us he was willing to admit that before God our whole enterprise from the day we put on fig leaves and went to work had been no better than pitiful.

I'm like that with a class in school.[11]

Robert Frost is also "like that" in "The Death of the Hired Man," the poem wherein "mercy tempers justice," [12] just as in *A Masque of Mercy* the Keeper ends the play by concluding that "Nothing can make injustice just but mercy."

One of Robert Frost's constellations of intention can be found in the cluster of poems dealing with justice and mercy. A bright and an early star in that constellation, "The Death of the Hired Man" "is the drama of man's justice and woman's mercy and the pull between both values when set against the simplest and deepest of claims—the dignity of man. The essence of the poem lies in the pull and in its resolution as mercy tempers justice." [13] Mary represents mercy, and Warren speaks for justice. One is New Testament; the other, Old. One is reasonable; the other, beyond reason.

Notes to *A Post Mortem on "The Death of the Hired Man"* by NANCY VOGEL

1. Frost to Thomas B. Mosher, July 17, 1913, *Selected Letters of Robert Frost*, ed. Lawrance Thompson (New York: Holt, Rinehart and Winston, Inc., 1964), 83–84.
2. Martin Joos has listed five styles of language in *The Five Clocks* (New York: Harcourt, Brace and World, Inc., 1967): intimate, casual, consultative, formal, and frozen. The characteristics of the various styles as presented here are drawn from Joos's discussion, pp. 11, 29, 34.

3. The circumstances can be found in Richard Poirier, "Robert Frost: The Art of Poetry II," *The Paris Review*, XXIV (Summer-Fall 1960) 100–101.

4. Reuben A. Brower, *The Poetry of Robert Frost: Constellations of Intention* (New York: Oxford University Press, 1963), 216.

5. Joos, 41, 43.

6. *Selected Prose of Robert Frost*, ed. Hyde Cox and Edward Connery Lathem (New York: Holt, Rinehart and Winston, Inc., 1966), 19.

7. Joos, 65.

8. For a discussion of the catenative construction, see W. F. Twaddell's *The English Verb Auxiliaries* (Providence: Brown University Press, 1963), 22–24.

9. Joos, 51–52.

10. Wilbert Snow, "The Robert Frost I Knew," *The Texas Quarterly*, XI (Autumn 1968), 23. I am indebted to Professor Lawrance Thompson's account of the Frost-Snow correspondence in *Robert Frost: The Years of Triumph* (New York: Holt, Rinehart and Winston, Inc., 1970), 656–57.

11. Snow, 33.

12. Brower, 162.

13. *Ibid.*

Like "Pythagoras' Comparison of the Universe with Number": A Frost-Tennyson Correlation

R. F. FLEISSNER

> "Keats got Tennyson going and Tennyson got
> Matthew Arnold going and they got us all going."
>
> Robert Frost, from an unpublished lecture at the New School
> for Social Research as preserved by G. Taggard,
> in the Dartmouth College Library.

WITH the possible exception of Hardy, Tennyson was Robert Frost's favorite Victorian poet. Whatever direct influence Tennyson had on Frost, the two lyrics that seem to reveal the closest relationship are Tennyson's "The Hesperides" and Frost's "The Gold Hesperidee." Purely from a metrical standpoint, Tennyson's lyric may appear to have no real similarity to Frost's poem. The apparent looseness of Tennyson's rhyme scheme hardly resembles Frost's tight structure—or at least so it at first seems. From a numerological perspective, however, there is more than meets the eye. A thematic approach to the subject of number should reveal a comparable anagogical quality in each poem as vital as is the basic connection between numerology and religious writings, a "mystical" significance which has part of its origin in the just proportions of aesthetics.

In a previous paper,[1] I have examined the linkage of "The Hesperides" to Coleridge, "Kubla Khan" in particular, with regard to the reference to number in both works. Though Tennyson's debt to Keats was, to be sure, more pronounced than his various homages to Coleridge, echoes of Coleridge are evident as well. We should expect a poet imbrued with the temptation of the lotus, as Tennyson was (save in "Ulysses"), to express some debt to DeQuincey and Coleridge, both addicts of a similar drug. In "The Hesperides," the "melody o' the Lybian lotusflute" conjures up memories of Coleridge's Abyssinian dulcimer; the allusion to "cedarshade" four lines further on connects with the "cedarn cover" of "Kubla Khan"; the

Tennysonian caveat, "(Let it not be preached abroad)," hauntingly summons up the ending of Coleridge's dream-vision with the cautionary admonition "Beware! Beware! Weave a circle." Yet the verbal correspondences are less important than the groundwork for the "awful mystery" of Tennyson's poem in the incantatory numerology of "Kubla Khan." That Frost alluded to both "Kubla Khan" [2] and "The Lotos-Eaters" [3] lends incentive to the present study.

And for whatever evidence the fact may provide, the Robert Frost Library of New York University contains an edition of Tennyson's *Poetic and Dramatic Works* (Boston: Houghton Mifflin, 1899) with a strong penciled checkmark alongside "The Hesperides." There is no other such mark in the volume.

The principal connection between "The Hesperides" and "The Gold Hesperidee," considering Frost's Scottish penchant for "the fact" (as in "Mowing"), is the conjunction of the numbers *five* and *three* and their implications. In Tennyson's poem, the esoteric symbolism of these numbers may be more obvious, though not so self-evident as to preclude its having been misread or exaggerated. It is curious that these two numbers, when added up, equal the so-called sacred ogdoad, though that particular summation is relevant with Frost only in this connection: if we take the first eight stanzas as the story proper, wherein five and three have an apparently realistic meaning only, and then add the last two stanzas, which draw the religious conclusion of which five and three were hidden signs, then the ogdoad is also structurally important here. What is more significant, however, is that three may be considered a component of five, as the male digit which, when added to the female digit two, produces the marital union of five. It is probable that five is the key nummer, even as it is in the published version of "Kubla Khan" to which "The Hesperides," as I have shown, is indebted. The line "Five and three make an awful mystery" does not have to be taken to mean "five *plus* three," which presumably would require the verb *makes* rather than *make*. So let us be satisfied with the meaning that three works together with five, as part of the larger number, and term this relationship the five/three cluster. This combination also emerges in Frost's poem, but the more significant use of the key number five is its multiple in the overall structure of "The Gold Hesperidee," a ten-stanza poem.

As to the matter of conscious intent, was Tennyson aware that five is a key digit in numerological history? Did he know, for instance, that the principle of analogy has manifested itself this way in "pentagonal symmetry," a leading illustration of a five-unit cluster at work in Nature? There is evidence that he did, even as his Egyptian interests mirror Egypt as a basis for numerological thought, revealed purportedly in the construction of the pyramids. Moreover, experimental psychology suggests a natural proclivity for the Golden Section Proportion, and for the pentagonal symmetry intimately allied with it, exists in man's unconscious (a point to be examined more fully later). Since man is a part of Nature, he is obliged to conform to its laws regardless of his specific intentions. Stretching this point a bit, the cluster T-e-n found in the first syllable of the poet's name tempts us to link the pun with a Tennysonian use of a multiple of five; and for all we know it may have tempted Tennyson too, though not explicitly in "The Hesperides." Punning surely could have tempted Frost, who, we may easily believe, was capable of divining such hidden nameplay unconsciously, even as he was fond of echoing his own surname (incidentally containing five letters) in his own poetry as, indeed, noticeably enough in the initial line of a stanza of "The Gold Hesperidee." (As Theodore Maynard once put it, rather too cavalierly perhaps, "If I had to sum up Frost with a word I would use the word 'frost.' Winter lies over all his landscape.")[4] Likewise, Frost's use of "Tennysonian" inspiration may thus be factually evident in his use of ten stanzas, a very unusual number for him.

Before considering the importance of ten in "The Gold Hesperidee," let us ask, as we did of Tennyson, whether Frost was aware of such neopythagorean mysticism. Since he deliberately called himself a "good Greek," perhaps he was more of a conscious follower of Pythagoras than we might at first imagine. In his essay "Education by Poetry," he wrote:

Once on a time all the Greeks were busy telling each other what the All was—or was like unto. All was three elements, air, earth, and water (we once thought it was ninety elements; now we think it is only one). All was substance, said another. All was change, said a third. But best and most fruitful was Pythagoras' comparison of the universe with number. Number of what? Number of feet, pounds, and seconds was the answer, and we had science and all that has followed in science. The metaphor has held and held. . . .[5]

In addition to this statement, Reginald L. Cook has assured me of Frost's feeling that science and poetry have in common a mutual concern with numerical progression. With a poet as interested in the classics as Frost was, we expect that. He naturally associated metrics with counting, as in a reference to Dekker's "Golden Numbers" or to Herrick's "Noble Numbers." The Herrick connection is worth considering, for Frost also knew of Herrick's "Hesperides." Did his mind associate number with a "Hesperidian formula"? We might recall that he alluded also, epigraphically, to Ridgely Torrence's "Hesperides," a collection of poetry which begins, interestingly, with a lyric about the mythic apples of gold which, though presented in a modern idiom, is dimly reminiscent of Tennyson's poem.[6]

That Frost was specifically interested in three and five seems clear to me from other, unrelated writings too. For example, in his essay "On Emerson" he refers to the mysticism of three as Trinitarian. In a single poem ("How Hard to Keep . . .") he frequently repeated the term *quintessence* (lines 41, 42, 43, 44, 51, 87, 88), with its current meaning, of course; but also, I think, the repetition indicates that the original mythical meaning captivated him.[7] It seems plausible that Frost was acquainted with the original meaning of the term as the *Quinta Essentia* or Fifth Element, a significance augmented through the major numerological belief in the traditional Four Elements as adding up to a multiple of five (namely, $1+2+3+4=10$).

Let us now investigate the specific use Frost and Tennyson made of the five/three cluster to see what possible interrelationships may have developed. Tennyson's initial reference has already been cited: "Five and three/(Let it not be preached abroad)make an awful mystery" (XI. ll. 28–29). His second is the following:

> *Five* links, a golden chain are we,
> Hesper, the dragon, and sisters *three*
> Bound about the golden tree.
>
> (XI. ll. 65–67, also 106 108)

The analogous portion in Frost's poem is at the very beginning:

Square Matthew Hale's young grafted apple tree
Began to blossom at the age of *five*;
And after having entertained the bee,
And cast its flowers and all the stems but *three*,
It set itself to keep those *three* alive;
And downy wax the *three* began to thrive.

(Italics added to both quotations)

In itself, this may hardly seem a significant cluster, but we should bear in mind that the theme is ultimately religious, at least inasmuch as church is mentioned soon thereafter, clearing the air, so to speak, for mystical analysis, the final two stanzas alluding to sin, worship, and God. The parenthetic aside there, "(The meaning of the passage had been hid)," recalls the one in Tennyson's poem, "(Let it not be preached abroad)"—at least as much as the Tennyson line itself thematically echoes the aside in Coleridge ("Beware! Beware! . . .") pointed out earlier. These lines evoke esoteric subsurface meanings which we suspect then also in the poem's seemingly realistic beginning. We are confronted with a Frostian secret that "knows," whereas the uninitiated layman is capable only of supposing.

Before proceeding further, we might consider how else the two poems are related, so that we shall not be treating the numerological factor in vacuo, as it were. The setting of the Tennyson poem is the non plus ultra of romantic longing: a starry night, a blue bay bordered by weighty cliffs, "bloombright slopes," "cedarshade," and filled with a mysterious singing, "like the voices in a dream," which follows the traveler as his boat heads for the outer sea. By contrast, Frost's setting is a small one-cow, one-pig farm with an orchard near a country road. Spring, summer, and fall are indicated only through the blossoming of a young apple tree, five years old, its three growing apples, a bit of foliage in the wind. Farmer Hale, however, is also inwardly a traveler; he is out for more than a good crop. For he is spellbound by his young grafted tree and its produce, three apples with a mysteriously promising name. The drab environment is forgotten in a fairyland of expectation; "the voices in a dream" are replaced by Matthew's subtle observations as to how the tiny "downy wax" apples turn "with a little twist" "from looking up [as blossoms] and being kissed to looking down and yet not being sad." A holy number, three, is presumably assuring him that they will not be bruised, but will ripen and be his.

Most of Tennyson's poem is taken up by the song the traveler hears as though in a dream; it is about five guardians of a sacred tree, three of whom (the singers themselves) are fairies, daughters of Hesper, the evening star. The fifth is a dragon curled about the tree's root. What they watch and protect is a mystery, the "treasure of the West." The theme is that if the East can steal the fruit, "the world will be otherwise," for the East stands for bright daylight, the enemy of dreams and their fulfillment of longing.

Frost's Matthew Hale experiences what Tennyson's traveler in a dreamworld fears but does not know: his wonderful apples disappear; they are not protected by a holy trinity. His response is a private "ritual" dance on his hat before church. This humorous ending to his own "dream" does not save him, however, from the consequences. He knows finally that he worshipped golden apples as the Jews falsely worshipped the golden calf. Yet God's grace saves him from ridicule; no one sees his dance of wrath. Humbly, therefore, he returns to the fold. Thus romanticism yields to the real world in which the orchard yields a crop for sale and winter storage, and Matthew's earnestness replaces his once mysterious longing.

Considered in this light, the chain of events of "The Gold Hesperidee" is simple, almost a parody of the esoteric. Matthew shows his son, who incidentally happens to be the same age as the tree (the number five again), the developing apples and warns against touching them. The father finds first two apples, then three, and reflects on the latter number as a mystical digit over which pagan fate (here in the form of parasites) would have no authority. But behind the slight humor of this rationalization is the subtlety that the true numerological significance lies not in the number three alone here, and this is more important than the momentary identification of religion with superstition, a familiar Frostian predilection. When Matthew, just before going to church, finds the apples no longer there, his silent dance on his hat is a cover-up for a deeper meaning: the ceremony for those who only suppose while the Secret is doing the knowing. On the surface, the Secret is what happened to the missing apples. But far beneath the surface the secret of the Secret lurks: the problem of the identity of the Ineffable, or (I suspect) the *Ding-an-sich*, the Kantian expression of inscrutability to which the English romantic tradition and its Victorian followers were to such an extent indebted.

The "Eden myth" permeates so much of world literature, as Robert Penn Warren and mythic critics like Northrop Frye have suggested, that it is fair to say that, up to a point, there is an Edenic theme in both the Tennyson and the Frost poems. "The Gold Hesperidee," with its wry humor, hardly operates on the level of pure Nature poetry. It is primarily about human nature, within a particularly Puritan context. The droll effect is itself somewhat stiffly Puritan. There is deliberate symbolism in such a line as that indicating "the name Gold Hesperidee was right." But "right" in what sense, apart from the good flavor of apples? Clearly it also relates to its namesake, the mythically "guarded" apples. But in terms of what occurs in the poem, the title is ironic. There is no dragon guarding the apples. An allusion to the myth of Eden is apparently evident in the green/gold cluster ("And what was green would by and by be gold"), a figure reiterated slightly differently in the penultimate stanza; for the same color theme is used in Frost's shorter lyric "Nothing Gold Can Stay" where the allusion to Eden is made explicit.

One basis for the division into ten stanzas may be that Frost had in the back of his mind an awareness of the Ten Commandments, perhaps especially "thou shalt not steal" and "thou shalt have no other gods before Me." Another is that, in terms of the poet's "good Greek" instincts, he was subtly probing into the hidden significance of the neopythagorean mysteries of ten as symbolic of forces beyond human control (the macrocosm) in contradistinction to five as a standard symbol of the tree, the boy, and Nature in general (the microcosm). That the first nine digits in our number system form a unit with the number ten before the cycle recurs was no arbitrary invention. It is notable that five stands as a midpoint between one and nine and that ten is a multiple of it; thus it has a dominantly double function, one that cannot be assigned to just another number.

The importance of five as a "midpoint" number probably has fostered its association with the principle of the Golden Mean, though the basis is largely mathematical in terms of the construction of the division into extreme and mean ratio with the regular pentagram. The Mean has been considered an aesthetic expression of a primarily mathematical formulation. To some extent, the Mean is also a concept in ethics; but in general, as a principle of moderation, it has more secular than dogmatically ethical meaning.

The Euclidean division of a line into extreme and mean ratio, what has sometimes been called the construction of the Golden Section, is the basis of the principle of the Mean, though the latter has been loosely associated with a via media in the *Ethics* of Aristotle. The close proximity of the proportion to the laws of natural growth has revealed that Nature furnishes a mathematical basis for human action, whether conscious or not. That Frost was familiar with some of this lore is evident from his devotion to Lucretius and the *De Rerum Natura*. Frost also knew of Aristotle's philosophy, as is evident from the "Peripatetic" reference in "The Bear," for example, though the allusion is largely jocular there (the poem being, to some extent, a parody of Pope's poetry);[8] he knew of Horace and probably of his *aurea mediocritas*. He was very likely familiar with a multitude of other allusions to the Mean in classical writings, usually summed up in the phrase "nothing too much." The important point, then, is that when Frost did intuit the Golden Mean in his poetry, as Tristram Coffin, in particular, and also Lawrance Thompson, have averred, he was harking back not only to Aristotle and Horace, not merely to the perfect Mean between excess and defect, but also to the whole classical tradition, stemming from the Pythagoreans and Euclid, that Aristotle was only bringing to the fore. This is the meaning behind Frost's being a "good Greek."

A clear-cut example of Frost's use of the Mean is "The Middleness of the Road," a good illustration of his deliberate refusal to be romantic or regionally realistic. The poem may at first seem to amount to an apologia for middle-of-the-road politics, to "muddling through" in the middle, but the thought behind the image is what is important. The poem is related to Frost's other "road" poems, particularly "Stopping by Woods on a Snowy Evening" and

"The Road Not Taken." In both, a choice is being set up, and the speaker has to make a decision. After weighing the possibilities, he arrives at a solution of sorts, not a radical or dogmatic one. The decision is, certainly in part, motivated by concern for temperance or the ideal of the Mean. The effect is more Greek than Hebraic or Puritan, to allude to Arnold's well-known distinction in *Culture and Anarchy*. (Inasmuch as Arnold, whom Frost also admired, believed so strongly in a healthy combination of these two drives, it would be worthwhile to see how they complement each other in "The Gold Hesperidee.") In "Stopping by Woods" the speaker has his errands and must move on; in "The Road Not Taken" he reserves the road he does not take for "another day," but for the time being he accepts the more challenging path. These decisions are in accord with the principle of not acting in extremes. In "Stopping by Woods" the danger is excess (to linger too long looking in); in "The Road Not Taken" it is defect (as the title already would suggest, though the application is ironic). Tristram Coffin, interestingly, identified the Mean in Frost with the Golden Rule: "The world is torn between extremes of the good. The wise man, and the good, tries to keep to the middle of the road, going his way in a third direction. . . . This is a New England farmer-poet's conception of the Golden Mean. . . . The Golden Mean is like the Golden Rule." [9] And Thompson refers to Frost's common sense position in the Golden Mean.[10] But, as I hope to have shown, the basis is more mathematical and aesthetic than ethical as such.

Does not Frost's very title, "The Gold Hesperidee," allude to the Golden Proportion—even by analogy to five as the so-called Golden Number? If so, does it perhaps also signify the Golden Mean as an ethical principle? Yes, the classic virtue of temperance is hinted at in the last line ("To walk a graver man restrained in wrath") after Matthew has acted quite intemperately by trampling so deliberately upon his hat (though even there the ritual involved is surely preferable to the venting of anger in a more excessive way). This is what lends the poem some of its humor, yet it is also that which shows an aesthetic basis of the principle of the Mean.

It is time now to consider some of the psychological bases for the Golden Proportion and related pentad-mysticism. Psychologists have experimented with the Golden Mean Proportion for some time in relation to the "conative theory of affection," and the bulk of the conclusions have revealed that there is a decided leaning toward acceptance of the formula (designated a/b=b/a+b) in the human psyche. Certainly the research of Fechner, Angier, Lalo, and others deserves to be weighed with great care, despite the qualifications posed by C. O. Weber.[11] The Golden Proportion cannot be expressed in terms of finite numbers; it is difficult, therefore, if not impossible, to stipulate how close we ought to arrive at a proportion that is in itself incommensurable. For example, it may well be that the octet-sestet division of the Petrarchan sonnet is based on the Golden Proportion in Nature (as intuited in Art), and Frost could have become aware of the intrinsic properties of the Mean through contemplation of this form. That the digits eight and six do not quite accord with the Fibonacci Number Series, which Matila Ghyka relates to the Golden Section and related pentagonal symmetry in his invaluable volume *The Geometry of Art and Life*,[12] is beside the point, for a sonnet needs to have a symmetrical rhyme pattern in the sestet, and the pentad therefore has to be accommodated to the closest number, six. In a situation where symmetry is not so explicitly needed, in the length of a metrical line for instance, the pentad has figured prominently, as revealed by the popularity of the five-beat line or iambic pentameter. Likewise, in "The Gold Hesperidee" each stanza has six lines to accord with the symmetrical effect of the end-rhymes. That the number comes close to five is, in itself, of sufficient significance, since five is an approximation of an incommensurable Golden Number that is the basis of Golden Proportionality.

Frost does use pentameter in this poem, and a word should be added on the five-beat line as a manifestation of the Golden Number. The use of pentameter has been defended on the grounds that a human being's "span of perception" may not permit him to see more than five units at any given time as a fixed cluster. The point is that once the span is larger than five units, the Gestalt is disturbed, and there is a breakdown into smaller units. To take an obvious example, French hexameter breaks down into two groups of three units each, separated by the caesura. Perhaps one reason that the next unit-cluster, seven, has so often been related to the Bible and theology is simply that it is not always taken as a cluster psychologically. In a similar manner, eight breaks down into five and three, two digits in the Fibonacci Number Series which we have seen intimately connected in Frost's and Tennyson's poems. The sequence is 1, 2, 3, 5, 8 . . . , whereby each digit after the second represents the sum of the two preceding digits, hence approximating the Golden Section Proportion in which the shorter segment of a line is to the longer segment as the longer is to the sum of the two, or the whole line. Dante's singular preference for the number nine breaks down into three threes and so has been not improperly dubbed the Trinity of Trinities. Finally ten itself breaks down psychologically into two separate units, each of which contains the Golden Number Five. As a correlation to this arrangement, we have the moralistic division of Frost's ten-stanza poem into eight stanzas (the ogdoad) and two (a kind of couplet ending).

The "conative theory of affection" is related to the psychology of the "span of perception." Since man's conative perception of the pentad in pentagonal symmetry and the interrelated Golden Section is absolutely essential to realize how both Tennyson and Frost were subject to forces outside their consciousness, let us examine this idea briefly. The theory is that the human being's striving for form is capable of being measured, that the aesthetic study of conation is on a par with a study of cognition. Fechner set up a number of geometrical forms, including the Golden Section Rectangle (g.s.r.) and queried his subjects about their preferences. The subjects had no conscious knowledge of the aesthetic proportions of the figures involved, but they tended to select the g.s.r. as the most pleasing. Fechner's conclusions were reaffirmed by independent studies. One demurrer worth citing is C. O. Weber's, whose series of experiments with only female students at Wells College, concluded that the g.s.r. was not the modal selection. The modal choice was rather a figure that had no reputation at all in the history of aesthetics. Professor Weber's main conclusion was that the unconscious mind simply prefers the asymmetrical to the symmetrical, but not necessarily any particular asymmetrical form. Yet he did concede that the g.s.r. came in a close second. Since he worked with a relatively small number of subjects, two assumptions seem warranted: that if many more tests were given to the students, or if the tests were given to appreciably more students, the first modal choice would again be the g.s.r.; though, since the g.s.r. cannot be constructed exactly, owing to the incommensurability of the proportion, drawing the line for determining exact response to it is impossible.

The conclusion, therefore, can only be that it would make little difference whether or not Frost was consciously aware of the implications of the Golden Number and Proportion in writing "The Gold Hesperidee." For experiments have demonstrated that preference for the mathematical basis of the Golden Section, upon which the Mean and possibly to some extent the Golden Rule are based, is part of the order of Nature itself and inherent in the very process of growth. It manifests itself, as Ghyka and many others have shown, in such natural forms as nautilus sea shells, maple leaves, and perhaps most conspicuously in the five fingers of the human hand and foot. That Frost utilized the key Fibonacci numbers of five and three in the poem points to further intuitive, unconscious selectivity. The stanza count, the use of pentameter, the repetition of the key digit five in separate references: these all confirm his manner of selection. But what strengthens the whole case immeasurably is the antecedent use of such numerology in Tennyson's "The Hesperides."

Basically, then, the Tennyson/Frost correlation deals with the references to three and five in both poems—particularly to five, since three is to be seen as a principal component of the other digit envisaged as the neopythagorean "nuptial number," namely the marriage of two and three as female and male. Moreover, three and five are prime digits in the key number system of Fibonacci, which Ghyka shows as basic to the principle of the Golden Section as manifest in Nature and Art. While experiments have demonstrated that such "golden proportionality" is indigenous to human psychology, it is possible that Frost obtained his use of these numbers in "The Gold Hesperidee" through his cognizance of Tennyson's "The Hesperides," especially since other links between these two lyrics are also evident, and since there is external evidence in favor of Frost's having been impressed by Tennyson's poem. Further substantiation for this correlation is to be found in Ridgely Torrence's Hesperidian poetry, to which Frost referred in an epigraph to "A Passing Glimpse." As a recent biographer of Torrence has remarked, "The fact that this poem was the only time Frost made such a gesture enhances its place as one of the highest honors Torrence received during his career." [13] He adds: "It is interesting, too, that Torrence used the golden apples of the Hesperides as his symbol for the goal of human aspiration. It seems likely that he derived this idea from Tennyson's poem, which describes the apples as 'the treasure/Of the wisdom of the West.'" [14] Frost's friendship with Torrence and specific allusion to the Torrentian version of the Hesperidian theme may have been responsible for his own acquaintance with the poem of Tennyson's that influenced Torrence. On the other hand, I should be callous if I did not concede that Tennyson, Torrence, and Frost all could have arrived at analogous conclusions intuitively and independently. Still another possibility, more remote yet worth pondering, is that the use of the three-five combination by Coleridge in "Kubla Khan" [15] stimulated Tennyson in "The Hesperides," as the poem certainly did elsewhere,[16] and thus, indirectly, Frost. In my brief excursion into the mazes of neopythagoreanism in this paper, in order to help validate the Tennyson-Frost relationship thematically, I have not meant to pose as a numerologist as such, but rather to work with numbers which have had principally a bearing on psychology and on Nature study. My purpose has been to show how Frost's awareness and use of number provide a helpful measurement, a new dimension, for applying his theory of the metaphorical basis of poetry.

Notes to *Like "Pythagoras' Comparison of the Universe with Number": a Frost-Tennyson Parallel* by R. F. FLEISSNER

1. R. F. Fleissner, "Tennyson's Hesperidean Xanadu: The Anagogical Thread," *Research Studies*, XXXIX (March 1971), 40–46. Citations are to *The Poems of Tennyson*, ed. Christopher Ricks (London: Longman Group Limited, 1969).
2. See, for example, Frost's introduction ("A Romantic Chasm") to the English edition of *A Masque of Reason*, republished in *Selected Prose of Robert Frost*, ed. Hyde Cox and Edward Connery Lathem (New York: Holt, Rinehart and Winston, 1966), 75–78.
3. Lawrance Thompson, *Robert Frost: The Early Years, 1874–1915* (New York:

Holt, Rinehart and Winston, 1966), 347. That Frost taught "the lyrics of . . . Tennyson" at Pinkerton Academy surely meant the inclusion of his more popular poetry, such as "The Lotos-Eaters," along with, possibly, "The Hesperides."

4. Theodore Maynard, "The 'Poet of Frost,'" *Literary Digest*, LVI (July 17, 1920), 32–33.

5. *Selected Prose*, 37.

6. Frost was a friend of the Torrence family of Xenia, Ohio, whose residence is a few miles from my office at Central State University, and with whom I established contact in preparing this paper. I also wish to acknowledge here the gracious assistance of Reginald L. Cook, Rabbi Victor Reichert, Alastair Fowler, Edward Connery Lathem, William Sutton, and C. O. Weber. Visits with these gentlemen-scholars have taught me a great deal. I cite Professor Cook's conversation at Middlebury with his kind permission.

7. I am indebted to Professor Tharpe for having brought this point to my attention.

8. See Lawrance Thompson, *Robert Frost: The Years of Triumph, 1915–1938* (New York: Holt, Rinehart and Winston, 1970), 630.

9. *New Poetry of New England: Frost and Robinson* (Baltimore: Johns Hopkins University Press, 1938), 133.

10. Thus, in *Fire and Ice* (New York: Henry Holt and Company, 1942), 150, Lawrance Thompson speaks of "a classical moderation in the Golden Mean" in Frost's poetry.

11. E.g., C. O. Weber, "Theories of Affection and Aesthetics of Visual Form," *Psychological Review*, XXXIV (1927), 206–19; "The Aesthetics of Rectangles and Theories of Affection," *Journal of Applied Psychology*, XV (1931), 310–18.

12. Matila Ghyka, *The Geometry of Art and Life* (New York: Sheed and Ward, 1946). A good recent article on the pentad, though strictly from a numerological perspective, is Russell A. Peck's "Numerology and Chaucer's *Troilus and Criseyde*," *Mosaic*, V (Summer 1972), 1–29, especially because he relates five to ten structurally; Peck somewhat "anticipates" my forthcoming article, "The Wife of Bath's Five," *The Chaucer Review*, III, no. 3.

13. John M. Clum, *Ridgely Torrence* (New York: Twayne Publ., 1972), 132–33.

14. *Ibid.*, 122.

15. See my short article, "The Mystical Meaning of Five: A Notelet on 'Kubla Khan,'" *English Studies*, XLVI (1965), 45. A further study of mine on the meaning of five in modern poetry also has some relevance: "Homage to the Pentad: Williams's 'The Great Figure,'" *Notes on Contemporary Literature* (West Georgia College), I (September 1971), 2–6.

16. E.g. in "The Palace of Art." See Christopher Ricks, *Tennyson* (New York: Collier Books, 1972), 92–93.

"The Black Cottage:" Robert Frost and the Jeffersonian Ideal of Equality

MARGARET V. ALLEN

IT might seem that the serene world of Jeffersonian rationalism is a kind of consciousness wholly alien to the dark vision of Robert Frost's *North of Boston*. What have those ancient assertions about human freedom and equality to do with these poems, where the characters are besieged by fears, loneliness, uncomprehended compulsions and even insanity? Yet the familiar sentence from the Declaration of Independence, "All men are created equal," does find its way into one of the poems in a dramatic and unexpected fashion. "The Black Cottage" raises the question of whether Frost assented to that ideal or whether, as a skeptic, he was able neither to affirm nor deny it. In other words, what did Frost think and feel about a concept that has, since Jefferson's time, been deeply imbedded in American awareness and given shape to so many American laws and institutions?

"The Black Cottage" contains the ambiguities which beset all of Frost's attempts to confront these questions, ambiguities which he never wholly resolved. The method of the poem is the familiar Frost technique of the dramatic dialectic, in which two contrasting characters embody opposing views. One of these affirms the ideal of equality, and has lived by it. The other is skeptical, admitting the possibility that the ideal is outmoded, too simplistic for a complex age, or even false. A third character, remaining neutral, functions as a narrator and audience.

This narrator is walking one day with a minister on a deserted country lane, when they chance to pass an old cottage, dark with age, wet with newly fallen rain. The cottage is uninhabited. Its owner was a woman whose husband was killed in the Civil War, and whose two grown sons live far away, although they have not sold the little house nor its furnishings since she died. Together, the minister and his companion peer through the window, then enter the cottage, as if to enter the life of the woman who once lived there.

A crude crayon portrait of the woman's husband hangs on the wall, made from a daguerreotype before he went to war. The minister, whose monologue comprises most of the poem, describes how the woman lived on for many years in the forsaken little cottage that the world had passed by. She liked to talk about the war, and she had seen Garrison and Whittier.

> One wasn't long in learning that she thought,
> Whatever else the Civil War was for,
> It wasn't just to keep the States together,
> Nor just to free the slaves, though it did both.
> She wouldn't have believed those ends enough
> To have given outright for them all she gave.
> Her giving somehow touched the principle
> That all men are created free and equal.

The minister indulges in a little philosophizing about her belief. Is it true? It is easier, he thinks, "to decide it simply isn't true." The woman, he implies, was an innocent. In her sheltered obscure life she hardly ever saw any blacks, and never other races, but her simple or simplistic assumption was that they all must be alike, because made by the same hand. "All men are created equal" was self-evident to her.

The minister then muses on the woman's equally "quaint" religious notions. She believed in hell, it seems, a belief the minister himself had long ago abandoned, like most of his congregation, to whom the words of the Creed, "descended into Hades," had come to seem outrageously pagan. "And well, if they weren't true why keep right on/Saying them like the heathen? We could drop them."

At this point the minister's talk moves away from the woman. The easy, relaxed conversational rhythms of the poem, which reflect the minister's easy, relaxed approach to religion, gradually give way to tighter, more stately rhythms. His subject becomes mutability itself, and he speaks of his own deepest longings for a realm not subject to change.

> As I sit here, and oftentimes, I wish
> I could be monarch of a desert land

I could devote and dedicate forever
To the truths we keep coming back and back to.
So desert it would have to be, so walled
By mountain ranges half in summer snow,
No one would covet it or think it worth
The pains of conquering to force change on.
Scattered oases where men dwelt, but mostly
Sand dunes held loosely in tamarisk
Blown over and over themselves in idleness.
Sand grains should sugar in the natal dew
The babe born to the desert, the sandstorm
Retard mid-waste my cowering caravans—

Abruptly he breaks off. The conclusion of the poem is swift:

"There are bees in this wall." He struck the
                              clapboards,
Fierce heads looked out; small bodies pivoted.
We rose to go. Sunset blazed on the windows.

Clearly, this is not a poem primarily about political ideas. Rather, it dramatizes three conflicts which are intimately related to political and religious thinking. Skepticism is set against faith; wordly knowledge and worldly sophistication against ideals; and change against the never-changing.

The woman personifies an older America, with her Calvinist religion, her emotional ties to Civil War days, her Yankee independence. No clinging vine, she had her own ideas, and lived alone, not with her sons. "She valued the considerate neglect/She had at some cost taught them after years." Seen through the minister's eyes, she is a sweet old creature, her bonnet nodding as she dozes in the front pew of his church. Her beliefs seem to belong to another time, a time of America's own age of innocence before the Civil War, for they are "so removed/From the world's view today of all those things." The cottage itself is an image of isolation and decay, set among overgrown grass, the boards warped, the old-fashioned furniture dusty, the clapboard walls usurped by bees. The modish minister suggests that the woman could hold to her idea that "all men are created free and equal" because she was secluded from the realities of racial strife, racial differences. The inescapable implication is that her kind of devotion to an idea is the symptom or the result of a life isolated from the world—and from change. A secluded New England cottage hardly placed her at the hub of society's concerns, in the minister's view, and she was impervious to what the people in the West or the South might have been saying. She was childlike, naive and changeless, and so she commands respect but does not evoke the desire to emulate, nor does she have much for the modern age to live by.

Or does she? One of the poem's artistic triumphs is the double view of the woman of the cottage. Some of the sharpest ironies of the poem emerge when, instead of falling in with the minister's view of her, we consider him instead. One of these ironies is that the minister, whom one might expect to be a man of faith, is instead the skeptic. The woman has vastly more faith than he does. What comfort in time of bereavement, one wonders, could he ever offer to match the faith that sustained her life? The highest wisdom of the minister is: adjust to the times, for they change. He is willing to revise the Creed to accommodate the more liberal beliefs of his congregation, particularly the young members. But so great is his desire to please all that to please the woman he retains the phrase about Hades. Does it matter so much after all? he thinks.

The minister is a realist. Commenting on the old crayon picture of the husband, he says "I doubt/If such unlifelike lines kept power to stir/Anything in her after all the years." He doesn't see that the woman had no need of an exact likeness in a frame in order to cherish her husband's image in her heart. Her love for her dead husband was not dependent on objects. As she would speak of the war, she would half lean, half kneel against the lounge beside it, a gesture of worship that proclaimed the power of her intangible faith and love, and their merging in her own mind with the ideal, "All men are created free and equal."

The minister seems hardly to understand that kind of devotion. His allegiance is to the future, to the young progressive members of his congregation. His interest in the past is so dim that he does not distinguish Gettysburg from Fredericksburg. "He fell at Gettysburg or Fredericksburg,/I ought to know—it makes a difference which:/Fredericksburg wasn't Gettysburg, of course," he says of the soldier husband, in lines which Randall Jarrell has called "the most touchingly and hauntingly prosaic of lines about the passing away of this world." [1]

The minister's skepticism about religious beliefs is paralleled by his skepticism about Jeffersonian ideals. "All men are created free and equal" may not be true, he muses. "I heard a fellow say so." One begins to suspect that the minister is willing to call this or any proposition untrue, if only enough people hold that it is untrue. One adapts, after all, and truths do come in and out of favor, after all, and one must keep up with the times, after all. Still, the minister recognizes that this potent ideal was "planted/Where it will trouble us a thousand years./Each age will have to reconsider it." And he is sophisticated enough to recognize the possibility that the ideal may after all be "the force that would at last prevail."

It is the minister's deep uncertainties about what is true and untrue, as well as his wordly-wise knowledge of the need to change and adjust, that engender his longing for the desert land, for a region where change comes so slowly it seems not to come at all. He longs for truth to be absolute, not cyclical. His mind knows that truths return again, but his heart longs for the realm of the un-changing. As he articulates his vision, the taut power of his language shows its intensity in his imagination.

Still, the "latter wisdom of the world" forbids such fantasies, and so he does not allow himself to become lost in them too long. A peremptory rap at the boards shocks his listener and himself back to the more usual mundane state of mind. In a series of staccato sentences, the reader too is brought abruptly back from the visionary land ringed by snow-covered mountains, symbolizing permanence, to the visible world where the sun is setting, a reminder of change and mortality.

Between these two characters, the old woman growing old and dying in her remote cottage, and the practical modern-thinking minister, there could hardly be a more complete contrast. She is one of those characters of *North of Boston* of whom Lionel Trilling has asked, "When ever have people been so isolated, so lightning-blasted, so tried down and calcined by life, so reduced, each in his own way, to some last irreducible core of being?" [2] She seems to embody an older American heritage on which the sun has set, one which has succumbed to the inevitable processes of change and disintegration. There are many obvious similarities in "The Black Cottage" to Frost's later and better known "Directive." Both poems portray isolation, extinction, and the encroaching wilderness. In both poems, the setting of a decaying house suggests another age, juxtaposed to a confused too-rapidly-changing contemporary world. The minister visits the black cottage in the same spirit in which "Directive" leads the reader "Back now out of all this too much for us/Back in a time made simple by the loss/Of detail. . . ." The motive power of both poems is a longing for stable truths, a longing to be "whole again beyond confusion."

There are persuasive reasons for believing that Frost himself is closer to the minister's viewpoint, primarily because of his skepticism about orthodox religious beliefs, but also because of his self-admitted political conservatism that forbade easy assent to popularized slogans about freedom and equality. Frost, like the minister, was tormented by epistemological uncertainties, and was often unsure what was worth believing in, or whether anything was. Frost gives to his fictitious minister the expression of one of his own persistent longings, the longing for stability amid flux, for continuity amid frightening change, for truths large enough and constant enough to compel transcendent devotion. Yvor Winters has called Frost an Emersonian Romantic who had become skeptical and uncertain;[3] and considering the likenesses between Frost and the minister, it seems that here are the stronger affinities.

Then are we obliged to conclude, with the minister, that the old woman is a nostalgic relic of an ancient time and ancient faiths inadequate to modern confusions? Rather, I think the contrary may be true. Frost's dialectic in "The Black Cottage" endows the woman with such a resilient vitality that she cannot be so readily dismissed. In fact, the fervor of her ideals is the most powerful element in the poem. The skeptic may smile condescendingly, fashionable currents of opinion may pass her by, but "she had her own idea of things." One is almost prepared to say that her idea of things, and her devotion, have outlasted her own death. In this respect, Frost the poet is more like the woman, less like the minister, for a poet too gives his deepest allegiance to intangible things, and by his ideals forges something that endures beyond his own death. Though she is dead and her cottage is at last yielding to the encroachments of nature, the woman remains a dominant presence in the room and in the poem. At the end, her faith seems as enduring and as constant as nature itself—and as likely to triumph over the minister's skepticism and confusion.

Frost once wrote, in a letter to Elizabeth Shepley Sergeant:

The one thing I boast I can't be, is disillusioned. Anything I ever thought I still think. Any poet I ever liked I still like. It is noticeable, I go back on no one. It is merely that others go back on me. I take nothing back. I don't even grow. My favorite theory is that we are given this speed swifter than any stream of light time or water for the sole purpose of standing still like a water beetle in any stream of light time or water off any shore we please.[4]

Frost, like the woman of the poem, experienced isolation, loss and terror, but in these words there are echoes of her granite unyieldingness and no trace at all of the skeptical minister's credo of adaptability.

Frost's political conservatism, what Louise Bogan has called "the ancient conservatism of the man who depends on the earth for his living"[5]—or, in Frost's case, his sympathies and fondness for those who do—will at first suggest that Jeffersonian ideals in their undiluted form were too radical for him. Frost knew too much about the abuses of freedom to assent very readily to any abstract principles which lavished it indiscriminately on so many who used it so badly, so selfishly. It is a theme he touches on, querulously or whimsically, again and again in his poems. "Everyone asks for freedom for himself,/The man free love, the businessman free trade,/The writer and talker free speech and free press," he says in "Build Soil." In "A Case for Jefferson," Frost wonders what Jefferson would have made of a man for whom "the love of country means/Blowing it all to smithereens/And having it all made over new." Jeffersonianism in his mind was alarmingly close to anarchy.

Frost sometimes was perplexed by the definition of freedom, or the limitations of freedom. In "How Hard It Is to Keep from Being King . . . ," he says,

The freedom they seek is by politics,
Forever voting and haranguing for it.
The reason artists show so little interest
In public freedom is because the freedom
They've come to feel the need of is a kind
No one can give them. . . .

One has the impression that he was more troubled by that "hard mystery of Jefferson's" about men being born free and equal than he was sustained, supported or inspired by it. He was not prepared to reject it, but there were difficulties in accepting it. Part of the reason for Frost's confusion on the subject was that he identified the Jeffersonian slogans with the liberal intellectuals to whom they have so often been shibboleths. Frost's distrust of the liberal mentality is well known: he could not agree with their belief in progress, in science, in government planning and control, nor could he approve their complacent conviction of their own enlightenment, and their intolerance of all who disagreed with them about the methods of achieving their liberal goals for society. Frost was afraid that freedom and equality for all would be forced down the throats of all by state planning and regulation—and thus he was often wary of the words themselves. Yet this same suspicion of central government and centralized power, his preference for an agricultural society, even his belief that rural life produced better citizens—all these are Jeffersonian concepts, and Frost must have understood that fact.

Ultimately it is not possible to identify Frost exclusively with either the woman or the minister of "The Black Cottage," for there was much of him in both. The form of the dramatic dialectic enabled him to depict the conflicts more clearly, but not to resolve them. He knew, like the minister, that the Jeffersonian ideal of equality was one that would be around a long time, for every generation to struggle with anew.

The poem itself is Frost's tribute to the strength of that ideal, and an expression of his own uncertainties about it. His fundamental question is the question still left at the end of the poem: can the Jeffersonian ideal survive the realities of twentieth-century experience, with its accelerating change, its fragmentation of experience, its disintegration of religious sensibility? Of the many dramas of the poem, not the least is that today, for us as for Frost, the question remains unanswered.

Notes to *"The Black Cottage": Robert Frost and the Jeffersonian Ideal of Equality* by MARGARET V. ALLEN

1. Randall Jarrell, "To the Laodiceans," from *Poetry and the Age* (New York: Knopf, 1953), 54.
2. Lionel Trilling, "A Speech on Robert Frost: A Cultural Episode," *Partisan Review*, XXVI (Summer 1959), 451.
3. Yvor Winters, "Robert Frost: or, the Spiritual Drifter as Poet," in *The Function of Criticism* (Denver: A. Swallow, 1957), 159, 162.
4. Frost to Elizabeth Shepley Sergeant, quoted in James M. Cox, "Introduction," in *Robert Frost: A Collection of Critical Essays* (Englewood Cliffs, N.J.: Prentice Hall, 1962), 13–14.
5. Louise Bogan, *Achievements in American Poetry 1900–1950* (Chicago: Henry Regnery Co., 1951), 49.

The Meaning of Frost's "Build Soil"

LAURENCE PERRINE

It takes all sorts of in- and outdoor schooling
To get adapted to my kind of fooling.

So wrote Robert Frost in his last book, and the truth of the warning is amply evidenced by the errant readings that have been made of many of his poems. "Build Soil," for instance, modulates continuosly through literal statement, irony, overstatement, metaphor, and symbol, and it is not always easy to determine, in this mixture of seriousness and playfulness, the precise weight to attach to any given utterance. In this paper I mean, first, to give a general account of the poem and, second, to correct some misinterpretations that have been made of it, by very competent critics.

Subtitled "A political pastoral," the poem is a dialogue (a parody, as Lawrance Thompson and John Lynen point out, of Virgil's first eclogue)[1] between Tityrus, a poet-farmer, who is really Frost himself, and Meliboeus, a potato-farmer who has fallen on hard times and is taking up sheep-farming. Meliboeus is chiefly an interlocutor, seeking solutions to his plight, whose function is to give Tityrus an opportunity to expound his views. The poem is a didactic one, but written with wit, imagination, and verve. It was first publicly read by Frost at Columbia University on May 31, 1932, during the Great Depression, one month before Franklin D. Roosevelt was first nominated by his party convention for the Presidency. Roosevelt during his campaign for the nomination had proposed, among other measures, a farm relief program. For Frost Roosevelt's welfare programs represented socialism, and the basic political issue of the poem is the comparative merits of socialism and individualism. By socialism I here mean the attempt to maximize human welfare through social controls. By individualism I mean the attempt to maximize human welfare through freeing individual initiative.

In the poem Frost embraces neither wholly, but his bias is toward individualism.

In paraphrase and summary the argument of the poem is as follows:

1. (Lines 1–52) In writing of politics, the poet must deal with universals, not specifics. [This observation is in response to Meliboeus's urging Tityrus to "Get in a poem toward the next election."]

2. (Lines 53–66) Though times are bad, they are not "revolutionary bad." [Frost believed that all times are bad; but, taking a long view of history, he refused to be swept off his feet by temporary alarms and newspaper predictions of "the worst." The present crisis, he feels, should not cause us to panic. Compare "The Lesson for Today" and "Take Something Like a Star."]

3. (Lines 67–91) The term "socialism" is an abstraction. There is no such thing as "pure socialism" but only different kinds and degrees of socialism. Socialism is an element in every government. [Since all government organizes people socially, all government is to some extent socialistic. One cannot therefore be rationally opposed to socialism but only to certain kinds or degrees of it.]

4. (Lines 92–125) Ambition already has been socialized. Greed has been partly curbed or socialized and may need to be curbed further. But ingenuity ought not to be curbed. [Ambition has been curbed by democratic political processes designed to prevent total power from being wielded by a Caesar, a Napoleon, or a Hitler. Greed has been curbed through fair-trade laws, antitrust legislation, and the like. But ingenuity, Tityrus implies, should not be curbed, though he *says* just the opposite, speaking ironically. The irony will be demonstrated below.]

5. (Lines 126–30) A dictator who "let things take their course" could then "claim the credit for the outcome."

6. (Lines 131–292) A proper balance should be maintained between self-cultivation and social engagement, and the former should precede the latter. Development of a rich individuality in human beings is a precondition of significant human achievement and of a rich and abundant social life. Self-cultivation is especially needed at the present time, which is too much preoccupied with external social activity and too little with the interior life. [Again Frost takes a long view of history. "We're always too much out or too much

in," Tityrus says; at present we're "too much out." We were "too much in" during the middle ages, when holy hermits lived in caves studying exclusively their own spiritual self-perfection. In modern times the inner life has suffered from overemphasis on the external and material.]

The most badly misunderstood passage in "Build Soil" is that on ingenuity (lines 92–125), which I quote in part:

> But the worst one of all to leave uncurbed,
> Unsocialized, is ingenuity:
> Which for no sordid self-aggrandizement,
> For nothing but its own blind satisfaction
> (In this it is as much like hate as love),
> Works in the dark as much against as for us.
>
> . . . .
>
> None should be as ingenious as he could,
> Not if I had my say. Bounds should be set
> To ingenuity for being so cruel
> In bringing change unheralded on the unready.

Malcolm Cowley in "The Case Against Mr. Frost" declares that Frost "objects . . . to new inventions (saying that ingenuity should be held in check)." [2] The opposite of Cowley's assertion is true. That the passage is intended ironically *ought* to be clear from Tityrus's solemnly ranking ingenuity with ambition and greed and calling ingenuity "the worst." But there are other clues as well. That ingenuity works "For nothing but its own blind satisfaction"— that is, is disinterested, is its own end—ought to be seen as a mark for it rather than against it, putting it in a class with love (and therefore necessarily with hate). When Tityrus goes on to say that if he were dictator, he'd "let things take their course" and then "claim the credit for the outcome," he is implying that the results of *un*-checked ingenuity are generally more good than bad. In setting the stage for his declaration that ingenuity should be checked, he admits that inventions may have bad effects as well as good (line 77). The chemist who synthesizes wool from jute may "put ten thousand farmers out of sheep," including his friend Meliboeus. But, for Frost, life by its nature is hazardous, and cannot be made safe for all. All human achievement demands risk-taking. Meliboeus in his sheep-farming venture must risk being put out of work by the invention of synthetic wool. "Everyone wants freedom for himself," and if Meliboeus wants freedom for his own ingenuity, he must leave the "chemist at Columbia" free to use his. The charge that Frost objected to new inventions is ridiculous. Among his lifelong heroes were the Wright brothers, whom he honors in "The Wrights' Biplane" in the same volume as "Build Soil." His later poem "Kitty Hawk" celebrates not only the Wright brothers' first flight but the United States's first putting a man into space: the poem is indeed a celebration of man's technological ingenuity. If Frost distrusted socialism, it was exactly because he *feared* it might curb ingenuity.[3]

Tityrus's assertion that, if he were dictator, he'd "let things take their course" and then "claim the credit for the outcome" has also been misinterpreted and unfairly criticized. George W. Nitchie calls it "anti-intellectual." [4] On the contrary, it represents a belief that greater good will come from freeing the intellects of men than in imposing on them the "superior" intellect of the dictator. Yvor Winters decries the assertion as "a statement of belief in an unrestrained laissez-faire system . . . a belief that if things were left alone they must come right." [5] But Winters takes as purely literal statement what is really playful overstatement. Tityrus has already conceded, at least implicitly, his support of some restraints on ambition and on greed. He therefore *cannot* favor unrestrained laissez-faire. What he does imply is that an unrestrained laissez-faire system would have better results than a completely controlled system. If he were dictator, he would leave his subjects free; that is, for Frost the best *dictator* is no dictator. But the best *government* is a democratic government, which puts a curb on ambition. That Tityrus's remark is not to be taken at literal face value is indicated by his reference to it as one of "the things I say against myself" (line 131).

The last two interpretations I wish to discuss, though quite different, may be conveniently grouped together. The first is minor. Reuben Brower calls Meliboeus a liberal-socialist.[6] In truth, Meliboeus has no fixed viewpoint. He is a poor farmer, with an inquiring mind, seeking a solution to his economic problems. He raises questions rather than advocates a position. At the end of the poem he follows Tityrus's counsel by going home to his farm to think things out for himself. That is, he becomes Tityrus's disciple by practicing self-reliance, both in thinking and in labor. One becomes a true disciple of Frost, as of Emerson or Whitman, not by becoming a follower but by becoming a self-determining individual. And here we encounter a more serious misunderstanding. Yvor Winters scornfully condemns Tityrus's last speech (see especially lines 249–56) as being opposed to "commerce of minds." "It does not occur to Frost that he might learn from his betters and improve himself. . . . There is the implication that his personal 'thought-flow' is valuable merely because it is his own, that it should remain uncontaminated." [7] Again, Winters reads Frost too solemnly. What the passage really demonstrates is a willingness to be stimulated by superior brilliance but a refusal to be overwhelmed by it. No matter how brilliant the thought of another person, Frost would contend (and so would I), one must do his own thinking, reach his own conclusions. Throughout his life Frost engaged in the "commerce of minds" through conversation and through reading. Meliboeus, after voluntarily seeking out and submitting himself to the superior brilliance of Tityrus, quite properly at the end of the poem goes home to form his own conclusions.

The central philosophical and didactic thesis of Frost's poem is contained in the injunction to "Build Soil." The advice is symbolical, and has implications for farming, for personal and national development, for politics and economics, and for writing poetry. Just as the building of good soil is necessary for the production of healthy and abundant crops, Tityrus argues, so the development of a rich individuality in human beings is necessary for significant social interaction, and so the development of a rich national life is necessary for significant international engagement, and so the development of a rich mind is necessary for writing good poetry. The great danger of modern life is that we rush into the social arena too fast, take our crops to market too soon. We desperately need to "build soil," to practice self-cultivation more intensely. Frost's advice is not unlike that of Matthew Arnold in his famous essay "The Function of Criticism at the Present Time":

Let us try a more disinterested mode of seeing [things]; let us betake ourselves more to the serener life of the mind and spirit. This life, too, may have its excesses and dangers; but they are not for us at present. Let us think of quietly enlarging our stock of true and fresh ideas, and not, as soon as we get an idea or half an idea, be running out with it into the street, and trying to make it rule there. Our ideas will, in the end, shape the world all the better for maturing a little.[8]

On a spectrum of political opinion, Frost's position was essentially conservative. But his was a responsible conservatism, not a mindless reactionaryism. It was based on considered philosophical principles. It was rooted firmly in the tradition of individualism and self-reliance preached by Emerson and Thoreau. One need not agree with it. But one must respect it.

Notes to *The Meaning of Frost's "Build Soil"* by LAURENCE PERRINE

1. Lawrance Thompson, *Fire and Ice: The Art and Thought of Robert Frost* (New York: Henry Holt, 1942), 153–54; John F. Lynen, *The Pastoral Art of Robert Frost* (New Haven: Yale University Press, 1960), 127.

2. Malcolm Cowley, "The Case Against Mr. Frost," II, *New Republic*, CXI (September 18, 1944), 345. The passage is also taken literally by the anonymous reviewer of Frost's *Complete Poems* in the (London) *Times Literary Supplement*, March 9, 1951, p. 148.

3. There is a certain irony, apparently unrecognized by Frost, in the fact that the American effort which put Alan Shepard into space was a socialized one. "Kitty Hawk" was written many years after "Build Soil," however, and is not concerned with socialism.

4. George W. Nitchie, *Human Values in the Poetry of Robert Frost* (Durham, N.C.: Duke University Press, 1960), 86–87.

5. Yvor Winters, "Robert Frost: or, the Spiritual Drifter as Poet," *The Function of Criticism: Problems and Exercises* (Denver: Alan Swallow, 1957), 169; reprinted in James M. Cox, ed., *Robert Frost: A Collection of Critical Essays* (Englewood Cliffs, N.J.: Prentice-Hall, 1962), 66.

6. Reuben A. Brower, *The Poetry of Robert Frost* (New York: Oxford University Press, 1963), 208.

7. Winters, "Frost: Spiritual Drifter," 170; Cox, *Frost: Critical Essays*, 67.

8. *The Complete Prose Works of Matthew Arnold*, ed. R. H. Super (Ann Arbor: University of Michigan Press, 1962), III, 282.

CONTEXTS

Frost has continued to seem like a New Englander, even as critics have pointed out the breadth of his concerns. The willingness to find Emerson and Whittier anticipating his settings and themes attests to the nostalgia engendered by his deceptively pastoral country. Perry Westbrook's very able essay, often on subjects other than Frost, shows much of the realism about New England people and places that Frost had to know well. The following essays deal with more specific matters of source and influence. Peter Hays deals with the interesting possibility that Frost's unusual notation of *New Hampshire* reveals something of the private Frost because the paraphernalia of that volume satirized Eliot's use of notes to "The Waste Land." Lloyd Dendinger, whose defense of Frost's ambiguity is very well done in other publications, here takes up another aspect of Emerson's influence.

Donald Crowley studies an influence from Hawthorne, specifically on "The Wood-Pile," that may be very significant in Frost's work. The essay by Edward Stone coincidentally supports this thesis. Despite the limitation suggested in the title, Professor Stone's essay discusses several possible sources in Hawthorne's work besides the desert place that has, also coincidentally, attracted essays herein.

J. T.

Robert Frost's New England

PERRY D. WESTBROOK

I

WHEN in the autumn of 1900 Robert Frost moved onto his newly acquired farm at Derry, New Hampshire, he was already intimately "acquainted with the night." A dropout from Dartmouth and Harvard, an indifferent success in his early efforts at poultry-farming, and an almost totally unpublished would-be poet, he had recently endured the death of his first child, aged four, and had been shattered by the knowledge that his mother was dying of cancer. He himself was afflicted with various physical symptoms, probably psychosomatic, and was depressed to the point of entertaining thoughts of suicide. His five years as a full-time farmer at Derry effected great improvement in his physical and mental health, but his profits from the venture were meagre and, though he published a scattering of poems and prose pieces, the latter in poultry magazines, his literary ambitions remained far short of fulfilment. Nor did his switch in 1906 from farming to teaching, first in an academy in Derry and later in a normal school at Plymouth, New Hampshire, further his literary career, though it did improve his disastrous finances. When he went to England to live in 1912, he was still a failure, so far as recognition goes, in what he considered his one true calling, that of poet.

Yet the early years in rural New England, especially those on the Derry farm, were crucial in Frost's intellectual, spiritual, and artistic development. During this period he formulated his personal philosophy, insofar as he had one; wrote some of the most notable of the poems later to be published in *A Boy's Will, North of Boston*, and subsequent volumes; and accumulated material and memories that found expression in poems to be written decades afterward. In 1952, at the age of seventy-eight, Frost wrote: "I might say the core of all my writing was probably the five free years I had there on the farm down the road a mile or two from Derry Village toward Law-

rence. The only thing we had plenty of was time and seclusion,"
then added, "it turned out as right as a doctor's prescription." [1]
Those years, indeed, he frequently referred to as "the most sacred
in his entire life." [2] The fact is that at the Derry farm Frost had
come into his own, as he expressed it in a poem in *A Boy's Will*, but
the spiritual and artistic maturation begun there continued in his
years of teaching at Derry and Plymouth and later in Franconia,
New Hampshire, where he lived for a time after his return from
England.

II

In pondering what influences contributed to the development of
Frost as man and poet during the New Hampshire years, one should
look closely—though not exclusively, of course—at the social and
cultural conditions of the rural New England in which he lived.
Frost was not a native New Englander. He was born and spent his
first eleven years—surely the most impressionable in anyone's life—
in San Francisco. Furthermore, only one of his parents, his father,
was by birth and ancestry a New Englander: his mother was a
native of Scotland who had lived in Pennsylvania and Ohio before
her marriage. It was not until Isabelle Frost went east with her children in 1885, after her husband's death, that Robert got his first taste
of rural New England, visiting and working on a relative's farm in
Amherst, New Hampshire. He experienced further, but incomplete,
exposure to country and village life during later summers of farm
work and while residing in Salem, New Hampshire, where his
mother and later he himself taught school. But during much of his
adolescence and young manhood he lived and worked at various
jobs in the mill city of Lawrence, about as unrural as any place
could be. Only after he moved to Derry in 1900, following a brief
try at poultry raising in Methuen, Massachusetts (a suburb of Lawrence), did Frost really learn what a farmer's life is like.

Rural New England in 1900 was culturally and economically in
a state of ruin. Many farms, sometimes whole villages, had been
abandoned during the past fifty years as the inhabitants emigrated
to the west or to factory towns where regular wages would provide a surer and better living than would the stony soil. The plight

of the New England countryside had become a cause for national concern. Articles describing it were appearing in such periodicals as *The Atlantic Monthly*, the *New England Magazine*, and *The Century*, and it is most probable that Frost had read some of these dismal accounts of largescale desertion of the land and of poverty and outright degeneracy among those who remained. Conditions were at their worst back in the hills and mountains, but no region was unaffected.[3] Derry, with its proximity to the large mill towns of the Merrimack Valley, would be in a somewhat favored locality but would be by no means exempt from the general blight. In Plymouth, New Hampshire, where Frost taught in 1911–1912, and in the White and Green Mountains, where he vacationed during the summers before his trip to England and where he lived the year around after his return, he would have observed decadence in its most advanced stages.

Among those who could not or would not leave New England, some of course did not succumb to hopelessness or degeneracy, but continued to live by the Puritan principles that had been their forefathers' support in settling these sterile regions. One need not rehearse the Calvinist convictions that underlay the New England way of life for three hundred or so years after the landing of the first Puritans. We need only remind ourselves that one of the points of faith was that God would not desert His elect, though He might test them by the sternest of trials, which the true Christian must accept as part of a divinely prearranged program culminating in salvation and eternal life. The problem was to know whether one was elect; but there were evidences, so-called, and among the most important was submission to God's will, no matter what afflictions He might send. God's plan for the world and its inhabitants was held to be an orderly one, and the true believer must persevere in assurance of this. In later years, even among persons who were not theologically strict Calvinists, the old beliefs and values would survive and would prove supportive even in an environment where failure and decay were everywhere evident.

In his childhood Frost absorbed the religion of his mother, which he describes as a mixture of Presbyterianism, Unitarianism, and Swedenborgianism.[4] Unlikely as this combination may sound, it left its mark on Frost, who frequently proclaimed himself a Puritan but readily admitted a large debt to Emerson, also a favorite of his mother. Actually Frost never became a member of, or regularly attended, any church; yet in his personal life and beliefs he was quite devout and orthodox, as opposed to his wife, who was an outright agnostic. His religious views, of course, changed from time to time. Periods of skepticism alternated with periods of faith; philosophies such as those of William James and Henri Bergson, as he became acquainted with them, modified his outlook. Yet during the years in New Hampshire his thinking was, in some respects, extremely close to Calvinistic orthodoxy. Two early poems make this clear.

The first, "The Trial by Existence," the idea for which came to him while he was still in high school and which was published in *The Independent* while he was teaching at Pinkerton Academy in Derry, explains individual human lives as a series of ordeals accepted prenatally by souls freely choosing and fully aware of all that they must endure on earth. These arrangements, made in heaven with God, are not remembered by the souls once they are incarnated on earth, for the knowledge of having made a free choice would detract from the severity of the test.

Jonathan Edwards himself might be fascinated by this solution of the problem of free will and necessity, and indeed Frost's fantasy bears some resemblance to Edwards' tenet that one wills in accordance with one's choice but does not control one's choices, which are predestined (to Frost they were freely made but not remembered). Frost's poem was doubtlessly not influenced directly by Edwards or any other theologian. Its significance lies in its concern with the problem of the will, which so exercised religious thinkers in the Augustinian and Calvinistic tradition, and in its assumption that life is a testing ground that has to be endured for the greater glory of God, even if the end result is eternal damnation.[5] The notion that each soul has freely entered into an agreement with God to undergo the testing suggests the covenant-based theology of the early Puritans.

The second poem, "Acceptance," though written much later, develops a related theme—submission, without murmur, to whatever condition and vicissitudes life may subject us to. Using the example of the birds, which accept as a matter of course the daily changes from light to darkness, Frost ends the poem with the adjuration:

"Let the night be too dark for me to see
Into the future. Let what will be, be."

In "The Trial by Existence" Frost emphasizes the soul's ignorance of the origins of its earthly lot; in "Acceptance" he emphasizes its ignorance of the future. Yet both suggest a certainty—the presence in the universe of some sort of directing power that controls our lives.[6]

Resignation then to the lot, albeit mostly unknown, that God has assigned to each of us is a cornerstone of Frost's philosophy or religion. Other traditional Christian facets in his outlook keep appearing throughout his life not only in his poetry but also in his letters and conversation. Thus the question of salvation is one of his chief concerns; and in harmony with the teachings of his mother's Presbyterian and his father's Congregational forebears, he considered divine grace to be the only means of achieving salvation.[7] Yet, though God gives grace freely to those whom He more or less arbitrarily chooses for this favor, He expects the fortunate recipients to placate Him by offerings of the best that each is capable of doing and being. Frost's offering would be his poetry, which he deeply feared might "not prove acceptable" in God's sight.[8] In his moments of self-denigration, he strongly resembles those Puritan diarists whose most passionate passages tended to be assertions of their own vileness.

"I have all the dead New England things . . . ,"[9] Frost once said, but those things were not really dead. They survived not only in him but also in many New Englanders and Americans all across the land. Indeed Frost did not entirely deplore his heritage of residual Calvinism. He found that to a certain degree it answered his spiritual needs; and as an admirer of William James, he found in this heritage a sufficient justification for his beliefs. Furthermore, he was frequently a champion of New England, especially of its past, and by no means denigrated its contribution to the national culture.[10]

III

In his poems about backcountry people, in *North of Boston* and later volumes, Frost, deliberately or not, presents a gallery of portraits from a place and time that one writer has described as "the terminal moraine of New England Puritanism." [11] On these pages we find records of the cultural rubble, the glacial erratics, and the residue of an era that is past—that has melted away, but not without adding its currents to the streams of the future. Let there be no mistake. Frost in his travels about New England, in his rambles along backroads and among the hills, had seen the cellar holes of abandoned farmhouses, the miles of stone walls gridding whole townships long since reverted to forest, and the tottering and fallen stones of family graveyards. Some of his most poignant lyrics—"The Census-Taker," "Ghost House," "The Black Cottage," "Directive"— attest to his acute awareness of the desolation and decay that had overspread the New England countryside. But he was even more keenly aware of the closelipped, rather aloof people who still remained in the region, and he became deeply concerned about their successes and failures in coping with a harsh and deteriorating physical and social environment. He was not the first to experience this concern.

We have seen that around the turn of the century rural New England had become a major preoccupation with sociologists and journalists and that their dismal findings were printed in the major periodicals of the time. A generation earlier, writers of fiction and poetry had begun publishing pictures of life and people in the hinterland and along the remoter stretches of the coast, and the hues in which they painted had tended to grow more and more sombre as the end of the century approached. Whittier and Harriet Beecher Stowe, writing about mid-century, had presented rosy versions of village and farm life.[12] Theirs, in the main, was a region of contented and harmonious communities and households where the old virtues, the harmless, happy folkways, the quaint speech, the pursuit of wholesome livelihoods, the observance of the old religion, and the democracy of town-meeting government still obtained. But in the last two decades of the century, when dissolution was becoming catastrophic, two other writers—Rose Terry

Cooke of Connecticut and Mary E. Wilkins Freeman of Massachusetts and Vermont—had a very different report to make. In the villages and on the farms—what was left of both—they found meanness, vindictiveness, narrowness, psychosis, and grinding poverty. Of the two, Mary Wilkins Freeman was the better artist and the one more conscious of the significance of her subject matter. A New England villager herself, descended on both sides from seventeenth-century Puritans, she was fully as discerning as Frost in her efforts to analyze and understand what was happening to the people of rural New England. More assiduous than Frost in her probing of hereditary traits, she said of her tales in *A Humble Romance and Other Stories*, her first volume of fiction: "They are studies of the descendants of the Massachusetts Bay colonists, in whom can still be seen traces of those features of will and conscience, so strong as to be almost exaggerations and deformities, which characterised their ancestors." [13] In many of her tales, indeed, she depicts the New England will and conscience as warped to the point of disease—for example in "A Conflict Ended," "An Honest Soul," [14] or the novel *Pembroke*, which last is perhaps the most profound study of New England village life yet to be written.

But even the gloomiest writers of fiction or nonfiction took into account those rural New Englanders who had not sunk into some form of degeneracy. Thus in certain stories by Mary Wilkins Freeman, the will, though likely to be hypertrophied, finds constructive outlets and becomes a positive force in meeting adversity, as in her "Louisa" and "A Taste of Honey." [15] Sarah Orne Jewett, Mrs. Freeman's contemporary, wrote more frequently but by no means exclusively, in this optimistic vein, repeatedly giving emphasis to those elements in the post-Puritan character that make for survival and perhaps growth. *The Country of the Pointed Firs* amply exhibits her faith in the perennial health of New England village life. Yet even this volume contains some pathologically eccentric characters, like the recluse Joanna Todd and the hallucinating Captain Littlepage. The robust spiritual strengths of Elmiry Todd or Esther Hight are by no means universal in the New England of Sarah Orne Jewett's fiction.

In the 1890's while Sarah Orne Jewett and Mary Wilkins Freeman were at the peak of their popularity and of their very impressive literary powers, Edwin Arlington Robinson read Mrs. Freeman's *Pembroke* and was deeply impressed. To what extent his early poems were influenced by it cannot be accurately gauged, but he must have found in it a confirmation of his observations of his own hometown of Gardiner, Maine, which is the Tilbury Town of his poems. In a rather large gallery of Tilbury Town portraits almost all (the two farmers in "Isaac and Archibald" are notable exceptions) are of eccentrics, misfits, or failures. Obsessions (which Mrs. Freeman would have classed as disorders of the will) afflict many of his people: miserliness in "Aaron Stark," alcoholism in "Mr. Flood's Party," lechery in "John Evereldown," self-destruction in "Richard Cory." Whatever their abnormalities, few of these characters have learned to cope with life in the decaying social and economic conditions of Tilbury Town.

One could list other authors, more or less contemporaries of Frost, who wrote primarily about New England country and village people. Among them was Alice Brown (1857–1948), a native of Hampton Falls, New Hampshire, only a few miles from Frost's Derry; and Dorothy Canfield Fisher, who for years was Frost's neighbor in Vermont. It is impossible to determine how much of the work of any of these New England authors Frost read. There is good evidence that he knew and admired E. A. Robinson's work at least by 1913. We cannot be so sure about the fiction writers; but since they published prolifically in periodicals and in book form, it is hardly likely that he did not have an acquaintance with the work of at least some of them.[16] Indeed only a determined nonreader—which Frost was not—could be entirely ignorant of their work. But even if he had read nothing by any of them, he is of their company—though admittedly his work as a whole transcends their "local-colorist" limitations.

IV

As in the writings of these fellow New Englanders, some of Frost's country people are defeated by their environment and by hereditary traits. Among such victims is the housewife in "A Servant to Servants," a character modeled on a farm woman, with a history of mental illness, whom Frost had met at Willoughby Lake in Vermont in 1909. The situation is totally plausible and realistic. The incidence of insanity, especially among women, in the rural areas of Northern New England, was the highest in the nation. The woman in Frost's poem has spent time in a state hospital and expects soon to return there. Mental illness runs in her family, and she tells of her demented uncle who had been kept in a cage in the attic of his house. (She herself prefers the asylum.) In addition to her inheritance of unfavorable genes, she has been afflicted by a rigid Calvinistic conscience—a legacy from her Puritan forefathers—which manifests itself as a grim sense of duty toward her husband and in a conviction that she was predestined to an existence of grinding toil alternating with periods of collapse. Except for the view of the lake from her kitchen window—and the view has ceased to delight her—her life is as devoid of beauty as of hope. Nor is her husband, whom she serves in accord with the most rigid Biblical injunctions, a source of comfort. His communication with her is limited to platitudes. The woman tells her story in a monotone which intensifies in dreariness as she progresses. Her words are restrained, as the culture which she represents demands, but for the reader her restraint serves only to dramatize her plight.

Similarly bleak depictions of sick or desperate women, presented in equally subdued tones of voice and color, are common in the fiction of Mary Wilkins Freeman—for example, in "A New England Nun" or "Sister Liddy," [17] and their male counterparts may be found in the early poems of E. A. Robinson. "A Servant to Servants" takes its place alongside the more memorable character studies of these and other New England writers. In subject matter and mood it is far from unique; even its form, that of the dramatic monologue, is paralleled in certain tales by Mary Wilkins Freeman, such as "On the Walpole Road." [18]

Two other poems by Frost deal as poignantly with the lot of women on New England farms. "Home Burial" records the emotional collapse of a wife whose inarticulate husband—he too communicates mainly in platitudes—has just buried their child in the family graveyard. "The Hill Wife," a series of short lyrics, traces the psychological deterioration and eventual flight of a childless woman isolated on a remote farm.

These women have succumbed to neurosis or worse under environmental and inner stresses. Three other women in Frost's early poetry suffer the collapse of morality so frequently commented on by the journalists and sociologists writing about rural New England. The narrative poem, "The Witch of Coös," tells a story of adultery and murder; and though Frost's treatment is somewhat ironic, his tale is not entirely improbable. Indeed, Thompson says that Frost later found the anecdote in a local history.[19] The motif of witchcraft in the poem, though presented as a folk superstition, is not out of place in a primitive New England setting. The same is true of the dramatic monologue, "The Pauper Witch of Grafton," which depicts a woman utterly without morals and glorying in her own vindictiveness. Finally, in "The Fear" Frost dramatizes the guilt of a woman who has left her husband and is living with another man.

It is the presence of some poems like these in *North of Boston* that induced Amy Lowell to designate that volume as "a very sad book," [20] a remark that infuriated Frost. But Amy Lowell was at least partly right. Decay and collapse of character, not to mention of a whole culture, *are* sad. As a summer resident of Dublin, New Hampshire, Amy Lowell knew rural New England, and in one poem at least, "The Day that Was that Day," [21] portrayed a woman as desperate as the wife in "A Servant to Servants." Moreover, the fact that, in the "sad" poems, Frost focused on women provides an even closer association with the "recorders of the New England decline," [22] as Fred Pattee has called writers like Mary Wilkins Freeman, Rose Terry Cooke, and Sarah Orne Jewett. Social and cultural disintegration was particularly hard on women—at least according to these writers—for it was more difficult for women to escape their immediate circumstances by moving west or to a factory town.

V

But many—perhaps the majority—of Frost's poems depicting rural character record less depressing lives and situations and celebrate

qualities that make for survival and perhaps fulfilment and which
have their origin in the Puritan heritage quite as clearly as do the sick
consciences and the sense of doom that destroy the wife in "A Servant to Servants." In direct contrast to her, indeed, is the widow
described in "The Black Cottage," a poem that Frost wrote during
the Derry years and which was inspired by an actual woman inhabiting such a cottage near the Frost farm. As the minister in the
poem tells it, the widow, living alone for many years, is a bulwark
of the old beliefs, not only religious but political, and her presence
in the community is a restraint on the minister and prevents him
from altering the traditional creed in order to conform to theological liberalism. The cottage, like so many New England buildings
of the time, was black because it had never been painted. Like its
occupant it stood for the unvarnished truths by which the early settlers lived and from which the widow and, through her, the contemporary community still drew spiritual strength. She resembles
certain strong and secure characters in Sarah Orne Jewett's work—
for example, Mrs. Blackett in *The Country of the Pointed Firs*, who
is spiritually rooted deep in the New England past.

Akin to the widow's traditionalism is a New England capacity—
as the regional authors see it—to endure and surmount whatever
obstacles God, nature, or chance may raise. Among Frost's characters so endowed, the most obvious is the farmer in the punning,
half-humorous "Brown's Descent," who faces undaunted the three-
mile walk back to his barn after his icy *descent* across his meadows
and thus demonstrates the continued soundness of his Yankee *descent*, despite the sociologists' assurances of the *descent* of rural New
Englanders into decadence—an opinion from which both Brown and
Frost *dissent*.[23]

Another character who belies the theory of New England decadence is the preacher Meserve in "Snow," a poem suggested to
Frost by an anecdote he heard in Franconia, New Hampshire.
Meserve triumphs in an ordeal he need not have encountered. He
deliberately chooses to battle his way home along a country road
in a blizzard in the middle of the night—partly, it seems, to gauge
the extent to which God will help one of His own. Frost, who was a
prey to fears of the night and storms, would have admired Meserve's

determination and confidence. Characters endowed with similar self-reliance abound in the New England fiction of the period, though most do not fling themselves so nonchalantly into dangerous situations. Sarah Orne Jewett's Joanna Todd, Esther Hight in *The Country of the Pointed Firs*, and the heroines of the stories "Aunt Cynthy Dallett" and "Farmer Finch," [24] are examples, as are the lead women in Mary Wilkins Freeman's "Louisa" and "A Taste of Honey."

VI

Perhaps what impressed Frost most about his rural acquaintances was their attitude toward work. A major Puritan tenet had been that each person must find the calling for which God intended him and then pursue that calling to the best of his ability.[25] It soon became obvious to Frost and those who knew him that his true vocation was not farming, at which he was pretty much of a failure. If he had been called to anything it was to poetry, as he had known from adolescence onward. The problem was to find some way to support his family while exercising his God-given talent. He did not achieve a total commitment of his time and energies to poetry until he went to England in 1913, but in the preceding years in New Hampshire he had been formulating a very definite attitude toward work—one which would aid him in making his final commitment.

In Puritan and post-Puritan New England the pursuit of the work for which one is best suited was a means of achieving self-respect and the approval of God and society. In Frost's "The Death of the Hired Man," written in Derry, a farm laborer draws his sense of self-worth from his humble but useful skills, especially his knack of loading a hay wagon. By this ability also he wins the respect and affection of the farmer and his wife for whom he has worked in the past. Thus they take him in at the end of his life, recognizing that he has a sort of claim on them. The college boy who has worked with him in the fields studied Latin for the fun of it. Such absence of serious purpose offended the hired man, whose mastery of the art of hayloading was the justification (almost in the Calvinist sense) of his life.

The semi-humorous "The Code" extends Frost's commentary

on the New England countryman's feeling about his work. If one has attained excellence in some useful and honorable calling, he has earned immunity from the merest suggestion, even by his employer, as to how he should do his job. An accomplished farmhand deserves and demands not only total confidence in his abilities but also the deference due to any kind of excellence. For this reason the hired men on New England farms have always eaten at their employers' tables and have otherwise been treated as equals.[26]

VII

Frost has said that God is the only source of salvation—[27] a fundamental tenet of Puritan theology. Each individual in this most important of earthly concerns—the search for salvation—stands in total isolation from his fellows, unreachable by their help. In the moment of death, when the soul faces its God, it is alone; and no past association nor good works will avail. In New England there have been many literary expressions of this aloneness of the soul in its relationship to God and man. Perhaps the most stunning statement of it is Emily Dickinson's poem beginning "This Consciousness that is aware." Another justly famous poem on the same subject is E. A. Robinson's "The Man Against the Sky." Frost's "An Old Man's Winter Night" ranks with both as a presentation of existential isolation.

The prose writers, too, wrote copiously on this theme. Persons living alone, dependent on their own inner assets, provided a stock situation for authors like Sarah Orne Jewett, Mary Wilkins Freeman, and Alice Brown; and of course the whole purpose of Thoreau's *Walden*, a favorite of Frost's, was to explore the spiritual resources that can be tapped entirely from within. Thoreau's conclusion was that these resources, under the proper discipline and conditions, are almost limitless. Others were not so sanguine. For example, Mrs. Freeman, whose pages abound in recluses, found that, far from releasing hidden strengths, solitude frequently stunted or warped the spirit, as in "A New England Nun." One of the few of her stories dealing with a male recluse, "A Solitary," [28] provides an interesting comparison with Frost's "An Old Man's Winter Night." In this tale, Nicholas Gunn has convinced himself that most misery stems from human relationships, especially with those one loves. Accordingly he has secluded himself in a cabin outside his village and lives on corn meal mush and water, foregoing even the comfort of a fire when he is not cooking. His will, becoming more and more warped, is directed toward the end of making himself wretched. But at last, one bitterly cold, moonlit January night—the scene closely resembles that in "An Old Man's Winter Night" except that there is no heat in the stove—a sick and destitute neighbor knocks on his door and asks to be taken in. Grudgingly Nicholas admits him and builds a fire, under the influence of which both the house and Nicholas's heart begin to grow warm. The upshot is that the neighbor has found a permanent home, and Nicholas, abandoning his hermit's ways, finds new meaning in existence. For Mary Wilkins Freeman, prolonged solitude destroys the soul, as happens so often with her spinsters who live alone with perhaps a cat, a canary, or a chained dog.

Sarah Orne Jewett is not so pessimistic as regards the solitary life. Poor Joanna in *The Country of the Pointed Firs* has, like Nicholas Gunn, suffered in a relationship with a person she has loved, but unlike Nicholas she is convinced that she has committed the unpardonable sin by rebelling against God in her misfortune. As a result, she has isolated herself winter and summer as the only inhabitant of a bleak, offshore island. The selectmen and the local parson fail in their efforts to induce her to return to her village. Still, despite her terrible feelings of guilt, she achieves a life of dignity and wins the respect, if not the approval, of the townspeople. Warped she may be, but she develops a sustaining strength of spirit. A Jewett character who lives in more nearly complete inner and outer harmony is Aunt Cynthy Dallett, whose lonely cottage is far up a mountainside. Only in extreme old age does she submit to living with a companion. A personification of wholesome and happy self-dependence, she resembles Frost's widow in "The Black Cottage" as an inspiration to the folk who look up to her from the valley below and see in her a living proof of the benefits of total reliance on Self and God. Aunt Cynthy—unlike Frost's widow, whose self-reliance is seasoned with a touch of plain obstinacy—has been idealized beyond the bounds of credibility; but she represents a not uncommon type in New England local-color fiction.

An even more idealized case is found in Dorothy Canfield Fisher's "Old Man Warner," [29] the story of an elderly Vermonter who, defying the pleas of friends and town officials, lives out decades of advanced old age on a remote farm and finally dies alone in mid-winter. Old Man Warner becomes a legend in his own lifetime, as one who exemplified the independence supposedly characteristic of Vermonters. But he is an even more unconvincing character than Jewett's Aunt Cynthy Dallett—because Dorothy Canfield Fisher has failed to take into account the feebleness and other miseries that any one attaining Old Man Warner's tremendous age is bound to suffer. Even a Vermonter, during the course of almost a century of living, must endure some of the ills of the flesh and spirit.

Robert Frost's "An Old Man's Winter Night" avoids Mrs. Fisher's and Miss Jewett's sentimentalizing of the solitary life as well as Mrs. Freeman's rejection of it as destructive to mind and soul. In Frost's poem moralizing is as absent as it is in Emily Dickinson's "This Consciousness that is aware. . . ." The old man survives the winter night—that is all, and that is enough. He is not an inspiration to the neighborhood, like Old Man Warner or Aunt Cynthy Dallett. He is "a light . . . to no one but himself." He represents no mastery over the elements. He does not "keep a house, /a farm, a countryside." Rather they keep him as he sleeps amidst the pounding of the winter gale. He is content to let nature control the scene:

> He consigned to the moon—such as she was,
> So late-arising—to the broken moon,
> As better than the sun in any case
> For such a charge, his snow upon the roof,
> His icicles along the wall to keep;
> And slept.

Acceptance, resignation enable the old man to sleep through the long boisterous night, while the logs shift and the embers burn low in the stove, like the fires of his life.

In this poem Robert Frost has captured, as others in the multitudinous group of New England regional writers have seldom done, the very essence of the late Puritan spirit that lingered on in the desolate and half-deserted New England countryside. The old man is not tragic, not heroic, not pathetic. He possesses dignity, as does the humble laborer in "The Death of the Hired Man"—the dignity of a being composed of spirit as well as body surviving in a hostile environment. For this, indeed, was the last lesson of Puritanism that persisted in backcountry New England. Each man and woman, endowed with an immortal soul, is fated on this earth to endure a pilgrimage to salvation or damnation. Each soul must go its solitary way—"Attended by a single Hound/It's own identity," [30] in Emily Dickinson's words—and it must go undaunted by circumstances and acquiescing in the tests of strength and faith that God visits upon it. "All out-of-doors" may look "darkly in," but looks need not terrify. What is required is faith, like Meserve's faith in "Snow," that what is inside, God helping, will withstand all assaults from without. This is the major positive theme of Robert Frost's poetry depicting New England country men and women—indeed of all his poetry and that of most other great poets.

Notes to *Robert Frost's New England* by PERRY D. WESTBROOK

1. *Selected Letters of Robert Frost*, ed. Lawrance Thompson (New York: Holt, Rinehart and Winston, 1964), 552. In the same letter, Frost writes: "[In Derry] I wrote more than half of my first book much more than half of my second and even quite a little of my third" (punctuation is Frost's). Though Frost's estimates may not be entirely reliable, it is clear that such important poems as "The Death of the Hired Man," "The Black Cottage," "The Housekeeper," "An Old Man's Winter Night," "Hyla Brook," and parts of "The Hill Wife" were composed at Derry.

2. Lawrance Thompson, *Robert Frost: The Years of Triumph, 1915–1938* (New York: Holt, Rinehart and Winston, 1970), 507.

3. For a detailed study of economic and social conditions in rural New England during the first half of Frost's writing career, see Harold Fisher Wilson, *The Hill Country of Northern New England: Its Social and Economic History, 1790–1930* (New York: Columbia University Press, 1936). The bibliography in this volume lists hundreds of articles, books, and official reports dealing with the problems of the region. Edith Wharton's *Summer* (New York: Appleton and Company, 1917) gives the grimmest of all treatments of New England rural degeneracy.

4. *Selected Letters*, 226.

5. Thompson, *Frost: Years of Triumph*, 593–94. See George W. Nitchie, *Human Values in the Poetry of Robert Frost* (Durham, N.C.: Duke University Press, 1960), 141, 146–47, 180, for comments on Frost's respect for, and partial adoption of, the lingering Calvinistic values of rural New England.

6. Sidney Cox in *A Swinger of Birches: A Portrait of Robert Frost* (New York: New York University Press, 1957), 78–79, discusses Frost's feeling that some divinity might have been shaping his life.

7. *Selected Letters*, 596; Thompson, *Frost: Years of Triumph*, 568–69.

8. *Selected Letters*, 525. See also Frost's *A Masque of Mercy*.

9. *Selected Letters*, 221.

10. Thompson, *Frost: Years of Triumph*, 77, 483.

11. F. L. Pattee, *Side-Lights on American Literature* (New York: The Century Company, 1922). The quotation is a chapter heading.

12. An exception is Whittier's "Among the Hills," one of the first pieces of New England local-color writing to admit that all was not well among the hill people.

13. See Perry D. Westbrook, *Mary Wilkins Freeman* (New York: Twayne Publishers, 1967), 34. For a discussion of the whole group of authors, see P. D. Westbrook, *Acres of Flint: Writers of Rural New England* (Washington, D.C.: The Scarecrow Press, 1951).

14. Both stories appear in Mary Wilkins Freemen's first collection of short fiction, *A Humble Romance and Other Stories* (New York: Harper and Brothers, 1887).

15. "Louisa" is in Mary Wilkins Freeman, *A New England Nun and Other Stories* (New York: Harper and Brothers, 1891); "A Taste of Honey" is in Freeman, *A Humble Romance and Other Stories*.

16. Nitchie (*Human Values*, 117–18) is among the few critics to comment on the relationship of Frost's poetry with the New England local colorists writing contemporaneously with him.

17. Both tales are in Freeman, *A New England Nun and Other Stories*.

18. In Freeman, *A Humble Romance and Other Stories*.

19. See *Selected Letters*, 473.

20. Amy Lowell, *Tendencies in Modern American Poetry* (Boston: Houghton Mifflin Company, 1917), 105. Robert P. Tristam Coffin, in *New Poetry of New England* (Baltimore: The Johns Hopkins Press, 1938), passim, gives attention to the cultural decline of New England during the period of Frost's development as a poet. W. G. O'Donnell in "Robert Frost and New England: A Revaluation," *Yale Review*, XXXVII (1948), 698–712, also emphasizes the decadence of New England but discerningly adds that Frost, though realizing that "much of the older New England had been lost," felt that "something had survived, that a vitality had remained which was strong enough to meet the challenge of new and potentially disastrous conditions" (710).

21. Amy Lowell, *East Wind* (Boston: Houghton Mifflin Company, 1926).

22. The phrase is the heading of the very interesting Chapter XI in Fred Lewis Pattee, *A History of American Literature Since 1870* (New York: The Century Company, 1915).

23. Another pun occurs in the subtitle to the poem in which Frost describes Brown's descent as the Willy-Nilly Slide. The allusion is to the famous Willey Landslide that occurred in Crawford Notch in the White Mountains of New Hampshire in 1826 and destroyed the entire Willey family.

24. "Aunt Cynthy Dallett" is in Sarah Orne Jewett, *The Queen's Twin and Other Stories* (Boston: Houghton Mifflin and Company, 1899); "Farmer Finch" is in Sarah Orne Jewett, *A White Heron and Other Stories* (Boston: Houghton Mifflin and Company, 1886).

25. The classic statement on the subject is John Cotton's sermon "Christian Calling," found in *The American Puritans*, ed. Perry Miller (Garden City, N.Y.: Doubleday & Company, 1956).

26. See Coffin (*New Poetry of New England*, 67–69) for a discussion of the status of hired help on New England farms.

27. *Selected Letters*, 596.

28. In Freeman, *A New England Nun and Other Stories*.

29. In Dorothy Canfield Fisher, *Raw Material* (New York: Harcourt, Brace and Company, 1923); or in Perry D. Westbrook, *Seacoast and Upland: A New England Anthology* (South Brunswick and New York: A. S. Barnes and Company, 1972).

30. *The Poems of Emily Dickinson*, ed. Thomas H. Johnson (Cambridge, Mass.: Harvard University Press, 1958), 623. The apostrophe in *it's* is Emily Dickinson's.

Two Landscapes: Frost's and Eliot's

PETER L. HAYS

As published originally in 1923, Robert Frost's volume *New Hampshire* was, like Caesar's Gaul, divided into three parts and, like a scholarly article, decorated with footnotes. As Lawrance Thompson describes it, Frost

> did have fun with his academic relationships by adding to "New Hampshire" passages which served as undeveloped hints which needed explaining. These passages justified his use of mock-scholarly footnotes containing merely the titles of the so-called "explanatory poems." His next decision was to give the book a three-part structure: Part One would be devoted exclusively to the title poem, Part Two would be the "explanatory poems" grouped as "Notes," and Part Three would be lyrics which could be referred to on the title page as "Grace Notes" in the sense that they were added for pure ornamentation.[1]

The "academic relationships" to which Thompson refers are Frost's years of teaching at Amherst and the University of Michigan in 1920–1923, immediately preceding publication of *New Hampshire*.

For those who have never seen an early edition, superscript numerals appeared over certain words, and at the bottom of the page these numbers referred by title and sometimes line number to Notes poems. Thus "The having anything to sell" (l. 7) was linked with the poem "The Ax-Helve." [2] The line "She has one witch—old style. She lives in Colebrook" (l. 125), refers to "The Witch of Coös." In the *Collected Poems* of 1930 and all subsequent editions of "New Hampshire," all of the footnotes are eliminated. The footnotes are indeed "mock scholarly," and the Notes poems not really explanatory. "Place for a Third" and "I Will Sing You One-O" are printed as notes, but there are no footnotes to them in "New Hampshire." The line "She has a touch of gold. New Hampshire gold—" (l. 107) is annotated as referring to line five of "A Star in a Stoneboat," which reads: "And saving that its weight [that of a cold meteorite a farmer finds] suggested gold,/... He noticed nothing in it to remark." Yet, the Grace Notes section of the book contains the lovely "Nothing Gold Can Stay." The line noted as referring to "Paul's Wife" is "The way the wiry gang-boss liked the logjam" (l. 345); a more appropriate reference point would be "Pre-primitives of the white race, dawn people,/Like those who furnished Adam's sons with wives" (ll. 78–79)—lines that bear no footnotes. At one point in the poem, Frost says, "I'd sure had no such friends in Massachusetts/As Hall of Windham, Gay of Atkinson..." (ll. 258–59). The last phrase is noted as having reference to the poem "The Ax-Helve," but close perusal of that poem shows neither Gay nor Atkinson. One has to read a biography of Frost to find that the Baptiste in the poem is drawn from Frost's French-Canadian neighbor at Derry, Napoleon Guay or Gay. The line "I'd hate to be a runaway from nature" (l. 397) bears no superscript numeral, though it does provide a gloss on the Grace Notes poem "The Runaway." On the other hand, at the passage "There [New Hampshire] quality makes up for quantity" (l. 148), one is referred to specific lines in three poems, line 57 of "The Census-Taker," line 26 of "The Star-Splitter," and line 21 of "Star in a Stoneboat." The line alluding to quality in "Census-Taker" reads, "The place is desert ..."; in "Star-Splitter," "There where he moved the rocks to plow the ground"; and in "Stoneboat," "The very nature of the soil was hot." None of these references casts light on either "New Hampshire" or the Notes poems. The notes do indeed mock scholastic pedantry, but not all pedants, in Frost's mind, dwelt in academic halls.

Later in his life he denounced poetry accompanied by footnotes,[3] and in January of 1923, the year *New Hampshire* was published, he denounced the poet whose footnoted *The Waste Land* had appeared just weeks earlier: T. S. Eliot. Frost was in New York during the University of Michigan's Christmas vacation and on January 6 attended a party including Carl Van Doren (who was later to publish "The Star-Splitter" in *Century Magazine*), Christopher Morley, and other literati. Burton Rascoe, literary editor of the New York *Tribune*, who was also present, printed this record of what occurred:

[Morley] read some pieces he said were imitations of "The Waste Land" and other modern poems.[4] If what he read bears the slightest resemblance to "The Waste Land," then I'm the Prophet Jeremiah and all his lamentations.

   ...Frost and I left the party together and went to Grand Central Station, where we talked for half an hour about Ezra Pound, T. S. Eliot, Conrad Aiken, and Amy Lowell. . . .

   Frost himself has little sympathy with Eliot's work. . . .

   "I don't like obscurity in poetry," he told me. . . .[5]

In response to Rascoe's publication of these remarks, Frost wrote a vituperative letter (which he sent instead to Louis Untermeyer), denouncing Rascoe and insisting that he had meant Eliot's "obscuration," not his obscurity, but nowhere in the tirade does he retract his criticism of Eliot. As Thompson says, "Eliot's newly published poem had already created such a splash that Frost was made nervous and jealous by this newcomer's rapidly increasing fame. . . . Frost quickly sided with those who found ways of trying to dismiss both Eliot and Joyce as pretentious fakers." [6] Frost's sense of rivalry and competition with fellow poets is too well known to need much arguing here; Thompson cites his feelings for Masters, Robinson, Lowell, Sandburg, Eliot, and others, devoting subheadings in the indexes of each biographical volume, as well as the *Selected Letters*, to "Enemies," "Jealousy," or "Vindictiveness." So I suggest that the mock-scholarly footnotes in *New Hampshire* that go nowhere and explain little or nothing, the Notes poems that have not been footnoted, the Grace Notes poems that make better notes than those referred to, and even the criticism of modern "Matthew Arnoldism" are satirical thrusts at T. S. Eliot.

   Besides Frost's jealousy of any successful contemporary poet, especially one fourteen years his junior, he had other, truly coincidental ties to Eliot. Frost's freshman English instructor at Harvard was Eliot's brother-in-law, Alfred D. Sheffield, known as Sheffy or "the bearded lady." Sheffield rejected some poems which Frost submitted as writing exercises.[7] At that time, Frost's first child was still alive, but the boy, named Elliot (or Eliot, according to Mrs. Sergeant) died in 1900, before his fourth birthday. In addition, Frost was descended from Nicholas Frost, who came to America in

1634, and who lived in Eliot, Maine, as Frost well knew, for he wrote a poem entitled "Genealogical" about Nicholas' son Charles, a New England Indian killer who "lies/Under a notable bowlder in Eliot, Maine." [8] By the time *The Waste Land* was published, the name Eliot must have touched a host of chords in Frost's consciousness.

Admittedly, the evidence that Frost is mocking Eliot is only circumstantial, but the list of common points is indeed impressive, even if we accept Frost's statement that the manuscript on deposit at the Jones Library at Amherst is the first draft of "New Hampshire" as he wrote it in July of 1922,[9] a claim that I find doubtful. But more of that subsequently. First, if "New Hampshire" and its footnotes are intended as a burlesque of *The Waste Land*, Frost must be more of a parodist than is generally known, and this is the case. Thompson lists some twelve parodies in *The Early Years* (pp. 623–24), starting from Frost's first poem when he was fourteen, and including parodies of Poe, *Ossian*, Coleridge's *Rime of the Ancient Mariner*, and two burlesques of Pound's free verse. One, written in July of 1913, begins,

> My nose is out of joint
> For my father-in-letters—
> My father mind you—
> Has been brought to bed of another poet,
> And I am not nine months old.[10]

The new poet whom his "father-in-letters" Pound had adopted, less than nine months after the publication of Frost's first book of verse, was Hilda Doolittle, who found Pound's imagism and tutelage much more amenable than Frost did. Frost left England in February, 1915; Pound had met Eliot the preceding fall, September, 1914, and was soon promoting him, as he did all the promising talent he discovered. In 1917, Frost wrote Untermeyer a limerick on the demise of *The Seven Arts;* in 1918, he responded to a request by Vachel Lindsay for a poem commemorating John L. Sullivan with "John L. Sullivan Enters Heaven," a parody of Lindsay's "General William Booth Enters Into Heaven" (John L. Sullivan may have provided Frost with his line in "New Hampshire" [l. 299] about "John L. Darwin"); and later the same year, he wrote an elaborate parody in a letter to Untermeyer.[11] And the final parodic stimulus, as I have noted before, could well have been Christopher Morley's parody of *The Waste Land* in January, 1923.

Frost began *New Hampshire* in 1922. He reports that, during one night in July, he wrote the long title poem and then, after a walk at dawn, wrote "Stopping by Woods." The manuscript of the long poem, as he says he wrote it that night, is at the Jones Library, Amherst, and is remarkably clean for a first draft. The form of "New Hampshire" is based on Horatian satire; the substance grew out of a talk Frost gave before the Ann Arbor Rotary in the spring of 1922. In *The Nation* during that time, there was a "series of critical articles . . . explaining what was wrong with commercialism in state after state. Edmund Wilson had written one of these, describing what was wrong with New Jersey." Frost was invited to contribute to the series and did not, but "he was tempted to accept, so that he could reverse the trend and praise one or both of his favorite states." [12] He considered it snobbery either to denounce buying and selling as ignoble and demeaning or, like the Communists, to condemn it as a pernicious aspect of competitive capitalism. He must have found it particularly ironic that in "Gerontion" (1919) and "The Waste Land," Eliot, then working for Lloyd's of London, should have denounced commerce as detracting people from concerns of the spirit. And so in "New Hampshire," working from Horace's model, he mocked such snobbery by ironically portraying New Hampshire as too scarcely endowed to produce anything, except poems, in commercial quantities. En route, he also mocked the snobbery of Emerson, who said, "The God who made New Hampshire/Taunted the lofty land with little men" (ll. 218–19), and of Amy Lowell, who had "given up [her] summer place in Dublin," New Hampshire, because "she couldn't stand the people in it" (ll. 222, 224). But then Frost breaks his characteristic rustic pose to become quite literary:

> I may as well confess myself the author
> Of several books against the world in general.
> To take them as against a special state
> Or even nation's to restrict my meaning.
>
> . . . .
>
> Being the creature of literature I am,
> I shall not lack for pain to keep me awake.

Kit Marlowe taught me how to say my prayers:
"Why, this is Hell, nor am I out of it."
Samoa, Russia, Ireland I complain of,
No less than England, France and Italy.

(ll. 228–31, 240–45)

Eliot too finds the spiritual infection pandemic.

Toward the end of "New Hampshire," Frost, his recent confessions of erudition notwithstanding, takes up his familiar anti-intellectualism to attack "a New York alec" from the "new school of the pseudo-phallic" (ll. 358–59). He also attacks Matthew Arnold in a twenty-three line passage which, like a poor man's "Waste Land," fits together fragments from two of Shakespeare's plays—*As You Like It* and *Macbeth*—and from three of Arnold's poems—"In Harmony with Nature," "Sohrab and Rustum," and "The Scholar Gypsy." Yet only Arnold is mentioned by name, and in disparaging contexts. Why this gratuitous attack on Arnold, who was one of Frost's favorite poets, one whose works he had memorized as a youth and had communicated his own affection for to his children?[13] Two years before Frost wrote "New Hampshire," Eliot had published his first book of critical essays. I think that Frost is obliquely attacking Eliot through Arnold. The wisecracks in "New Hampshire about "a grove of trees," "dendrophobia," "improvised/Altars the woods are full of nowadays," "worship under green trees in the open," and "the groves [that] were God's first temples" (ll. 368–92) are indirect references to Eliot's *The Sacred Wood* (1920), which mentioned Arnold prominently in the introduction and the initial essay.

There are other pieces of evidence, also circumstantial and less substantial. "New Hampshire" was originally written, according to Thompson, in July of 1922 and revised only slightly for publication in the summer of 1923, after *The Waste Land* had come out.[14] Thompson specifically speaks of Frost's addition of passages to serve as hooks upon which to hang Notes poems. But no lines or phrases appear in the published poem that are not in the draft. In fact, the alterations on the manuscript are so few and so minor that it is hard to believe it constitutes a first draft of a long and complex poem. And the changes between the manuscript and the published poem are, again, negligible, reinforcing my belief that the manuscript on hand is not actually a first draft. There is no record in the Jones Library to testify when the manuscript was donated. I believe that did not occur until after the publication of *The Waste Land* and that the holograph manuscript is not a first attempt at all but an intermediate version, one to which the lines to be foot-noted have already been added, and added in form to respond to T. S. Eliot.

The Notes poems—except for "An Empty Threat"—had all been previously published, some as long as six years before, and did not explain anything, so the lines that referred to them could say any-thing Frost wanted them to say, directly pertinent to the Notes poems or not. Thus I find it interesting that although two witches are described in "New Hampshire," each of the witch poems is foot-noted separately: the gruesome witch of Coös appropriately by line 125, "She [New Hampshire] has one witch—old style. She lives in Colebrook" (a city in Coös County); "The Pauper Witch" by an irrelevant allusion to election night in Franconia. "The Waste Land" also has one witch, "old style," Sibyl of Cumae, and an-other, Mme. Sosostris, whose fortune-telling Frost may be parody-ing with his description of a much younger witch, "new style," with "a gift of reading letters locked in boxes," a talent recognized by the "S'ciety for Psychical Research." In the first line of his poem, Frost changed "A Lady from New York" to "A Lady from the South," like Marie who goes south in the winter; in line 20 of "New Hampshire," Frost speaks of graveyards, and Part I of "The Waste Land" is "The Burial of the Dead." Part IV of Eliot's poem, as well as lines 419–20, speak of sailing, and Frost mentions Cap-tain John Smith sailing by New Hampshire's coast (l. 74). Both poems refer to polar expeditions: Frost to Stefansson (l. 22), Eliot to Shackleton (his own footnote to line 360). Both, of course, prom-inently feature mountains. And both allude to Dostoevski: Eliot in his note to lines 368–76, Frost in line 275.

And one last piece of circumstantial evidence. At the same time as *The Dial* publication of "The Waste Land," Louis Untermeyer published a second issue of his *A Miscellany of American Poe-try*, containing his own "long pseudo-Oriental tapestry of a poem, 'Roast Leviathan.'" In response to Untermeyer's poem, itself some-

thing of a parody of Job, Frost wrote Untermeyer in November,
1922:

Your Roast is good. Now go ahead and cook in some form or other
everything in the Bible. You be serious for a while and I'll be your
parodist. Ghost Toasties or Manna Rechauffé; Fermented Scapegoat's
Milk....
I am at present hard at work translating one language into another.
I wish I could see you on my way through New York [the forthcoming January visit] for as I have often told you I had rather see you
once than write to you an hundred thousand times—Biblical an. You
see how thinking of the Bible can corrupt the style.[15]

Of course, Frost's references to the Bible and to parody may have
been called up only by Untermeyer's poem, but they could also
have been aroused by Eliot's poem and Frost's desire to mock Eliot
by parodying him; his announcement on the arrangement of *New
Hampshire* with initial poem and Notes was made just three months
later. He certainly might be alluding to "The Waste Land" with
his "translating one language into another"; none of the biographical
sources offers any explanation.

Ten years after the publication of Frost's book, Eliot wrote his
own portrait of "New Hampshire," published in 1934. By then
Eliot's tone is more lyric than it was in "The Waste Land," as
Frost's had already been in his portrait, especially in the Grace Notes
section. But in "The Waste Land" Eliot sees mainly man's greed,
lust, commercialism, hollowness, and lack of spirituality; his tone,
there, is one of despair. In *New Hampshire* Frost also recorded
greed and lust and hollowness, even murder, but the book moves
from satire to lyricism, it celebrates growth in nature and communication among men, and it shows individuals—in "Star in a Stoneboat" and "The Star-Splitter"—contemplating their roles in the universe, asking those questions Eliot's characters did not dare and
"could not/Speak" (ll. 38–39). In answer to the small-minded
criticism of Emerson and Lowell, Frost shows his New Hampshire
characters as various as men anywhere, acknowledging only that
"For art's sake, one could almost wish them worse/Rather than
better" (ll. 266–67). I believe he structured *New Hampshire* as
he did, not only to mock Eliot's pedantry and "obscuration," but

also to counter Eliot's pervasive pessimistic tone. And in answer to Eliot's despair, Frost juxtaposes the harmonious music of his verse, his humor, and this statement from the man who was "census-taker to the waste": "It must be I want life to go on living" (The Census-Taker," ll. 9 and 64).

Notes to *Two Landscapes: Frost's and Eliot's* by PETER L. HAYS

1. Lawrance Thompson, *Robert Frost: The Years of Triumph* (New York: Holt, Rinehart and Winston, 1970), 239. Cf. Elizabeth Shepley Sergeant, *Robert Frost: Trial by Existence* (New York: Holt, Rinehart and Winston, 1960), 267–68.

2. All quotations from *New Hampshire* and line references to it are taken from *The Poetry of Robert Frost*, ed. Edward Connery Lathem (New York: Holt, Rinehart and Winston, 1969).

3. Robert Frost, "The Prerequisites," in *Selected Prose of Robert Frost*, ed. Hyde Cox and Edward Connery Lathem (New York: Collier Books, 1968), 96.

4. Eliot's poem appeared without notes in the November issue of *The Dial*, published, thinks Valerie Eliot, around October 15, 1922. The book version, with notes, was issued on December 15, 1922, and was in a second printing by February 1923. T. S. Eliot, *The Waste Land: A Facsimile and Transcript*, ed. Valerie Eliot (London: Faber & Faber, 1971), xxiv and xxv.

5. Burton Rascoe, "A Bookman's Day Book," New York *Tribune* (January 13, 1923). Reprinted by Thompson, *Years of Triumph*, 220; and by Edward Connery Lathem, ed., *Interviews with Robert Frost* (New York: Holt, Rinehart and Winston, 1966), 40–41.

6. Thompson, *The Years of Triumph*, 219–20. Cf. Sergeant, *Trial by Existence*, 256.

7. Sergeant, *Trial by Existence*, 53; Lawrance Thompson, *The Early Years* (New York: Holt, Rinehart and Winston, 1966), 234–36.

8. *Selected Letters of Robert Frost*, ed. Lawrance Thompson (New York: Holt, Rinehart and Winston, 1964), 599, 604.

9. Thompson claims that it is the first draft (*The Years of Triumph*, 596, n. 15). I want to thank the Jones Library Curator, W. D. Sayer, for her very kind and very prompt help.

10. Thompson, *The Early Years*, 420.

11. *The Letters of Robert Frost to Louis Untermeyer*, ed. Louis Untermeyer (New York: Holt, Rinehart and Winston, 1963), 64–69.

12. Thompson, *The Years of Triumph*, 231. Although this explanation seems generally accepted by Frost's biographers—*The Nation* articles in spring 1922 and the Rotary talk that June—it should be pointed out that as early as 1915, Frost was offering to talk on "New Hampshire Gold," "a homily on the exceptional in life and poetry" (*Selected Letters*, 198).

13. Thompson, *The Early Years*, 608, 500, 304. Thompson suggests that Frost is attacking "Arnold's implied assertion that it is impossible to achieve a harmonious relationship between man and Nature, or, thereby, between man and God" (*The Years of Triumph*, 596, n. 14).

14. Thompson, *The Years of Triumph*, 231–39. Cf. Sergeant, *Trial by Existence*, 249–50.

15. *Letters to Louis Untermeyer*, 152–57.

Emerson's Influence on Frost Through Howells

LLOYD N. DENDINGER

A TTEMPTS to explain the nature and extent of Emerson's influence on Frost have been crucial to the major assessments of the poet's achievement. William Dean Howells was one of the principal transmuters of that influence, and the affinities between some of his critical dicta and Frost's poetry significantly clarify the nature of Frost's Emersonianism.

A valuable study of the Frost-Emerson relationship has been made by Alvan S. Ryan, who, stimulated by the Lionel Trilling-J. Donald Adams episode of 1959, postulates a middle ground for Frost between the positions defined by those two critics.[1] Ryan sees the validity of both views, that of Trilling who sees Frost as a terrifying, "Sophoclean" poet, and that of Adams who insists on Frost's affirmative Emersonianism, but Ryan feels that these assessments apply to the extremes of Frost's "spectrum" rather than to the main body of it. He concerns himself particularly with the distinctions to be made between the visions of Frost and Emerson:

> Between Frost's early and late poetry, there is no such shift of emphasis from impulse or spontaneity to the recognition of evil and limitation as is found in Emerson's essays. Frost has kept the dialogue between feeling and thought through nearly all of his poetry, most nearly in his dramatic monologues, but also in his briefer lyrics. It is chiefly because of this that he is not Emersonian; his interpretations of experience—in his own words, his momentary stays against confusion—are not those of either Emerson, though they are nearer to Emerson's later than to his earlier phase.[2]

Closing his study, Ryan uses the terms "dialectical" and "dramatic" to describe those central characteristics of Frost's vision which make it most clearly an "unEmersonian" vision.

The distinctions between Frost and Emerson which Ryan makes are all valid. The two poets have obviously different views of the poet's role; their theories of poetry are similar but far from identical; their poetry is only very superficially alike; and most fundamental of all, Emerson ultimately comes to a philosophical position which Frost never approaches, a positive, affirmative position dependent upon a transcendental ontology. The clearly demonstrable nature of these differences forces one to look deeper for an explanation of the vitality of the question about the extent of Frost's indebtedness to Emerson. The "naturalness" of Frost's voice provides the most obvious basis of his association with traditional English verse and with Emerson in particular. The simple direct diction and the natural speech rhythms of that voice are obviously related to Frost's choice of subject matter, to his New England regionalism, even though he is, of course, not a dialect poet. And that regionalism in the broader sense, like the voice which it gives rise to, naturally calls up an association with Emerson, with the earlier poet of New England. But there is a deeper significance to this association which delineates a complex but unbroken line of development from Emerson to Frost.

The development of nineteenth- and twentieth-century American poetry parallels that of English poetry of the same period, and the relationship between Wordsworth and Thomas Hardy is in a very fundamental sense very much like the relationship between Emerson and Frost. The poet's central problem by the end of the nineteenth century was to learn, in the words of one of Frost's poems, "what to make of a diminished thing," that is, of the relatively diminished stature of post-Darwinian man. The cultural responses to Darwin and later to Freud and Einstein, even if one thinks more specifically in terms of poetic responses, are, of course, too complex to be treated incidentally. But there were among the significant responses in terms of the poetry produced in the first half of the twentieth century three clearly definable patterns. There were those who, like T. S. Eliot, implicitly denied the significance of nineteenth- and twentieth-century science by assuming that the traditional values and attitudes of Christian civilization were as valid in the modern wasteland as they had ever been; there were those like Yeats and Wallace Stevens who created their personal myths to replace what they felt had been lost; and there were those like

Hardy and Robinson and Frost who attempted neither to deny the loss nor to replace it with personal myth but rather to make poetry out of the diminished thing itself. That Frost's poetry is not predominantly dark poetry, in the vein of Hardy's "for life I have never cared greatly," is explainable in terms of the modifications in Emersonian thought made toward the end of the nineteenth century by the champions of realism, particularly by William Dean Howells.

Emerson's transcendentalism, with its roots in English and German romanticism, differs from its sources significantly because of the political and social climate of America in Emerson's lifetime. It was a climate controlled by a vigorous, often ambivalent, but largely optimistic faith in the democratic process and in the future of the democratic state. Emerson's "American Scholar" address is a romantic manifesto based upon the fundamental romantic proposition that "in proportion as a man has any thing in him divine, the firmament flows before him and takes his signet and form." But it is also a nationalistic tract—in the words of Oliver Wendell Holmes, America's "declaration of literary independence." The mixture of transcendental idealism and practical political considerations is not, of course, unique in Emerson; rather, it is an important factor in establishing his affinity with someone like Thomas Carlyle in particular, the significant difference being that the same general conditions which drove the Englishman to frustration and despair ultimately led the American to an optimistic faith in the worth and dignity of the individual human being. It is a characteristic of Emerson's thought and of his prose style that his expression of this faith is often transferable back and forth, as it were, between the terms of transcendentalism and those of political and social reform. It is an easy and natural step, that is, from the concept of the manifold unity of being in the Oversoul to the concept of the equality of all men in the democratic state. In the last quarter of the nineteenth century this step was taken with something approaching finality by the proponents of realism, particularly as their theories found expression in the writings of William Dean Howells.

From Emerson's "I embrace the common, I explore and sit at the feet of the familiar, the low" ("American Scholar") through

Howells' "the finest poetry is not ashamed of the plainest fact" [3] to Frost's *North of Boston* is an unbroken and obvious enough line of development. But there has been development; and the common and the low in Frost's poetry are not, as they were for Emerson, signs of anything beyond themselves; they are "realistic" by Howells' definition of that term because they are "bound to no thesis." For Emerson in "The American Scholar," the literary interest in his time in "the near, the low, the common" was an encouraging sign:

What would we know the meaning of? The meal in the firkin; the milk in the pan; the ballad in the street; the news of the boat; the glance of the eye; the form and the gait of the body;—show me the ultimate reason of these matters; show me the sublime presence of the highest spiritual cause lurking, as always it does lurk, in these suburbs and extremities of nature; let me see every trifle bristling with the polarity that ranges it instantly on an eternal law . . . and the world lies no longer a dull miscellany and lumber-room, but has form and order; there is no trifle, there is no puzzle, but one design unites and animates the farthest pinnacle and the lowest trench.

The focus of Howells' realistic theories is precisely the same as that of Emerson's thought here except for one highly significant difference: Howells drops the references to "ultimate" reasons and to the unity of the design. Where Emerson speaks in terms of a transcendental rationale for his aesthetic theories, Howells speaks in terms of social and economic need: "Literature, which was once of the cloister, the school, has become more and more of the forum and incidentally of the market place. But it is actuated now by as high and noble motives as ever it was in the history of the world; and I think that in turning from the vain endeavor of creating beauty and devoting itself to the effort of ascertaining life it is actuated by a clearer motive than before." [4]

Howells knew and liked Frost's poetry, praising *North of Boston* by comparing it favorably with the work of the prose realists. Frost respected Howells and spoke in a letter to Hamlin Garland of the "great debt" he owed Howells.[5] But the importance of the relationship between the two does not rest upon any very close association, and there seems to be no basis for talking of influence. The importance arises rather from the applicability of Howells' thought to Frost's poetry and the light which such application throws upon the poet's relationship to Emerson. Howells' exceptions, for example, to Zola's distortions of reality contain a definition of art which applies as specifically as any that can be brought to bear upon Frost's poetry:

Each of the [Rougon-Macquart] series is bound to a thesis, but reality is bound to no thesis. You cannot say where it begins or where it leaves off; and it will not allow you to say precisely what its meaning or argument is.... Life is no more symmetrical than a tree, and the effort of art to give it balance and proportion is to make it as false in effect as a tree clipped and trained to a certain shape.[6]

This central aesthetic principle, based upon the distinction between "thesis" and "reality," establishes the fundamental common ground between Howells and Frost. But the affinities between the two men are made clear in various ways. Precisely the same kind of objection was raised in the 1920's about Howells' failure to explore the dark side of human experience as was to be raised in time against Frost. Howells was accused of prudery; Frost of timidity, of excessive caution. But by Howells' definition of realism, the "dark" side of life, particularly as it is manifested in the sexual depravity which received so much attention from the naturalists of his time, represents only a fractional portion of human experience. Defending his attitude about the restrained treatment of sex in the novel, he explained that unconventional sexual behavior might not come within the scheme of a particular novel, and "that so far from maiming or mutilating itself in ignoring" such experiences, "it was all the more faithfully representative of the tone of modern life in dealing with love that was chaste...."[7] Frost, in a tone very much like that of Howells, on one occasion championed Longfellow on the basis of his moral uprightness, claiming that "inspiration doesn't lie in the mud; it lies in the clean and wholesome life of the ordinary man." He professed here, too, to be "ordinary," to "like the middle way," and to like "to talk to the man who walks the middle way with me."[8] And on still another occasion, in "New Hampshire," Frost catches in humorous, epigrammatic verse the central note of Howells' views of the middle way, of the mean reality between the extremes of tragedy and unqualified joy.

How are we to write
The Russian novel in America
As long as life goes so unterribly?
There is the pinch from which our only outcry
In literature to date is heard to come.
We get what little misery we can
Out of not having cause for misery.

The early responses to Frost's poetry, particularly to *North of Boston*, emphasize, by their repeated specific comparisons of his poetry with the prose realists, Frost's relationship to Howells. But this is a fairly obvious relationship based upon the poet's regionalism and his "realistic" objectivity, a relationship which becomes more valuable when pressed beyond this relatively superficial level. Howells' definition of reality applies to the whole body of Frost's poetry, not only to his specifically New England regional pieces. His definition of reality, of "poor real life," explains Frost's frame of mind, his "middle" position, which is in turn responsible for the vital ambiguity permeating his poetry. The realist's position as defined by Howells and manifested in the poetry of Frost is one distinctly American attempt to make the most of a diminished thing. It is a middle position, a mean between the extremes of romantic idealism on the one hand and naturalistic determinism on the other. It is Emersonian in its affirmation of the goodness of life and of the worth of individual effort in the realization of that good; it differs clearly and emphatically from Emerson's thought in its absence of a transcendental rationale and in the recognition by its proponents of the positive nature of evil.

In a letter to Lawrance Thompson, speculating about the validity of Lionel Trilling's view of his poetry, Frost made the following specific comparisons of himself with Emerson:

At least he [Trilling] seemed to see that I am as strong on badness as I am on goodness. Emerson's defect was that he was of the great tradition of Monists. He could see the "good of evil born" but he couldn't bring himself to say the evil of good born. He was an Abominable Snowman of the top-lofty peaks. . . . Arnold thought him a voice oracular. ("A voice oracular has pealed today.") I couldn't go as far as that because I am a Dualist and I don't see how Mathew Arnold could because he was a Dualist too.[9]

Frost is not properly an Emersonian poet, but he is, in a very real sense, in the Emersonian tradition. While neither he nor Howells relegates evil as Emerson does to the role of a negative entity, to "non-being," neither do they go to the other extreme of denying human dignity and value. Frost's repeated definition of the basis of that dignity and that value is cautious and restrained; he is dealing with a changed and changing tradition at the heart of which is a diminished concept of man. But because for Frost man's dignity is only diminished, not denied, he gives evidence of a faith which reflects his fundamental affinity with Emerson. Unlike Emerson, Frost saw "much in nature against us." But his sense of balance, his "realist's" view of human experience, prompted him to admit the validity of the opposite view that there is also much in nature on the side of man. In "Our Hold on the Planet" is the realist's balance, which results from a synthesis of Emersonian optimism and naturalistic despair:

> There is much in nature against us. But we forget:
> Take nature altogether since time began,
> Including human nature, in peace and war,
> And it must be a little more in favor of man,
> Say a fraction of one percent at the very least,
> Or our number living wouldn't be steadily more,
> Our hold on the planet wouldn't have so increased.

Frost's refusal to fit his perceptions of reality into the pattern of a thesis is fundamental to his widespread appeal, finding expression, as it does, in his poetry in a widely varied range of responses to experience. There is something of Emerson in Frost as there is something of Sophocles, and so the poet is admired by both Lionel Trilling and J. Donald Adams. But this basis of the popularity is also the basis of the most serious criticism of Frost on the part of those who object to his lack of a comprehensive view of modern man in terms of a system or a myth. The most persistent charge brought against Frost has been that his vision is limited, that the body of his poetry constitutes not a synthesis of experience but a collection of fragments, of, at best, in the poet's own words, "momentary stay[s] against confusion." [10]

Two book-length studies since 1959 which continue the debate about the restrictions of Frost's subject matter are John F. Lynen's *The Pastoral Art of Robert Frost*, 1960, and George W. Nitchie's *Human Values in the Poetry of Robert Frost*, 1960. Lynen's thesis is that Frost does have the equivalent of a unifying myth in terms of the pastoral tradition, that "the concept of pastoral reveals the unity in the diverse elements of Frost's art" (p. 8), and that his "retreat" from the modern city to the agrarian world is of "a special sort" which does not result in his turning away from the problems of the world of today (p. 175). Lynen closes his study with a long quotation from Frost's "Directive," which he introduces with the following summary of his thesis: "[Frost] has explored wide and manifold ranges of being by viewing reality within the mirror of the natural and unchanging world of rural life. Pastoralism, whether in Frost or in the poets of the Arcadian tradition, will always at first appear to involve an escape from the world as we know it, but actually it is an exploration upstream, past the city with its riverside factories and shipping, on against the current of time and change to the clear waters of the source . . ." (p. 189).

George Nitchie, seeing Frost in much the same light as does Lynen, seeing, for example, that nature for Frost "is primarily an evasion according to plan, a condition of strategic withdrawal" (p. 22), does not agree that in the final analysis there is a unified vision giving direction to all of the poetry. Rather he places the emphasis upon the fragmentary nature of the vision:

Frost's world is fragmentary and meaningless—fragmentary *because* meaningless, except as an alien entanglement that our wills must confront. It is, once more, 'the vast chaos of all I have lived through,' within which a poem may exist but only as 'a momentary stay against confusion.' One thinks of Oscar Wilde's impressions, of the Imagists' reverential fragments, and if the conjunction of Frost and Wilde is startling, that is partly because Frost has been less consistent than Wilde in abiding by his professed principles; the shining gate may be there after all; the sphere of art and the sphere of morality, or of metaphysics, may not be absolutely distinct and separate. But Frost will not commit himself. And without such commitment, Frost offers us no tragic acceptance— only the drumlin woodchuck's canny adjustment. (p. 218)

Lynen and Nitchie both make valuable contributions to our

understanding of Frost's poetic method, Lynen in terms of the pastoral motif and Nitchie in terms of the Edenic myth. They bring into the 1960's, with considerable consistency, the duality inherent in the appraisals of the poet since Ezra Pound's qualified praise in 1913 of *A Boy's Will*. Nitchie's case is the more persuasive of the two, for the truth of the matter is that Frost does not have a system in any of the usual senses of that word, not even the pastoral tradition, in spite of the fact that, as Lynen so ably demonstrates, many of his poems can be intelligently and meaningfully read in light of that tradition. For it is a tradition imposed upon the poetry from without, not a carefully conceived structure giving shape to the poetic development from year to year. On the other hand, Nitchie's emphasis upon Frost's lack of commitment is not altogether satisfactory. Although the terminology is troublesome, Frost has made a "commitment," the difficulty arising from the fact that his commitment is to "non-commitment." The difference between this view and that of Nitchie and of Yvor Winters, among others, is to make Frost something other than a spiritual drifter. He has made a choice and a commitment. One is, of course, free to consider that choice a very bad one, even a disastrous one, but the evidence clearly indicates that the choice was made early and never substantially changed. And it is the nature of this choice which makes Frost the most modern of poets.

Frost's regionalism, his affinities with William Dean Howells and the prose realists, provided him with the means of making poetry of the materials of an age that was forcing upon other poets the decision to turn away from it, to turn backward in time to tradition or to turn inward to the creation of individual myth. Frost's achievement is not that he is a better poet than Eliot or Yeats but that he found a way other than theirs of writing poetry in the twentieth century. Yeats and Eliot and even Wallace Stevens, the poets most often held up as the most modern of modern poets, all follow the pattern of the nineteenth century of "replacing" what had been lost to the poet as a result of the scientific, industrial, and political revolutions of the age. Precisely what it was that had been lost is difficult to define. "Faith" is the best word, though, of course, too general to be fully satisfactory. But it is the loss being lamented as early as Wordsworth's cry that he would rather be a "pagan suckl'd in some creed outworn" so that he might have glimpses that would make him "less forlorn." It is the loss lamented in "Dover Beach" and in "Stanzas from the Grande Chartreuse" where the poet finds himself between two worlds "one dead,/The other powerless to be born." It is the loss most forlornly felt by J. Alfred Prufrock who has "heard the mermaids singing, each to each," and who is about as sure as Prufrock can be that they will not sing to him. Frost's modernity rests primarily in the fact that, having experienced the loss affecting his contemporaries, he turns neither to Eliot's "chambers of the sea" nor to Yeats' prophetic vision of some "rough beast, its hour come round at last," slouching "towards Bethlehem to be born," but rather to the "real" world, to what Howells would describe as the "poor real life" of the largely impoverished countryside of New England. It is a view of life sometimes sinister, even tragic; it is a view sometimes characterized by unqualified joy; but as it is first of all a view of life "bound to no thesis," it is largely an ambivalent view focusing for the most part upon the large body of experiences between the extremes.

Notes to *Emerson's Influence on Frost through Howells* by LLOYD N. DENDINGER

1. Alvan S. Ryan, "Frost and Emerson: Voice and Vision," *Massachusetts Review*, I (Fall 1959), 5–23.

2. *Ibid.*, 17–18.

3. Quoted in "Norwegian Romances," in *Criticism and Fiction and Other Essays*, ed. Clara M. and Rudolph Kirk (New York: New York University Press, 1959), 105.

4. William Dean Howells, "Seventy-fifth Birthday Speech," in *Criticism and Fiction and Other Essays*, p. 369.

5. *Selected Letters of Robert Frost*, ed. Lawrance Thompson (New York: Holt, Rinehart and Winston, 1964), 265.

6. William Dean Howells, *Prefaces to Contemporaries*, ed. G. Arms, et al. (Gainesville, Fla.: Scholars Facsimiles and Reprints, 1957), 91–92.

7. William Dean Howells, *Criticism and Fiction* (New York: Harper and Brothers, 1893), 149.

8. Frost, in an interview with Rose C. Feld entitled "Robert Frost Relieves His Mind," *New York Times Book Review*, October 21, 1923, p. 2.

9. *Selected Letters*, 584.

10. *Complete Poems of Robert Frost* (New York: Henry Holt and Company, 1949), vi.

Other "Desert Places": Frost and Hawthorne

EDWARD STONE

Robert Frost's "Desert Places" has been a part of the American consciousness for so long that the wording of its title does not pique our curiosity. Yet familiarity should not render us insensitive to that strange adjective, for it is not a word such as Frost characteristically uses. In fact, the title itself may have been borrowed for the occasion. Certainly a comparison of Frost's poem with the source of its title discloses various coincidences. These are interesting enough to justify, in turn, a consideration of the relationship of certain others of his poems to the art that furnished the metaphor in question. Frost's poetry can thus be viewed in a light that has been suggested before but not explored with any particularity.

Why does this most conversational of major modern American poets say *desert*? Predominantly a confession, this brief poem begins with a dignity, almost a solemnity, and ends with a colloquialism (*scare*), almost a jocularity—the two extremes of usage even meeting in the poem's last line. Since we cannot allow the word solely on the grounds of scansion, we might wonder why, instead of some synonym for the *deserted* which is his meaning, he chose *desert*, which is not only archaic but has come to carry during the present century the much narrower literal meaning of the noun *desert*—of an area hot and sandy and therefore completely inappropriate to the landscape of a poem about snow on an arable northern field. (By way of contrast, his use in "The Census-Taker" of *desert* for *deserted* is appropriate, for the context—liturgical phraseology—is itself archaic.)

True, the snow is rapidly transforming an easily distinguishable late autumn landscape into an undifferentiated, unrelieved midwinter whiteness that might appear to a poet like the featureless countenance of a desert; and such a countenance of nature might dismay the poet with its lifelessness and impersonality, as the white

275

western American desert dismayed Mark Twain in *Roughing It* or
Frank Norris in *McTeague*. But Frost is using *desert* chiefly in its
other, antique, sense—as an adjective. And modern readers, properly
consenting to Frost's quiet restoring to the modern noun the adjective's properties from days of old—the meaning deserted, forsaken, abandoned, desolate, and lonely—may well puzzle over the
choice of the archaism.

The answer, I think, is that Frost did not create the two-word
image of his title, but appropriated it; took it from a context so apt
and familiar that he may have considered the choice in keeping
with the homeliness of his other titles: after all, what American of
his generation had not read Nathaniel Hawthorne's *The Scarlet
Letter*?

The Puritan magistrate had not foreseen that punishing Hester
Prynne with a physical stigma of her sin would isolate her yet further from society. Nor did he see that this isolation would cause
even more harm. Hester chooses to stay and bear her shame, instead of leaving Boston, but again she bears it in a way of her own
choosing. She goes to live in a little cottage at some distance from
the town and surrounded by "a clump of stubby trees"; these "did
not so much conceal the cottage from view, as seem to denote that
here was some object which would fain have been, or at least ought
to be, concealed." In this "little, lonesome dwelling," Hawthorne
writes, Hester began her new, isolated existence. She is, then, separated from the view of the townspeople by a growth of trees. But
this separation, we learn, is to conceal not the incriminating letter
so much as an "object" truly in need of concealment from Boston—
namely, a new and dangerous way of thinking. This launching forth
into strange seas of thought comes from the loneliness that arises
from both society-inflicted ostracism and self-inflicted seclusion.

Readers of Hawthorne (and Chaucer) will recognize the association between the evil of freethinking and the isolation of the forest.
The forest is where Hawthorne's young goodman named Brown
rushes after he has yielded to despair at the apparent universality of
evil. It is also the place Hester has in mind when she asks Chillingworth, " 'Art thou like the Black Man that haunts the forest round
about us?' " (Ironically, it is Hester herself whom Dimmesdale

much later identifies with the Black Man in the forest: back in town after consenting to Hester's plan to run away with her and once again in command of his thoughts, he wonders, " 'Did I make a contract with him in the forest?' ") Well might Hester ask this: Chillingworth has just told her that a little while ago he "came out of the vast and dismal forest, and entered this settlement of Christian men" only after a year's residence there, where he—a necromancer of old—evidently lived both comfortably and profitably with the pagan Indians. This concept of the dark wilderness as the haunt of evil, F. O. Matthiessen notes in *American Renaissance*, came to Hawthorne "from the days of Cotton Mather, who held that 'the New Englanders are a people of God settled in those which were once the devil's territories.' " In *The Scarlet Letter* itself, the Mistress Hibbins who tells Hester, " 'I have been to the forest so many times' " is a well-known witch.

This is the *selva selvaggia* of Dante's faltering faith, and its beasts threaten Hester Prynne as well. "Standing alone in the world,—alone as to any dependence on society ... alone, and hopeless of retrieving her position . . . .—she cast away the fragments of a broken chain. The world's law was no law for her mind," Hawthorne tells us. Earlier he had noted that she was "as much alone as if she inhabited another sphere. . . . She stood apart from mortal interests." Separated from humanity, in her *lone*liness (Hawthorne tolls the word like a mourning bell!) she succumbs to the license of the free thought of the day. She has "imbibed" the "freedom of speculation" of Anne Hutchinson, which her age considered "a deadlier crime" than adultery. "In her lonesome cottage ... thoughts visited her . . . , shadowy guests . . . perilous as demons," and Hester "wandered without a clew in the dark labyrinth of mind; now turned aside by an insurmountable precipice; now starting back from a deep chasm. There was wild and ghastly scenery all around her, and a home and comfort nowhere."

Now the ghastly scenery that surrounds Hester is what Hawthorne's generation referred to as *desert places*. The "chorus of the desert" in "Young Goodman Brown" actually refers to a congregation deep in a forest. Seven years after the novel opens, when Hester and Dimmesdale meet in the forest, Hawthorne refers to the broken-spirited minister as "this poor pilgrim, on his dreary and desert path" in the forest, just after he has used the very phrase of Frost's title in his description of Hester's state of mind: "She had wandered, without rule or guidance, in a moral wilderness; as vast, as intricate and shadowy, as the untamed forest, amid the gloom of which they were now holding a colloquy that was to decide their fate. Her intellect and heart had their homes, as it were, in desert places. . . ."

In this metaphor, then, we have presented the basic component parts of her situation, as given and repeated by the author: the *forest* creating an inner rebellion of mind and heart against orthodoxy, creating—actually, being infected by—a heresy that is a natural outgrowth of loneliness. But since her predicament now is itself an outgrowth of a forbidden tendency (passion), we can see that the New Thought (*intellect*) finds its home in *desert places* as an extension or concomitant of her original freedom of conduct (*heart*). And if Robert Frost chose to title his poem with a phrase borrowed verbatim from Hawthorne's novel, as I think he did, it was because his situation in the poem bears a strikingly interesting similarity to Hester Prynne's. There are with him, as with her, two sources of despair and a set of factors, symbolically visualized, conducive to them.

There is a difference of kind between poet and fictional character, but not of degree. Hester's was a rebellion of passion that, accentuated by loneliness, was directed into an intellectual channel. Hester, like Anne Hutchinson, entertains the heresies that emigrated to the New World with the Puritans. Frost's rebelliousness is not accounted for. Light years, infinity, expanding and limitless universe—these were scaring modern Pascals just as the original New Thought had scared John Donne, but Frost's faith is assailed by terrors described merely as "so much nearer home" than what Hawthorne had described as "the vacant regions of the atmosphere." What these terrors are, Frost does not say; but he provides the mirror in which he sees them. And the circumstances here closely resemble those of Hester's plight.

The something in Frost's poem that is to be concealed is, as in Hawthorne's novel, concealed by a clump of trees ("The woods around it have it, it is theirs") which again are to be thought of as the natural habitat of the father of doubt, the Devil. For it is through this forest that Frost looks at the field rapidly disappearing under a snowy shroud far more responsible for his despair than the New Geometry could be. The forest encloses *his* desert places just as it had enclosed Hester's. (Or young goodman Brown's: Brown, after he has given way to despair, looking *from a woods* and *into a clearing*, sees "at one extremity of an open space, hemmed in by the dark wall of the forest" the altar of none other than the Devil.) In both poem and novel the intimate abode of an abstraction, an illicit, proscribed thought (Frost's atheism, Hester's single sexual standard) is projected concretely as a place hidden from society's view (a field surrounded by woods, a remote cottage concealed from view by a clump of trees). The snow is what in Frost's poem will by night time so completely efface all signs of life, of movement and of contour as to reinforce his freethinking ("my own desert places"), his awareness of a world of darkness of intention ("benighted")—in short, the same Despair that had been one of Hester's teachers during the seven isolated years. Hester's rebellion has passional roots; Frost's, metaphysical, for he rejects the most fundamental of beliefs —the belief in Design ("no expression, nothing to express"); yet they are both spiritual outcasts nursing in private a view that separates them from society. Indeed, sexual sin and intellectual sin are equally intemperate: "the wildness of her nature" matches the wildness of his heresy, which would consign him to the ring of the intellectually violent in Dante's hell. Unlike Dimmesdale, who during his earlier vigil, in Elizabeth Barrett Browning's words, "through the midnight air /Beat upward to God's throne in loud access /Of shrieking and reproach," Hester and Frost are weighted down with a grief that is mute because it is hopeless: "Full desertness," we read in "Grief,"

> In souls as countries, lieth silent-bare
> Under the blanching, vertical eye-glare
> Of the absolute Heavens. . . .

Like Ivan Karamazov, or Thomas Mann's Jesuit, Leo Naphta, Frost dismisses the problems posed by non-Euclidean geometry as irrelevant to his three-dimensional consciousness and, it may be supposed, confesses to disbelief in such articles of faith (the divinity of Jesus and the immortality of the human soul) as the giddy mind of Hester's paramour flirts with briefly after his talk with her in the forest. But then, has Hester herself not come to reject all "human institutions, and whatever priests or legislators had established. . ."? And most significantly, this twentieth-century response to the Devil's insinuations is greatly accentuated by the one factor that more than any other had led to Hester's grief: four times in rapid succession Frost tells us of the desert places' *loneliness* and of his own. (It is even possible that his sardonic phrase "benighted snow" is also an echo, of the "benighted wilderness" of Hawthorne's "The Maypole of Merrymount" and "Young Goodman Brown.")

If my assumption is correct, then Frost in effect offered his title as a quotation. Yet this he would have done only, I think, if the phrase quoted was one that he could count on being recognized, if the richness that his poem would gain from the literary association was to be perceived. Obviously this has not been so: the quotation from *The Scarlet Letter* has nearly escaped notice.[1] Of course, we understand him quite well nonetheless. Then, too, possibly his intention, all along, was more private. Perhaps, having recognized his own plight in Hester's, he had simply wanted to admit to himself, at least, how frequently—as Mrs. Nancy Westerfield puts it—we think in quotation marks.

We can also observe Frost using the materials—this time, the stuff of myth—that Hawthorne had used in writing a *Mosses From an Old Manse* story as forgotten as *The Scarlet Letter* is familiar. In this instance both writers are reaching back (Hawthorne consciously) into the public domain of the artist—the Pygmalion-Galatea myth; but the two writers depart from the myth in precisely the same ways, inducing us to wonder whether Frost found his suggestion, at least in part, for "Paul's Wife" in Hawthorne's "Drowne's Wooden Image." Other similarities also are visible. Perhaps Paul's wife, that lovely creature who springs into life from a log, is out of Ovid by Hawthorne.

Frost's Paul is, of course, a figure from western myth: he is Paul Bunyan, several of whose feats actually come in for mention in the poem; but although the story of Paul's wife is told by a fellow lumberjack and the poem is swathed in horselaugh and horseplay, the Bunyan feat that identifies "Paul's Wife" is completely unrelated to the outrageous and the gross Bunyan myth. It is, in fact, essentially an act (and its consequences) of ineffable delicacy and so recognized, as much by the crude logger-informant Murphy as the woodcarver Drowne's feat is recognized by the colonial American painter, Copley. Into the lives of both lumberjack demigod and proper Bostonian comes the moment of love that lights up the surrounding darkness and then goes glimmering. In keeping with the feats, the wonders, of Paul's repertory is the "yarn" that Murphy relates: in the mill that day the pine log Paul was helping push through the saw was, for a marvel, hollow; to it Paul returned in the evening to extract a fragile, shapeless, skinlike pith that, when immersed in the nearby pond, emerged some distance away as a lumbercamp Venus ("Her wet hair heavy on her like a helmet") to the smitten view of her frontier sculptor. Drowne, in his Boston water's-edge shop, sculpting an oak log into a figurehead for a friend, releases a hamadryad from the heart of her tree home, and "it was only necessary to remove the strange shapelessness that had incrusted her, and reveal the grace and loveliness of a divinity"; passionately Drowne stretches his arms toward it "as if he would have embraced and drawn it to his heart." The "bewitching coquetry," the "mirthful mischief," of Drowne's exotic maid are reproduced in Frost's, who, after she has caught her first breath, laughs, then walks off "talking to herself or Paul." And the report that Drowne "had been seen kneeling at the feet of the oaken lady, and gazing with a lover's passionate ardor into the face that his own hands had created" is repeated in Murphy's account of Paul "Falling in love across the twilight mill-pond," of sculptor and creation sitting together "keeping house" in a small niche halfway up a cliff. Whether because of loggers' jests or because of true owners' claims, both girls literally disappear—Paul's like a firefly and Drowne's onto the water outside his door—from lovers who cannot hold them. So ends Drowne's "brief season of excitement, kindled by love," and he returns to his commissions, executed now as before, dully and without enthusiasm. Although Paul returns to camp, he will not tolerate even the mention of his wife by a stranger, for real love had actually kindled his life once. Although Hawthorne ends his story with a Frostian, common sense, alternative reading of his miracle, he cannot dim the wonder his tale has worked, a wonder that envelopes "Paul's Wife" completely. Perhaps Frost's epic buffoon's one-and-only love was actually carved from oak, rather than pine, after all?

Even elsewhere identical objects will engage the vision of both men, with meditations resulting. Frost's "The Wood-Pile" and the chapter in *The Blithedale Romance*[2] entitled "The Masqueraders" find poet and novelist alone, far from town, contemplating an abandoned pile of firewood in the forest. It was, Frost recalls, "a cord of maple, cut and split/And piled—and measured, four by four by eight." The wood is already gray, the bark loose, the pile sunken and encircled by vines. In his flight from the masqueraders, Miles Coverdale tell us, "I stumbled over a heap of logs and sticks that had been cut for firewood, a great while ago, by some former possessor of the soil, and piled up square, in order to be carted or sledded away to the farm-house." They lay there decaying, autumn after autumn, under each year's fall of leaves and growth of moss. The solemn, almost sullen poet finds the object of his wonder in a bleak frozen swamp on a gray day of winter, and the excited figure from fiction stumbles upon his woodpile in the dense foliage of a September wood. Hawthorne's character, discovering that he is strangely affected, imagines the long-dead woodman and his family coming back to the woodpile after fifty years or more of absence; whereas Frost, trying to determine the woodman's motive for leaving unused the efforts of his axe, does not say "elves." Surely, it would seem, Hawthorne's ghoulish whimsy, his conjuring up a vision of the ghosts trying to remove the chill of their graves by making a fire of the mossy wood, cannot be made to consort with Frost's vision of Enterprise, of "Someone who lived in turning to fresh tasks." As Robert Penn Warren once noted, in a 1928 review in *The New Republic*, if both New Englanders "had their eyes fixed on the past," it was "in profoundly different ways," for Frost "replaces imagination by 'sensibility,' tragedy by a certain pathos rather finely tempered by common sense." And yet the image with which Frost's musing ends this experience—of the long-abandoned pile of wood as somehow warming the frozen swamp "With the slow smokeless burning of decay"—is no more common-sensical than Hawthorne's supernatural one. Through the haze of years and wonder, both men view the remote, discarded firewood akindle, warming the chilled bones of dead men or a swamp frozen in winter.

Elsewhere both writers conceive of summer as the reckless, the prodigal of the seasons of the year. The impression that summer gives of immediacy, of glory in its own luxuriance, Hawthorne expresses in another *Mosses* piece, "Buds and Bird Voices": "Summer works in the present, and thinks not of the future." This impressionistic reading of the season being rather unusual among poets, I find it significant that it reappears in Frost's "Spring Pools." Here Frost warns the buds to "think twice" about their power to darken nature and become summer woods. By banishing spring, he implies, they invite their own end in turn.

Like nature, the city provides both Hawthorne and Frost identical prosy materials to be transformed by the imagination into poetry, even into symbolism; and the correspondences at times can be close. As artists they reveal a characteristic convergence upon the raw materials that "fancy will magnify"—in Hawthorne's phrase—and as characteristic a divergence as thinkers, or believers. It is true that "Birches," Frost's statement of his lover's quarrel with the world, can seem a versified epitome of "The Hall of Fantasy," that routine processional piece from *Mosses* which Matthiessen found significant as a statement of the "normal balance" in Hawthorne between the claims on him of reality and ideality. The Hall is exactly the sanctuary from the world's thorns that is the swinging out on the birch limb; and the admission that "earth's the right place for love" has been foreshadowed in Hawthorne's awareness that to destroy the earth would be to forfeit "that very earthliness which no other sphere or state of existence can renew or compensate." But Frost's quarrel with the other sphere ran much deeper. Of Melville's indictment of that sphere ("the invisible spheres were formed in fright") we can find echoes in Frost, but not in Hawthorne.

Early in *The Blithedale Romance*, Miles Coverdale, reminiscing, feels that in joining the colony of social reformers at Blithedale farm he had at least attested to his idealism, to his once having "faith and

force enough to form generous hopes of the world's destiny,—yes!—
and to do what in me lay for their accomplishment; even to the extent
of quitting a warm fireside, flinging away a freshly lighted cigar, and
travelling far beyond the strike of city clocks, through a drifting
snow-storm." Visible in such ironic selfmockery and nostalgic self-
assurance is an antithesis that Hawthorne elaborates into metaphors of
security and despondency—those twin poles of the poetic consciousness—and that we find Frost turning to as though by affinity. We associate clocks that strike in a city with the regularity and thus the
assurances to our peace of mind that the concerted effort of society
provides; drifting snowstorms we think of as civilization's undisci-
plined natural adversary, struggling to wrest from it men's minds as
well as their bodies. Like clocks, city lights. When they and the
pavement end, our security ends. To walk out beyond them, literally,
is to venture into the dark; metaphorically, into the sinister and forbidding, because unseen and unknown. Both Hawthorne and Frost
go to its margin. The obscure "Night Sketches" from *Twice-Told
Tales* discloses Hawthorne setting out into the rainy night, his spirits
depressed because he has shielded himself from the night by reading. But actually facing it is even worse: "I look upward, and discern no sky, not even a fathomable void, but only a black, impenetrable nothingness, as though heaven and all its lights were blotted
from the system of the universe." "I have walked out in rain—and
back in rain," Frost writes in "Acquainted with the Night," where
the title becomes a refrain that speaks for itself, tightlipped but con-
veying the same spiritual depression. Hawthorne goes to the edge of
this unfathomable void, this impenetrable nothingness: "Now I have
reached the utmost limits of the town, where the last lamp struggles
feebly with the darkness, like the farthest star that stands sentinel
on the borders of uncreated space." And Frost: "I have outwalked
the furthest city light." Hawthorne's sketch ends with the watchman figure. His lantern throws light on the ground all around him,
and he "passes fearlessly into the unknown gloom" of fear, disbelief,
and attendant perils to the spirit, his light (his faith) banishing these.
To this figure, Hawthorne's own relationship is equivocal. He proclaims that "the impenetrable obscurity . . . can be dispelled only
by radiance from above"; that if "we, night wanderers through a

stormy and dismal world . . . bear the lamp of Faith," it will guide us to heaven; even so, the fearless watchman, faithemboldened, is last seen venturing into a gloom "whither I will not follow him." Laodicean though this confession may sound, it is practically a statement of belief compared with Frost's. His poem also contains a watchman; but Frost, in passing the watchman on his rounds, confesses to having "dropped my eyes, unwilling to explain." In fact, the "luminary clock against the sky" in his poem, so far from Miles Coverdale's comfortable symbol of civilization's creature comforts, peers through the darkness from the starlike distance of Crane's verse or Hardy's fiction: in proclaiming that "the time was neither wrong nor right," it relegates human endeavor to the irrelevance of the naturalistic philosophy—a gloom into which the doubting Hawthorne cannot follow.

Nor can he, after all, despite the frequent chiming of the two mens' thoughts—which is to say, their fears—and even their language. Their paths and visions merge, then part. The power of blackness, not really in Hawthorne (where Melville thought he saw it), is central to Frost's thinking. Nowhere can this be seen more clearly than in their reaction to the death of the year in the blackness of snow.

It seems to be true, for example, that not only does Frost's "The Onset" thematically recapitulate Hawthorne's "Main Street" (in the *Snow-Image* volume) and "Snow-Flakes" (in *Twice-Told Tales*): it even expresses their oscillation between faith and doubt by the same metaphors. To each writer the church building becomes the object by which to measure the depth and power of annihilation of life contained in the first snowfall of the year and to which he can look for whatever comfort is forthcoming. The spire, because it remains uncovered, affords solace to the spirit. The Hawthorne of "Main Street" broods as he notes that the storm has "annihilated all the visible distinctions of human property," and wonders whether, "indeed, the race be not extinct, and it be worth our while to go on with the march of life, over the cold and desolate expanse that lies before us"; yet, noting that the spire of the meetinghouse is still discernible, he can tell himself that "matters are not so desperate as they appear." So Frost, looking upon the first snow falling as he would look upon the approach of death and the defeat of man's work for good causes, can tell himself in "The Onset" that "winter death has never tried/The earth but it has failed," of which truth there is no better proof than the survival and emergence in the spring of all forms of life, the church building prominent among them.

But otherwise their reactions are by no means the same. To Hawthorne in "Snow-Flakes" there is a "melancholy bleakness" in the winter scene, including "the withered grass-plat" that is still discernible, that fortunately will give way to the beauty of "the fleecy garb of her winter's wear" that Mother Earth is now putting on, as the snow falls; and although that garb, lasting all winter, becomes an "immitigable deity who tyrannizes over forest, country side, and town," who requires occasional human sacrifice in the form of frozen humans, still the tyrant is due our thanks: the Malthusian Hawthorne muses that severity of weather engenders "our unyielding strength of character," makes for the companionship and cheer of sleigh rides, firelight, and "all the home enjoyments, and the kindred virtues, which flourish in a frozen soil." Meanwhile, as evening descends over "the comfortless scene," a view of the snowbirds frolicking in the tempest, and the thought that they have chosen to remain when they might have followed summer southwards, is enough to cheer Hawthorne's spirits. But to Frost in "Desert Places" the "few weeds and stubble" still showing on the frozen landscape are his last acquaintance with life as he watches snow beginning to cover his world; for when it has finished its work it will present a complete whiteness that has "no expression, nothing to express." Gone is the surge of religious feeling that rises above the loss of faith in "The Onset." Nothing can redeem the blackness here and in "Design," which plummet to a despair from which Hawthorne would have recoiled. Such thoughts—that the face of Nature would ever have nothing to express, that there is a part of Nature, however minute, not included in some master plan of creation—Hawthorne entertained privately only to reject in his fiction. Into his notebooks he wrote his doubts about God's benevolence or the hereafter as he watched death overcome his mother; still, like Ishmael surveying the black-bordered marble tables masoned into the walls of the Whaleman's Chapel in New Bedford, Hawthorne could minister Father Mapple-like to his own despair. Imagining the demise of his imaginary self in the *jeu d'esprit* "Monsieur du Miroir" in the *Mosses* volume, Hawthorne could say: "He will pass into the dark realm of nothingness, but will not find me there." And we, in turn, can say: not himself, but his fellow-artist descendant, Robert Frost.

To think of the one in terms of the other, nevertheless, seems natural, even inevitable, as the literary criticism of our times will surely continue to demonstrate. I have cited the Robert Penn Warren review, "Hawthorne, Anderson, and Frost." In his introduction to *The Oxford Book of American Verse*, Mattheissen also finds an essential distinction between fiction writer and poet, here in the course of developing the series of contrasts that he sees between Frost and T. S. Eliot, the "central figures" in the history of modern American poetry. As "the poet of individualism," Frost is "in the Emersonian tradition," whereas Eliot, with his greater awareness "of the weakness of individualism, of the need of the individual to find completion in something larger than himself," is "in the darker vein of Hawthorne." But whereas this explains Dimmesdale's destiny (as well as Holgrave's and Hollingsworth's), it does not explain Hester Prynne's; and the Frost of "Desert Places," among other poems, is surely in the darkest vein imaginable. Nor is it inconceivable that, in borrowing his title, Frost himself first sensed this affinity.

Though his universe can be the terrifying place that Lionel Trilling finds it, and that Hawthorne's is not, Frost's vision, we have seen, frequently mirrors Hawthorne's. In addition, Robert Frost has certainly enriched the modern consciousness with a variety of other poetic effects, and for some of these too it is tempting to believe that he reached back a century into the New England tradition, into the treasury of Nathaniel Hawthorne.

Notes to *Other "Desert Places": Frost and Hawthorne* by EDWARD STONE

1. Only Professor James Ellis appears to have recognized Frost's source. In his note [*The English Record*, XV (April 1965), 15–17], he finds in Frost's choice of the Hawthorne phrase a "recognition of man's capacity for moral evil."

2. Elsewhere in this volume Professor J. Donald Crowley explores the use Frost seems to have made of various Hawthorne notebook entries in writing "The Wood-Pile." The *Blithedale Romance* passage I discuss above is itself a fictional use of one of these entries.

Hawthorne and Frost: The Making of a Poem

J. DONALD CROWLEY

"He [Melville] seems rather weak on the brain side. But as you say never mind. We may admire him more wrong than almost anybody but Hawthorne right" (Frost to Lawrance Thompson about *Billy Budd*).[1]

Mᴏʀᴇ than any other of our writers, Hawthorne and Frost are commonly viewed as preeminently New England artists and personalities whose works epitomize large aspects of the New England character. Both, clearly, are radical symbolists. Perhaps the touchstone of Hawthorne's art is that passage in "The Custom-House" where, pretending to actually examine the old, faded scarlet letter, he writes: "Certainly, there was some deep meaning in it, most worthy of interpretation, and which, as it were, streamed forth from the mystic symbol, subtly communicating itself to my sensibilities, but evading the analysis of my mind." And Frost, in his turn, is known for his cryptic explanation that he wrote poetry because it "provides the one permissible way of saying one thing and meaning another." [2]

The nature and direction of their symbolism obviously share, too, an interest in what Henry James called "the deeper psychology": at the center of their art is the persistent engagement of the fundamental question of the relationship between the mind and reality. The landscapes they present us with, often Wyeth-like in their simplicity and austerity, are impressively mental and moral rather than picturesque. And one often has the sense that the wooded paths Frost's personas take us through have been explored before by young Goodman Brown, Hester Prynne, Miles Coverdale, or Hawthorne himself.

The critical responses to the works of the two men likewise have a striking similarity. Lionel Trilling's celebration of Frost as "a terrifying poet" is reminiscent of Melville's praise of Hawthorne's

288

"power of blackness" and Emily Dickinson's fascination that, as she puts it, "Hawthorne appalls, entices—". Various other readers, in turn, have leveled virtually the same critical charge at both, seeing in Hawthorne's romances and Frost's pastoral art a disturbing withdrawal from the terms of actual contemporary "realistic" life. Neither in their lives nor in their writings were Hawthorne and Frost social activists. Apolitical and philosophical by temperament, both men were deeply skeptical of liberal reform and generally antagonistic to political and social reformers. Politics, Frost said, is "an extravagance about *grievances*" and poetry "an extravagance about *grief*" (449). And Frost, like Hawthorne, preferred to focus on irremediable griefs, often those griefs having to do with a sense of loss that defined the New England past. Even the most devoted students of Hawthorne find themselves cringing a bit at the writer's caustic attitude toward Abolitionist friends; and Frost's anti-New Deal posture in poems such as "Build Soil" continues to arouse bewilderment, embarrassment, and anger. In spite of their general disaffection from political realities, both men paradoxically came to have a political visibility, Hawthorne as U.S. Consul at Liverpool and Frost as a good will ambassador-at-large. Finally, no other New England writers have cultivated as habitually—and teasingly—their public images as popular authors as have Hawthorne and Frost.

If there is indeed no substantial relationship between the two writers, Providence would seem to be firing a lot of blank cartridges, especially for the literary historian given to wonder whether design governs even in things so small. I use the list of similarities merely by way of preface and to suggest that, given the number of source studies about Frost's poems, it is somewhat curious that very little has been written to claim that Hawthorne is one of Frost's literary forebears. Wordsworth is most often mentioned, and next to him in the direct bloodline are Emerson, Thoreau, and Longfellow. Much more removed are Bryant, Whittier, Hardy, and Browning.

Hawthorne, however, is also there, in the background. I would like to demonstrate this by talking primarily about one of Frost's poems, "The Wood-Pile," and the specific sources that Hawthorne's *American Notebooks* provided for it and then, briefly, about the larger matter of Hawthorne's influence on Frost and the reasons

why Frost found the Hawthornian temper and mode so congenial
to him. The genetic relationship between the notebook passages
and the poem points conclusively to the fact that Frost's "discovery"
of Hawthorne amounts to a pivotal influence on the poet's early
work and suggests some of those deep affinities which led to Frost's
admiration for "Hawthorne right."

I

"The Wood-Pile" was first published in 1914 in Frost's second collection, *North of Boston*. Frost was forty at the time; Hawthorne
had been dead for fifty years. The poem has not received the critical attention it deserves, even though it has been called his first great
nature poem and even though Frost himself thought so highly of it
that as late as 1942 he included it in a group of sixteen pieces he called
his finest creative achievements (377).

> Out walking in the frozen swamp one gray day,
> I paused and said, "I will turn back from here.
> No, I will go on farther—and we shall see."
> The hard snow held me, save where now and then
> One foot went through. The view was all in lines
> Straight up and down of tall slim trees
> Too much alike to mark or name a place by
> So as to say for certain I was here
> Or somewhere else: I was just far from home.
> A small bird flew before me. He was careful
> To put a tree between us when he lighted,
> And say no word to tell me who he was
> Who was so foolish as to think what *he* thought.
> He thought that I was after him for a feather—
> The white one in his tail; like one who takes
> Everything said as personal to himself.
> One flight out sideways would have undeceived him.
> And then there was a pile of wood for which
> I forgot him and let his little fear
> Carry him off the way I might have gone,
> Without so much as wishing him good-night.
> He went behind it to make his last stand.
> It was a cord of maple, cut and split
> And piled—and measured, four by four by eight.
> And not another like it could I see.

No runner tracks in this year's snow looped near it.
And it was older sure than this year's cutting,
Or even last year's or the year's before.
The wood was gray and the bark warping off it
And the pile somewhat sunken. Clematis
Had wound strings round and round it like a bundle.
What held it, though, on one side was a tree
Still growing, and on one a stake and prop,
These latter about to fall. I thought that only
Someone who lived in turning to fresh tasks
Could so forget his handiwork on which
He spent himself, the labor of his ax,
And leave it there far from a useful fireplace
To warm the frozen swamp as best it could
With the slow smokeless burning of decay.

"The Wood-Pile" is thoroughly typical of many of Frost's mature nature poems. At once narrative and dramatic, the poem seems astonishingly clear even on first encounter. There at its center are the solitary speaker, a familiar figure, and his story, this one—like Frost's others—told in the inevitably simple, straightforward and calm, almost laconic language that characterizes dozens of Frost's other narrative lines. There is the typical stripped minimum of physical action—walking. Here, as elsewhere, the walking is seemingly aimless, has no manifest destination: it is an epitome of Frost's conviction that "Calculation is usually no part in the first step of any walk" (402). But, again as elsewhere, however much the walking appears to lack direction, it is clearly mysterious in that it radiates a high sense of personal destiny. "Every poem," Frost once remarked, "is an epitome of the great predicament; a figure of the will braving alien entanglements" (401). The speaker simply appears in our field of vision and—to use Yvor Winters' negative criticism in a positive way—seems to be "spiritually drifting." There is the familiar winter landscape, bleak, desolate, initially amorphous and forbidding. There is the appearance of the small bird and the speaker's curious pretense of talking with such creatures. There is the woodpile itself, like the tuft of flowers, the mending wall, the road not taken, the west-running brook, so enigmatically and hypnotically *there*. And there is the almost dreamlike state of meditation it induces, in some ways calling to mind the sleepy vision of "After Apple-Picking." Finally, there is what Frost called "the vocal imagination," the speaker's voice, his style: that particular quality of sound "which indicates how the writer takes himself and what he is saying..., the way he carries himself toward his ideas and deeds" (403). Frost once joked: "Let the sound of [Robert Louis] Stevenson go through your mind empty and you will realize that he never took himself other than as an amusement. Do the same with Swinburne and you will see that he took himself as a wonder" (298). In "The Wood-Pile" Frost clearly takes himself neither simply as an amusement nor as a wonder but as both.

On another level of its structure, beneath the relaxed surface of the language, the poem progresses by way of a series, almost a system, of oppositions, ambiguities, and contrarieties that might be called Hawthornian. "In order to know where we are," Frost has noted, "we must know opposites." [3] The "frozen swamp" is the first obvious instance of this characteristic structural phenomenon and suggests immediately multiple ambiguities in the external landscape: hardness-softness, cold-heat, solidity-fluidity, stability-instability, a surface level and a dimension—as yet untouched but present—beneath the surface. All this is registered against the blankness, the flatness of the minimally specified "one gray day." In the first line, then, we have concentrated an action, a place, a time. There is also a typically Frostian subtlety in the simple prepositions surrounding the action and thus wrapping it in still another operative ambiguity: "Out walking in"—the phrase is so solidly idiomatic, so much a mode of common speech, that all its powers of suggestion (namely, the juxtaposition of externality and internality) are playfully hidden, buried beneath the plainness of the words themselves. This particular tension is elaborated in the relationships between lines 1 and 2. Whereas the first line addresses itself to a continuous physical action and the external landscape, the second is concerned with a pause and a turning inward to the mind of the persona and his fearful response to that landscape. The speaker's decision to "turn back" emphasizes the sharp disjunction existing between this particular mind and this particular reality. The fear and confusion are isolated only momentarily, however, since they are immediately answered to by the courage of the counter-resolution of line 3. There, as the grammatical shift from "I" to "we" signifies, it is not Frost's purpose to annihilate the fear but to use it: the fear and the courage, the will to proceed and the hesitancy to do it, now almost formally define two dimensions of the persona. He has become at once his own reassuring guide and cautious initiate. And since it is the "we" who shall see, what is to be discovered will be informed by both. Still another ironic opposition is in Frost's use of the negative qualifier "No" to decisively introduce the positive affirmation of "going on" and thus to undermine the negative preference to "turn back." It is as if there is in the persona's emotions a mathematical logic in which two negatives interpenetrate to form a positive. The playful blending of "amusement" and "wonder" here illustrates what Reuben Brower calls Frost's "delight of saying the ordinary thing and discovering that it is art." [4]

We might at this juncture turn back to ask what gives rise to the fear in the first place. The question leads back to that "frozen swamp" and to the realization that the place is forbidding and inscrutable because it suggests nature in its least regenerate aspects. It is essentially primordial, totally unformed. Hinting as it does at a sweeping geological sense of time and age, it provides another, prehistoric tension with the fragile minuteness and ephemerality of the mere "one gray day."

In line 4 the speaker, going on, now, as it were, gives himself to the place. He is no longer "out" altogether but in some sense "in." The distance between mind and reality is now diminished even to the point of tactile intimacy implied in the word "held." He who would see submits willingly to being acted upon by the still undefined force within that which he would see. But the explicit oppositions and tensions persist: in the "now" and the "then," the one foot and the implied other, the "here" and the "Somewhere else." Even the syntax displays similarly precarious balances: "The hard snow held me" announces a categorical, absolute condition, and points to a sureness of footing and, concomitantly, an intellectual and emotional security. But the line moves on by way of a concessive clause that turns back on the earlier statement and attaches exceptional circumstances contrary to it. The sentence contains elaborated images of impenetrability and penetrability that are quietly paradoxical because of the conditions they are associated with. The impenetrability suggests sureness and constancy, the penetrability doubt and instability, even danger. What normally seem to be positive and negative connotations are equally mixed in each of these syntactical units, then, and they are joined in fact by a conjunction—"save"—whose playful punning transforms the usual logic of "except" and suggests that the categories of positive and negative have again interpenetrated. To see is, of course, to penetrate into the truth or meaning of a phenomenon or thing. In a Frost poem, however, to see is always to know that there is a point at which the thing to be seen resists and defies penetrability, a point of its being beyond which it is alas unknowable. "The Wood-Pile," like "Neither Out Far nor In Deep," is from this angle a metaphor about the process of penetration and the ultimate limits of that process: a metaphor about the process of the interpenetration of him who sees and that which is seen. It is at once, like so much of Hawthorne's work, an exploration into the wilderness and into the self, a journey at once out and in.

What the persona sees in lines 5 to 9 is merely a "view," since he has as yet penetrated very little—only enough, in fact, to be confronted with an overwhelmingly confusing verticality. He sees merely one-dimensional lines without shape, and the measure of his plight is that he cannot find a language to give a name to the place. But, although he is thus suspended between his desire for certainty and the fact of his fearful uncertainty, his uneasiness and doubt are now informed by his awareness of them. Trying to solve the riddle of the landscape, he comes to know something not so much about that landscape as about himself. He is, he says, "just far from home." If "just" points up the severe, even terrifying, limits of his knowledge at this point of the process, it also simultaneously emphasizes his diminished anxiety regarding those limits. The word at once generates a sense of terror and dispels it. The effect is almost that the terrors of "homelessness," of being lost in undifferentiated space, comprise a condition the speaker has known before and finds so persistent and multifarious as to demand his constant re-engagement.

The small bird now appears, and in a way that seems equally fortuitous and gratuitous. The speaker responds immediately by recognizing it as a dramatic projection of his own fearfulness. In the following lines, the bird's activity adds a horizontal dimension to the speaker's growing spatial consciousness; and, giving the scene intersecting lines, if not shape, it permits the speaker to have for the first time a perspective. Again, the process moves by way of the artful opposition between bird and tree and the little joke by which physical laws seem overturned: the bird "puts" a tree—that is, assigns it a specific material place—between itself and the speaker. The bird is clearly what the speaker has come so far to know best, and he comes to know it by way of what he has previously come to know about himself. As Frost's deliberately confusing pronoun references in lines 12 and 13 imply, the speaker intimately identifies with the bird at the same time he tries to assert his superiority to it. The condition that allows him this intimacy, however, is his physical separation from the bird, marked by the one tree standing between subject and object. The tree, like the mending wall, signifies one of those barriers without which the world would, for Frost, not make sense. The speaker's teasing identification with the bird leads to his awareness of himself as the source of the bird's fearfulness; and this, in turn, clarifies his own relationship with the larger, unredeemed scene, the source of his own fear, which is thus brought further under the control of consciousness. The speaker's awareness is now many-layered, and he now has words for what is at stake. The bird's white tail feather is, of course, that by which he is what he is: it is the unmistakable mark of his irreducible identity and, paradoxically, the sign of his surrender. His fear of its loss turns back on and elucidates the speaker's recognition of his homelessness. "Home" is now understood to mean that point in space where one is at ease, where the self "belongs," where identity is safe.

Counterbalancing the gradual emergence of clarity and shape in the landscape is the gradually emerging personality of the speaker: at every stage of the poem, we know the speaker only to that extent which the speaker himself has come to know and understand the landscape. Frost once remarked that if the style of a poem "is with outer seriousness, it must be with inner humor. If it is with outer humor, it must be with inner seriousness. Neither one alone without the other under it will do" (351). The cautious sobriety and reserve within the vocal imagination as it initially addressed the outer terror are now cut across by a tone of humorous self-parody as the speaker engages in reflection. Now he can indulge in the quietly extravagant joke of a pathetic fallacy—"like one who takes/ Everything said as personal to himself." Now too, however, the speaker's enlarged awareness and confidence are juxtaposed to, and measured by, his own self-deception. The speaker is himself deceived in thinking that the way for the bird to become "undeceived" is simply to flee the scene—to go "the way I might have gone." The bird, given free play, does not flee but, willing to get lost in order, apparently, to find itself, goes behind the woodpile. He seeks it out as a refuge, a home, in a final effort to discover and preserve identity in this place. Bird and man now embrace the woodpile, bind it by both courage and fear; and what the speaker sees there is conditioned, then, by his awareness of the bird on the opposite side. The logic of this perceptual symmetry, of course, is that the pile of wood has consolations to offer the man—consolations against the threat of formlessness, mindlessness, absence of order. And consolations there are indeed, in the lovely wholeness, the solid three-dimensionality of the woodpile. Here is, at last, the physical universe filled out in shapely and substantial form, caught in a moment of exacting perception that sees into it with a clarity and completeness incorporating at once modes of analysis and synthesis, modes of physical labor and intellectual love: "It was a cord of maple, cut and split/And piled—and measured, four by four by eight." The moment of perception constitutes a symbolic reenactment of the original building of the woodpile. The cutting and splitting and piling refer us simultaneously to the *fact* of the pile of wood and to that *process* by which it came to be. The speaker imaginatively duplicates all of the separate, divisible stages of the process of physical activity and then, in an evaluative act of measuring, finds a language—"four by four by eight"—that expresses perfectly the fact of its fully unitary and integrated wholeness of being. Process and fact, energy and form, coalesce and become one in a single continuous act of perception, and in that act the courage and fear have themselves been transformed into love and meditative forgetfulness.

The moment is a perfect illustration of Frost's distinction between what it means to believe in things and what it means, on the other hand, to believe things in (339). The latter is the special task of him who would be poet and person. In this symbolic reenactment, the speaker believes into existence an entity which was potentially there in the emerging but partial lines of the earlier stages of his journey inward. The woodpile, according to Frost's poetic theory, had its beginnings "in something more felt than known" (339). While in one sense, then, the speaker only "reveals" and "discovers" the wood-pile, in another he can be said to have "made" it. We have here what William James, in "Humanism and Truth," called a quasi-paradox: "A fact virtually pre-exists when every condition of its realization save one is already there. In this case the condition lacking is the act of the counting and comparing mind.... Undeniably something comes by the counting that was not there before. And yet that some-thing was *always true*. In one sense you create it, and in another sense you *find* it." [5]

Like the white tail feather, the woodpile is totally singular. It is a far larger, more elaborate and complex symbol of individual form and identity. In its four-by-four-by-eightness there is a marvellous solidity as well as form, a substantiality that makes it not only pal-pable but, at least initially, permanent. In its apparent permanence it has a homeostatic capacity that heroically confronts the ephem-eral and formless flux of the entropic environment. But just as soon as the speaker has become aware of its shape and form—its *thereness* —he is compelled, notice, to describe it in terms of what is *not* there: "And not another like it could I see." Thus, in the very process of celebrating the magnificence of its being, he uses language, has a per-ception, that points ironically to a sad sense of the diminishedness of things. Frost was himself fascinated by what he called "carrying numbers into the realm of space and at the same time into the realm of time" (333). In the same essay, he later quotes Einstein that "In the neighborhood of matter space is something like curved" (334). What Frost has done in "making his count" of the woodpile's dimen-sions is to carry those numbers into time, and in doing so he has transformed the straightness and angularity of the landscape into curves, into roundness and sphericity. This transformation is initially hinted at, I think, in the multiple suggestiveness of "cord," which is not only the specific name given to 128 cubic feet of fuel wood but, here, a pun on the mathematical term denoting a straight line which joins two points on an arc or curve. The change wrought in the speaker's perception of the scene is a brilliant poetic realization of Frost's conviction that "We are what we are by elimination and by deflection from the straight line." [6]

Once he exists in a definitively three-dimensional physical universe, the speaker muses on the fourth dimension in trying to penetrate further into the meaning of the physical fact. Immediately, he meditates on—has a creative vision about—what is not there, what is quintessentially impalpable and increasingly indefinite, what is further and further back in time and of completely mysterious origin. Whereas the physical journey moves forward in space, its ultimate outcome is an inward journey, a meditation, which is a heightened mode of "turning back from here," an action no longer informed by fear alone. The implied and emergent curves of the woodpile the speaker's vision now makes explicit in the imagined loops of the runner tracks he cannot see; and these imagined curves in turn lead the speaker back into an awareness of the actual curved lines explicit in the woodpile itself: the warping bark, the sunkenness, the strings of clematis circling round and round. But the Hawthornian tensions and polarities, of which those curves are the ultimate expression, persist: between the imagined facts and the observable realities, in the references to different points in time, between the one side and the other, between what the clematis had done, what the tree is still doing, what the stake and prop are about to do. All these details catch, in a single, powerful image, a moment of process in which exquisite physical and spiritual form and imminent formlessness, growth and decay, stasis and flux fully interpenetrate, the implications of each participating in and giving value to the other. Now, although the speaker is completely at home in this place, his meditation does not lead to any reassuring consolation or benevolent resolution that would cancel these tensions and contrarieties; instead, it reaffirms and heightens them. For if the speaker's turning inward to the mind is a turning outward to the imagined identity of the woodcutter, and thus implies a consoling movement from solitude to human relationship, it also leads simultaneously to the speaker's recognition of his still distant separation from that imagined home with the "useful fireplace." The very process by which the speaker, along with the frozen swamp, has been warmed by the wood-cutter's selfless and forgetful act of love issues in no comfortable, Emersonian notion of transcendent compensation. The condition of distance, of being "far from home," still attaches, as does the implied need to continually "turn to fresh tasks." Space and time have indeed been redeemed within the process of the speaker's vision to the extent that the woodpile as fact and process—as seemingly senseless material waste—is now endowed with a poignant significance and spiritual usefulness. But the implications of that redemption presuppose the necessity of continual other ones at different times, in different places. Seeing the woodpile in all its magnificence, the speaker sees also that its heat warms "only as best it could." And while there are duration, clarity, and beauty in the "slow, smokeless burning," they are apprehended in a vision that focuses on the inexorable fact of decay. The woodpile and the loving vision it induces only momentarily stay the confusion of a universe moving toward nothingness.

The condition of lostness, of homelessness, is not finally overcome; we are, at the end, still more aware of tensions than of unities. Whatever triumph there is lies in the fact that homelessness has now been defined and formalized by intelligence and love, by the process of growing awareness by which the woodpile and the poem have simultaneously come to be. In one sense, Frost himself provides the best gloss on the way the poem works when he says that "it makes us remember what we didn't know we knew" (394). He would agree with William James, I think, that "All homes are in finite experience" and that "finite experience as such is homeless." [7] The process of the poem does not take us from an attitude of fearful doubt to one of certainty in the immutable. Instead, it begins with a *felt* doubt that arises out of the formless inscrutability of a new place and takes us to an affirmation of that doubt, which, now formalized, persists even after the loveliest but inevitably mutable forms of that place are fully understood. Frost's persona cannot stay there at the woodpile: his existence, it is clear, presupposes the necessity of perpetually walking on to an endless series of other new places equally unformed.

What he walks on to, conscious all the while of the roads he does not take, is most often, as Frost says in "Directive," "a house that is no more a house/Upon a farm that is no more a farm/... in a town that is no more a town."

II

Although there are difficulties in dating exactly Frost's early work, there is no question that "The Wood-Pile" is one of the first poems to exhibit most of those elements that can be said to comprise his mature style. And while it would be a mistake to claim that those elements share an exclusive similarity with what we recognize as Hawthorne's typical manner, there is every reason to believe that Frost saw in Hawthorne's work, no less than in the work of other writers, important grist for his mill. Frost's great admiration for Hawthorne—his sense of "Hawthorne right"—stemmed from his purposeful study of the romancer. Indeed, the following passage from *The American Notebooks*, dated September 7, 1850, begins to suggest strongly that Hawthorne's work had a crucial importance for Frost's development:

In a wood, a heap or pile of logs and sticks, that had been cut for firewood, and piled up square, in order to be carted away to the house when convenience served,—or, rather, to be sledded in sleighing time. But the moss had accumulated on them, and leaves falling over them from year to year and decaying, a kind of soil had quite covered them, although the softened outline of the woodpile was perceptible in the green mound. It was perhaps fifty years—perhaps more—since the woodman had cut and piled those logs and sticks, intending them for his winter fires. But he probably needs no fire now. There was something strangely interesting in this circumstance. Imagine the long-dead woodman, and his long-dead wife and family, and the old man who was a little child when the wood was cut, coming back from their graves, and trying to make a fire with this mossy fuel.[8]

One is struck, first, by the obvious similarities between many of the details in the poem and the notebook entry and, secondly, by the strong possibility that other, superficially different, details in the notebooks had made their way into Frost's poem: for example, the

woodpile as a mounded, green grave and Hawthorne's Gothic speculation on the return of the family to the site. One is also struck, of
course, by how much more high drama Frost has in his poem and by
the ways in which he had clearly transformed those materials he
had made use of. Hawthorne's vague recognition of "something
strangely interesting in this circumstance" contrasts vividly with
Frost's fully achieved exploration of that idea in the poem. Frost's
own explanation of the uses to which he put books is instructive here:
"I'm afraid all I see in books and going around is ideas to emulate—
to try if I can't have the like of. The only thing that can disappoint
me in the head is my own failure to learn to make metaphor. My
ambition has been to have it said of me: He made a few connections." [9] In "The Wood-Pile" Frost had clearly succeeded in
creating his metaphor, and he had done so by making numerous connections from various notebook entries. Hawthorne's following remarks, dated February 12, [1851], occur several pages later in the
Notebooks:

A walk across the lake. A heavy rain, some days ago, has melted a good
deal of the snow on the intervening descent between our house and the
lake; but many drifts, depths, and levels yet remain; and there is a frozen
crust, sufficient to bear a man's weight, and very slippery....Bare, brown
spaces of grass here and there, but still so infrequent as only to diversify
the scene a little..., spaces where the snow was more imperfectly dis-
solved than elsewhere; little crackling spots, where a thin surface of ice,
over the real mass, crumples beneath one's foot; the track of a line of
footsteps, most of them vaguely formed, but some quite perfectly, where
a person passed across the lake while its surface was in a state of slush, but
which are now as hard as adamant, and remind one of the traces discovered by geologists in rocks that hardened thousands of ages ago. It
seems as if the person passed when the lake was in an intermediate state
between ice and water. (398–99)

Two pages later, there is this entry of February 18:

The lake is still of adamantine substance, but all round the borders there
is a watery margin, altogether strewed or covered with thick and broken
ice, so that I could not venture on it.... A chickadee was calling in the
woods yesterday,—the only small bird I have taken note of yet. (401)

Hawthorne is absorbed, in these entries, with the phenomena of the changing seasons. There are numerous images of death, decay, and dormancy in the February passages, and these are interspersed with remarks about the strangeness of the winter's beauty. In his March 31st entry, Hawthorne notes: "Nevertheless, the general impression is of life, not death. One feels that a new season has begun" (404–405). Taken together, these passages, fragmentary as they are, generate a sense of that sort of intense focus on the essential ambiguity of things which we think of as the signature of Hawthorne's highest art.

Frost, I believe, had read *The American Notebooks* very carefully —carefully enough to synthesize and reshape not only the details of the woodpile itself, but nuances and aspects of Hawthorne's basic intellectual posture, from these various entries within a dozen pages of one another. Frost not only found his woodpile started for him there; he found a preliminary sketch of his frozen swamp—with its different depths, its treacherous footing, its undiversified scene—as well as a sense of the distance between home and swamp. I suspect he even found his little bird there—almost certainly a junko—which he was poetically wise enough to leave nameless. Hawthorne's chickadee, in its size, its basic coloring, and especially its timid, nervous behavior, is a perfect prototype for Frost's bird.

"The Wood-Pile" is one of the poems Frost wrote while in England from 1912 to 1915. It is likely, I think, that Frost would have felt there a deep New England kinship with the romancer, and, perhaps feeling far from home himself, he may have found Hawthorne's notebooks a way of getting into touch again with the New England scene. Lending credence to such a possibility is the fact that Frost would use Emerson's and Thoreau's works in much the same way. "A Drumlin Woodchuck," for example, is a meditation on a theme from *Walden*, and, as Reuben Brower has pointed out, "Neither Out Far nor In Deep" is a reworking of a brief paragraph in Emerson's journals.[10] In addition, there is evidence that one of the central sources Frost drew on for "Desert Places" is Chapter XVIII of *The Scarlet Letter*, where Hawthorne writes that Hester's "intellect and heart had their home, as it were, in desert places." [11] And then there is Frost's own crusty confession that it was his habit to make such deliberate borrowings. In a commencement address given at Dartmouth, he indulged himself in a tirade against the ideal of speed reading and spoke of the need for the reader to give himself over completely to his books: "I'm going to tell you," he said, "that every single one of my poems is probably one of these adaptations that I've made. I've taken whatever you give me and made it what I want it to be. That's what every one of the poems is" (420–21). The fact that there are so many close parallels between "The Wood-Pile" and the notebook entries and the fact that Frost was, to a larger extent than is commonly thought, a self-declared "book poet" lead to the conclusion that he could not have written this particular poem in this particular way without first having absorbed those Hawthorne notes. In writing "The Wood-Pile," Frost had followed a version of the advice he gave to a young poet, Charles Foster: "Make a business for a while of having ideas. You might well have ten or a dozen this winter. . . . Emerson built his essays out of note-book ideas like that" (319). In that poem, as in later ones, Frost, using Hawthorne's "note-book ideas," had indeed "made a few connections," had created one of his "adaptations," a fully integrated metaphor all his own.

But there is still the larger—ultimately more interesting—question of the significance of the relationship between Hawthorne and Frost in what might be called the history of consciousness. Why is it that, for Frost, Hawthorne is so "right"? I would like to sketch briefly two related ways in which Hawthorne might be said to be a central influence on Frost and to share genuine affinities with him. Most critics agree that it was in his second collection that Frost discovered the basic terms of his familiar dramatic mode. *North of Boston* differs from *A Boy's Will* in that it owes much less to the manner of the Wordsworthian lyric. What Frost had found was new resonances in his "vocal imagination." The collection was subtitled "A Book of People," and one of the added dimensions of the Frostian voice lay in his ability to capture the patterns and rhythms of country speech in dialogues. That Hawthorne had absolutely nothing to do with this aspect of Frost's growth is obvious: all of Hawthorne's characters speak in stiffly formal "literary" language. But Frost had also hit upon new tones in his central poetic voice: more definitively American tones which combined more fully the possibilities of "outer seriousness" and "inner humor," "inner seriousness" and "outer humor." He discovered what he later called "the still small voice:" "the still small voice," he said, "is the only one I'm susceptible to" (317). And it is here that Hawthorne had much to offer. The Hawthornian dimension of the Frostian voice can be heard when that typical qualifying tone of reserve, light wit, and half-serious self-parody cuts across the weighty, expansive, and visionary nuances of utterance. The effect in the styles of both writers involves a constant and at times gentle skepticism, a genial irony, often focusing on the very authenticity of the fictional and poetic processes themselves. There is at the bottom of that ironic tone a strain of the antipoetic in both Hawthorne and Frost, a need to test the limits of art and the nature of its relationship with reality. Such testing Hawthorne repeatedly carried on in his prefaces, and he seems often to have been compelled to make it the chief donnée of his fiction. When Hawthorne, at the end of, say, "My Kinsman, Major Molineux," calls upon the child's fairy-tale man-in-the-moon, he is testing those limits much as does Frost when, at the end of "For Once, Then, Something," he audaciously juxtaposes to "Truth" a mere "pebble of quartz" and dares to imply that they are of equal value.

I have said that there is in all this a distinctly, if not exclusively, American tone. The irony common to Hawthorne and Frost stems from an urge to express the deepest matters in the form of a quiet joke and has many of its roots in the American condition of homelessness. It was Henry James, in his study of Hawthorne, who first suggested the relationship between that condition and the emergence of an indigenous American style. Hawthorne, as James saw him—and as Hawthorne himself often thought—lacked the raw materials necessary to the writer of fiction; and James goes on to enumerate "the items of high civilization" necessary for the novelist but "absent from the texture of American life." Many of those items are homes—there are "no palaces, no castles, nor manors, nor old country-houses, nor parsonages, nor thatched cottages, nor ivied ruins." [12] What James is getting at is the absence of home in the largest sense, the lack of a defined, reliable institutionalized civilization that clearly exists prior to the individual. He goes on to say that, though these things are left out, "The American knows that a good deal remains

... that is his secret, his joke, as one may say. It would be cruel, in this terrible denudation, to deny him the consolation of his national gift, that 'American humour' " (56). The humor, he later implies, is generated by the fact that in America "The individual counts for more" because "his standards are [not] fixed by the general consent of the society in which he lives" (61).

Now all of Hawthorne's New England contemporaries responded, of course, to this condition of homelessness. Emerson, especially in his early essays, invariably responded with a rapturous idealism, hitching his wagon to a star and intoning with Olympian confidence: "Build therefore your own world." His was the expansive voice— expansive but usually unironic and rarely humorous—that played a major role in informing one register of Frost's tone. Frost's praise of Emerson's "Uriel" as "the greatest Western poem yet" is well known, but Frost recognized a crucial difference between his poetry and Emerson's. Commenting on Emerson's line, "Unit and universe are round," Frost remarked: "Another poem could be made from that, to the effect that ideally in thought only is a circle round. In practice, in nature, the circle becomes an oval. As a circle it has one center—Good. As an oval it has two centers—Good and Evil." [13] The four-by-four-by-eightness of Frost's woodpile might be said to constitute the figure of the poem Frost would have made from "Uriel." The dimensions of the woodpile suggest the oval, not the circle, and they suggest Hawthorne, not Emerson. That issue of homelessness was never out of Frost's mind. He once listed *Robinson Crusoe* as a very favorite book, saying, "I never tire of being shown how the limited can make snug in the limitless" (355). And he ranked just below that book Thoreau's *Walden*: "Crusoe was cast away; Thoreau was self-cast away. Both found themselves sufficient." Thoreau's response to homelessness was, as our critical commonplace has it, to test Emersonian idealism by confronting the meannesses of real life at Walden, and there is in his response an authentic American tone. But, although Frost found Thoreau's modulations equal to many of his own purposes, there is in the Thoreauvian voice an ultimate confidence in the solid bottom's being everywhere, in the making snug in the limitless, that Frost often questions and goes beyond. If Thoreau, unlike Emerson, was often capable of humor, Frost's concept of humor as "the beginning of doubt" is distinctly un-Thoreauvian. As "The Wood-Pile," "Desert Places," "An Old Man's Winter's Night"—to name but a few—suggest, Frost was, like Hawthorne, interested in confronting the bleaker question of the ultimate impossibility of satisfactorily making snug, of ever finally overcoming homelessness.

Hawthorne was, in his private life, plagued, on the one hand, by a strong desire to establish a home for himself and his family and, on the other, by a restlessness that kept him moving constantly from place to place. The man who had written of the urgent and curious home-feeling he had felt for Salem complained shortly before his death that it is foolish "for mortal man to do anything more than pitch a tent." [14] His fiction, from first to last, is permeated with house images, and he seems to have spent his creative energies attempting to render dramatically a happily making snug. One thinks of Hester, isolated in her cottage, equidistant from village, wilderness, and ocean alike and belonging to none; of Robin Molineux, bereft of his past home in the wilderness and his future home in the city; of young Goodman Brown who, though he walks out of the midnight forest, can never really go home again; of poor Mrs. Wakefield, whose husband just picks up and walks away for twenty years for no earthly reason; of Roger Malvin, journeying to a new home in the wilderness only to create there instead the grave of his only son; of Miles Coverdale, cast out into a driving snow or perched Paul Pry-like in his tree branch; of Peter Goldthwaite, who tears down his ancestral home in a vain effort to find a fortune with which to build his dream house; of the guilt-stained house with seven gables; of the desperate yearnings which the heroes of the unfinished fragments have for "their old home" in England, yearnings which Hawthorne clearly found artistically unmanageable. Nearly all of Hawthorne's characters are psychic wanderers, people literally far from worldly or spiritual homes.

But if images of ungraspable homes are one of the chief données of Hawthorne's fiction, the house is also the Hawthornian metaphor for fiction itself, for the very shape and possibility of fiction. In his prefaces he tried repeatedly to create a home for art in "a neutral territory, somewhere between the real world and fairy-land, where the Actual and the Imaginary may meet, and each imbue itself with the other." That he was not easy with this sort of definition is attested to by his sense of disappointment and frustration with his work and his wish that he could write realistic novels. "When we see how little we can express," he lamented, "it is a wonder that any man ever takes up pen a second time." He continually questioned the legitimacy of this "neutral territory." Desiring on the one hand to build his own house of fiction, he found himself rejecting on the other the very possibility of doing so. Thus the condition of homelessness is not only a central theme in Hawthorne's art: it is the source of that doubt he had about his ability to create fiction. The battle he had to fight, then—given the condition of homelessness, this absence of civilization which James speaks of—was not simply to create fiction but, as Terence Martin has said, "to create the conditions of fiction." [15] Hawthorne's style is that of the "still small voice" which mediates between a pragmatically minded audience and an imaginative fictionality that the voice itself often has difficulty sustaining belief in. As Hawthorne said in "The Artist of the Beautiful," "Ideals, which grow up within the imagination and appear so lovely to it and of a value beyond whatever men call valuable, are exposed to be shattered and annihilated by contact with the practical. It is requisite for the ideal artist to possess a force of character that seems hardly compatible with its delicacy; he must keep faith in himself while the incredulous world assails him with its utter disbelief." Many of Hawthorne's energies were burned up in his efforts to protect the imaginary from such shattering contact with the actual, exhausted in his attempts to create convincingly real homes in the realm of romance when sharing his audience's disbelief in that possibility. In the process, his fiction often suffers from an incompleteness.

Now Frost, as I see him, responds most characteristically to the condition of homelessness on Hawthorne's level, the level of its most besetting trials. Whereas Hawthorne often found his art compromised by his uneasiness about the disjunction between the Actual and the Imaginary, Frost, as his achievement in "The Wood-Pile" suggests, engaged the question so as to savor these conflicts between the imagination and the real. The largest part of the reason he could do so lay, unquestionably, in his own talent and temperament; but part of the reason lay in the fact that Hawthorne, like the wood-cutter of Frost's poem, had gone into the woods before him, had hacked and hewed his way through the wilderness and discovered something of what woodpiles are made of and how they are made. In doing so, Hawthorne helped create for Frost that "rich fund of suggestion" demanded for a genuinely American poetry which, as James pointed out, no one had managed to create for Hawthorne. "The Wood-Pile," then—and its relationship with Hawthorne's *American Notebooks*—has a special place in our literary history and in the development of an American consciousness. Using as his "germ" Hawthorne's journal entries and transforming for his own purposes qualities in Hawthorne's vocal imagination, Frost, in an early and consummate work of art, has redeemed some part of that incompleteness we have come to sense in much of Hawthorne's work. In doing so, Frost discovered—or discovered once more—many of the essential terms of his mature style. And he discovered also a livelier, subtler, more powerful way of saying what he had already said bluntly in "The Tuft of Flowers"—that "Men work together.../Whether they work together or apart."

Notes to *Hawthorne and Frost: The Making of a Poem* by J. DONALD CROWLEY

1. *Selected Letters of Robert Frost*, ed. Lawrance Thompson (New York: Holt, Rinehart and Winston, 1964), 553.

2. *Robert Frost: Poetry and Prose*, ed. Edward C. Lathem and Lawrance Thompson (New York: Holt, Rinehart and Winston, 1972), 332. Unless otherwise noted, all further citations of Frost's prose are to this edition, and page references are given in the text.

3. Quoted in Lawrance Thompson, *Robert Frost: The Years of Triumph, 1915–1938* (New York: Holt, Rinehart and Winston, 1970), 425.

4. Reuben A. Brower, *The Poetry of Robert Frost: Constellations of Intention* (New York: Oxford University Press, 1963), 11.

5. William James, *The Meaning of Truth* (New York: Longmans, Green, and Co., 1909), 93–94.

6. *The Letters of Robert Frost to Louis Untermeyer* ed. Louis Untermeyer (New York: Holt, Rinehart and Winston, 1963), 189.

7. William James, *Pragmatism: A New Name For Some Old Ways Of Thinking* (Longmans, Green, and Co., 1907), 260.

8. *The Complete Works of Nathaniel Hawthorne* (Cambridge, Mass.: Houghton Mifflin & Co., 1883), IX, 392–93. This is, of course, the edition of *The American Notebooks* that Frost would have had access to.

9. *The Letters of Robert Frost to Louis Untermeyer*, 189.

10. Brower, *The Poetry of Robert Frost*, 150.

11. James Ellis, "Frost's 'Desert Places' and Hawthorne," *The English Record*,

XV (April 1965), 15–17. For two other analyses of the relationship between Hawthorne's romance and Frost's poem, see the essays of Edward Stone and A. J. von Frank in the present volume.

12. Henry James, *Hawthorne*, ed. Tony Tanner (New York: St. Martin's Press, 1967), 55.

13. *Selected Prose of Robert Frost*, ed. Hyde Cox and Edward Connery Lathem (New York: The Macmillan Company, 1968), 118.

14. *Letters of Hawthorne to W. D. Ticknor, 1851–1864* (Newark: Carteret Book Club, 1910), 115.

15. Terence Martin, *Nathaniel Hawthorne* (New Haven: College & University Press, 1965), 45.

METHOD
AND THEORY

The focus of these essays is central to any serious appreciation of Frost's achievement in poetry. Other sorts of critical scrutiny, those that are primarily biographical or interpretive, for instance, tend necessarily toward either a narrowing of inquiry that can become cryptic or a breadth of scope that risks vagueness and overgeneralization. And any explication, no matter how limited its objectives, requires a critical background well rooted in an understanding of both the larger poetic aesthetic of a given poet and the characteristic poetic techniques evidenced in the poet's canon.

These several essays endeavor to provide, individually and collectively, that very background. They examine, in varying depth and scope, the aesthetic "strategies" embodied in Robert Frost's poetry and the more particular "tactics" most commonly employed in Frost's poems.

Frank Lentricchia locates Frost with respect to modern aesthetic thought, pointing toward a satisfactory resolution of the seeming contradictions of Kantian Romanticism and "commonsense realism," two strains readily evident in Frost's poetry. This resolution, or "bridge," is defined as a philosophical and epistemological pragmatism, its source the thought of William James. Lentricchia's essay discusses the "landscape" of Frost's poems as a whole, isolating the coherence Frost creates in the relationship between the individual mind and the "real" world of objective phenomena. The essay illustrates its conclusions with an examination of Frost's "All Revelation."

George Monteiro discusses "Design," published in 1922, as a poetic archetype in the Frost canon. In the sonnet, Monteiro sees the paradigm of Frost's characteristic symbolism; and in the examination of this symbolism, the author indicates the "darker implications" manifest in the commonplace "argument from design," thus illuminating another aspect of the larger terms of Frost's "philosophy" and, hence, his aesthetic. This insight is developed through a close reading of the extensive and productive revisions Frost undertook in the creation of this remarkable sonnet.

Donald Greiner shifts the reader's attention to Frost's concept of just what "metaphor" is, and to how this concept can be seen as significantly operative in the poet's canon. Greiner goes on to discuss the relationship that, in the case of Frost and his audience, must necessarily exist between poet and reader. Drawing on Frost's own critical essays, Greiner explores the particular consistency of metaphor in the canon.

Lewis Miller contends that a dramatic structure united the contents of Frost's first book of poems. The tangibility of this structure is seen as a function of the progressive development, in dramatic contexts, of the various personae in the poems in this volume. Miller finds here a "personal" voice unlike the more conventional personae in the later poems. Still, the author finds significant continuity between the earliest and the latest work in the body of Frost's poetry.

The matter of continuity and wholeness in Frost's canon is treated by Stephen Warner. He closely examines Frost's final volume, *In The Clearing*, centering his discussion around the poem "Kitty Hawk," which he sees as providing the volume's essential structure. From his reading of this and other major poems in the book, and by cross reference with many of the important earlier poems, Warner argues for Frost's affirmation of the successful completion of his poetic intentions, as announced in his earliest work. Thus, the Frost canon is seen as describing a coherent aesthetic movement from beginning to end, a coherence of which Frost was manifestly conscious.

As we move from a consideration of theory per se to an overview of Frost's symbolism, to metaphor, to poetic personae, we have moved, however gradually, from a consideration of Frost's poetic "strategy" toward one of his poetic "tactics." This alteration in our frame of reference is largely only implicit in the essay by Sister Mary Finnegan, which treats a single long poem, "How Hard It Is to Keep from Being King. . . ." The poem, which appears in Frost's last volume, is examined as a covert statement of many of the mature poet's own political and literary principles. In addition, the author cites the poem's numerous sources and analogues for the purpose of demonstrating how Frost employed his version of the story as a vehicle by which the central characters might espouse the poet's own views.

The narrowing of critical scrutiny to the scope of "tactics" is made a good deal more explicit by Kenneth Rosen. He shows, with some particularity, the poet, guided by a coherent concept of literature and its audience, revising in the direction of greater brevity, compression, and focus.

Finally, Joseph Garrison comes to grips with a most precise (perhaps *the* most precise) problem of poetic "tactics," that of prosody, of prosodic control and manipulation. This essay's central contribution is its necessary reminder that the craft of poetry requires, after all, an *ear* (on the part of both poet and reader) rather than an *eye*. Garrison asserts the sharp limitations of purely philosophical or literary critical approaches to poetry. He illustrates the dramatic involvement of the personae in Frost's poems with the ostensible subjects of those poems. This observation leads to a significantly heightened awareness of the tonal dimension of the language of Frost's poems— including such particular matters as the poet's use of rhyme. In short, this essay, while incorporating larger elements like persona, treats the prosody of the poems that controls their meaning (excepting metrical prosody) with the aim of a *total* appreciation of the poet's achievement.

These essays exhibit a species of circularity, tracing a route that begins with a scrutiny of personae in the poetry of Robert Frost and ends (with however many significant differences) in a like consideration. As a whole, the essays following hereafter do provide an essential frame of critical reference within which narrower and more isolated studies may, do, and should properly operate.

G. W.

Robert Frost and Modern Literary Theory

FRANK LENTRICCHIA

I offer this essay as a theoretical prologue to the study of Robert Frost's poetry and poetics. My key figures and terms are familiar to students of post-Kantian literary theory, but their presence in a study of Frost is likely to appear odd to the many who, with J. Hillis Miller, tend to think that Robert Frost, wherever else he may be located, must most definitely be excluded from the company of the great modern poets. The single most damaging and question-begging critical opinion about Frost today has not been rigorously formulated; it is simply a widespread and casual assumption among the cognoscenti of literary theory that Frost cannot bear sustained theoretical contemplation. I am urging, on the contrary, that the difficulty in Frost's poetics is not absence of depth and modernist sophistication, but too much subtlety. Thus far (and surely to his credit) he has successfully eluded the easy generalizations of the schools.

I find that the most striking feature of Frost's thought is that it unifies what at the surface appear to be mutually exclusive dimensions of the modern literary mind. At the center of Frost's theory is the idea we find in Kant and the Romantics that our mental acts constitute the world of our experience. This notion of mind leads, of course, to the Romantic insistence that the poet's imagination is creative, that poems do not imitate a fully structured, antecedent reality, but rather inform chaos with structure and meaning. Yet, right alongside the Romanticism in Frost stands, paradoxically, the philosophy of common sense realism which posits a real world "out there," independent of our acts of perception. What I take to be the unifying principle in Frost's thinking has its basis in the pragmatism of William James. It is peculiarly the strength of James, that great philosophical mediator, to recognize a difficult real world which plays some determinative role in our lives, while also allowing for the possibility of the active consciousness to carve out, to a certain extent, the world of its desire.

315

Throughout the essay, I use "landscape" because I believe the concept holds together the divergent philosophical directions in Frost's poetics. The following passage from J. H. Van Den Berg, *The Phenomenological Approach to Psychiatry*, elucidates the definition of both "phenomenology" and "landscape": "The relationship of man and world is so profound, that it is an error to separate them. If we do, then man ceases to be man and the world to be the world. The world is no conglomeration of mere objects to be described in the language of physical science. The world is our home, our habitat, the materialization of our subjectivity. Who wants to become acquainted with man, should listen to the language spoken by the things in his existence. Who wants to describe man should make an analysis of the 'landscape' within which he demonstrates, explains and reveals himself." [1] "Landscape" suggests both a configuration of objects really there in nature and the phenomenological notion that any particular landscape is coherent because the mind of the artist makes it so. And, finally, I shall argue that the special qualities of coherence and the peculiar dominance of this or that object in the landscape are reflections of the artist's subjectivity, his deepest inclinations as a person. "Landscapes" are clues to the essential expression of the poet.

I

As my point of departure I choose Frost's strange and surprising poem "All Revelation":

> A head thrusts in as for the view,
> But where it is it thrusts in from
> Or what it is it thrusts into
> By that Cyb'laean avenue,
> And what can of its coming come,
>
> And whither it will be withdrawn,
> And what take hence or leave behind,
> These things the mind has pondered on
> A moment and still asking gone.
> Strange apparition of the mind!
>
> But the impervious geode
> Was entered, and its inner crust

Of crystals with a ray cathode
At every point and facet glowed
In answer to the mental thrust.

Eyes seeking the response of eyes
Bring out the stars, bring out the flowers,
Thus concentrating earth and skies
So none need be afraid of size.
All revelation has been ours.

Frost's subject in "All Revelation" is a common poetic and philosophical subject after Kant and the Romantics; it is strange and surprising only within the context of most traditional critical thought about Robert Frost. His subject is the act of the mind, the dynamic thrust of consciousness which he evokes in his metaphor of the cathode ray. Because the glowing effect inside the dark cavity of the geode originates from the action of the cathode ray itself, our vision of the geode's interior is inescapably mediated by our very instrument of scientific cognition. Frost shrewdly manages, however, with the first four words of the poem ("A head thrusts in") to suggest that the action of the cathode ray is figurative of human perception in general. In the third stanza the cathode ray emerges as a metaphor for the tendency of human consciousness to be excursive, to reach out, grasp, and shape its world. Frost's metaphoric expansion of the cathode ray is paralleled by his metaphoric expansion of the geode itself. Initially only a "stone nodule," the dictionary signification, Frost makes it mean by the end of the poem something like "our world," "external reality in general." Reuben Brower points out how precise Frost's metaphor is: "geode," in its etymological derivation, means "earth-like"; and this meaning is solidly re-inforced in the phrase "Cyb'laean avenue" (from Cybele, goddess of earth).[2]

One way of reading "All Revelation," then, is to see it as a poet's confronting of the leading idea of post-Kantian epistemology: that the mind is in some part constructive of the world. But there are other, complicating philosophical features in the poem which, once perceived, make a simple Kantian reading impossible to sustain. In the first stanza, for example, a number of questions are bracketed that many traditional philosophers make the central concern of their quests. For Frost, though, the question of the origins of mind

("Where it is it thrusts in from"); the question of the nature of the objective world considered as a thing in itself ("what it is it thrusts into"); and the question of the final and enduring value of the constitutive acts of the mind ("what can of its coming come")—all of these are questions that can be answered only provisionally, if at all. The suggestion is fairly strong, in fact, that when such questions are taken to the metaphysical level they have little pragmatic value for Frost: "These things the mind has pondered on/A moment and still asking gone."

The third and fourth stanzas of the poem particularize a rich philosophical paradox which is crucial to Frost's poems and poetics. By affirming contrary philosophical propositions—by insisting, on the one hand, that consciousness insinuates itself into the world, in part constituting that world (the geode *was* entered, the crystals do "answer" to the "mental thrust"); and by insisting as well (with realists) that the object is out there, independent of the mind (the geode is "impervious," to use Frost's word, and resists flagrant transformation)—Frost asks us to accept a position logically impure and ambiguous, but, for a poet, a position more exciting than what we usually find in either Kantian idealism or common sense realism. When in the last stanza Frost does question the value of this peculiar meeting of mind and object (this "strange apparition"), his answer is pragmatic. Stars and flowers, earth and skies, are there: but consciousness shapes its environment in order to concentrate "the immensities" ("So none need be afraid of size"), make them manageable for the self and thereby supply a psychic need to feel in our confrontations with nature that we are not hopelessly lost and adrift in a world that engulfs and drowns us. The constructive acts of consciousness make the world answer, as Nietzsche reminds us in his extension of Kant, to the desires of our emotional nature; and, specifically, in this poem, to the desire for human continuity and mutuality—"Eyes seeking the response of eyes"—within an inhuman environment.

"All revelation has been ours," reads the last line. It is we who reveal the world—as we desire to see it revealed—and by so doing we reveal the revealing self, we reveal ourselves. It is a characteristic of Frost's poetic stance that he is generally able to maintain the perilous balance which he achieves in "All Revelation," where he can somehow move in and out of the constituting mind. From the "inside" he achieves the kind of vision of a "better nature" demanded by his psychic needs—a vision which I would locate within his "redemptive" act of consciousness. From the "outside" he achieves an ironic self-consciousness which tells him that constitutive visions of a better na-ture are "apparitions" in the sense of "illusions." The act of ironic consciousness enables Frost to maintain his double vision, his skepti-cism, and his common sense which let nature be, as it is, and which are, as it turns out, often as psychically healthgiving as his more romantic acts of redemption.

II

On the American intellectual scene at the turn of the century there were basically three philosophical alternatives open to the young Robert Frost: the way of naturalism, which denied creativity and autonomy to human consciousness; the way of Josiah Royce's ideal-ism which guaranteed creative freedom but only within the context of metaphysics that a young, emerging modern mind could not ac-cept; or the via media of William James' pragmatism, which saved the autonomy of consciousness without asking, at the same time, for an acceptance of something like the early Emerson's view of nature and self. Those "redemptive" and "ironic" thrusts of consciousness embedded in "All Revelation," and repeatedly revealed in Frost's poems and urged by his poetics, are illuminatively reflected in the philosophy and psychology of James, who provided Frost with the chief intellectual adventure of his brief Harvard experience at the end of the 1890's.

What was probably basic to the appeal of James for Frost, and for a number of minds that came to maturity at the turn of our cen-tury, was that naturalistic toughness which kept James from floating out of time in search for resolutions to human dilemmas. Yet for all his storied hostility toward his Harvard colleague Josiah Royce and toward various idealistic positions, James showed faith—usually as-sociated with a post-Kantian view of mind—in the creative potential of human consciousness which would establish the priority of the human act even in time. James' concept of the freedom of the human act of mind liberates the self from the subjection to the shaping dictates of material reality that seemed demanded by later nineteenth-century naturalism. Joseph Blau has put it this way: James "was a man whose training in the hard-headedness of science never completely subdued his soft-hearted belief that men are not merely automata, strictly determined in a mechanical world, but are, at least to some degree, the makers and shapers of their world." [3] I would characterize the principle of James' philosophical mediation between the tough-mindedness of naturalism and the tender-mindedness of Royce's idealism as "aesthetic": a term by which I mean to suggest that he predicates a freely creative activity of mind. It is doubtful that James' frequent recourse to metaphors which characterize the molding power of consciousness as an artistic process could have failed to catch the eye of the young Robert Frost, then in his formative poetic years.

We might imagine that James' pragmatist reconciliation of scientific naturalism and Royce's idealism saved for Frost the truths of two distinct but not utterly incompatible philosophical traditions. From Royce's Kantian tradition James could accept the proposition that mind actively participates in the constitution of the world of fact without also accepting Royce's idealistic theory of timeless mental categories, or his theory of the Absolute, or his theory that evil is a privation, or his notion that the eternal and temporal orders are continuous. In James's philosophical modernism such issues were dead. And certainly they were dead for Frost. From those of tough-minded persuasion, James could accept the skeptical and common sense view of the world of objects as indeed "out there," as hard, dense, and often dangerous. It is a fundamental postulate of his discussion of the "stream of consciousness" that the objects of consciousness belong to a shareable and independent order. [4] Putting together the Kantian and realist views James could posit an objective world that is yet always caressed and bathed in human consciousness, receiving its final touches from the excursive tendency of consciousness to reach out beyond itself and by so doing insinuate its needs and shapes into the given world.

Though the full philosophical context of his existential phenomenology seems not relevant to Frost's poems, Jean Paul Sartre, who admired James deeply, eloquently articulated a perception of a peculiar duality within human experience which points us to the very center of Frost's poems and James' pragmatism.

Each of our perceptions is accompanied by the consciousness that human reality is a "revealer," that is, it is through human reality that "there is" being, or, to put it differently, that man is the means by which things are manifested. It is our presence in the world which multiplies relations. It is we who set up a relationship between this tree and that bit of sky. Thanks to us, that star which has been dead for millennia, that quarter moon, and that dark river are disclosed in the unity of a landscape.... With each of our acts, the world reveals to us a new face. But, if we know that we are directors of being, we also know that we are not its producers. If we turn away from this landscape, it will sink back; there is no one mad enough to think that it is going to be annihilated. It is we who shall be annihilated, and the earth will remain in its lethargy until another consciousness comes along to awaken it. Thus, to our inner certainty of being "revealers" is added that of being inessential in relation to the thing revealed.[5]

The epistemological emphasis in James which places a premium on the power of human subjectivity to "reveal" and "build out" the world of experience was consistently articulated in his various books. In the first volume of the *Principles of Psychology* (1890) he put it this way: "Out of what is in itself an indistinguishable, swarming *continuum*, devoid of distinction or emphasis, our senses make for us, by attending to this notion and ignoring that, a world full of contrasts, of sharp accents, of abrupt changes, of picturesque light and shade." [6] In another attempt to explain the nature of our perception of the world he said: "if we pass to its aesthetic department, our law is still more obvious.... The mind, in short, works on the data it receives very much as a sculptor works on his block of stone." [7] Still, even as he puts forth a view clearly post-Kantian in its suggestion of a creative function for consciousness, James, in his proto-existentialism, refused to accept Kant's importation into the act of knowledge of intersubjective categories of consciousness because he believed that prereflective consciousness was not transpersonal but irreducibly private and that its various constructions of the world flowed from a contingent subjectivity, the interests of an embodied self evolving through time and pressured by place. James separated himself from neo-Kantianism once and for all when he refused to take the notion of the constitutive power of consciousness to what he called the solipsistic conclusion of Kant and the neo-Kantians. Standing now with the tough-minded, he wrote that, for Kant, "Reality becomes a mere empty locus, or unknowable, the so-called Noumenon, the manifold of phenomenon is in the mind. We, on the contrary, put the Mutiplicity with the Reality outside...." [8] Without slighting the creative self, James affirms an insight of philosophical realism which the mainstream of post-Kantian idealism cannot affirm: that the pluralistic richness and particularity of the world stands recalcitrantly there, independent of mind, coercing our attention. The basic Kantian insight that man brings meaning into the world in a creative act has been transferred from a static idealistic setting—the eternal geometry of consciousness—to an existential one: the empirical self in a real world.

James envisions the drama of consciousness beginning when mind is confronted by a world which in its destructive unintelligibility seems to call out for a creative intelligence: "the visible surfaces of heaven and earth refuse to be brought by us into any intelligible unity at all. Every phenomenon that we would praise there exists cheek by jowl with some contrary phenomenon...." Such a vision of the face of reality is "poisonous," James concluded—ultimately fatal to psychological serenity—and therefore intolerable. The preservation of our "mental sanity" [9] is directly dependent upon the mind's power to transform its environment, to create for itself something not already there, to take that romantic leap beyond the function that traditional empiricism normally assigned to it. In short, the creative act of the mind in James' philosophy defines the self as the redeemer of brute fact and chaos into human value, pattern, and significance.

III

The crucial metaphor for the creative act of mind in James, that of the process of the sculptor,[10] is strikingly reflected in passages in Frost's letters: "My object is true form—is and always will be.... I fight to be allowed to sit cross-legged on the old flint pile and flake a lump into an artifact." Or, more explicitly still: "I thank the Lord for crudity which is rawness, which is raw material. . . . A real artist delights in roughness for what he can do to it. He's the brute who can knock the corners off the marble block. . . ." [11]

Sometimes this sculpting act of consciousness becomes literary in character as it avails itself to the poet's technique. Given our modern fascination for the amalgamatory, ordering powers of metaphor we cannot help recalling Johnson on Cowley, Coleridge on imagination, Eliot on Marvell, and on to the dearest concerns of New Critics and neo-New Critics, when we meet with this in James: "Purely objective truth, truth in whose establishment the function of giving human satisfaction in marrying previous parts of experience with newer parts played no role whatsoever, is nowhere to be found. . . . 'to be true' *means* only to perform this marriage-function." [12]

When James spoke of the "marriage-function" of consciousness he implicitly analogized the creative act of the mind to the dynamic, integrative process of metaphoric activity. For Frost, the metaphoric act of the mind, one of his favorite philosophical themes,[13] is basically a shaping and order-making process. "The only materialist," as he put it, "is the man who gets lost in his material without a gathering metaphor to throw it into shape and order. He is the lost soul." Metaphoric activity is indigenous, Frost frequently suggested, not only to poetic thinking but to all thinking: "Poetry is simply made of metaphor. So also is philosophy—and science, too, for that matter. . . ." One of his more extensive remarks on metaphor occurs in a letter to Louis Untermeyer:

. . . isn't it a poetical strangeness that while the world was going full blast on the Darwinian metaphors of evolution, survival values and the Devil take the hindmost, a polemical Jew in exile was working up the metaphor of the state's being like a family to displace them from mind and give us a new figure to live by. Marx had the strength not to be overawed by the metaphor in vogue. Life is like battle. But so is it also like shelter. . . . We are all toadies to the fashionable metaphor of the hour. Great is he who imposes the metaphor. . . . There are no logical steps from one to the other. There is no logical connection.[14]

The metaphoric integrations of great thinkers become (for ordinary men) the structures—the "world hypotheses," as Stephen Pepper put it—which condition and frame our understanding of the world of experience. The integrations of metaphor have immediate consequences for our lives. Though it is widely assumed that he evaded the pressures of modern philosophical thought, Frost's epistemological stand on metaphor is precisely parallel to the positions taken by Nietzsche and Hans Vaihinger, two philosophers whose thought is central to the history of modernism.

In a suggestive passage from *Pragmatism* James evokes his sense of human experience as "intolerably confused and gothic," "multitudinous beyond imagination, tangled, muddy, painful and perplexed." [15] The proper response to such a situation, his epistemological principles seem to suggest, is a creative act. In what is probably his fullest single statement on the nature and value of creative activity, the "Letter to *The Amherst Student*," Frost evokes a sense of reality close to what James had evoked in the passage just quoted. Reality in Frost is often projected in psychological language as a place of "excruciations," of "hugeness and confusion," of "black and utter chaos." And the proper response to it is the "figure of order," the "little form which I assert upon it." The order created by any act of consciousness for James and the order created by a specifically artistic act of consciousness for Frost yield similarly therapeutic values. James calls it an inner "ease, peace," and "rest," while Frost sees the process of aesthetic composition as "composing to the spirit," as a release from excruciations. [16] It is ultimately, however, a quality of Frost's tough-mindedness—he places the chaos and the confusion outside the mind, as James had in his criticism of Kant—which underscores the existential urgency of composition, the need for the form-making power of artistic consciousness to come into play.

IV

In the limited post-Kantianism of James and Frost ("limited" because injected with a powerful dose of common sense) consciousness confronts objects which sit out there in a shareable public world. Those objects are not created by the poet's imagination or by the mind of any other human being. We would not be surprised to find in the poems of a man who, say, spent most of his formative and mature years in the countryside of New Hampshire and Vermont, as did Robert Frost, and who shared Frost's literary and philosophical predilections, a recognizably common landscape. The consciousness of our hypothetical poet could have focused, presumably, upon a similar set of objects; his poetic landscape, therefore, would be marked by similar fixed features. So far the tenets of literary realism supply all of the critical procedures that we need. But if we assume that each consciousness is at some level utterly distinct and private—and that is a chief point of the psychology of James and of common sense—then we must assume, as well, that the objects of the perceived world will radiate a different, a special subjective presence, will cohere in ways contingent upon the particular consciousness which has apprehended those objects, and, in apprehending them, enveloped them with the interiority of the perceiving self. The act of perception which represents the landscape is affectively suffused. James supplies a good example for this point. The phenomenon of the "eternal recurrence of the common order," he says, "which so fills a Whitman with mystic satisfaction, is to a Schopenhauer . . . the feeling of an 'awful inner emptiness' from out of which he views it all." [17]

If the world's furniture is partially shaped and revealed by consciousness, then we can expect to find in the world evoked by a particular writer's ouevre that the furniture—or phenomena—of his imagined world will reveal, or radiate, his revealing consciousness, to extend the theoretical implications of the last line of "All Revelation." And now we have taken a considerable step beyond literary realism because we need a method which can help us grasp the intersection of literature's objective (or mimetic) dimension with its radically subjective (or expressive) one. Georges Poulet has summarized this matter quite clearly:

Every thought, to be sure, is a thought *of* something. It is turned invincibly towards the somewhere else, toward the outside. Issuing from itself, it appears to leap over a void, meet certain obstacles, explore certain surfaces, and envelop or invade certain objects. It describes and recounts to itself all these objects, and these accounts or these descriptions constitute the inexhaustible objective aspect of literature. But every thought is also simply a thought. It is that which exists in itself, isolatedly, mentally. Whatever its objects may be, thought can never place them, think them, except in the interior of itself.[18]

The following passage from James on the privacy of personal consciousness reveals that the leap from Frost to Poulet is really no leap at all:

Each of these minds keeps its own thoughts to itself. There is no giving or bartering between them. No thought even comes into direct *sight* of a thought in another personal consciousness than its own. Absolute insulation, irreducible pluralism, is the law. It seems as if the elementary psychic fact were not *thought* or *this thought* or *that thought*, but *my thought*, every thought being *owned*. Neither contemporaneity, nor proximity in space, nor similarity of quality and content are able to fuse thoughts together which are sundered by this barrier of belonging to different personal minds. The breaches between such thoughts are the most absolute breaches in nature.[19]

V

The literary critic may cull from William James some three suggestions to help him close the chasm between the poetry and self of Robert Frost. First, the objects of the perceiver's world are marked by the privacy of his apprehending consciousness; as Van Den Berg puts it, the world is the "materialization of our subjectivity." Secondly, the various objects marked by consciousness are also ordered or arranged by consciousness, and those very arrangements or "landscapes" will be revelations of the poet's needs, his way of looking at things, his personal identity; the constituted landscapes of consciousness thus become keys to interior landscapes, the unique psychological structures of Frost's experience. Thirdly, because consciousness is continuous, the self maintains its identity through time, thereby insuring that the individual poems in the Frost canon, though spread out through the poet's private and public history, are enveloped by a guiding presence which guarantees the wholeness of the poetic corpus.

Studying Robert Frost's interior self as pure interiority is impossible. But we have his poems, and, within them, we have the dominant, fixed objects in his poetic landscape: the things in the real world which he then transferred to and transformed in the poetic medium where they become, inevitably, objects in a poetic landscape. Whether the object is mediated by the consciousness of the lyric "I," or whether the object is mediated by Frost's more fully dramatized selves—the personae of his longer dialogues and monologues —the psychic life of Robert Frost himself is what is ultimately evoked by those fixed objects in his poetic landscape. Philosophically suggested in America by William James, this neo-Romantic expressive poetic that I am urging for Frost is elaborately detailed in the European phenomenological tradition and by several recent American critics. Its basic assumption is that the unique subjectivity *behind* the poem invades the poem itself despite the conventionalizing social and aesthetic forces, the various determinations of his culture at work to dissolve the poet's individual identity as a person. As a critical concept "landscape" becomes synonymous with the poem itself and means always this double thing: not a simple configuration of objects, "out there" in inhuman otherness, but a configuration of objects thoroughly intermeshed with the poet's self. For "poem" read: a linguistic preservation of that landscape-caressing act of consciousness.

"Tree at My Window" is Frost's self-conscious treatment of landscapes, interior and exterior:

> Tree at my window, window tree,
> My sash is lowered when night comes on;
> But let there never be curtain drawn
> Between you and me.
>
> Vague dream-head lifted out of the ground,
> And thing next most diffuse to cloud,
> Not all your light tongues talking aloud
> Could be profound.
>
> But, tree, I have seen you taken and tossed,
> And if you have seen me when I slept,
> You have seen me when I was taken and swept
> And all but lost.
>
> That day she put our heads together,
> Fate had her imagination about her,
> Your head so much concerned with outer,
> Mine with inner, weather.

Something in Frost wants to distinguish landscapes, to mark off "inner" from "outer," subject from object, human from nonhuman; perhaps it is because Frost feels so strongly that the outer landscape is not congenial to the self: the sash, at night, must be lowered, we must stay enclosed for our own good. All of which is to say that this poem, like so many poems by Frost, is grounded in a tough realist's view of things. Yet Frost gives us no unnavigable gulf between subject and object. The sash must be lowered, of course, but the curtain must never be drawn across the window. Thus, between self and not–self Frost places a transparency which allows for an interaction of sorts, as enclosed self and weathered tree take creative looks at one another. The tree, self-like, dreams and speaks; the self, tree-like, is swept and tossed. The intentional, other-directed subjectivity of the poet marks the exterior landscape by naming it "window tree" and "dream-head;" in so naming it he reveals not a deeper "something" interfused with the landscape and with the self, as Wordsworth believed, but only the character of his excursive subjectivity, a subjectivity constituted in the very interaction, the naturalizing of "inner" and the humanizing of "outer."

Frost's subjectivity is in an important (though not metaphysical) sense, romantic; it expresses itself dominantly as a dream-energy which wants to transform (by entering) the landscape it encounters. It tends to be redemptive, though it may be counterredemptive; it desires that all objects become subjects, but only to a point. For the essential Frost is also comic and ironic, and he will allow redemption to go only so far. The "dream-head" is, after all, "vague," the "light tongues" speak meaninglessly because they "utter" nonhuman sound. The poet of ironic consciousness will insist, in a direct thrust at his own redemptive self and at the noumenal confidence of the early Romantics, on the pure object-hood of nature, and in so insisting preserve the integrity of the single, simple subject against the big world beyond self. And that, too, in Frost's poetry, is a lesson derived from the interaction of subjectivity with its environment. The flowing of subject into object is presented by Frost modestly and cautiously—i.e., humorously—as a datum of consciousness (this is the way it feels sometimes) and not as evidence for a metaphysical monism (this is the way it really is with the universe). So, objects will remain objects, even when they are enclosed in subjectivity; subjects will remain subjects, even when they are weathered.

Frost's complex sense of the interrelations and distinctions of interior and exterior landscapes in "Tree at My Window" urges us to modify the Cartesianism that we find in the statements of Poulet and James on the nature of a personal consciousness. If James, anticipating Poulet, appears to refer to Descartes' meditations for the sense of personal consciousness as pure, fully constituted spiritual substance, utterly self-contained and forever inaccessible to the outside and all spatio-temporal definition, then we must correct James with James. For it is one of James' first principles of psychology that consciousness is an outgoing, pragmatic energy that acts upon its environment, and defines itself by its acts. Attempting to mediate extremes, to formulate a position between the Cartesian sense of a subjectivity which is never related, or relatable to an outer environment, and the naturalistic sense of a subjectivity which is nothing but a derivative form of the objective environment, James suggests that the inner citadel of selfhood, the unique subjective character of a personal consciousness, has a real status, but that it can be grasped and known only as it expresses itself, as it is impelled outward to interaction with objective conditions by the pragmatic energy at the very core of consciousness. John Dewey, an admirer of James, would come to say that selfhood is a mere potentiality until it is "both formed and brought to consciousness through interaction with an environment." [20]

In a full-length study I would explore the aesthetic and philosophical dimensions of Frost's poems within the more inclusive context of post-Kantian literary theory in order to define the modern intellectual environment of those poems. In recent organicist theories, the stress is heavily on the shaping force of the poetic medium, on the idea that the discourse of poetry is a special mode of language which reveals a unique world. Extending the range of organicist aesthetic theory with the insights of the phenomenological tradition, the poem becomes a preservation—i.e., a "preserve"—which sustains for our contemplative pleasure the distinctive world—the very life—of the poet's consciousness. If, as James would insist, ordinary consciousness, or mere perception, shapes out the self's world, then for Frost, who is decidedly organicist in his bias, the shaping instrument is decisively language itself. Language, the poem itself, discloses the "inner weather" of Frost's subjective universe in the intersection of self and landscape.

Frost's Jamesian view of self and his organicist tendency in poetics pose a difficult and fascinating question. The question is this: what is the nature and value of that self-sufficient poetic world, which is shaped in language by a constitutive act of his consciousness, vis-à-vis the real world which James and Frost accept as stubbornly there, independent of consciousness? Guided by Frost's Jamesian sympathies and by the several theoretical problems implicitly posed by the poems, I would isolate his response to this key question of modern aesthetics while placing him against the background of some typical modernist answers. At every important theoretical juncture, the significant measurement of Frost's participation in and dissent from major modern theories of imagination is his Jamesian commitment to the powers and limits of human consciousness to recreate its world in accordance with the needs and desires of self. Frost's poetics, his conceptual landscape, as it were, is congruent with the patterns of experience, the interior landscape that I find revealed in his poems; and that very congruency seems to me to be convincing evidence that, the important negative criticism of Yvor Winters and George Nitchie to the contrary, Frost's sensibility is profoundly unified.[21]

Though Frost read William James, and through James came into contact with a number of the salient themes of modernist philosophy and aesthetics, I do not suggest that Frost was "influenced" in the sense that historicists used to say that imaginative writers were "shaped" by the "intellectual backgrounds of the times." Modernism becomes the historical ambience of Frost's work only in the sense that it is what one comes to conceptually if one moves outward from Frost's poems in an attempt to define the ideational milieu of the kinds of consciousness and experience found in Frost.

So Frost is not modernist because he holds self-consciously to certain ideas which we identify with this or that modern philosopher. There are few ideas as such in Frost. Properly speaking, Frost's poems do not "belong" to the intellectual environment we call the "modern mind" because the "modern mind" does not have independent, Platonic existence. It is a thing that his poems have helped to create. The perspectives of modern philosophy and aesthetics are conceptual abstractions from that dense, preideational, primary data of human experience which Frost renders from the inside, as lived.

More than most modern poets Frost needs to have some sort of historical context deliberately constructed for him. (The poems need nothing. It is we, as historical creatures, seeking historical understanding, who need to construct such contexts.) Unlike Stevens, Frost only rarely deals directly with the issues of post-Kantian epistemology; unlike Crane, Williams, and Auden, he only rarely situates us in the modern urban environment; unlike Pound and Eliot he does not measure in any richly allusive way the modern moment against tradition and the past. And, from the point of view of language and metrical experiment, Frost seems very traditional indeed. In two of the best books about him, he is presented as inhabiting a sort of timeless world. John Lynen sees Frost in the venerable tradition of pastoralism. Reuben Brower, drawing his comparisons from the range of world literature, relates him to the tradition of tough-minded, unflinching writers who see things as they are and do not hesitate to tell the score. Lynen and Brower are both persuasive. Frost inhabits a timeless world as do all poets of high quality. Yet Frost did not exist in a vacuum, and his poems do not present an ahistorical consciousness. What I would call his "implicit poetics" is one way of entering history, of locating the poet in time; "implicit poetics" is a regulative principle which does not help much in explicating the poems, but which does help us to "generalize" the experiential patterns of those poems, and hence to extend the significance of the poems for our times.

Notes to *Robert Frost and Modern Literary Theory* by FRANK LENTRICCHIA

1. J. H. Van Den Berg, *The Phenomenological Approach to Psychiatry* (Springfield: Charles C. Thomas, 1955), 32.

2. Reuben Brower, *The Poetry of Robert Frost* (New York: Oxford University Press, 1963), 140.

3. Joseph Blau, in introduction to *Pragmatism and Other Essays* (New York: Washington Square Press, 1963), xv. The historical relations of Frost and James are traced by Lawrance Thompson in *Robert Frost: The Early Years, 1874–1915* (New York: Holt, Rinehart and Winston, 1966).

4. William James, *Psychology* (New York: Fawcett Publications, 1963), Chap. XI.

5. Jean Paul Sartre, *What is Literature?* trans. Bernard Frechtman (New York: Harper & Row, 1965), 32–33.

6. William James, *The Principles of Psychology* (New York: Dover Publications, 1950), I, 284.

7. *Ibid.*, 287, 288.

8. *Ibid.*, 363.

9. William James, *The Will to Believe and Other Essays in Popular Philosophy* (New York: Dover Publications, 1956), 41, 42, 118.

10. For further examples of James's recourse to aesthetic metaphor see: *Pragmatism: A New Way For Some Old Ways of Thinking* (New York: Longmans, Green, & Co., 1907), 61, 64, 65, 256–57, 258; cited below as *Pragmatism; A Pluralistic Universe* (New York: Longmans, Green, & Co., 1942), 9–10. For further examples see *The Meaning of Truth: A Sequel to "Pragmatism"* (New York: Longmans, Green, & Co., 1909), 58, 80.

11. *Selected Letters of Robert Frost*, ed. Lawrance Thompson (New York: Holt, Rinehart and Winston, 1964), 381, 465.

12. James, *Pragmatism*, 64.

13. See: *Selected Letters*, 215; *The Letters of Robert Frost to Louis Untermeyer*, ed. Louis Untermeyer (New York: Holt, Rinehart and Winston, 1963), 189; *Selected Prose of Robert Frost*, ed. Hyde Cox and Edward Connery Lathem (New York: Holt, Rinehart and Winston, 1966), 24, 35, 37–38, 39, 40–41, 49–50; Sidney Cox, *A Swinger of Birches: A Portrait of Robert Frost* (New York: Collier Books, 1957), 18–19, 44, 46, 76.

14. For the quotations in order, see *Selected Prose*, 41; Lawrance Thompson, *Robert Frost: The Years of Triumph, 1915–1938* (New York: Holt, Rinehart and Winston, 1970), 401; *Selected Prose*, 24; Untermeyer, 285.

15. James, *Pragmatism*, 21, 22.

16. For the quotations in order, see *Selected Prose*, 106, 107; quoted in *A Swinger of Birches*, 121.

17. James, *Pragmatism and Other Essays*, 263.

18. Georges Poulet, *The Interior Distance*, trans. Elliot Coleman (Ann Arbor: University of Michigan, 1964), vii.

19. James, *Psychology*, 148.

20. John Dewey, *Art as Experience* (New York: Capricorn Books, 1958), 282.

21. This is the central complaint of George Nitchie, *Human Values in the Poetry of Robert Frost* (Durham: Duke University, 1960).

Robert Frost's Metaphysical Sonnet

GEORGE MONTEIRO

Published rather inauspiciously in the same year that saw the appearance of T. S. Eliot's "The Waste Land," Robert Frost's sonnet "Design" has wonderfully ridden out the long years. Its reputation has so grown that the poem now flourishes fully apace with its lengthy rival as one of the century's most explosive poetic statements on the metaphysics of darkness.[1] Indeed, historically "Design" can be located rightfully somewhere between the visionary expanse of "The Waste Land" and the mind-stretching speculations of Herman Melville's chapter on "The Whiteness of the Whale" in *Moby-Dick* (1851), a book whose rediscovery came several years after Frost had independently examined the poetic-philosophical relationship between metaphors of whiteness and the idea of cosmic design. In paradigm, "Design" expresses those perplexing fears spawned and scattered by evidence which indicates that (1) human existence continues without supportive design and ultimate purpose, or (2) human existence is subject to a design of unmitigated natural evil. The details of the poem appear to sustain these complementary readings without choosing between them.

No student of Frost's poetry can afford to ignore the implications of "Design." For one thing, it is one of those rare poems, archetypal to the entire oeuvre of a poet, which in brief compass offers a valuable key to a poet's richness and reach. Although it would be rash to insist that "Design" answers all the important questions about Frost's thought overall, it is equally true that to ignore this key to the truths of the poet's inner being would be most unfortunate.

"Design" is Frost's most carefully shaped investigation of the darker implications of the classical argument from design. The poem did not spring fully formed from a single bout with the Muse. The manuscript evidence bespeaks the contrary. In 1912, apparently to get the poem on record as well as to try it on a sympathetic reader, Frost forwarded an early version to an old friend, calling it a sonnet for his " 'Moth and Butterfly' book." [2] Although he did not choose to publish that early version, the manuscript copy preserved among the Susan Hayes Ward papers enables us to trace Frost's philosophical-aesthetic development as he reworked his poem and rethought his ideas over a period of ten years.

Frost's extant manuscript version bears a title, "In White," which, though it indicates the poem's principal image and motif, does not have the thematic resonance of the simpler and more direct later title, "Design." [3] A more explicit title for the final version of the poem, but a far less effective one, it strikes me, would combine the two. "Design in White," a melded title, arty and somewhat arch, would compromise Frost's theme. Rather, concerned with any and all designs which would foster poetic and philosophic resonance, Frost revised his poem in the direction of line-by-line concision and toward making each image appropriate and every word totally functional.

Here is the 1912 manuscript version, "In White,":

A dented spider like a snow drop white	(1)
On a white Heal-all, holding up a moth	(2)
Like a white piece of lifeless satin cloth—	(3)
Saw ever curious eye so strange a sight?—	(4)
Portent in little, assorted death and blight	(5)
Like the ingredients of a witches' broth?—	(6)
The beady spider, the flower like a froth,	(7)
And the moth carried like a paper kite.	(8)
What had that flower to do with being white,	(9)
The blue prunella every child's delight.	(10)
What brought the kindred spider to that height?	(11)
(Make we no thesis of the miller's plight.)	(12)
What but design of darkness and of night?	(13)
Design, design! Do I use the word aright? [4]	(14)

This early version of the poem is to be compared with the final version published first in 1922, and later gathered by Frost into his sixth volume of poetry, *A Further Range* (1936):

I found a dimpled spider, fat and white,	(1)
On a white heal-all, holding up a moth	(2)
Like a white piece of rigid satin cloth—	(3)
Assorted characters of death and blight	(4)
Mixed ready to begin the morning right,	(5)

Like the ingredients of a witches' broth— (6)
A snow-drop spider, a flower like a froth, (7)
And dead wings carried like a paper kite. (8)
What had that flower to do with being white, (9)
The wayside blue and innocent heal-all? (10)
What brought the kindred spider to that height, (11)
Then steered the white moth thither in the night? (12)
What but design of darkness to appall?— (13)
If design govern in a thing so small.[5] (14)

Frost's revisions turn the poem to narrative and away from naked lyric, thereby enhancing the mystery which surrounds the incident he wishes to describe. In removing his personal experience to the past, the poet is able to suggest as well that he has been brooding on the meaning of the tableau of spider, moth and ritual death which he has observed, even though he has failed to come to a conclusive answer (at least for himself) on the question of design. The introduction of the poet's personal voice (as subject) into the first line, moreover, turns the spider into the object of sight and contemplation. It gives the poet more prominence than he had in the manuscript version, which begins with a sentence fragment (no verb) in apposition to the noun "sight" in the fourth line.

There is not much that survives intact from one version of the poem to the other. Notably, only the ninth line of the early version— "What had that flower to do with being white"—survives without change in "Design." Lines two, six and eleven are largely repeated, with changes only in capitalization or line-end punctuation. The remaining ten lines, however, offer substantive changes, which must be taken up line by line.

The simile in the first line, "A dented spider like a snow drop white," which is purely and neutrally descriptive, disappears along with another descriptive word "dented." In their place Frost offers three adjectives: "dimpled," "fat," and "white." The first two are unexpectedly appropriate to this murderous spider. Cannily placed in the poem, these terms are normally far more appropriate to a baby than an insect. So, replacing neutrally descriptive terms by terms that normally would seek another context and would offer a different sentiment, Frost both announces his theme and reveals that his approach is basically ironic. In line three the moth, described "Like a white piece of lifeless cloth—" becomes "rigid satin cloth." "Lifeless" is only vaguely descriptive of the moth's state; but it is not at all accurately descriptive of the tableau of the spider holding up the moth. The moth may in fact be "lifeless," but the poem is more accurately descriptive to compare the moth to "rigid" cloth. Hovering over this image is the hint of rigor mortis and that satin fabric which customarily lines the inside of coffins.[6]

Line four in the manuscript version is rather limp, lifeless. The semirhetorical question "Saw ever curious eye so strange a sight?" seriously deflects the central argument of the poem. In the final version Frost moves the second half of the original fifth line, "assorted death and blight," up to line four, and extends it to "Assorted characters of death and blight," thereby introducing the important metaphor of kitchen domesticity that he will pursue through line seven. So, too, does he decide to drop the first phrase of line five ("Portent in little"), this time, I would suggest, because "portent" strikes us as too potent a word for the poem at this point. Line six stays almost intact, except that it no longer asks a question. Indeed, the two questions which dominate the octave in the manuscript version are strategically dropped, so that the only questions come in the sestet closing the poem. Lines four through seven are intended, then, to suggest kitchens, cakes and cookies ("Assorted," "ingredients," and "Mixed ready")—all as if drummed up by advertisers "to begin the morning right." The only sour note is that the whole thing resembles "the ingredients of a witches' broth." Still, it is *broth* and not *brew* (as we might expect in everyday witchcraft); *broth* echoes the culinary metaphor.

The single change in line seven turns "beady spider" into "snowdrop spider," picking up the adjective which Frost had discarded from his original first line. At this point the earlier poem was still fundamentally descriptive, but something was needed, apparently, to keep the idea of coldness and death before us. "Snow-drop" accomplishes this. "Beady," however, does something else. The word, less than precisely descriptive, is morally loaded. A seemingly less neutral word would keep the poem from becoming at all moralistic. In the last line of the octave "moth" turns into "dead wings," but the simile "like a paper kite" is happily retained. The simile carries us back to the implicitly "childlike" description of the spider in the opening line. "Dead wings," on the other hand, moves toward precision, for it is not the "moth" in its entirety that looks like "a paper kite": it is only its "dead wings." Furthermore, both "wings" and "kite" suggest the idea of flight; the image of white "dead wings" moves toward paradox.

The ninth line ("What had that flower to do with being white,") is retained intact. That much about his basic poem Frost had been sure of all along. But if the appositive clause which constitutes the tenth line ("The blue prunella every child's delight") adds the new information that the heal-all is also known as the prunella, it nevertheless adds nothing to the argument of the poem. Indeed, because the content of the lines is not at all functional other than as a bit of incidental information, it can do no more than disrupt the poem's discourse. On the other hand, repeating the fact that it is a "heal-all" despite its not being blue (as are most heal-alls) pushes the argument a step further. The next line is substantially the same. But the twelfth line of the manuscript version is dropped completely, and fittingly so. "(Make we no thesis of the miller's plight)" is wasteful and repetitive, seeming to exist only for the final word ("plight") which maintains the pattern of the same end rhyme throughout the six lines of the sestet. In replacing the entire line, Frost chooses to deepen the question he asks about the tableau he has witnessed. Not only does he ask, "What brought the kindred spider to that height," but also what "Then *steered* the *white* moth thither in the *night?*" (italics added). What power, then, actually "steered" the moth (white) in the darkness of "night" to a heal-all which is preternaturally "white"? Rather than the somewhat disingenuous admonition that avoids making a thesis out of this tableau, Frost chooses to extend the mystery of the "witches' broth" that he has cautiously witnessed.[7]

In the penultimate line of the poem the first five words are retained ("What but design of darkness"), but the last three words ("and of night") are revised: "to appall?" In the original, "of night" merely repeats the idea in the phrase "of darkness." There is a relatively pointless, if harmless, repetition of meaning. But the phrase "darkness to appall" suggests the appalling effect that the close conjunction of two ideas—"darkness" and "design"—might well have.

Moreover, "appall" is a particularly suitable word, in that it suggests both a specific color or the lack of color (pallor) and death (pall).

Because it, too, is inconclusive and somewhat wasteful, the last line of the manuscript poem gives way to a conditional clause in the final version. "Design, design! Do I use the word aright?" is crudely rhythmic, but the simple device of ending a poem with a disingenuous question does little toward formally resolving the poem. On the other hand, to end the poem with the tentative clause "if design govern in a thing so small" offers thematic resolution even as it enhances poetic resonance. "Govern" develops from "steered," of course, which in turn grows out of "brought." The effect is cumulative.

Our conclusion is that a comparison of the earlier definitive versions of "Design" helps to define the poet's final intention. It remained fundamentally consistent. From version to version Frost worked towards a clarification of his idea that the philosophical argument from design was endemically ironic. Another conclusion. Both the first published version of the poem (1922) and the manuscript version (1912) are in sonnet form. Despite internal revisions and the reshaping of several lines, the overall poetic form remained the same over the years. That the poem was conceived in the form of a sonnet, I would propose, is the poet's final irony, for the strict formal design which characterizes the sonnet apes and mimes the internal argument of the poem.[8] Does the same guiding power, the steering force, which works through the tableau of spider, moth and stylized death, work through the poetic process as well? After so much whiteness, have we experienced, after all, still another variant of that scriptural blackness of darkness which fascinated so many American writers, including Poe and Melville? These questions—good ones, I think—are no more rhetorical than the question which closes Frost's chilling sonnet.

Notes to *Robert Frost's Metaphysical Sonnet* by GEORGE MONTEIRO

1. Frost's confidence in his poem is suggested by his insisting to Untermeyer at the time: "You'll want Design." See *The Letters of Robert Frost to Louis Untermeyer* (New York: Holt, Rinehart and Winston, 1963), 143.

2. *Selected Letters of Robert Frost*, ed. Lawrance Thompson (New York: Holt, Rinehart and Winston, 1964), 45.

3. The "In White" manuscript, now at the Huntington Library, San Marino, Cali-

fornia, was published first in Reginald L. Cook, *The Dimensions of Robert Frost* (New York: Rinehart and Co., 1958), 85. It was subsequently republished, with slight differences in transcription, in Lawrance Thompson's *Robert Frost: The Early Years, 1874–1915* (New York: Holt, Rinehart and Winston, 1966), 582.

4. Cook, *Dimensions*, 85.

5. *The Poetry of Robert Frost*, ed. Edward Connery Lathem (New York: Holt, Rinehart and Winston, 1969), 302. Three commentaries on "Design" are indispensable: Randall Jarrell, *Poetry and the Age* (New York: Alfred A. Knopf, 1953), 50–53; Reuben A. Brower, *The Poetry of Robert Frost: Constellations of Intention* (New York: Oxford University Press, 1963), 104–108; and Hyatt H. Waggoner, *American Poets, From the Puritans to the Present* (Boston: Houghton Mifflin Co., 1968), 4 and passim. For a cogent and persuasive presentation of the argument that "Design" shows the influence of William James's *Pragmatism*, see Thompson, *Frost: Early Years*, 383–87.

6. See Brower, *Poetry of Robert Frost*, 105.

7. Thompson suggests that the lines "What brought the kindred spider to that height, / Then steered the white moth thither in the night?" are a mock-echo of the well-known lines of William Cullen Bryant's poem on providential design, "To a Waterfowl": "He who, from zone to zone, / Guides through the boundless sky thy certain flight . . ." (*Frost: Early Years*, 582).

8. Frost's puckish attitude toward the sonnet form is instructive. "The sonnet is the strictest form I have behaved in," he wrote to Untermeyer, "and that mainly by pretending it wasn't a sonnet" (*Letters to Untermeyer*, 381).

"Our Singing Strength": The Texture of Voice in the Poetry of Robert Frost

JOSEPH M. GARRISON, JR.

CRITICISM of Robert Frost continues to be indebted to Randall Jarrell (*Poetry and the Age*) for his cogent appreciation. Thanks to him, the myth of the "simple" Frost began to vanish. What appeared subsequently has been salutary; it has also been debilitating. On the one hand, explication of text has insured Frost's reputation as a craftsman; on the other hand, it has dulled our responsiveness to the centrality of the speaking voice in his poems and has limited our understanding of the nature of his complexities. Although we pay lip service to Frost's theory of "the sound of sense," [1] we do not bring it into constructive play in our critical dealings with the poet. Commentaries take frequent notice of the "personality" of the voice in a given poem and certainly approach different poems as being spoken by different voices, but they do not seriously consider how these voices affect our assessment of the speaker and his relationship to the oral presence of the poem. My objection is made not only for the purpose of thematic enrichment; it also bears upon larger questions and is germane to Frost's thoughts on the arts of reading and knowing.

There are two kinds of readers, Frost said, "eye readers" and "true readers." The former "get the meaning by glances. But they are bad readers because they miss the best part of what a good writer puts into his work." The "true reader," however, is able to "get the variety that makes it fun to write and read. *The ear does it.* The ear is the only true writer and the only true reader" (SL, 113). Mindful of this caveat, Frost frequently read the works of other writers aloud, both to himself and to his family. In speaking of Melville, for example, he protests against "a certain air of nouveau richeness" and remarks that he "began to notice it years ago when I read Typee aloud at home" (SL, 554). Then, too, there is the habit of dramatic colloquy in his letters, written as if he were determined to lift his correspondence from the visual confines of the page. In one of these colloquies, he actually transcribes a line from "Into My Own" backwards, thereby calling attention to the limitations of horizontal (and left-to-right) conditioning: " 'eurt saw thguoht I lla fo erus erom ylnO' " (SL, 66). His essays, speeches, and prefaces insist upon the vocalization of poetic language. Hence, writing must release "the speaking tone of voice somehow entangled in the words and fastened to the page for the ear of the imagination." [2]

Anyone who has read Frost will observe nothing new in what I have said thus far; we agree that he is a poet of the spoken word. But our agreement does not always carry over into our discussion of his poems. We do not let his theory inform our practice; and insofar as we fail to meet him on his own terms, we are guilty of the charges which he leveled against American academe for being "professionally literary" (SL, 146). Frost hated the priority of "research for the sake of erudition" (ibid.). The problem, as he saw it, was method; and he frequently expressed his desire to formulate a radically modified pedagogy, evident, among other places, in a quip about his teaching of philosophy at Amherst: "As a first exercise ... I sent them out with lanterns to find the originals in life of the half dozen philosophies we talk and write" (SL, 295). The poet's words charge us to "find the originals" in his poems.

In view of the abundance of incisive criticism of Frost's work, particularly during the last ten years, it may seem ungrateful and naive to reissue the charge. Nonetheless, I contend that Frost is not being studied in the most productive ways and that teachers and critics are not utilizing his richest resources. A recent essay by Eben Bass is a case in point.[3] In discussing poems which he has selected to illustrate his interpretation of "Frost's Poetry of Fear," he draws abstract and synoptic conclusions, as if the ability to state what a poem is "about" or what it "says" or "shows" were the final critical objective. I concede that a poem needs to be brought to conceptual heel, if only for the sake of comparison with the ideological content of other poems. But in most poems—and particularly in Frost's—the sorting out process affords only a preliminary glimpse; it should prepare for a consideration of voice. Commenting on "Desert Places," Professor Bass observes that "Frost does not ... mistake his own loneliness for humanity's. The 'desert' of 'Desert Places' is his own personal fear."

The possibility of confusing personal and corporate fear is not really at issue in this poem; it is not the seed out of which the poem grows. Moreover, it does not relate the poem resonantly to Frost's other poems about fear. As I read "Desert Places," the poem concerns, fundamentally, the *attitudes* of the speaker toward his own "desert places." The poem is remarkable because of the subtle and rich ways in which the voice and texture of the poem reveal these attitudes. Our understanding of the speaker's reflections upon his fear must finally lodge in the tone of the closing lines; we must be able to incorporate the pun ("where no human race is") and the feminine rhymes ("spaces," "race is," "places") into our interpretation. "Desert Places" does not present an "abstracted fear," to use Professor Bass's phrase; it is an experience in fear, with all things held very tentatively at the end—so tentatively, in fact, that we are persuaded that the speaker really has something to fear. When fear is real, it cannot be utterly mastered; our mastery will always be, at best, "a momentary stay against confusion" (SP, 18).

My concern with voice in Frost's poetry is not exclusively literary. Although I am aware that a poet should not be used as a means to an end—should not become a public utility—I suggest that Frost's theory of "Vocal Reality" (SL, 241) should make pedagogical sense to teachers and readers who have been conditioned by the visual priorities of a highly sophisticated print culture, including, of course, the media of television. In his stunning investigation of language and its relationships to sound, Walter J. Ong characterizes our situation: "We are the most abject prisoners of the literate culture in which we have matured. Even with the greatest effort, contemporary man finds it exceedingly difficult, and in many instances quite impossible, to sense what the spoken word actually is. He feels it as a modification of something which normally is or ought to be written." [4] The effects of this privation are self-evident: it inclines us "to overrate verbatim repetition or record," and it creates the illusion that "if one has the exact words someone has uttered, one has by that very fact his exact meaning." Frost's theory of poetry is a corrective, a way out of the linear bondage of typography and a way into what he considered the life's blood of a poem, "the intonation entangled somehow in the syntax idiom and meaning of a sentence" (SL, 107). His poetry, therefore, can promote the development of an urgently needed liberating art, the art of hearing language as utterance. And that art will enable us to make more telling distinctions among the life experiences which are dramatized in literature; it can regulate, for example, our compulsion to *look for* images. In a culture which seems determined to produce indiscriminate exercise of mind and will, Frost shows us how to find "Our Singing Strength." But he must be read and taught in a new way, according to his principle that "words exist in the mouth, not in books" (SL, 108).

A poem such as "Into My Own" does not pose any straining visual problems. Its figurative language is fairly conventional and straightforward. An "eye reader" of this poem will probably conclude that the speaker advocates radical self-reliance and expresses a desire to reject the world. The superficiality of this level of meaning is certainly inconsistent with Frost's claim that he was "not undesigning" (SL, 84). Although we should not assume that all of his poems are successful expressions of his "way of coming at things" (SL, 189), we know that he considered himself a difficult and complex poet, boasting on one occasion that "not half a dozen people can tell who was hit and where he was hit by my Road Not Taken" (SL, 190). One comment from his preface to the *Memoirs of the Notorious Stephen Burroughs* suggests something of the nature of Frost's distinctive complexities: "*He* knew how to put the reverse on a ball so that when it was going it was also coming" (SP, 84). The speaker in "Into My Own" is both "going" and "coming" at the same time. When the poem was published in *A Boy's Will* in 1913, Frost added a thumbnail description of the argument. "*The youth*," he wrote, "*is persuaded that he will be rather more than less himself for having forsworn the world.*" I am particularly interested in the words "*is persuaded.*" A boy would not have to "persuade" himself (or "be persuaded") into that view. It would be a natural stance for him and would be in keeping with the egocentric priorities of youth. My interpretation of the poem does not hinge upon Frost's gloss; but, conceivably, "Into My Own" is not as simple as it seems to be. The last two lines of the poem have many connotative possibilities, depending upon tone and placement of emphasis: "They would not find me changed from him they knew—/Only more sure of all I thought was true." If the primary emphasis falls upon "more sure," the rest of the line will get short measure—the appeal to self-integrity will remain foremost in the ear. But if the verb "thought" rings strong in the line (and both the metrics and the pattern of mono-syllabic words favor it), the poem opens up in a hauntingly provoca-tive way: it implies that the speaker's eventual confirmation of the rightness of his choice will be absolutely dependent upon being found by his friends. In other words, the poem flirts with "the fear that men won't understand us and we shall be cut off from them" (SP, 60) and presents a speaker who wants to learn to live fearlessly with the hazards of misunderstanding, preferring that way of life to other modes. He wishes to be able to live in a world which has neither "open land" (no solution of guaranteed rescue or comfort) nor "highway where the slow wheel pours the sand" (no solution of dogged endurance in the continuum of time). He wishes to undergo an ultimate test of all that he thinks is true and have his faithful thought ratified by people who would seek him out, wishing to know if he still "held them dear." Their anxiousness about his absence, the question which they would ask when they had "overtaken" him, and the speaker's implied response that he still most certainly does hold them "dear"—these manifestations of human concern, of the capacities to need, to feel, and to communicate, would bring the speaker "Into My Own"; he would then know that what he "thought was true" is true.

Frost's "Design" lends itself to further illustration of the centrality of voice in his poetry. Most interpretations of this sonnet emphasize the rich layerings of language in the octave, including the evil-innocence mixture of the diction ("dimpled spider," "white heal-all," and "dead wings"). They also attend to the last line of the poem and stress its dark teleological doubts: "If design govern in a thing so small." In a conclusion which is representative of many readings, Reuben A. Brower says that "the soothingly humorous hesitation points to something many readers may find less agreeable than design of darkness, to no order whatever." [5] The poem may invite a choice between a lesser of two evils, but I think that Frost wants us to go a little deeper into his words and structure and modify our understanding of the conclusion with a recognition of the "small" and ordered "design" of the poem as a poem and the ways in which that "design" qualifies the poet's speculations. Again, the tone of the speaker's voice, particularly its progression within the poem, is crucial. The sestet does not prepare for "soothingly humorous hesitation." If that attitude were actually present at the end of the poem, the speaker would be a rationalizing intelligence who succumbs to the logic of the absolutist's mentality; and Frost would be playing with that situation. The poem, however, seems to have more urgent concerns. Having devoted the octave to his curious fascination with the predicament of the moth, the speaker asks some very real and obviously sympathetic questions and tries to formulate an answer:

> What had that flower to do with being white,
> The wayside blue and innocent heal-all?
> What brought the kindred spider to that height,
> Then steered the white moth thither in the night?
> What but design of darkness to appall?—
> If design govern in a thing so small.

An answer is found in the last two lines, and it gives credibility to the speaker's tone. Since the poem itself evidences a "design" that *does* "govern in a thing so small" as a sonnet, the "design" of the poem attests to the fact that all "design" is not necessarily the "design of darkness to appall." The "design of darkness" may exist, or may seem to exist insofar as men perceive it; but there is also the "design" of art, "not of cunning and craft, mind you, but of real art; that believing the thing into existence, saying as you go more than you even hoped you were going to be able to say, and coming with surprise to an end that you foreknew only with some sort of emotion" (SP, 46). What enables the speaker to undermine his fear of the omnipresence of malevolent purpose (or the harder alternative of pure chance) is his recognition of the *purpose* of his poem and his knowledge that the coincidence or "design" of the three white things does not controvert his artistic "design." The stakes are high, indeed; but they seem to have less to do with the implications of the fate of the moth than with our ability to "treat the word as a point of many departures." In the concluding sentence of his introduction to the English edition of *A Masque of Reason*, Frost tells us that "the future of the world may depend on your keeping in practice with each other's quips and figures" (SP, 78). And his comment applies as well to his own "Design."

Since my primary concerns are the general principles of reading Frost—emphasizing oral content as a way of promoting a fresh approach to his work—I will add some very specific methodological examples, selecting my details from a few familiar poems. My aim is not inclusiveness, and I will not enter into a full discussion of the implications of my suggestions. I will assume that I have already demonstrated a convincing application of my thesis and that what is needed at this point is a cumulative identification of further instances where voice not only provides a fruitful entrée to the poem but also throws it into a more demanding interpretive context. These desiderata have the sanction of Frost's testimony that his poems "are all set to trip the reader head foremost into the boundless. . . . Forward, you understand, *and* in the dark. I may leave my toys in the wrong place and so in vain. It is my intention we are speaking of—my innate mischievousness" (SL, 344).

Many of Frost's poems, of course, express his "mischievousness," but his best pranks always "leave something to learn later" (SP, 29). "Fire and Ice" is such a poem. Lawrance Thompson observes that, like other of Frost's epigrams, it reaches its goal through the "ironic balance . . . of a twofold consideration." [6] Charting conclusions from this generalization, the speaker's laconic tone would be read as a counterpoint for the rash alarmism of those who would state, categorically, that "the world will end in fire"; his emotional distance from his subject would be understood as a tempered love, lying between the extremes of "fire" and "ice." The alternatives of "fire" and "ice," however, are simply the subjects of the speaker's statements. The primary "clarification" of the poem is made not in what the speaker says but in the way in which he says it, ironically revealing, perhaps, a third theory about the end of the world. The last word in the poem is "suffice," rhymed with "ice" and "twice." The tight-lipped and brittle sound of that rhyme teases me. I hear the speaker protecting himself—in the face of a contemplated cataclysm—with the studied indifference of wit for wit's sake. And I suggest that Frost is offering this attitude as the most disturbing prospect in the poem. Moreover, once that meaning has come through, we recognize that the speaker's indifference to the way in which the world will end, including the cold notion that it may *have to end* "twice," is his own version of the cynical assumption of those who say that the world *will end* (either "in fire" or "in ice") and who would be motivated to a sense of concern and urgency only by the prospect of anticipating or actually confronting its end.

Similarly, the last stanza of "Come In" leads us to suspect that the poem does not depict the progression of a conclusive mastery of temptation, whether that mastery be the result of the speaker's recognition of his self-deception ("I meant not even if asked,/And I hadn't been") or the result of his choice of self-determination. For me, the poem should not be read as the record of an experience in which a man acquires "complete control of his human integrity." [7] In other poems, and in his prose as well, Frost's tough realism challenges the naive assumption that human victories—even our small acts of courage—are securely won. The choices of rhyme in "Come In," and the delicate variations of tone, suggest that Frost is addressing himself to matters of control. The first stanza of the poem presents a model of tight, end-stopped, heavily metered, and counterbalanced lines; the fifth stanza introduces the possibility of a loss of control in the reference to "lament." As an alternative to these two extremes, the last stanza defines control as a precarious ordering of experience, held together by the near rhyme of "in" and "been" (as compared, for example, with "hark" and "dark") and vibrating with the complex overtones of its conclusion. The speaker would not "come in" because there were no bearings in the "pillared dark." But the final lines of the poem entertain the notion that he has withstood the temptation to abandon control in this instance—and the struggle is convincingly voiced in stanzas two through four—only to discover that this temptation, given the others which he will be confronted with, is a negligible threat to his sense of commitment. He actually does not know what we would have done had he been *asked* "to come in," and he seems to sense that his life from this point on will necessarily include an element of risk. The end of the poem is honest and in accordance with the speaker's acceptance of his own limitations:

> But no, I was out for stars:
> I would not come in.
> I meant not even if asked,
> And I hadn't been.

In "The Road Not Taken," Frost also entrusts richness to rhyme. The human content of the poem may be said to follow the oral contours of the word "difference" in its rhyme with "hence," as contrasted to the rhyme of "both" and "undergrowth" in the first stanza. As Frost said, a poem "finds its own name as it goes and discovers the best waiting for it in some final phrase at once wise and sad—the happy-sad blend of the drinking song" (SP, 19). To add a further brief example, "Dust of Snow" works its magic in the unexpected break in meter in the last line. We expect the poem to conclude with "Of a day I'd rued." But the poet does not sustain the dominant iambic dimeter pattern of the other lines of the poem. His meter emphasizes the fact that it was *the speaker* who had "rued" the day and that the problem of failure, regret, or anxiety was the result of being preoccupied with self. The crow gives the speaker an appreciation of the particularity and preciousness of external things and apprises him, at the same time, of his error:

> The way a crow
> Shook down on me
> The dust of snow
> From a hemlock tree
>
> Has given my heart
> A change of mood
> And saved some part
> Of a day I had rued.

The nuances of the spoken word make heavy demands of the reader, but Frost has good reasons for making these demands.

The centrality of voice in Frost's poetry is ultimately related to his respect for his reader's integrity and freedom. "The heart sinks," he said, "when robbed of the chance to see for itself what a poem is all about" (SP, 96). For Frost, "the greatest reward of all was self-esteem" (SP, 101); he found great pleasure in "fathoming depths for myself" (SP, 114), a privilege which he also protected for his reader. Hence, the poet frequently refers to "the right reader of a good poem" (SP, 71), a reader who would have "the nice ability to tell always when a poem is being figurative and when it is not being figurative" (SL, 557) and who would know that "strongly spent is synonymous with kept" (SP, 24). These priorities establish a clear connection between voice and metaphor in Frost's poetry. The last lines of "Directive" will help me draw my conclusion:

> Your destination and your destiny's
> A brook that was the water of the house,
> Cold as a spring as yet so near its source,
> Too lofty and original to rage.
> (We know the valley streams that when aroused
> Will leave their tatters hung on barb and thorn.)
> I have kept hidden in the instep arch
> Of an old cedar at the waterside
> A broken drinking goblet like the Grail
> Under a spell so the wrong ones can't find it,
> So can't get saved, as Saint Mark says they mustn't.
> (I stole the goblet from the children's playhouse.)
> Here are your waters and your watering place.
> Drink and be whole again beyond confusion.

As the poem tells us, the water from the "brook," drunk from the right "goblet," will make us "whole again beyond confusion." Frost is very specific about the properties of the saving water: "Cold as a spring as yet so near its source,/Too lofty and original to rage." This is a metaphor for the sake of metaphor; but it also directs us to search for the fresh reality of language at its "source"—the moment of utterance. In another metaphor, one from his essay on "The Figure a Poem Makes," Frost associates the "source" with smell: "Read it a hundred times: it will forever keep its freshness as metal keeps its fragrance" (SP, 20). He should have the last word:

> Well, something for a snowstorm to have shown
> The country's singing strength thus brought together,
> That though repressed and moody with the weather
> Was nonetheless there ready to be freed
> And sing the wild flowers up from root and seed.

Notes to *"Our Singing Strength"; The Texture of Voice in the Poetry of Robert Frost* by JOSEPH M. GARRISON, JR.

1. *Selected Letters of Robert Frost,* ed. Lawrance Thompson (New York: Holt, Rinehart and Winston, 1964), 79. Other references to this work are in the text as SL.

2. *Selected Prose of Robert Frost,* ed. Hyde Cox and Edward Connery Lathem (New York: Holt, Rinehart and Winston, 1966), 13–14. Other references to this work are in the text as SP.

3. Eben Bass, "Frost's Poetry of Fear," *American Literature,* XLIII (January 1972), 606.

4. Walter J. Ong, *The Presence of the Word: Some Prolegomena for Cultural and Religious History* (New Haven: Yale University Press, 1967), 19. The next quotation is p. 32.

5. Reuben A. Brower, *The Poetry of Robert Frost: Constellations of Intention* (New York: Oxford University Press, 1963), 107.

6. Lawrance Thompson, *Fire and Ice: The Art and Thought of Robert Frost* (New York: Holt, Rinehart and Winston, 1961), 170.

7. John Robert Doyle, Jr., *The Poetry of Robert Frost: An Analysis* (New York: Hafner and Johannesburg: Witwatersrand University, 1962), 196.

Design and Drama in *A Boy's Will*

LEWIS H. MILLER, JR.

ESPITE the reservations of some critics,[1] most of the poems in *A Boy's Will*, Frost's first volume, meet the requirements of design and drama that Frost, throughout his long career, articulated in his prose and exhibited in his poetry. Frost's continued preoccupation with "large design," with the emergence of "any broken or dotted continuity or any fragment of a figure" from the accumulative context of his poems is of a piece with his pervasive concern for the dramatic in poetry: "Everything written is as good as it is dramatic.... A least lyric alone may have a hard time, but it can make a beginning, and lyric will be piled on lyric till all are easily heard as sung or spoken by a person in a scene—in character, in a setting."[2] The design of *A Boy's Will* is both thematic and dramatic, and it is unique to the Frost canon in its portrayal of a young, often immature speaker who develops and ripens as the poems unfold. At the same time, there are several thematic strands in *A Boy's Will* which prefigure the dynamics of later, more mature volumes. Thus, Frost's first volume can be viewed as both a proving ground for the Frost with whom we are perhaps most familiar and as a poetic accomplishment worthy in its own right of close examination.

The first poem in *A Boy's Will*, "Into My Own," explicitly sets forth the symbolic counters with which the poet is to play throughout the volume: on the one hand, the wild, dark, unlimited vista of the forest; on the other, the tamed, domestic, and limited realm of human society. It is between these poles that Frost's speaker in *A Boy's Will* so frequently attempts to come into his own; and it is between these poles that the more seasoned speaker of poems like "The Wood-Pile" or "Stopping by Woods on a Snowy Evening" *does* come into his own by reconciling and transcending the strong, conflicting claims upon him. The final lines of "Into My Own" appear to confirm the import of the poem's title by asserting a distinct gain in self-knowledge:

351

> They would not find me changed from him they knew—
> Only more sure of all I thought was true.[3]

But readers cannot be sure. The self-assurance in these lines suggests a bravado rarely found in Frost; indeed, the tone of the entire poem is blatantly callow and, as such, has disturbed readers who come to *A Boy's Will* with expectations aroused by the seasoned speakers of the later lyrics. Yet to recognize and accept this poem's self-conscious and petulant idiom is to appreciate a distinct part of its charm and of its drama. For the speaker here is an adolescent who, in typically youthful fashion, confronts the world with an opinionated, defiant stance filled with unresolved contradictions and cross-purposes. Or to use Frost's own characterization of the young man between the ages of fifteen and twenty: he "knows more about himself than he is able to prove to anyone." [4] Rather than "prove" anything, the speaker of "Into My Own" talks from an exaggerated height of self-sufficiency and daring:

> One of my wishes is that those dark trees,
> So old and firm they scarcely show the breeze,
> Were not, as 'twere, the merest mask of gloom,
> But stretched away unto the edge of doom.
>
> I should not be withheld but that some day
> Into their vastness I should steal away,
> Fearless of ever finding open land,
> Or highway where the slow wheel pours the sand.

The menace implicit in "mask of gloom" is dismissed with a "merest" shrug in the youthful speaker's flaunting rejection of human intercourse and in his cocky insistence that his area of escape be not only dark but vast and unending, extending indefinitely into both space and time as the Shakespearean phrase suggests. Such a stance would be quite offensive were it not for the ironic qualifications Frost has written into the poem. Although the youth's wish verges on the momentous (perhaps the eschatological), his earnest commitment to a journey toward the "edge of doom" is called into question by his own admission, in the opening line, that what he describes is only *"one* of my wishes." Thus, readers of "Into My Own" are pertinently reminded of the presence of "a boy's will," a will which is, after all, the wind's. Frost's title, which is taken from Longfellow's refrain, "A boy's will is the wind's will" (in "My Lost Youth"), serves to prepare for the false starts and sudden shifts of direction in "Into My Own." For it is a boy who speaks here, and despite his professed antipathy to clearings, he is no Leatherstocking. His repeated use of the conditional tense also undermines his brash determination to "steal away"; and where his rhetoric is most convincing, in the final line of the second quatrain where starkness of detail obtrudes itself to become metonymically suggestive, where his projected journey is presented as a deliberate rejection of civilization, progress, and even the sands of time—he is unable to hold fast to his vision:

> I do not see why I should e'er turn back,
> Or those should not set forth upon my track
> To overtake me, who should miss me here
> And long to know if still I held them dear.

The "sonnet" turns here as with the wind. The youth who would not be "withheld" from his program of total escape now reveals his propensity to hold on and his need to be held, as he envisages a reunion with friends and family who have solicitously pursued him into the forest. Unlike the old, firm trees that "scarcely show the breeze," the speaker of "Into My Own" is a sapling.

In "Ghost House," the lyric which directly follows "Into My Own," adolescent role experimentation continues as the speaker rather deliberately assumes a posture which is patently macabre in its exclusion of the living for the dead. The poem is uneven and is, I believe, deserving of the silence accorded it by Frost's critics. It does, however, enumerate what is to become another of Frost's major preoccupations: the ease with which nonhuman forces reclaim and absorb man's efforts in staking out a claim for order and survival. Frost is to treat this theme more thoroughly and complexly in such ghost-house poems as "The Need of Being Versed in Country Things" and "Directive." For our immediate purposes, as we allow "lyric to be piled on lyric," "Ghost House" is important for its presentation, however muted, of the speaker's state of mind. In spite of his ready assumption of nature's point of view (e.g. "The footpath down to the well is healed") and his explicit cultivation of a "society" which has been obliterated, his instincts are healthy; he is obviously *not* "happy in society of his choosing." (Frost's original 1913 gloss for "Ghost House" asserts ironically: "He is happy in society of his own choosing.") The "strangely aching heart," the wistful glance at the "close-keeping . . . lass and lad" reveal romantic longings, an awareness of which should facilitate entry into the amorous context of the lyric which follows, a context which seems strangely to have eluded readers of *A Boy's Will.* Indeed, for one who has claimed that all of his poems are love poems, Frost has received little credit for his extensive treatment of the grand passion throughout his poetry.

Frost's commentators have generally ignored "My November Guest" and its place in *A Boy's Will.* Reuben Brower alludes briefly to the early poem as a means of pointing up the pervasive sadness in the later poem, "Directive": "Sorrow is a less consoling companion than in 'My November Guest'; she has now become a presence more deeply and more painfully affecting." [5] Of interest here is Mr. Brower's tacit assumption about the addressee of Frost's early poem; he views "My Sorrow" as an abstract "presence," an element, perhaps, of the speaker's own psyche. But "My November Guest" is more than a mood-piece announcing the speaker's "love of bare November days." The lyric, one of the finest in *A Boy's Will,* is quite convincingly a love poem; and "My Sorrow" is no reference to an allegorical personage but a term of endearment addressed with teasing, third-person obliquity to a lady. The wistful adolescent of "Ghost House" has become the lighthearted suitor.

In its playfulness and decorum "My November Guest" approaches the "goodly temperature" of Spenser's *Amoretti* and should be read in such a spirit. The poem moves from the controlled expression of the speaker's desire: "My Sorrow, when she's here with me" (would she were here more often); to the mock-complaint of: "Her pleasure will not let me stay./She talks and I am fain to list"—where the archaisms underscore the speaker's own awareness of his conventional role as the put-upon lover; to the playful criticism implicit in his use of the verb "vex": "She thinks I have no eye for these,/And vexes me for reason why." Rather than revel in desolation or gloom for its own sake—as in the two previous poems—the speaker's ultimate purpose is to invoke the bare November scene as an occasion for compliment:

> Not yesterday I learned to know
> The love of bare November days
> Before the coming of the snow,
> But it were vain to tell her so,
> And they are better for her praise.

The final line, casually appended by "and," tells all. The speaker's eye has all along been approvingly on the lady; and the light, patronizing boast of "Not yesterday I learned to know" is for her benefit—so too the extra-duty "vain" which reflects both the speaker's humble silence and the lady's unwillingness to listen to him. Thus, throughout the poem, the cold, colorless November landscape has served as a foil for the warm and colorful relationship so decorously defined by the speaker. Such a relationship, however, is not to remain immune to outside incursions; once the November guest becomes "bride" (in "Love and a Question"), the self-contained joys of young love are starkly called into question.

Although "Love and a Question" is marred by a distinct heavy-handedness in Frost's handling of allegorical detail, the epithalamic situation in the ballad is charged with emotional currents that often lurk effectively beneath the narrative surface. The opening stanza, with its allegorical presentation of the "Stranger," hints of the forces which imperil the cozy security defined by the bridal house. Burdened with "care," and bearing also an offshoot of the half-dead realm of nature ("a green-white stick"), the solitary visitor, like his less allegorical counterparts in "The Death of the Hired Man," "The Fear," or "Snow," poses a threat to the comfort, stability, and order of "home." As the focus shifts rapidly from the outer gloom ("green-white," "littered," "blue") to the inner hearth ("rose-red"), we sense a growing burden within the bridegroom himself until, finally, the Stranger looms before us as "woe," a portion of the bridegroom's own divided consciousness.

For unlike the defiant youth of "Into My Own" or the self-assured lover of "My November Guest," the bridegroom is all too aware of the conflicting demands upon him. Under the shadow of the

Stranger, he can no more ignore the "weary" road outside than his passionate bride within:

> The bridegroom looked at the weary road,
>   Yet saw but her within,
> And wished her heart in a case of gold
>   And pinned with a silver pin.

The fragility and tentativeness of the yet-to-be consummated relationship is implicit in the bridegroom's wish: he would protect her heart and secure it before admitting the chilling air of the outside world. Yet, it is a central irony of the poem that the outer gloom, the winter wind, or "woe," has unquestionably entered the bridal house through the bridegroom's own intense awareness of it. The poem ends inconclusively with the bridegroom unable to reconcile his aroused awareness of the outer world with his commitment to the unquestioning seclusion of the glowing coal and the heart's desire.

I turn now to "A Late Walk," the third in a series of love poems which invoke the barrenness of a late autumnal landscape. The speaker is not the carefree suitor—"in love with being misunderstood" (Frost's gloss)—of "My November Guest"; rather, he is a married lover burdened with the "care" acknowledged in "Love and a Question" and acutely aware that his responsiveness to the outer scene intensifies and objectifies his own troubled thoughts and feelings. In the strained Emersonianism of this poem, nature quite explicitly "wears the colors of the spirit" so that the same sort of scene which elicited "pleasure" in "My November Guest" points here toward loss, destruction, and sadness. Indeed, the first half of this lyric is comprised of so copious a presentation of natural objects piled heavily upon one another to define the speaker's autumnal mood that shuffling through the "headless aftermath" and past the tangled garden ground, with "whir," "wither," "sober," "sadder," wears poetic faith thin. What begins to save the poem from the speaker's wallowing in his own forced misery is the third stanza with its exaggerated example of Emerson's "occult relation between man and the vegetable," and the speaker's revelation—"I doubt not"—of his own awareness of the fanciful level he has attained. The final stanza offers a bittersweet consolation with control and grace:

> I end not far from my going forth,
>> By picking the faded blue
>> Of the last remaining aster flower
>> To carry again to you.

The tone here is quite complex—modulating between a sadness residing in the "faded blue" of the aster, and the buoyancy of a lover's ritual of which the aster is "again" a part. But the most effective touch in the poem is the delayed and unexpected direct address to "you." It is the "you" which has put an end to the speaker's going forth in sadness; it is the "you" which is—and over the years has been—dependably there to receive and understand the final, redeeming gesture. And the impact of the direct address is all the more emphatic as we come to it not only through the labyrinth of "A Late Walk," but also through the accumulated pressure of its absence in the oblique, third-person reference to "My Sorrow" ("My November Guest") and in the impersonal, yet subjective, ballad-narrative of "Love and a Question."

From the late autumnal scene of "A Late Walk," *A Boy's Will* thrusts headlong into winter, the season of reflection and contemplation as Thoreau once viewed it but, for Frost's speaker, a season which serves to provoke and intensify conflict. In "Stars," snow-whiteness points, as it does in the later lyrics "The Onset" and "Desert Places," toward meaninglessness and extinction. There is little comfort to be taken from stars which are not only blind to human purpose but are viewed as the expressionless eyes of a divinity which is itself stone deaf and dumb. And in "Storm Fear," a grossly underrated lyric, Frost's treatment of winter is chillingly extended to the unsettled inner weather of his speaker.

Unlike the majestic arrival of Emerson's snowstorm, "announced by all the trumpets of the sky," the wind and snow of Frost's "Storm Fear" arrive surreptitiously under the cloak of night:

> When the wind works against us in the dark,
> And pelts with snow
> The lower-chamber window on the east,
> And whispers with a sort of stifled bark,
> The beast,
> "Come out! Come out!"—

> It costs no inward struggle not to go,
> Ah, no!

These lines generate a dark sense of furtive entanglement on the part of nonhuman forces working insidiously against man. Yet the drama unfolded in this poem moves through and beyond a distinct opposition between Man and Nature, the Me and the Not-Me. Immediately one is struck by the curious tonal disruptions in the two one-foot lines: "The beast," and "Ah, no!" The one punctures the portentousness of the first four lines by intruding a tone of lighthearted scorn; the other, through an exclamatory insistence rare in Frost, suggests the opposite of what it disclaims. What these lines have most significantly in common is their revelation of the speaker's uncertainty and ambivalence in regard to the storm he describes. The tensions here are thus within the speaker himself who is doing his rhetorical best to persuade himself of the ease with which he can reject the storm's "Come out! Come out!"—while all along "the beast" is that part of him which interprets the wind's whisper as an invitation. Such a dual commitment is reminiscent of the speaker's predicament in "Love and a Question." Here, although it is not a new, uncertain relationship which is besieged, but an established "us," the winter wind strikes where it is most to be feared—"the lower chamber window on the east"—and works against the uncertain fire within:

> I count our strength,
> Two and a child,
> Those of us not asleep subdued to mark
> How the cold creeps as the fire dies at length—
> How drifts are piled,
> Dooryard and road ungraded,
> Till even the comforting barn grows far away,
> And my heart owns a doubt
> Whether 'tis in us to arise with day
> And save ourselves unaided.

The sparse, impersonal language—"Two and a child/Those of us not asleep . . ."—is chilling in its revelation of the extent to which the speaker's own fire has died at length. Here, without question, "woe" has entered the house, has entered as the cold creeps into the speaker's heart and renders it susceptible to "doubt." For the "storm fear" of this poem is more than a fear of the outer elements; it is the speaker's fear of his own wintry isolation from those who hold him dear and, consequently, a fear of the numbing estrangement to which "two and a child" have been "subdued." Thus, the final lines of the poem, far from summarizing "a simple matter of black and white, of surviving or not surviving," [6] point insistently toward the emotional depths to which the speaker's "doubt" has taken him: in his "heart" he senses the disintegration of home and family, and he comes to the stark realization that only from within ("in us") can help arrive—which is to say that if the disruptive "beast" remains unexorcized, if the "two" of the poem cannot work things out within and between themselves, if they cannot save themselves "unaided," they cannot save themselves.

"Storm Fear" is truly a disturbing poem, and in its bleak depiction of the wild and random forces which threaten to undermine the stronghold of marriage, it anticipates the sudden and terrifying severance of "ties" in such a later poem as "The Hill Wife." For in dealing with what his detractors view as a reductive context—man in and against nature—Frost, even in his earliest volume, makes it his business to deal also with the universal conflict of man against himself.

In "Love and a Question," "Storm Fear," and, more implicitly in "Into My Own" and "A Late Walk," Frost has revealed distinct and opposing aspects of his speaker's personality. One aspect comprises an acceptance and appreciation of the warm, comforting order defined by bride, family or fireside, while the other affects a strong propensity for a cold, unbounded freedom implicit in the decaying disorder of nature and the turbulent winter wind. "Wind and Window Flower" effectively picks up this thread by treating with sustained impersonality what readers of *A Boy's Will* can and should view as a very personal gesture. The opening stanza, by enjoining all lovers to "forget" their own love and to listen to the story about to be unfolded, suggests that the narrator fully believes in the uniqueness of the love he is about to sing. Although the narrative appears to deal objectively, though fancifully, with nonhuman activity, it is crucial to an understanding of the poem and of its place in *A Boy's Will* that we read "She a window flower,/And he a winter breeze" as figurative language which defines a specific human relationship of which the narrator-protagonist is a part. Stanza three, for example, in which "he" marks "her" through the window-pane, offers Frost's earliest use of the "window-pane" motif, a motif which, throughout his career, he was to endow with a variety of significances. In order to gain an ordered perspective on that which defies order, Frost's speakers are often instinctively attracted, as in "Home Burial" or "A Servant to Servants," to "window-views." In "Wind and Window Flower," the motif provides a metaphorical representation of an insurmountable distance that may occur between lovers despite physical proximity. This central metaphor shows the narrative as a whole to be a parable that the speaker offers specifically to his lady. For all his objectivity, the narrator of this "story of modern love" (Frost's rubric) cannot refrain from revealing his personal involvement—his close connection with the "winter wind" of which he speaks, and his own impatience with his flower's intractability:

> He was a winter wind,
>   Concerned with ice and snow,
> Dead weeds and unmated birds,
>   And little of love could know.

We cannot take the final line of this stanza at face value since the main thrust of this poem is towards a demonstration of the "love" which this line denies. In this stanza, the narrator assumes what he takes to be the lady's point of view in regard to her lover, a point of view the narrator does not accept and therefore presents ironically for her benefit. Indeed, the winter wind does know love, but a love directed at one whose allure and whose survival depend upon conditions inimical to "ice and snow/Dead weeds and unmated birds." The domestic containment of what was once wild—as in the "caged yellow bird"—defines the window flower's plight, and to remove her from the warm stove-window light would be fatal. Of this the narrator-wooer is well aware; yet, like the wind, he persists in his hopes of prevailing upon her for a flight beyond the window glass; he would have both the tamed and the wild at once. And the impossibility of satisfying such a desire is poignantly recognized in the concluding stanza of the poem:

But the flower leaned aside
    And thought of naught to say,
And morning found the breeze
    A hundred miles away.

There is finally "naught" to be said; for with a window-pane so fixedly between them, the lovers might just as well be separated by a hundred miles.

The appeal "To the Thawing Wind" marks a turning point in the sequence of poems which have stressed the threatening chill of winter outside as well as the wintry weather within Frost's speaker, whose isolation would seem (in "Storm Fear" and "Wind and Window Flower") to have become intolerable. The "loud Southwester" (Shelley's "azure sister" to the "wild West Wind") brings with it promise of renewal and growth both to the "buried flower" and to the speaker himself who, for the first time, casts himself in the role of the poet. Indeed, precisely the poet in him has led the protagonist of "Love and a Question," "Storm Fear," or "Wind and Window Flower" to an insatiate yet firmly qualified attraction for the out-of-doors. Calling upon the "violence of the elements" (Frost's gloss) to melt his window glass, the "poet" in "To the Thawing Wind" commits himself almost totally to a position which he heretofore either felt compelled to resist or accepted woefully. The rejected invitation of the wind in "Storm Fear,"—"come out! come out!"—is here solicited and accepted, as the poet invokes the Southwest wind to change him by thawing his wintry isolation. For, in his fancy, the speaker envisages a situation in which both aspects of his opposing self might be satisfied: by asking the thawing wind to "melt the glass and *leave the sticks*" (italics mine), he reveals once again his desire for immediate contact with the wild and unbounded, but also his attachment (like the hermit to his crucifix) to some hallmark of order and security.

With the coming of spring, the "window flower" can thrive out-of-doors, and the poet's yearning for the world beyond the window-glass can be fulfilled without complication. Thus the speaker of "A Prayer in Spring" emerges from his isolation and asks for a momentary stay in which he and she (the "us") would be kept "all simply in the springing of the year." Behind this almost saccharine appreciation of the natural world and the wish for simple, immediate absorption of "us" in the experience of spring, lies an urgency on the part of the speaker which emerges not only from his repeated entreaties ("Oh, give us pleasure") but also from the context which his language defines. For, notwithstanding the Christian context into which Frost's official biographer places the poem,[7] this lyric is finally a poem of "carpe diem." If not blatantly sexual, the first two stanzas suggest fertility, growth, gestation (flowers, bees, "springing," "dilating"), while stanza three, with its exact appreciation of the humming bird, is no less evocative with its inward "thrust," a word Frost is to use in "Meeting and Passing" and "All Revelation" with similar physical force. The concluding stanza, despite its reference to God, is anything but pious, as the speaker explicitly equates human love with the natural events he has graphically depicted:

> For this is love and nothing else is love,
> The which it is reserved for God above
> To sanctify to what far ends He will,
> But which it only needs that we fulfill.

God is invoked here only to be dismissed as irrelevant: He "sanctifies" for His own "far ends" the procreative urge of nature; but "we" can "fulfill" it here and now (think not of the "uncertain harvest") by completing on the human level that process which is taking place so naturally among the birds and the bees.

Few mortals can continue long "all simply in the springing of the year"; those complexities and conflicts so Edenically absent from "A Prayer in Spring" soon reappear. In "Flower-Gathering," a springtime companion-piece to the autumnal "A Late Walk," a growing tension between lovers is manifest in the speaker's insistent questionings and his listener's utter silence ("Are you dumb because you know me not,/Or dumb because you know?"). And although in the final lines of this poem the solitary wanderer dramatically redeems his position in respect to his lady by placing a lover's value on the flowers he brings back, a marked strain in his rhetoric belies reconciliation. In the summer poem, "Rose Pogonias," a confining, hothouse atmosphere detracts from whatever pleasure the lovers take in bowing together "in the burning"; and with the brief exception of the five-lined poem, "In Neglect," the lover who waits dreamily "afield at dusk," who retreats into sexual fantasies "In a Vale," or who unconvincingly denies, in "A Dream Pang," that he "dwelt aloof," might just as well be "a hundred miles away." Indeed, "The Vantage Point," by depicting the speaker's close, sensuous engagement with nature, reveals the extraordinary distance from which the speaker can view all of mankind. Yet the lyric which concludes the series of poems we have been considering (a series which Frost originally designated as "Part I" of *A Boy's Will*), expresses with utmost dignity and conviction a mature and heartfelt intimacy between man and wife.

The pervasive lightheartedness of "Going for Water," its insouciant celebration of a deeply shared moment in nature, sets it apart from a group of love lyrics in *A Boy's Will* which have presented a dreamy-eyed and sometimes tormented youth whose attraction to woods and flowers, ice and snow, has often dissociated him emotionally or physically, if only "for the ages of a day," from his married lover. In this poem, "a late walk" is its own consolation, and any barrenness in the autumn scene is vitalized by the buoyant tone of the speaker who, in recounting the performance of a simple country task, moves beyond the practical aspects of "pail and can" to reveal the extent to which two lovers are as one.

The poem is unique to *A Boy's Will* in its unqualified compliment to both lovers for being what they are. What lifts it out of the ordinary is its exquisite decorum in invoking objective details to express and contain enthusiasm. The heightened facts of the concluding stanza could not be more appropriate:

> A note as from a single place,
> A slender tinkling fall that made
> Now drops that floated on the pool
> Like pearls, and now a silver blade.

The stark simplicity of language almost conceals the artfulness of these synesthetic images. By focusing on "the moon and running water," subjects which Frost described as overworked and "hard to do anything with," the poet manages to affirm, with quiet originality, both the individual integrity of his protagonists, man and wife, and the perfection of their union. For from the delicate intermingling of sound and sight emerges a confluence of feminine and masculine configurations: the fragile, passive drops "like pearls" and the assertive "silver blade," though separate, are parts of the same "tinkling fall." Here lies the treasure hoard of these gnome-like lovers (see stanza 4), a rare find uncovered by their jointly attuned senses—and with the help of the moon. Incited to their task by a delight in their joint ownership of the fields and woods (stanza 2), the lovers conclude their journey by making the brook theirs too; in the process, they achieve and display a serene self-possession, "a note as from a single place."

The "large design" we have been tracing in *A Boy's Will* breaks off rather suddenly with the meditative, philosophizing poems which immediately succeed "Part I"; the tensions or crosscurrents which provide the "drama" of a major portion of the preceding lyrics are conspicuously absent—and the poems suffer. Frost's speaker (with the exception, perhaps, of his role in "The Tuft of Flowers") comes dangerously close to shedding his individuality, which is to say that the poems "Revelation," "The Trial by Existence," "Pan With Us," and "The Demiurge's Laugh" are *not* "easily heard as sung or spoken by a person in a scene—in character, in a setting." Frost recognized the danger of too much philosophizing in poetry, of "flirting with the entelechies," [8] and in his final cluster of poems in *A Boy's Will* (originally "Part III"), he again offers us drama. The conflict within the speaker of "In Hardwood Groves," for example, emerges steadily until reason and emotion, head and heart, clash urgently and effectively in the twice repeated "*must*." And "A Line-Storm Song," with its speaker's persistent supplication of his lady to "come forth into the storm and rout," offers once again a dramatic situation in which love raises a loaded question. But it is in the much neglected poem, "Reluctance," that the "broken or dotted continuity" of large design in *A Boy's Will* is brought to a rounded conclusion.

The opening, retrospective lines of "Reluctance" describe a journey very similar to the one projected by the speaker of "Into My Own:"

> Out through the fields and the woods
> And over the walls I have wended;
> I have climbed the hills of view

And looked at the world, and descended;
I have come by the highway home,
And lo, it is ended.

The tone of voice tells us a good deal about the speaker: he is resigned, subdued, anything but flamboyant; and in spite of a trace of
sadness in his voice, he accepts, with a wise passiveness, the limitations set upon his experience. No longer "Fearless of ever finding
open land,/Or highway, . . ." he has "come by the highway home";
in so doing, he demonstrates his recognition of the implausibility,
the impossibility of a boundless journey. Earlier the possibility of
"ends" had been dismissed with a cavalier flourish; here there is "reluctance" because ends are so explicitly confronted—and accepted.
Coming into his own through a mature and reasoned appreciation
of limits, the speaker, with reluctance, accepts both the passing of
the seasons and the passing of his own youth, a time when, in fearless
abandon, he could and did acquiesce to the "drift of things" *without* reluctance, since the "heart" and "reason" were not then at odds
and since "the feet" did not then question "Whither?" Now, however, like the dead leaves that "lie huddled and still/No longer blown
hither and thither" (stanza 3), the speaker's will is no longer the
wind's. The defiant adolescent of "Into My Own" has ripened into
manhood.

Particularly striking about this "poem of experience" is the isolated position of its speaker and his own trenchant awareness of this
isolation. Earlier, from the isolation imposed by "storm fear," he
could at least speak of "those of us not asleep"; now he suggests
(stanza 2) that only he will be awake to the torturous "scraping
and creeping" of the oak leaves over the snow—"when others are
sleeping." Earlier he could subdue the isolation of "a late walk"
through a lover's gesture ("By picking the faded blue/Of the last
remaining aster flower/To carry again to you"); now he recognizes
that the possibility for such reconciliation is "gone" with the "last
lone aster." Thus, even "love" (the word sneaks chillingly into the
final line of the poem) has its end; and to the seasoned speaker confronting a dead, crusted world, nothing is left but the insistent refusal
to bow and accept what reason knows. Yet this, Frost would have
us believe, is everything: our mere reluctance to go with the drift

of things is heroic proof of our humanity; like the resistant white wave in "West-Running Brook," it is "most us." It is most Frost.

Despite the maturity of the speaker in "Reluctance," the poem's self-conscious deliberation is typical of a majority of the lyrics in *A Boy's Will* where Frost's "I" rarely reaches the objectivity and distance of later poems. Indeed, it is tempting to look through the lyrics of *A Boy's Will* to the headstrong youth whose bittersweet courtship and marriage is so boldly depicted in Lawrance Thompson's *Robert Frost: The Early Years*. Frost himself once wrote that "a poem would be no good that hadn't doors"; but he was quick to add: "I wouldn't leave them open though." [9] In *A Boy's Will*, Frost does not discourage entry as he does in his next volume, *North of Boston*, where he willfully bolts his doors by writing dramatic monologues and dialogues. Even in his lyric-narratives (e.g. "After Apple-Picking"), he assumes a voice more assured and steady and less transparent than the personal, self-reflexive idiom of his first volume. This is not to say that Frost was to cast aside the wealth of self-dramatizations he so explicitly offers in *A Boy's Will*—the petulant adolescent, the brooding melancholic, the lighthearted suitor, the nature lover, the husband burdened with care, the solitary wanderer—but that he worked toward and achieved, in individual poems, a greater integration and compression. Consequently, the tone deepens. Rather than "speak and tell us where" he is, the vintage Frost moves with Yankee cunning through and out of his poems, leaving final judgments, if any can be made, to his readers. The explicit assertions of *A Boy's Will*, as in the final stanza of "Reluctance," are superseded by subtle modulations of tone which often hold opposing points of view in masterful suspension. In the sonnet "Mowing," for example, Frost acknowledges the hard fact of the scythe's indiscriminate cutting edge with so perfect a tonal balance of acceptance and reluctance that the mower's "love" cannot be separated from either his "earnest" determination to perform his task or from his tender appreciation of the nature he disrupts.

The fact that "Mowing" appears in *A Boy's Will* should caution us against making easy distinctions between "early" and "late" Frost. For Frost's poetic development defies neat categories. Thus, we should not be surprised to find in the concluding lyric to his final volume, *In the Clearing*, distinctive ties, thematic and dramatic, with the large design of *A Boy's Will*:

> In winter in the woods alone
> Against the trees I go.
> I mark a maple for my own
> And lay the maple low.
>
> At four o'clock I shoulder ax,
> And in the afterglow
> I link a line of shadowy tracks
> Across the tinted snow.
>
> I see for Nature no defeat
> In one tree's overthrow
> Or for myself in my retreat
> For yet another blow.

This is no defiant adolescent speaking, although the defiance is there all the same—as are the symbolic demarcations and gestures with which readers of *A Boy's Will* should be familiar. In this his final poem, Frost seems to be answering those readers of his poetry who assert that he fails to thrust into the threatening wilderness of nature and of the self but instead retreats to the comforts of the farm or sunny pastures. As we know from *A Boy's Will*, Frost, from the start of his career, was no runaway from the dark side of human or nonhuman nature. And in his last poetic statement, he pertinently reminds us that for him "retreat" is only one part of a strategy which enables him to strike an effective "blow" against chaos and confusion. Frost did not supply a title for this poem, but he might have called it "Into My Own."

Notes to *Design and Drama in* A Boy's Will by LEWIS H. MILLER, JR.

1. See William G. O'Donnell, "Robert Frost and New England," *Yale Review*, XXXVII (1948), 701–702; John F. Lynen, *The Pastoral Art of Robert Frost* (New Haven: Yale University Press, 1960), 18–19; George W. Nitchie, *Human Values in the Poetry of Robert Frost* (Durham: Duke University Press, 1960), passim; and Donald T. Haynes, "The Narrative Unity of *A Boy's Will*," *PMLA*, LXXXVII (1972), 462.

2. For Frost's discussion of "large design," see his letter to Whit Burnett, July 26, 1942, in *Selected Letters of Robert Frost*, ed. Lawrance Thompson (New York: Holt, Rinehart and Winston, 1964), 501; for Frost's discussion of "drama," see his "Preface to *A Way Out*," in *Selected Prose of Robert Frost*, ed. Hyde Cox and

E. C. Lathem (New York: Holt, Rinehart and Winston, 1966), 13.

3. While I quote from *The Poetry of Robert Frost*, I prefer the *Complete Poems of Robert Frost* (New York: Henry Holt and Co., 1949) for the reasons outlined in my review of Mr. Lathem's edition in *The Massachusetts Review*, Summer 1970, 602–604.

4. Robert Frost, "Education by Poetry," in *Selected Prose*, 44.

5. Reuben Brower, *The Poetry of Robert Frost* (New York: Oxford University Press, 1963), 240.

6. Nitchie, *Human Values*, 17.

7. Lawrance Thompson, *Robert Frost: The Early Years* (New York: Holt, Rinehart and Winston, 1966), 324.

8. *Selected Letters*, 202.

9. Thompson, *Frost: Early Years*, 397.

Visions and Revisions: An Early Version of Robert Frost's "Our Doom to Bloom"

KENNETH ROSEN

Edward Connery Lathem notes in *The Poetry of Robert Frost* that "Our Doom to Bloom" was first published "without Robinson Jeffers quote, as 'Doom to Bloom' in booklet form, being RF's 1950 Christmas poem" to his friends. Professor Lawrance Thompson also suggests, in a letter of January 18, 1972, that this poem originally occurs in the manuscript of Frost's poem entitled "How Hard It Is to Keep from Being King When It's in You and in the Situation," published in 1951, and that the first public printing of the "Doom to Bloom" poem was in a very small book published by the House of Books in New York City. All presently available evidence, therefore, suggests that the work I propose to deal with in this paper is an early and heretofore unpublished version of Frost's 1950 Christmas poem.

In 1949 Frost wrote a letter to a young law student named Edward Munce.[1] The letter was, for the most part, a copy of the poem ("On a Tree Fallen Across the Road") that Frost had selected to send to his friends as his holiday greeting card of the 1949 season. Added to this printed copy, however, was the following prose and poetry, written in Frost's own hand:

Odd thing, but I was just toying with some verses for a lawyer when you burst in on me with your news of what was about to become of you. The verses went or set off to go like this:

> Cumaean Sibyl, charming Ogress,
> What are the simple facts of Progress
> That I may handle with reliance
> In consultation with my clients?
>
> The Sibyl said, go back to Rome
> And tell your clientele at home
> That if its not a mere illusion
> All there is to it is diffusion—

Of coats oats votes to all mankind,
Of even more than half a mind,
Of wealth enough to give relief
From all but the more dainty grief

The fear of the conservative
Is that for every gift we give
We may be taking more away
But that is not for us to say.

The state is like a bud whose doom
To spread wide open and perfume
There's no way for it to evade
Unless 'twould rather wilt than fade.

Soon you will be a lawyer God willing, next with my consent a member of Congress. By then this poem will begin to take on meaning for you as a lawyer become law-giver like Cleisthenes for instance or Franklin Roosevelt the diffusionists. The pleasure of hearing again from a favorite pupil prompts me to a longer letter than I have written anyone for years.

Every yours,
Robert Frost

See that I don't lose track of you but don't expect another such letter till I come of age

There are obvious limitations inherent in comparing the early holograph version and the printed version of 1950, but I believe a few significant suggestions may be offered in the course of such a comparison.

The 1949 version has no title and consists of five stanzas of four lines each. Frost cut the poem to four stanzas and added the title "Doom to Bloom" in the printed version of a year later. The versions of the poem printed after 1963 all have the title "Our Doom to Bloom," are prefaced by "Shine, perishing republic" quoted from Robinson Jeffers, and consist of sixteen lines with no stanza divisions. What may be worth noting here is the gradual consolidation and limitation imposed upon the original handwritten lines to Munce. What began in 1949 as a somewhat rambling and universal statement about the mythic nature of political progress finally becomes a carefully focused poem about America, our perishing republic.

Except for a single word ("trade on" substituted for "handle")

and two minor points of punctuation, the first two stanzas of the early version are unchanged in the later printed versions. The third stanza, however, is almost completely reworked. By 1950 this stanza has been tightened up, and Frost's reference to the essentially diffusionist nature of contemporary politics, also noted in the prose comment to Munce about the Greek law-giver Cleisthenes and America's Franklin Roosevelt, has been carefully turned to the essential agreement among modern liberals and conservatives that the state exists primarily to institute such things as proportional representation among the Greek tribes or New Deal gifts to the masses. The third stanza, clear evidence of Frost's view of populists such as Cleisthenes and Roosevelt, determines the printed version's final focus:

> Of coats, oats, votes, to all mankind.
> In the Surviving Book we find
> That liberal, or conservative,
> The state's one function is to give.

The fourth stanza of the early version is completely deleted in later printings of the poem. It seems quite logical to assume that Frost was simply clarifying the political argument by such a deletion, but a closer look at the original fourth stanza may suggest a slightly more subtle motivation. The four lines of the stanza are strangely parochial. They deal with only one side of the ostensibly political coin that is being examined in this poem. The rather philosophical fear of the conservative is stressed here, and Frost's own fears in this area are thereby suggested; but the force of the poem is diminished by the obvious imbalance created by the fourth stanza. After the important third stanza sets the focus, the absence of the liberal voice in the fourth stanza serves to distort that focus. Rather than rely on the direct statement of the fourth stanza, Frost seems to have chosen not to elaborate on either faction mentioned in stanza three. What may be viewed as a serious artistic intrusion in the early version of the poem is thereby avoided in later versions.

The fifth stanza of the early handwritten version becomes the fourth and final stanza of the 1950 poem. In revising the fifth stanza Frost seems to have chosen, once again, to delete the direct statement in favor of a clearer focus and a less rigid and less fatalistic emphasis.

In the early version the state is, "like a bud," doomed "to spread wide open," but the finality suggested in the poem's title is somewhat tempered by Frost's revision of this final stanza:

> The bud must bloom till blowsy blown
> Its petals loosen and are strown;
> And that's a fate it can't evade
> Unless 'twould rather wilt than fade.

The state is still the work's subject, and the state is still part of an inevitable process, but this final revision allows the reader some latitude by focusing on the rather connotative nature of "the bud" instead of on the more specific noun used in the early version.

The discovery of this early version of one of Robert Frost's poems may be of particular critical significance when considered in the context of Frost's work as a whole. Even a brief comparative reading based upon such a discovery may at least suggest some valuable insights into the nature of Frost's artistic procedure. It certainly invites responsible critical speculation about both the political and the aesthetic assumptions of one of America's most important literary figures.

Notes to *Visions and Revisions: An Early Version of Robert Frost's "Our Doom to Bloom"* by KENNETH ROSEN

1. This letter, along with several others written by Frost, is part of the Special Collections section of the Boyd Lee Spahr Library at Dickinson College, and it is with the permission of that section that I now offer the material following in text for publication. Mrs. Martha Slotten first brought the manuscript to my attention, and both she and Professor Charles Sellers have offered me encouragement and professional advice when it was most needed.

Frost's handwriting occasionally borders on the illegible, and I am deeply indebted to Professor Robert Sider for his assistance in figuring out that the word in the manuscript is "Cleisthenes."

Robert Frost's Dark Woods and the Function of Metaphor

DONALD J. GREINER

ANY reader familiar with the scope of Robert Frost's poetry knows that certain metaphors dot his work more consistently than others. Even a cursory glance at the poems reveals that woods and stars are the focal points for patterns of imagery in all of Frost's books. The meaning of these two basic metaphors is not always consistent—hence the caution necessary when a reader suggests that woods and stars mean this or that. Yet these metaphors, plus certain others, such as the wall or the retreat, recur with such consistency, even though their meanings are inconsistent, that examination of them is justified. Of importance equal with what these metaphors might mean is what the term "metaphor" means to Frost. Several perceptive critics have approached the problem through the poet's admitted admiration of Emerson, pointing out Frost's agreement with Emerson's insistence upon the primary value of correspondence and analogy.[1] Both poets hope to show connections between apparently disparate objects and to help the reader recognize analogies which he could have thought of himself but did not. This is not to say that Frost and Emerson completely agree upon the function of metaphor. Emerson believes that poetry should express spirit, while Frost is more concerned with the material fact. Growing naturally from Emerson's preoccupation with spiritual values is his belief that metaphor should illustrate the unity of creation, especially a beneficent unity. Frost could not disagree more. His use of metaphor is more limited in the sense that, unlike Emerson, he does not rely on metaphor to suggest the final unity of all objects. He sets down his thoughts on metaphor most completely in his letters and in "Education by Poetry: A Meditative Monologue." [2] We shall refer to these primary sources as we determine what metaphor means to Frost and the ways he puts it to work in some of his more puzzling, yet popular, poems.

Using the term in its broadest sense, Frost defines all figurative language as metaphor: "I have wanted in late years to go further and further in making metaphor the whole of thinking. I find some one now and then to agree with me that all thinking, except mathematical thinking, is metaphorical, or all thinking except scientific thinking. The mathematical might be difficult for me to bring in, but the scientific is easy enough." Frost suggests here that most thinking and communication take place via allusion and indirection. The expression of a correspondence is one function of metaphor, but Frost feels just as strongly about a second use. Metaphor permits him to suggest this correspondence rather than pinpoint it with direct statement. He hopes to enhance a common object by making it more figurative than it is at first sight. What this idea really amounts to is a different vantage point from which to view the object. Once the new figure or correspondence is determined, indirect expression by means of metaphor secures it in the poem. If all thinking except mathematical thinking is metaphorical, it follows that the reader must be at home with figurative language if the correspondence is to be communicated. Use of private metaphor, of course, cuts off the poet from any meaningful relationship with his reader. Frost's dislike of extremely esoteric poetry is well known. But, he insists again and again, some of the burden rests upon the reader, for not all figurative language or illustration of correspondence can be dismissed as private imagery: "What I am pointing out is that unless you are at home in the metaphor, unless you have had your proper poetical education in the metaphor, you are not safe anywhere. Because you are not at ease with figurative values: you don't know the metaphor in its strength and its weakness. You don't know how far you may expect to ride it and when it may break down with you. You are not safe in science; you are not safe in history."

Ideally, the intelligent reader will be surprised and pleased when he finds a metaphorical notation of a connection he had not anticipated, but he will not be mystified as to meaning and/or significance. Similarly, the metaphor should be a new illustration of a familiar object rather than an introduction of material utterly foreign to the initiated reader. Frost's case for metaphor revolves around recognition. To be a poet, the writer must have an analogizing mind that is capable of recognizing something new about a familiar sight and of suggesting it by way of figurative language. The reader, on the other hand, must be sufficiently schooled in metaphorical expression that he can pick up the figure when he comes across it. The desired communication is a nice balance between writer and reader. Frost writes to John Bartlett: "In literature it is our business to give people the thing that will make them say, 'Oh yes I know what you mean.' It is never to tell them something they dont know, but something they know and hadnt thought of saying. It must be something they recognize." [3] He goes on to illustrate by calling attention to his short poem "A Patch of Old Snow." The setting of this poem is simple enough: a patch of snow that is dotted with dirt. The juxtaposition of the off-white background with the black specks reminds the poet of an old newspaper, and he realizes that a patch of dirty snow is just as useless as yesterday's news. Yet this simple setting *is* the poem—the eight lines are the metaphor. They exist for Frost primarily as a means to communicate an analogy he has recognized: "Now [the scene in this poem] is no good except for what I may call certain points of recognition in it: patch of old snow in a corner of the wall,—you know what that is. You know what a blow-away newspaper is. You know the curious dirt on old snow and last of all you know how easily you forget what you read in papers."

A much better example is the sonnet "The Silken Tent." All fourteen lines are a single extended metaphor expressed in one extraordinary sentence so that this metaphor forms the poem. Essentially a love poem, "The Silken Tent" illustrates the woman's steadfastness by comparing her to a tent standing in a field. The poem's brilliance is revealed in the successful way Frost treats a difficult subject: how a woman can be bound to one love and yet maintain her freedom. The tent metaphor works perfectly, for the poet knows that we have all seen a tent sway with the breeze. With the center pole hidden, it seems to stand alone, in total freedom, until the sway causes the guy ropes to exert gentle pressure, and we realize that the tent is free within the limits of its definition:

> She is as in a field a silken tent
> At midday when a sunny summer breeze
> Has dried the dew and all its ropes relent,
> So that in guys it gently sways at ease. . . .

The center pole which provides direction for the tent is a metaphor for the woman's soul. Were it not for her soul, life's circumstances as well as her own feminine nature, both suggested by the capricious breeze, might weaken her ties of love. Although she is not "strictly held," she is, like the tent, "loosely bound" with countless ties that are revealed when capriciousness calls pressure into play:

> And only by one's going slightly taut
> In the capriciousness of summer air
> Is of the slightest bondage made aware.

Although the poem is one extended metaphor, the metaphorical expression is composed of several levels that contribute to the whole. The woman is a silken tent, silken to suggest femininity as opposed to the rough canvas of most tents. The "ties of love and thought" are the guy ropes; the soul is the center pole; and the whims of personality are the capricious breezes that cause the tent to sway, consequently calling attention to the pole and guys. The metaphor's various levels mesh to compose a perfect lyric. Frost knows that, as with "A Patch of Old Snow," we will recognize the analogy as a new way of looking at a common object. He uses metaphor to renew old material much the same way that he relies on voice tones to refresh old words.

Frost likes to refer to these unexpected, but common, correspondences as "enthusiasm tamed by metaphor." He means that metaphor gives shape to inspiration, or expression, or emotion. The word "tamed" is interesting because it suggests that the unformed thought is often wild, or as capricious as, say, the wind in "The Silken Tent." We recall his statement from the well-known essay "The Figure a Poem Makes": "Then there is this wildness whereof it is spoken. Granted again that it has an equal claim with sound to being a poem's better half." Thus while a poet may recognize correspondences, his recognition will fail in poetry if it is expressed as an uncontrolled outpouring. It will lack form and direction, and it will, like most enthusiasm, diminish with time. Frost writes that he is not afraid of enthusiasm but that he would distinguish two kinds. One is a blinding or deafening enthusiasm which is foreign to poetry and which he names, with characteristic humor, "sunset raving." When face to face with something inspiring, the poet who is caught by this enthusiasm can express himself with no more meaning than the raves of "oh" and "ah." But the enthusiasm which Frost approves of is "tamed" by metaphor so that meaningful expression is possible. As if playing with his readers, he defines this taming process with another metaphor: enthusiasm tamed by metaphor corresponds to the way a prism tones down a bright light:

But the enthusiasm I mean is taken through the prism of the intellect and spread on the screen in a color, all the way from hyperbole at one end—or overstatement, at one end—to understatement at the other end. It is a long strip of dark lines and many colors. Such enthusiasm is one object of all teaching in poetry.... I would be willing to throw away everything else but that: enthusiasm tamed by metaphor. Let me rest the case there.... I do not think anybody ever knows the discreet use of metaphor, his own and other people's, the discreet handling of metaphor, unless he has been properly educated in poetry.

Providing a sensible means to control the poet's zeal, metaphor also serves as a meeting place for the intellect and enthusiasm.

Originality counts too, of course, but it is the originality of renewal. The originality, the freshness, is in the analogy and in the surprise of recognizing a connection between common objects such as a woman and a tent so that both assume new meaning. New trivial metaphors do more to distinguish a poem than borrowed great ones. Frost writes in his essay "The Constant Symbol" that a poem is nothing if it fails to suggest a new metaphor, great or small: "There are many other things I have found myself saying about poetry, but the chiefest of these is that it is metaphor, saying one thing and meaning another, saying one thing in terms of another, the pleasure of ulteriority. Poetry is simply made of metaphor.... Every poem is a new metaphor inside or it is nothing." Defending slight metaphors, such as the one expressed in "A Patch of Old Snow," he goes on in "Education by Poetry" to argue that slight metaphors represent the initial steps toward great thoughts or commitments. His thinking here is certainly Emersonian. In "The Poet," Emerson insists that trivial things have significant metaphorical value if they are expressed through an original correspondence. Seen in this light, not only triv-

ial objects, but even the base and obscene can illustrate a new analogy: "Small and mean things serve as well as great symbols. . . . The
poorest experience is rich enough for all the purposes of expressing
thought. Why covet a knowledge of new facts? Day and night,
house and garden, a few books, a few actions, serve us as well as
would all trades and all spectacles. We are far from having exhausted
the significance of the few symbols we use. We can come to use
them yet with a terrible simplicity." [4] Emerson's optimism and his
assurance that the oversoul will render the meanest experience meaningful are evident here. Frost rejects the religious implications, but
he echoes Emerson when he writes that poetry begins in trivial metaphors and then "goes on to the profoundest thinking that we have."

Especially important in Frost's definition of metaphor is his belief that metaphor functions as a kind of form. Trivial or elaborate,
all metaphors provide form for the recognition of correspondence,
and, as such, they are "stays" against confusion. The very act of
metaphorical expression, for example, tames the confusion caused by
the raving type of enthusiasm. But like all form in Frost's poetics, be
it a smoke ring or a poem, metaphor is only a momentary stay. It is
a "living thing . . . as life itself," but it eventually breaks down. Yet
this potential failure is the "beauty" of working with figurative language. The poet pits his skill against the metaphor to see how much
it can carry, to determine how far the analogy can go before it becomes farfetched and cracks under the burden. "All metaphor," he
writes, "breaks down somewhere. That is the beauty of it. It is touch
and go with the metaphor, and until you have lived with it long
enough you don't know when it is going. You don't know how
much you can get out of it and when it will cease to yield."

Frost illustrates the process of metaphor crumbling when he reports a conversation with a man who suggested that the universe was
like a machine. After listening to the analogy, Frost asked if the man
had ever seen a machine without a lever or pedal or button with
which to operate and control it. The poet's point is, of course, that
the universe is not like a machine, that it is, in fact, quite different.
The man was willing to carry his analogy only so far, but close examination exposes its instability. Frost feels that a better metaphor
would be to liken the universe to a growing plant. He calls it the

"metaphor of evolution" and admits the brilliance of it. But even this metaphor breaks down when carried to an extreme in discussions of the evolution of, for example, candy or elevators.

A poetical expression of the inability of metaphor to carry too heavy a load is seen in "A Missive Missile." Finding a pebble marked with two red dots and a "ripple streak," the poet wonders if the pebble's design bears a message from the pre-Ice Age era in an attempt to communicate across the centuries. He tries to formulate a correspondence between the design and possible meanings, and he offers two interpretations:

> But what imperfectly appears
> Is whether the two dots were tears,
> Two teardrops, one for either eye,
> And the wave line a shaken sigh.
> But no, the color used is red.
> Not tears but drops of blood instead.
> The line must be a jagged blade.
> The sender must have had to die,
> And wanted someone now to know
> His death was sacrificial-votive.

He is unsure, however, whether or not the pebble's figure can bear such interpretations, and he wonders if all attempts metaphorically to express the design will fail. Yet the definite design nags at him as he muses:

> How anyone can fail to see
> Where perfectly in form and tint
> The metaphor, the symbol lies!

But no metaphor is acceptable unless he limits it to his own private meaning. Both his earlier interpretations and any metaphor he devises in the future will prove unsatisfactory. The span of time between the moment of marking the pebble and this discovery of it is too great to permit meaningful figurative expression.

Metaphorical expression is, of course, oblique; and Frost, like any good poet, names indirection as one of the joys of working with figurative language. For this reason he refuses to answer readers who press him for the "meaning" of a particularly intriguing poem like "Stopping by Woods" or "After Apple-Picking." It is not that he desires to withhold the meaning, to keep it hidden as if the poem were a private communication with the self, but only that poetry, often described by Frost as "simply" metaphor, falls apart when the language is too straightforward. The poet maintains a kind of zigzag course through the act of composition, and he hopes the reader will be willing to follow: "Poetry provides the one permissible way of saying one thing and meaning another." Frost insists that he is not trying to prove anything when he writes metaphorically. Rather, he wants to suggest a correspondence by indirection or to invite the reader to take another look at a common object. He violates his own principle in his later "editorials," but in most of his poetry metaphor is the primary means of communication.

This is another reason why his notion of "sentence sounds" is so vital. By using voice tones, he can convey the desired impression of fear, sarcasm, and so on and still avoid the direct commentary that he dislikes. The reader again plays a key role, for he must be at home with the idea of voice tones if he hopes to follow the poem. A precise use of words, free of nonessentials, clarifies metaphor and tone so that suggestiveness is successful. Answering a friendly critic's complaint that he omitted words, Frost replies, "I give you credit for being able to supply words plainly understood. Dialogue would be unendurable if all words had to be said outright for complete construction." [5] This technique functions significantly in the longer poems in which metaphor joins colloquially clipped dialogue to suggest meaning. Almost any example will serve as illustration, from the end of "Home Burial" with the husband's threat of forceful action to keep Amy home, to "Snow" with Mrs. Cole's growing impatience at Meserve's presence despite her genuine concern for his safety. One of the most dramatic and famous examples is found in "The Death of the Hired Man." Toward the end of the poem, Warren enters the house to talk with Silas after Mary has persuaded him to sympathize with the broken man and offer him his old job. Silas' death will come as no surprise because the poem's title clearly tells us what Warren will find. The poem's focus, however, is not on what will happen but on the way Frost communicates the death. Suspense is sacrificed for inevitability, and our attention is drawn away from the hired man of the title to the actions, opinions, and emotions of Warren and Mary. What matters is not so much that Silas will die but that Mary's sympathy for him has broken through Warren's demands for justice. Frost suggests Silas' death with a perfect metaphor when he describes Mary watching a cloud and the moon while waiting for Warren's return from the house. The cloud "hits" the moon, momentarily blotting out its light, and we know that Silas has died. This metaphorical hint is then reinforced by the action. Warren returns, "too soon," with the news of what he has found. When Mary questions him, only one word is needed to convey the full impact of the situation because the cloud-moon metaphor has already done the work:

> Warren returned—too soon, it seemed to her—
> Slipped to her side, caught up her hand and waited.
> "Warren?" she questioned.
>   "Dead," was all he answered.

Frost assumes that the careful reader will note how metaphor and dialogue function together.

Keeping in mind Frost's thoughts on metaphor, we should now examine one of the basic metaphors which consistently appears in his poetry. Ask any knowledgeable reader of Frost what one metaphor shows up more often than any other, and he will answer "woods." This metaphor has intrigued the critics since it first appeared in the first poem of Frost's first book, "Into My Own" in *A Boy's Will*, and many articles have been written to suggest interpretations. One critic writes that the woods symbolize "nature itself with its challenge and fascination." [6] The woods draw the poet-figure to them and hold him spellbound for a moment before he returns to the world of man. Another critic feels that the woods are the "alien entanglements" which Frost must face and against which he matches his strength. In this reading, the woods pose a serious threat, but the poet risks the meeting because he fashions his poems from it. [7] A third interpretation argues that in a few poems the creative impulse can be equated with the woods, and that the mood associated with woods grows darker in the later poems. [8] A more recent article places Frost's use of woods in the whole tradition of American literature, from *The Deerslayer* through *Huckleberry Finn* to

Go Down, Moses, as part of the wilderness theme and the irrational choice which escape to the wilderness suggests.[9] Despite these various readings, two common points can be found in nearly every discussion of the woods metaphor in Frost's poetry: the woods throw a spell on the poet-figure which invites him to forsake his daily business, and the woods are nearly always dark.

We should begin with a discussion of the spellbinding power of the woods because most interpretations of poems like "Stopping by Woods," "The Sound of Trees," and "Come In" comment upon the poet-figure's almost mystical attraction to the trees.[10] "Stopping by Woods" is the focal point of this particular reading of Frost because it contains most of the elements to be found in the group of poems that inspires the interpretation. Finding himself alone between the opposing worlds of nature and man, the traveler stops to watch the woods fill up with snow. Even his horse knows that one does not normally stop so far from the village, especially on the "darkest evening of the year." But any fear of isolation which the traveler might have gives way before the pull of his casual interest in the scene. Natural interest, though, soon becomes fascination as the woods, with the help of "easy wind and downy flake," begin to weave their spell. The woods seem to offer a place of revery, a welcome interlude from the promises that should be kept. But while the woods are lovely, they are also "dark and deep." The apparently measureless domain of the woods neutralizes for a moment the traveler's definite commitment to the village before he breaks the spell and moves on toward town. He rejects the mysteries which the woods offer to keep the undefined promises awaiting him in the village. Or at least he seems to free himself from the woods. This is the standard reading of the woods metaphor in "Stopping by Woods on a Snowy Evening." It is highly probable, however, that the conflict remains unresolved as the poem ends. The repetition of the last two lines ("And miles to go before I sleep") has generally been interpreted to mean that the narrator is stressing his obligation to the village as he turns his back on the trees, but perhaps this repetition should be read in conjunction with the repeated rhyme sound in the last stanza. The sound of the final quatrain is hypnotic, and as such it joins the other sound of "easy wind and downy flake" as the force which lulls the traveler to stop short of the village. The traveler wants to believe that his place is with his promises, but the hypnotic, repetitive sound of the final stanza suggests that his vow will be neutralized by his inaction. If this interpretation has merit, then the poet-figure at the end of "Stopping by Woods" remains in the clearing between village and woods, with the spell of the woods off-setting his awareness of promises.

This pattern, or variations on it, structures most of the poems in which the woods metaphor functions importantly. The poet-figure is alone; he is stationed between the dark woods and man; he feels the pull of both, momentarily entertaining the invitation which the mysterious woods seem to offer; he would like to free himself from his cares; and the central question is whether or not he can reject the spell and accept his burdens or "promises." The same problems are faced in "Come In," a poem which is nearly always discussed along with "Stopping by Woods." Here the loveliness of the woods is represented by a thrush's song, and the darkness is suggested by the fact that it is too late in the evening for the bird to "better its perch for the night. . . ." The music and the woods cast their spell with an invitation to enter the dark and "lament." But approaching no closer than the edge of the trees, the poet-figure rejects the call by turning toward the stars. At this moment the poem's ambiguity is established—what do the stars represent? In refusing to enter the dark woods, the narrator turns toward another kind of isolation and, perhaps, loneliness as suggested by the star. There is certainly no hint in "Come In" that he has decided to return to society or to any obligations which he may have, but the fact remains that he does not enter the trees or "lament" in the "pillared dark." The mood of revery, of fascination bordering on hypnotism, is absent in "Come In," but the conflict is the same as that in "Stopping by Woods." "The Sound of Trees" is an example of a variation on this theme although the basic outline of the conflict remains intact. In this poem the narrator wonders why we tolerate the constant sound of trees when other noises so close to our homes would be resented. Frost uses the word "suffer" to suggest the seriousness of the problem. Significantly, the trees again act as a metaphor for the forces which would pull us away from our daily business:

> We suffer them by the day
> Till we lose all measure of pace,
> And fixity in our joys,
> And acquire a listening air.

The narrator listens to the noise and decides that although the trees talk of going, they will never leave the scene. A parallel is thus established between these trees and the narrators of "Stopping by Woods" and "Come In" who would like to enter the dark woods but who resist the pull. But it is here that Frost subtly varies the pattern of this metaphor. For while the trees may talk of going but never get away, this narrator vows to pack up and leave the "measure of pace":

> I shall make the reckless choice
> Some day when they are in voice
> And tossing so as to scare
> The white clouds over them on.
> I shall have less to say,
> But I shall be gone.

His declaration of freedom from his "promises," however, is ironic because of the identification established between himself and the trees. He has done no more than adopt the tree's pose—constantly talking of going but never making more than the first few moves. The spell of the woods seems complete at the end of this poem, but its intactness is an illusion. The narrator fools himself if he believes that he rejects his obligations.

Clearly, Frost varies the meaning of his woods metaphor. His insistence on allusion and indirection, his use of common objects for metaphorical significance, and his demand that the reader "be at home" in metaphor when thinking or reading are all at work in these illustrations of the woods metaphor. The meaning of the woods is never consistent. Indeed, the only consistency which the reader can be sure of is that Frost varies the significance of his most famous metaphor. For example, although the spell of the trees is contested in "Stopping by Woods" and "Come In," the woods often function as a metaphor for that place to which the poet-figure can retreat away from the pressures of reality. Retreat does not mean escape. Many readers believe that the traveler rejects both total escape and retreat in "Stopping by Woods," but in several of the woods poems, periodic retreat is necessary to compose the self before returning to humanity. Frost was quite careful about the arrangement of individual poems in his books, and it is significant that "Into My Own," the first poem in the first book (*A Boy's Will*), is a poem of retreat to the woods, just as the last poem, unnamed, is in the last book (*In the Clearing*). The moods of the two poems are different, but the settings and themes are similar. "Into My Own" is a poem of youth's rebellion, an almost defiant declaration of independence from those who would miss him if he left. Once again the trees are dark, and the narrator vows to go his own way as he retreats into the woods, a metaphor for himself. The woods are also vast, as he hopes his inward state is, stretching all the way to "the edge of doom." Absolutely sure of himself, the immature narrator declares that he will find nothing new, only support for his already formed opinions:

> They would not find me changed from him they knew—
> Only more sure of all I thought was true.

Such confidence is lacking in the final unnamed poem. This is a lyric of old age in which the narrator shoulders his axe for a last retreat to the woods. He goes alone, of course, and in keeping with the poem's mood, the images suggest age: winter, late afternoon, shadowy tracks. Yet this is not a poem of defeat or death. The woods function as a dual metaphor—as nature and as a place to forget daily cares—just as they do in "Into My Own." But this narrator is wiser; he is not so sure of his beliefs. All he knows is that he cannot defeat nature, nor can it beat him:

> I see for Nature no defeat
> In one tree's overthrow
> Or for myself in my retreat
> For yet another blow.

All the mystery of the dark woods rests in that final word "blow." Is his retreat planned solely to cast a blow against nature by cutting down one tree, or does he suspect that he will also receive a blow from the woods in return? Here is the metaphor's ambiguity stated in four short lines, and it is this ambiguous nature of woods, their loveliness, their darkness and deepness, that so fascinates Frost.

The point is that the woods do not grant any special refuge to the poet. Their beauty and stillness seem to offer a place where solace can be found away from the cares of everyday reality, but the consistent darkness of Frost's woods suggests that the narrator is not always sure of what he will find if he chooses to enter the trees. One possible reading of the darkness is death, surely a valid, but not the only, interpretation of the hypnotic spell. The pattern of the woods metaphor outlined above, and variations on it, holds for most of the poems in which trees play a significant role, but the woods themselves do not always bring the same response in the narrator. Nearly always lovely and dark, the trees represent that place in which the narrator might find or lose himself. In "On Going Unnoticed" and "An Encounter," the poet-figure finds himself lost when he crosses the edge of the clearing to enter the trees. In the latter poem the lostness is merely physical. Sorry that he ever left the road, the narrator finds himself nearly suffocated by the crush of natural growth. Because he sees a telephone pole, a sure sign of humanity's presence, we never fear for him, but he nevertheless loses his way. "On Going Unnoticed" is a more fearful poem. This narrator enters the woods for the specific purpose of determining his own significance, but he makes the mistake of measuring himself against the apparently infinite life of the forest. He finds that even the coral-root flower counts for more in the woods than he and that his loudest shout is paltry when compared to the tumult of the leaves. Never once lost in a physical sense, the narrator experiences a greater shock. He learns that his life span is no more than a "little hour" while the woods "sweep leafily on. . . ." His discovery opposes that of the confident youth of "Into My Own," for these woods do not reveal what he had hoped to find. Man passes through life unnoticed by the solid, eternal forest.

That place of potential solace suggested by the woods in "Stopping by Woods" can turn out to be a place of violence and a cause of fear. In "The Draft Horse," the narrator finds himself in a setting a little like that in "Stopping by Woods." He has a companion with him, but he is in a horse-drawn buggy passing through the dark woods late at night. The key difference between the two poems is that this narrator is literally in the forest, a fact which clearly matters. Viewed from a distance as "lovely, dark and deep" in one poem, the forest is a "pitch-dark limitless grove" when entered in the other poem. Similarly, the horse in "Stopping by Woods" is alert and almost human in its awareness of the poet-figure's predicament, whereas the horse in "The Draft Horse" is described as "too heavy" and as a "ponderous beast." Every detail in "The Draft Horse" is against the narrator and his companion. The lantern will not burn; the buggy is too frail; the horse is too heavy; and the woods are too dark and limitless. In a beautifully incongruous matter-of-fact tone, Frost describes how a man comes out of the trees and deliberately stabs the horse. No warning has been given, and the word "deliberately" suggests that violent death is waiting specifically for them once they enter the woods. The ambiguity of the violent situation is established in the third stanza:

> The ponderous beast went down
> With a crack of a broken shaft.
> And the night drew through the trees
> In one long invidious draft.

We are not quite sure whether the night is resentful about the killing or about the human presence in the forest. This narrator knows that he is up against a greater force than he, but he does not question the apparently senseless death:

> The most unquestioning pair
> That ever accepted fate
> And the least disposed to ascribe
> Any more than we had to to hate,
>
> We assumed that the man himself
> Or someone he had to obey
> Wanted us to get down
> And walk the rest of the way.

His acceptance is, of course, ironic, for it is tempered by the almost humorous, matter-of-fact expression of their blind fatalism.

The threat of natural forces can, then, be represented by the woods as well as by the storm in Frost's poetry. The metaphor works because of the mysterious, dark characteristics which seem impenetrable to human questioning. Losing their loveliness, the dark trees become a metaphor for fear, desolation, or possible violence. Rather than long to enter the woods in these poems, the individuals hope to escape the power which the dark, impersonal trees seem to have.

This discussion of the woods metaphor shows that Frost makes significant variations from the general pattern of hypnotic pull and eventual rejection which most of us remember when we think of his deep, dark woods. The tone associated with the metaphor is nearly always consistent. It usually suggests the impulse to retreat, or sadness, or mystery, or outright terror—dark tones in keeping with the darkness of the woods. But Frost's uses of the metaphor are so varied that no one interpretation can be successfully applied. Yet, the woods metaphor remains the best concrete illustration of his more general conclusions about the function of metaphor, particularly those expressed in his letters and in "Education by Poetry." Revealing his analogizing mind, this metaphor shows how the true poet simultaneously recognizes something new in a common object, uses figurative language to suggest the correspondence, and demands that the reader be educated enough in poetry to pick up the unanticipated metaphorical notation.

Notes to *Robert Frost's Dark Woods and the Function of Metaphor* by DONALD J. GREINER

1. See Lawrance Thompson, *Emerson and Frost: Critics of Their Times* (Philadelphia: The Philobiblon Club, 1940); Reginald Cook, "Emerson and Frost: A Parallel of Seers," *New England Quarterly*, XXXI (June 1958), 200–217; and Alvan S. Ryan, "Frost and Emerson: Voice and Vision," *Massachusetts Review*, I (October 1959), 5–23.

2. See Robert Frost, *Selected Prose of Robert Frost*, ed. Hyde Cox and Edward Connery Lathem (New York: Holt, Rinehart and Winston, 1966). Prose quotations not otherwise cited are from this essay.

3. *Selected Letters of Robert Frost*, ed. Lawrance Thompson (New York: Holt, Rinehart and Winston, 1964), 111.

4. *Complete Works*, ed. Edward W. Emerson (New York: Houghton Mifflin, 1903), II, 17–18.

5. *Selected Letters*, 370–71.

6. J. McBride Dabbs, "Robert Frost and the Dark Woods," *Yale Review*, XXIII (March 1934), 514–20.

7. James M. Cox, "Robert Frost and the Edge of the Clearing," *Virginia Quarterly Review*, XXXV (Winter 1959), 73–88.

8. John T. Ogilvie, "From Woods to Stars: A Pattern of Imagery in Robert Frost's Poetry," *South Atlantic Quarterly*, LVIII (Winter 1959), 64–76.

9. Lloyd N. Dendinger, "The Irrational Appeal of Frost's Dark Deep Woods," *Southern Review*, n. s. II (October 1966), 822–29.

10. See James G. Hepburn, "Robert Frost and His Critics," *New England Quarterly*, XXXV (September 1962), 367–76 for a full discussion of the problems of interpretation in these poems.

Frost Remakes an Ancient Story

SISTER MARY JEREMY FINNEGAN

Among the poems in Frost's last volume, *In the Clearing*, one in particular repays close examination. Frost had read this poem, cumbrously entitled "How Hard It Is to Keep from Being King When It's in You and in the Situation," on May 25, 1950, at the annual ceremonial of the American Academy of Arts and Letters and the National Institute of Arts and Letters. As the Blashfield Address it was published in the Proceeedings of the Academy.[1] In 1951 the poem was issued in a limited edition under the shortened title, *Hard Not to Be King* (N.Y.: House of Books, Ltd.).

Written in the marvelously flexible blank verse that is Frost's hallmark, it characteristically combines narrative and reflection. The poem is a virtuoso display of dramatic dialogue, a highly original redaction of an ancient tale, and a statement of some of Frost's political and literary convictions.

The work begins with a brisk conversation between a king and his son who have decided to abdicate. The former fears that in spite of his departure, he cannot escape his duty: "For hard it is to keep from being King/When it's in you and in the situation." At his own instigation he is sold into slavery by his son in order that with the money thus realized, the youth may either set himself up in business or become a poet. To his purchaser, a palace eunuch, the erstwhile king declares: "I know the quintessence of many things." Assigned to help in the royal kitchen, he rises rapidly in the favor of Darius, the king, first by his culinary expertise and then by his revelation that a certain pearl is worthless because it contains a live worm. The king is so impressed by his slave's acumen that he summons him to a private conference to ask, "Why am I unhappy?" The immediate answer is "You're not where you belong. You're not a King/Of royal blood. Your father was a cook." After his mother admits the truth of the assertion, Darius demands to know how his slave discovered it. Reminding the king that he has invariably given a banquet as a reward for services that a true king would have repaid by a title of nobility, the slave says, "Your one idea was food./None but a cook's son could be so food-minded."

In this first, purely narrative section of the poem, Frost has made his own a story of great antiquity. The basic plot identifies it as one of a general class of wisdom stories originating in the East. Among its various versions the following may be cited:

In the tenth-century *Mas 'Udi*, the story of the Sons of Nizar relates that after demonstrating their sagacity by several deductions, the youths declare that the king entertaining them is illegitimate. His mother acknowledges that this is true.[2] In the preclassical Persian narrative, *The History of the Forty Vizers*, compiled by Sheykh-zada, one of the stories tells of a physician who cures the mysterious illness of a prince. He accomplishes this by persuading the queen to admit that her son's father is not the king, but a young man, presumably a member of one of the wandering Turkman tribes. The physician then orders that the boy be fed some of the favorite foods of these tribes, whereupon he recovers.[3] In the second story of the thirteenth-century *Cento Novelle Antiche*, a Greek prisoner shows the king that a supposedly valuable jewel contains a live worm. Subsequently, the king, suspecting his own legitimacy, consults the prisoner and learns that he himself is a baker's son. The prisoner has deduced this from the fact that all his services to the king have been repaid by gifts of bread.[4] In the Old French and Middle English versions of *The Seven Sages of Rome*, the nephew of Hippocrates examines the sick prince of Hungary and from this inspection deduces that the child is misbegotten. The queen confesses that the father is the earl (or in some versions the king) of Naverne.[5]

At least three other analogues have been recorded from oral narration. A folktale, "The Wit of the Four Brothers," reports that a rajah is considered baseborn because the shadow of a "washerman" fell on his mother before her purification on the sixth day after his birth.[6] "The Tale of the Akhun" tells how the youngest of four wise brothers shows the king that a beautiful ruby is valueless because there is a live worm in it.[7] A Punjab folktale relates that a blind beggar deduces that the king's father was a trader because the king's rewards were so niggardly.[8]

Whereas all these stories deal with deduction, the protagonists are variously a group of brothers, a physician, or a beggar. Sir Richard Burton has observed that "the story of the brothers who were so very 'knowing' is common in most countries, with occasional local modifications." He adds that the knowledge of the "quintessence of things" is less often concentrated in a single person.[9] Ordinarily the subjects of deduction are a supposedly flawless jewel which contains an animal of some sort, and the illegitimacy of a royal person.

Of all the versions of the story the one closest to Frost's is in *The Thousand Nights and a Night* as translated by Burton. Entitled "The Tale of the King Who Knew the Quintessence of Things," it is in the "Supplemental Nights."[10] Other translators of this story designate the animal in the pearl as "a boring worm"; Frost follows Burton in adding "a teredo."

Dialogue, informal comments, place names, and other supplemental details enliven Frost's version of the ancient tale. He has, moreover, made the poem uniquely his by recasting elements of the plot and extending the story through a long discussion of the duties of a ruler and the uses of freedom in the realms of government and literature. He has also developed the role of the wise king's son far beyond that of the prototype in *The Thousand Nights and a Night*.

The differences between Frost's poem and the Eastern original are noteworthy. The first is the dissimilar motivation for the abdication of the wise king. While in the old story he leaves his kingdom for religious reasons, "to flee from the sin of sovranty to Allah the Most High," and his son also desires "to take refuge with the Almighty," Frost gives both a somewhat cavalier attitude: "The King said to his son: 'Enough of this!/The Kingdom's yours to finish as you please.'" The Prince refuses the offer: " 'Sire, I've been looking on and I don't like/The looks of empire here. I'm leaving with you.' "

In Frost's poem the two leave "in the guise of men," a mysterious detail not in the original. Later, when the king orders his son to sell him as a slave, Frost has him say, "My price/Should be enough to set you up in business—/Or making verse if that is what you're bent on." In the older story he had said: "Receive my price and do with it whatso thou willest." Frost makes a radical alteration by empha-

sizing the king's fear that he cannot escape the obligations of his
sovereignty:

> I needn't think I have escaped my duty
> For hard it is to keep from being King
> When it's in you and in the situation.

It will be remembered that in the original story the king fled "to
escape the sin of sovranty."

In the older narrative there are no proper names except for
"Mameluke," which is not ordinarily capitalized when it denotes a
slave. Frost names the illegitimate king Darius. He also adds color
and contemporaneity by introducing the names of stars (Aldebaran,
Capella, Sirius, Rigel, Bellatrix, Betelgeuse); of places (Xanadu,
Rhodes, Punt, Mosul, Cos, Ctesiphon); and of persons (Julius Cae-
sar, Brutus, Washington, Madison, Haman, Omar, Homer, Tissa-
phernes, Marx, Christ, Pericles, Aspasia, Whitman, and Sandburg).
References to Carnegie grants, jet departure, atomic smithereens, and
the Seven Freedoms (Will, Trade, Verse, Thought, Love, Speech,
Coinage) effect a telescoping of time similar to that in Frost's
"Masque of Reason" and "Masque of Mercy."

Contrasting with the grave and dignified style of his source is the
informality of the dialogue in Frost's poem:

> "Let's not get superstitious, Sire," the Prince said.
> "We should have brought the crown along to pawn."
>
> "You're right," the ex-King said, "we'll need some money."

The informality is heightened by offhand comments, sometimes
parenthetical:

> The King sat favoring one pearl for its bigness,
> And then the other for its costliness
> (He seems to have felt limited to one).
>
> . . . .
> (The King was temperamental like his cook,
> But nobody had noticed the connection).
>
> . . . .
> His mother didn't like the way he put it,
> "But yes," she said, "some day I'll tell you, dear."

Frost's love of word-play emerges in several passages: "I'm a Rhodes scholar—/I was at college in the Isle of Rhodes." "His name is Omar. I as a Rhodes scholar/Pronounce it Homer with a Cockney rough." "Tell them Iamb, Jehovah said, and meant it."

Much of the freedom and variety of effect illustrated by such examples depends on alterations of the basic plot. Frost's changes may be thus summarized:

1) The father of the king is his own cook; in the original he is simply "a baker."

2) In the earlier story Darius rewarded the ex-king by increasing his rations; in Frost's poem the reward is a succession of feasts, culminating in an all-night banquet.

3) An episode in which the ex-king proves himself a judge of horses is reduced to a summary account leading into an implication of cowardice on the part of Darius.

4) The king's mother in Frost's poem is casual and nonchalant in acknowledging her adultery; in the original she explains that her motive was to provide an heir for the kingdom, her husband being old and impotent.

5) In the older story the prince is not mentioned after he has sold his father; in Frost's version he not only reappears as a poet in rags, but his speech constitutes the final section of the poem.

6) Finally, whereas the original story ends with the ex-king rewarded for his wisdom by great wealth and advancement to high estate, Frost has him succeed to the throne of the illegitimate king. The latter is humiliated, self-condemned to execution, and led off by the headsman "the Asiatic way/Into oblivion without a lawyer."

Frost makes an easy transition from the disclosure of Darius' illegitimacy to the discussion that follows it. The ex-king says:

> "None but a cook's son could be so food-minded.
>
> . . . .
>
> I'll bet you anything that's all as King
> You think of for your people—feeding them."

In answer to Darius' rejoinder, "Haven't I read somewhere/There is no act more kingly than to give?" the ex-king says firmly, "Yes, but give character and not just food." At this point the king begins to sound like Frost himself. In an interview after his return from Russia in 1962 where he had discussed democracy with Khrushchev, the poet said: "... bread and butter, yes; but that's not the top thing. The top thing to bestow is character." [11]

When Darius pleads for further instruction on how to rule wisely ("In case I should decide to reign some more") the ex-king explains that although a king should make his people "as happy as is good for them," it must not be "without consultation with their wishes." This course inevitably leads to progress, which unfortunately cannot be arrested "at a good point for pliant permanence/Where Madison attempted to arrest it." This speech is also a reflection of Frost's opinion as he gave it on September 29, 1959, in a panel on "The Future of Man." On that occasion he said: "Since we all agree that we're now smart enough to go on with what we are in an evolutionary way, we ought to be smart enough to stop where we are. And I'm in favor of stopping where we are because I like all this uncertainty that we live in, between being members and being individuals." [12]

In the poem, however, the king draws the pessimistic conclusion that a nation has to rotate "From King to Mob to King to Mob to King/Until the eddy of it eddies out." "So much for Progress," Darius comments meekly.

His next request is for a maxim about freedom: "What has it got to do with character?" In response, the ex-king turns to his poet-son who, having found the price for his father's slavery insufficient, is now a beggar. ("Poetry has always been a beggar," says Frost.) [13] "He'll tell you about Freedom. He writes free verse, I'm told." Before the son can reply, however, the ex-king continues his admonitions to Darius, warning him against seeking freedom by submitting to enslavement to any leader's truth, "Christ's or Karl Marx'." His conclusion is "The only certain freedom's in departure." This sentiment is reminiscent of Old Pike's speech in Frost's poem, "From Plane to Plane": "A man has got to keep his extrication," and later in the same poem: "Everyone has to keep his extrication." Associating this idea with the problem of sovereignty, the ex-king identifies it as the determination of

"just how strict
The lack of liberty, the squeeze of law

And discipline should be in school and state
To insure a jet departure of our going
Like a pip shot from 'twixt our pinching fingers."

The last line did not appear in the first two publications of the poem; it is in the final version as printed in *In The Clearing*. It is interesting to compare it with a quotation from an interview with Frost in *Life*, September 29, 1959: "School is for *discipline*. A student is an orange pip between my fingers: if I pinch him he'll go far." [14]

Far from being encouraged, Darius is so disheartened by "all this facility" that he decides on his own execution and says to the son, "I guess . . . I'll press your father into being King."

The son's reply constitutes the remainder of the poem and culminates in his moral ascendancy over both Darius and his father. He first discloses the latter's real rank: "Don't let him fool you: he's a King already"; and then goes on to say, "But though almost all-wise, he makes mistakes." His father, evidently no reader of his son's works, had said, "He writes free verse, I'm told." This rankles. "I write real verse in numbers. . . ." His subsequent description of strict and loose iambic corresponds exactly to Frost's own explicitly stated theory and practice. A few examples will illustrate: The first is from an interview in the New York *Times*, October 21, 1923: "I do not write free verse; I write blank verse. I must have the pulse beat of rhythm." [15] In a taped interview, "The Craft of Poetry," he remarked: "You know, I've given offense by saying I'd as soon write free verse as play tennis with the net down." [16] Frost's comment on meter is also familiar. One instance of it is found in "The Figure a Poem Makes": "All that can be done with words is soon told. So also with meters—particularly in our language where there are virtually but two, strict iambic and loose iambic." [17]

The prince-poet's disparagement of free verse as "really cherished prose" is likewise familiar to Frost's readers, as is his laconic dismissal: "It has its beauty, only I don't write it."

Taking up the theme of freedom, the prince explains that the freedom artists need is different from that sought by the public. Artists need "the freedom of their own material." Among Frost's own pronouncements, are the remarks on "Meet the Press," December 23,

1956: "Your real anxiety, day by day, is your own freedom of your own material." [18] In "The Figure a Poem Makes" he reiterates the statement: "All I would keep for myself is the freedom of my material—the condition of body and mind now and then to summon aptly from the great chaos of all I have lived through." [19]

In the poem, the ex-king's son interprets his father's "freedom of departure" as the artist's "freedom to flash off into wild connections." His excitement when he makes his "wild connections" is uniquely satisfying: "Once to have known it, nothing else will do./Our days all pass awaiting its return." Carried away by the recollection of this creative ecstasy, the prince suddenly returns to the present: "Let's see, where are we? Oh, we're in transition,/Changing an old King for another old one." He adds dryly that despite all the contemporary talk about the hope of youth, "No one is nominating me for King."

Although, he says, his father superstitiously blames the stars for his enforced return to sovereignty, they are not responsible: rather, "his display/Of more than royal attributes betrayed him." This leads directly into the third and final statement of the leitmotif: "How hard it is to keep from being King/When it's in you and in the situation." The poem ends with the prince's reflective comment: "And that is half the trouble with the world/(Or more than half I'm half inclined to say)."

In his review of *In the Clearing*, William Meredith writes: ". . . a poet speaks through many characters. He has many visions of the things that concern him. The subjects to which he returns, as Richard Wilbur has observed, are those which vex him." [20] In both characters, the king and his poet-son, Frost has provided himself with means of dramatic ventriloquism. Each persona becomes a medium for the expression of some of the poet's own convictions. Frost's achievement, more largely stated, is the dramatic transformation of a simple ancient narrative into a psychologically complex one with contemporary overtones of political and literary implications.

Notes to *Frost Remakes an Ancient Story* by SISTER MARY JEREMY FINNEGAN

1. *Proceedings*, 2nd series, No. 1 (New York, 1951), 28–38.
2. Barbier de Meynard et Pavet de Courteille, trans., *Les Prairies d'Or*, Société Asiatique (Paris, 1965), secs. 1093–1101.

3. E. J. W. Gibb, trans., "The Lady's Second Story" (London, 1886), 37–41.

4. *Libro di Novelle et di Bel Parlar Gentile* (Florence, 1572), 4–5.

5. Killis Campbell, "A Study of the Romance of the *Seven Sages* with Special Reference to the Middle English Versions," *PMLA*, XIV (1899), 1–107.

6. Recorded by Pandit Ramgharib Chaube, *North Indian Notes and Queries*, III (1893), 85–86.

7. Sir Aurel Stein and Sir George Grierson, *Hatim's Tales: Kashmiri Stories and Songs*, Recorded with the assistance of Pandit Govind Kaul, Indian Text Series, (London, 1923), 85–87.

8. *Folk-Lore*, XXXVI (1925), 364–65.

9. Sir Richard Burton, *Supplemental Nights to the Book of a Thousand Nights and a Night* (London, 1903), II, 322.

10. *Ibid.*, "The Third Night of the Month," I, 212–17.

11. Edward C. Lathem, ed., *Interviews with Robert Frost* (New York, 1966), 289.

12. *Ibid.*, 213.

13. *Ibid.*, 232.

14. *Ibid.*, 270.

15. *Ibid.*, 52.

16. *Ibid.*, 203.

17. Frost, *Complete Poems* (New York: Holt, Rinehart and Winston, 1964), v.

18. Lathem, *Interviews with Robert Frost*, 155.

19. Frost, *Complete Poems*, vii.

20. William Meredith, Review of *In the Clearing*, *Poetry*, CI (1962), 201.

Robert Frost in the Clearing:
The Risk of Spirit in Substantiation

STEPHEN D. WARNER

I*n the Clearing* represents Robert Frost's final statement, and its title, organization, and individual poems reflect a conscious review, with significant reaffirmations, of the younger poet. Frost had advanced by withdrawing into a dark wood of the self, the famous index of which was "Into My Own." Frost, in that poem "Fearless of ever finding open land," predicted that those who pursued him "would not find me changed from him they knew—/Only more sure of all I thought was true." This was the principal assertion opening *A Boy's Will*, Frost's first published volume. And in the final volume, as if in answer to that early claim, Frost announced himself *In the Clearing*. But, as Frost surely knew, to be in the clearing was not necessarily to be out of the woods. An earlier American folk figure, Natty Bumppo, had addressed himself to the same problem at the conclusion of *The Pioneers*: "I don't call these woods, Madam Effingham, where I lose myself every day of my life in the clearings." The passage and its inversion are instructive as an index to Frost's resolution of his own career through *In the Clearing*, a resolution which may be seen most clearly by analyzing, in order, the volume's title, central poem, and major orbital pieces.

I

To read the collection simply as the poet's examination of the prophesies of *A Boy's Will* may seem too simple. The argument against oversimplicity when dealing with poetry urges a cautious ambivalence. Here, however, three arguments may be based on the epigraph, the frontispiece, and the dedication to the original volume. Never one to give a critic easy purchase, Frost renders his title ambivalent by the epigraph "And wait to watch the water clear, I may" from "The Pasture," which served as frontispiece to the *Complete Poems*. That poem speaks of watching "the water clear" as the result of raking away the leaves. To pursue the image in parallel terms, such an action equates with removing "those dark trees" that seemed in "Into My Own" to be "the merest mask of gloom." The parallel is obscure but useful. The mask of gloom is gone from *In the Clearing* (especially if we literalize the title and the line), and we can see now that the gloom had been gradually disappearing since *A Boy's Will*. As I will demonstrate later, the dominant tone in *In the Clearing* is light and self-confident, often capricious.

The frontispiece, the second piece of evidence, echoes a faith which grew to supplant the earlier gloom. Frost quotes as frontispiece the central portion of "Kitty Hawk," the central poem of the collection, and echoes the earlier theme of "The Trial by Existence" —a companion piece to "Into My Own" in *A Boy's Will*. He omits from the frontispiece an aside in "Kitty Hawk" on our national penetration into matter and joins the two originally separated statements into a single statement of faith:

> But God's own descent
> Into flesh was meant
> As a demonstration
> That the supreme merit
> Lay in risking spirit
> In substantiation.
> Spirit enters flesh
> And for all it's worth
> Charges into earth
> In birth after birth
> Ever fresh and fresh.
> We may take the view
> That its derring-do
> Thought of in the large
> Was one mighty charge
> On our human part
> Of the soul's ethereal
> Into the material.

The lines parallel the substantive testament of "The Trial by Existence." While much of that earlier poem deals with our inability to remember the choice, the burden of the poem argues the same risk of spirit in substantiation as in the above quotation:

> And from a cliff top is proclaimed
> The gathering of the souls for birth,

> The trial by existence named,
>   The obscuration upon earth.

And in a later stanza:

> Nor is there wanting in the press
>   Some spirit to stand simply forth,
> Heroic in its nakedness,
>   Against the uttermost of earth.
> The tale of earth's unhonored things
>   Sounds nobler there than 'neath the sun;
> And the mind whirls and the heart sings,
>   And a shout greets the daring one.

But again the parallel seems dangerously simple. What of the difference in tones? Why the surrender of the archaisms and line inversions if "Kitty Hawk" is also a statement of faith? Where are the solemnity and impersonal detachment represented in "The Trial by Existence"?

Gone, as they have been going since the poet's arrival at public prominence. Every poem in *In the Clearing* explicitly or implicitly demonstrates a playfulness and confidence lacking in the early poetry. Frost had changed his attitude toward his material, not the material itself. Confirmed in his earlier attitudes, Frost provides the third piece of evidence for arguing affirmation as the thrust of *In the Clearing*. The dedication to the volume provides a curious combination of documents: a disposition of effects, and a salutation to the reader.

DEDICATION

Letters in prose to
Louis Untermeyer, Sidney Cox, and John Bartlett
for them to dispose of as they please;
these to you in verse for keeps

Like a codicil in a will, the dedication presents *In the Clearing* as a bequest. Labeling these poems his "letters" to the reader, Frost writes from the end of the journey "Into My Own" these letters which, when read, reveal Frost indeed not changed from him we knew.

How then shall we read the title and accept the collection? I argue that the collection seems a conscious response to an earlier Frost "fearless of ever finding open land" who, having found it, writes to affirm his earlier vision and direction. The volume also solves, once and for all, the question of what *type* of sigh will accompany the later retelling of "The Road Not Taken":

> I shall be telling this with a [satisfied] sigh
> Somewhere ages and ages hence:
> Two roads diverged in a wood, and I—
> I took the one less traveled by,
> And that has made all the difference.

II

As straightforward as this approach to the collection seems, it still overlooks the Frostian paradox behind the title. Although the metaphor of the title seems to argue that the poet has arrived and is willing to reveal himself, the title itself echoes the title of the third poem in the collection, "A Cabin in the Clearing." Thus the title seems to associate the poet-persona with inhabitants of a clearing who know neither who nor where they are.

> MIST. I don't believe the sleepers in this house
> Know where they are.
> SMOKE. They've been here long enough
> To push the woods back from around the house
> And part them in the middle with a path.
> MIST. And still I doubt if they know where they are.
> And I begin to fear they never will.
> All they maintain the path for is the comfort
> Of visiting with the equally bewildered.
> Nearer in plight their neighbors are than distance.

The pairing of volume title and poem seems at first to pose a rather startling contradiction if we assume Frost to have reached a metaphorically comparable location.

The key to unraveling the difficulty resides in what Roy Harvey Pearce called in *The Continuity of American Poetry* a strength in Frost's verse that results from living with failure: a strength of discerning one's self as living with conditions which limit rather than those which permit.[1] Frost himself spoke of such a possibility in loss during a 1958 speech in Redlands, California: "God seems to be something which wants us to win. In tennis. Or poetry. Or marriage.

Of course, somebody must lose. That's when you step up to the spiritual plane." [2] Like the inhabitants of the cabin who live "In the fond faith accumulated fact/Will of itself take fire and light the world up," we struggle against loss to reach that spiritual plane. To enforce the ambiguity of the line and title, MIST declares "No one—not I—would give them up for lost/Simply because they don't know where they are."

Lest the line seem an accidental ambiguity, it should be noted that the poem which follows "A Cabin in the Clearing" echoes a line from "Directive" and, in that echo, confesses the volume's willful and final exercise of the poet's will. "Closed for Good" leaves the persona to talk "naught/Perhaps but to a tree"—that tree which in "Directive" hides "a broken drinking goblet like the Grail" for those who accept the call to "pull in your ladder road behind you/ And put up CLOSED to all but me." Without too great a leap of the imagination, "Closed for Good" seems a whimsical affirmation of "Directive." This truncated version of that poem from the *Complete Poems* appeared in *In the Clearing*:

> They come not back with steed
> And chariot to chide
> My slowness with their speed
> And scare me to one side.
> They have found other scenes
> For haste and other means.
>
> They leave the road to me
> To walk in saying naught
> Perhaps but to a tree
> Inaudibly in thought,
> "From you the road receives
> A priming coat of leaves.
>
> "And soon for lack of sun,
> The prospects are in white
> It will be further done,
> But with a coat so light
> The shape of leaves will show
> Beneath the spread of snow."
>
> And so on into winter
> Till even I have ceased

> To come as a foot printer,
> And only some slight beast
> So mousy or so foxy
> Shall print there as my proxy.

Indeed, we have not found Frost changed from all he knew; rather, "Closed for Good" indicates we've not followed at all!

Where, then, must we turn our steps? "Kitty Hawk," the central poem of *In the Clearing*, marks the retrospective path and also structures the collection. The other poems circle "Kitty Hawk" like pieces broken from that sun. The use of a longer poem in this way is reminiscent of "New Hampshire" with its footnote references to the other pieces in the 1923 *New Hampshire*. Seen as a pair, both poems act as central symbol and subject, but "Kitty Hawk" is more autobiographical and historical and evidences an entirely different perspective.

"Kitty Hawk" may be summarized as a portrait of the young poet in the dark wood, his arrival in the clearing, and the application of an essential personal and universal principle. "Part One" depicts the errant poet poised for flight into the romantic sublime—outside of time and into the unknown:

> It was on my tongue
> To have up and sung
> The initial flight
> I can see now might—
> Should have been—my own
> Into the unknown,
> Into the sublime
> Off these sands of Time
> Time had seen amass
> From his hourglass.

This deliberate rendering of the Wright brothers' romantic venture away from the earth allows Frost, in considering his early failure in his own proposed flight, to juxtapose his own most unromantic sublime.

The irony of Frost's failed romantic flight from Kitty Hawk is that in failing he succeeded:

> Once I told the Master,[3]
> Later when we met,

> I'd been here one night
> As a young Alastor
> When the scene was set
> For some kind of flight
> Long before he flew it.

Frost was poised for two flights—into the sublime, but away from the failures, disappointments, and despair of his material existence. The experience becomes, in retrospect, the first personal confirmation of the truths of "The Trial by Existence" and a demonstration that the spirit is tested and tempered in the fire of existence, of life, and not by removal into Arcadian sublime (which is perhaps why Frost's woods are no Arcadia).

The coincidence of flight from Kitty Hawk for poet and the Wright brothers (and thus the nation and mankind) serves Frost as the necessary circumstance to parallel and reflect upon the ventures attempted and achieved. "Part Two" makes this Frost-Orville Wright-mankind-America comparison explicit:

> Neither you nor I
> Ever thought to fly.
> Oh, but fly we did,
> Literally fly.

The last line, with its probable pun on "literarily," refers to an actual physical elevation in flight, the transition from the experience and adventure of the poet's youth to the mechanical ability of man to literally take wing and fly. It is from the vantage point of that elevation that Frost proclaims "I saw it all," again reversing the perspective from literal flight to an elevated poetic *Aufklaerung*.

From this perspective is delivered a restatement of the principles set forth in "The Trial by Existence" and quoted earlier during the discussion of the frontispiece. The lines represent an orthodoxy subject to broad application: from our living "deeper into matter" to our penetration of space (which might be considered "but further matter"). Interestingly enough, this entire section echoes Joseph Campbell's discussion of rebirth archetypes for the hero: "Full circle, from the tomb of the womb to the womb of the tomb, we come: an ambiguous, enigmatical incursion into a world of solid matter that is soon to melt from us, like the substance of a dream. And, looking back at what had promised to be our own unique, unpredictable, and dangerous adventure, all we find in the end is such a series of standard metamorphoses as men and women have undergone in every quarter of the world, in all recorded centuries, and under every odd disguise of civilization." [4]

Frost continues "Kitty Hawk" with a rehearsal of national history, a parallel passage to the development of the poet in "Part One." The trek West Northwest is concluded with a stone-skipping leap: from England to America, across the face of America, and into space. It is to Frost the typically Western "design for living/Deeper into matter" rather than romantic removal into the sublime.

With "Talk Aloft," the first subsection of "Part Two," Frost shifts from elevated poetic perspective to the literal elevation of flight. The opening lines of the section deny the value of venture for venture's sake and recall the lines from "Mowing": "The fact is the sweetest dream that labor knows."

> Someone says the Lord
> Says our reaching toward
> Is its own reward.
> One would like to know
> Where God says it, though.
>
> We don't like that much.

The counterplay of fact and value is enforced by the rhyme reference from "We don't like that much" to the earlier "We would want to touch/Not to mention clutch" at the end of the previous section. The passage rejects the romantic ideal.

The "Talk Aloft" portion emphasizes through parallels the cyclical nature of flight and the cyclical nature of the venture into existence, echoing the earlier lines from "Part Two" as quoted in the frontispiece. Apparently Frost has sufficiently reconciled himself to science to accept its vehicles for personal and national ventures into further matter, but they are still subject to a higher law:

> Though our kiting ships
> Prove but flying chips
> From the science shop
> And when motors stop

> They may have to drop
> Short of anywhere. . . .

Nature's law, the law of gravity, applies the force that completes the cycle. We have, however, made "a pass/At the infinite" and given it a rational order and wholeness.

This order and wholeness is derived from "The Holiness of Wholeness," the title of the next subsection, which is composed of two essentials: first, focusing on man as the central figure—playing the "royal role" and giving character to the whole as Kennedy did ("For John F. Kennedy His Inauguration") and Darius didn't ("How Hard It Is to Keep from Being King When It's in You and in the Situation"); and second, grasping some part which "by craft or art" may be given wholeness.

The latter element represents a significant affirmation in Frost, for in the volume *New Hampshire* the relation of part to whole was stated with a representative pessimism in "A Star in a Stoneboat:"

> Such as it is, it promises the prize
> Of the one world complete in any size
> That I am like to compass, fool or wise.

Frost grasped then only the part and could not conceive of using that part to render a reflective wholeness, except as an isolated yet note-connected portion of the central poem "New Hampshire."

In *In the Clearing*, Frost was able to apply the part to the whole in life and in the universe while earlier he could do so only partially and only through eccentric regionalism.[5] In "Kitty Hawk" Frost was no longer intimidated by the larger realm outside the part because of his elevation to a perspective from which

> We may get control
> If not of the whole
> Of at least some part
> Where not too immense,
> So by craft or art
> We can give the part
> Wholeness in a sense.

Thus the fear that suits us best is the fear that "We come nowhere near/Getting thought expressed." This is the equivalent of the poet's finding "A meaning I was supposed to seek,/And finding, wasn't supposed to speak" in "One More Brevity." This last is the new meaning represented by the part, and goes about poetry's business of expressing the ineffable.

In an address delivered on the eve of the volume's publication Frost said:

I was thinking the other day that perhaps the most important thing in me . . . is what I have said in this last book that all there is to life is getting a meaning into a lot of material. Religion or getting a lot of pointed meanings, getting sharp, pointed meaning into the material.
In a poem, I say:

> But God's own descent
> Into flesh was meant
> As a demonstration
> That the supreme merit
> Lay in risking spirit
> In substantiation.

An accumulation of knowledge will not burst into flame [see "A Cabin in the Clearing"]. You have to do something about it, and that is what poetry is about; that is what philosophy is about; that is what politics is about.[6]

It is that meaning, the truth of "The Trial by Existence" and its application on a national scale, that Frost has put in this last collection.

"The Mixture Mechanic," central to the last portion of "Kitty Hawk," is the mixture of machine and man as artisan. This is the royal pair who, "Like a king and queen," venture into the center of the flux of matter to keep it stirred, not to run like the dendrophobiac in "New Hampshire." This "mixture mechanic" gives sense to the universe and

> Undertake[s] to tell her
> What in being stellar
> She's supposed to mean.

Thus the part again gives meaning to the whole, as Frost saw his own role as poet to the nation. In the same publication-eve address, Frost said: "Isn't it wonderful to put me in a thing as big as the USA?" I don't consider it unfair or ungenerous to find in this statement Frost's estimation of his role as giving meaning to America just as the "mixture mechanic" gives meaning to the universe. Finding the meaning in the part that was Robert Frost enabled the poet to give meaning and wholeness to the nation and to the universe. And the wholeness was comprehended not only by going into himself but ultimately by going outside and above.

In the last lines of "Kitty Hawk" Frost acknowledges his allegory and the relevance of the flight:

> God of the machine,
> Peregrine machine,
> Some still think is Satan,
> Unto you the thanks
> For this token flight.

The lines express the poet's gratitude for the perspective of flight from which he "Saw it all." They recognize the importance of his own early experience, of the elevated perspective he achieved and from which the volume was written, and the "token" or allegorical use made of that flight.

III

A major effect of this new perspective in Frost's poetry is the light assurance of the verse, the playfulness and nursery rhyme tenor in *In the Clearing* that often approach doggerel. "Lines Written in Dejection on the Eve of Great Success" and "The Milky Way Is a Cowpath" are rich with this quality, and in "A-Wishing Well" the nursery rhyme becomes explicit with " 'I wish I may, I wish I might'/ Give the earth another satellite." The line also echoes the launching outward of his vision.

In "The Objection to Being Stepped On" the animus in man's tools, so strong in "Out, Out—," and at the end of "The Ax-Helve," is no longer a sacred cow and can be milked lightly and confidently of all its poetic value. It is the new Frost Nashing his teeth on his old gnawing doubts.

"Away!" evidences the growth in two ways. The antecedent lines from "Misgiving" are infused with doubt and a flat perspective. The persona is unable to foresee positively or clearly the inevitable end, and yet echoes once again the cycles and options from "The Trial by Existence." Here the dare is to die and return whence he came.

> I only hope that when I am free,
> As they are free, to go in quest
> Of the knowledge beyond the bounds of life
> It may not seem better to me to rest.

Compared to these lines, the self-assurance in the parallel from "Away!" is effusive:

> Unless I'm wrong
> I but obey
> The urge of a song:
> I'm—bound—away!
> And I may return
> If dissatisfied
> With what I learn
> From having died.

The poem is the last of a series of antecedent verses: "The Demiurge's Laugh," "The Road Not Taken," "Stopping by Woods on a Snowy Evening," "On a Tree Fallen Across the Road," "Desert Places" and "Directive." They record Frost's survival on the road through the dark wood. To read the opening stanza of "Away!" with the emphasis on the first word contrasts the poem with past attitudes and past walks:

> Now I out walking
> The world desert,
> And my shoe and my stocking
> Do me no hurt.

Similar references to the past and to antecedent poems expand and help explicate "Closed for Good." Previously published in *Complete Poems*, the first and last stanzas of the poem were omitted from *In the Clearing*. The omitted stanzas strengthen the link to the earlier "Directive" and clarify, in the context of the earlier poem, the relevance of the title "Closed for Good" to the poem's content:

> Much as I own I owe
> The passers of the past
> Because their to and fro
> Has cut this road to last,

> I owe them more today
> Because they've gone away
>
> . . . .
>
> How often is the case
> I thus pay men a debt
> For having left a place
> And still do not forget
> To pay them some sweet share
> For having once been there.[7]

In "Directive" Frost proposed a means by which the wholeness beyond confusion might be obtained:

> And if you're lost enough to find yourself
> By now, pull in your ladder road behind you
> And put a sign up CLOSED to all but me.
> Then make yourself at home.

The lines again encompass the cycles of "birth after birth/Ever fresh and fresh" of "Kitty Hawk" and, earlier, "The Trial by Existence." Following a road made by "the passers of the past," the reader closes the path to all but the speaker. This path moves ultimately to the fountain of wholeness beyond confusion: the "ladder road" through the woods is the same that raised Frost to the elevated poetic perspective of *In the Clearing*.

Even the volume's couplets demonstrate the new confidence derived from the new perspective. "Forgive, O Lord, my little jokes on Thee" replaces subservience to deities with a joking familiarity between peers: the poet has become master of his own element. "From Iron" is the capsulized statement of the broadly articulated motif underlying almost every poem Frost wrote. But perhaps the most concrete statement of poetic attitude is the last couplet, a teasing warning that "It takes all sorts of in-and outdoor schooling/To get adapted to my kind of fooling." Thus the need to be versed in country things is paralleled by the same need in poetic things; or, don't surrender to pathetic or poetic fallacies!

But perspective does not solve all problems or resolve all paradoxes. There are still unanswered questions such as the waste of "Pod of the Milkweed," the depressing poles of existence in "We vainly wrestle with the blind belief," and the life-struggle which strengthens the irony of having originally printed *In the Clearing* on paper clearly watermarked "Utopian."

The real value of the volume is the new confidence reflected through the tone and statement of the poems. They affirm the truths of earlier poems through a broadened application and an elevated perspective. Frost's career became the "parabolic curve" (the pun in "The Milky Way Is a Cowpath") that didn't overshoot the moon but plunged back into matter to complete the cycle explicit in his early orthodoxy.

For Frost that personal cycle is completed in the last poem of *In the Clearing*. "In winter in the woods alone" links the "shadowy tracks/Across the tinted snow" (an echo of "Closed for Good") with his "retreat/For yet another blow." This retreat is the same as his retreat from romantic flight at Kitty Hawk, the plunge into matter through the return to life. It is the truth of "The Trial by Existence": "And so the choice must be again,/But the last choice is still the same." For Frost, it was the risk of spirit in substantiation.

Notes to *Robert Frost in the Clearing: The Risk of Spirit in Substantiation* by STEPHEN D. WARNER

1. Roy Harvey Pearce, *The Continuity of American Poetry* (Princeton: Princeton University Press, 1961), 278.

2. Quoted in Lawrance Thompson's *Robert Frost: The Early Years, 1874–1915* (New York: Holt, Rinehart & Winston, 1966), 573–74.

3. The "Master" is Orville Wright, the surviving brother in 1932 at the Kitty Hawk dedication by Herbert Hoover of the memorial spire to the Wright brothers' achievement. The autobiographical references in the poem are enlarged upon in chapter 16 of Thompson's *The Early Years*.

4. Joseph Campbell, *The Hero with a Thousand Faces* (Princeton: Princeton University Press, 1949), 12–13.

5. Frost ends "New Hampshire"
>   It's restful to arrive at a decision,
>   And restful just to think about New Hampshire.
>   At present I am living in Vermont
and dedicates the volume to Vermont and Michigan.

6. "Robert Frost at Eighty-Eight," *New Republic*, April 9, 1962, pp. 20–21.

7. Lathem restores the opening verse but still omits the final. See his note on variations, p. 574.

RELIGION

The dominance of nature as theme in Frost's poetry makes religion appear to be of secondary importance, despite the fact that "Trial by Existence" was one of the first poems Frost published and one that he retained in the various collections published during his lifetime. His complex background further obscures the question, as does his general unwillingness to promulgate a creed. While critics have usually agreed that Frost revealed a puritanic background in his life as well as his work, they find neither specifically puritanic nor specifically Christian doctrines outlined. His mother's Swedenborgian interests, which were such as to lead Frost to say that he was brought up in that religion, only complicate the question further. Frost seems far more pragmatist than mystic, however. Publication of the two masques, dealing with traditionally enigmatic questions of theology, were at first more puzzling than revealing, especially since they seemed unlike Frost—less than serious and perhaps a little sacrilegious. Rabbi Reichert recalls an incident in which the casual mention of Frost elicits a response about "that atheist!"

Rabbi Reichert's long friendship with Frost makes his informal essay one of the most poetically justified in this volume. It avers that Frost was a devout man and suggests that his approach to religion was through the concepts of a puritanic Old Testament. Alfred Ferguson discusses, however, the Christian paradox of the fortunate fall, a theme to which Frost returns throughout his work.

Peter Stanlis, another old friend of Frost, writes a sensitive discussion of the quite serious themes of the masques which convincingly supports the idea that, whatever Frost's belief, doubts or faith, he was in fact earnest and devout in his attempts to investigate the relationship between Man and Deity. A concern that continues throughout a lifetime attests quite by itself to a man's seriousness. If Frost remains ambiguous, we may pay him the respect of supposing that it was because he was honest enough never to claim to know the truth about ultimate matters.

J. T.

The Faith of Robert Frost

VICTOR E. REICHERT

STUDENTS of American Literature who have a special interest in Robert Frost are familiar with the massive studies of America's beloved poet that have come from the pen of Professor Lawrance Thompson of Princeton University. They know that many years ago Frost chose Thompson to be his official biographer. An early study of Frost's poetry by Thompson was called *Fire and Ice*. Then, after Frost died on January 29, 1963, Thompson published 566 "Selected Letters." The weighty volume of *Selected Letters of Robert Frost* has a detailed chronology, genealogy, and analytical index as well as Professor Thompson's annotations and interpretative notes. Following this formidable volume came the first two volumes of the Frost biography: *The Early Years* and *The Years of Triumph*. What is not widely known is that when Thompson was trying to complete his third and final volume, to be called *The Years of Glory*, he was suddenly stricken. Professor Thompson and I, brought together by Robert Frost, have been friends for a long time. With this background, you will understand my feelings, when, one day during this past summer, returning to the School House, our summer home in Ripton, Vermont, I found the following note stuck in our School House door:

21 August 1972

Dear Rabbi Reichert,

Professor Lawrance Thompson asked me to look you up when I was passing through Ripton. In case you may not have heard, he's had a second brain operation this summer and is rather ill—I should say *quite* ill. Before the second operation he had what amounted to his second stroke.

With the help of Mrs. Thompson and one of his graduate students at Princeton (me) he's working on Volume Three of The Biography of Robert Frost. I thought to ask you (when I saw you) if you could help Professor Thompson unravel Frost's complicated set of religious beliefs by writing down some of your recollections concerning the degree to which Frost was a religious believer.

Sorry I missed you—I've got miles to go before I sleep.

Yours respectfully
(signed)   Roy H. Winnick

If you find you have time to write to Professor Thompson, his address is: 611 Lake Drive, Princeton, N.J. 08540

August 31, 1972
The School House
Ripton, Vermont 05766

Dear Larry:

Ever since Louise and I returned from Cincinnati and Buffalo—where Jonathan at the moment teaches Physics at the State University—a note from Roy H. Winnick stuck in the School House door has been silently reproaching me.

Now I lay aside the clutter on my desk and hope that nothing will break in while I chat with you. You are putting up a valiant battle, I know. Deep down, I'm betting on you. And while I don't have any special inside line to the snowy haired Ancient of Days, I'm letting Him know in no uncertain terms that there's at least one rabbi who is asking for a repetition of Isaiah 38.

I am always loath to trust my memory without eye-witness written support but you were there when Bishop Hobson presided at the Memorial Service for Robert at Amherst and may remember this. Bishop Henry W. Hobson said that on the plane coming to Amherst he met a man who knew him and asked where he was going.

"To Amherst to conduct a memorial service for Robert Frost."

"What, that atheist!"

Bishop Hobson countered:

"You're mistaken. Robert Frost was no atheist. What you don't understand and Frost did was that God has a sense of humor!"

Bishop Hobson was right. Only one with the playful intimacy of a naughty grandchild could be bold enough to say:

> Forgive, O Lord, my little jokes on Thee,
> And I'll forgive Thy great big one on me.

In our School House Cottage Guest Book, the first to write in it (a handsome gift of David and Marilyn) was Robert Frost. In his clear, bold hand, he penned that mischievous couplet. And he wrote beneath: "August First, 1959 at Ripton."

A few pages later, August 2, 1959, we have the Thompsons: Janet, Ellie, Nat, Joel, Tom. And on August 4, 1959 Lawrance.

While I am still in our Guest Book at Ripton, you might remember that you came by on Monday, September 2, 1968 and wrote these words:

Dear Victor and Louise:

I'm tempted to write a summary of how far back the three of us can go in our memories of each other. All I'll do here is say we started by arguing over my review of *A Masque of Reason*. Then we proceeded by admitting—by my admitting that I was *wrong*, in that review; I was *real* wrong. [The word "real" you underlined twice.]

Thanks, still, for helping me out.

Affectionately
Larry

You may have forgotten that you ever wrote that note in our Guest Book. I treasure it as a window into your soul. What an eloquent revelation it is of your own great spirit. I have all but forgotten now how I would have differed with you. But how great you were to say that your review—which I think bothered Robert Frost—did not grasp, did not quite grasp, Frost's deep intent.

Look again at the *Masque of Reason* and you can see that Frost knows that real religion must go beyond the barter level. You cannot ask a material reward for a spiritual loyalty. Frost understands the tremendous breakthrough that the Book of Job represents in the history of religion when he has God thanking Job for helping Him

> Establish once for all the principle
> There's no connection man can reason out
> Between his just deserts and what he gets.
> Virtue may fail and wickedness succeed.
>
> . . . .
>
> But it was of the essence of the trial
> You shouldn't understand it at the time.
> It had to seem unmeaning to have meaning.

And later, Job's wife is asking:

> For instance, is there such a thing as Progress?
> Job says there's no such thing as Earth's becoming
> An easier place for man to save his soul in.
> Except as a hard place to save his soul in,
> A trial ground where he can try himself
> And find out whether he is any good,
> It would be meaningless. It might as well
> Be Heaven at once and have it over with.

I don't want to get into further exegesis of Frost's *Masque of Reason* but I hate to let go before mentioning the cryptic reference to Ralph Waldo Emerson's "Uriel":

> Yet I suppose what seems to us confusion
> Is not confusion, but the form of forms,
> The serpent's tail stuck down the serpent's throat,
> Which is the symbol of eternity
> And also of the way all things come round,
> Or of how rays return upon themselves,
> To quote the greatest Western poem yet.
> Though I hold rays deteriorate to nothing:
> First white, then red, then ultrared, then out.

The idea of immortality is not left out of Frost's *Masque of Reason*. Again, Job is saying to God:

> You could end this by simply coming out
> And saying plainly and unequivocally
> Whether there's any part of man immortal.
> Yet You don't speak. Let fools bemuse themselves
> By being baffled for the sake of being.
> I'm sick of the whole artificial puzzle.

Did I ever tell you of the words Frost said to me the last time we were together? It was here in the School House, Ripton. Frost had come back from Russia and there was a gathering in our Ripton home. Suddenly, out of nowhere, sitting side by side and chatting, Frost said to me, "Victor, what do you think are the chances of life after death?"

I teased Frost by reminding him that when you ask a Jew a question, you don't get an answer; just another question. In the Book of Job, God never answers Job. Instead, God belabors Job with one great question after another. So I said to Robert, "What do you think?" Frost became deeply silent and then he said to me, "With so many ladders going up everywhere, there must be something for them to lean against."

I never forgot that poignant remark. Here was Frost, deep in his eighties, wistful about the prospect ahead. And what an image it suggetsed of Jacob's ladder with the angels ascending and descending. And how it contrasted with those lines in "The Strong Are Saying Nothing":

> There may be little or much beyond the grave,
> But the strong are saying nothing until they see.

There is not the slightest doubt in my mind about the deep, deep religious nature of Robert Frost. But you must approach his religious complexities through one of his great heroes, Ralph Waldo Emerson. He once called him one of the four greatest Americans. And since Frost adored his mother, who was a religious seeker and finally came to Swedenborg by way of Emerson's essay, something of the mysticism of his mother remained with him all his life. Of his constant reading of the King James version of the Bible there is overwhelming evidence.

One summer, when I was giving special attention to the Hebrew difficulties of the Book of Hosea, Frost inadvertently supplied me with the clue to the meaning of what seemed to me then great obscurity. The passage was in the twelfth chapter of the Book of Hosea, verse ten in the King James version (verse eleven in the Hebrew Massoretic text). It reads: "I have also spoken by the prophets, and I have multiplied visions, and used similitudes, by the ministry of the prophets."

I could not fathom the meaning of "used similitudes by the ministry of the prophets." It happened that Frost was giving one of his talks and reading at the Little Theater to some writers. That day he said to them: "Our object [as poets—a word you know he regarded as a praise word for others to say of him but not to say of himself] is to entertain you [the reader] with the play of things we hope you already know."

Suddenly a light dawned on me. Hosea, some twenty-seven hundred years before, was saying the same truth. The gift of God to the prophet, poet, the eternal man, is the gift of making metaphor. That "by the ministry of"—in Hebrew, simply "U'V'yad" (literally "by the hand of")—really meant that the endowment, the divine endowment to the prophet, the poet, is the art of the play of things. Later, I showed the passage to Robert. He was delighted. In my Limited Edition, Frost wrote: "You and I Victor 'have multiplied visions and used similitudes' as Hosea would have us. Thank you for showing me the Bible of it." Robert/At Ripton/Sept 4 57

When in 1964 I published a second edition of the *Tower of David*, Vermont Books, Middlebury, Vermont, which I dedicated "In affectionate remembrance of Robert Frost," Dike Blair, the publisher, reproduced in Robert's strong hand those words.

I have always regarded as the high point in my thirty-five years as rabbi of Rockdale Temple, Bene Israel, Cincinnati, Ohio, the time when Robert Frost preached in my pulpit. The date, October 10, 1946. James Adams, interviewing me for the *Cincinnati Post and Times-Star*, August 2, 1969 (page 8) correctly says that this was a high point for me when Robert Frost, having come down from Kenyon College with Gordon Chalmers, sitting in our living room on Red Bud Avenue, said spontaneously to me that he would preach for me the next day.

That sermon, spoken by Robert Frost, on the First Day of the Feast of Tabernacles, Thursday morning, October 10, 1946, and beautifully printed by Joe Blumenthal of the Spiral Press, New York, is now a prized collector's item. But its importance lies in the fact that Frost here for the first time, to my imperfect knowledge, clearly gives his view of religion.

After saying that courage is great but wisdom is better, he goes on:

> Now religion always seems to me to come round to something beyond wisdom. It's a straining of the spirit forward to a wisdom beyond wisdom. Many men have the kind of wisdom that will do well enough in the day's work, you know, living along, fighting battles, going to wars, beating each other, striving with each other, in war or in peace—sufficient wisdom. They take their own side, naturally, and do well enough. But if they have religious natures, they constantly, inside, they constantly tremble a little with the fear of God. And the fear of God always has meant the fear that one's wisdom, one's own wisdom, one's own human wisdom is not quite acceptable in His sight. Always I hear that word acceptable—acceptable about offerings like *that* [An enormous cornucopia graced the pulpit, filled with all sorts of vegetables and fruits. There were some very beautiful pineapples and oranges in particular that showed on top to which Frost alluded in the first part of the sermon, saying that it was only a little like Vermont, "we can't raise too many of those fruits in Vermont"]—like offerings of mine. Always the fear that it may not quite be acceptable. That, I take it, is the fear of God, and is with every religious nature, always.

The Frost sermon is a most important window into the soul of the poet, mostly because it was spoken without previous planning on my part or Frost's. It happened spontaneously. When Frost said he would preach for me, he jumped up, asked Louise to give him two raw eggs, which he put into his little bag where he carried his manuscript poems, and said, "Take me back to my hotel."

Later he was to stay in our home, when he visited the Queen City to receive honorary doctorates from both the University of Cincinnati, and later from the Hebrew Union College, the Seminary for the Reform Jewish Rabbinate.

I had a glimpse of Frost's inward piety that morning he preached. A gentle lady, a German refugee, always asked to say the blessings over the palm branch, the willow, the myrtle and the esrog (citron) under the Sukkah, when the service was at an end. As she stood there reverently, and softly, inaudibly saying those ancient Hebrew benedictions, my eyes caught Frost, his head bowed in complete sympathy with hers. I have never forgotten that look on Frost's face.

Dear Larry, I hope these vagrant, fleeting memories will be of some help to you. Please forgive the long delay in reaching you. God bless you. Fondly.

> Victor E.

What should I add to last summer's letter to Professor Thompson? It is a mistake to call Robert Frost's religious beliefs any more complicated than the whole remarkable and tough texture of his mind and soul. No one of us is ever free from the complexity of changing mood and the unresting tides of outward circumstance and inward tensions. What gladdens our hearts and places us in everlasting debt to Frost is that as poet he fashioned a strategy of mirth and an upreach to the stars to vanquish the defeating foes of doom and darkness.

The volume *Steeple Bush* (1947) is full of examples of Frost's steadfast spiritual purpose, as indeed is the whole sweep of his eleven books from *A Boy's Will* through *In the Clearing*. "Astrometaphysical" illustrates my point as easily as many more familiar ones. Listen to the poem. Read it aloud.

Or consider the poem "Away!" (*In the Clearing*, 1962). The fact that Frost was not a churchgoer, as Professor Cook of Middlebury College tells us in his superb *The Dimensions of Robert Frost*, did not mean that he stayed out of the Bible. On the contrary, Frost loved the Scriptures and liked to call himself an Old Testament Christian. He was soaked in the King James version and might have agreed with John Livingston Lowes that it is the noblest monument of English prose. Once, I remember, when the Arabs were giving so much trouble to the Israelis, it was Robert Frost who reminded me that as far back as Nehemiah there was difficulty. For when that great Persian Jew sought to restore Jerusalem that lay in waste and to build up its walls, it was, among others, Geshem the Arabian who laughed him and his people to scorn.

It would be risky to single out certain places in the Bible as having a favored fascination for Frost, especially since the two Masques rest so solidly upon the Book of Job (*A Masque of Reason*) and Jonah and the Sermon on the Mount (*A Masque of Mercy*). Yet there are several poems like "The Ax-Helve" ("The snake stood up for evil in the Garden"); "Once by the Pacific" ("There would be more than ocean–water broken/Before God's last *Put out the Light* was spoken"); "Nothing Gold Can Stay" ("So Eden sank to grief"). And in *A Masque of Reason*, where God is praising Job for setting him free to reign, God says:

> My forte is truth,
> Or metaphysics, long the world's reproach
> For standing still in one place true forever;
> While science goes self-superseding on.
> Look at how far we've left the current science
> Of Genesis behind. The wisdom there, though,
> Is just as good as when I uttered it.

There must be other examples that escape me, but I can hazard the guess that the early chapters of Genesis had a haunting attraction for Frost. The poem "Away!" is another fine example of how Frost uses the strategy of mirth, with echoes of Eden, to deal with what he describes in the great dramatic poem "West-Running Brook" as "The universal cataract of death/That spends to nothingness."

"Touch a poem lightly," Frost liked to say. Yet I ask you to notice, in that last four lines of "Away!" the significant word "learn." You might say that Frost's whole life was an adventure in learning. I remember once telling Frost about the great medieval French Jew known as Rashi (1040–1105). The name is an acronym for Rabbi Solomon ben Isaac. Rashi is indispensable for our understanding of the Babylonian Talmud and is the most famous Jewish commentator on the Hebrew Bible. Frost said, "Got any book about Rashi?" I said I did and I sent him my copy of Maurice Liber's study of Rashi, translated from the French by Adèle Szold and published by the Jewish Publication Society of America in 1906. What particularly appealed to Frost was the fact that Rashi had influenced the celebrated Franciscan monk, Nicholas de Lyra (ca. 1292–1340), and he in turn the great leader of the Reformation, Martin Luther. There was the parodied proverb in Latin: *si Lyra non lyrasset, Lutherius non saltasset*. Then too Frost was delighted to learn of Rashi's amazing gift for clear and concise comment on the scriptural text.

Do you know what? I thought no more about Rashi until deep in the winter a card came from Kathleen Morrison saying that Frost had been reading the book with intense care. Nor was that the end of the matter. One day, the following summer, at Bread Loaf, I could not believe my ears when, out of the blue, Frost, speaking to a group, began talking about Rashi. Since Frost was a great baseball fan and a highly competitive baseball player himself, at first I thought he was talking about the famous player, Raschi. But no. It was the immortal eleventh century French commentator on the Bible and the Talmud. And Frost knew what he was talking about!

No one could long be in the presence of Robert Frost without feeling the intellectual force of this man. For one thing, he would startle you with his amazingly accurate and retentive memory. Once, hearing a rabbinic comment on a passage in the Book of Genesis on the reason why Ephron the Hittite's Hebrew name is spelled defectively when he reveals his true, greedy character to the patriarch Abraham, Frost held on to that homily long after the rabbi had forgotten he had ever told it to Frost. The incident occurred in the old and original Rockdale Temple one November. Winter passed and spring. The following summer, in Ripton, far from Cincinnati, Frost, walking and talking, abruptly said, "Why, he's just like Ephron." We were discussing an untrustworthy person whom we both agreed was false. The Ephron comparison didn't register. "Ephron who?" "Why, don't you remember! Ephron the Hittite who sold for an outrageous sum to Abraham the cave of Machpelah in Hebron where he could bury Sarah. And you told me that the ancient Hebrew sages of the Talmud say that a letter in his Hebrew name is missing to hint at the blemish in his character which is now revealed. He spoke much, that Ephron, but even a little he did not do!"

Tenacious memory and deep thrusting mind! Remember that marvelous line in the poem "Mowing":

> The fact is the sweetest dream that labor knows.
> My long scythe whispered and left the hay to make.

Frost would have approved the saying of Abraham Ibn Ezra (1092–1167) immortalized by Robert Browning in Rabbi Ben Ezra. The great Spanish Jewish genius used to say that the real angel between God and man is his intellect, his mind. And listen to Frost in the poem "A Considerable Speck (*Microscopic*)" with his wonderful compassion for this "living mite/With inclinations it could call its own."

> Since it was nothing I knew evil of
> I let it lie there till I hope it slept.

I have a mind myself and recognize
Mind when I meet with it in any guise.
No one can know how glad I am to find
On any sheet the least display of mind.

If these memories of Frost's interest in a Bible commentator named Rashi and a Hittite called Ephron seem trivial and farfetched in respect to Frost's religious beliefs, perhaps they are relevant in throwing light upon that search for truth which Louis Untermeyer believed to be Frost's central passion. "Truth is the seal of God" said the sages of the Talmud. Those who come closest to truth come nearest to God. Frost, like one of his heroes in the Hebrew Scripture, promethean Job, was a stormer of heaven.

In a letter to his lifelong friend, Louis Untermeyer, written from South Shaftsbury, Vermont, January 6, 1929, he wrote: "Well to hell with nearly everything. With everything but poetry, politics and true religion—and a few friends and relatives—a very few. And I forgot farming."

"Did you ever have a revelation?" Robert asked once in walking about Bread Loaf.

"What about you?" I countered.

A long interval of silence as we noiselessly paced, in our canvas, rubber-soled tennis shoes, those white slabs of Vermont marble that often reminded me of misplaced grave stones. Of some such stone as the ones we were walking on, Frost had penned in "The Lesson for Today," "I would have written of me on my stone:/I had a lover's quarrel with the world." I thought of those lines as we walked on those stones that fronted the old Bread Loaf Inn. Then at last Frost said, "I've had insights that have come to me when I was riding high. Call them 'nature favors.' An owl that banked as it turned in its flight made me feel as if I'd been 'spoken to—favored.'" The poems "Dust of Snow" and "A Passing Glimpse" flashed through my mind.

Reading again that remarkable section of Professor Cook's analysis of Frost's religious beliefs (*The Dimensions of Robert Frost*, pp. 188–94), I find myself in such complete agreement with Professor Cook ("Doc" to all of us who love and respect this distinguished scholar of Middlebury College) that I freely confess that you would not have to read through my rambling recollections to get at the core of Frost's religious convictions.

Yet I would not close without reminding you of the vital star figure that you find from first to last in *The Poetry of Robert Frost*. The star imagery in Frost's poems dazzles like the Milky Way. Stars keep shining through Frost's poems, suggesting splendors of infinity and intimations of the Divine. Frost talks about stars the way the more orthodox in religion speak of God. Frost chooses star light as Isaiah chose God to say that the mind stayed on Him, He keeps in perfect peace.

Robert Frost knew a great deal about the stars. You would expect a poet to know star mythology. Frost surprised and pleased astronomers with his more precise knowledge of the science of the skies. Frost employed the star symbol to communicate the ideals of living in which he believed. Frost wanted men and nations to hold each other apart in their places as the stars do. He was on the side of constancy and the search for the absolute, however unattainable. He believed that we should live with a certain height of aim, the calm of courage, the poise of a man who is self-possessed, who values the worth of incorruptibility. Frost sees in the stars the suggestion of the light of reason and common sense. But the stars call also for endurance and commitment.

All his life, Frost was out for stars. He refused to come into the dark and lament. Though he had looked into the dark abyss of the human soul, and was well familiar with his own desert places, he steadily turned his back on despair and doom and steadfastly followed the starlight of affirmation, aspiration and dedication.

In this sense, Frost stays Old Testament Biblical and Hebrew prophetic. Because Frost was full of fun and the joy of living, he liked to break loose from the phylacteries of rigid creed and frozen theological dogma. The sassiness of Frost can be seen in his rebellion against falseness wherever he found it. His spiritual forbears here may be uncovered in the patriarchal Abraham and Job, in the uncompromising strength of Amos, the compassion of Hosea, the massive integrity of Micah. These men too lived in dark, evil days, but they did not teach cowardice or despair.

Let me close by affirming that Frost was never fooled into pretending to know more about the inscrutable ways of God than man in his finite frailty can ever comprehend about the Infinite. This humility Frost phrased in many ways but none more compactly than in that epigrammatic couplet called "The Secret Sits":

> We dance round in a ring and suppose,
> But the Secret sits in the middle and knows.

Frost and the Paradox of the Fortunate Fall

ALFRED R. FERGUSON

ALWAYS central to Frost's poetry has been his delight in word play of all sorts, in metaphor, pun, and paradox. As he once noted, "poetry begins in trivial metaphors, pretty metaphors, 'grace' metaphors, and goes on to the profoundest thinking we have. Poetry provides the one permissible way of saying one thing and meaning another." [1] Paradox, particularly, provided him with verbal and intellectual tensions in which "oppositions became almost unions" and through which the reader was forced to deal with the "two-endedness of things." [2] He praised what he thought of as the "counter-wisdom" [3] of Emerson's "Uriel" with its apparent contradiction that "Evil will bless, and ice will burn." The "counter-wisdom" is part of what Frost called "my kind of fooling," [4] the kind of wit that appears in "West-Running Brook," for example, in which the stream itself is a thing of contraries, standing still and yet running away, black water in a white wave, moving so that "the fall of most of it is always/Raising a little, sending up a little."

Translated to another and more memorable image, the fall that is always a rise, an ascent-descent, shifts to more than verbal play when linked to the image of Eden, to the tree of knowledge, and to the connection between sinful man and the incarnate God. It then becomes the paradox of *felix culpa*, a part of the Edenic myth of Adam's fall as prelude to Christ's triumphant rise from the second garden, Gethsemane. In March of 1941 Frost wrote to Louis Untermeyer to report that he had been having "good talk" on the "two-word phrase *felix culpa*." [5] Actually the fortunate fall had been providing him with metaphor and matter for his own poetry for years. Again and again Frost focused his attention on the connections between evil and good, between fate and choice. In the late "Kitty Hawk" Frost links the choice in the garden by which man fell into sin (an act which "Pulpiteers will censure") with the coming of the second Adam (the Christ) and the consequent promise of

427

salvation. The sinful choice becomes an act of hope rather than despair; the moment "When we took that fall/From the apple tree" is in reality "our instinctive venture," that is to say, a moment of experience leading toward greater humanity and making possible the triumph of the descent of God into man. The apparent fall leads to the high value:

> But God's own descent
> Into flesh was meant
> As a demonstration
> That the supreme merit
> Lay in risking spirit
> In substantiation. ("Kitty Hawk")

Though Frost seldom creates such explicit theological and Christian overtones, he does often seem to accept St. Ambrose's conviction that "Sin is more fruitful than innocence." [6] Certainly, by linking, as he does, the fall, the apple tree, the high human virtue of the act of choice, and God's choice of descent into man, he emphasizes the paradox of *felix culpa*. Normally the connection of the fall and the rise is for Frost less a theological concern than a metaphor to suggest a precarious equilibrium between good and evil or stasis and dynamism. Through the metaphor Frost can accept the reality of error and pain yet cling to affirmation. He adopts the reaction to the fortunate fall which Lovejoy calls most common—to consider it less in relation to Adam's sin than in the light of its final results. [7] From the fourth century "Exultet," which explained the choice in the garden as the first step to "deserve so great a redeemer," on to the charming medieval lyric "Adam lay yboundin," the consequences of the fall, final grace rather than present guilt, were stressed:

> Ne hadde the appil take ben, the appil taken ben,
> Ne hadde never our Lady a ben hevene quen.
> Blissed be the time that appil take was,
> Therfore we mown singen *Deo Gratias*.

And Milton pointed out, in his version of the fall, the majesty of Adam standing before the Archangel Michael saying:

> O goodness infinite, goodness immense!
> That all this good of evil shall produce,

And evil turn to good. . . .
                  . . . full of doubt I stand,
Whether I should repent me now of sin
By mee done and occasion'd, or rejoice
Much more, that much more good thereof shall spring. . . .
                  (*Paradise Lost*, XII, 469–76)

The emphasis on the "fortunate" in the fall is, we must remember, only a part of Frost's final concern, not with theology but with metaphor. In his many references to the garden, to the fall, to the apple tree, he should never be taken too seriously. That is, he has warned us that to be at ease with "figurative values" we must judge the strength and the weakness of metaphor, realizing how far it may be carried before it breaks down.[8] He has insisted, as Reginald Cook has pointed out, on making idea and poem dependent finally upon metaphor and identifying the problem of the poet as the need to attain a delicate balance of thought in which ideas are embodied in adequate language. The poem becomes an interrelationship in which words and things cut across one another, " 'making a connection in the mind.' " [9] Eden, the fall, and man's act of choice provide such a connection. The metaphor or the connection in the mind is of more importance than are the theological implications of sin (Frost tends to ignore what Milton's Adam spoke of as "sin by me done or occasioned"); and the paradox of the fortunate fall becomes a device by which the poet and the reader balance precariously between the polarities of good and evil. Paradise is perfection; man is a human and fallen creature. As an inhabitant of the world of growth and process, man must wake from his paradisiacal dream to the reality of the world after the fall.

That Frost accepts the human condition as imperfect and diminished seems clear enough. In "The Lesson for Today" he notes wryly that "The groundwork of all faith is human woe" and suggests that man's real choice is simply "how to take the curse, tragic or comic." To live under the curse as an outcast from Eden is the condition not only of man. All things are temporal; the very earth itself is "liable to the fate/Of meaninglessly being broken off." In reality we live not in an unchanging paradise but in a world of death—which is also, of course, a world of growth and life. Though Frost is not transcen-

dental as was Whitman, urging us to see the possibilities of "lovely
and soothing death," he does link death and life as a part of the
process of the whole. He is thoroughly "acquainted with the night,"
as well as his "own desert places," and impressed by the need to "be
prepared for rage" ("Once by the Pacific"). Evil is a part of process
and of life. As he phrased it in "Quandary,"

> Never have I been sad or glad
> That there was such a thing as bad.
> There had to be, I understood,
> For there to have been any good.

Inevitably there will be casual destructive accident as in "Out,
Out—." Inevitably there will be the fall to failure, visible both to
Frost and to his witch Abishag, who learned that "Too many fall
from great and good/For you to doubt the likelihood" ("Provide,
Provide"). Paradise was one-dimensional; the world is bipolar, shows
death and life. In an unusually direct statement of opposites in tension, Frost described the poles of good and evil, which in "Quandary" led to the development of discrimination and of brains ("We
learned from the forbidden fruit/For brains there is no substitute"):

> I sang of death. . . .
> . . . .
> Oh, should a child be left unwarned
> That any song in which he mourned
> Would be as if he prophesied?
> It were unworthy of the tongue
> To let the half of life alone
> And play the good without the ill.
>   ("The Wind and the Rain")

But no matter how much Frost is moved by Emerson's wisdom in
"The Tragic," Frost knows that "He has seen but half the universe
who never has been shown the house of Pain." [10] No matter how
much he is shaken by the cosmic chill and by the "design of darkness to appall" ("Design"), he is affirmative and expects the paradox
of good rising from evil. Man learns from his troubles, as Adam
found life more meaningful outside the garden than in it. Man is in
exile, and his strategy must be to learn " 'how the limited can make
snug the limitless.' "[11] Like the poet moving within the frame of

verse or the tennis player operating within the lines of the court, the human being will find in the limits or boundaries both challenge and charm. Experience, age, seasons, change—all are limits within which we must learn to live—and all are as acceptable as the dreams of innocence, youth, or the stasis of Eden. To Frost the bud is no more significant than the ripe fruit; indeed stasis usually seems far less valuable than process. Obstacles, guilt, choice, death and decay are proper segments of earthly experience. For Frost as for Edgar in *King Lear*, wisdom is knowing that "Ripeness is all." The garden gives way to the world with its "shocks and changes we need to keep us sane" ("On Looking Up by Chance at the Constellations").

In Frost's most typical work, personae and reader move within a rich ambiguity, often reminiscent of Emerson's polarity. We balance between stasis and process, heaven and earth, wish and reality. In "Birches," for instance, the imagined flight toward perfection is induced by the very real irritation of life like a "pathless wood" whose twigs slash the unprotected face. The swinger of birches soars on the branch "to get away from earth awhile"; but if separation from earth means that heaven found is earth lost, the poet rejects the flight. Let the flexible tree bend back again to the ground; for "Earth's the right place for love: /I don't know where it's likely to go better."

The child riding the birch in imagination, the prelapsarian parents —these may know simple innocence; but for awakened man, the fall has intervened; the garden is irretrievably lost. For full humanity, man needs pain as well as pleasure, needs not only untroubled joy but also the "moment overcast" ("The Oven Bird"). Frost might well have echoed Emerson's remark, "There are moods in which we court suffering, in the hope that here at least we shall find reality, sharp peaks and edges of truth." [12] Indeed, he left his own version of the link between reality and pain in "To Earthward":

> Now no joy but lacks salt,
> That is not dashed with pain
> And weariness and fault....

From Eden, Adam and Eve, marred but humanized by sin, walked hand in hand out of myth into the real world which lay open before them "where to choose" (*Paradise Lost*, XII, 646). Frost, like Milton, accepts the results of the fall: the seasons, change, error, choice, the human condition. He knows that "nothing gold can stay," that Paradise must and should give way to mutability and the cycle of growth, for the choice and sin in Eden not only "Brought death into the world, and all our woe" (*Paradise Lost*, I, 3), but produced process as well.

To accept the concept of change as necessary and as good, to approve of the movement from bud to ripe fruit to decay involves both an emotional and a rational response. Emotionally one may find change heart-rending and the admission of its inevitability a kind of treason, as Frost sees in "Reluctance":

> Ah, when to the heart of man
> Was it ever less than a treason
> To go with the drift of things,
> To yield with a grace to reason,
> And bow and accept the end
> Of a love or a season?

The treason of accepting with grace what is, rather than demanding what no longer can be, is inherent in a world of limitations and leads Frost back to time and to his muted version of the fortunate fall. As William Moynihan has pointed out, Frost has relatively few poems about spring and summer; and even of those he has, almost a third by overtones evoke the coming of fall or winter, of harvest and mowing, of the completion of the year's cycle. Spring and summer seem to suggest "the transient, the unreal." [13] The beginning of time is the perpetual spring and summer of Eden; fall, whether the petal-fall, the leaf-fall, or "that other fall we name the fall" forces us toward the reality of process, of limit, of pain. Through it we learn "what to make of a diminished thing" ("The Oven Bird"). Our maturation teaches us, as Frost reminds us in "Hyla Brook," to accept what is, to "love the things we love for what they are." So all dreams must finally take into account the fall that leads into death as well as the spring of life, ripening as well as bud. The change of rise and fall may be upsetting, but it belongs properly to earth if not to paradise, as Frost points out explicitly:

> Before the leaves can mount again
> To fill the trees with another shade,

They must go down past things coming up.
They must go down into the dark decayed.

They *must* be pierced by flowers and put
Beneath the feet of dancing flowers.
However it is in some other world
I know that this is the way in ours.
                    ("In Hardwood Groves")

A part of the fortune of the fall is the development of process over stasis. Spring must give way to high summer even though the latter for flowers is to the former as "one to ten" ("The Oven Bird"); April pools must vanish and be blotted up by the trees if leaves are to "darken nature and be summer woods" ("Spring Pools"); if bud is to transform into leaf or if flower is to become fruit, there must be time, change, and death, temporary if not endless. Eden was changeless and static, even Frost's "A Winter Eden," whose frozen replica of paradise is lifted toward heaven by its "plane of snow." In the frozen moment, living experience is delayed or reversed in meaning. The beasts eat in obvious parody the bark of "some wild apple tree" rather than its nonexistent fruit. In the immobilized world the birds are all "loveless" because "So near to Paradise all pairing ends"; this utopia is too sterile and transitory "To make it worth life's while to wake and sport." Winter Eden, like any other Eden, is a dream and as unreal as the world seen by the two lovers in "A Boundless Moment," who, as Nina Baym has suggested,[14] walk in the March woods thinking of the magic May flower named "Paradise-in-Bloom." What they actually find in the woods of dream is deceptive—a young beech tree white with "last year's leaves," that is to say, not a paradisiac flower but a tree complete with decay as well as growth.

Both nature and man reveal a world of imperfection. Although John Lynen suggests that as a pastoral poet Frost tends to romanticize the natural world and make it better than the world of men,[15] Frost is actually as uneasy as was Milton with any idealized nature. "Range-Finding," for example, offers an ironic similarity between the follies of man and the ferocities of the insect; here are not only the gentle butterfly and the ground bird but also the predatory spider waiting to destroy the fly quite as efficiently and unemotionally as the bullet would destroy the man. The spider responds to the tug on his web but withdraws sullenly, disappointed by a signal that marked ballistic death instead of insect food. In nature as in man the fall has left its mark: "Earth felt the wound, and Nature from her seat . . . gave signs of woe" (*Paradise Lost*, IX, 782–83).

The wounds in nature and the flaws in man are acceptable or at least endurable aspects of the human condition, reflecting the consequences of freedom and choice. A longing for Paradise is simply romantic nostalgia for an impossible prehuman state. Yet the yearning is so intense that the world lies forever, as Frost notes in "The Grindstone," under the shadow of the "ruinous live apple tree." And even the harvester in "After Apple-Picking" starts from a ladder "sticking through a tree/Toward heaven still," though he and all other human beings are "overtired/Of the great harvest" of what Milton called "the fruit/Of that forbidden tree" (*Paradise Lost*, I, 1–2). What will trouble the sleep of the apple-picker is the fact of mortality, the introduction of death, change, and loss into the garden through the tree of knowledge. But that Eden was lost is clearly in Frost's eyes a good, not an ill; the descent into flesh leads to a larger humanity. Like Brown, who "bowed with grace to natural law" ("Brown's Descent"), we learn to act within limits, to stretch our strength against difficulties, to escape from wishful thinking into what Frost speaks of as "An Answer":

> But Islands of the Blessèd, bless you, son,
> I never came upon a blessèd one.

Instead of the pure clear light of Paradise, man after Eden is faced with the challenge of darkness into which he must bring his light—even if it is only a "flickering, human pathetic light" maintained with "a Godforsaken brute despair" ("On the Heart's Beginning to Cloud the Mind"). Time and mortality supply "zones whose laws must be obeyed" ("There Are Roughly Zones"). The emphasis on necessity, zones, and laws echoes Emerson's chapter on discipline in *Nature* and has somewhat the same affirmative value for experience. Like the monkeys in "At Woodward's Gardens," we learn by trial and by error that "It's knowing what to do with things that counts." Frost is praising the courage and will to act, to choose. Both as poet and as person he found value in the process, in the struggle: "Every poem," he wrote, "is an epitome of the great predicament; a figure of the will braving alien entanglements." [16]

The symbol for alien entanglements is frequently, for Frost, the ruinous apple tree. Neither man nor beast is safe from the results; for the cow, the fall may be repeated at every apple time. Then she will "make no more of a wall than an open gate,/And think no more of wall-builders than fools." But let me quote the whole passage to indicate the humor with which the poet mocks the effect of eating the apple:

> Having tasted fruit,
> She scorns a pasture withering to the root.
> She runs from tree to tree where lie and sweeten
> The windfalls spiked with stubble and worm-eaten.
> She leaves them bitten when she has to fly.
> She bellows on a knoll against the sky.
> Her udder shrivels and the milk goes dry.
>   ("The Cow in Apple Time")

Yet, though tasting the fruit may lead to madness, to live in the garden is impossible and inhuman. Driven from it man is challenged; and acting with what Goethe would call resignation without apathy, he may be partially victorious. In "A-Wishing Well" Frost develops the image of a man's virtue; to try, to persist, to endure and so become "practically inexterminate"; in "Our Hold on the Planet" he uses again the metaphor of man gripping earth or reality and committing himself to hope and to action:

> We may doubt the just proportion of good to ill.
> There is much in nature against us. But we forget:
> Take nature altogether since time began,
>
> . . . .
> And it must be a little more in favor of man,
> Say a fraction of one percent at the very least. . . .

By a "fraction of one percent at least" Nature is on the side of man. That is hope enough to make life on earth more exciting than the stasis of Paradise. To insist only on the perfect bud, on the full brook, on the singing bird is to ask far more than a fractional support. And such a demand for apparent perfection is blindness since it ignores the real though diminished virtue of the shadowed leaf and the bird that "knows in singing not to sing" ("The Oven Bird"). Even decay (or death) fits into the pattern and completes it, assures us of lines and of limits, a whole not a part:

> I bade men tell me which in brief,
> Which is fairer, flower or leaf.
> They did not have the wit to say,
> Leaves by night and flowers by day.
> Leaves and bark, leaves and bark,
>
> To lean against and hear in the dark.
> Petals I may have once pursued.
> Leaves are all my darker mood.
> ("Leaves Compared with Flowers")

The "darker mood" fits earth and fact rather than dream and Eden. To Frost the assurance that life is complex, that evil may well spring from good or vice versa, is often more of an intellectual than an emotional quandary. As an ironist he sees with a double vision, feels the balance of opposites, operates by humor, by juggling and tension. Truth he finds uneasily resting in delicate equipoise, as metaphorically described in "The Armful," as he carries what Thoreau would have called his "grossest groceries":

> And the whole pile is slipping, bottles, buns—
> Extremes too hard to comprehend at once,
> Yet nothing I should care to leave behind.
> With all I have to hold with, hand and mind
> And heart, if need be, I will do my best
> To keep their building balanced at my breast.

This is, of course, Frost fooling; but it seriously undermines any expectation of the perfect or the unified. To juggle, to choose, accept the incomplete or precarious, to wish "May something go always unharvested" ("Unharvested")—this is the typically Frostian response.

Perhaps no single poem more fully embodies the ambiguous balance between paradisiac good and the paradoxically more fruitful human good than "Nothing Gold Can Stay," a poem in which the metaphors of Eden and the Fall cohere with the idea of *felix culpa*. Six versions of the poem exist, the first sent to George R. Elliott in

March, 1920, in three eight-line stanzas under the title "Nothing Golden Stays." [17] In this version the poem lacked any Edenic metaphor, reading in the three last lines, "In autumn she achieves/A still more golden blaze/But nothing golden stays." [18] In its first published version, however, in *The Yale Review* (October 1923), under the present title, the poet caught both the moment of transitory perfection and the sense that the Edenic ideal must give way to earthly dying beauty:

> Nature's first green is gold,
> Her hardest hue to hold.
> Her early leaf's a flower;
> But only so an hour.
> Then leaf subsides to leaf.
> So Eden sank to grief,
> So dawn goes down to day.
> Nothing gold can stay.

The poem begins at once in paradox: "green is gold ... leaf's a flower." At once, common knowledge, precise observation, and the implications of ancient associations are brought into conflicting play. Green is the first mark of spring, the assurance of life; yet in fact the first flush of vegetation for the New England birch and the willow is not green but the haze of delicate gold. Hence green is a theory or sign of spring; gold is the fact. Gold, precious and permanent as a metal, is here not considered as a metal but as a color. Its hue is described as hard to hold, as evanescent as wealth itelf.

In the second couplet of the heavily end-stopped poem, paradox is emphasized again, this time in the terms of leaf and flower instead of green and gold. The earliest leaf unfolds in beauty like a flower; but in spite of its appearance, it is leaf, with all the special function of its being, instead of flower. Yet as apparent flower (the comparison is metaphoric rather than a simile—that is, leaf *is* flower, not leaf resembles or is like flower), the leaf exists in disguise only a moment and then moves on to its true state as leaf. In terms of the two parallel paradoxes, we find the green which appears as gold becoming the real green of leaf; the leaf which appears to be flower with all the possible color of flower becomes the true green of leaf. Our expectations are borne out: apparent gold shifts to green; apparent flower subsides into leaf. But in each case an emotional loss is involved in the changed conditions. The hue of gold with all its value associations of richness and color cannot be preserved. Nor can flower, delicate and evanescent in its beauty, last long; hence we are touched by melancholy when gold changes to green and flower changes to leaf (actually "subsides" or sinks or falls into leaf). Yet in terms of the poem, the thing which metamorphoses into its true self (gold to green of life and flower into leaf which gives life to the tree or plant) undergoes only an apparent or seeming fall. The subsiding is like the jut of water in "West-Running Brook," a fall which is a rise into a new value. It is with this movement of paradox that Frost arrives at the final term of his argument, developing the parallel between acts within nature and acts within myth. "So Eden sank to grief" with the same imperceptible movement that transformed gold to green and made flower subside to leaf. By analogy the third term in the poem takes on the character of the first two; gold is green; flower is leaf; Eden is grief. In every case the second element is actually a value, a part of a natural process by which the cycle of fuller life is completed.

Thus by the very movement and order of the poem, we are induced to accept each change as a shift to good rather than as a decrease in value; yet each change involves a seeming diminution, a fall stressed in the verbs "subsides" and "sank" as well as in the implicit loss in color and beauty. The sense of a fall which is actually a part of an inherent order of nature, of the nature of the object, rather than being forced unintelligibly and externally, is reinforced as the final natural metaphor recapitulates the first three movements of the argument: "So dawn goes down to day." The pattern of paradox is assured; the fall is really no fall to be mourned. It is a *felix culpa* and light-bringing. Our whole human experience makes us aware that dawn is tentative, lovely, but incomplete and evanescent. Our expectation is that dawn does not "go down" to day, but comes up, as in Kipling's famous phrase, "like thunder," into the satisfying warmth of sunlight and full life. The hesistant perfections of gold, of flower, of Eden, and finally of dawn are linked to parallel terms which are set in verbal contexts of diminished value. Yet in each case the parallel term is potentially of larger worth. If the reader accepts green leaf and the full sunlight of day as finally more attractive than the transitory golden flower and the rose flush of a brief dawn, he must also accept the Edenic sinking into grief as a rise into a larger life. In each case the temporary and partial becomes more long-lived and complete; the natural cycle that turns from flower to leaf, from dawn to day, balances each loss by a real gain. Eden's fall is a blessing in the same fashion, an entry into fuller life and greater light. Frost, both through language and through structure, has emphasized in "Nothing Gold Can Stay" not merely the melancholy of transitory beauty—of Paradise—but an affirmation of the fortunate fall.

Here is Frost's most evocative use of the *felix culpa* metaphor. The subsidence, the sinking, the going down is, by the logic of the poem, a blessed increase if we are to follow the cycle of flower, leaf, bud, fruit, into the full life that includes loss, grief, and change.

Notes to *Frost and the Paradox of the Fortunate Fall* by ALFRED R. FERGUSON

1. Robert Frost, "Education by Poetry: A Meditative Monologue," *Amherst Alumni Council News*, IV (March 1931), Supplement, 6–7.

2. Sidney Cox, *A Swinger of Birches: A Portrait of Robert Frost* (New York: New York University Press, 1958), 20.

3. In *A Masque of Reason* (1. 344) Frost quoted from "Uriel," omitting the name of the poem but referring to it as "the greatest Western poem yet." Cf. his article on Emerson in *Daedalus*, LXXXVIII (Fall 1959), 717. The paradox of fire and ice in "Uriel" may have been a stimulus to his own "Fire and Ice."

4. *The Poetry of Robert Frost*, ed. Edward Connery Lathem (New York: Holt, Rinehart and Winston, 1969), 470. For "counter-wisdom," see R. L. Cook, *The Dimensions of Robert Frost* (New York: Rinehart, 1958), 177.

5. *The Letters of Robert Frost to Louis Untermeyer*, ed. Louis Untermeyer (New York: Holt, Rinehart and Winston, 1963), 327.

6. Arthur O. Lovejoy, "Milton and the Paradox of the Fortunate Fall," *ELH*, IV (September 1937), 162.

7. *Ibid.*

8. Frost, "Education by Poetry ...," 8–9.

9. Cook, 60.

10. *Complete Works of Ralph Waldo Emerson* (Boston: Houghton Mifflin, 1903–1904, Centenary Edition), XII, 405.

11. Emerson, quoted from Frost in Cook, 144.

12. Emerson, *Complete Works*, "Experience," III, 48.

13. William Moynihan, "Fall and Winter in Frost," *MLN*, LXXIII (May 1958), 348–49.

14. Nina Baym, "An Approach to Robert Frost's Nature Poetry," *American Quarterly*, XVII (Winter 1965), 717.

15. John Lynen, *The Pastoral Art of Robert Frost* (New Haven: Yale University Press, 1960), 156.

16. Frost, "The Constant Symbol," *The Atlantic Monthly*, CLXXVIII (October 1946), 50.

17. Lawrance Thompson, *Robert Frost: The Years of Triumph, 1915–1938* (New York: Holt, Rinehart and Winston, 1970), 565.

18. See Louis Mertins, *Robert Frost: Life and Talks-Walking* (Norman, Okla.: University of Oklahoma Press, 1965), 218. Cf. Sister Benetta Quinn, "Symbolic Landscape in Frost's 'Nothing Gold Can Stay,' " *English Journal*, LV (1966), 623.

Robert Frost's Masques
and the Classic American Tradition

PETER J. STANLIS

I. FROST'S AMERICAN TRAITS
AND THE MASQUES

Robert Frost has frequently been described by both his critics and his admirers as the most American of modern American poets. The first writer to comment on Frost's uniquely American traits was Ezra Pound. In London, right after he had read the galley sheets of Frost's first book of poems, *A Boy's Will*, in March 1913, and even before the book had appeared, Pound wrote to his friend Alice C. Henderson that his new friend was "vurry Amur'k'n, with I think, the seeds of grace." Pound's remark was most perceptive, because "the seeds of grace" that made Frost an unusually original and gifted poet were planted and had sprung from a soil and national sensibility that was indeed uniquely American. In July 1962, at Bread Loaf, Frost confirmed Pound's insight in an aphorism: "All literature begins with geography." [1] The subjects of the thirty-one brief lyrics in *A Boy's Will* were mainly from American and particularly from New England rural scenes, and contained Frost's sensory observations, feelings, and reflections as an idealistic young American, on the seasons, stars, storms, the wind, flowers, and other common objects of nature and rural life, together with a few of the poet's convictions concerning God, love, science, and other such related subjects.

In addition to his subjects and themes, Frost's early poems were in their language and speech rhythms American adaptations of the forms, techniques and conventions of Romantic and Victorian poetry. The colloquial idiom and simple diction of Frost's first poems were decidedly in the American grain, more in the spirit of Whitman than of Wordsworth. Several critics have remarked on the essentially American character of Frost's use of English, not only in his early poems but throughout his literary career. Lawrance Thompson has noted that ". . . Frost's entire work is deeply rooted in the American, even in the most vital Puritan, idiom. It is 'native to the grain,' and yet thoroughly original." [2] Louis Untermeyer also considered Frost "the most American of poets" because of his "characteristically plain utterance" and "the conversational tone of speech" in his poetry.[3]

The pastorals and eclogues of Frost's second book, *North of Boston* (1914), were so strongly stamped in their subjects, themes, language and rhythms of speech with Frost's regional and national temper that Ezra Pound, in his review in *Poetry* (December 1914), called them "American Georgics." Frost's originality in adapting and assimilating the Classical eclogues and pastorals of Theocritus, Horace, and Virgil to his personal New England-American idiom in effect created a new genre for modern poetry, in which blank verse, used for description and dialogue, was combined with the narrative ease and discursiveness of prose fiction, and with the concise dramatic power of the stage, to create an intense psychological human drama.

The native American tradition in subjects, themes, forms, techniques, and language, so evident in Frost's first two books of poetry, was enormously enriched and extended by the five volumes of poetry he published between *North of Boston* and his two masques, published in 1945 and 1947. During these three decades Frost adapted a great variety of poetic forms to his American character and sensibility. Frost once remarked that "the most American trait is Americanniness," [4] which even in its playful wit suggests that improvised shrewdness and conscious Yankee humor provided the poet with a regional-universal perspective toward life most appropriate for dealing with unreconciled oppositions, for double-edged dramatic ironies, for saying the whole of a theme in terms of a part contained in an image, for harmonizing the eternal "two-endedness of things," such as the conflicting claims of justice and mercy. Frost's "Americanniness" consisted of his skill in handling the complex contraries of life in such a simple and apparently artless style that his poetry became widely read by discriminating intellectuals and uncritical common readers alike. It took the sophisticated Freudian undiscriminating intellectuals a whole generation to discover the "real" Frost, but Americans who were not myopic symbol hunters appreciated Frost, each according to his lights, almost immediately. In 1957 Frost admitted to "having become . . . an almost national poet. . . ." [5] Undoubtedly, as some critics have claimed, Frost's wide popularity was a reflection of certain common American traits shaping the national character: "Frost is important as a kind of American culture hero, as an index of certain persistent American characteristics." [6] Lionel Trilling has said the same thing in terms of the main tradition of American literature: "Robert Frost is doing in his poems what [D. H.] Lawrence says the great writers of the classic American tradition did." [7]

Frost's *A Masque of Reason* (1945) and *A Masque of Mercy* (1947) mark yet another leap in his refinements of earlier subjects, themes, techniques, language, and form. Of the three great all-inclusive subjects treated by poets—God, man, and nature—Frost's central subject is always man. A human perspective and human values always provide Frost's point of view toward his subject. He is more a humanist than a theologian or a naturalist in his philosophy, although his humanism in any given poem may incline either way. In *A Boy's Will* Frost was primarily concerned with man's relationship to external nature; and in *North of Boston*, subtitled "A Book of People," his central concern was man's relationship to man. The five volumes which followed were all devoted to further explorations of these two complex sets of relationships. But in his two masques, for the first time in his life as a writer, Frost dealt extensively and exclusively with man's relationship with God. The bulk of this article will explore the various aspects of Frost's themes, techniques, and language in the masques, but before analyzing these elements it will be useful to consider briefly the masque as a form of poetic drama, and what Frost did with it.

How do Frost's masques compare with the masque as a conscious literary and dramatic form in English literature? Clearly, they are a world apart from the somewhat profligate popular court masques introduced as "Twelfth Night" for Henry VIII in 1512, with their masked dancers, carnival amusements and revels with the audience. Nor are Frost's plays related to the mummery pantomimes or folk masques, since his characters wear no masks and speak much dialogue. Also, in their simplicity Frost's plays are the antithesis of the elaborate and lavish spectacle plays put on by Ben Jonson (1572–1637) and Inigo Jones (1573–1652) during the early years of James I's reign. Like the first Jonson-Jones collaboration, *Of Blacknesse* (1605), Frost's two masques have for their setting a fixed scene in perspective, with no procession of actors. The irreverent wit and humor in Frost's *A Masque of Reason* has its earliest analogue in Ben Jonson's antimasque in *The Masque of Queenes* (1609), whose comic interlude parodied the main plot and theme. But unlike Jonson's, Frost's wit and humor are integrated within the dialogue, and are an organic part of the main plot and theme rather than mere commentaries on them. In his dialogue Frost has the epigrammatic conciseness of Jonson. Unlike the figures in most English masques, the characters in Frost's two plays are not mythological; they are stark prototypes of human or spiritual personalities, symbolic of established moral ideals, whose set speeches, like those by characters in medieval morality plays, subordinate the dramatic conflict and action wholly to an allegorical dialogue of ideas. Like Milton's *Comus* (acted 1634, published 1637), which is more a pastoral drama than a masque, Frost's two plays depend more on poetry than on spectacle, and like Milton his main purpose is to state a serious theological and moral principle about an important religious or philosophical problem.[8] But all things considered, Frost's masques owe less to his English sources than to his own resources in the classic American tradition of literature; his masques are uniquely modern adaptations of a poetic-drama form which has been almost entirely discarded since the middle of the seventeenth century.[9] Although Frost had a brief "juvenile dream of Broadway" for *A Masque of Reason*, he was in the end "content ... with the pair of masques as poems ...,"[10] and it is as closet drama that they should be considered.

II. A MASQUE OF REASON (1945)

Frost's *A Masque of Reason* is a dramatic explication of Old Testament justice, contained in the forty-two chapters of The Book of Job, as understood by modern man in a modern setting. At the end of the masque Frost wrote: "Here endeth chapter forty-three of Job." This is Frost's bland and ironic way of saying that no one can understand his masque without a complete knowledge of The Book of Job, and also, in light of his theme, that his masque is a prophetic-like satire on modern man's excessive confidence in his own reason.

In the opening scene ("A fair oasis in the purest desert"), Job and his wife, Thyatira, awake to find God caught in the branches of the Burning Bush (the Christmas Tree), which, ironically, gives not a light of Old Testament revelation, but "a strange light" of New Testament Christianity, of spirit entangled in matter, or religion organized and refined by art, so that "the Tree is troubled" by God's being "caught in the branches." [11] Job's comment on the Christmas tree ornaments extends this point through a parody of Yeats' rhetoric in "Sailing to Byzantium" and through a probable allusion to T. S. Eliot's "Sweeney Among the Nightingales:"

> The ornaments the Greek artificers
> Made for the Emperor Alexius,
> The Star of Bethlehem, the pomegranates,
> The birds, seem all on fire with Paradise.
> And hark, the gold enameled nightingales
> Are singing.

In *A Masque of Mercy* Frost again criticized Yeats through a long speech by Paul, condemning Yeats for having

> Once charged the Nazarene with having brought
> A darkness out of Asia that had crossed
> Old Attic grace and Spartan discipline
> With violence.

Frost then defends Christ against Yeats' charge by noting that Christ introduced "The mercy on the Sin against the Sermon," whose "origin was love." [12] But in *A Masque of Reason* Frost omitted consideration of mercy in the conflict between justice and mercy.

When God finally gets disentangled from the Christmas tree Job's wife remarks:

> It's God.
> I'd know Him by Blake's picture anywhere,

to which, later, God responds: "The best, I'm told, I ever have had taken." God sets up a plywood flat, prefabricated throne (obviously a parody on conventional notions of the throne of God, as held by pious literalists, and also in keeping with modern efficiency in construction), and Job's wife guesses the throne is "for an Olympic Tournament,/Or Court of Love," but which Job assumes is for Judgment Day. Job looks for a forthcoming verdict on himself, and being a student of English literature, he bids his wife: "Suffer yourself to be admired, my love/As Waller says." All these Biblical, classical and courtly love allusions, linked by historical and literary anachronisms and verbal buffooneries, immediately establish the mixed comic-tragic ingredients and tone of the whole masque. It is obvious from the very beginning of the masque that Frost's method involves an ironical, mocking, comic treatment of the serious and tragic theme of Job's suffering of injustice. Throughout the masque the whimsical situational comedy, the witty quips, playful puns and double entendres, indulged in by Job, his wife and even by God, underscore Frost's mock-serious treatment of the Biblical characters, who think and talk like modern Americans, and give an externally light tone to the serious internal discourse at the heart of the theme.

There are many things in both the manner and the matter of Frost's masque deliberately calculated to raise the temperature of sincere and conventional religious believers who are hopelessly humorless—and even more that of sincere and militantly devout agnostics or freethinking atheists who have an undoubting confidence in man's self-sufficient reason. Unfortunately for Frost, his comic and satirical technique has been the chief source of misunderstanding of his masques. Too many readers have ignored Frost's dictum that in good writing "the way of understanding is partly mirth," and that when writing "is with outer humor, it must be with inner seriousness." Frost's statement in the amended preface to E. A. Robinson's *King Jasper*, that "the style is the way a man takes himself," best explains the function of comic wit and irony in his masques. The terrible tragedies that overwhelmed his family—the early deaths of his parents and several of his children, the mental affliction of his sister, the suicide of his son Carol, and other sorrows that pursued him into late life—were enough to make him the modern living embodiment of

Job. On August 9, 1947, when his daughter Irma was about to be confined in a mental institution, Frost wrote to Louis Untermeyer: "Cast your eye back over my family luck and perhaps you will wonder if I haven't had pretty near enough." Then he added: "That is for the angels to say." [13]

Frost's implicit religious faith included both evil and good, and therefore both the tragic and comic sense toward life. This belief required him to assume a God-like, cosmic, stoical detachment toward all of life, even in matters in which he was most personally involved and intensely committed, so that he could grasp the tragic as tragic but also in terms of the comic, and understand sorrow in terms of laughter and irony. In this way of taking himself Frost was unique. Louis Untermeyer wrote of this trait in Frost: "His was a high stoicism which could mask unhappiness in playfulness, which could even delight in darkness. . . ." [Frost] was "one who could tease and be tortured, renounce and be reconciled." [14] Certainly, Frost never lost his balance between the tragic and the comic. Although the theme of his masque is centered in the serious tragedy and unhappiness of Job, Frost's method is playful, like the casual, bantering, whimsical, frolicsome, tongue-in-cheek teasing of one who has a lover's quarrel with the world. His masque is ironical in tone, with levity-gravity and light-somber qualities that at once intensify God's arbitrary injustice to Job, and balance it off with the perverse relief of laughter. To Frost, God is a comic wit who cares for man, at once detached and concerned. He is not only the source of revelation but also the master of revels.

Most critics of *A Masque of Reason* have failed to perceive the function of the comic elements, and have dismissed the masque as a serious artistic lapse. According to Randall Jarrell, "*A Masque of Reason* . . . is a frivolous, trivial, and bewilderingly corny affair, full of jokes inexplicable except as the contemptuous patter of an old magician certain that *he* can get away with anything in the world." [15] This singularly obtuse criticism is typical of many critics who cannot understand how comedy, even low comedy, can heighten the sense of high tragedy in Job's affliction. Yvor Winters stated that Frost's comic "details . . . are offered merely for the shock of cleverness; the details are irrelevant to any theme discernible in the poem," and he concluded that the masque is among Frost's "feeblest and least serious efforts." [16] It is ironical that critics who fall far short of Frost's all-inclusive comic-tragic view of the tragedy of man's temporal life should insist from the one-dimensional base of their high seriousness that his wit and humor and comic view of man are sadly misplaced in the masque.[17]

A more valid criticism of Frost's use of comedy in the masque is that it is not always well integrated with the dialogue and dramatic action of the serious theme. This is partly the result of Frost's indiscriminate mixing of things sacred and profane, which has been questioned as bad taste—a sacrilege against the religious sensibility of Christians and Jews. Even here a distinction needs to be made. Frost's comedy is not directed against traditional religious orthodoxy regarding the justice or mercy of God, but against the conventional social respectability of devout but humorless prudes. But it is even more sharply directed against antireligious or nonreligious rationalists. Those readers whose rigid religious faith does not permit spoofing, bantering, and raillery between man and God fail to understand that it is the very intimacy of Job and his wife with God that allows them such liberties in speech. Their dialogue is like gossip, like the fierce spontaneous give and take of a domestic quarrel, where an assumed and intense love allows for great liberties in the expression of resentments or demands. There is nothing unctious or reserved about the faith of Job and his wife. If God is a real person He should be spoken to as a real person, not as a remote and bloodless abstraction.

The whole question in comic relief is whether it fulfills its dramatic purpose artistically. Since most of the comedy is provided by Thyatira, Job's shrewd and sharp-tongued wife, in her remarks to Job, God, and Satan, an examination of her function in the play will clarify Frost's skill in comedy. Clearly, Job's wife is a blood descendant of Mother Eve, by way of the shrew in medieval and Tudor drama. She is proud to acknowledge that the Witch of Endor was a friend of hers. She has the advanced and militant social consciousness of a pre–World War I Bloomer girl or a Women's Liberation advocate. In the modern setting of Frost's masque Job's wife is an emancipated and sophisticated American woman, the prototype of the most ardent member of the League of Women Voters. But she is also a tangled skein of contradictions. She is convinced that God (being Male) has it in for women, and asks Him if it stands to reason (her reason, not God's)

> That women prophets should be burned as witches,
> Whereas men prophets are received with honor.

Her complaint against this injustice is particularly ludicrous, because it follows immediately after God's long speech to Job on why men have to endure injustices they can't explain, for reasons God does not have to give. Thyatira's complaint is the comic equivalent of Job's serious case against God.

But, it turns out, she wasn't really listening to the exchange between Job and God, because philosophical discourse doesn't interest her. In a tone of disdainful superiority Thyatira says: "You don't catch women trying to be Plato." Job confirms this to God:

> And she's a woman: she's not interested
> In general ideas and principles.

Thyatira's interests are "Witch-women's rights," so that the moment Satan appears, "like a sapphire wasp/That flickers mica wings," she promptly sits up and says:

> Well, if we aren't all here,
> Including me, the only Dramatis
> Personae needed to enact the problem.

After so many eons of time, as Eve's undoubted and unrepentent daughter, she still feels a deep kinship with old Nick. When Satan first speaks she responds:

> That strain again! Give me excess of it!
> As dulcet as a pagan temple gong!

Although this is said in light mock-seriousness, Job's wife is in truth a perverse feminine Romantic to the bitter-sweet end, and says of Satan:

> He's very real to me
> And always will be.—Please don't go. Stay, stay
> But to the evensong, and having played
> Together we will go with you along.

> There are who won't have had enough of you
> If you go now.

Romantic love and sensual delight are supreme for Job's wife. In her rapport with Satan and her emotive anxiety to receive with honor the prince of evil wizards, she has forgotten completely her intellectual concern about witch women's rights and the differences between men and women prophets. Could anything be more charming and disarming than Frost's portrait of Job's wife? Other than a modern naive intellectual critic would any male—pagan or religious —claim that the comedy she provides has no place in the drama of the masque?

Job's wife supplies the comic subplot for the serious theme centered in the dialogue between Job and God. Her comic role adds an ironical dimension to the main theme. It is ironical that Job, the rational and philosophical male, is less virulent in asking God for explanations that satisfy his reason than Thyatira, the nonphilosophical and emotional female, who is quick to insist "to know the reason why" God allows irrational and unjust events to happen:

> All You can seem to do is lose Your temper
> When reason-hungry mortals ask for reasons.
> Of course, in the abstract high singular
> There isn't any universal reason;
> And no one but a man would think there was.
> You don't catch women trying to be Plato.
> Still there must be lots of unsystematic
> Stray scraps of palliative reason
> It wouldn't hurt You to vouchsafe the faithful.

Job's wife is in a profound sense more reasonable and more religious in rejecting hope or belief in an "abstract" or "universal" reason than men philosophers whose very attempt to find a universal reason is itself a kind of irrational madness.

Frost's serious theme in the masque can best be understood by reference to The Book of Job, the most disturbing book to Judaic orthodoxy in the Old Testament. Its challenge to the Mosaic law contained in the first five books (the Pentateuch), through Deuteronomy, puzzled and disturbed the pious among the orthodox. In Deuteronomy, God is angry at men who are incredulous and disobedient against His commandments. But in The Book of Job much discontent against God is expressed by Job, who has been true to God's law yet has suffered many terrible and apparently meaningless afflictions. But in his acceptance of God's injustice Job helped to change God's old relationship to man. Frost has God acknowledge this to Job:

> I have no doubt
> You realize by now the part you played
> To stultify the Deuteronomist
> And change the tenor of religious thought.

In a long speech by God, which contains much that is essential to that part of the theme which is concerned with justifying God's ways to man, and reveals the essence of Frost's own "Old Testament Christianity," Job is made to realize how he stultified the Deuteronomist:

> I've had you on my mind a thousand years
> To thank you someday for the way you helped me
> Establish once for all the principle
> There's no connection man can reason out
> Between his just deserts and what he gets.
> Virtue may fail and wickedness succeed.
> 'Twas a great demonstration we put on.
> . . . .
> Too long I've owed you this apology
> For the apparently unmeaning sorrow
> You were afflicted with in those old days.
> But it was of the essence of the trial
> You shouldn't understand it at the time.
> It had to seem unmeaning to have meaning.
> . . . .
> My thanks are to you for releasing me
> From moral bondage to the human race.
> The only free will there at first was man's,
> Who could do good or evil as he chose.
> I had no choice but I must follow him
> With forfeits and rewards he understood—
> Unless I liked to suffer loss of worship.
> I had to prosper good and punish evil.
> You changed all that. You set me free to reign.

Yvor Winters' comment on this vital passage sets it in its correct (religious) historical perspective: "So far as the ideas in this passage are concerned, the passage belongs to the fideistic tradition of New England Calvinism; the ideas can be found in more than one passage in Jonathan Edwards, as well as elsewhere." [18]

In that part of his theme which justifies the mysterious and irrational ways of God to man, Frost added little beyond Scripture or Milton's treatment in *Paradise Lost*. Job's endurance of an apparently meaningless evil which released God from the end of adhering to strict poetic justice was not original with Frost. God's reply to Job's insistence to know "plainly and unequivocally" why God hurt him so is sifted through many delays and witty equivocations, before God gives His shocking reason: "I was just showing off to the Devil." But this aesthetic shock, which is something both more and less than Job can understand, is finally shown to be based on the less shocking idea that "the Devil's . . . God's best inspiration," which in turn rests upon the platitude that God and man cannot exist in a meaningful moral relationship without both good and evil, including evils inexplicable by human finite reason. For mankind this means that spiritual salvation can come only through a perpetual trial by existence, a struggle to endure even unreasonable afflictions and to triumph over them through a personal implicit faith in God.[19] This defense of the ancient ways of God to man comes close to an orthodoxy that is common to both Judaism and historical Christianity.

If Frost's main object had been merely to justify the ways of God's justice to man it would have been more appropriate to call his play *A Masque of Justice*. One excellent critic, Marion Montgomery, has noted that the main thrust of Frost's theme is a criticism of the human error of reading man's own rational nature into God. He asks: "Is man's reason sufficient to overcome the wall between himself and God?" His answer is—not without God's help—which is the traditional answer of Judaism and Christianity in their doctrines of grace. He concludes: "The theme of the poem, then, is that understanding is dependent not only upon reason, but upon faith as well, a faith which helps the finite mind accept the mystery its reason will not completely explain." [20] So far as it goes this is excellent criticism, because it interprets the masque as centered in man's reason rather than in God's justice. But it falls short of a full statement of Frost's theme, which is not merely that man should add faith to his reason, but that modern man's excessive faith in his own reason, his lack of doubt or intellectual skepticism toward his reason, leaves little or no room for any religious faith and ends in the cardinal sin of pride. Frost called his play *A Masque of Reason* not only because he rejected man's finite reason as insufficient to understand and accept the mystery of God's justice, but even more because in essence his masque was a satire on faith in reason as such, a severe condemnation of modern man's proud and delusive Faustian ways toward God.

Frost certainly recognized that there are rational and creative powers in man that give form and meaning through science and art to Nature, and that these probes into the infinite in search of truth are among the chief glories of human nature. In "Neither Out Far nor In Deep," in man's search for "wherever the truth may be—," Frost had written:

> They cannot look out far.
> They cannot look in deep.
> But when was that ever a bar
> To any watch they keep?

Compared to the infinite perfection of God's power and knowledge the rational and creative powers of man are very limited, though the recognition of his limitations does not prevent man from persisting in his search for truth. The satire in *A Masque of Reason* is directed against modern man's failure to recognize the severe limitations of his finite reason.

In light of this interpretation of Frost's main theme, one of the most crucial passages in his masque is this speech by God:

> Job and I together
> Found out the discipline man needed most
> Was to learn his submission to unreason;
> And that for man's own sake as well as mine. . . .

There is nothing in man's "submission to unreason" contrary to Frost's lifelong belief that man should strive to find "truth" wherever it is by all the power of his limited reason. Job finally comes to understand this paradox when he replies to God:

> Yet I suppose what seems to us confusion
> Is not confusion, but the form of forms,
> The serpent's tail stuck down the serpent's throat,
> Which is the symbol of eternity
> And also of the way all things come round,
> Or of how rays return upon themselves,
> To quote the greatest Western poem yet.

The only critic who has interpreted Frost's masque with reference to Emerson, Reuben A. Brower,[21] has made no use of the allusion to Emerson's poem "Uriel" beyond comparing parallel images. Yet this passage, and the lines in "Uriel" to which they allude,

> In vain produced, all rays return;
> Evil will bless, and ice will burn...

are crucial to an understanding of Frost's satirical theme.

Several critics have noted that Frost's philosophy has many important points in common with Emerson,[22] particularly his love of seeking truth in "a world of conflicts, clear to the limit," and his ability to contain vast inconsistencies within himself, to perceive "how rays return upon themselves" and finally harmonize in "the form of forms." But much as Frost agreed with Emerson's philosophy, and admired his skill with words, there was one very crucial difference between them concerning the problem of good and evil. In "Uriel" Emerson had written that "The bounds of good and ill were rent;" and that "Uriel's voice" shamed the evil Angels' "veiling wings . . . out of the good of evil born." In a letter to Lawrance Thompson (July 11, 1959), Frost referred directly to these lines and stated concisely how radically he differed from Emerson's optimistic view of good and evil: "Emerson's defect was that he was of the great tradition of Monists. He could see the 'good of evil born' but he couldn't bring himself to say the evil of good born. He was an Abominable Snowman of the top-lofty peaks. . . . Arnold thought him a voice oracular. ('A voice oracular has pealed today.') I couldn't go as far as that because I am a Dualist. . . ."[23] Frost's ethical dualism included a view of reality in which good and evil were both real, so that evil was born of good as well as good of evil. Emerson's ethical monism made good (God) the only reality to man, and he explained evil not as real in itself but only as the absence of good, so that in the end Emerson explained evil by explaining it away altogether. In Frost's masque God, Job and Job's wife all refer to evil (the Devil) as real, though Satan has a very small part in the play.

Frost's contention that Satan's "originality" in doing evil is "God's best inspiration" implies that great evil provokes God to create an opposing complementary good. In this sense Satan is not only God's great antagonist but also His collaborator in making good and evil meaningful to man.[24] In Judaic and Christian religion Satan's originality, in first defying God, was built upon the false premise that his will and reason were superior to God's and should prevail. This is precisely the same premise upon which the modern rationalist builds his faith in progress through physical science. The evil that comes of good for modern man is his Faustian pride, which is the result of his originality and inventiveness and great success in advancing his knowledge and his power over the laws and processes of physical nature, until he imagines that he can eliminate all temporal evil and achieve salvation through his own self-sufficient reason, without God. This is what from Frost's point of view so frequently underlies modern man's facile optimism, his denial of original sin, that is, of the natural limitations inherent in his finite and fallible nature, and his boundless faith that his private reason is sufficient to create a heaven on earth. Although in religion Frost referred to himself as "an old dissenter,"[25] and wrote "I believe I am safely secular till the last go down...,"[26] he was sharply critical of modern secular rationalists whose dissent made their own private reason a substitute for religion. In a letter written a few days before his death Frost alluded to the combined themes of his two masques, and denied emphatically that man's salvation can come of man: "Why will the quidnuncs always be hoping for a salvation man will never have from anyone but God? I was just saying today how Christ posed Himself the whole problem and died for it. How can we be just in a world that needs mercy and merciful in a world that needs justice."[27]

In *A Masque of Reason* Frost's Old Testament religious orthodoxy is voiced most explicitly by God, who makes it plain that in any conflict between the old, unchanging moral wisdom of Genesis and the claims of modern science, with its novelty and current change, the ethical norms of traditional revelation are still the fountain of wisdom:

> My forte is truth,
> Or metaphysics, long the world's reproach
> For standing still in one place true forever;
> While science goes self-superseding on.
> Look at how far we've left the current science
> Of Genesis behind. The wisdom there, though,
> Is just as good as when I uttered it.
> Still, novelty has doubtless an attraction.

Frost wrote this passage on the flyleaf of a student's book in 1945, and then added below it: "Really Robert Frost's though by him ascribed to someone higher up." [28] Although Job and even Job's wife express some of Frost's deepest personal convictions, the ideas, viewpoint and tone of God in the masque are practically identical with Frost's philosophy.

Perhaps nothing could be more antithetical than the philosophy of modern secular man, with his faith in reason, and Frost's satire on reason based upon a theology which derives from Old Testament religious orthodoxy. Where the modern rationalist makes man's reason supreme and simply eliminates God as irrelevant to his temporal or spiritual salvation, Frost exalts the omnipotence of God's arbitrary justice and makes man's reason appear peevish and impotent by comparison. To those moderns who are infatuated with the dynamics of an ever-changing society, and believe in the idea of scientific progress through education, politics, and technology, including ethical "progress" for man, Frost's Old Testament theology and insistence that the world is always a hard place in which to save man's soul must appear as an unforgiveable heresy against modern man's faith in himself. Perhaps this explains why so many modern critics have gotten so little out of Frost's masque.

Frost accepted completely the superiority of God's mysterious ways and the limitations and fallibility of man's reason. His hard principles are so well fitted to the voices and exploratory dialogue of his characters in the masque that they appear natural and easy in delivery, perhaps even too easy. This is probably what is behind the charge of some critics that Frost is "smug"; he accepts unflinchingly the fact that there are terrible evils in the world about which man can do little. But the charge of smugness can cut both ways; perhaps the critics themselves are smug in assuming that modern man is God and can remove all unreasonable evils from the world. Only a critic victimized by his pride in his own reason would accuse Frost of dramatizing a philosophy of irrational despair. In *A Masque of Reason* Frost's explicit theme is Job's quarrel with God for afflicting him with undeserved evils. But implicit throughout the masque is Frost's own lover's quarrel with smug modern man for not remembering original sin and his fallen state, and for presumptuously assuming the supreme position in the universe. Implicit in Frost's satire against man's presumptuous reason is God's soul-shattering question to Job, in chapter thirty-eight: "Where wast thou when I laid the foundations of the earth?" In this light the humor and comedy in the masque may well be taken as Frost's amusement that men who forget their own finiteness and limitations should at once deny or question the infinite wisdom of God and yet expect heavenly miracles on earth from the manipulation of their social machinery, from their programs of education, science, and government. Far from being frivolous and irresponsible, as so many critics have charged, *A Masque of Reason* is the purest example in the whole of Frost's writings of his serious case against modern man's fondest delusions about himself. In this masque Frost's intellectual skepticism toward man's reason as an instrument adequate to explain the moral mystery at the core of life is as rigorous and profound, within its dramatic medium, as anything found in the philosophical poems of Donne and Dryden and the prose of Swift and Dr. Johnson. Indeed, *A Masque of Reason* places Frost squarely in the great tradition of Pyrrhonism in English thought and literature.

In 1956, as if in sharp answer to the plot, theme, and method of Frost's *A Masque of Reason*, Archibald MacLeish wrote *J.B.*, also a philosophical drama in verse based on a modern adaptation of The Book of Job. In MacLeish's play, two broken-down actors, Zuss and Nickles, are reduced to being vendors in a circus. They find themselves after closing time on an empty sideshow stage, where a drama on Job, God, and Satan has been performed. They put on the masks and begin to read the parts, Zuss speaking for God and

Nickles for Satan. Much of the play consists of their comments on offstage or sidestage flashback scenes centered in J.B., the main character. He is shown first as a devoted husband of Sarah and father of five children, a wealthy banker, a virtuous and admired man, who in a series of tragic scenes loses everything except his embittered wife, and is reduced to rags and sores. J.B. becomes the modern prototype of Job, a symbol of suffering humanity in a meaningless universe.

The differences in theme and technique between MacLeish's play and Frost's masque clarify by contrast the Bible-centered orthodoxy of Frost's argument from one which rests upon faith in modern man's reason. MacLeish's play is psychological, naturalistic and humanitarian, and stresses that a deep sense of guilt distinguishes man from other forms of animal life. Frost's masque is theological, theistic, and humanistic, and the problem of guilt is subsumed by the larger problem of justifying the ways of God to man and by the satire on man's pride and reason. There is no humor in MacLeish's play. In contrast to Job's wife in Frost's masque, J.B.'s wife is an almost desperately serious woman, deeply concerned with her husband's suffering and misfortunes and morally outraged by the idea that God is just. When she says to J.B. of their dead children,

> They are
> Dead and they were innocent: I will not
> Let you sacrifice their deaths
> To make injustice justice and God good![29]

she summarizes the case of the modern secular skeptic against God's ultimate justice. Her skepticism is reinforced by the sarcastic remarks of Nickles on the worsening fate of J.B., who persists like Job in keeping faith in God. Nickles' sarcasm is as close as MacLeish comes to wit as a vehicle for sharpening the theme.

J.B. differs from Frost's Job in seeing all the evils he suffers as a matter of pure chance, rather than as direct or indirect expressions of the Divine will. J.B. believes he should love God, but he rejects the injustices of the world as a trial by existence of man's courage and faith in God's inexplicable will, or His ultimate mercy to man—which are precisely the themes advanced in Frost's masques. MacLeish appeals to man's natural reason and finally to love between men; Frost to man's courage and to supernatural faith. MacLeish inspires confidence to endure through knowledge and understanding, even in a meaningless universe; Frost reveals skepticism that man's natural reason is capable of piercing through the design of God's plan. The grand theme of *J.B.* is identical with Matthew Arnold's "Dover Beach." When Sarah says to J.B., "You wanted justice and there was none/Only love," [30] MacLeish makes it clear that this does not include love from God to man: "He does not love. He is." [31] Most concisely, MacLeish's theme is that only human love redeems man from God's injustice. In contrast, Frost's theme exalts in man a redemptive reverence for God's unknown will and possible love even in the face of terrible and unmerited tragedy. But it is in *A Masque of Mercy* that Frost makes God's love for man the ultimate basis of hope and faith in life.

III. A MASQUE OF MERCY (1947)

In a letter to G. R. Elliott (April 22, 1947), written right after he had completed *A Masque of Mercy*, Frost wrote a significant passage that combines the central motifs of both his masques, his "two New England Biblicals," and applied them to himself in his trial by existence since the First World War:

Two world wars and a few private catastrophes have made a man of me who doesn't mind blame. Neither for my sins of omission nor commission am I afraid of being punished. All that is past like a vision of Dante or Gustave Doré. My fear of God has settled down into a deep inward fear that my best offering may not prove acceptable in his sight. My approach to the New Testament is rather through Jerewsalem than through Rome and Canterbury.[32]

This passage is a perfect transition from Frost's exploration of Old Testament justice in *A Masque of Reason* to the other side of the same theological coin, the claims of New Testament mercy as set forth in *A Masque of Mercy*. As a "masque" it is that rarest of literary forms, a city eclogue engrafted upon a dramatic fantasy.

The setting of *A Masque of Mercy* is a bookstore late at night in New York City. There are four characters, all innocent, but each is harassed by a personal spiritual problem involving love and faith toward God or man within the justice-mercy contradiction.[33] The first speaker, Jesse Bel, proprietress of the bookstore, is somewhat like Job's wife in *A Masque of Reason*, a shrewd, hardheaded, bored, slightly alcoholic woman, under psychiatric care because she can't love God, her husband, or her psychiatrist. Her husband is My Brother's Keeper, called "Keeper," a modern pagan-religious man who says he would "rather be lost in the woods/Than found in church." The third character is Paul the Apostle, whom Keeper calls "the Exegete,"—"the fellow who theologized/Christ almost out of Christianity." Finally, there is Jonas Dove or Jonah, whom Paul identifies as "the universal fugitive" running away from God's "mercy-justice contradiction." Keeper and Paul divide the serious debate between them, and each at various times expresses Frost's own convictions on justice and mercy. Jonah, like Job, appears as a man unjustly treated by God, and his case provides the essential drama in *A Masque of Mercy*.

The Book of Jonah contains the first notable instance in the Old Testament of God's mercy to sinful man: God spared the wicked city of Nineveh because the people repented and because the city contained many innocent women and children—"More than sixscore thousand persons that cannot discern between their right hand and their left hand." But God's mercy raised a serious moral problem. His ultimate forgiveness of wicked men is as great a mystery as His temporal afflictions upon the innocent. His mercy, that forgiveness which derives from His love, violates the strict logic of poetic justice in favor of man. If Job's punishment despite his obedience to the moral law makes God appear unjust, God's mercy in forgiving sinners who break His law also appears as a violation of strict justice, even if done in order to spare the innocent. In essence this is the viewpoint of Jonas in the early part of the masque.

The occasion for the drama is provided by Jonah's refusal to act as a chosen prophet to the God of the Old Testament, a wrathful God of strict justice, because Jonah fears that God has become softened into a New Testament God of mercy. Jonah has lost his faith in God because he cannot trust God to be strictly just, that is, unmerciful to the wicked. Jonah has refused seven times to prophesy the destruction of Nineveh, and has fled from God, because he fears that God will sacrifice his public reputation as His prophet rather than be unmerciful and punish the wicked:

> I've lost my faith in God to carry out
> The threats He makes against the city evil.
> I can't trust God to be unmerciful.

When Paul asks Jonah, "What would you have God if not merciful?" Jonah replies: "Just." After noting that not trusting God to be unmerciful is "the beginning of all wisdom," Paul confronts Jonah with the New Testament case against God's temporal justice:

> I'm going to make you see
> How relatively little justice matters.

Paul opens his argument by noting that "after doing Justice justice," first "the Gospels" and then later

> Milton's pentameters go on to say,
> But Mercy first and last shall brightest shine—
> Not only last, but first, you will observe....

But before Paul can bring Jonah to realize that no man in his right senses would demand God's justice for himself when he could have His mercy, there is some dramatic give and take between Keeper and Paul on the claims of justice and mercy in the practical affairs of modern man.

In its subsidiary theme, *A Masque of Mercy* makes it clear that Frost believed the main problem of modern man is not commutative justice in the courts of equity, between one individual and another, but a conflict over social distributive justice and the various means by which it is brought about. In a long soliloquy Paul draws out the range of possibilities for the redistribution of wealth in the modern world:

> The rich in seeing nothing but injustice
> In their impoverishment by revolution
> Are right. But 'twas intentional injustice.
> It was their justice being mercy-crossed.

This is the kind of revolution favored by Keeper, whose political views are a summary of the leveling social legislation of Franklin D. Roosevelt's "New Deal":

> The revolution Keeper's bringing on
> Is nothing but an outbreak of mass mercy,
> Too long pent up in rigorous convention—
> A holy impulse towards redistribution.
> To set out to homogenize mankind
> So that the cream could never rise again
> Required someone who laughingly could play
> With the idea of justice in the courts,
> Could mock at riches in the right it claims
> To count on justice to be merely just.

The main question in bringing about distributive justice "is the form/ Of outrage—violence—that breaks across it." In violent total revolutions, such as Communism, justice is "evil-crossed." Paul concludes:

> And if you've got to see your justice crossed
> (And you've got to) which will you prefer
> To see it, evil-crossed or mercy-crossed?

Although Keeper somewhat flippantly offers a third alternative, to have justice "star-crossed," in fact Keeper and Paul meet on common grounds in their politics by both favoring a distributive justice that is "mercy-crossed." [34] Keeper rejects an "evil-crossed" total revolution:

> No revolution I brought on would aim
> At anything but change of personnel.

Similarly, Keeper sees the religious basis of Paul's politics in having justice "mercy-crossed" as originating in the basic law of the New Testament. After Paul has said,

> Christ came to introduce a break with logic
> That made all other outrage seem as child's play:
> The Mercy on the Sin against the Sermon,

Keeper summarizes how justice in the temporal order of man's practical affairs is seen from the viewpoint of New Testament Christianity:

> Paul's constant theme. The Sermon on the Mount
> Is just a frame-up to insure the failure
> Of all of us, so all of us will be
> Thrown prostrate at the Mercy Seat for Mercy.

Paul in effect concedes that Keeper's summary is valid when he says:

> Mercy is only to the undeserving.
> But such we all are made in the sight of God.

This long and involved digression into the justice-mercy contradiction in modern politics seems at first very remote from the spiritual problem first posed by Jonah. But it is in fact a concrete illustration of the essential problem of the masque, applied to historical conditions and circumstances that are familiar to modern man.

The religious-political discussion between Paul and Keeper is not a violent difference in principle, but a mild difference in degree from a difference in method. As Keeper says:

> Our disagreement when we disagree, Paul,
> Lies in our different approach to Christ,
> Yours more through Rome, mine more through Palestine.

From this passage, with reference to Frost's letter to G. R. Elliott, it would seem that Keeper speaks more for Frost than Paul. But the characters are not always consistent with themselves as dramatic vehicles for expressing Frost's own ideas, which are about equally divided between Keeper and Paul.[35]

Apparently Jonah, who says little after the opening scenes, has listened intently to the discussion between Paul and Keeper, because in the midst of it he says:

> I think my trouble's with the crisises
> Where mercy-crossed to me seemed evil-crossed.

As their discussion proceeds Jonah remarks further: "My trouble has been with my sense of justice"; and then near the end of the action, he adds, "I think I may have got God wrong entirely." After Paul convinces Jonah that God's tempering justice with mercy is in harmony with His omnipotence and love, Jonah has the whole justice-mercy mystery applied to him in his favor by Paul's ironical prayerful appeal: "Mercy on him for having asked for justice."

Jonah's complete change in viewpoint concerning justice and mercy finds an exact parallel in Keeper, but within a secular rather than a Scriptural frame of reference. Jesse Bel had chided Jonah early in the play for his lack of faith in God's justice:

> Your courage failed. The saddest thing in life
> Is that the best thing in it should be courage.

Keeper also laughs at Jonah, but in the end he discovers that he too has lacked courage and faith, not regarding God's justice but His mercy:

> My failure is no different from Jonah's.
> We both have lacked the courage in the heart
> To overcome the fear within the soul
> And go ahead to any accomplishment.
> Courage is what it takes and takes the more of
> Because the deeper fear is so eternal.

Keeper's distinction between the pagan virtue, physical courage, and the Christian virtue, spiritual fear, exalts fear above courage:

> Courage is of the heart by derivation,
> And great it is. But fear is of the soul.

"The deeper fear" that "is so eternal" is not so much the fear that the trial by existence which is man's life on earth has no final meaning, as that it does have meaning but that men as individuals will fail to measure up to what God expects of them.

In what is probably the most vital passage in the masque, Paul defines God's mercy not as the forgiveness of sins or failure,[36] but as His acceptance as a free gift of the best sacrifice man has to offer:

> Yes, there you have it at the root of things.
> We have to stay afraid deep in our souls
> Our sacrifice—the best we have to offer,
> And not our worst nor second best, our best,
> Our very best, our lives laid down like Jonah's,
> Our lives laid down in war and peace—may not
> Be found acceptable in Heaven's sight.
> And that they may be is the only prayer
> Worth praying. May my sacrifice
> Be found acceptable in Heaven's sight.[37]

Because of the uncertainty of God's ultimate justice or mercy man is compelled throughout his life "to stay afraid" deep in his soul, a fear that goes beyond the necessary elemental pagan virtue of courage. As a basis for humility and maximum effort in an absolute commitment to life, this passage is in essence Christian and Hebraic, and reconciles the justice of the Old Testament with the mercy of the New Testament. In the masque this reconciliation is summarized in the final line, spoken by Keeper: "Nothing can make injustice just but mercy." The religious orthodoxy at the end of *A Masque of Mercy* is at once more subtle and more obvious than in *A Masque of Reason*; more subtle because of Frost's originality in what God's mercy means, and more obvious because the theme of the masque is more congenial to modern man's New Testament emphasis upon a God of love. Yet both masques make the same stress on the limitations of man's knowledge regarding God's ultimate purposes, and the need for implicit faith in God. To Frost, God always remains an invisible reality of the ideal spiritual perfection toward which man aspires, with courage and daring and a full, free commitment, and with the softer virtues of love, faith and humility. Frost's *A Masque of Mercy* has no systematic theology or creed or dogma or revealed path to personal salvation. Instead, it reaffirms from a New Testament viewpoint the same austere sense of right-mindedness and courage found in *A Masque of Reason*. Its drama is verbal debate and quite didactic. It advocates living the trial by existence with daring and faith, on the highest level of which man is capable, and in the assurance that when this is done the rest belongs to heaven.

The masques are unique among Frost's poems because they are the culmination in form, technique, and theme of much that Frost has written. James M. Cox has noted the climactic position of the masques in form: "Frost has clearly moved toward comedy and wit—from lyric through narrative toward satire, and finally to masque." [38] Readers who wish to understand the truly significant place of the masques in the themes of Frost's poetry would have to compare them with many of his earlier poems. "The Trial by Existence" is in many ways an early anticipation of elements in the theme of the masques. The theme of love's contrarieties in "The Death of the Hired Man" is centered in the same conflicting claims between justice and mercy. The contrarieties between transcendent and immanent love in "West-Running Brook" bear comparison with aspects of the masques. The voice tones and patterns of imagery and arguments of the poet-philosophers in "New Hampshire" and "The Lesson for Today" also throw light on the masques. Frost's views toward the ambiguities in traditional religion and modern science could be fruitfully explored by comparing the masques with such poems as "The Demiurge's Laugh," "Neither Out Far nor In Deep," "All Revelation," "For Once, Then, Something," "Desert Places," and "Design." Indeed, all of Frost's poems on science should be read in the light of Lawrance Thompson's suggestive insight: "Also echoed throughout the masque is the related Bergsonian concept of a continuously creative process which develops the universe." [39] Only after many such comparisons in form, technique, imagery and theme would we see the full extent to which Frost's masques are in the classic tradition of American literature.

Notes to *Robert Frost's Masques and the Classic American Tradition*
   by PETER J. STALIS

1. A conversation between Robert Frost and Peter Stanlis, Bread Loaf, Vermont, July 6, 1962.

2. Lawrance Thompson, *Robert Frost* (Minneapolis: University of Minnesota Press, 1959), 41.

3. Louis Untermeyer, *Robert Frost: A Backward Look* (Reference Department: The Library of Congress, 1964), 2.

4. A conversation between Robert Frost and a group of students at Bread Loaf, July 1962.

5. Robert Frost to Louis Untermeyer, April 16, 1957, in *The Letters of Robert Frost to Louis Untermeyer*, ed. Louis Untermeyer (New York: Holt, Rinehart and Winston, 1963), 369. See also Frost's letter to Lawrance Thompson, also on April 16, 1957, in *Selected Letters of Robert Frost*, ed. Lawrance Thompson (New York: Holt, Rinehart and Winston, 1964), 566 (cited below as *Selected Letters*).

6. G. W. Nitchie, "A Momentary Stay Against Confusion," in *Robert Frost: A Collection of Critical Essays*, ed. James M. Cox (Englewood Cliffs: Prentice-Hall, 1962), 174. See also 175.

7. Lionel Trilling, "A Speech on Robert Frost: A Cultural Episode," in Cox, *Frost: Critical Essays*, 156. On a vital aspect of the poet's philosophy, Trilling contends that Frost "admires will in the degree that he suspects mind," and that Frost "stands at the center of American thought about American culture because ... he expresses the chronic American belief that there exists an opposition between reality and mind and that one must enlist oneself in the party of reality" (*The Liberal Imagination*, Anchor Books, 5, 10).

8. While he was a teacher of English and drama at Pinkerton Academy in Derry, New Hampshire, Frost had his students put on Milton's *Comus*. See *Letters to Untermeyer*, 357–58.

9. In the twentieth century the only notable masques produced in the United States and England were Percy Mackaye's *Masque of St. Louis,* performed in 1914 in St. Louis, and some early seventeenth century masques performed in 1916 at Stratford during the tercentenary of Shakespeare.

10. *Letters to Untermeyer*, 333–34.

11. Frost believed that the embodiment of spirit in matter was the manifestation of true religion, and that the highest reaches of poetry were the attempt to say spirit

in terms of matter. In "Kitty Hawk" he expressed this idea in a passage celebrating Christ's incarnation:

> But God's own descent
> Into flesh was meant
> As a demonstration
> That the supreme merit
> Lay in risking spirit
> In substantiation.

But Frost's theism, like Abraham Lincoln's, was not sectarian; he believed it could be best fulfilled individually, not through institutions. Frost once remarked to Peter Stanlis (Bread Loaf, July 1942), that "[T. S.] Eliot is more churchy than I am, but I am more religious than Eliot."

12. One critic, wholly missing the point of Frost's parody and criticism of Yeats, even contends that in *A Masque of Mercy* "Keeper's failure" in courage "is also Frost's; and that failure helps to explain, perhaps, Frost's irritated awareness of Yeats in the masques...." G. W. Nitchie, "A Momentary Stay Against Confusion," Cox, *Frost: Critical Essays*, 167.

13. *Letters to Untermeyer*, 346.

14. *Ibid.*, 388.

15. Randall Jarrell, "The Other Frost," in *Robert Frost: An Introduction*, ed. Robert A. Greenberg and James G. Hepburn (New York: Holt, Rinehart and Winston, 1961), 131.

16. Yvor Winters, "Robert Frost: or, the Spiritual Drifter as Poet," in Cox, *Frost: Critical Essays*, 71, 79.

17. See for example Radcliffe Squires, *The Major Themes of Robert Frost* (Ann Arbor: University of Michigan Press, 1963), 80–83.

18. Winters, "Spiritual Drifter," 71–72. The fideistic tradition of theology is also found in some of the works of Donne, Dryden, Swift and Dr. Johnson.

19. Job's wife speaks a passage which combines ideas expressed in Frost's "The Trial by Existence" and "The Lesson for Today":

> Job says there's no such thing as Earth's becoming
> An easier place for man to save his soul in.
> Except as a hard place to save his soul in,
> A trial ground where he can try himself
> And find out whether he is any good,
> It would be meaningless. It might as well
> Be Heaven at once and have it over with.

20. Marion Montgomery, "Robert Frost and His Use of Barriers," Cox, *Frost: Critical Essays*, 142–43.

21. Reuben A. Brower, *The Poetry of Robert Frost* (New York: Oxford University Press, 1963), 164, 215–18.

22. See for example Reginald L. Cook, "Emerson and Frost: A Parallel of Seers," *New England Quarterly*, XXXI (June 1958), 216–17.

23. *Selected Letters*, 584.

24. In one of his latest poems, "Quandary," Frost amplifies the necessary relationship between good and evil:

> Never have I been sad or glad
> That there was such a thing as bad.
> There had to be, I understood,
> For there to have been any good.
> It was by having been contrasted
> That good and bad so long had lasted.

25. *Letters to Untermeyer*, 340.

26. *Ibid.*, 331.

27. Frost to G. R. and Alma Elliott, January 12, 1963, in *Selected Letters*, 596.

28. See Elizabeth S. Sergeant, *Robert Frost: The Trial by Existence* (New York: Holt, Rinehart and Winston, 1960), 372.

29. Archibald MacLeish, *J.B.* (Boston: Houghton Mifflin, 1956), scene 8.

30. *Ibid.*, scene 11.

31. *Ibid.*

32. *Selected Letters*, 525–26. See also Frost's letter to Lawrance Thompson, 530.

33. The contradiction between justice and mercy is an old subject for debate in Christianity. See for example Godfrey Goodman, *The Fall of Man* (1616), and the reply by George Hakewill, *An Apologie of the Power and Providence of God* (1627).

34. Frost's own views toward "New Deal" politics were in other poems far harsher than what is expressed in *A Masque of Mercy*, where his secondary theme contradicts the criticism of Malcolm Cowley that Frost had no vision of social justice: "there is little in his work to suggest Christian charity or universal brotherhood under God." "The Case Against Mr. Frost," in Cox, *Frost: Critical Essays*, 41; see also, 40, 42–43.

35. The omission of Geneva as an approach to Christ is significant. In this connection Reuben Brower has said: "Frost has remarked that the people who have best understood the *Masques* were Roman Catholics and Jews" *Poetry of Frost*, 212.

36. This conventional view of the mercy in God's judgment is Marion Montgomery's interpretation. He sees Frost's God as " 'that which man is sure cares, and will save him, no matter how many times or how completely he has failed.' " "Robert Frost and His Use of Barriers," in Cox, *Frost: Critical Essays*, 150.

37. Frost discovered this ending for *A Masque of Mercy* while preaching on Psalm 19 at the Rockdale Avenue Temple in Cincinnati, Ohio, on October 10, 1946. See *Selected Letters*, 555–56.

38. James M. Cox, "Introduction," in Cox, *Frost: Critical Essays*, 14.

39. Thompson, *Robert Frost*, 31.

BIOGRAPHY AND REMINISCENCE

Even casual students of Frost will know that, during the last decade, the major point of disagreement among those discussing Frost was the man himself. While those who were at first astonished have gradually adjusted to the revelations of Lawrance Thompson's excellent work, the tendency still is to praise the man as well as the poet. If some persons find Frost to be censurable in his private life, they have not chosen to speak out for the collection presented in this centennial volume. Instead, those who had long associations with Frost continue to admire him in all respects. Dorothy Tyler, one who knew Frost for many years, writes a genial account of Frost's relationships in Michigan. Wade Van Dore, who describes himself as Frost's hired man, generally defends the man against all criticism and in the essay here printed shows ways in which the character of the man influenced the work. William Gahagan's informal essay is by implication a further defense, since Mr. Gahagan is president of California Friends of Robert Frost. William Evans has found a few unpublished pages showing the youthful Frost's sense of humor (and of irony).

John Ciardi's talk deals with both reminiscence and critical estimate. His reasonableness speaks for the critic as well as for Frost.

J. T.

Ciardi on Frost: An Interview

EDWARD CIFELLI

CIFELLI: Lionel Trilling once called Robert Frost a "terrifying" poet; and since the remark threatened some popular images of Robert Frost, a series of shock waves followed it. What do you think about the exchange?

CIARDI: The occasion was a dinner to honor Frost on his 80th—or was it his 85th?—birthday. I'm not sure now, the years blur. Trilling arose and paid what he meant to be a heartfelt tribute. Then J. Donald Adams, not a man on whom my admirations have focused, wrote an angry reply in the *Times*, and a small wrangle of letters followed. It seemed to me Adams objected to exactly the wrong things. Trilling confessed that he had not taken Frost seriously as a poet until two or three years before the dinner and that he had then realized suddenly that Frost was more poet than he had granted. His remarks on that point reminded me of a series of articles Randall Jarrell did for the *Partisan Review* sometime back in the forties. Jarrell was floating around in the quarry at the University of Indiana (he was at the summer school of critics) and found lines, passages, and whole poems of Frost going through his head without ever having memorized them. And in this setting it suddenly occurred to him, "By God, this man really *is* a poet!" I think the conclusion was right. I have a vision of him arising dripping from the water and running to the *Partisan Review* with three momentous installments of this news. But it also occurred to me—though I have no quarrel with what he had to say—that he took his own sweet time about discovering Frost.

I found myself wondering if this did not say something about the new criticism. Eliot, of course, scores superbly at the new criticism. He invented the terms of it. Or the occasion for it. He invented a criticism to be applied to his own poems, and I see the new criticism as an offshoot of Eliot's. The academic critics, the new critics, ate their own weight daily in symbols. They had a hawk's eye for a subtlety. Somehow that blinded them to Frost, whose surfaces seem simple but who has enormous depths underneath these seemingly simple surfaces. And I think there was a kind of distrust of even seeming simplicity in them that weakens their positions as critics. It doesn't take away from the good they did, but it does indicate a defect. I think that is one point of objection that might have been made to Trilling's remarks.

I also think it was extraordinarily insensitive of him to have said that he never really sensed what Frost was about until he came to him through D. H. Lawrence. Anyone who had the slightest inkling of Frost's set of mind would have recoiled; there was a tremendous coil of Puritanism at the core of Frost. Frost thought of D. H. Lawrence as an amoral man and even might have been tempted to say that he was a sexual deviant; at least he was not what Frost would think of as a "proper" man. It certainly was not a comparison that Frost would welcome. Trilling then called him a "terrifying poet." I think he said a terrifying poet "in the Sophoclean sense." Certainly it can offend no man to be compared to Sophocles. J. Donald Adams jumped on the "terrifying" thing, and tried to make Frost, as I recall, into an image of more sweetness and light than this implied. But I think the force of Frost is that terrifying depth that's underneath even what seemed to be the sweet surfaces or the simple surfaces.

Frost had a deep-rooted life-sense. It included a sense of death, the ways in which a life can go sour, and of the choices that are forced upon a man that are not in any sense pretty. I suppose "pretty" might be a key to it. I like to argue that the pretty is never the beautiful. There is some sort of Gresham's law of aesthetics in which the pretty drives out the beautiful. And the beautiful drives out the pretty. They cannot coexist.

CIFELLI: You'd say, with many others I expect, that Frost's reputation suffers when you see him only as a regional poet, the sage of New England. Is that correct?

CIARDI: Yes. Frost had regional surfaces but he reached out. He went through a series of periods really. Almost all of the poems for which we know him best were written by about the time he was thirty and stored up in notebooks and then leaked out from them bit by bit. As a matter of fact, when the last book, *In The Clearing*, appeared, there were two poems about driving in a carriage, and I was *sure* those were early poems. I called Lawrance Thompson in Princeton. Thompson had access to the notebooks, "Larry," I said, "didn't Robert reach back into the early notebooks for these two poems?" He said that he sure did, that they had been in the notebooks something like sixty years. He mined those.

I think there's a middle period in which he wrote what he called his "editorials." They're clever, they're neat. Frost was always a superb craftsman. I think those were the poems of his later years, but I think they substituted a kind of clever competence for the throb and passion of the early poems.

And then I think at the very end, Frost went into a third period in which he became bardic.

CIFELLI: And you objected to that?

CIARDI: No. No. I think it was a fine expansive movement. I wish he'd been around to carry it a little further. He became the poet of America. I think quite tellingly. His poem on Kitty Hawk does not grab me as some of the earlier things did, but there are marvelous passages in the others. In the Columbus poem, for instance:

> If I had had my chance when young
> I should have had Columbus sung
> As a god who had given us
> A more than Moses' exodus.
>
> But all he did was spread the room
> Of our enacting out the doom
> Of being in each other's way,
> And so put off the weary day
> When we would have to put our mind
> On how to crowd but still be kind.

This is Frost speaking for America. In his late years he had a great deal to say about what he called "this position America has given me." He tried to speak as the poet of America. He was proud of the inauguration affair. I'm sure he felt truly humiliated by the fact that the sun glaring on the paper did not allow him to read the poem he had prepared for the occasion. It's as if one were called up for the supreme star act and goofed it, and he must have felt very,

very deeply his stage failure on that occasion. And yet he did think of himself at the end as the poet of America. The speaker of the American idea. And in a sense Kennedy appointed him for this purpose, an unofficial appointment.

CIFELLI: Do you think that the poems of his third stage, his "bardic" period, produced as fine a body of work as the earlier stages?

CIARDI: I find things I like very much in it. I don't think there's anything to equal "Stopping by Woods on a Snowy Evening," "Death of the Hired Man," "Home Burial," and those early fantastically caught, emotionally explosive lyrics that had all the passion and all the fire of this self-consuming young man. Frost in a sense, in a true sense, and I imply no denigration, was a nineteenth-century poet who lived a long time into the twentieth century. He had written most of his poems by 1900 or within the next ten years. Had he died young we would have thought of him as far back in the progression. He went on and kept mining those notebooks he had filled when he was younger and kept publishing them as if he had just written them.

CIFELLI: That touches on an interesting and important point—the extent to which he is really a twentieth-century poet.

CIARDI: I think he tried to become a twentieth-century poet in those poems I have called the editorials and in the bardic poems, "Kitty Hawk" and "America Is Hard to See" foremost among them. But he was born in another tradition. Frost was intensely puritanical. I think he also had a very strong sexual impulse, and these two things set up a contest of forces. A contest of forces produces the turmoil, the energy and the agony out of which the poems came. I don't want to make it that patly Freudian; it was *one* of the sources of energy. But I do think Frost lived his life at a level of passion not generally sensed. I think few people live at that intensity.

I was not intimate with Frost; I could not pretend to that. He was kind to me over many years but I cannot speak as one intimately acquainted. I speak as an admirer. And I had the privilege of knowing him, usually at the Bread Loaf Writers' Conference, for about 25 years. Away from Bread Loaf, I'd see him here and there when he came to lecture. I admire his poetry—I've had an enormous charge out of it—and admire the man. I do not think of Frost as many people do, as a white-haired old saint. He was not a white-haired old saint. He could in season be a mean old son-of-a-bitch. That's part of the man's energy. The best way I've found to say it (and I mean it as an admiration): he had a magmatic mass at his core. He burned at a higher heat than is commonly known. When this man erupted, it produced the glories. It was Mount Frost, the volcano. But volcanos also have their sulfurous sidestinks.

And they're both a product of that enormous inner energy. What's that poem? He says [in "To Earthward"]

> When stiff and sore and scarred
> I take away my hand
> From leaning on it hard
> In grass and sand,
>
> The hurt is not enough:
> I long for weight and strength
> To feel the earth as rough
> To all my length.

He was not faking that. There was an enormous intensity in him. Sometimes it was for the subject, and sometimes it was for his own life as he reviewed it. I've heard him say vehemently when someone mentioned a now practically forgotten poet who was in ascendence when Frost was still unknown—he'd say "Yes, while *I* stood waiting." And there was passion and anger in the fact that he had been slighted so long. He had to wait till he was almost forty to be recognized and that burned him. Frost was a man capable of burning.

At times he construed small insults into cause for real rages. And sometimes even when no insult was meant. I was not there, but I've had reported to me the occasion at Bread Loaf (before I began attending) when he drove even Archibald MacLeish, one of the most equable men I've ever known, not to anger, but in a sense to resistance. MacLeish arose after an exchange and said, "Don't worry, Robert, you are still the master." Which was his gentlemanly way of retiring from the argument. But Frost was insistent, you see, he wanted to be recognized. He doted on admiration. These are the sidestinks. They're still characteristics of a true volcano.

He loved to sit after an evening, with a circle of people on the floor while he sat in a chair and played the wise man, usually reciting lines of stories he had practiced and rehearsed for purposes of his own. He tended to pick up a little motif and play it for a year or so, and if you heard him on several occasions you would hear him repeating himself, always as if it had just come to him. But after all, he was called on to perform in public so often he had to have—what shall I call it?—some standardized "Material" to use over and over. I've had to play the same game myself at times, running my mouth through long-since memorized impromptus.

A sad story about the decline of a great man occurs—I think it was the last time or almost the last time I saw him, his last year at Bread Loaf. He announced that he wasn't strong enough to do the full program he had done in the past, and he said he would either come up and give an afternoon talk, or he would autograph the books people had bought. Either would take an afternoon's work. People had bought so many books that we elected to satisfy them by getting the books signed. And there were crates of them. We used my office at the Bread Loaf Writers' Conference and stacked them up there and had a little chain going. One person would take the books out of the crate and hand them to Kay Morrison who was Frost's confidant, advisor, general factotum, secretary, arranger of everything, a marvelous person, and she would look at the names on the slip of paper inserted in the book and remind Frost of any relationship that might exist—that's so-and-so's grandson, you know, and you ought to mention such-and-such—and Frost would write that in the book, and I would take it out from under him and hand it to somebody else to put in a box. It got to be a long session on a sunny, warm, lazy afternoon. Frost took off his coat and sat there in suspenders, and from time to time somebody would bring him a lemonade as I had prearranged, and he would sit and reminisce for a while, and it was very *en famille* and friendly, and finally he got through the stack of books and was just reminiscing about this, that, and the other. As a matter of fact, I think we were talking about his marvelous dog, a border collie named Gilly, as we started out the door.

This is, I think a slightly funny story, a rather sad story, about the decline of a great man. The point may well be that he is a great man, and the decline happens to us all. Frost had spent so much time on stage that it was at least partly possible to say that except in very intimate and relaxed circumstances, he was never *off* stage. He was always playing the role he had learned to perform, a rather coy one at times. (I guess I'm in a parenthesis again, but he had once taught Latin at Lowell High School. He read the Latin poets. I've never heard him mention one of them in a lecture. I once heard him say, "Oh, I could quote you some Chaucer, but I'm not supposed to know about that." He liked to play country boy; he found that a rewarding platform presence, and in his later years he got to feeling very strongly, as I said earlier, about this "position the country has given me." He was consultant in poetry at the Library of Congress and he always called a press conference when he went there and announced his latest thoughts. And he reveled in this. It's one of the ego rewards of a remarkable life, and why shouldn't the man have them?)

As we came out of the office that afternoon he caught sight of one small, white-haired lady coming through the door, and suddenly he turned off the conversation about Gilly or whatever it was and said, waving his hands in the air, "And I'll *tell* them in Washington." Then he turned to that little old lady from Dubuque and raised his voice and with a kind of false heartiness said, "Oh, hello there!" And he picked up this Washington theme he had suddenly thrown into the air. He *snowed* that poor old gal. Here she was in the presence of the great man in a blizzard of blither. He walked her around the corner, and she went one way, and he went out the door, still waving and performing: "You can be sure I'll *tell* them when I get down there." Pontificating, he took three steps and turned to me and in a totally different voice said, "Who the hell's that?" He wasn't kidding himself, in a way. He liked to play the role. He relished it.

All I'm saying is that he was an extremely complicated man and it was something of a revelation to see this little quirk in his character. It doesn't lessen the mountain or lessen the heat of the eruption. Remember this is a man of 85 or 86. He would never have played that role that way some years earlier. Reserve judgment until you get to be 85 or 86 and see what you have left to go on.

CIFELLI: This may not be a fair question, but if you had to pick between the short lyrics and the dramatic monologues and dialogues, do you think he was better at one than the other? Do you think ultimately his reputation will rest with one or the other?

CIARDI: I don't see how you can separate one from the other. The speaking voice tends to run through them in much the same way. "They would not find me changed from him they knew—only more sure of all I thought was true." I've never been sure, quite sure, of the resonance of those particular lines. I think there were probably more changes than that earlier lyric foresaw. But the voice of "Home Burial," of "The Witch of Coös," of "Death of the Hired Man," of all those marvelous narrative, dramatic monologues. ("Mending Wall," is that a lyric, or is it a monologue? It divides between the two.) No, I'd say that in both ranges the best forms are undiminishable, and in an astonishing quantity, an astonishing high level of performance. Frost was never in a hurry to publish. Things had to suit his ear before he would let them into print.

CIFELLI: Sentence sounds and natural speech rhythms were extraordinarily important to him, as I know they are to you in your own poetry.

CIARDI: Of course they are. I think they have to be to every poet. I recall Frost saying at one time that he showed some of his poems earlier in life to someone, I've forgotten who, and the man said, "This isn't poetry, it's talk." And Frost, feeling partly rebuffed and partly moved to angry insistence—he was a tough, stubborn man—thought to himself, or so he reported, "All right, if it's talk, I'll make it the best talk anybody ever heard."

CIFELLI: Capturing the human voice, then, was part of it?

CIARDI: Very much part of his poetic purpose, part of his ego purpose. And he was not always as magnificent in person as in his poems, but then you expect a good artist to be at his best within his medium. His medium is an enlargement of himself. If one reads his letters to Louis Untermeyer, I don't see how he can fail to realize that Frost politicked shamelessly for recognition when he thought he needed it to advance his position as a poet. He paid court to Amy Lowell. Then in his letters to Untermeyer—I can't quote the words, I'm remembering, and I hope I'm not remembering incorrectly, I think

I have it right—he wrote "Do we have to put up with her any longer?" "Can we get anything more out of her?" was the implication. Also that he strongly disliked her and disapproved of her. Again, at this period he had a great deal to say about calling on Braithwaite, who did an anthology, and almost humbling himself—no, he wouldn't have humbled himself—but paying court to Braithwaite because he thought that was a recognition. When he became more secure in himself that changed. It became a more ritual sense. And he was a ritualist.

I'm trying to describe Frost as a man who was punctilious in his ritual. He liked to decide when a door was to be opened, and nothing would get his back up sooner than to have somebody push in against a door he would rather keep closed. For many years at Bread Loaf I kept my distance. I didn't want to thrust myself upon him. We had little conversations now and then, but always I was an extremely junior member of whatever was going. There were many people around who had known him longer and much better. But when I was appointed director of the conference some 15 or 16 years later, I got a letter from him. I suspect that Kay Morrison prompted the letter. As nearly as I recall it, he began with "Dear John, You read my poems, I read yours, what's this about your asking if"—I had a poem in which I said "Does God believe in me?"—and Frost said, "There you are, the fair-haired boy, director, professor, publisher, poet, asking questions like that." He's half kidding. He's being playful, friendly, but the real occasion of the letter was the fact that he signed it "Robert," which was his way of saying, "All right, you may now call me Robert, instead of Mr. Frost." And it was a ritual arrangement: *he* would say when. I was, of course, grateful for the letter. I hadn't pushed against his door; he had opened it. I flew down to Florida, to West Miami Beach to interview him for *SR* on his 80th birthday, and we had long discussions there. I put up at the local hotel, took him out to dinner. He absolutely insisted on paying the dinner check, and when I went to pay the motel check, he paid it. I pointed out that Good Heavens, I was on the *Saturday Review* expense account; there was no need for it. He said, "You came down to see me, and you are my guest. That's the way I was brought up."

CIFELLI: I don't know now how we got onto that story about lollipops. Something to do with the film I expect, but would you tell that story again, for the record?

CIARDI: Oh, I think it's a rather charming anecdote of the way things were put away in his mind without comment, but not lost. One year at Bread Loaf, they had a showing in Ripton, which is a little hamlet a few miles down the mountain—a showing of a film about Frost. I think it was the United States Information Service film and the director had been no end artsy-craftsy about it in glorious, living technicolor. With all the cameras grinding and all the overcolored scenery flashing to make this as pretty as marzipan (I'm thinking of the difference between the pretty and the beautiful again), the director had Frost dodder out of his cabin. I think Frost was uncomfortable making this film. He distrusted the way it was handled. He thumbed a milkweed pod, wandered over to a fence, looked out across the distance, and the camera played on his face. Then the director did all sorts of pretty things: there was a sequence in which a horse came down a road and the handyman—I've forgotten his first name, his last name was Dragon; he was one of the Dragon family of Ripton (they had served as dragoons in the Revolution) —was driving a wagon, a flatbed, but you don't see him. The camera is focused into a puddle, and he appears when the horse walks into the puddle and smashes it. Then they had a prettied up scene of "my little horse must think it queer to stop without a farmhouse near." And when they got to "he gives his harness bells a shake, to ask if there is some mistake," sure enough there was a "tinkle, tinkle, tinkle" of sleighbells! It just ground on that way—clouds in the sky, treetops, focusing on a flower, focusing on Robert Frost's face. We sat through the showing and went back to Bread Loaf. Frost was in an easy chair and I was sitting in a chair not far away, and he turned to me and said, "What did you think of it?" I said, "Frankly, I didn't like it." He said, "Why?" I said, "As nearly as I can say it, it's because Robert Frost is not a lollipop." He said nothing—"Hm," or something of the sort and went on to talk of other things. But a year later in another context, he turned to me and said, "It's as you say, I'm not a lollipop!" I was fascinated by the way he had stored that and said nothing about it at the time but let it out a year later.

I think, too—again I cannot speak as an intimate, but as an attendant—that up to the time when he was about 80, Frost had feuds going. He was afraid of—he acted as if he was afraid of—being insulted. Once at Bread Loaf, he tossed a quip at Bernard DeVoto, and DeVoto picked it up, I thought very deftly, without malice, and dumped it back on Frost's lap so that the honors were left with DeVoto. Frost hated that. The next day, as I was told later, he walked up and down the hillside attended by Kay Morrison, taking a stick and beating saplings to death while he cussed DeVoto. One of the sidestinks of that volcano. He was capable of meanness. Morton Zabel had written something that offended Frost. Henry Holt was about to publish it. Frost walked into Holt's office, or announced by mail or whatever, "If you publish that book by Zabel, you'll never publish another thing by me." The company had committed itself to publish the book so the firm had to make arrangements to have another publisher bring it out—another sidestink. When he got to be 80, I think a new feeling came over him, as if he had decided that perhaps he was wrong in having let his intensity make these divisions and having estranged people who turned out in retrospect to be important to him. And I had a sense, I can't really locate this, of his going out of himself to try to patch fences. He became a much gentler, a much kinder man.

CIFELLI: He's fortunate to have lived long enough to be able to do this.

CIARDI: May I! Well, I don't think I've honored myself enough to fume and feud about it.

CIFELLI: I wanted you to say something about your essay on "Stopping by Woods." It's fifteen years now since it was written. The piece came out with a bang, and it's still around and talked about. Do you still hold with the points you made in that essay?

CIARDI: It was not written for any bang. I was poetry editor for the *Saturday Review*, and I was writing about poetry, and in some context I came up with that essay. There was a lot of talk about the virtues of reading widely, which I approve. But what about the virtues of reading in depth? Now had I taken this point into any reasonable classroom, it would have been, I hope, a good, but basically a fairly ordinary exercise in exegesis. The class would have assumed that I was not trying to replace the poem but to describe it. I never have tried *pre*scriptive criticism, never told poets what to do and what not to do. I value *de*scriptive criticism. A man who has read a poem very carefully sets down his reflections and responses to it, in a disciplined way, one hopes, in order to show a less practiced reader what that reader might find in the poem if he looked closely, instead of simply taking a free-association bath in it, as one can go to the music hall and simply respond to the tonalities and the shaking of the hall and the vibrations of the air while paying no attention to the musical structure and to the tradition and to the subtleties of the music. I set out within a limited space to point out some of the things I thought I had seen and had responded to in the poem.

I got back a flood of letters, angry letters, that divided into two categories. One was, "Get your big muddy feet off that miracle" (that would be my categorical tag for it). Which is to say, any discussion of a beautiful object subtracts from the beauty of the object. I have to dismiss that as nonsense. The other group of letters seemed to run, "Frost wrote only"—what is it?—"16 lines. And you have used up so many columns writing about it. There are only 132 words in the poem, and you have used over a thousand in talking about it, and how silly can you get." What is the premise there? That criticism should not be longer than the thing criticized? Of course criticism is a hobbling and fumbling thing that comes after the object and has to isolate things that happen simultaneously in order to talk about them, always on the assumption that the reader will have the good sense to put them back together within their simultaneity and be able to respond to them, in some way, with a better recognition.

Frost, himself, objected to one thing in the essay, and I should have foreseen that. I said at one point (I was describing the dramatic action of the surface of the poem) the horse stops. Frost looks into the woods. It is the shortest evening of the year, that's December 22nd; it's dark; it's late; the snow is falling; the situation is full of a sense of oblivion. And Frost is drawn to it. How nice to go into the woods and let the snow cover one over. That's why I think those lines toward the very end should read "The woods *are* lovely, dark and deep," not "The *woods* are lovely." "The woods *are* indeed lovely, dark and deep." And what is that dark and deep? At first I tried to compare it to what scuba divers call the rapture of the deep. A number of divers have died inexplicably while scuba diving, and the theory was that having reached the point where their instruments said it's time to make it to the surface if you're going to get back, they were tempted to take a stroke further and a stroke further until they didn't have enough air left to get back to the top. They were thought to be hypnotized by the beauty of the thing and so drawn into oblivion. Now when it came time to publish the piece, there had to be a cut, and I began to think the scuba analogy a little flowery, so I made my cut there and reduced all that passage about scuba diving and the rapture of the deep to a question in a parenthesis. ("Is this then a poem about a"—I think I said—"*momentary* death wish"?) Frost does shrug off the mood in the next instant, as Frost would. "Death wish" is a phrase I should never have used. It sounds Freudian. And just as Frost got his back up when Trilling mentioned D. H. Lawrence, any Freudian terminology would get his back up. I wasn't thinking at the moment. I was thinking only of getting the piece to fit the space, and making the cut come out right. For two, two and a half, three years thereafter, Frost went around lecturing saying, "Ciardi says I've got a death wish. No such thing. That's not what the poem was about." Well, there are other ways of interpreting it, but I cannot surrender my interpretation that for a moment he felt the tug of "allness," which is another way of saying "oblivion," and how sweet oblivion would be, how sweet it would be to lie down and let yourself get covered over. And even though you shrug it away in the next instant, that is the experience of a momentary death wish.

While I have them in mind, I might tell a couple of very minor anecdotes that I don't think have been written up. For whatever it's worth, there was the occasion of, I think, the dumbest question ever asked a distinguished speaker following a lecture. One year at Bread Loaf, Frost came up from his farm for an afternoon give-and-take. As you know, he had published a number of books called Selected Poems, Collected Poems, Complete Poems, and as time went by he would do a new book and there would be a new edition of this Complete Poems or Collected Poems. When he finished reading one after-

noon, someone arose and said—(in this context, I guess she had been
in the bookstore and seen all these different books, and books are
expensive, and she didn't want to spend her money foolishly)—she
said, "Mr. Frost, is it safe to buy the Complete Poems *now*?" I've
never seen Frost so nonplussed in my life! He shook his head as if
someone had just belted him. He didn't lose his composure, but I
guess he was expressing disgust more than amazement. I guess he had
had enough experience in not being really stunned by human stu-
pidity. He shook his head and leaned into the microphone and said,
"I don't give a damn whether you buy the book or not."

Another occasion I think was a little odd and rather endearing. At
the end Frost began to go deaf. But he was too proud to wear a hearing aid. He didn't like to wear glasses though he needed them to read.
When you're in your 80's, you begin to be in your 80's. Nevertheless,
he had his sense of pride, and he wasn't going to wear a hearing aid.
Therefore, at the end of a lecture, at Bread Loaf, I would sneak up
behind him, field the questions from the floor, and shout them into his
right ear, which was his good one. And he accepted this without any
objections. Somehow this arrangement was less obvious than a hearing aid. And it soothed his pride.

But, you see, unless you have these little quirks and cantankers, what
have you got to go on when you get that old? I never knew Frost in
his prime, but from what I've read and from photos I've seen, he
was an extraordinarily powerful man. We hate to give up our stub-
bornness and identity. Who wants to decline into old age without
railing against it a bit?

CIFELLI: Did Frost, in any of his roles, see himself as a teacher?

CIARDI: He taught at Lowell High School, taught Latin. He did
various residencies. He was at the University of Florida for many
years. I think it was there his wife died, if I recall.

CIFELLI: Of course, also at Amherst and Michigan.

CIARDI: Some at Amherst, a little at Michigan, quite a bit at Dartmouth. I think Frost was in one sense a teacher, a kind of inspirational
presence; he was a magnificent talker. I don't think he was capable
of being a teacher, and I say this tentatively as a guess, in terms of
generating a truly sympathetic interest in the problems of the student. He told one story once, and I would guess it to be perhaps typi-

cal of his attitude. Frost was not a man to divide his attention. This is a theme that runs through a lot of his poems. Why should he give away what is his? One of the very early poems is about the bridegroom on his wedding night when a tramp comes by. "The bridegroom thought it little to give/A dole of bread, a purse,/A heartfelt prayer for the poor of God,/Or for the rich a curse." The question there is "But whether or not a man was asked/To mar the love of two/By harboring woe in the bridal house,/The bridegroom wished he knew." But Frost's answer to that would always be, "Yes, I know. I don't harbor him. I send him on down the road." I think this comes out again in "Two Tramps in Mud Time."

I think it was Perrine who published a piece recently in some journal. His interpretation is that Frost *allows* the tramps to chop the wood. I think the whole point of the poem (I've read his interpretation; it makes no sense to me), I think the whole point of the poem is that Frost does *not*. How's that thing go?

> Nothing on either side was said.
> They knew they had but to stay their stay
> And all their logic would fill my head:
>   [He recognized what they were doing
>   and thinking.]
>
> As that I had no right to play
> With what was another man's work for gain.
> My right might be love but theirs was need.
> And where the two exist in twain
> Theirs was the better right—agreed.
>   [I'll grant them that, if the two could
>   be separated. Add then a huge thing
>   that I think Perrine ignores: *but.*]
>
> But yield who will to their separation,
> My object in living is to unite
> My avocation and my vocation
> As my two eyes make one in sight.
>   [They have a better right if the two are
>   separate, *but* I will not yield to their
>   separation—that's part of my life.]
>
> Only where love and need are one,
> And the work is play for mortal stakes,

> [That's not just play: that negates play
> in the preceding stanza.]

> Is the deed ever really done
> For Heaven and the future's sakes.

I think that is absolutely conclusive. Everything he sets up in the next to the last stanza and agrees to as their argument is rebutted and denied in the last stanza. I think Perrine has badly misinterpreted that poem. I don't know where he got derailed, or maybe *I'm* derailed, but I feel very strongly that this, moreover, compared to the body of all his work, is Frost's position. *No one invades him.* And so back to the teaching question.

He would not let himself be invaded by a student. In my own small way I know something about invasion. The last years when I was teaching, I had things piled up on my desk, but I had student papers to work on. And I found myself in a terrible state of division. If I worked on my papers, I felt I was cheating my students. If I worked on their papers, I knew damn well I was cheating myself. Finally, rather than go through this division of—what shall I say?—spirit, I decided not to teach anymore. I don't think Frost would have been willing to give himself. I think it's well that he did not, because he had more to give within the selfishness of his self-concern than he did within the gentleness and outgoingness of being a sympathetic teacher. A different sort of person.

The story I started to mention, before I got lost in all these parentheses, is one he told about, I believe, Dartmouth when he asked the students to write some papers. I don't know whether this actually happened, but it's a nice story and he liked to tell it. He said he walked in a week later and held up the papers and said, "Is anybody especially proud of what he wrote here?" He got no answer. So he threw them all in the wastebasket: "If you don't care about your writing, why should I?" A rather lovely trick.

Frost was full of marvelous perceptions. He would pick up an idea as if it were a stick and begin to whittle it. Sometimes he just ended up with a pile of shavings. More usually he ended up with a shape. It was quite impressive. There was also the fact that if you heard him ten more times, the chances were you'd hear the same lecture again.

I don't know what he would do if he tried to give a series of lectures over a semester. He had some marvelously chosen conversational gambits and he liked to play them. Sometimes, just great openings. He returned to Bread Loaf one summer with a phrase he relished. He said in his way, "There you are again. I've been thinking about you. I've been wondering what has happened to you and what has occurred to you." And he played this difference between *happened* and *occurred* very sweetly throughout. That's a poet's way of handling words. Frost rewarded the listening, even when he went over and over and over and over the same material in different lectures at different places—or in the same lecture at different places. For example, there were two or three years in which he lectured at various places, at Bread Loaf and at Harvard, and there were two or three other places I heard him. Was one of them Tufts? I don't know. But over the period I heard this same gambit many, many times.

Frost, I should explain, wanted a Nobel prize. It was the last accolade that he had not acquired and he wanted it. A little story on this point: He was staying with Selman A. Waksman at Rutgers. Waksman was the Nobel prize winner in—is it chemistry or microbiology?—for having developed aureomycin. And Mrs. Waksman, a vivacious birdlike little girl from Vienna, who used to be a singer, came bouncing in at one point and said to him, "Mr. Frost, Mr. Frost! T. S. Eliot just won the Nobel Prize!" And Frost said, "Hah! so'd Pearl Buck." There's a kind of stored-up anger in this "Eliot huh?" The other thing is I think his anger was partly justified in that Eliot had had the academic ascendency over him for so many years. Partly because Eliot was so *teachable* a poet by the new critics. If you discuss Frost, you have to discuss poetry. If you discuss "The Waste Land," after reading two or three books, or just one, F. O. Matthiessen's *The Achievement of T. S. Eliot*, you have enough material to guarantee that you can go in and stun a class of undergraduates with your brilliance for fifteen or twenty lectures. You can quote so many different languages, the legends, the grail, the ring cycle, Dante, you see; you have a chance to use all your erudition, glossy or deep as the case may be, but you have a chance to sound brilliant. Frost gives you a harder go at teaching. You're down to the language itself without this enormous paraphernalia of footnotes, and

I think perhaps—I can't say this as an assertion, but I know that Frost was greedy about his reputation and his place; he wanted to be at the top—that the attention paid to T. S. Eliot rankled a bit. And though he was grateful to Ezra Pound for having discovered him and though he was instrumental in getting Pound released from St. Elizabeth's, which he took occasion to claim as his doing after others had tried and failed, in a sense that was paying off a debt so that he was even. In a sense. We all have cross-motives. But he used to love to tell his Ezra Pound story with one eye on the Nobel Prize. The recital went on for years, and it always followed the same pattern. It was always after a lecture when he was in a chair with his circle of attendants on the floor, and it always started with Frost saying he was thinking of writing a book called *The Shadow of Frank Flynn*. By the time he got through, it turned out that Frank Flynn, a poet no one knew anything about (at least I didn't, nor did anyone I asked) was the master of imagism, the founder of imagism, of free verse. But Ezra Pound came along and stole it from him. Now this makes Ezra Pound the thief of a ghost. What does it leave *him* with? So Ezra Pound is knocked out of the way as no more then a marauder who had taken the genius of this unknown Frank Flynn and developed his reputation on it. And having demolished Ezra Pound, Frost always concluded in the same way. He would say, "But Pound was a great teacher. Two of his students won the Nobel Prize: Tom Eliot and Willie Yeats." Now you see, that disposes of them, as I sense it, disposes of them as pupils of this thief of nothing. And Frost would not take Wallace Stevens seriously as a competitor; he refused to, and refused to take William Carlos Williams seriously as a competitor. At one time, people had forced Carl Sandburg on his attention, and he *always* went out of his way to run Sandburg down. But now if he gets rid of Pound and Yeats and Eliot, in his view, who's left? You see the object of the game? There is, of course, a touch of clay on everybody's feet. I'm not trying to demolish Frost as he tried to demolish Ezra Pound. I'm trying to report on what I think I observed as a quirk in the man.

There are a few related anecdotes that might fit in there. I mentioned that he disliked Carl Sandburg. You could get Frost furious at any time by suggesting that he and Sandburg were equal entities.

It was in an effort to insult Sandburg that Frost first coined his mot that "Free verse is like playing tennis with the net down." Teachers have used that sentence in many ways without knowing it was really a slur at Sandburg. Frost also liked to tell about an incident in Washington. He had gone down for one of his visits as poet in residence; he didn't stay the whole year. He'd go to Washington for a week or two at a time, and someone would give a reception for him. He said of one of them, "I was sitting over by the fireplace,"—this is as nearly as I can reconstruct the story as he told it. I won't swear to it word for word, but I think I have it firmly in mind—he said, "I was sitting by the fireplace talking to Edmunds [I think he said] when *Carl* walked in" (Frost almost snarled the word *Carl*). He said, "You know the way he dresses, that hair of his and those ties. Everything about him is studied—except his poetry." He said, "I turned to Edmunds" [if it was Edmunds, I think it was], "I turned to Edmunds and I said" (Sandburg had written a book, as you know, called *Slabs of the Sunburnt West*), "I said—I shouldn't have said it but I'm glad I did—I said, 'Here comes that slob from the sunburnt west.'" He liked to tell that story.

He also like to tell one about Wallace Stevens in Florida. He told it as if he had scored a victory. I'm not sure he had, not even as he told it. They were talking together one night and Stevens said, "Trouble with you, Frost, is you write on subjects." Frost reported himself as snapping back: "Trouble with you, Stevens, is you write bric-a-brac." A rather good critical piece could be done on the difference between subjects and bric-a-brac. Frost's poems, in a sense, required some prior knowledge of New England. By the time you've read him two or three times, of course, you've *got* the New England legend. He has built it in. Stevens *invented* the universe about which he wrote. Frost also invented the universe about which he wrote, but he borrowed an existing ethos and mythos as the surface of his invention. Stevens, it could be argued, is the pure creator. Frost could never have written, as Stevens did—I'll probably misquote but not egregiously—"The sound of that slick sonata coming across the lawn makes music seem to be a nature, a place which itself gives rise to everything else." That was Stevens' bric-a-brac, and bric-a-brac is not a fair term for it. It's a question of two ways of seeing and saying, and Frost's is not necessarily the better way, though his little story always implied that of course it was.

CIFELLI: Frost's notion of form in a poem—organic form, I expect is a fair term—is well known. He says, I believe, that poems begin as a "lump in the throat," as an emotion rather than an idea. And yet you look at the poetry, all so neatly and tightly organized and structured, and it seems to belie that organic principle that he says he wrote according to. What do you think about that?

CIARDI: Well, Frost—I'm not sure about it—I think Frost worked by ear. And the glory of that is that he had a superb ear. A certainty about it. Also, the reticence, secretiveness to hold his poems a long long time until he was sure of them. And not to let anything out until he was, in fact, sure of it. In that way he didn't publish his mistakes as many another has done, certainly as I have done. At one time, when he was busy promoting his own reputation, he liked to talk about "the method." Eliot had a "method" and everyone was talking about it. Why shouldn't Frost have one and get his share of the talk? Some of those letters to Louis Untermeyer talk about "the method" as if Frost had invented a new way of writing poetry.

I think he had something better than "method." He had a superb ear, and the imagination to go with it. And the prop room, the subject matters, the dramatic situations to go with it. Did Frost do anything new? Or did he carry established methods to a perfection of a sort no one else has ever come close to? I would tend to believe, by and large, that he was not an innovator, though I think he did as much as any man to tune the metrics of the twentieth century to the spoken voice. He found a true equivalent for the talking voice he had in mind within his metrics. If you want to make method out of that, I think that is really what you mean by oral imagination. And my summary would be (at least tentatively, till I've had time to recheck my feelings, but I think they'd come out this way) that Frost was not basically an innovator, but a man who carried established methods to new heights, which is perhaps in itself an innovation.

CIFELLI: I remember in your essay on "Stopping by Woods," one of the important points that you make is that he couldn't possibly have known that he would repeat the last line until he actually did, that he had gotten himself into trouble.

CIARDI: Oh, of course, but that's not just about Frost. Frost is a glorious example of this principle. A poem is a context looking for its own conclusion. You don't know where it's coming out. Somebody asked a French poet once—who said he was writing a poem—"What's it about?" He said, "I don't know, I haven't finished it." In a sense, it's almost as if a shipwrecked sailor landed on an island and set out to explore it. He doesn't know what island it is, but he knows he's on it. Except that in poetry, of course, it's not a preexisting physical island you're determining. You're imagining the island and being imagined back by it. So we're back to Wallace Stevens. "It makes the music seem to be a nature, a place which itself gives rise to everything else." The way I think of it is that a poem is a context in which the poet is constantly making choices, and each choice he makes is partly in answer to an obligation he has picked up along the way that was not in his head when he started, and often, if not always, itself the making or the beginning of a new obligation that has to be answered. And when all these obligations come on in the act of writing the poem have been met, and hopefully, with that fine excess Keats speaks of, that's the end of the poem, and knowing when you've found the end is tremendously important.

CIFELLI: Hyatt Waggoner suggested recently that some critics have "defended" Frost by saying that he wrote some of the darkest poems ever written by an American. Do you agree with that?

CIARDI: I think that he did write some of the darkest poems ever written by an American. I also think Hyatt Waggoner is a very acute critic.

Remember that Frost grew up in a period of rhetorical poetry, and had the good sense, the natural sense, the poet's sense, to avoid merely rhetorical poetry, and to come up with haunted poetry. Frost was a self-haunted man. He was also an enormously self-preoccupied man. One of the sadnesses of a great life is that I think he was a tragic parent. I think partly for the same reasons that would make him not in the long run a good teacher, though he could be like a shower of stars for a series of lectures. In which book is the incident retold? Is it in Thompson? Of his son who was a troubled man, who had tried farming and failed and tried some other things and failed. He sat down with his father one night for a long anguished talk. And the image I have is of Frost being self-assured and maybe even pontificating a bit as he reasoned away all of his son's doubts. At the conclusion of which the son said, "Father, I have failed even in argument," and went into his room and blew out his brains.

Frost was aware from the very beginning that he was an instrument of great possibility, or at least that thought dawned on him early. He felt the power of his genius. And it absorbed, it shut him off from things a man with less intensity and less genius might have been ready to go out to. He was sealed in by his own gift in a sense. That's a terrible price, but in a sense, as a father, I don't think he had enough outgoingness. Lawrance provides the footnote, too, as a kind of footnote to his life, and it's a dark note in a great life, that the disease from which his wife died—what was she, 58 or so?—was the result of the fact that he got her pregnant when she was 56. It seems to me it could have been an unfortunate accident, yet there's the possibility that Frost would demand his gratification and take it. I don't know how to answer that but from one dark side of his nature it could be read one way; from another, the great side of his nature, it could be read another, and there were both sides of this enormous man's nature.

The measure of the poetry comes down, finally, to one man at a time, at some midnight of his consciousness, sitting down with a book and being gripped by it. Now, what do we mean by a dark poem? I think that's an interesting question. Is there any such thing as an unhappy or a pessimistic poem? I think it could be argued that the act of writing a poem well has to be a joyous act, no matter what your subject matter. The subject matter can be tragic, but the act of finding what strikes you as a true equivalence has to be joyous.

CIFELLI: Is that like your poem "The Gift?"

CIARDI: Yes, in a sense. But perhaps a better example would be Keats, "When I Have Fears That I May Cease to Be." Here's a young genius, in the fullness of his intellectual powers feeling his lungs go and knowing that he will die soon. Maybe part of this same feeling was that he would never live long enough to become as dull as the old Tennyson, which is a relief perhaps, but the poem is all about a real death:

> When I have fears that I may cease to be
>   Before my pen has gleaned my teeming brain,
> Before high-piled books, in charact'ry,
>   Hold like rich garners the full-ripened grain;
> When I behold, upon the night's starred face,
>   Huge cloudy symbols of a high romance,
> And think that I may never live to trace
>   Their shadows, with the magic hand of chance.

That is joyous writing! The man may be talking about his own death, but he has to register the facts, say to himself, "John, boy, you've got yourself an image!" At the very end he said,

> And when I feel, fair creature of an hour,
>   That I shall never look upon thee more,
> Never have relish in the faery power
>   Of unreflecting love!—then on the shore
> Of the wide world I stand alone, and think
> Till Love and Fame to nothingness do sink.

He seems to be saying that love doesn't matter, fame doesn't matter; by an easy poetic extension, nothing matters, except that the rhyme scheme matters, the sonnet form matters, the symmetries he has worked within the form matter; in those are elements of joy. The emotion of a poem is not in its subject matter. It is in finding an equivalence for the subject matter; because of something in perhaps our evolutionary natures, we take pleasure in what strikes us as a true emotional equivalence of anything.

There were also dark depths of Frost's own passions. He was a torn person. He had strong puritanical impulses, and like every other man he had lecherous impulses, and these, I have to guess, got into tangles inside him. He was absorbed with his great gift; he was also a perceptive man. I think he recognized that he had failed in some of his life commitments, and this gnawed him. His son committed suicide, his daughter married a man from Montana, who later became mayor of Billings, and some yokel prairie doctor didn't wash his hands at childbirth, and she died of puerperal fever. Frost and his wife raced out to Montana and got her to the Mayo Clinic, and they did their best, but she died. These are frustrations and darknesses. And his wife died. Frost was deep in depression following her death. These are the trials of a life. Frost was not the man to be pollyanna about them. He had to drink his grief. He had to swallow the poison and take it into himself, because in some sense it was his proof of life. He had to taste his disappointment, live with it.

CIFELLI: Was he the kind of griever that the man is in "Home Burial?"

CIARDI: Certainly, part of Frost is in that man. A thing to be done must be done. And the wife can't follow what a man has to do.

I suppose one of her great regrets in "Home Burial" is that he made the dirt fly as he dug the grave. Well, how the hell *does* a farmer dig? With a memorial silver spoon laying each grieving spoonful up on the edge of the grave? You have to get in there and swing. That's what his life has been. He's down in the soil doing what he's been doing all of his life, in the one way he knows how. And she takes this as insensitivity in him. I would certainly think, I'd have to look at the poem again very closely before committing myself, but my impression, not having seen the poem for some time, is that Frost's sympathies are *all* with the man. He does his best to try to hold this together and overcome her womanish grief. He says, "It's the grief in you speaking out." He comes in with the mud still on his boots. But he's been coming in from the fields all his life with mud on his boots.

There's reticence. One can share grief with those closest to him. But he doesn't spill it on others. And of course, Frost also had his poems as an outlet. But the depths of grief are also closely related to the depths of passion. Frost was passion's man. In grief and in passion he is still a genius, one of the great geniuses of our language. And, like it or not, a poet is a man forever thinking of poetry. My friend Miller Williams has a fine poem on that subject ("Let Me Tell You"). When you go to your father's grave, when you go to your father's funeral, you're trying to think of the line in which you'll express your feelings. You have to be, you're a poet. The poem ends with "If there is a heaven/he will forgive you/if the line you found was a good line./It does not have to be worth the dying." A number of writers have gone on record with this sense of their own division, of feeling a thing passionately. And yet with one side of the mind, a long conditioning in the medium, reaching for how they will treat it because they have to treat it. Because that's part of the commitment. I think it's ridiculous to assume that Frost is simply a passionate man with certain darknesses and certain confusions in him. He was that, plus a master poet forever in the presence of his medium.

A "Day" in the Life of Robert Lee Frost—1874

G. WILLIAM GAHAGAN

"A pleasant greeting to you, young candidate for immortality," read the beginning sentence of the *Daily Alta Californian*'s New Year editorial entitled "How Are You, 1874?" If he had not worked for a rival newspaper—the *Evening Bulletin* of San Francisco—a young, ambitious reporter and editorial writer by the name of William Prescott Frost, Jr., might have written this particular greeting. He and Isabelle Moodie Frost were expecting their own child to whom they might have spoken as the editorial did to the New Year: "You, 1874, come as a weakling is very apt to come, with a moistened face. Nature's tear drops hang upon your brow like pearls in a Caucasian's ear. We welcome you as the father welcomes children born to him, hoping for the best, scarcely entertaining a thought that evil, or error, or disappointment can ever sully the clean, clear page of the fresh, blank volume!"

Robert Frost had difficulty getting his first U.S. Passport. He simply did not have a birth certificate. Frost did not even know exactly where he was born and when. He would say that for a while there was a question as to whether the year was 1875 or 1874 but that he was certain that where he was born was "up on Washington Street in San Francisco on Nob Hill somewhere." The city's earthquake and fire in 1906 had destroyed most of the records. Nowhere in the city's newspapers is there a line by way of a birth announcement. Even in the current records of the Swedenborgian Church in San Francisco, where someone duly recorded that Robert Lee Frost was baptized on July 10, 1881, the modern script of the present pastor of this lovely little church on Lyon Street in Pacific Heights notes that "Robert Frost was a great American poet, born in San Francisco on March 26, 1875!"

Frost once declared that he had been baptized twice in this First Society of the New Jerusalem church on O'Farrell Street. If alive today, the Reverend John Doughty would refute the claim, for in the now faded and worn Official Registry, still used for baptisms, marriages, funerals, and the listing of new members, the names of the family of Robert Frost are entered in Rev. Doughty's elegant script under Baptisms, except for Frost's father. The poet's name is listed only once, together with his mother as "Belle Moodie Frost," and his younger sister, "Jeannie Florence, born June 25th, 1876 in Lawrence, Mass."

Why the birth of Mr. Frost was not recorded in the vital statistics columns in the public press is a mystery, for his father could easily have listed the great event of his young married life. Nor did the other major papers in the city—*Daily Alta Californian, Chronicle, Call* or *Examiner*—carry the item. Yet Frost's father sent the news on eventually to the Harvard Alumni offices, and this is the only official record of the actual and accurate birthday. Perhaps the young journalist was still recovering from his celebration of his first child's coming into the world, for he regarded whisky as "strong man's food," and it is also on record that he greeted the doctor at the Frost residence by waving a Colt revolver at him and shouting that if anything happened to his wife Belle the physician would never leave alive!

Exactly where such a scene took place is puzzling, too. In Bishop's *San Francisco City Directory* for 1874, W. P. Frost, Jr. is listed as "journalist, No. 14 Eddy Street." This is near one of the busiest intersections in the United States—at Powell and Market Streets in downtown San Francisco. Here the cable cars begin their colorful, exciting and uncertain roundtrip to Fisherman's Wharf. Here the so-called Day and Night office of the seven-story Bank of America building dominates the northwest corner, extending up Eddy Street to Anna Place, an alley that borders on a sordid parking lot.

St. Anne's Building once stood on this site, and it was a handsome edifice that faced the magnificent Baldwin Hotel across the street at Powell. Both buildings were victims of the 1906 fire. Anna Lane is listed in the 1874 directory as 14 Eddy Street, so it is conceivable that a house stood on this alley corner. (Temperance Hall was then located at 18½ Eddy, and it was the scene of many eloquent pleas by visiting antibooze crusaders.)

But Mr. Frost may not have been born there. Twelve addresses were listed for the parents during their eleven-year period in San Francisco. The *Bulletin* of March 26 of 1874 had a classified announcement that "An experienced nurse girl is wanted to bring up a child on the bottle," but it gave no address. One can only guess that at the next listed directory address—1530 Sacramento Street—between Larkin and Hyde Streets, the man who would one day be the first poet to speak at a Presidential inauguration was born.

Accompanying this memorable event, there were countless fascinating news stories and advertisements in the daily press of March 26th. One reads of "The Great Ship—Successful Launching of the Largest Ship ever Built in America—in Philadelphia—the City of Pekin—intended for the Pacific Mail Co.'s Line—420 feet—accommodations for 1,370 passengers."

Down in Tucson, "Eleven Apaches were Killed and Thirty Odd Squaws were made prisoners in action by a company of White Mt. Soldiers under a Major Randall." A full column advertisement on the *Alta*'s front page reviewed the recent "Lecture 'Beauty and the Beast' " by the famous humorist Josh Billings and ran an announcement of his lecture for that evening.

Next to this was an advertisement of a "Mme. Zeitska's French, German and English Institute for Young Ladies at No. 55–56 South Park." Robert Frost's parents sent him to this school, where he lasted only one day! He referred to it later in one of his letters to Louis Untermeyer as a "very expensive Montessori education at Madame Zitsker's in San Francisco circa 1880—year Garfield was elected."

On that memorable day, March 26th, other interesting news stories were recorded which would have delighted Robert Frost in his mature years. Under "Brief Mention," was a paragraph about a "Rascally fellow, parambulating about the 8th Ward, selling to ladies, through intimidation, what purports to be copies of an old Revolutionary paper." And beneath the item was a report that "A gamin, arrested yesterday for stoning a Chinaman, had been addicted to the use of tobacco since the age of 7 years, and he now takes the essence of 10 papers of rind cut per day. He has fits," the brief article concluded, "when deprived of his allowance of the weed."

On the more Frostian side, "Pacific Slopes Brevities," reported that "Wool is falling off the sheep in Mendocino County," and that

"Thirty young ladies, who intend to leave April 2d from Indiana shortly, on a praying tour to San Francisco, with the intent of praying out the alcoholic establishments along the way, will arrive here in 1890!"

"Territories," a short column in Frost's father's newspaper, *The Evening Bulletin*, reported that "Wild Flowers are blooming in profusion under the influence of the beautiful weather which we have recently been favored with, and the fields have assumed a beautiful carpet of green. Pic-nic talk is in the air."

The press of March 26th announced a new weekly in Oakland—the *Semi-Tropical Press*. Ralph Waldo Emerson was "reported" as the new rector at Glasgow University. A man named John Pierce was fined $50 for stealing a loaf of bread and a copy of *The Alta* from a doorstep in the Western addition of the city. The gas and water companies of nearby Vallejo were at loggerheads. One claimed that in a certain locality the escaping water rotted the gas pipes; the other claimed that the escaping gas rotted the water. (Mr. Frost once told me of an old New England proverb—"Reading Rots the Brain.")

Three houses were for sale—on a sixty by sixty-nine foot lot at Leavenworth and California Streets for an asking price of $14,500. (The Frost family's last home in San Francisco was 1404 Leavenworth. Mr. Frost told me of the chickens they used to have in the backyard.) One could pick up a seven-room home on Clementina Street for $3,100. Countless "respectable girls wanted situations." The Great French Mail Balloon was scheduled to ascend at Woodward's Gardens on the following weekend. (It so happened that, on the ascent, one of the men who assisted in the inflation of the colorful balloon became asphyxiated, and "it took him several days to recover, after not having been discovered for one full day." (Mr. Frost and his little sister Jeannie spent many happy days at Woodward's Gardens, and of course there is the delightful Frost poem "At Woodward's Gardens.")

The young man missed seeing "Caoutcheuc—the Hairless Horse from Australia—on display on Sutter street. - Bet. Montgomery and Kearny sts. opp the Lick Hotel." It was ".25 admission for adults with children half price—one bit."

This particular March 26 marked the 27th anniversary of the arrival of the "Low Chow," one of the three vessels to bring 1,000 enlisted men as volunteers to serve in the Mexican War—the famous regiment under the command of Col. J. D. Stevenson. This same issue of the *Bulletin* printed a poem by Keats entitled "Life." It spoke of a young boy who climbed up into an elm tree to get a better look at the world, "riding the springy branches."

A Dr. Clark had written an essay—"Sex in Education"—which was bitterly attacked by Julia Ward Howe, who accused him of "brutality and cowardice and intruding into the sacred domain of womanly privacy." She denied that "in educating a woman's brain, you starved her body!"

A terse comment under "International News" in that issue of the *Evening Bulletin* pointed out editorially that "Bismark has the gout. Now is France's Opportunity!" Mark Twain was tendered a welcome supper in Connecticut by old friends, but the bill for the event, amounting to $208, was sent to Twain. "He paid it," concluded the report.

Tennyson's new poem, "A Welcome to the Duke and Duchess of Edinborough," occupied a *Chronicle* frontpage position, and the farewell appearance of a Miss Neilson in Bulwer's three-act play, "The Lady of Lyons," at the California Theatre, was emblazoned in an advertisement, near which one was informed that Miss Neilson Note Paper, "Juliet or Rosalind," was available for sale.

"New Mexico," the *Chronicle* editorialized, "wants to become a state," and, it went on, "as a state, it would make another rotten borough like Nevada." "Nativities" reported that "Nothing exhibits more clearly than the death record the cosmopolitan character of our city. Forty-five out of every 100 who died last year were natives of foreign countries; Ireland leading the way, with China a close second."

The *Bulletin* announced a benefit scheduled for "Mrs. Martha Cobourn and her fatherless children in Platt's Hall for April 7th evening, at which time Albertine and Mabel McCabe will sing an Italian duet by I. Pescatori." A report told of a priest: "Father Powers was fined $250 for assault and battery against an insane woman. He paid his fine in double eagles, and hastily left the court room."

Los Angeles oranges were seventy-five cents a dozen, with butter, "Calif. Fresh," averaging thirty to forty cents a pound. Eggs, fresh, were twenty to thirty cents a dozen. The wheat crop had risen twenty-five percent over the '73 crop. Spanish lessons were available at $120 the year.

The schooner "Ada May" cleared for Guaymas with an assorted cargo valued at $11,600, about $7,500 of which was destined for Tucson, Arizona territory, to go by special train from the seaport. The San Francisco stock market was $1,800,000 over the previous week's sales of $5,687,600. The *Chronicle* reported a circulation on March 26th of 32,775 at ten cents a copy, and included under its Crime columns: "A Chinaman yesterday was convicted of stealing bacon, notwithstanding the plea of his attorney that his client had stolen a ham, not bacon."

Nothing had been heard from an overdue steamer "Colina," although underwriters were still quite willing to write upon her. It was a bad day for all mining stocks, with "gold showing a further hardening tendency, closing at 112½ in New York. Quick silver declined two points to 30¼."

In that year of 1874, the first practical operating unit of the typewriter was shown in both public notice and advertising columns of the *Evening Bulletin*. Patented in 1868 by three Milwaukee investors, the "speed-writing" machine was being manufactured by E. Remington & Sons, of Ilion, New York, makers of guns.

Scarlet fever prevailed that year; and on March 9th, ex-President Fillmore died. French and German lessons and language classes in the public schools were banned, except for six schools. Public protest followed this drastic action, and "a citizen's committee screamed vehemently in vain."

Cyrus Field came into the city from the East, with high hopes of developing a Pacific Ocean cable. James Lick left two million dollars for public purposes, and the great horse Occident, used in the famous Muybridge series of experimental photos to see whether a horse's hooves were completely off the ground in full stride, won a straight three-heat trotting match from his arch rival Fullerton at the Bay District Fairgrounds.

"Four thousand, two hundred and four vessels visited the San Francisco Port, an increase of 597 over 1873. Sixty-two thousand souls, from outside sources, swelled the tide of immigration, pouring in with velocity." A prediction expected a population of 400,000 by 1878, though the city did not reach that peak until the turn of the century.

Mayor Otis' salary was set at $3,000 per annum, and he was to serve as president of the Laurel Hill (Lone Mountain) cemetery, with a Mr. W. C. Ralston as treasurer. In 1873, a total of 671 new brick and frame buildings went up, but in 1874, a total of 2,159 were erected, "many of them elegant and stylish."

Alva Edison introduced to the world in 1874 the quadruplex telegraph that carried four messages on one wire. The *Bulletin* was unhappy about the new Palace Hotel on Market Street at Montgomery. An editorial called "A Vast Pile," conceivably written by W. P. Frost, Jr., stated that "The Palace Hotel may now be contemplated. The huge pile has steadily risen, day by day. The building, probably the largest public edifice in the world, violates many of our traditions. It is seven stories high, while all else is five!"

Henry George, the crusading editor of *The Evening Post*, was at the height of his career as a fearless journalist. He was soon to become one of W. P. Frost's great friends as well as his employer, for George wooed Frost to join the *Post* as city editor in 1875.

In an editorial on July Fourth, George said, "The great American Republic must be a republic in fact as well as form; a Christian republic in the full sense and meaning of the words, until the time shall come when warships and standing armies, and paupers and prisons, and men toiling from sunrise to dusk, and women brutalized by want and children robbed of their childhood shall be things of the dark past."

This author of *Progress and Poverty*, an international bestseller at the end of the '70's, had earlier insisted that the U.S. Army was too large, and suggested that "it be trimmed to 2,000 to 3,000 well-paid, hand-picked men, all treated and imbued with the spirit of equal opportunity."

A Grand Calico Ball for the benefit of the Ladies United Aid Society was advertised in the *Bulletin* in October. Ballenkamp's Full Orchestra was to play, and tickets were $5, "admitting one gentleman and TWO Ladies."

On the final day of 1874, a *Bulletin* editorial entitled "Old and the New" summed up the year as follows: "It has not been marked by notable events. There have been no great wars. We have had remarkable prosperity on the Pacific Coast, but the New Year dawns suspiciously."

A letter to the paper asked "What has Russia done for America? What has she done for mankind? Nay, what has she done for her own people that any American should be in sympathy with her Asiatic encroachment?"

Across the Atlantic, under the heading of "Births" the *Times* listed: "On the 30th November, at Blenheim Palace, the Lady Randolph Churchill, prematurely, a son."

Robert Lee Frost was nine months old. It was a little early for his father to take him to see the $30,000 shining brass fence surrounding the mansion of James Flood on Nob Hill near the Frost "home." But "this young candidate for immortality" was to be a fence builder and repairer himself, hopefully making good neighbors.

A Literary Friendship:
Robert Frost and Carl Burell

WILLIAM R. EVANS

ONE of the marks of being a major poet is that your life and even your friends' lives are made known to the circle of your admirers. Aficionados know about Johnson and Mrs. Thrale, Emily Dickinson and Thomas Higginson, Yeats and Dorothy Wellesley. But relatively few people have even heard of Carl Burell and his relationship to Robert Frost. Burell is not mentioned in Elizabeth Shepley Sargent's biography. Thompson, in his mighty work, talks about Burell but fails to stress the full significance of his impact on Frost. For thirteen years, Burell played a unique role in the poet's life. Between 1889 and 1902, Burell was the friend and confidant of Frost at four important points in his life: the high school years of 1889 to 1892; the summer of 1895 when Frost and Elinor, taking a delayed honeymoon, lived at Allenstown, New Hampshire, in the cottage Burell found for them; the Harvard years of 1897 to 1899, during which Frost corresponded with Burell in a series of mock-poetic, whimsical letters; and finally in the years 1900 to 1902, when Burell helped Frost run the farm at Derry. Burell knew Frost well before the poet was famous. He encouraged Frost to write poetry. And he is one of the few friends about whom Frost wrote poems. Perhaps no one except Elinor was so influential on Frost in his formative years as poet.

Burell was probably the first living poet Frost ever knew outside his immediate family. Although most of the poems of Burell are obvious, sentimental, and crudely wrought, full of commonplace ideas, Frost followed his example in March of 1890 to become an amateur poet.[1] Burell introduced Frost to a lifelong interest, botany. In addition, Burell was the direct inspiration for some of Frost's early poems, "The Quest of the Purple-Fringed," "An Encounter," and, most importantly, the dramatic dialogue, "The Self-Seeker."

Who was this man? A forgotten poet, a farmer, a humanitarian, and a decisive force on perhaps the greatest twentieth-century

American poet. The facts about Carl Burell's life are relatively few. Lawrance Thompson states that Frost met Burell in the fall of 1888 when Frost entered Lawrence High School and that their friendship began the following year. Frost was fourteen; Burell, who had been a manual laborer for some time after graduation from eighth grade, was almost twenty-four, a senior in high school. Both Frost and Burell were odd men out: Frost, because he was a shy newcomer and a Westerner; Burell, because of his age, his clumsiness, his slight speech impediment, and his unusual interests. His hobbies included poetry and botany; he was interested in books ranging from philosophy to evolution, religious skepticism, and atheism. Perhaps Frost's intellectual curiosity and independent spirit attracted him, a newcomer, to Burell, an eccentric figure to many of their peers.

The friendship between the two men took root. Burell showed Frost his personal library, which included some of the books that were to move Frost deeply, especially one of them, Richard Anthony Proctor's *Our Place Among Infinities*.[2] Burell must have talked long and enthusiastically with Frost about Burell's great interest in botany, a science upon which Frost draws heavily in his poetic imagery. An avid gardener and a wide-roaming practical naturalist, Burell sought out wild flowers, particularly orchids.

Burell also showed his carefully kept file of his own published works to Frost, and it is probable that this record caused Frost to begin writing and publishing poetry. Frost himself, reminiscing in 1925, said, "I remember probably almost better than anything else in my high school days the poems of my rivals. The poems of my fellow poets had as much influence on me as anything my teachers ever said or did."[3] Evidence indicates that Burell was Frost's principal "rival," but also friendly confederate, in writing poetry. Although Thompson believes the two built their friendship more on the grounds of loneliness than anything else,[4] I suggest the roots were deeper.

Burell, who had a lively sense of humor and appreciated Artemus Ward, Josh Billings, Petroleum V. Nasby, and Mark Twain, introduced Frost to their works, part of his own collection of books. Years later, Frost remembered the good times Burell and he had enjoyed: "Those were the days when Carl Burell and I in my Uncle's house in Lawrence laughed loud and long at Phoenix Shillaber, Artemas Ward, Mark Twain and the other jokesmiths indescriminately." [5]

Underneath the humor, Burell, like Frost, was concerned with religious questions. His profound but unconventional spiritual convictions represented many stages between belief and disbelief. Burell's poems, a record of the dark night of his soul, are filled with phrases describing such things as "the disguise" of Christ and the "fatal seeds" of faith.[6] Plunging into the depths of belief, he depicted his relationship with an ultimate being as a catastrophic encounter. Frost's own spiritual beliefs were complex. Like Frost, Burell sought matrix without convolution in an incantation of choice.

The ties that bound the two men during their high school years— an interest in writing poetry, in botany, in humor, in questions of belief—held strong, though their paths diverged. Frost was graduated from high school and entered Dartmouth in 1892. Misfortune struck Burell. His parents died suddenly, and Burell had to assume the responsibility of caring for his grandfather. Burell, who had taken the entrance examinations for Harvard, was unable, because of financial pressures, to be graduated from high school in 1890. He had to go to work.

While Frost studied at Dartmouth, their friendship continued. Frost, during his freshman year, traveled to Sutton, Vermont, to celebrate Thanksgiving with Burell and his grandfather. And the story has been told of how Burell visited Frost in December, 1892, and ended up cleaning his grate and carting away the ashes Frost had allowed to build up in his room in Wentworth Hall.[7]

The next period in which Frost and Burell were together for an extended time was the summer of 1896, a happy experience that, unfortunately, ended in near tragedy. Frost and his bride, taking a delayed honeymoon, vacationed in a cottage at Allenstown, New Hampshire, and Burell worked in a box factory in nearby Pembroke. Burell and Frost, sometimes with Elinor but more often not (because she was pregnant), went botanizing. The two friends spent long hours in the fields and bogs in quest of wood anemones, star grass, gentians, and wild orchids, especially the rare purple orchis. Burell knew the way orchids pollinated and reproduced themselves, and his homespun narratives delighted Frost and Elinor.[8] Life seemed idyllic until one day at the box factory Burell had a nearly fatal accident. His feet were so badly crushed that it was feared they would have to be amputated. Although they were not, Burell limped for the rest of his life. Relatively indifferent to money, he accepted what Frost felt was a shamefully small amount from the insurance company.[9] Seventeen years later, in "The Self-Seeker," Frost examines that accident and its full implications, as we shall see.

When Frost entered Harvard in the fall of 1897, the friendship was hearty. Away from his literary friend, Frost sent Burell a series of humorous epistles. Writing in a journalistic style, Frost needled the man he was so fond of. These letters underline the closeness of their friendship: Burell was a friend Frost could kid with, someone who appreciated his "kind of foolin'," someone he could relax and joke with. Playful and childlike, Frost calls Burell "Coebee" and "A Young Man from Podunk." In all, Frost sent Burell six "whimsical literary productions," now preserved in manuscript at Baker Library, Dartmouth College. The youthful joy and camaraderie of these charming pieces demonstrate the early stages of Frost's humor.

Life is Boxes and Other Tight Places,[10] by "Shooks," is typical of these productions. Probably written in 1897, possibly it was meant as a Christmas greeting for Burell. Previously unpublished, it is reprinted in its entirety here:

The Box Wonderful

Once a boxmaker made a box with three sides so that its cross section was an equilateral triangle, and when he saw what he had done, he was greatly amazed, for never had he seen before a box that had not at least four sides not counting ends, and having considered sometime whether in any way he might improve the box and having satisfied himself that it was perfect, he called his friends together to see it in the shop where he had made it and to inquire of them what he should call it.

Now as the neighbors were most of them boxmakers, for the first day none but boxmakers attended his exibition, and *as* boxmakers and seeing it with the eyes of boxmakers they all with one accord marvelled at the box that had only three sides which they were all agreed was not a box, though what to call it they did not for the life of them know.

On the second day it was the same, the visitors were all box-makers, and on the night of the second day the artist went to bed confirmed in the belief, by the failure of so many to find a name for his creation, that he had transcended the bounds of nature and by the daring of his conception once more asserted for the race the supremacy of mind over matter, genius over talent.

On the third day however there came a disconcerting individual who insisted that if this idea of reducing the number of sides of a box were carried to its logical conclusion, boxes would have to be made with only one side, to which though the boxmaker retorted that that was not naming the box and it was not a box anyway, and though he concealed for the moment his displeasure, it was with a heart not quite content that he went to bed on the night of the third day.

But the final pricking of the bubble of his pride was on the fourth day when a farmer came and with mind untrammeled by the technicalities of boxmaking surveyed the box and allowed that it wasn't a box, or granting that it might for convenience roughly and inaccurately be called a box still it was for all the world like a hen-coop—and that was what *he* would name it, was it right and what was the reward.

An Apotheosis

At noon of a summer day the boxmaker sat in the open door of the factory eating his lunch from a tinplated pail. Ten minutes before the buzz saws little and big in the room behind him had slowed abruptly and showed their teeth. The rest of the laborers had gone to the houses scattered about the village for their dinners. Silence reigned. The boxmaker was alone with his thoughts and his doughnuts.

He was looking absently down the sunlit road in the direction of the station when he saw a man descend from the platform where he must have lain concealed ever since the nine o'clock train went up in the morning. For reasons obvious to a box-maker it was certain that he could not have reached the station except by that train. But on second thought the boxmaker could not remember that the nine o'clock train went up. If not, how to account for [sic] of the stranger? and what was his business in Pembroke? The boxmaker was soon to see.

For instead of passing on by the factory, as from the clear state of the boxmaker's concience he might have been expected to do, he faced suddenly about when opposite and advanced into the yard. Then it was seen that he wore a wide open waterlily and on the side of his head a greenish derby hat. For a moment the shy boxmaker had his mind's eye on a pile of shavings in the room behind him as a place of refuge. But he was saved the necessity of flight by the strangers stranger actions. That gentleman paused at a distance of fifty paces and spreading out both arms and all ten fingers toward the boxmaker, distinctly apostrophized him thus:–

"Come where glory waits thee–thou art claimed by notoriety!"

Something in the stranger's style of dress and address reminded the boxmaker of notoriety he knew not why.

"Come!" he repeated, "You are the author of poems?"

The boxmaker could not deny it. He cast down his eyes into the greesy depths of the pail between his knees and faltered, "Yes."

"Come!" insisted the stranger.

The boxmaker was at a loss for a satisfactory answer. He expostulated weakly:–

"But sir I do not care for notoriety."

"Not fame?" cried the stranger as if in astonishment at something unheard of.

"Not that kind."

"Nor revenge?"

At this the boxmaker was visably moved but only to ask what was the connection, but discovering one for himself he desisted. The other fancying he had made an impression repeated, "Come you shall have revenge!"

"Now when I come to think of it I do not care for revenge now. And anyway it would be a poor sort of revenge on my enimies merely to become notorious."

"Then you shall have female adulation!!"

The boxmaker rose from his seat. The stranger turned to lead the way.

"But I am not quite sure that I care for that either."

"O yes you do," said the stranger presuming on the uncertainty in the others tone, "You know you do!"

"Well then wait till I burn the mill."

"What for?"

"I'm done with it."

"You mean you've got no more use for it?"

"Yes."

"And its yours?"

The Stranger thought he caught the answer "No" but as the destruction of mill did not concern him and he fancied it was some sort of poetic justice he did not exercise himself greatly but waited until the boxmaker rejoined him when he lead him down the valley and so out into the world.

The stranger was probably Dean Howells.

Ad Astra

One at least of the degraded creatures who dragged out their lives at the workbenches of the box factory had visions of better things. Having concieved a hope of a world beyond Pembroke where one might live without labor, he now addressed his poor imperfectly developed faculties to devising a way to attain that world. Impute it to his youth and his hard condition if his plans for escaping from the intolerable slavery of boxmaking did not include his fellowmen.

He was employed in the upper story of the factory in an out-of-the-way corner and there with pitiful simplicity he built himself the best box that had ever been built in the establishment except as a sample copy and slowly and painfully calked it with chewing-gum. The "arrowy" Suncook shot through the valley just missing the factory on the left and the youth reasoned and reasoned correctly there must be a very large place somewhere to receive as much water as went by which place would be the place of his dreams.

So with the cunning that is the last intelligence of the imbecile he dragged his box undetected down to the river launched it and put out into the stream.

The day was wild and windy and the black ruffled water scarcely reflected the white scud overhead. In the frail craft knelt the frail boy the merest framework of a lovely youth with the dimmest of dim blue eyes and tow hair. Before setting sail he had provisioned with a great number of cigar-butts and as the day wore on and he made little progress, crossing rudderless from bank to bank whirling in the eddies, he made great inroads on his store gulping the bitter morsels down ravenously.

He was not out of sight of the factory but all was going well when suddenly to his dismay the box sprung a leak in the bottom, the chewing-gum having been displaced by the pressure of the water. At this juncture the factory set up an awful whistling and he realized that doubtless he had been missed or even sighted at a distance on his voyage. The was nothing for it but to abandon the box and make good his escape as he could. Where there was no choice there was no hesitation. The support of box was withdrawn from under him and he found himself in the deep-flowing water.

The rest is soon told. The youth made his peace on the best terms possible with the God of the Adventists and just as a group of hatless coatless and breathless men appeared on either bank of the river, threw up his meanly shod feet in the wind and expired. Further down he grounded on a sandbar and was fished out and burried close by with scant ceremony as one who had left to others what he should have done himself.

"The Box Wonderful," while playful is also satirical. If the box is read as a symbol for poetry, Frost is mocking Burell's creative originality. If the wonderful box is read as a Freudian symbol, then Frost is mocking Burell's lonely, apparently womanless existence, a lack Burell himself in his poetry mourned.

In "An Apotheosis," Frost satirizes Burell the ambitious poet. The Boxmaker, alone with his thoughts and his doughnuts, is approached by the mysterious satanic stranger. The stranger's appearance also suggests Oscar Wilde, then at the height of his notoriety—the famous trial had occurred in 1895. (Frost ironically says the stranger may be William Dean Howells, a writer quite unlike Wilde.) The stranger tempts Burell with fame, revenge, and "female adulation," three desires Frost himself may have had.

The title of "Ad Astra" reflects another aspect of Burell's influence on Frost. From high school days, Frost had been an enthusiastic amateur astronomer, an interest enkindled by Burell's lending him a copy of Proctor's *Our Place Among Infinities*, a study of religion and astronomy. In "Ad Astra," Frost, perhaps using Burell as a *doppelgänger*, emphasizes that although the youth worked in a box factory, he had "visions of better things." In the narrative, the box is a means of escape which ultimately becomes a coffin. The youth, possibly Frost himself, is rebuked for leaving "to others what he should have done himself." Possibly in this work Frost is disguising the fact that the battle being fought is in his own breast. Perhaps he is not really rebuking the youth (or Burell) whose ambitions were less than his own. Perhaps he is condemning himself for progressing so slowly toward the goal that burned in him: to be famous.

After a nearly disastrous encounter with the Department of Modern Languages at Harvard, Frost concluded his formal education. Through a beneficial financial arrangement with his grandfather, Frost, in 1900, was able to take over a small farm at Derry, New Hampshire. The poet, who knew little about running a farm, was helped by Carl Burell and Burell's grandfather who came to live with him. Working the land together, Frost and Burell for two years had extensive opportunities to talk long hours about their passionate enthusiasms: botany, poetry, and God.

Frost's "An Encounter" is probably the outgrowth of their long conversations. Here Frost substantiates in metaphysical terms a dramatic encounter with Christ. A Donne-like image, the telephone pole, as Christ with yellow wires, flames out grotesquely at a reader prepared for snowy fields and apple orchards. Although nothing undeniably specific in "An Encounter" indicates the narrator is talking of Burell in the poem, it is unlikely that at this point in his life Frost could associate wandering "out of beaten ways" to seek "The orchid Calypso" with anyone but Burell.[11] It was also at this time that Frost and Burell were arguing with each other about atheism, and it may be that the poem is Frost's affirmation of the Risen Christ.

"The Quest of the Purple-Fringed," probably written in 1896, although not published until 1901 as "Quest of the Orchis," describes an orchid-hunting expedition in which a guide, possibly Burell,[12] leads the narrator to find something ultimately greater than a rare purple-spired flower. This poem may be Frost's implied thanks to the man who had introduced him to the writing of poetry.

Following the death of his grandfather, Burell left the farm in 1902 and found work in other parts of New England. Although some further correspondence ensued, that departure apparently marks the end of the relationship. Frost sailed for England in 1912, and when he returned, he sent Burell a copy of the recently published *North of Boston*. Strangely enough, Burell, in his thank-you note, made no reference to Frost's poem "The Self-Seeker," in which Burell's accident in the box factory is central; instead, Burell elatedly spoke of the excellent notices *North of Boston* had received in the *Literary Digest* and mentioned that "The Wood-Pile" was his favorite poem in the collection.[13]

The friendship had more or less closed when Frost returned from England, but one unpublished incident, which unfortunately cannot be dated, in the relationship should be recorded since it reveals the high spirits of the friends. In answer to an inquiry, the severely handicapped Burell wrote in 1935 to Mrs. Edna Davis Romig. Part of the letter is reprinted here just as Burell typed it, with a few corrections made in the spelling for the sake of clarity:

One thing—incident comes to my mind that will interest you ROB and SULLIVAN (now very prominent doctor) had spent the evening with me, some time after midnight we concluded we ought to separate ROB & I were sure SULLIVAN ought to be escorted home so we did our Duty but when we had got SULLIVAN home, SULLIVAN & I decided we ought to escort ROB home When we got ROB home, HE & SULLIVAN decided I must be escorted home—we should still be at the game if a policeman hadn't advised us to "GO HOME AT ONCE" [14]

The reasons for the break in the friendship are complex: some are obvious; others possibly can never be known. Returning to New England in 1915, Frost was no longer the struggling farmer-poet, but a man who dined with *Atlantic* editors and corresponded with famous poets in England. Burell and Frost were no longer on the same level; each went his own way. One became the unacknowledged poet laureate of America; the other, a practicing humanitarian.

The later years of Burell are somewhat difficult to discern, except for a few facts. Very probably he made his livelihood working on farms and doing odd jobs. In 1908 he married Florence Dudley, but he had no children. All his life he kept a prose journal called "Calendula Gardensis," which is a record of his interest in God, nature, life, and his own personality.[15]

On August 4, 1936, Burell wrote: "Not till I went to San Francisco in 92 did I realize I could not get away from myself and not till I had married Florence in 1908 did I realize that God was ever and always with ME." This entry, made when he was nearly seventy-two, goes on to say that he realized God was helping him spiritually, not materially, as he had first hoped. He ends with words that are typical of the man: "My garden never forgets to grow (in growing season). I must never forget to love—at all seasons and in all places, GROW IN USEFULNESS, GROW IN BEAUTY, GROW IN LOVE." [16]

The subsequent years of Burell's life, apparently, were filled with questioning, searching, and love. After the death of Florence Dudley, Burell married Ethelyn Williams, an invalid and president of the Maine, New Hampshire, and Vermont Branch of the Shut-In Society. He helped her with her work and, following her death, assumed the presidency of the group. His own obituary in the Manchester *Leader* of June 13, 1938, featuring a picture of the elderly man in his attic office, states that he was "untiring" in helping the home-bound to receive records, puzzles, knitting materials, and books. A friend of mankind, he chose perfection of the life rather than art. Yet he continued to write throughout his life, mainly for himself and for a few friends.

As a poet, Burell is decidedly minor. Like so many amateurs, he states what many men feel but few can express artistically. However, at the time Frost met him, Burell was the superior writer. A number of his poems, which had been published in local papers, reveal the rudiments of style in his ability to rhyme. He treated traditional themes: the delights of spring, the pangs of unrequited love, a faith in God. Perhaps the best of his poems is one he wrote in 1892, when Frost was a senior at Lawrence High School and Burell, no longer a student, was living with his grandfather. Entitled "The

Philosopher's Dream," the poem shows Burell at his symbolic best.

In the poem an aged philosopher meditates on "Modern science and ancient lore," material he has spent his life studying. His philosophy has become flawless; he has found "The purpose of life and the secret of death." But troubled by memories of his youth, he admits to himself that wisdom has not brought joy. Suddenly he remembers the girl he had loved in his youth, but this memory saddens him. Impulsively, he gathers all his books and throws them on the fire. As he watches his lifetime work burn, a phoenix suddenly rises from the ashes. The bird is the young girl he had loved. In a silvery voice, she gives him her message, and he dies. His spirit has fled with his vision: "A heap of ashes and a smell of smoke/Was all't was left of his life's work." But the message is ineradicable. Only love makes life worth living.[17]

Burell put "The Philosopher's Dream" with other poems he was proud of into a homemade book, dated 1892, called *My Beautiful, Beautiful, Good and True*. The title seems almost embarrassingly amateurish until its origin in Plato is recalled. (Burell had studied Greek, and occasionally, in large, awkwardly shaped letters, laced his poetry with a Greek word or phrase.) Plato held beauty, truth, and goodness to be the three greatest virtues. A Platonist, Burell was also an intermittent Christian. His writings and his humanitarian efforts suggest that he lived a life of faith, hope, and charity, virtues in Burell that perhaps Frost celebrates in the poem about his former mentor, "The Self-Seeker." As indicated earlier, the poem had its origin in the terrible accident Burell had suffered in the box factory in 1896.

The poem, which made its first appearance in *North of Boston*, has failed to generate much enthusiasm among scholars.[18] This failure is strange because the poem, as it unfolds the story of a man who has lost his two feet in a factory accident, exemplifies Frost's gift for writing pastoral drama. "The Self-Seeker" also indicates how gravely impressed Frost had been by Burell's near disaster in the factory: Frost had stored that accident in his mind for seventeen years until he shaped it into the poem.

The first hurdle to jump in reading "The Self-Seeker" is the title, which initially suggests egotism and selfishness. But the narrative demonstrates that the title has another meaning: we must seek out our true selves before we can deal with others. The self-seeker is the self-reliant man willing to search himself out, even if his discoveries are unpleasant. His opposite runs away from himself unable to bear the disturbing revelations.

Four distinct characters stand out in the drama. The "Broken One" (surely ironic on one level of meaning) is perhaps Burell himself after the disaster has occurred. His friend Willis is the observer, perhaps Frost himself. Anne is the little girl who brings Ram's Horn orchids to the injured man. The Lawyer is the villain, the representative of a heartless society. Although a sardonic humor operates early in the poem—the Broken One speaks of selling his amputated feet for "Five hundred dollars for the pair"—the dominant tone is sorrowful and compassionate. For the man who loved to search for wild orchids, it is tragic to lose his feet. Philosophically, Willis the observer hovers between the Broken One's idealism tempered by reality and the Lawyer's crass materialism. The Broken One is resigned to his fate. The Lawyer takes advantage of the Broken One's attitude by offering a settlement of five hundred dollars. A drama in miniature, the poem makes us "see" in the Conradian sense. We see not only a man injured for life, but also loss, pain, and tragedy tempered by loyalty, kindness, and love. Here again the flower is symbolic: the Ram's Horn orchid the child Anne brings to the Broken One is beauty and reality. Throughout his work, Frost examines the coexistence of ugliness and beauty, materialism and spirituality, the real and the ideal; and in "The Self-Seeker" Frost dramatizes and synthesizes, with extraordinary insight, the conflicting elements in life.

Perhaps Frost in writing the poem was acknowledging his debt to Carl Burell and implying his gratitude for their friendship. We can never know with certainty. But as we review the entire Frost-Burell relationship, one consideration emerges strongly. As Frost's friend, Burell was a highly personal influence and a strong poetic one. Frost as a poet described, either openly or in various disguises, aspects of his own interior landscape. That landscape was not entirely shaped by himself, but by several others: his mother, his wife, his children, and his friends. Carl Burell was the first of those friends.

Notes to *A Literary Friendship: Robert Frost and Carl Burell*
by WILLIAM R. EVANS

1. Lawrance Thompson, *Robert Frost: The Early Years, 1874–1915* (New York: Holt, Rinehart and Winston, 1966), 93, describes how Frost's first poem, "La Noche Triste," came to be written and published.

2. *Ibid.*, 90.

3. James A. Batal, "Poet Robert Frost Tells of His High School Days in Lawrence," Lawrence *Telegram*, March 28, 1925, p. 14, as quoted in *The Early Years*, 503, n. 11.

4. Thompson, *The Early Years*, 89.

5. *Selected Letters of Robert Frost*, ed. Lawrance Thompson (New York: Holt, Rinehart and Winston, 1964), 530. (The erratic spelling and lack of punctuation are Frost's.)

6. Carl Burell, "We May See Jesus Even Now" and "Solum Auxilium" in *My Beautiful, Beautiful, Good and True* (1892), 90, 170. Original typescript in Baker Library, Dartmouth College, Hanover, New Hampshire. I wish here to express my gratitude to Edward Connery Lathem, Dean of Dartmouth College Libraries, for permission to consult this and other material and for all the kindnesses he and his staff extended to me.

7. Lawrance Thompson, "Robert Frost and Carl Burell," *Dartmouth College Library Bulletin*, VI (NS), No. 3 (April 1966), 65–73.

8. Thompson, *The Early Years*, 218.

9. *Ibid.*, 220.

10. The original manuscript, of which the reproduction here is an accurate transcript, including the errors, is in The Robert Frost Collection, Baker Library. Saved from destruction by the heroic efforts of Edward Connery Lathem, it is reproduced here through the courtesy of Alfred C. Edwards, trustee of Frost's literary estate.

11. Thompson, *The Early Years*, 223. Thompson connects Burell with "The Encounter."

12. *Ibid.*, 217; 223–24.

13. Carl Burell to Frost, May 17, 1915, in Baker Library.

14. Carl Burell to Mrs. Edna Davis Romig, March 5, 1935, in Baker Library.

15. Carl Burell, "Calendula Gardensis." Original typescript in Baker Library.

16. *Ibid.*, XLV.

17. Burell, *My Beautiful, Beautiful*, 23–26.

18. John F. Lynen, *The Pastoral Art of Robert Frost* (New Haven: Yale University Press, 1960), 113, lists "The Self-Seeker" as one of Frost's "Dramatic Dialogues," but says: "I would not rank 'The Self-Seeker'... among Frost's best poems." George W. Nitchie, *Human Values in the Poetry of Robert Frost* (Durham, N.C.: Duke University Press, 1960), refers often to the poem in his discussion of recurring themes and values in Frost but makes no value judgment on it. Radcliffe Squires, *The Major Themes of Robert Frost* (Ann Arbor: University of Michigan Press, 1963), 77, says that "The Self-Seeker" does "not reflect anything which ever happened to Frost directly." Reginald L. Cook, *The Dimensions of Robert Frost* (New York: Holt, Rinehart and Winston, 1958) and Reuben A. Brower, *The Poetry of Robert Frost, Constellations of Intention* (New York: Oxford University Press, 1963), refer to the poem only in passing.

Frost's Last Three Visits to Michigan

DOROTHY TYLER

W<small>HEN</small> he was 88 years old, in his final year of life, in 1962, Robert Frost came home to Michigan three times, in April and June to Ann Arbor, and in November to Detroit. "Came home?" Yes, for it was no mere figure of speech that he was at home in Michigan from his first year in residence at the University of Michigan in 1921–22 till he returned for those final visits forty years later.

Some of the friends he had known so many years before were still there, and he tried to see them all, and succeeded fairly well. He had been invited to Ann Arbor earlier in the year, but could not come, for he was suffering from one of those bouts of pneumonia that had been his lot through the years.[1] But he began to recover, as he had recovered so many times before. In March a telephone call to Mrs. Theodore Morrison, his devoted friend and aide in his later years, who was attending him in Florida, brought the encouraging news that he could come—though not until early April.

There was a dramatic difference between Frost's earlier arrivals in Ann Arbor, in the 1920s, and the reception he received in April, 1962. In 1921 he was known, to be sure, but he came both as poet and teacher from the small, liberal arts college for men in Amherst, Massachusetts, to a university, even then large, in an Ann Arbor that had many professional schools whose students were interested mainly in subjects other than the arts.[2] Some professional students were aware of Frost's presence, and he valued their interest; but even some students in English language and literature, who were to have a career in that field, had no contact with him during his several years at Michigan, as I discovered on questioning them later. Now all was changed, and not only the whole University community but the entire Detroit area was interested in seeing and hearing Frost.

Of the preparations after it was certain that Frost would come, the student, James M. Seff, who, as chairman of the committee that sponsored the Creative Arts Festival, was responsible for the poet's coming, wrote: "He came the week after his 88th birthday party in Washington, and the week before his visit his picture was all over everything, including *Life's* cover. We sold tickets for five afternoons, and in that period of time sold out Hill Auditorium SRO. I think we could have filled the Stadium."

It was true. In the lobby of Hill Auditorium before the performance I saw a great crowd milling about, looking for tickets at any price. Offering three tickets to a man in the crowd—for reserved seats had been set aside for a few guests—I was greeted with a look of astonishment because I asked only for the price printed on them. And Hill Auditorium accommodates nearly 5,000 seated, besides the standers allowed. They were all there that evening.

Let young Mr. Seff tell of the meeting at Metro Detroit Airport: "I had never seen the way the University treated honored guests before, and I was impressed. They provided us with a chauffered limousine to meet him at the airport. He was the last off the plane—spryly, but on the arm of an attractive stewardess. I met him on the field, introduced myself and offered my arm. But Frost didn't need it, and declined. It was my first and last attempt to treat him like an old man. He wasn't one."

There was talk on the way to Ann Arbor and Inglis House, where the University houses its important visitors. It was mostly Frost talk, for—though he had told them that he was hard of hearing, and they must interrupt when they had anything to say or ask—"We mostly listened. He had things to say."

Donald Hall, poet and faculty member, was at Inglis House to greet Frost. It was a happy thought to have him there, for Frost and Hall had known each other for many years, and Frost cherished the younger poets who were his friends.[3] Later, a warm and friendly Frost sat in a big leather chair and talked to Hall and the small group of students gathered to receive him. As he had been instructed by Mrs. Morrison, James Seff "hustled Frost off to bed" at eleven o'clock.

Even to read or remember the records of the next two days of Frost's program and presence is to wonder at the energy expended, the number of persons encountered, the prodigal giving of himself that characterized the poet's last years. Frost had agreed to appear not only at Hill Auditorium, but also at a press conference and at a luncheon given in his honor.

The press conference was held on the afternoon of April 2 in the Regents Room of the Administration Building, the place "a clutter of lights and reporters." Frost complained about the lights, as he had at President Kennedy's Inauguration—the comparison is inevitable. He sat at one end of a big table, with Donald Hall at his left, "bellowing into his ear," as he recalled, the questions asked by reporters. University station WUOM kept a tape of the conference. At the back of the room sat a group of administrators and their secretaries who had come in to see the show. Thereby hangs an amusing story, for Frost, who had had difficulty "seeing much" in the bright lights, walked back, when he had almost reached the end of the hall after the conference, to "a very pretty girl who was watching him" from the sidelines. He took her hand and thanked her for coming to the conference. It was not the first time he had taken notice of a pretty girl,[4] though it may possibly have been the last.

That afternoon Donald Hall and his wife Kirby took Frost for a drive around Ann Arbor. He must have observed many changes, both on the campus, including its new North Campus, and in the city, much bigger than the one he had known. Did he ask to see the sites of his former houses—three of them? Not one of them was there in 1962—neither the D'Ooge house where he had lived in 1921–22, nor the house of Professor I. N. Demmon, on the other side of Washtenaw Avenue, where he lived in 1922–23—both situated among fraternity houses—nor the Greek Revival house on Pontiac Road[5] where he lived in 1925–26, and, indeed, until early 1927. He was pleased, however, about the fate of the house on Pontiac Road, for it had been taken to Henry Ford's Greenfield Village, where it is known as "The Ann Arbor House," and Frost's living there is recorded.

The appearance of Frost in Hill Auditorium that evening was an episode in "The Years of Glory," as Lawrance Thompson would call them. Donald Hall and James Seff took him there from Inglis House, and left him in an anteroom—for Frost always required a period of contemplation and preparation before such an appearance

—while they checked the amplification and the WUOM videotape cameras.

A few minutes later, after Seff had spoken to the great crowd about the Michigan Union's Cultural Program and its part in bringing Frost to them, and had introduced Donald Hall as the one who was to present Frost himself, he stood with the poet, waiting to tell him when to come on stage.

When the signal was given, and Frost walked to the podium, what a moment was there! A wave of feeling swept through the crowd, and they rose to their feet as one, in a great spontaneous tribute to man and poet. I, who was one of them, have never experienced another such emotional response of mind and heart uniting so many at one time into a single soul, expressing their feeling for the man before them. Frost had brought them together into the heart of the mystery, and surely he must have felt it.

Donald Hall, the perfect choice for the task, then introduced Frost. He called him *"Life's* Cover Boy," [6] which obviously delighted both poet and audience. What did Frost say then? It was, as Maugham would say, "the mixture as before," but with a rich sauce of Michigan memories spicing his discourse. Of the several well-loved poems he "said," one was "Acquainted with the Night," and he recalled that the "one luminary clock against the sky" was in Ann Arbor. It may well have been, for the big illuminated clock on the Michigan Central station, remembered by generations of Michigan students, was in the valley on the old stone building. It was just around the corner from the house on Pontiac Road where the Frost family lived in 1925, down the hill and over the railroad bridge he must have crossed many times.

Of that Greek Revival house—which Frost referred to as "hen and chicks" architecture, spreading his arms in imitation of a hen's wings protecting her nestlings—had he not been a poultry farmer in Derry?—he spoke with affection. As I have noted, he was gratified that it was now in Greenfield Village, where it is visited by thousands every year. In its original setting, hard by Ann Arbor's oldest cemetery, which surely he had visited, Frost was probably happier than in any other of his Ann Arbor homes. Even so, he left it often in the hours of darkness, sometimes to walk with Jean Paul Slusser,[7] who then lived nearby and would later build a house on the site of Frost's home.

He spoke of his poem "The Witch of Coös," which he had written while he was in the first year at Michigan, living in the D'Ooge house. He recalled that he had shown it to Witter Bynner, who was visiting him at the time and meeting with students, at Frost's urging.[8] Bynner was pleased when I told him of this reference. He spoke also of his first coming to Michigan by invitation of President Marion LeRoy Burton and of his departure under President Clarence Cook Little.

"Getting him through the crowd and back to Inglis House was a job," said Seff, though almost no one had been allowed backstage, and the only book he signed was for a lad of seven named Robert Frost. ("We denied everyone last night," said Frost at the luncheon on the following day, but he was pleased to make an exception for his namesake.)

The day was not yet over. Frost, who ate little before a platform appearance, had agreed (through Kay Morrison) to an informal supper with a few students. The number was eventually twelve, some from the Michigan Union committee, others "some of the best kids who were then writing poems, including Tom Clark." [9] The menu favored by Frost at such a time became widely known: scrambled eggs, vanilla ice cream, and Seven Up—all served up at Inglis House in an elegant manner and with the best crystal set out. After dinner the group moved to the living room, where Frost sat in the same leather chair he had occupied the night before. There was Frost-and-student talk, but it was remembered that he had mentioned Ezra Pound, speaking kindly of him, and before he went up to bed had signed books for the group. "We sat and talked, looking for all the world like a photo from an old Amherst College *Bulletin*," Seff remembered,[10] "in the best of spirits and the warmest of atmospheres."

Frost had written to his son Carol in 1933 that in connection with his "lectures" it was "the sociability" involved that laid him out,[11] and Elinor Frost had often noted the illnesses that followed such appearances.

Nevertheless, he had asked especially for a luncheon at which he could meet "old friends" of his earlier Michigan years, and telegrams had gone to several and letters to others.[12] They were all there, it appeared, to do him honor, to the number of about twelve. From the faculty and administration were Ralph A. Sawyer, famed physicist, Dean of the Graduate School, and, as Frost probably knew, a graduate of Dartmouth; and Erich A. Walter, of the President's Office (President Harlan H. Hatcher was then in South America for the Ford Foundation), who had been Professor in what is now the Department of English during Frost's several years at the University of Michigan. Stella Brunt Osborn, who had been an editor of *Whimsies* during Frost's earlier years in Ann Arbor and later became wife, then widow, of former Governor Chase S. Osborn, donor of the first Frost fellowship, had come from Washington for the reading and the luncheon. Mrs. Campbell Bonner and Mrs. Roy W. Cowden were there. Fred L. Black, personnel and public relations man for Henry Ford Sr., and Mrs. Black were there. Two graduate students had been invited, Konstantinos Lardas, poet, and a Japanese student named Ken Akiyama, now of Doshisha University, Kyoto, and until recently editor of *East-West Review*. And, on each side of Frost at the table were his later students Mary E. Cooley and myself, both delighted to be there.

"You must help me," said Frost, as we sat beside him and he adjusted his hearing aid. No doubt the excellent food, so well served, was eaten, but most memorable were all the people and subjects mentioned there. Let me recall a few of them.

Mr. Black mentioned that Frost, in his early years at Michigan, had been offered, and presumably had taken, a ride in one of the early Ford planes.[13] Frost said, when asked, that he greatly preferred "a good train" to the plane (on which he had arrived and would return), but that "there wasn't always time." Mary Cooley said that the poem "The Draft Horse" (*In the Clearing*) "made her blood run cold." He nodded appreciatively. His new book, I said, I would review for *The Detroit News*. "Be careful!" he said. (I was!) "Read it!" he said. (I did.)

He said to Mrs. Bonner that—and he nodded to the two of us on either side—he was sorry the third, her daughter, Sue Bonner Walcutt, could not be with us. She answered that her daughter would have liked to be present. (Actually, she lived near him in Cambridge and saw him there.) He asked about Lawrence Conrad, who had been important to him in the early years and had typed the manuscript of *New Hampshire*.[14] His memories seemed intact. As Mary Cooley said of those days, "Who would want to be anywhere else when Robert Frost was living in Ann Arbor, consorting amiably with the student editors of the *Inlander*?" We relived them —those days of consorting—in miniature during that luncheon.

The pity was that so many of his best Ann Arbor friends were then dead: Roy W. Cowden, Dean Joseph Bursley, Morris P. Tilley (but his daughter Lois and her daughter were at the luncheon), Campbell Bonner (whose hospitality he had so often enjoyed), Charles Horton Cooley,[15] father of Mary Cooley, and President Burton(whose daughter and her husband, novelist George R. Stewart, had entertained him in California).

After the luncheon Mrs. Cowden came to greet Frost more intimately. In her warmhearted way she reminded him of a time, long ago, when he had come to their home on one of his late jaunts ("Acquainted with the Night"), and he and Professor Cowden, agreeing that the motto of the University under President Little might be "more mice, fewer men," had also agreed that a cup of tea might be welcome when the hour approached midnight. Frost enjoyed the memory. And he signed books for us.[16]

That afternoon, when James Seff escorted him to Metro Airport in a University car, there was a somewhat irascible encounter with an autograph seeker. Frost refused adamantly, saying that since his picture had been on the cover of *Life* people came to him in restaurants asking him to sign menus, and that these people "didn't know a whit about poetry anyway." The abashed seeker after his signature, hurt and taken aback, then produced a copy of the *Complete Poems*. "The poet softened immediately," said Seff, "and signed the book."

One would not be far afield to suspect that Frost made his April trip to Ann Arbor in part to nail down a higher honorary degree than the A.M. awarded him in 1922. Kathleen Morrison had mentioned to James Seff, in a preliminary telephone call, that Frost, who had honorary degrees from all over the world, was sorry that the University of Michigan, "which he loved so dearly," had never given him a doctorate. Seff mentioned it to Mr. Walter, who said that the Regents, whom he served as Secretary, might award such a degree in the near future.

Frost, at the luncheon for "old friends," awaited his moment. It came at the end, when the guests were departing. That A.M. degree, said Frost, made a poor showing among all the honorary doctorates he held. Mary Cooley wrote, "It was good to have Robert Frost come back to Ann Arbor, and to have him tell us during lunch at Inglis House that he thought the University should upgrade his honorary degree, and to have the University administration respond amiably to his suggestion."

He had, indeed, taken the right moment. Looking a bit thunderstruck, Dean Sawyer paused in the doorway to hear Frost's speech. Erich Walter, who had already heard of this idea, was still sitting beside Frost, keeping his expression to himself. Some of us were more amused than surprised.

Of that earlier honorary master's degree, Mr. Walter wrote: "In 1922 the A.M. degree was still commonly used as an honorary one; now it would seem unthinkable. . . . In anticipation of the 1962 Commencement, Mr. Frost and I had a talk. I was able to tell him about the invitation that was about to be sent him. With the merry twinkle that could light up his eyes, he said, 'I've had about all the degrees on the shelf except the LL.D. It would be nice to have that one.' So I took that bit of information to the committee on honorary degrees and recommended that we award Mr. Frost the degree he would like." [17]

And it was so, as the Bible would say. In relation to that event it is of interest to recall the 1922 citation:

ROBERT FROST. Poet and teacher. By birth a Californian; from residence since early youth a New Englander. Trained at Dartmouth and Harvard; yet more truly a fashioner of his own education through sympathetic and penetrating studies of man and nature, preserving the fruits of his meditations in verse of individuality and imaginative insight. As Fellow in Creative Arts, a welcome sojourner in our academic community —wise, gracious, and stimulating. (From University of Michigan Records)

In June Frost returned to Ann Arbor and was again a guest at Inglis House. It is strange to recall now that Theodore Roethke

(1908–1963), poet Michigan born and educated, also received an honorary doctorate at the same time. He was intended to represent the "field" of poetry at that Commencement. As it happened, most attention and publicity went to Frost and Cantiflas (Mario Moreno), "the clown gifted with a paradoxical wisdom," who was awarded a Doctor of Humanities degree. They were photographed together, a rare coincidence.

The happily worded citation, written by the late Professor Alexander Allison, echoes the friendship of Frost and the University in all the forty years intervening between 1922 and 1962:

DOCTOR OF LAW

ROBERT FROST, A.M. (Hon.), 1922; poet. Since an instinct for order and the power of vividly apprehending value are necessary to the commonwealth, and since poets possess these gifts in eminent degree, a man may become known as a public personage and a statesman by virtue solely of the long exercise of poetic genius. Such a man is Robert Frost, among poets distinctively American easily chief, and now by presidental action and spontaneous popular consent our nation's laureate. Setting aside the negative force of Shelley's dictum, that poets are the unacknowledged legislators of the world, the University happily acknowledges the public offices of this sometime poet-in-residence and frequent and most welcome guest in the degree now conferred on him, Doctor of Laws.[18]

Frost must have liked that one. He wrote to President Hatcher later, thanking him, and admitting that he had asked for the degree. He was always one to acknowledge his sins of omission and commission. And whatever the public celebrations had been, Mary Cooley was there to walk with him in the garden of Inglis House. It would be the last time. A good friend[19] had said that Frost liked to go only to places where he knew people and had old friends. There was no lack of them in Michigan.

He knew people and had a few friends in Detroit, and some of the writers for the *Detroit Free Press* and the *Detroit News* had been following his career and character for a long time. Moreover, he had a friend, Peter Stanlis, on the University of Detroit faculty, whom he had known from Bread Loaf days, and had promised to make an appearance at his university. (He had shown great interest in the poems written by the students of Stanlis, and little in Stanlis' important works on Edmund Burke!)[20]

When he knew Frost was coming, Charles E. Feinberg, famed Whitman collector, who had met the poet in New York, invited him to be his guest at his spacious house and garden on Boston Boulevard. There, said Feinberg, he would be more comfortable and could be better taken care of than in the hotel Frost suggested. It was well that he accepted, for—in what was almost a repetition of his experience in Russia in August, and a portent of his last illness and death— Frost was to be very ill on this occasion.[21]

But he would carry through. As he had told Witter Bynner[22] in a letter apologizing for not writing a promised preface, he had seldom or never missed a personal appointment. So it was this time. Looking back upon the occasion, one wonders how he withstood all the pressures. In his later years he was in a giving mood, and, moreover, wanted as much credit for poetry as he could build up in the country. He "could give all to time," he said, with a few exceptions. That was part of the answer.

On Tuesday, November 13, Frost "held court," as Louis Cook had it, and rightly, in Feinberg's home. Cook introduced his report in the *Detroit Free Press*[23] with a description as apt as any I have seen. "The years are crusted on Robert Frost like rust on an old boiler, but the fire inside is as bright as ever." It was repeated in an editorial on Frost's death, and the color reproduction of Gardner Cox's final portrait of Frost on *The Atlantic*'s cover (September 1963) bore out its truth. As the magazine commented: "It was characteristic of Robert Frost that in his mid-eighties he should stand up to the most demanding occasions of his career."

Never at a loss for something quotable to say, Frost outshone himself at that particular "press conference"—the term was an odd one to apply to his performances. Said Cook, he beamed on all and "read with enigmatic interest some poems written in his honor by three University of Detroit students." For the benefit of the young people around him, "most of them interested in how to become successful poets," he said:

I would not go into any of the arts unless you can stand a bump on the snout.

Homer was a beggar in seven cities, all of which claimed later to be his birthplace. But when he was alive he sat at the foot of the table, or under it, with the dogs.

It's funny. Poetry is the worst paid, and it endures the longest. We have to toady.

Nowadays we toady to universities. It's hard. Hard to figure out where a university's toes are.

"He grinned," Cook reported. "Frost doesn't often pun, but he's shameless when he does."

Frost had fairly recently returned from Russia and was still full of the subject. Of present Russian poets he said: "One of the charms of translation is that I don't know if their poetry is good, and they don't know whether mine is. Sort of left us even."

When someone suggested that Frost should be invited back sometime, he chuckled and said: "You better hurry." He knew his time was short, however much he may have wanted "another blow," and to live until the nation's 200th birthday. He would, after all, have been 102 at that time.

On the afternoon of November 13 Frost was granted an honorary degree, Doctor of Humane Letters, at a convocation held at the University of Detroit, with "Dr. Peter J. Stanlis, who has known Frost 23 years," giving the main address. Frost, if he heard it, must have liked it when Stanlis said that "the revelations of poetry are at least as significant as those of science and history, and quite on a par with the revelations of religion. The ordered beauty of the universe and man, and all that is disordered and tragic and comic in it, is part of the province of the poet." [24]

"U. of D. Honors an Impish Frost," *The Detroit News* headline read. "Looking out of place," wrote Anthony Ripley, "Robert Frost sat in academic robes. . . . The 88-year-old best-selling poet sat with his legs spread like a country boy. His mortarboard was just enough askew to show some small impish rebellion, but not enough to disturb the crowds of students who watched him. . . . Being a practical man, he carried his own red-and-white honorary degree hood and unfolded it at the proper moment."

Said Frost, when the Very Reverend Laurence V. Britt, University President, presented the degree, "I'm greatly pleased that you would want me to get this hood. I've been given a lot of hoods lately. . . ." Then he twisted a line from the title of one of the poems in his new collection, *In the Clearing*, and remarked, "How hard it is to keep from being educated when it's in you and in the situation!"

In the anteroom at the time of the convocation there was a meeting, arranged by Peter Stanlis, with Anne Bursley Steed, daughter of Dean Joseph Bursley, in whose parents' Ann Arbor home Frost and his wife had been guests many times, beginning in 1922. Mrs. Steed, living in Dearborn, said that her son David had met Frost at Lake Forest Academy.[25] It was not the only instance in which Frost was remembered and honored by the second and third generations of his friends.

It had been touch and go whether Frost would be able to appear for the long announced appearance in Detroit. On the morning of the big day the Feinbergs' maid had knocked several times on his bedroom door, without response. After waiting for a time Charles Feinberg himself had gone upstairs to inquire. He found Frost looking very ill. He thought he had suffered a heart attack. Not until about one o'clock was he able to say that the show would go on. Once more he had bounced back, in one of his almost miraculous recoveries.

Was it then that he took the walk he mentioned that evening? Sometime between degree granting and evening appearance he had taken one of his famous walks—this one in the big city of Detroit, and in a section at that time still holding much of its handsome appearance. From Boston Boulevard he had walked about two miles to the New Center, with its beautiful General Motors and Fisher Buildings. On the way, he said, he had met only two pedestrians.

At the time of Frost's death more particulars of his walk were remembered.

The death of poet Robert Frost at 88 Tuesday spurred University of Detroit's Bill Rabe to reminiscing about the last Detroit visit of the great writer. Bill tells of Frost dropping in for a look at the Fisher Theater, noting its handsomeness and remarking, "You should have a beautiful place in which to say beautiful things." The date was Nov. 13 and theater manager Joe Nederlander, knowing Frost's U-D poetry reading next night was a 9,500-seat sell-out, told him, "Mr. Frost, you're the hottest ticket to hit this town since 'South Pacific.'" To which Frost replied, with a thought for the musical's heroine, Nellie Forbush, "Yes, but I don't have to wash my hair every night."

Nederlander invited the legendary New Englander to set a spell and watch the rest of the current attraction, "Lord Pengo," but Frost graciously declined. Said he, "If I was only 85, I might; but I have to get my sleep." [26]

Frost was always good copy. As to when that walk was taken, accounts differ. He said it was on the day of the "big show," not the day before.

Some doubts had been expressed in advance about a poet's being able to draw an audience big enough to justify reserving the University of Detroit's Memorial Building. Frost had been confident. "We'll lay them in the aisles," he promised. No one thought at the time that the prediction would come true, almost literally. It was to be Frost's largest audience, the estimates ranging from 8,500 to 9,500. Said Fr. Britt, "A poet has outdrawn some of the finest athletic teams in this country."

Leaving early for the appearance, for Frost always required a short period of meditation alone before he faced an audience, Charles Feinberg remembered that Frost was astonished by the fleets of chartered buses and the many cars that hindered their approach to the campus, some miles to the north. "It was our own traffic jam," said Feinberg. So great was the press that the show was half an hour late in starting.

What did he say? He read poems, he made remarks about poetry, politics, critics, Mother Goose, big cities, the country, walking, walls —all with the full Frostian flavor. It was televised and taped and remembered.

Most remarkable of all was the response of the audience. Frost had only to walk from the wings to the podium, to lean on the podium, to bring a roar of applause and delight from the wall-to-wall audience. It was more than showmanship, it was a personal magic called charisma, before the word was spoiled by overuse. For more than an hour he held his vast audience spellbound, and they left with rapture on their faces, as if they had had a religious experience. Perhaps they had. It was easier to remember later the substance of his sayings.

On cities: "I count cities as trophies of my life if I've talked in them and especially if I've slept in them and walked in them—alone. The country is a fine place, often mentioned in my poems, but my books sell chiefly in the city. These big cities give me confidence. They hold the continent down."

On politics (he had said as much before): "I never dared be radical when young for fear of being conservative when old."

If he said much that he had said before, including the saying of familiar poems that he had begun to slight by giving them less than the voice quality they deserved—including "Spring Pools," "The Courage to Be New," and others—he was saying it to a new and young audience, with whom he had the courage to be old and new at the same time.

Was it then or earlier that he quoted Emily Dickinson, as he often did? After all, those two American poets had lived near each other in a beautiful New England village, Amherst, where there is now a Robert Frost Library. He quoted Emily's poem:

> The heart asks pleasure first,
> And then, excuse from pain;
> And then, those little anodynes
> That deaden suffering;
>
> And then, to go to sleep;
> And then, if it should be
> The will of its Inquisitor,
> The liberty to die.

A student had come to him after he had quoted it once, he said, and commented seriously: "We Americans don't think thoughts like that, do we?" Said Frost: "That boy died as a missionary among the headhunters of Brazil."

In an interval the University of Detroit chorus sang "The Gift Outright," Frost's poem set to music by Don Large, conductor of the chorus. And to save the poet further strain and calls for encores, the Alma Mater was sung at the last, to put an end to the long evening.

On the morrow, in Charles Feinberg's company, Frost left by train for Chicago, to attend the 50th anniversary dinner of *Poetry* which had played so large a part in his career. "I'm going over to help them sell a few magazines," he said.

Two years after Frost's death in January, 1963, Donald Hall of the University of Michigan recalled both poet and poetry to audiences in Ann Arbor, Detroit, New York (Off Broadway), and the campus circuit with a play titled "An Evening's Frost." Will Geer portrayed the poet.

That was in 1965. Now the year is 1973, and Frost's biographer, Lawrance Thompson, is himself dead. So, indeed, are Frost's sons-in-law, Willard Fraser and Joseph Ballantine. Can it be that Frost's own 100th birthday will be observed in 1974? It is so, and a hundred vivid memories survive to tell me that I and others in Michigan who knew him so long and so well will see him no more. "And did you once see Shelley plain?"

Writing to me in 1967, when volume two of the biography was going forward, Lawrance Thompson noticed that "there are fewer and fewer people . . . who actually knew Frost, 'on the ground.' And do you notice that people already begin to speak to you in a different way when they can say, 'So you actually *knew* Robert Frost?' When the kids say that to me, I hear it as though they were saying, 'So you actually *knew* George Washington.' "

Soon there will be even fewer of those who knew the living Frost. Even I, who keep him in a memory ever green, am beginning to wonder: "Who was that man, after all? Who was he?" For there is a mystery about great men, great poets, and all the books only deepen the mystery.

Notes to *Frost's Last Three Visits to Michigan* by DOROTHY TYLER

These pages on Frost's last three visits to Michigan are carved, so to speak, from a large file of materials intended to provide the substance for a book, "Robert Frost in Michigan." In reading those letters and notes for this essay, I am impressed by the one-to-one relationship of Frost to many persons who knew him well, all of whom owned some portion of a man who, nevertheless, was not owned by anyone. These pages are offered in full knowledge of that essential fact.

1. All information referring to the Michigan Union program comes from a typescript, James M. Seff, Berkeley, California, to me, October 12, 1965. Mr. Seff credits Mary E. Cooley with the suggestion that Frost might come, "and it is really due in part to her that all of this came about."

2. The contrast between Amherst and Ann Arbor in Frost's experience was made clear on a visit to the Jones Library in Amherst, when the late Charles R. Green showed the Frost and Dickinson rooms in the Library to me.

3. Donald Hall, professor and author of several volumes of poems, including *A Roof of Tiger Lilies* (Viking, 1964), a biography of sculptor Henry Moore, and the play *An Evening's Frost* (1965). He knew Frost first when, at age 16, a teacher at Exeter Academy suggested that he attend the Bread Loaf Writer's Conference (Middlebury College) in which Frost played so prominent a role. He knew Frost while a student at Harvard, and also met him in California. "They were great together," wrote Seff of their meeting in Ann Arbor, which Hall said was "their best ever." Later in 1962 Hall saw Frost in Vermont—their last meeting.

4. For an earlier occasion on which Frost took note of a pretty girl, see Ruth Lechlitner's account in Lawrance Thompson, *Robert Frost: The Years of Triumph, 1915–1938* (New York: Holt, Rinehart and Winston, 1970), 576.

5. At that time 1223 Pontiac Road. Now "Pontiac Street," no doubt to avoid confusion with the Pontiac Road leading to Detroit.

6. *Life*, March 30, 1962. "America's Ageless Poet ROBERT FROST: Seven Poems from His Wonderful New Book" (Cover portrait and title).

7. Jean Paul Slusser, artist and formerly professor of Fine Arts, University of Michigan. His residence at 1223 Pontiac Street was built on the site of Frost's house, now in Greenfield Village, Henry Ford Museum. Slusser in an interesting letter to me (Ann Arbor, November 20, 1963), places the "one luminary clock against the sky" on the old Washtenaw County Courthouse, "standing in its square in the heart of town." Slusser believes that Frost's poem, "Spring Pools," was suggested by his watercolor sketch of the Huron River in floodtide, which he showed to Frost. (The sketch no longer exists.) Frost purchased from him a watercolor of a bridge and a set of five linoleum prints, all scenes in Sicily "in or about Taormina, Lipari, or Palermo" from a sketching tour there about 1925.

8. There is an interesting series of nine letters from Frost to Witter Bynner (1881–1968) in the Harvard College Library, copies of which were made available to me by Lawrance Thompson. When I wrote Bynner about Frost's reference to him in April, 1962, he wrote from Santa Fe: "It is pleasant of you to have written me the note about Frost's reference to those old days. I wish I were seeing him these new days" (see Thompson, *The Years of Triumph*, 670 for notes on the Frost-Bynner friendship).

9. Tom Clark, poet (b. Chicago, 1941), author of *Stones* (Harper & Row, 1968).

10. Seff Typescript.

11. *Family Letters of Robert and Elinor Frost*, ed. Arnold Grade (Albany: State University of New York Press, 1972), 154.

12. Among the Ann Arborites present were Lois Tilley Schneider (now the wife of the Rev. Henry Lewis) and her daughter ("I know my daughter will never forget it," she wrote in a note to me). Mrs. Lewis was the daughter of Professor Morris Palmer Tilley (1876–1947), University of Michigan Professor who knew Frost from his early Franconia days.

13. Fred L. Black (now deceased) was with Ford for twenty-three years, including administrative positions with the Henry Ford Museum for eight years. He had known Frost from 1926, or earlier. When I mentioned to Black that Horace H. Rackham had been donor of Frost's 1922–23 fellowship at Michigan, he commented, "Well, that was Ford money, too."

14. Though at that moment I could not tell Frost where Lawrence H. Conrad was (I nodded, however, when he asked whether I remembered him), I later learned that he was Professor of English, Upper Montclair (N.J.) Teachers College (now retired).

15. Charles Horton Cooley (1864–1929), eminent sociologist. When Mary E. Cooley sent Frost a copy of *Life and the Student* (Knopf, 1927), he wrote that, if he ever gave up doing his own thinking, he would let CHC do it for him! (I quote from memory.)

16. Frost's inscription in my copy of *In the Clearing* reminded me of the change in his runic handwriting from the time he inscribed *A Boy's Will* for me in 1927 with his poem "Fiat Nox."

17. Erich A. Walter, to Dorothy Tyler, May 5, 1973.

18. Citation from University Records, Honorary Degrees, June, 1962. Erich A. Walter writes: "Alexander Allison, Professor of English, and my assistant, wrote the citation. I think it one of his best (and he wrote some very good ones)."

19. Wade Van Dore. Among the guests at a Sunday noon dinner at Inglis House in June, 1962, "for a few intimates and at his request" was Jean Paul Slusser (see note 7). Slusser writes an interesting note on Frost: "What always impressed me most about Robert Frost's person was his keen and—yes—crafty way of looking at you sidewise, rather laughingly from under deep brows, and at the same time his persistent pursuit, in his rather twanging and somewhat countrified voice, of the theme of his thought. His voice would go on and on, over hill and dale, until he had had his way and come to his conclusion. He seemed to me eternally young, or maybe both very young and very old, probably of no age at all, and this was true even the last time I was near him—in spite of the marks of time on his face and figure."

20. So Peter Stanlis told me during an interview at his home in Trenton, Michigan. For the past several years he has been on the faculty of Rockford College in Illinois.

21. Charles E. Feinberg, host to Frost during these days in Detroit, told me of Frost's illness at this time. It was Feinberg who arranged Frost's trip to Israel in 1961, and who gave the Hebrew University Library in Jerusalem some fifty bibliophile items relating to Frost.

22. Frost to Witter Bynner, August 29, 1925, in possession of Harvard College Library. Frost never wrote the preface!

23. Louis Cook, *Detroit Free Press*, November 14, 1962.

24. Anthony Ripley, "U. of D. Honors an Impish Frost," *Detroit News*, November 14, 1962.

25. From a telephone conversation with Mrs. Steed, daughter of Dean Joseph Bursley. Her sister, Mrs. Angst of Lansing, wrote me a charming letter about her memories of the Frosts' visits to the Bursley home.

26. Ken Barnard, "Frost Fast with Quip," *Detroit Free Press*, January 31, 1963.

The Subtlety of Robert Frost

WADE VAN DORE

"I could say 'Elves' to him/But it's not elves exactly, and I'd rather/He said it for himself."

Only when it seemed necessary did Robert Frost say and write things "right out." He preferred his meanings to appear like light glancing off threads of gossamer or shed onto his friends and readers with the same delicate haze that blueberries leave on the fingers when one touches or picks them. This preference was mainly due to what Lawrance Thompson called the poet's "excruciating sensibilities." Frost went about in the world as if he and everyone in it wore transparent clothing and as if there were no means to assuage the shocks of intimacy that such a nakedness engendered. So acute were his senses that, sometimes when I was with him, I wondered if he might be a "mutation"—a human being comparable to what in the plant world is called a "sport." There was always a leaflike sheen about him that seemed to come not so much from outward light as from a kind of rare intelligence. Actually, he was too sentient for his own comfort! Thus, he resorted to subtlety as a cushion against unavoidable human contact.

He was like the birds in "The Exposed Nest," when the mowing machine cut away the grass and revealed "too much world at once." So world-sensitive was he that the first time an occasion came up for him to read a poem in public, he couldn't do it. An acquaintance read "A Tuft of Flowers," and this incident secured his first important job—teaching at Pinkerton Academy. Another time when there was no getting out of making an appearance, he put pebbles in his shoes so that the physical pain could help alleviate his mental anguish. In time, such reading and lecturing became easier, but always he was inclined to recoil from "too much world at once" and too much intimacy. Country living was an escape, though he did love to be in the midst of nature more than he was willing to acknowledge. One day when we were making a new path through a fine grove of birches standing near the southeast corner of his newly purchased Gully farm in South Shaftsbury, with feeling he exclaimed, "I like doing this better than *anything!*"

At the time I thought this was a rather rash statement. I also felt very fortunate in being able to be alone with Frost during some of the happiest, most carefree days of his life. Imagine a high, green pasture, a clear, Vermont spring day, a big grove of white birches—and all this set off by the sight and proximity of Robert Frost! What more could one ask? As a matter of fact, I didn't ask for anything more at that time. I operated on an apex of reality as definite and satisfying as anything may be in this shop-smudged world. Poetry neatly printed on paper was of secondary importance during my Frost days, because I felt immersed in the very birth-stuff of poetry through having a great poet beside me. With us it was not a meeting of minds, but purely a mingling of acute life-consciousness, and this sentiment fostered in me a rare endorsement of *being*, of seeing and loving at the same moment a flower quivering beside a sparkling granite boulder, discovering a momentous trickle of water coming from what my friend called a "*spring*" spring—one that was certain to dry up before summer arrived with its onslaught of heat.

For those not familiar with it, the quotation at the beginning of this essay comes from "Mending Wall," the poem in which Frost describes his working with a native farmer neighbor, resetting stones in a wall from which, mysteriously, they had tumbled during the winter. No one could have been less insistent in his social traffickings than this poet. He forever wanted individuals to be able to say and do things without his direction. During all the seasons that I was with him as helper and companion, he never once tried to "boss" me, or urge me to do this or that in any situation. It seemed that he had an almost divine respect for the sensibilities of others. You would have thought that he saw everyone as a distinct unit of nature; and, when an individual did something patently "wrong," he saw the act as if it were a part of nature's secret plan that it *should* be done wrongly.

In "Revelation," Frost wrote: " 'Tis pity if the case require . . . / We speak the literal to inspire/The understanding of a friend." So habitually did Frost speak in an unliteral manner, it must have seemed a bit disgraceful to him to have to say a thing "right out." Though he dearly loved to talk, it was the squiggly nuances inside the voice tones, the loaded, enterprising silences between phrases, that most mattered. Thompson has noted that "The Road Not Taken" was a non-literal message to Frost's best friend, Edward Thomas. But Thomas failed to see the intimate point of the poem, and this was a disappointment to its author. Yet this poem became one of the poet's most beloved.

For years Frost was described as writing "simple poetry in a homely idiom." How was it possible to make this judgment when just the opposite was true? Though Frost greatly wanted to be understood, he desired that understanding be on his own level of finesse and intelligence. In "A Considerable Speck," inspired through noticing an almost microscopically small, yet seemingly intelligent, insect walking across a page of paper he was writing on, he asserted: "No one can know how glad I am to find/On any sheet the least display of mind."

Some claim that if a man becomes superior to those about him, he automatically wins the right to be a law unto himself. This sounds rather antidemocratic. In a society that seems to resent anyone rising above the level of an average television commercial, it can be uncomfortable for one who is so subtle that few can begin to comprehend or suspect his meanings. This fact was probably one of the biggest burdens that Frost had to bear. His fund of sensitivity and intelligence added up to a debit when it was assessed by critics who had little conception of his methods and aims. Even now, his "sound of sense" postulation waits to be closely examined or even performed by a student or critic.

In "Build Soil," Frost, in the person of Tityrus, says to Meliboeus the "potato man": "Don't let the things I say against myself/Betray you into taking sides against me. . . ." Our poet went so far in cultivating a teasing kind of subtlety that he couldn't at times resist trying to assume another's identity; or if not that, then disappear altogether. He once told me: "At times I've felt like paring my writing down until nothing was left but an exclamation mark—which could be seen as the shortest poem ever written. Often I have scary doubts about words. Didn't Thoreau say, 'If words were invented to conceal thought, then printing is a great improvement on a bad invention?' Or something like that. Writing is a kind of weakness, and once you get along in it, I expect the greatest thing would be not to write at all. Then we could hope the act of *non*-writing would be seen as the ultimate gesture—like that look a dying person can give instead of words. Maybe the best thing Eliot ever wrote was that about the world ending not with a bang but a whimper. Unless words are extensions of whimpers and terrifying screams they just can't be taken too seriously."

It was because of Frost's fear of exposure, along with guilt about the presumptuousness of using words, that sometimes made him want to "hide." A paper could be written on this aspect of the poet. He was like the small bird in "The Wood-Pile" that was always careful "To put a tree between us when he lighted." He wrote it out more forcibly in "Triple Bronze," in which he listed the items of defense fortunately erected between "too much and me." In this poem he failed to mention subtlety as a kind of armor, but it was one of his "walls." In his superb poem, "Directive," he says he kept a broken drinking "goblet" like "the Grail under a spell" hidden under an old cedar tree so that the "wrong ones" couldn't find it. Because his sensitivity was a burden, he was always conscious and wary of the "wrong" people in situations. This was another reason for practicing subtlety. If a reader couldn't decipher Frost's unique brand of subtlety, he was a "wrong" person that Frost didn't want to have around; but if he could decipher it, then he was a friend and ally well worth having and keeping.

This characteristic makes Frost sound exclusive, but here was exclusiveness of the kind practiced by Thoreau and Emerson. And, in order to retain this quality, Frost refused to wallow in mediocrity, or change "from hot to cold, from wet/To dry, from poor to rich, or back again" as he put it in "New Hampshire." He wasn't willing to rub shoulders with just anyone the way Whitman did, but he was always willing to squat on his heels and listen long to any off-beat person (especially a country one) relate colorful experiences, ideas, opinions.

Several times in different editions of his work Frost used the slight poem "The Pasture" as an invitation to readers to enter his books, his world. Here the phrase "you come too" has more of delicacy than subtlety in it. Similarly, another poem, "The Telephone," exerts an even greater delicacy while portraying the poet as a nature lover rather than a farmer. Going on a long country walk, in an hour "all still," he leans his head against a flower in order to learn if his wife is calling him through a flower she kept on her windowsill. Faintly, he hears her or "*someone*" say "*come.*" The poem seems slight, except for that italicized word, "*someone,*" which adds a dimension of mystery. This poem well illustrates the extreme delicacy and subtlety of Frost. Being able to communicate with his wife by using a flower for a telephone, he would have liked to do it with the whole world. My feeling is that, knowing he couldn't, he tried to subdue his natural inclination to try to perform that feat; however, there is hardly an early poem that doesn't contain a physical or mental subtlety; and, while the physical subtleties prevail, often it requires but little effort to translate them into mental or spiritual subtleties. Shakespeare says things for his readers or listeners—says them to save his audience the work of thinking and saying them for themselves. Frost, lush in boniness in an aura of bareness, requires readers to exert themselves and actually merge with his poetry; or we could say that he entices them into bringing their own thought-furniture into the bare, clean rooms of his hospitality.

Though fragment-subtleties abound, in the early poems especially, occasionally Frost made a whole poem a subtlety. The poem "Maple," filled with speculative undertones, is such a one. This poem turns on the influence that the unusual name "Maple," given to a girl, has on her life. Or sometimes he makes the title of the poem, such as "Out, Out—" contain the subtlety. Elizabeth Sergeant suggests in *Robert Frost: The Trial by Existence* that the title was derived from Shakespeare's "Out, out, brief candle," but, as one who often worked with buzzsaws, I claim it could have come from the fear such a saw instills in an attendant. To keep *out* of the snarling, terrifying saw's range is always in the consciousness of a worker, and in this connection nothing could be more effective and appropriate than Frost's use of the phrase in his title.

But of all the poems that are entirely subtleties, perhaps the most remarkable is "Paul's Wife." This Paul is Paul Bunyan, the mythical lumberjack, and right away a problem presents itself: how is one going to hang an aura of subtlety over a rough lumberjack? But Frost liked to work out such a problem; and, though he has some of Paul's fellow workers throw a bottle as a "brute tribute of respect to beauty," in a wonderful act of balancing various delicacies he is able to manage it. Inside a pine log, Paul discovered a length of pith that resembled a cast-off snake skin. When he removed the pith and immersed it in a nearby pond, it seemed to "melt" away, only to rise up further off "as a girl" with "wet hair heavy on her like a helmet." This girl Paul took for his wife; but, removing her to a secret place in the woods, he didn't want anyone to so much as mention her. If someone did, Paul immediately left camp and moved to another location.

Here one can analogize that Frost is pitting the value of nature against the worth of civilization, making out the latter to be crude, comparatively. Paul, as superior to ordinary men as wild strawberries are superior to cultivated ones, like a married Thoreau or a St. Francis, is unwilling to be subjected to social vulgarities. Frost has another lumberjack, Murphy, at the very end of the poem express the idea that "Paul/Wouldn't be spoken to about a wife/In any way that the world knew how to speak." It is my conviction that Frost, with his "excruciating sensibilities" or sensitivities, was like Paul—in fact, he almost certainly was writing about himself in this poem. So sentient and superior was he, it was hard for him to try to communicate with people in the way "the world knew how to speak."

Of all the keys then that might be used to unlock this poet, perhaps subtlety would be the best to use to gain entrance to his world. Take the poem, "Home Burial," which is full of subtlety—and heartache. A country wife, having lost what seems to have been an only child, is disconsolate. Because her husband has himself dug with a shovel the grave for the child, she believes he is unfeeling and unfit to remain with. She says to him: " 'I saw you from that very window there,/Making the gravel leap and leap in air,/Leap up, like that, like that, and land so lightly. . . .' " He, on the defensive, with deepest wisdom observes: " 'A man must partly give up being a man/With womenfolk' "; then, later: " 'I shall laugh the worst laugh I ever laughed./I'm cursed. God, if I don't believe I'm cursed.' " But with all his talk he cannot convince her that he loved the child as much as she did, and she exclaims: " '*You*—oh, you think the talk is all. I must go—/Somewhere out of this house. How can I make you—' " She is opening the door, and he exclaims, " 'Where do you mean to go? First tell me that./I'll follow and bring you back by force. I *will*—' "

Here, in common speech, without a trace of rhetoric, is domestic drama as moving to a reader versed in Frost's subtlety as anything in literature. To get his effects (and his listeners), Shakespeare resorted to the "sounding" phrase, which always lends at least a suspicion of falsity or insincerity. But Frost's method embraces the very heartbeat of honesty, suffering, joy. Knowing drama as he did, and being aware of its great potentials, it was as if he resolved to remove drama from the theater into our homes where it could be more intensely and intimately meaningful.

All is in exquisite balance in Frost, and reading him to the peak of his value is like climbing a birch tree in order to "swing" it, as he describes the performance in his famous poem "Birches." As anyone who has climbed to the top of a birch tree must know, getting there is like writing poetry, an act of precision and poise. In Frost's poem, the climbing boy is pictured in these words: "He always kept his poise/To the top branches, climbing carefully/With the same pains you use to fill a cup/Up to the brim, and even above the brim." (As a tree-swinging boy myself, I was also fascinated by the "skin" of water which allows one to fill a cup or spoon beyond its rim. We used to float needles on it!) As you step on "black branches" and rise high in the white tree, you may hold your breath in the same kind of excitement that Frost describes in his playing-with-fire poem, "The Bonfire." Balance, care, or subtlety is the thing. That and clear-headedness, because this is not a wine-time, but a cold spring-water-time. Perhaps it could be said to be something like trying to pin yourself as an angel on top of your Christmas tree; and, while doing angel- or bird-thinking, the big question is this: Are you going to choose the direction of your sudden downward flight by *not* going beyond the height where you can control or direct it; or, by rising on one more doubtful branch, are you going to leave that choice to the tree—or a chance breath of wind? If you do the first, you may call yourself in philosophy or science a determinist; if you decide on the second procedure, you are a transcendentalist, or a quantum-mechanics operator.

Frost described himself at the end of his poem as being in the second category. After declaring that "Earth's the right place for love," he says he'd like to climb *toward* heaven until the tree could no longer sustain his weight, "but dipped its top" and returned him with a rush back to the ground. And it is exactly with this sort of approach that one must read Frost if he would reach Frost's peak of subtlety. This poetry is not laid out before you, openly, like Whitman's. It is not "spectator" poetry, but poetry of implication. The reader is required to participate in it—become a poet himself while reading it.

Thus Frost is truly a seeder of new poets. Emerson claimed to be "a harbinger of poets to come," and Frost is one of the poets of that prophecy who, however, having the advantage of sophistication derived from modern science and psychology, has outdistanced the Concord philosopher-poet, and, in the subtle use of subtlety, possibly every poet. This device reveals the biggest difference that exists between him and Whitman. These two may properly be called the greatest American poets. Yet how dissimilar they are! If there are two sides to everything, we might liken the two poets to the two sides of the American dollar. However, I'd put Frost, not Whitman, on the front because of Frost's completeness, his taking into account all the complexities and subtleties of life, such as the element of humor (which Whitman didn't acknowledge), and making the very greatest use of them.

ROBERT FROST

No arrangement allows a place of honor for all essays. The last section was originally intended as an afterword in which the editor made a few remarks that closed the volume. But the other two essays in this section, written by men who very much appreciate Frost, are so perceptive as to deserve a section by themselves that is in some way specially entitled.

James Cox writes sensitively about the "compleat Frost" as a major figure in the great tradition that includes Emerson and Thoreau. John Lynen writes a relaxed study of "Directive" that both explicates the poem and shows the significance of its author. And so Robert Frost has much more than an afterword citing him as Man Thinking about the miracle and the mystery of what is.

J. T.

Robert Frost and the End of the New England Line

JAMES M. COX

THERE are probably many New England lines, but the one I shall pursue begins with Emerson, runs through Thoreau, and ends with Frost. I know of course that the line is older than Emerson. Certainly, enough scholars want to trace everything New England back to the Puritans; and it includes more than Emerson, Thoreau, and Frost. Not only are there the Schoolroom poets, Bryant, Longfellow, J. R. Lowell, Holmes, and Whittier. There is the incorrigible Emily Dickinson. Finally, many would no doubt argue that the line hasn't even ended. They would point out Robert Lowell, who dropped out of Harvard, went to school to Ransom and the Fugitives, became a conscientious objector in World War II, and converted to Catholicism. That's being Protestant in the great tradition. Certainly Emily Dickinson and Robert Lowell share much with Emerson, Thoreau, and Frost. They are rebels in the original revolutionary sense. So I don't wish to exclude them, these true New Englanders. Yet when I present Emerson, Thoreau, and Frost together, I think that the identity of my New England group is at once more sound and more clear than if I went on to include the Schoolroom poets or Emily Dickinson or Robert Lowell.

For Emerson, Thoreau, and Frost are in line—a line of descent. Each descendant refers directly back to his antecedent. Thoreau *is* Emerson's spiritual son. (To be sure, he is not the only son, for there is Whitman, who, by fostering another line, merely reminds us of what a mighty father Emerson was.) And Frost in turn looks back constantly to both Thoreau and Emerson. Again and again in his poetry as well as out of it, he is both directly and indirectly relating his work to theirs.

Emerson *is* the beginning. Beginning was at once his achievement and his problem. Rooted in the past as he was and deep in his descent from New England theology, he set about in *Nature* to assert an original relation between man and the universe. Looking out on the

Concord battlefield from his residence in the Old Manse sixty years after the Declaration of Independence, Emerson meant to free himself into his own new country in the West. Oliver Wendell Holmes was indeed speaking for his contemporaries when he observed that Emerson in "The American Scholar" had voiced their Declaration of Independence.

Already in *Nature* the essential Emersonian harmony was sounded. It was, as everyone knows, at once hortatory, oracular, and poetic, but the medium was the prose essay. Emerson wrote poetry, even inspired poetry, but it was the essay—the instantaneous effort, the abrupt surge of the idea assuming shape, direction and force—that was Emerson's form. And his line in the essay was a true sentence; that is, it was a thought carrying conviction in the form of a judgment sufficiently complete to put a genuine period to discursive movement. By stringing a series of such sentences in a line devoted to encircling a particular abstraction—be it nature, history, character, politics, self-reliance, love, or friendship—Emerson at his best could compress at the same time he possessed his subject.

Emerson was by inheritance, by training, and by temperament a preacher. To be sure, he left the ministry, but that act reflected a determination to spiritualize the secular in a new birth of religion. Throughout Emerson's essays, there sounds the evangelical admonition—a clarion call for action. But action for Emerson is really a reflection of the soul. That is why Emerson's primordial act is Man *seeing* Nature. If he truly sees nature, then he becomes a transparent eyeball, and if he becomes that, he can truly see nature. That is the first and last metaphor for Emerson.

Indeed, if the form of evangelical appeal provides the hortatory aspect of Emerson's harmony, the metaphoric charge in his style gives his admonitions oracular and poetic identity. Metaphor is no decoration for Emerson. As Jonathan Bishop rightly insists, metaphors are not keys to meaning so much as they *are* meaning—for a man's metaphors mean what they say. Metaphors are thus the substantive forms which constantly act out the content of the Emersonian style. Every metaphor is an expression, in the form of radically experienced or "read" perception, of the relation of man to nature. As the very words on the page convert eyesight to insight, so does the tyrannous imagination answer thought with metaphor. If there is no answer then, for Emerson, there has been no thought, since metaphors are the necessary as well as the inevitable equivalents of thought.

Given Emerson's assault upon discursive logic with metaphor, it is small wonder that narrative was all but annihilated. The closest Emerson comes in his essays to anything resembling narrative is parable so compressed that it assumes metaphoric rather than anecdotal identity in his sequences. And given Emerson's subordination not merely to the ideal but to the Idea, the writer's persona is never allowed to become personality as it does in Lamb's delightfully informal extended observations. For Emerson is never the observer precisely because his active will is driving him to be the Seer. The "I" of his essays is, in short, always striving to be the Eye. That, after all, is not only the point but the act of his initial eye metaphor.

Thus the self, if it is truly active, is for Emerson always becoming the soul. The "I" is becoming the Eye; and personality is becoming character. That is why it is not accidental but fatal that Emerson should have an essay on character. Anyone who knows his Emerson almost has to know what character in the Emersonian world has to be. First of all, character is inward. It is a quality of being before it is a form of behavior. It is, as Emerson insists, a latent power, "a reserve force which acts directly by presence, and without means." Though it is related to personality, character is also an expression of a given man's relation to Nature and the Oversoul. Finally, character is a dominant force, a prevailing quality which must be acknowledged by those around it. The very way in which Emerson defines character reveals how much he himself wants to possess it—for it is a forceful presence without which achievement and dominion are all but impossible. It is not too much to say that Emerson had a conscious desire to possess the very character of New England, thus embodying within himself those virtues which would at once invigorate and illuminate the region. And it is not too much to say that Emerson, more than anyone before him, expressed the ideal character of his region in his own eloquent presence.

Thus, when Emerson says in "Self-Reliance," "Trust thyself. Every heart vibrates to that iron string," we can still hear the authentic voice of the character of New England. There is the hortatory imperative; there is the aphoristic compression; and there is the metaphoric equivalent of the abrupt exhortation. All are bound together to form the essential Emersonian harmony, and hearing it we feel the deep identification of thought and action with virtue. We know that when we use the word *character* we have in mind at least two possibilities: first, a moral force which a person possesses; second, a dramatic or personal identity which a person is. Now Emerson by no means excludes the direct personal identity in his definition, but clearly he feels that the indwelling moral spirit takes precedence over the external presentation of self. It is after all this precedence which illuminates behavior and guarantees a prior dimension of personal behavior to that which can be called social.

There is no better way to see Emersonian character exemplified than by reading Thoreau. For Thoreau's very existence seems rooted in the prior presence of Emerson—so rooted that many Thoreauvians feel a compulsion to extricate their man from the domination of the father. They are not entirely wrong, for Thoreau felt the same urge, and though he remains clearly in the line of descent from Emerson, the identity of his own line is in good measure a sharp retort against the parent. Yet the retort is Emersonian in spirit. Emerson had not wanted disciples; whatever of god he had in him, and whatever influence he felt himself having on the young, his dream was of bringing forth self-reliant men. He wanted to be a prophet in the true sense, which meant that, rather than merely predicting the future, he was determined to call it into being. Thus, he called for an American Scholar, and there was Thoreau; and he called for an American poet, and there was Whitman.

Thoreau and Whitman were not echoes of but genuine responses to Emerson's prophetic call. Whereas Whitman expanded his Emersonian universe, Thoreau contracted and concentrated his inheritance. This contraction was not a shrinkage so much as it was a possession—a making of his world so much a part of him that whatever external nature he touched seemed an expression of himself. If Whitman set forth upon the open road and sought a passage to India, Thoreau came at last to find full sufficiency in a pond almost at his feet. The pond reflected Thoreau's essential self; at least that was the reflection in which Thoreau determined to cast his life.

Even to think about Thoreau's act of style and vision is to see the similarity and distinction between his work and Emerson's. Emerson had become the transparent eyeball—rather, had set that metaphor as his ideal act. Thoreau, on the other hand, says at the outset of *Walden* that, though other writers drop the first person singular, he intends to retain it. And so Thoreau in the very act of exemplifying the Emersonian ideal of self-reliance, begins to regain individuality and narrative. He sets himself in space; and, for all his emphasis on toeing the line of the present, he unfolds in time. It is no ordinary time and space that Thoreau inhabits, however, but an extended parable in which the "I" is related to universal man by virtue of its particularity and isolated atomic completeness rather than—as in Whitman's line—by its pervasiveness, enlargement, or containment. Whitman breaks down distinctions; Thoreau seeks them out. And so, as he brings Emersonian man into time, space, and particularized ego, he widens the gap between general and particular, between individual and universal. But that widening, instead of attenuating the relationship, actually sharpens and intensifies it. Thus, the more singular and eccentric the individual becomes, the more purely he must embody the ideal. Otherwise, he will fall into the mere role of village hermit or town loafer—that form of "character" which society tolerates with bemused indulgence. The Thoreauvian "I" is eccentric because he dramatizes in the very procedure of his consciousness the paradoxical resolution of what seem startling juxtapositions. Thus Walden, which is at the edge of the village, is made to seem far away—has become far away—precisely because the minds of the villagers have in effect moved away from it. In submitting to the social contract they have betrayed nature. And so, while Thoreau may seem recalcitrant, even whimsical, to the village, he is reestablishing and vitalizing the relationship between mind and nature. So, too, Thoreau does not become the transparent eyeball precisely because he keeps enough of his "I" to force Nature herself to become Earth's Eye—and Earth's Eye is, of course, Walden. As Earth's Eye, the pond becomes the mirror in which Thoreau can see his essential self. By treating man and nature as sufficiently separate entities, Thoreau can give to every relationship which affirms their essential identity both pungency and stringency. He thus tends to drive the two entities apart in order to generate their attraction. That very will to perceive duality in order to annihilate it with a startling counterthrust of unity results in the proliferation of paradoxes which at times annoyed Emerson and should annoy us. Yet Emerson saw and was grateful for the essential concreteness of Thoreau's style and vision. "In reading him," Emerson observed of Thoreau's journal, "I find the same thought, the same spirit that is in me, but he takes a step beyond, and illustrates by excellent images that which I should have conveyed in a sleepy generality. 'Tis as if I went into a gymnasium and saw youths leap, climb, and swing with a force unapproachable though their feats are only continuations of my initial grapplings and jumps." There, in all but naked family metaphor, is the father claiming paternity as he graciously but a trifle wistfully acknowledges the son's supersession of the parent. And the son transcends because he is the vigorous *embodiment*, the concrete presence, of the parent's spirit.

In order to embody the Emersonian ideal in the form of his own experience (and surely *Walden* is such an embodiment), Thoreau had to drive himself—the retained "I"—between man and nature in such a way that his very consciousness, which is to say his style, becomes the individuated act relating the two energies. That is why his retained "I" was visible to Emerson's eye as the concrete embodiment of the prior visionary ideal.

This individuality, standing out everywhere in Thoreau's style, makes it at once more paradoxical, more ironic, more droll, more recalcitrant, more eccentric, more "antisocial"—in a word, more *conceited*—than the style of Emerson. But if Thoreau's consciousness is more individuated than that of Emerson it is not therefore more revolutionary. For Emerson stands behind Thoreau as the great original, a source of exemplary awareness which makes a future not only possible but necessary. Thoreau is the great fact which Emerson's exhortation promised. His fine consciousness is nothing less than the presence of what was promise in Emerson.

Seeing Frost in relation to Emerson and Thoreau brings clarity of identity to all three writers. Born in March 1874, Frost emerges after the Civil War, the war which had at once fulfilled and killed both Emerson and Thoreau. Thoreau actually died of consumption while the war raged in the South. Though Emerson lived on till 1882, he was really finished as a writer by 1866, the date of "Terminus," his remarkable poem declaring the end of his creative force. The war was not of course the answer to the prayers of Emerson and Thoreau, but they had submitted sufficiently to abolitionism to be bound to the war against slavery. Both men knew that slavery of mind was possible in the abolitionist mentality as well as on the southern plantation; indeed there was always a sense in which neither man could submit to the perversions of reform idealism or patriotic idealism which inevitably occur in war. Yet just as clearly their admiration for Captain John Brown called for vengeance against the society which martyred the fierce prophet. No admirer of Thoreau could wish that he had outlived the war, yet who would have wished him not to see his America take up the struggle to free itself from chattel slavery. If Thoreau died away from the War, Emerson lived to harden in it—as Thoreau too might have had to harden had he lived through it. It was Emerson who wanted the harsher policies of reconstruction, not that such policies were necessarily wrong (we still do not know that they would have been wrong, though it is hardly more certain that they would have been right). It is simply that, as Emerson settled for war, he lost the instantaneous dialectic energy which animated his vision. Instead of Man in America, he descended into the American. The process had begun before the war, but the war provided a kind of excuse for Emerson to stop thinking. It was the history in which he complacently came to lodge. By the time Frost was born, Emerson had ceased to write except for occasions and eulogies. He was carted about to church and lectures as an all but dead memorial to the life he had once so keenly lived. In the month that Frost was born Emerson's literary activity consisted of little more than praising the memory of Charles Sumner. He had come to the threshold of the blessed forgetfulness which overtook him in his last years, the years when he serenely but helplessly obeyed his youthful exhortation to forget the past.

If Emerson had been the promise of New England, and Thoreau its pure but fiercely individual present, Frost was to be its memory, its tradition. As the embodiment of New England survival, Frost's form and line changed from prose to poetry. Traditional lyric, dramatic, and pastoral forms are at last embodied by a genuine New England voice. Emerson and Thoreau of course considered themselves poets, yet the very fact that their efforts at actual verse were weaker than their flights in prose indicated their restiveness in traditional poetic forms. Though Emerson in "Hamatreya" had sounded a blank verse that, though harsh, promised something of Frost's down-to-earth line, Pound is still right in commending Emerson for breaking the back of blank verse. Pound knew that in embracing tetrameter and trimeter, Emerson had deliberately sought to challenge the royal iambic line, so dominant in English verse. The journals of both Emerson and Thoreau abound with lamentations about the tameness of English poetry. Yet for all their calls and directions to themselves to write a wilder line, their own efforts at poetry never began to meet their own ideals.

It is Frost who from the beginning to the end of his life continued to find a voice authentically regional and at the same time genuinely poetic. Both Emerson and Thoreau had spoken for their region. Emerson had, as it were, called for the New England American to stand up for his country. Thoreau just as clearly had stood up. But their language, though it clearly assumed individual stylistic identity, did not take on a distinct Yankee aspect. We can see the New England Yankee in them, but we see the exemplary presence first. We are wrong to see them as Yankees. Even Thoreau, who shows, as Emerson observed, the decisive grasp of homely language, remains more identified with nature and principle than with time and space. Thus, concrete though he is and acutely individual in point of view and style, Thoreau does not come down to earth any more than he fully comes down to narrative. The narrative of *Walden*, the Thoreau of *Walden*, and even the Walden of *Walden* all stand in a binding, and even subsidiary, relation to the principles they represent. Thus Thoreau, particular though he is, stands for Man reflected by Nature; his linear time is encircled by the yearly cycle; similarly, Walden is the self-contained image of nature and God more than it is the Massachusetts pond. All this is obvious, but it can be forgotten in the praise of Thoreau the Yankee individualist, the concrete expression of the Emersonian ideal. The pond, the man, the experience are great because Thoreau made them stand for so much even as he sought their particularity. Their standing for so much is a measure of Thoreau's belief in their being ultimately representative rather than particular.

Now in Frost something quite distinct takes place. He assumes a much more Yankee identity than either Emerson or Thoreau had done. If he rises to poetry, he nonetheless brings language down to earth. As to his being a Yankee, we need to be careful, for Frost's name was Robert *Lee* Frost, his father having had enough Yankee perversity in him to name his son after the fallen southern leader. Moreover Frost was born in San Francisco, and made his way back to a decaying New England. He lived in that historical time when New England, particularly the New England north of Boston, for all its having been on the victorious side in the Civil War, lost almost as decisively and almost as much as the South had lost. It lost in population, industry, and wealth. What it got in return was a regional identity—precisely because it, almost as much as the South, had lost to a rapidly centralizing process. Local color writing after the Civil War reflected an instinctive emotional awareness of such a loss. Regions took shape as imaginative rural havens which still had "characters" inhabiting them as the "nation" plunged on toward incorporation, standardization, and federalization, those processes forever certified by the triumph of the urban and industrial North.

In determining to be a poet, Frost entered time and form in a way different from that pursued by Emerson and Thoreau. They had lived in forms in which idea precedes experience. Though each of them put pressure upon their ideas, their ideas nonetheless retain priority. Indeed it is the strategy of both Emerson and Thoreau to try their ideas so vigorously, to put so much earthly and experiential pressure upon them, that the idea, like Emerson's Sphinx, is brought to life to dance in mystery. Radical as Thoreau is when he says he wished to drive life into a corner to find whether it were mean or great, there is a closed option in his very conception. We may have no doubt about his having embarked upon such a radical experiment (indeed his language is itself the convincing experience he has brought back), but we can be just as sure that he began with an equally radical hypothesis that he would make good—that in other

words he would spiritualize nature more than he would be natural-
ized by it. He may want to run after a woodchuck, but in the end
he will forego the eating of meat to feast on the spirit. For Nature
is always for Thoreau, and for Emerson too, more spirit than matter.
It is the way man gets outside himself to find in the blessed universe
the God that is in him.

How different is Frost's relation to Nature and to his audience.
If his region is a historical emergence signifying a certain lostness
and pastness, a resistance toward everything that runs away, his
form is itself a means of keeping and marking time, rather than being
a means of asserting his relation to time or denying such a relation
by way of asserting the eternity of the moment. What, after all, is
the rhythm of the poem but a means of keeping time? The fact that
Frost welcomes such a rhythm is evident in his adherence to traditional forms. He eschews the free verse of Whitman because he
wants to be held in an older suspension. His whole poetic enterprise
is to breathe into the traditional forms not something newer than
they are, but something just as old. Thus, if the forms are familiar,
so will be the poet. Whatever is new in him will be new in the way
that the form can express such newness and still retain its traditional
identity. To be equal to the time of the form—that is Frost's kind of
democracy. And to be equal to it does not mean to accept it passively
but to embrace it fully. At his best, Frost does just this. He seems
literally to have embodied the forms, to have put himself into them
as if they were garments made to fit him. Lyric, dramatic monologue,
ballad, song, sonnet, pastoral eclogue, narrative verse, epigram, riddle, mock epic—all the poetic past is brought visibly down upon
him, not as burden but as inheritance for him to stand up in. What
is probably most remarkable about Frost's poetry is that the self
which stands up in all the forms is decisively continuous, gaining
coherence and singularity by virtue of the variety of play among
the forms of poetry. Tennyson, it is well to remember, had mastered
all the possibilities of English prosody, but the Tennysonian "self"
is not so decisive as Frost's. That is why Tennyson becomes the
spokesman of his age rather than the spokesman of himself.

The moment we confront this continuous self of Frost's, which
gained dominance as the poetry unfolded, we are facing Frost's

act of language. His language, as everyone knows, is colloquial and regional just as his identity is rural. Being rural, though it inevitably incorporates pastoral forms and attitudes, is something quite different from being pastoral. Frost is as much farmer poet as he is poet farmer. He equalizes those terms—or democratizes them, we might say—to the point of being able to reverse their order. Thus he can articulate himself as the two voices of poet and farmer which resonate both against and with each other to make a poem. "Mending Wall" is nothing less than the signal of just such a harmony—and it is a distinctly different harmony from that of Emerson or Thoreau. Emerson had exhorted his audience in "The American Scholar" to remain Man Thinking or Man on the Farm rather than descend into the role of mere thinker or farmer. But Frost is clearly willing to risk such descents of play. To hear the farmer, the poet must be near him; to hear the woman, the poet must all but give himself to her speech. All this amounts to coming down to earth. And such a descent of course risks folksiness. Indeed when Frost divides himself into poet and farmer, as he does in "Mending Wall," surely one of his self-defining poems, he runs the risk of being elfin and whimsical on the one hand or complacent and platitudinous on the other. The whimsical or mischievous voice is brought, by virtue of the ground of the poem—the *frost*-heaved stone fence—and also by virtue of the resistant platitude, to rise to the great vision of the poem wherein the farmer is seen to move "like an old stone savage armed." Once having carried himself into this metaphoric flight, the speaker comes back to earth. For Frost's whole imaginative enterprise, unlike Emerson's or Thoreau's, always has to retreat at the end. Here is flight that must not carry itself away; the feet must end securely on the ground; all metaphor is tentative rather than positive. *As if* is Frost's great virtue. Thus even the "bravest that are slain," in "Trial by Existence" (Frost's "Miltonic" poem), go to heaven only to find that their earthly valor commits them once more to the heavenly act of choosing human rather than angelic existence.

This whole commitment to earth is not idea, but act—act in the form of the colloquial poet who embodies the poems. What had been moral character in Emerson has taken the shape of regional character in Frost. The inner youthful ideal character extolled by

Emerson and exemplified by Thoreau becomes the increasingly "old character" of Robert Frost—a little bit wise, a little bit shrewd, a little bit deceptive, carrying his measure of common sense, platitude, joke, tease, and wisdom—carrying it to the measure of poetry.

In a lesser poet the regional, colloquial language would have amounted to nothing more than dialect or local color poetry. But Frost understood that colloquial language was something more than pungent and something greater than quaint. He heard in the rhythms of common, rural speech not only the tone but the intonation of poetry; he saw the vision of such a language. He realized, for example, the skepticism lying so deeply embedded in common speech as to constitute a stance of life. When we hear in everyday language such a statement as "I think it's going to rain," we feel the tone of the verb freeing the speaker from the formal meaning of the word into the informal and much more vague realm of uncertainty. The speaker is not truly *thinking*, we want to say, though the point is that he is not *formally* thinking. Instead he is casually and much more freely speculating, and speculating in such a way as to free himself from the responsibility of prediction or prophecy. This is of course the evasive side of such language, but then the speaker is, after all, dealing with the *weather*—that voice of nature which none can really interpret despite all the satellites, charts, and forecasts designed to predict or control it. Moreover, the speaker is acknowledging an aspect of thought which the formal definition of "think" excludes. Thus "I think it's going to rain" is really a much more precise and much less pretentious way of expressing the relation between man and weather than such wretched language of weather forecasts as, "There is a fifty per cent chance of rain tomorrow." Similarly, when we hear someone say, "I guess I'll go down to the post office," he is likely not "guessing" so much as he is really "going," yet in the tone of such a sentence there is the sound of a deeper sense—a casual, slightly guarded effort to avoid the determined action by keeping an area of free play between intention and act, between will and deed.

This free play, which seems to me close to the heart of so much colloquial speech, is surely the sign of a deep grace of life residing in those who naturally speak such language. Frost heard better than any American poet the sound of that deeper sense. Thus in "The Road Not Taken," the speaker, after contending that he took the less-traveled of two roads, says:

> Though as for that, the passing there
> Had worn them really about the same.

The "as for that" in the first line sounds the emphatic beat of the iambic line at the same time the sense of the phrase relaxes the certitude of the statement, and in the second line the "really" is at once the central as well as the truly colloquial term of the line. And that "really" does not mean *really* much more than it means *perhaps*, reminding us, if we need reminding, that Frost is not changing the meaning of colloquial speech so much as he is discovering it.

The discovery plays a remarkable part in giving Frost's poetry a genuinely new measure. Thus in Frost's blank verse there is often a falling away at the ends of lines sometimes accomplished by feminine endings, sometimes by deploying adverbs and prepositions to bear the burden of a line ending but in such a way as to lighten the weight of movement. Take these famous lines in "Birches":

> Such heaps of broken glass to sweep away
> You'd think the inner dome of heaven had fallen.

There the Shelleyan image from *Adonais* is brought down into playful description of an ice storm. "You'd think" is the fulcrum of the sentence and brings the heightened image into familiar and informal perspective. Later in the same poem, we read,

> I should prefer to have some boy bend them
> As he went out and in to fetch the cows.

The verb "fetch" gives the rural flavor, while the "should" gives what is at once colloquial, archaic, and conditional ease to the preference. The pronoun at the end of the line all but reverses the beat of the last iambic foot in the first line, and the prepositions are made to bear the stress in the second line, greatly accentuating the informal but nonetheless routine rural act of bringing in the cows. To hear these rhythms is to feel how marvelously Frost has bent blank verse to the point where the speaker can catch and be lifted by it.

It is just this sense of ease and grace of life which Frost's poetry sounds. I do not mean that there is no darkness in Frost. There of course is. But those who require the dark Frost in order to "elevate" him into the realm of "serious poetry" invariably miss the delicacy and depth of that fully conditional world where the very nature of experience is registered in language showing always a skeptical edge. That edge, by being slightly evasive about the significance or meaning of an act, is at the same time the instrument which produces the sharp and precise image or impression. It is as if by relinquishing his hold on the Emersonian unity behind nature, Frost had enabled himself greatly to increase his hold upon the earth.

Indeed Frost's skepticism and relativism, though they have deeply qualified the transcendental realm of Emerson and Thoreau, have if anything merely made his eye for nature more acute. They have seemingly relaxed his mind (part of that relaxation is a guise to put us off our guard), thereby releasing him to the possibilities of narrative and dramatic form. So relaxed, so at ease in his sharply defined and limited nature, Frost can apparently take life as it comes. I say apparently because Frost's ease is really a finely balanced poise between nature and society which relieves him from some of Thoreau's outright hostility to society and frees him to be, as he would put it, "not quite social." Poised though he is for flight into nature, he never quite flees. That is why there is a touch of fantasy in Frost's visions of solitude. He *knows* that he will stay in society to hear the endless talk-talk; that is why his threat to go to Hudson's Bay is empty; and that is why he says in "An Empty Threat,"

> Better defeat almost
> If seen clear
> Than life's victories of doubt.

That "almost" followed by the added conditional line beautifully illustrates Frost's mastery of the futile aspect of his dreams of freedom. The language itself is the balance of the speaker's life. Its colloquial ease makes him almost helplessly a social, even a sociable, animal. Its skepticism, which is inseparable from its ease, expresses the wild and furtive caution he has toward everything around him— toward nature, which in Frost's New England encroachingly threatens to repossess the fields that man once cultivated; and toward man, who, dissatisfied by his urban conquest of nature, stands acquisitively ready to seize the fields once again—this time in the name of escape from the cities.

Frost's skepticism is no mere antagonism to be satisfied by or expressed in an idea of unbelief. That is why polemical forms are insufficient for him. Frost's skepticism is a means of doubting unity enough to need another voice both to corroborate and express his own existence, and so releases him to dramatic form—the outright division of himself into a unified mimesis of opposing and harmonizing "other" voices. It is a means of doubting morality and spirit enough to convert principle to pleasure, thereby realizing himself more fully in story and song—which is to say narrative and poetry—than either Thoreau or Emerson could. Above all, it is a means of doubting himself enough to need humorous self-exposure as a defense against that part of himself which feels betrayed by his own skepticism.

The part of him which feels betrayed is surely the Emersonian self-belief and self-trust which Frost has so deeply inherited. Frost's colloquialism, skepticism, and humor are thus not inversions of Emerson but descents from him.

In 1924 Frost wrote a wonderful letter to Louis Untermeyer which tells all but everything. Embarking upon a discussion of style, he argued that style was not the man but rather the way a man "carries himself toward his ideas and deeds." He went on to say:

The style is out of his superfluity. It is the mind skating circles round itself as it moves forward. Emerson had one of the noblest least egotistical of styles. By comparison with it Thoreau's was conceited, Whitman's bumptious. Carlyle's way of taking himself simply infuriates me. Longfellow took himself with the gentlest twinkle. . . . I own any form of humor shows fear and inferiority. Irony is simply a kind of guardedness. So is a twinkle. It keeps the reader from criticism. Whittier, when he shows any style at all, is probably a greater person than Longfellow as he is lifted priestlike above consideration above the scornful. Belief is better than anything else, and it is best when rapt, above paying its respects to anybody's doubt whatsoever. At bottom the world isn't a joke. We only joke about it to avoid an issue with someone to let someone know that we know he's there with his questions: to disarm him by seeming to have heard and done justice to his side of the standing argument. Humor is the most engaging cowardice. With it myself I have been able to hold some of my enemy in play far out of gunshot.

When Frost speaks of belief being better than anything and being best when rapt, he is surely referring back through Whittier to that most noble, least egoistical style of Emerson. And when he speaks of the world being, at bottom, no joke, he is still acknowledging the Emersonian priority of rapt belief and also acknowledging that humor ultimately defers to that priority. Now when he goes on to say that his own humor is a kind of engaging cowardice to keep his enemies at play, though he is explicitly referring to contemporary poetic and social rivals, I think that he is implicitly referring to Emerson. For his humor is surely there to disarm even as it affirms the transcendental fathers.

Yet if Emerson has priority in Frost's own mind, Frost's irony and humor give him a dimension of humanity which Emerson's austerity precludes. If Frost looks at the world less boldly, he looks upon it more kindly because he is aware of his own weaknesses. If he has less virtue, he had more humor, which means that he can tell a joke as well as take one. If he has less belief in heaven, he has a stronger hold on the planet. God in Frost's skeptical universe, far from ceasing to exist, becomes the very principle of uncertainty—the force that may or could be the condition behind every conditional. And if Frost doubts the imagination and even poetry more than Emerson or Thoreau dared doubt it (perhaps it would be better to say that his doubt is an absence of their will to believe), his skepticism has brought him back in powerful touch with fancy, that faculty of associative play and pleasure which Coleridge so decisively depreciated. These are the gains—what we might call the purchases—on the path of descent. They are not points of refuge so much as they are strongholds where imaginative leverage can be powerfully exerted—where, in other words, the earth itself seems sufficient ground on which to stand and does not have to be transformed into symbolic nature. Relations with God may be more tentative, but relations with people, if not more happy, are certainly more necessary. And so, sweet though solitude remains, love is truly equal to it. Thus, what must be Frost's greatest lines—lines which reveal the grace and loss and gain of all Frost's life and language—are simply these:

Earth's the right place for love:
I don't know where it's likely to go better.

Du Côté de Chez Frost

To consider Frost's place in modern literature is to adopt, per-
force, a double perspective; for the modern world of Frost was the
world of Einstein and Eliot, of Mann and Stravinsky, a world which
ours includes but which, through time's distancing, we perceive as
but a part of a larger epoch that not only contains the eleven years
since Frost's death, but extends backward to include much of what,
through the invocation of that grand epithet, "Victorian," used to
be defined as safely historical. The modernity of Frost's time can
now be understood as modernism in its early classical phase, a phase
of witty formalism and acerb candor which began to be replaced
shortly after World War II by the now already somewhat deli-
quescent romantic phase initiated with the revival of picaresque fiction by Ellison, Bellow, and Salinger. With the arrival of the "Beat"
poets, hard upon this novelistic flowering, a new period had dawned,
in which formal indeterminacy and the submerging of aesthetics in
sociology would be leading features. Now intensity rather than
classical clarity was valued, and the artlessness of "open-ended"
forms served to make insistent a range of new questions. To what
end form? Meaning? The unity of the literary work? Surely the
things a poem was "about" mattered more, and these were to be
"lived" (as in Whitman, poet and reader "become" the objects they
jointly perceive). They were not to be contemplated, for that meant
"turning them into objects," which was so necessary a preliminary
to the "exploitation" of things that it might as well be regarded as
the same activity. Indeed there was a dark suspicion abroad that
the very words "form," "meaning," "unity," "literary work" were
double agents, pretending to serve as the names for real things when
they actually functioned as self-answering questions, self-fulfilling
prophecies, representing the literary aspect of what the Cold War
had schooled one to believe was a general entrapment.

562

While the root terms of classical modernism were being discredited in this way, the contrasts that set it off from the past were beginning to seem neither interesting nor especially tenable in the light of a finer historical realization of its indebtedness to the nineteenth century. Now Yeats was to be seen as the descendant of Shelley and Blake, and the prestige of Stevens grew as his wit and Protean emotional nature were overshadowed by the grandeur of his apocalyptic humanism. What had recently been called self-pity was now restored, free of Hardyesque liver spots, as a proper compassion for one's own difficulties, an attitude justified by certain convictions about the divinity of human nature.

Thus, by a repossession of the last third or so of the nineteenth century, the modern age has come to include the whole of Frost's life. And yet, for that very reason, it may now be well to remind ourselves of his historical remoteness—to recall that in the year of Frost's birth Donizetti and Metternich belonged to a more recent past than Alban Berg and Franklin Roosevelt do with respect to today, that Browning and Tennyson were still writing, Emerson and George Sand still living, and none of the major works of Hardy or James as yet published. Indeed Frost had already lived a third of his life by 1903, when *The Ambassadors* appeared, yet even at that date the advent of modernism was still some years in the future. The more that that movement has come to seem an episode in a more generously defined modern age, the less there seems to be to generalize upon, for the fewer are the features distinctively modern enough to define the field we premise. One might suppose that, like "reality" in the poems of Wallace Stevens, the "modern," though assuredly real, is forever beyond the mind's reach in that the very perception of it so transforms it (to all sorts of human benefit, admittedly) that it is no longer the thing we sought. Is Frost's relation to modern literature, then, a discussable—even a "thinkable"—subject? Without an unseemly effort to be definite, can one find some feature of the modern that, in Stevens' happy definition of modern poetry, "will suffice?" [1] Such a question gets the answer it deserves in the word chaos, a word so mercifully vague that, like the hole in the doughnut, its conceptual necessity need not trouble us. It seems to be universally agreed that the modern world has one certain feature, the lack of order consequent to the collapse of old organizing myths and/or faiths and the ethical codes that formerly expressed them.

Yet the modern sense of chaos is not, itself, chaotic; by its effects we can come to know something about it. In particular we can recognize its influence upon our idea of meaning, which it defines as a significance sought, rather than discovered. Thus meaning is transformed into a motive, a shaping force, and experience takes on the form of a quest—a search for discoveries that are self-reflexive in that they are not truths about things found, but truths about the process of seeking.

Thus the modern sense of chaos simultaneously psychologizes whatever questions are to be asked and temporalizes the answers. If what is to be found is the process of discovery, one consequence is that the seeking demands translation into psychological terms. To understand the issues, we must first understand the mind entertaining them. But, then, the answers that are found are projected outward into the world to be seen as actual events transpiring in time. For the answers are simply truths about the process of discovery. They are proved by being dramatized. We see them as real by seeing them as a step-by-step sequence of events that really happened or is happening.

In making some observations on "Directive," I will try to illustrate the import of this dual psychologizing and historicizing, as it manifests itself in some characteristically modern literary traits, traits which, it is my hope, will serve to place Frost in relation to classical modernist poetry. Stevens' "what will suffice" will be my light and guide, and "Directive" especially commends itself as an example in that this minimal particular is named in the poem's last word—"confusion." Let us start with this one, small element in this one poem, and see where it leads, we too being on a quest, though not, let us hope, more concerned with the style of our footing along the way than with the destination.

In "Directive" the destination is rather noisily announced:

> Here are your waters and your watering place.
> Drink and be whole again beyond confusion.

How oddly assuring this is; how certain we are that an answer to "confusion"—to chaos—is being provided! "Wholeness" holds the promise of a psychological curing and a cultural reintegration that would, as it were, put the world back together. Then, too, the ritualism of drinking from the pure waters of a source would seem to invite whatever conception of spiritual rebirth the reader feels inclined to impute to it. Yet just because the promise is so strongly put, there is also an invitation to look a little unkindly into its reverberant vaguenesses, questioning its take-your-choice spirituality, and, in view of Frost's distaste for easy answers, wondering about certain false notes. For example, "watering place" may suggest the source of the spiritual waters that Christ referred to when speaking to the Samaritan woman, but it may also suggest Bath or a cattle trough. The surmise that Frost is once again treating us to a dry chuckle from the cracker barrel only makes matters worse, for if the spiritual promises are ironically withdrawn, the poem would seem to end so pointlessly as to make our sense of a richly meaningful close a rather inexplicable phenomenon.

To be sure, we are being tested, very much as we are in "Crossing Brooklyn Ferry," when Whitman asks:

What I promis'd without mentioning it, have you not accepted?
What the study could not teach—what the preaching could not
    accomplish is accomplish'd, is it not?

Frost's closing lines must be appreciated as the goal of a quest fraught with trials that only the worthy reader will recognize as important tests. One has to be troubled by the properly Hamlet-like reflections that the things seen along the way can evoke, and ponder at the edge of the cellar hole of the "house in earnest" the sundry defeats of past human effort. Compared to one's regret at the playhouse, it is, as Reuben Brower remarks, "a more serious game to be told, 'Weep *that* out, lose yourself in *that*,' and drop the effort to make yourself at home in an alien world." [2] By the growing seriousness of such meditations we are eventually led to ponder the theological clue of the jesting allusion to St. Mark. As Christ explains: "To you has been given the secret of the kingdom of God, but for those outside everything is in parables; so that they may indeed see but not perceive, and may indeed hear but not understand; lest they should turn again and be forgiven," so in "Directive" the promise of wholeness is given only to those worthy of understanding the poem. "Watering place" is merely one of the more obvious tests of our worthiness in confronting Frost's ambiguous images. Like the star in "Choose Something Like A Star," each image "demands of us a certain height."

The testing aspect of the poem brings us to the point of junction between Frost's aesthetics and his ethics. In Louis Mertins' helpful *Robert Frost: Life and Talks-Walking* we find the poet declaring: "Just set a man against the elements. Let him battle. If he's worth his salt he'll make it. If not, it doesn't much matter. He's got to ride like ice on his own melting. He may make a botch of it, but nothing's irredeemable. I often come back to the woman who in the crowd touched the hem of Christ's garment. It was enough." [3] Frost often used the image of ice riding on its own melting to describe both the form of a poem and the way it is first written in the poet's mind; but here we see that it is also a metaphor for the ethical way of life. The way we should live and the way our minds move as we read a Frost poem are moral experiences in the same sense. Or can be and should be.

Yet the highest response to "Directive's" imagery will not necessarily be that which prefers the most noble interpretations. Perhaps the poem tests us rather perversely by leading us into temptation to ascertain whether we will choose higher meanings when low ones are the honest truth. I do not see anything demonstrably incorrect in the view that those who are made whole by drinking of the brook's waters are those who see the water as of the ordinary faucet variety. Such readers would prove their worthiness by their honesty and courage. For them the trials of the Grail quest are easily passable, armed as they are with the truth that their journey is just a walk in the country. Not ignoring the more threatful or exalting implications of the things along the way, they would let these play as fancy lights about the perimeter of common sense.

By a quarter rotation of such a reading, we find it turn serious, as it does in Robert Peters' comment that: "Through drinking from the goblet-Grail hidden in the cedar, we may come to the wisdom that the self alone is all we have—but that is enough; and by contemplating this stark need for a self-reliant view it is possible to become 'whole again beyond confusion.' " Yet in conceding that this experience is "a religious one," although "only in a broad, almost existential sense," [4] Peters allows for another quarter-turn, whereby the stoicism of facing the facts begins to look so brave as to appear inspirational "high seriousness" of the sort informing Reuben Brower's comment on the closing lines: "there is a Wordsworthian sense of healing power, of passing 'into our first world' and feeling a release and renewal in the act of doing so." [5] Taken in this spirit, the poem invites symbolic readings that Brower himself would shun—for example, Pearlanna Briggs's suggestion that one can interpret the poem as an allegory of Frost's own development. "Frost is saying, 'This is the ordeal by which I became a poet; if you would become a poet, you must undergo a like preparation.' " [6] While other Frost poems cannot prove, they can corroborate the idea that in "Directive," as in "Birches," "Mowing," "After Apple-Picking," or "Evening in a Sugar Orchard," something is being said about Frost as artist. Briggs seems mistaken in neglecting to admit that such allegory is but one dimension of the poem's meaning, but this is merely a partial error, for the allegory is surely "there."

To carry literalism further would seem more imprudent than wicked, as seems the case when Margaret M. Blum advances "A Theological Reading." "The main house," she suggests, represents an "earlier religion (possibly Judaism)," a religion "very near to the source of the living God, of fundamental truth." The playhouse represents Christianity, "closely associated with the main house," and also, "if at second-hand, nourished by the waters of the brook of Truth . . . Christian symbols may well aid one in finding the 'lofty and original' God who still abides despite the vitiating effect of time and institutionalism." [7] In spite of the narrowing explicitness of such a reading, Blum has something to tell us, for surely the contrast between the farm house and the playhouse suggests, among other things that between model and imitation; and this, together with the decay of institutionalized religion and the residual power of old religious symbols, is an aspect of the poem, as is Briggs's art allegory. Both of these critics are in harmony with the mood of high seriousness that Brower finds in the poem's ending. Indeed, Briggs's and Blum's readings seem aimed at giving content to that mood, which one wishes Brower had attempted.

The price of avoiding doing so is shown by the contradictory interpretation of Roy Harvey Pearce, who, while granting Frost all the artistry that Brower would claim for him, finds in his poetry, and in "Directive" in particular, not ennobling insight, but a final evasiveness. To Pearce the poem illustrates a limiting and pretty nearly damning escapism that is so central to Frost's thought as to form the very basis of his artistic techniques. Since the demonstration is one of the great moments of the criticism of American poetry, let me quote a few words from it. "Bartleby was driven to prison and suicide. Frost is driven to mountain and farm, to wholeness 'beyond confusion,' to life simplified." The poet's strategy is essentially that of retreat. "For Frost there is a new order, to be sure; but it is the product of a recovery and reconstitution, rather than of a reinvention and transformation of the old." The cause is Frost's drive towards two forms of achievement—an outward definiteness of image and feeling, and an inward freedom "to define, not to unleash himself." Though Pearce stresses the social cost, his main concern is with what Frost claims to win by such sacrifices—with the quality of the experience the last lines of "Directive" promise us. "Always in Frost there is the desire (or a temptation so strong as to be a desire) to 'go behind' something. And most always there is the failure to do so, and then the triumph in living with the failure and discovering that it is a condition of strength—the strength of discovering oneself as a person, limited by the conditions which can be made clearly to define oneself as a person. This is the subject which 'shall be fulfilled.' " [8] The last lines, then, give us a true experience, but an experience of perceiving no more beyond ourselves than a blank wall. Like Marvell's "green thought in a green shade," and the ultimate reduction of the subject-object relationship in *The Sun Also Rises*— "I swam with my eyes open and it was green and dark" [9]—being whole "beyond confusion" may sacrifice nearly everything to the sense of one's own immediate existence.

Where Brower finds a fulfilled significance, Pearce finds the numb-

ness of touching the noumenal, the effect of the parting of Racine's
Titus and Bérénice, the preternatural calm of Dickinson's "I wish I
were a hay." [10] Brower's fine sense of the rich allusiveness of the
poem makes his reading seem preferable to Briggs's and Blum's because it is more inclusive, but can it either answer or accommodate
itself to Pearce's objections? I find all the difference in the world
between Brower's "What Frost has saved from Wordsworth is
dramatic rediscovery of simplicity and the power to endure" [11] and
Pearce's "Confusion is stayed but from a distance. The distance is
such that the poet could not listen to us even if we did know how
to speak to him." [12] There is a contradiction, not of mere logic, but
of total response to the feel and mood and rhythm of the poem.
Brower speaks of an "inwardness of tone" that "tenderly includes
the reader";[13] Pearce declares that "The opening statement is marked
first by a groping, hesitant syntax, then by a series of strong paral-
lelisms. . . . Thus the poet hesitates and then confronts the modern
world." [14] Reginald Cook offers a comment that agrees with neither
but seems just as nearly true: "It is a poem of robust counsel," whose
prototype is Melville's "Lone Founts," not Wordsworth.[15]

Our problem is that of discovering a principle of inclusion that
will allow for the "real presence" of multiple meanings and tones,
even ones that seem totally at odds, and yet avoid a blurring and
final indefiniteness. For all the readings advance irresistible claims.
The poem does indeed end with a Wordsworthian sense of transfor-
mative insight; and it does also end with a discouragingly hermetic
riddling. It does offer "robust counsel," but also tenderly ruminative
reflections, while at the same time it seems an oratorial casting of
spells. Finally it does project specific allegorical suggestions concerning Frost's own career, the decline of Christianity, and the need for
self-reliance, although these seem but aspects of a wider field of
meaning.

There is an oft-practiced specious solution that appeals to our
sense that poetry is multivocal, the solution of admitting all, accepting contradictory interpretations without considering the differing
senses in which they hold true. One simply agrees that "watering
place" means (1) a source of spiritual grace, (2) a fashionable spa,
and (3) a drinking trough for cows, without discriminating between

the ways in which these meanings apply. But "watering place" is not like a bench that is also a table; it is more like a violinist who is also a socialist. "Is" plays different roles. The way the water the cows drink *is* and the way the water of a font *is* are quite dissimilar modes of existence. We are most apt to fail the test of "Directive," not by "reading things in" or making a poor choice among possible meanings for an image, but by failing to recognize the variety of ways of being of the things named and the multiple frames of reference within which they have their being. Yet we must do more than discriminate between a wide range of modalities and of contexts; we must be continually questioning how one mode or context relates to another. To study this is really to study the process of our own thought as it combines and arranges the multiple levels of meaning it perceives. We must, in sum, make this very process the object of our attention, seeing it, as from a distance, as a story the poem depicts.

Instead of assuming that there is a quest, on the poet's mere say-so, we must ask how the quest comes into being. To be sure, the poem is a "directive," telling us what to notice and how to feel about it, but the mere logic of this would not suffice were it not that in much subtler ways Frost convinces us that the images fit together as things seen in the course of a walk through a woodland, or as ideas naturally suggested by such sights. There has to be a dramatic credibility to our turn of thought as we imagine the glacier bracing its feet "against the arctic pole," just as the quarry-like road, the height of country, the playhouse, farmhouse, and cedar must seem to be arranged along our route through a spatially harmonious landscape.

Now to ask just how this is achieved is to embark on a search that is simultaneously inward and outward. On the one hand, the images are things as they are seen by an observer, and it is in his mind that they are brought to harmony. On the other hand, the objects, through their own intrinsic traits, lead us to perceive them as we do; and thus it is they that create the unity we see in the landscape. For example, we can take two views of the brook "so near its source" that it is "too lofty and original to rage." We can say that the analogies this image suggests—to lofty human character, for instance —result from the mind's creativity in so shaping the object in the process of perceiving it as to infuse it with an added human meaning.

Or we can say that the traits of the brook itself are such as to stimulate in the observer's mind such thoughts of elevated serenity and ennobling loftiness. To look inside is really to look outside, and vice versa: we examine our responses to objects to find the objective traits that inspired them, and we examine the objects to find what thoughts in ourselves they call forth.

Romanticism always "ups the ante"; its solitude tends to turn into alienation, its dream becomes hallucination, its sentiments shade off into compulsions. To the extent that Frost is a later Romantic nature poet, he works under the same obligation as Poe, Tennyson, or Swinburne, and must depict a much more rocky and recalcitrant landscape than the Lake Country if he is to show the creative imagination bringing it to harmony and meaning. Thus instead of a composed, time-mellowed setting, he pictures a raw one, full of angularities and oddities, a landscape more miscellaneous than organic, where agreeable intuitions are jostled by funny doubts. But though a good measure of the "anti-Romantic" leavens the Wordsworthianly rising assurance of "Directive," it is not there just to give the Romantic spirit a harder nut to crack. It is there to bring out, by the sharpest possible contrast, just what the process of unification is; to make the quest itself the main object of attention.

Taking a term from one of Frost's main sources, William James, let us observe our "will to believe" in the quest by noting how many obstructions Frost throws in its way. We accept the route of our journey even though we are told at the outset that the goal is in some sense nonexistent:

> ... a house that is no more a house
> Upon a farm that is no more a farm
> And in a town that is no more a town.

Nor are we puzzled by the advice: "pull in your ladder road behind you," even though we should have been forewarned of its doubtful reality. It "May seem as if it should have been a quarry"; and while in some places it seems to coincide with an actual road "marked by the wear of iron wagon wheels," it soon becomes inferential, a route suggested by things one typically, or perhaps only possibly, might see wherever, in this region, one happened to go. It may then be no more than a personally invented road, defined by the traveler's choice to walk now this way, now that, as he cuts across lots. A road recorded only in this traveler's recollection could, indeed, be pulled in behind him; but it may not even be retained by memory, if he is "lost enough" to find himself; if the self-discovery he is making is the result of spatial disorientation.

He no longer knows where he is, and thus even his immediate surroundings open upon uncertainties. The field "no bigger than a harness gall" is so very small a patch of land as to show, either how much "night seriousness" can make of a trifle, or how little a word can mean. We are close at many moments in this poem to the spirit of "The Jabberwocky" and the Duke's Shakespearean soliloquy in *Huckleberry Finn*. And this is not the least true when we learn of the "house in earnest." One assumes that "in earnest" means "actual," but, taking "earnest" to mean a pledge, one might more properly read "a house in earnest" as a hypothetical house, which we infer by guessing that the hole was its cellar. The same trickiness is manifest in the doubtful sequence in time implied by "First there's the children's house of make-believe," and "Then for the house that is no more a house." We are not really obliged to suppose that the one is seen before the other, since "first" could mean merely first from a logical standpoint, as childhood is prior to adult life, while "Then for the house" could be analogous to "then for a swim," where "then" claims only a connection in thought, and a merely appropriate rather than necessary connection, even there. Our impulse to make more orderly sense of the words than they in fact require becomes the more obvious when we reach the statement:

> Your destination and your destiny's
> A brook that was the water of the house.

We assume that the brook is a more explicit place than by its very nature a brook really can be, for it is natural to think that when the poet says "Here are your waters .../Drink," he refers to the brook just where it passes the old cedar, which in turn is close to the farmhouse. Yet we are reminded by the contrast between the brook upstream and downstream that, after all, "the water of the house" flows all along its course. Evidently our destiny can be the brookside at any point. And in asking how a point in space can also be a destiny, we find ourselves returning to the conception of the poem as test. As the cedar may not be near the house, and the poem does not require the quester to drink from the goblet, the locale that we take to be our goal will depend on ourselves. Just where it will be cannot be separated from the meaning this place holds for us. Our response to the locale, like our response to the words "watering place," will be a judgment upon us.

Frost's words create a significant indeterminacy of meaning that reveals the unity of the quest as something the reader creates, through the strength of his own preference, from inconclusive hints and syntactical equivocations. Our will to believe in the quest is an aspect of the same problem we confront in the multiple conflicting meanings of such images as the playhouse, the goblet, and the brook. Our faith in the reality of the dimension of space, to say nothing of its rational usefulness, depends upon the conviction that there is a real, human significance in being in one place rather than in another. Were all places alike, the idea of place would be both useless and inconceivable. But when we ask what is special about the traveler's place of destination we are simply asking what the meaning is of the objects that define that place—the brook, the cedar, the goblet, the water—or that lead up to it, as objects along our path. The mystery is the coherence of these images as aspects of the scene by the brookside, and, more generally, of the entire landscape we traverse. We can only assume that the setting is composed by a process more profound than the interrelations between the few particular images Frost mentions can account for, but which these illustrate and move our minds to complete. What it is merely plausible to believe, despite the legalistic loopholes I have mentioned, with respect to the arrangement of objects in space, must be necessitated, on a deeper level of thought, by a compulsive logic.

Here we approach at last the cluster of paradoxes upon which the poem is built. My thesis will be that all of them are manifestations of antinomies so habitual in our thinking that they have the power to make the poem's images continuous with those in real experience, thus giving us the illusion of having an experience as we read Frost's lines.

We begin with the paradox of "a time made simple by the loss/Of detail," an earlier time, putatively a time so primitive that it is time of a different sort, as a year in a child's life is different in kind from a year in adult experience. Yet this earlier time is to be conceived in terms of an image expressive of the passage of long periods of time. Its simplicity is like that of statuary and inscriptions whose details have been worn off by erosion, or like the eroded hills in which marble destined for a cemetery still awaits the sculptor. Early time is thus conceptualized with reference to its opposite, much later time, the time after centuries or millenia have passed. Furthermore, the time made simple is not really a time, but a place; it now is somewhere "back out of all this" that we are to go. Conversely the place will not be so much a spatial location as a "time" we will be "in," when we are "out of" the "now too much for us." From the notions that early is late, and time is space, we find ourselves led to the paradoxical unity of being and nonbeing:

> There is a house that is no more a house
> Upon a farm that is no more a farm
> And in a town that is no more a town.

Our guide "only has at heart" our "getting lost." To lose is to find, and vice versa. And it is really we who lose ourselves, for in submitting to his guidance we are acting on our own. Acting and being acted upon are the same. The near disappearance of the town is counterpoised by the survival in a book of the story of this event. Time destroys, but, as history, time preserves. The glacial markings run southeast, but therefore northwest, also. To push south, the glacier braced its feet "against the Arctic Pole."

The "coolness" that the glacier is said still to impart balances the idea of a scrupulously indirect social gesture against the feral connotations of "Panther Mountain," and there is a continuing antithesis of this sort in the succeeding imagery, where the wild, second-growth trees are personified as a silly drawing room set flustered by the traveler, whom they view as an intruder. His "serial ordeal," being stared at by "forty cellar holes/as if by eye pairs out of forty firkins," may suggest the trials of the Grail Knight, while alluding also to the forty thieves in the Arabian Nights, but it is expressed in the language of a social ordeal that the traveler should make light of by resorting to the classic challenge, "Where were they all not twenty years ago?" That will put the trees, whose excitement at the intruder "sends light rustle rushes to their leaves," in their place. The utterly natural suggests the over-artificial, just as we see the "cultivated" replaced by the wild in the plight of the "pecker-fretted apple trees."

The song about the former inhabitant, who may be just ahead with a buggyload of hay, is false yet true; he is long since dead, but we follow him in walking down the same country road, and in moving towards death as our life, too, passes. All flesh is grass (hay). The song, as an original invention, is then contrasted with its opposite, the venerable cliché—as in "high adventure," "high culture," and "high country." By contrasting the figurativeness of the first two with the literal meaning of the last, the speaker shows that "height" as an evaluative term and "height" as a descriptive term can either coincide or exist quite independently. We simply do not know whether it is a coincidence or a matter of necessary connection that makes the "height of the adventure" also the "height/Of country where two village cultures faded/Into each other." Similarly lostness has two aspects: the two village cultures are lost in the sense of disappearing forever; while the quester's lostness, though real enough, may be the means of its opposite—his finding himself.

Far from having disappeared, he is now about to make the road do so. But the road has ceased to be a road, in becoming a ladder, a means of ascension rather than transportation, though one sufficiently inclining from the true vertical to leave us wondering whether, as in Zeno's paradox, there is an absolute point at which a road is too steep to be a road, or whether there is an area of transition between road and ladder. And we may ask by way of analogy, how small a field may be and still deserve the name. If the only field has but the extent of a sore on a horse's back, and the road is so upright as to require rungs, then in using the words "field" and "road" the speaker seems to stress both the difference between a word's meaning and the thing it refers to, and the necessary connection between the two. We can call a ladder a road, different as they are, because some of "road's" meaning applies, and perhaps this is but an exaggerated case of the partial way any word corresponds to its object. On the other hand, we feel that the term is misapplied, because word and referent should more fully correspond.

In its make-believe nature, the playhouse is "no more a house" than the farmhouse, but its nonexistence is of an ideal rather than physical sort. Though it still stands it is not and never was a house. The playthings that once made the children "glad" are now, for that very reason, a cause of weeping. Conversely, the cellar-hole of the *real* house that *doesn't* exist, is ceasing to be a hole. As it fills with lilacs, it resembles a "dent in dough," but the flower of these bushes and the flour of the dough, are quite different, though they are pronounced the same. The brook, whose flow is the archetypal image for becoming, has two different natures at once: calm near its source, turbulent downstream. We can regard it as an image of change—from lofty to low, original to derivative, serene to raging, and so on—but we are also obliged to think of it as an image of static being, for the brook is all these states at once. That is why one has such a strong sense that the lines on the brook bring the poem to a point of resolution. The brook contains just such contradictions as the earlier images, but it bodies its contradictions forth in a physical way that much more fully manifests the conflicting elements as harmonious aspects of a system, necessary parts of that complex thing we call a brook.

The goblet is broken and stolen, but even so it is like the Grail, in its shape, which it still retains, though this shape is now visibly incomplete, in its function as a drinking vessel, though not as a reliquary for sacrificial blood, and in its being hidden, though not from Frost's readers, who are told where to seek it. "The wrong ones" do not include the thief who stole it. The theft is no sin, only make-believe; and in any case he cannot hide it from himself. For concealment no place could be better than the old cedar, a species of tree favored for burial grounds because, as an evergreen, it symbolizes immortality. And yet the cedar is so commonly used in cemeteries that it has become a death symbol too. A rooted, static object, like the chestnut tree of "Among School Children," it yet has an "instep arch" suggestive of the human foot, as Yeats' tree, through its blossoming, leads into the imagery of dancer and dance.

For as the journey is defined by its destination, so, conversely, the static object to which the quester's feet carry him is to be understood in terms of the movement towards it. The journey is implicit in the goal, though the goal itself does not move. This contrast of the static and dynamic is then brought to culmination in the penultimate line, where the "waters"—the brook as thing in the process of becoming—balance "watering place"—the brook as static entity.

These numerous antitheses, and many others which a more detailed reading could, doubtless, amply supply, bring the poem's images to harmony by establishing the principle that opposites are rational polarities. As north implies south, make-believe reality, the complex the simple, the old the new, the serene the turbulent, the literal the figurative, the natural the artificial, the nonexistent the actual, so the poem as a whole, is, for the reader, a continual involvement in the process of resolving apparent opposites into actual unities. In his "In Memory of W. B. Yeats: 1939," one of the many poems that probably lie behind "Directive," Auden declares that "poetry makes nothing happen; it survives/In the valley of its making.../A way of happening, a mouth." And as Auden, like Frost, draws upon the traditional association of water and poetic inspiration:

> In the deserts of the heart
> Let the healing fountain start[16]

so also both poets conceive of the survival of poetry in two senses, both of which suggest an affinity to the thought of Heidegger. First poetry survives in the world ("the valley of its making"), the total human situation out of which the poem, as it were, discloses itself, the ultimate context of the poet's life and our life, of his poem and of our reading of the poem. Second, the poem survives as "a way of happening" which, being a way or process, is repeatable. In this sense, the "valley of its making" is the "mouth" of any reader who, in having an experience with the poem (as Heidegger undertakes to have an experience with language) recreates, and thus, figuratively, speaks it. Each reading is a new historical event for the very reason that the process remains the same.

In "Directive" the way of happening is expressed in a series of antitheses so numerous and subtly interlinked that the reader's mind is continually engaged in a process of "composing" or creatively harmonizing miscellaneous sense data into rational wholes. We are led through a sequence of contrasts so constructed that the naturalness of accepting the first—that a complex present time implies a simple past time—commits us to accepting the second—that this simple past of the new and elementary is very old, indeed, and worn down through the years to its original elements—and this, in turn, induces acceptance of the third antithesis, and so on. Now our immersion in this ongoing process of reconciling antitheses provides the key to the problem of interpreting particular images. For an image, like an antithesis, is really a system of meanings. As in such contrasts as old-new, simple-complex, or natural-artificial there are a practically infinite number of states between the extremes, so in such an image as "drinking goblet" or "watering place" the opposed meanings (water glass-Grail; baptismal font-cow trough) are but the poles defining the outer limits of a whole range of meanings lying between them. Thus the goblet suggests the Eucharistic chalice, and a "watering place" as a fashionable spa falls within the spectrum that font and trough define. The wholeness of spiritual rebirth manifests itself on a more modest level at the springs of the Kurhaus, which produce recreation and health (Old English "hælþ" cognate with Old English "hal," modern "whole.")

All good poems contain meaning systems as complex and inclusive as these. What is distinctive in "Directive" is, first of all, the fact that the meaning systems of its key images are so consistently based on the same pattern throughout—the spectrum created by an antithesis—and, secondly, the point this use of the same pattern seems intended to make, which is that the modern chaos (the "now too much for us") is created, not by total fragmentation, but by the transformation of the world into a diversity of systems of thought. Thus to think of the meaning of Frost's images as meaning systems has the double advantage of clarifying his characteristically modern concern with processes of interpretation while at the same time allowing us to "pin down" images without making arbitrary choices between various aspects of meaning or denying their wide inclusiveness and complexity. One must suppose that with an image, as with the entire context of a poem, the more exact the meaning is the more nearly ineffable it must be, and thus the more hopeless is the task of the critic who imagines he can provide an exhaustive inventory of all it signifies. Criticism will be sufficiently precise if it grants that while a meaning system cannot contain simply anything that the whim of a reader may suggest, one can name but a few of the meanings it *does* contain. For a meaning system is a way of meaning, and one can only describe it as a process; one cannot name all that it can possibly mean. New meanings may come into view in the course of time, as happened when the Romantics discovered the brilliantly imaginative quality of Falstaff's mind and T. S. Eliot discerned the pattern of fertility cults underlying "The Tempest." Such discoveries transform the poem by bringing out its inherent possibilities more fully, and thus clarifying and enhancing, rather than superseding, earlier interpretations.

To say that some meanings are "there" and others merely "read in" is to assume a seriously misleading conception of poetic form as a thing analogous to an object in space, contained within the bounding line of its outer perimeter. But a poem does not have such a boundary hooping in its intrinsic properties and excluding everything else; and it does not, therefore, either "refer to" the things it means as things outside itself, or "contain" or embody its meanings. "In" and "out" are but crude and misleading metaphors indicating the degree to which there is, between the poem and some factor, a "bearing," pertinence, commensurateness, or harmony. The words of a poem and all that it means are both inside of and outside of it at once, like the sunshine on my roof and your lintel. As in reading "Directive" one quickly realizes that the opening words, "Back out," can't be read as a verb (e.g., to back out of a driveway) because this will not fit according to the rules of grammar, it is easy enough to see that the meaning as a process simply cannot involve this meaning as an element of the sentence. But it is actually the same with respect to the meaning "money" for "dough"; we cannot bring this to bear on the phrase "like a dent in dough," not because grammar forbids, but because analogous rules of process, the rules by which the rest of the poem's meanings interrelate, provide no way that such a reading could fit, even though "dent in dough" is respectable slang. Yet this wrong reading is "outside" the poem in about the same sense that Genghis Kahn is outside of contract bridge or paleontology. A process does not exclude everything that is not involved with it, in the same sense that an object in space excludes all that it does not contain.

The error that has kept Frost criticism still stalled, even in its fourth generation, in the debate between those who consider the poet a wise man and those who think him an escapist seems to consist in a hasty and unconsidered opinion about the nature of poetry. As a way of happening, form is neither a skeletal essence reducible to some profound idea of the poet, nor a particular occurrence, such as someone's reading of "Directive," nor a particular historical event pegged to the poet's life or to that of a period or movement. It is an activity whose field of experienced reality is forever being explored and realized. It can involve in its unfolding far more than is revealed to any reader or period. The facts of its genesis in the author and his age may illuminate but cannot fully explain its field; indeed these facts are themselves not to be fully known, literary history, like history proper, being an ongoing enterprise whose questions are never closed out and whose proven facts change their meaning in the light of later insights. Historical, like critical, understanding of a poem advances, therefore, by elaborating the field of meaning to be contemplated rather than by striding from lesser to greater certainty. The folly of the recently popular theory of "open-ended form" is that of attempting to escape visual metaphors by substituting one such metaphor, the cylinder, for another, the box, which hardly frees one's thoughts from the idea of form as a visually bounded object. How detached from or involved in modern life and all its complexities and difficulties Frost was is, when more carefully framed, a question of how much of this life the poems draw along with them and involve in their own processes of development. But this quantity is not to be weighed by the pound; it is not a question of the number of modern facts, conceived as particles to be counted, but of the engagement of dimensions of experience and modalities of consciousness that count more for their scope and reach than for their number. And to appreciate Frost's inclusiveness in these respects requires breaking out of the concept of form as an object with fixed limits. Years ago, in the era of Vorticism, Pound, in recommending the aesthetic theories of Jules Romaine as an antidote to critical obtuseness, quoted Romaine's important statement: "One ceases to believe that a definite limit is the indispensable means of existence. Where does la Place de la Trinité begin? ... A being (être) has a centre, or centres in harmony, but a being is not compelled to have limits." [17] Poetic form is such a unity of process as Pound described in calling the Image a Vortex "from which, and through which, and into which, ideas are constantly rushing." [18]

The Frost poem, like other typically modern poems, differs from earlier periods in that it not only actually functions in this way, but intentionally defines itself as a poem that would be in these terms. Its indeterminacy is not only a consequence of its rich complexity of meaning, that being of the very essence of all poetry; it is an indeterminacy that announces itself as a confessed enigma by an imperious confidence of tone, full of Miltonic organ notes so inflating to the reader's expectations as to make explicit their nonfulfillment. The promise to bring the reader to a state "beyond confusion" leaves him in the dark as to just what such a state would be like. The plentiful advice he receives gives him no practical enlightenment as to what to do. But if this induces the "blank wall" feelings that Pearce has mentioned, it also reveals some procedural truths. We learn, for example, that the contradictions of experience are not miscellaneous collisions, but contrasts between opposed limits within a system, that meaning can be a spectrum joining contrary thoughts, like old-new, or imaginary-real, and that, therefore, even the most harmonious thought naturally displays some tension within the elements of its system, and must generate some measure of doubt and of formlessness. To quote Pound again: "There is in inferior minds a passion for unity, that is, for a confusion and melting together of things which a good mind will want to keep distinct." [19] Even the greatest organizing cultural statements—*The Odyssey*, *The Divine Comedy*, *Paradise Lost*—give only putative answers concerning the unity of the world and the oneness of man's duty and his nature, answers which, when we try to specify their exact meanings, turn into fields of exploration, and cease to be answers at all. "Directive," as a modern poem, gives us answers designed to make the question as to the nature of answers and the conditions for finding them its central theme. If we cannot say what the goblet or the "watering place" mean, except by designating a certain system of ideas within which all possible meanings lie, a system we can only crudely sketch and never fully describe, I do not find this a nugatory conclusion. Rather it would seem to promise a better interpretation, and one in which the modernity of Frost's art is *mise en valeur*, an interpretation in which the richly varied content of the experience of walking through the woods is framed by a study of systems of meaning and of how these systems are related to each other.

The modern chaos is not a blur, but a tangle of all too clear and specific frames of reference, each being autonomous, since there is no over-all system in the form of a religious faith or organizing myth to assign to each of the others its proper sphere, function, and place in a scheme of values. At times Frost seems immaturely destructive in his delight in the creative opportunities of this disorder. "I am always interested in games. When I get a newspaper, I look at the front page first to see how they're behaving in Brazil. I know Brazil, I've been down there. Then I look at the editorial page, if its readable. Then I look at the sports page. Then I look at the zigzag on the stock exchange to see how the world's going." [20] Obviously Frost's maddening detachment, his indifference to important modern facts, his boasted safety as one too high to be touched by the ordinary mischances, are somewhat put on here to dramatize the fact that our realities are systems of thought and action that seem to have shrunk to mere games because there is no standard by which to measure their importance and our duty. Yet work therefore becomes "play for mortal stakes," since in acting we must submit to several systems of rules at once, and somehow strike a balance between their competing claims as to truth and use. It is a very sad fact that one cannot do more about a *coup d'état* in Rio than to wonder "how they're behaving" down there; sad as it is that the stock exchange and baseball seem equally frivolous games, which crowd out, say, the beggars of Calcutta and the methods of Jackson Pollock. In one of Sidney Cox's records of conversation, Frost is paraphrased as follows:

We all talk of facing facts. Not so many of us are concerned about how many facts we keep in view at once. When all the parts of Robert Frost—past, present, and concern for future—were not in play he was not free. All in play, he has been prevented from going the full length of any pity or recoil; earlier pities, earlier admirations, enthusiasms, joys, have checked the gesture. Meanwhile they intensified the experience. He is insufficiently objective to see only what at the instant is glaringly apparent. His objectivity has to reconcile the immediate object with all that is in his world.[21]

True, restraint and balance seem to be preferred to ardent commitment, but remembering the contrast between Hamlet and Laertes, does one not feel that the more noble course is to act deliberately, to realize, indeed, that in the modern world the thinking out of an act is its greater part? As Frost's "play" is a matter of bringing the whole of his consciousness "into play," so his past experience is a window upon "all that is in his world."

The portrayal of this process of self-realization in such poems as "Directive" is not escapism, but its opposite, an earnest commitment to the Sisyphean task of making sense in the face of chaos, of recognizing modes of unity even against the background of dissociations into which the wholes we perceive are always in the process of fading.

To be sure, self-realization is achieved by a journey backward in time, as many commentators have noted, but this journey is also, and, I think, more importantly, an analysis of time itself whereby we are shown that our movement through the landscape is also a passage through multiple frames of reference, as time is fragmented into the varieties of time proper to diverse systems of thought. The mere century or less since the region was farm country represents time as it is understood in the field of historical scholarship; but the time just beyond that, when the Indians camped by the brookside, brings us into the borderland between history and archaeology. A little further back and we enter the vast epochs of the anthropologist, whose definitions of pastness concern cultural phases rather than chronological limits, so that, for example, the stone age of forty thousand years ago is still, for him, the present in the Andean jungle.

Then, through the references to erosion and glaciation, we are ushered into the unimaginably long stretches of geological time, where the usual ideas of time's irreversible and progressive character tend to be displaced by a cyclical patterning suited to geology's interest in general laws and recurrent situations. Beyond this, there is the past of myth, which, as Brower has noted, is essentially atemporal. The Grail Legend stands off in a past, so remote that by its nature it transforms the images it reveals into eternal archetypes and thus seems to cancel time by summarizing it.

The quester of "Directive" becomes "lost" by recognizing the disarray of the innumerable systems. And he thereby "find[s] himself" by coming to the realization that the systems are the components of his own consciousness. Quite literally, where he is in space is also where he is in history. Whether he has studied geology, anthropology, history, archaeology, and mythology, they are aspects of the modern mind, so that as a man of our time he sees the visible landscape in such a way that, potentially, he could perceive it in terms of these communal systems of interpretation. Thus finding oneself means realizing one's place in culture as well as in history; for one's place is communal. Even history itself is a mode of interpretation and, therefore, an evolving social institution.

The self-discovery is a passage through "confusion" to a wholeness "beyond" it. "Confusion," from Latin "confundere," from "con" plus "fundere" (to pour), is a "pouring together" or, in Pound's words, a "melting together of things which a good mind will want to keep distinct." Being "whole again beyond confusion" is being free from false simplifications, accepting one's own and the world's endless complexity, realizing that answers cannot be more than partial and temporary syntheses.

Yet though the word, "beyond," indicates that salvation is to be found within nature, not by transcending it, it also brings to focus the essence of the case against Frost. One cannot free one's mind from the impression that for Frost there are still special places of retreat, backwoods regions which, while not literally beyond the reach of the modern world, are yet the outward manifestation of a state of mind that holds the "all this now too much for us" at a distance. "Directive" is a quiet poem, so dominated by easeful and pleasurable tonalities, that the stresses of the modern confusion, though keenly observed, are emotionally muted. This is characteristic of the low-keyed pastoral manner, its calm rural orchestration of the grand themes of politics, labor, love and war. Pearce's comment that Frost's protagonists "have only a dim sense, even that resisted mightily, of the transformations which the individual might have to undergo if he is to live fully in the modern world and still retain his identity as an individual" [22] seems a very telling point. For though the transformations are surely acknowledged in the poem—it shows effectively enough how the systems pull the self, now into one, now into another mode of perception, stance, role— it is also clear that here, by the brookside near the abandoned New England farm, an integrative experience can be achieved that one cannot preserve past the occasion or transfer to less remote places.

The key to the problem of Frost's escapism, be it apparent or actual, would seem, then, to be his faith in the ultimate and unquestionable reality of space as it is rendered in vanishing point perspective. Whereas his greatest contemporaries—Yeats, Pound, Eliot, Stevens, Auden, Thomas—are all clearly modernist in preferring sudden changes of visual focus and the mosaic effect of being simultaneously aware of differing modes of vision, of which the "realistic" is but one, Frost is strictly preimpressionist in all his more lengthy renderings of landscape. In "Directive" one can see how the visual realism that won for him so wide a "middle-brow" audience is achieved by noting that here, as in an academic landscape painting of the nineteenth century, the observer is held to a single point of view.

For the antitheses underlying the meaning systems of images are primarily ones involving the root contrasts of practical experience: first, such contrasts as govern one's motor reactions as one moves through space—backward-forward, high-low, present-absent, and so on; second, those which, like old-new, natural-artificial, dead-alive, are the rudimentary schemes of recognition enabling us to adjudge an object a quarry, a road, a cellar hole. The extended meanings tend to grow out of the spatially immediate practical ones. One feels that it is a plain fact of the foreground that the "lofty" brook is high up the slope from which it springs and that the idea of spiritual height is more distant, a mere suggestion. The goblet as visible object is merely a broken drinking glass that was evidently used as a toy, since it was found near the playhouse. That it is like the Grail is a confessedly forced metaphor, as are the "serial ordeal" as a backward reference to the trials of the Grail hero, and the more general allusion, thus established, to *The Waste Land*, with its restorative water symbols, its deserted chapel, and its Sanskrit "directive." With respect to the communal systems the poem engages—geology and the rest—the same holds true. The immediate sense data—glacial markings or a "height of country"—open upon a further range of immaterial theory, and mental association. The consistency with which the physically visible things in the landscape are contrasted with their associations, as more distant and more largely imaginary kinds of reality, authenticates the visual realism of the plenitude of space, in which there is a continuous flow of the near into the far, and of all into a harmony governed by the laws of perspective.

Because we are held so firmly within a scene made of humble facts about physical objects, the wider meanings of these things and the systems of thought they bring into play seem held off at the horizon's edge, as merely suggested or made-up things. Yet this pastoral distancing, even belittling, is an aspect of that resistance to unity which our sense of the wholeness of the quest triumphantly overrides. For all Frost's chuckles, the reader insists on being serious about serious matters—the Grail, T. S. Eliot, Christ's parables, the quest as archetypal myth, glaciation, and Patience on her monument, smiling at grief. The ultimate humor consists in the urbanely comic demonstration that the practical consciousness can only banish such matters to the background of amusing fancies for a time. That they refuse to remain there is manifested by the poem's constant explosions into kettle drum rumblings and oboe plaints. The reach of verbal connotations, like that of the imagery, positively drags the mind towards momentous significations. The more Frost pretends to impound such words as "ordeal," "goblet," "lofty," and "whole" within their minimal meanings (social embarrassment, water glass, and so on) the more the reader feels his mind launched into contexts far wider and more socially important than that within which one deliberates about crossing a stream.

Frost is not the less a modernist poet in that he holds the reader's
mind within the frame of one of its manifold perceptual systems,
the vision of perspective painting, and thus reveals the chaos of conflicting systems as it is seen from this standpoint. There is, to begin
with, the reassurance of "touching bottom," of finding that the
individual mind is always aware of a unity in its immediate visual
environment that serves to make this scene a center around which
further ranges of experience are organized. By dramatizing the mind's
act of composing its world, Frost brings the further ranges into
view, not only as remote areas lying off at a distance from the serene
pastoral foreground, but as the true "fields" of the mental processes
through which this foreground is built up and appreciated. Frost
does not depict actors engaged in specific political and social con-
troversies at particular moments in time. But he depicts engagement
in the modern world much more inclusively and complexly by im-
mersing the reader in the manifold systems of seeing and interpreting
that constitute the life of our time.

Allegations of escapism are not really justified by Frost's failure
to teach men what line to take on specific problems, for his greatest
contemporaries have not done this either. Yeats' political deeds must
seem ambiguous, at the least, to all but Irish minds; his best poems
treat them as tragically ambiguous. The example that Eliot and
Pound made of themselves, whether foolish or sinister, in their effort
to bring art to bear directly on political action, reveals nothing more
edifying than the marring of a few good verses. If Auden's politics
have been more benign, they have hardly been so pointed, seldom
successfully extending themselves beyond the generalized comments
and exhortations of humanistic satire. Williams is even less concerned
than Auden with giving advice as to how to vote or what government budgetary policies to pursue. The particulars of his urban landscapes, when not shaped to the purposes of love lyrics and nature
poems, provide the stuff for a sociological meditation that treats
social facts much as the Transcendentalists did. What is lacking in
Frost is not political wisdom, but the assertion that it is needed, not
an actual engagement in political and social questions, but an imaginative vision in which the world is seen as a place where such engagement would be laudatory and effective. Yet this does not by

itself explain the charge of escapism fully, since even Wallace Stevens is not much blamed nowadays for his indifference to social problems, though his far surpasses Frost's. But Frost, unlike Stevens, has made his unbelief in political action and his suspicion of social conscience articles of his creed. The skepticism that Stevens passes over in silence, Frost proclaims by way of glorifying self-reliant individualism. Most probably his opinions are wrong, but that does not make them evasive. We must distinguish between ignoring the modern world and holding to one grossly oversimplified idea about it when the majority holds to another.

I would grant that there is a certain narrowness of spirit in the zest with which Frost denounces politics as futile and the agonies of our time as minor manifestations of the age-old sufferings that have as often enhanced man's courage and creativity as they have defeated him. But setting aside an occasional meanness of tone in the poems that seems to come from this, one may ask whether Frost does not very poignantly comment upon the modern scene by stressing the discontinuity between private experience and communal life, by exploring with severe skepticism the question as to just how the self can be effective in the practical politics of a mass society without falling into the delusion that one or two systems make up the whole of reality, and by asking, as his dramatic poems so searchingly do, just where, as things now are, the conscience and consciousness of the community can reach fulfillment except within the mind of the worthy individual. I do not see how a poet can utter a much more direct "directive" to political action than Frost has voiced, if his advice is to be responsible and intelligent. For in a world as complex as ours, the acting of a good deed can have some chance of being truly good in its results only if it is founded upon and, indeed, practically inseparable from such a surveying of the areas of its influence as "Directive" presents.

Yet there is a far deeper level on which Frost's realism in picturing rural landscapes is revelatory of the modern age. We have seen that the modern sense of chaos defines truth as the quest for truth, on the supposition that what we can learn with certainty are truths about the process of discovery. And we have seen that such a conception of truth has the effect of merging subject and object. Thus "Directive" depicts a quest that is both inward and outward, the seeing of the landscape being at the same time a survey of modes of perception. The logical result one would expect is that the poem would conclude that reality is a process. And this is what the tenor of its philosophic ideas seems to declare. It is a poem that emphasizes the transformation of static objects into dynamic events, of essences into activities, of being into becoming. This exactly coincides with the modern scientific account of nature, in which the physical world is rendered indistinguishable from the scientific systems for perceiving and interpreting its phenomena. As the idea of matter has retreated behind the atomic particles of which our only experience is that which is obtained through systems of admeasurement and recording, it has become impossible to specify what lies beyond the reports the systems send back, except further systems. But though it is a practical impossibility to separate physical substance from scientific procedure, it is an indispensable hypothesis that they are really separate— that scientific inquiry is one thing and the physical world it explores is something else. The same is true in humanistic studies. For example, behind the Grail Legend, we discern the religions of the ancient Middle-East, and behind these primitive fertility cults, and behind these tribal beliefs. Yet we have to suppose that myths are about more than other myths.

Now in "Directive" we end in the same paradox—with a unity of self and world which tends to affirm the very dualism of subject and object that it claims to resolve. We end with the advice, "Be whole," but this advice is directed to the reader as the man by the brookside, an isolate self in an alien world. This outcome is representative of that which must necessarily follow from the modern mind's commitment to the historicizing of truth. One starts by assuming that since our world is a world composed of symbolic systems, one can only understand it by projecting the symbolic process itself into time to see it unfold there as an actual series of events which shows self and world as both reducible to the same thing—a congeries of systems. But to see this merging of self and world as an actual happening, one must keep the two separate. Were they to become totally identical, the event of their merging would cease. Asserting their separation is not merely an artistic requirement, but a requirement inherent in the idea of wholeness Frost is trying to express. The point is not just that he must picture a person in an objective scene if he is going to show how person and scene merge. It is that the concept of unity as an actual coming to oneness of things distinct is meaningless if the things aren't really distinct.

"Dasein" in the philosophy of Martin Heidegger resolves the subject-object duality on the theoretical level, overcoming the gulf between the mind thinking and the objects of its thoughts by replacing both with a state of "being-in-the-world." Instead of a self and a world, we have an evolving situation, a particular way of being in time. "Dasein's" world is not *its own*, nor is it *the* world. "Dasein" is one of the ways that being goes on. Frost, who in his earlier days was a teacher of philosophy, might well have come to know of the concept of "Dasein" by the time he wrote "Directive," whose probable sources in Eliot, Auden, and Pound suggest that it was written in the thirties or after. One must recollect that after about 1916 Frost associated mostly with academics and delighted in long intellectual conversations about "ideas," a taste according well with his platform career as poet-as-thinker in the Emersonian tradition. Often his conversations served as the preparatory stages of his lectures. Perhaps the reverse was also true.

But whether "Directive" reveals him consciously testing Heidegger's "Dasein" on his nerves, or, all innocent of Heidegger, exploring an analogous merger of self and world into "becoming," it is clear that his conscious mind doubts that such a unity could so establish itself as to free the imagination completely from its belief in the duality of self and world. In "Directive" and most of Frost's poems, the claims of epistemology are at least as good as those of metaphysics. Thus it would be quite characteristic for Frost to decide that whatever the truth of Heidegger's theory from the metaphysics viewpoint, the old dualism need not be abandoned, metaphysics itself being only one of the systems. At any rate "Directive" lays bare the fundamental irony of the historicizing habit of mind: the fact that if realities are ongoing processes they cannot display the rational unity that is intended by so defining them, and thus that in the attempt to synthesize subjectivity and objectivity in a whirl of action in time one has to have constant recourse to the old scenario of the self and the world.

But although these are restored, they are not as they formerly were. Though the poem ends with the image of a person alone, out in the woods, he has been transformed into the representative human being, and his special setting is now revealed as a microcosm, mirroring "all that is the case." Thus it was that the Frostian persona became a sort of institution, so much so that when some discrepancies between the poet and his image were forced upon the public mind by the revelation that the poet was actually chargeable with such rarely encountered human faults as egotism and envy, this was matter of great and anguished surprise. So much had everyone been persuaded that Frost's representativeness freed him from the faults of an ordinary individual, a delusion one would only expect to find among the suitors of some great patron. In "Directive," the representative self is shown to be all the more generalized in that it is divided between the speaker and the reader. By doing as he is told, the reader has the thoughts, sees the things, takes the points of view that characterize the speaker, insofar as we know anything about him. And when one considers that this is so of every reader, that we all, in the course of the poem's development, merge with Frost by coming to coincide with the idea of himself that his uttering of the poem's words suggests he has in mind, one can see how far the generalizing away of individuality has gone. It does not even matter whether the poet is talking to himself or to someone else, since soliloquy and dialogue are both equally dualistic. The only significant contrast is that between the functions of speaker and auditor, which can co-exist in a single person. The rhetorical form of the poem tends ultimately to suggest that even if it were true that being is such a unity as "Dasein," language would still be obliged to present it as a duality —as something one person names in talking to another person. Perhaps, then, the schema of speaker and auditor is an artificial contrast created by the very nature of language and perpetuated, therefore, by our efforts to discuss the subject. To be sure, language itself is but one of many systems, and though Frost probably felt that the fictions underlying it made the noblest and profoundest claim upon our belief, he would not sacrifice to these his delight in the "play" between language and other systems. What he valued most was what the modern age values most: the historicizing that creates the "play." Neither he nor the age has quite appreciated the price of it: the fanatical habit of thinking in terms of a generalized human situation. This is the other side of the coin of the modern historicizing. We would see everything historically, would examine all, even theories of seeing, under the aspect of time, to study their development as processes actually working themselves out; but to do this we must nourish an excessively abstract notion of the thinker and his situation, a notion that excludes the uniqueness of human beings and the unrepeatable nature of actual moments of time—the two things that history should cherish most. This is a great fault in Frost and a great fault in the modern age. It is a paradox well illustrated in Auden's *New Year Letter*, when, after declaring that a wider social consciousness is needed, since "No longer can we learn our good/From chances of a neighborhood" he moves straight from this to the conclusion that "Aloneness is man's real condition." [23] Man's? What has happened to you and me and the millions of other individual selves living or having lived in historical time? And to "the silken weavings of our afternoons," as Stevens would put it? [24] The "you" of Frost, the conservative individualist, seems to collectivize them as neatly as the chthonic boom of Heideggerian theory and the dialectic of scientific materialism.

The merits of a period are also its faults, and vice versa. If the poets of classical modernism practiced a harshly detached method of seeing, there is in it a special precision and clarification, especially concerning the philosophical assumptions underlying modern belief and their effects in endowing modern experience with its distinctively paradoxical qualities of loneliness yet vividness, of stressful uncertainty yet fascinating complexity. If the self has been pared down, in such poetry, from a real individual to a "Skinny sailor looking in the sea-glass," [25] as Stevens called his Crispin, the telescope of this questing voyager picks out an amazingly various range of things within the landscape of human experience. If we see fewer people than in earlier poetry, we see more of the dimensions and planes of the mental life of any one person, and see them the more directly related to philosophic belief, the less our frantically changeable age has allowed poets to explain them as the effects of social habit.

Job, in *A Masque of Reason*, is an all too sparely archetypal representation of suffering mankind, and God, as here depicted, cannot be seen, because he is the prisoner of the varied human icons of divinity, from the Christmas tree to Blake's engravings and Yeats' poetry. The problem Job faces is not the acceptance of his sufferings, but the acceptance of a God who cannot tell Job the reason, because He *is* the reason. The answer is not a verbal one spoken by someone else; it must be a recognition on Job's part, of God as God, an engagement in the process of beholding, witnessing. But there is also Thyatira, Job's wife, who declares that

> There isn't any universal reason;
> And no one but a man would think there was.

One recognizes a certain healthy good sense in her desire for no more than "unsystematic/Stray scraps of palliative reason." She alone, of the four characters, does not appear in the concluding snapshot. For it is she who takes the picture. The picture shows Job standing between God and Satan, and thus merged with the other two, as but one element in the essential human situation. Thyatira represents the detachment which is, in the artist and in every man, the necessary corollary of the engaged self. To have the merging, you must have the detachment. To place all within the context of historical change is yet to hold the historian and the world firmly outside of history.

Notes to *Du Côté de Chez Frost* by JOHN F. LYNEN

1. Wallace Stevens, *The Collected Poems of Wallace Stevens* (New York: Alfred A. Knopf, 1954), 239–40.

2. Reuben Brower, *The Poetry of Robert Frost: Constellations of Intention* (New York: Oxford University Press, 1963), 237.

3. Louis Mertins, *Robert Frost: Life and Talks-Walking* (Norman, Okla.: University of Oklahoma Press, 1965), 63.

4. Robert Peters, "The Truth of Frost's 'Directive,'" *Modern Language Notes*, LXXV (January 1960), 32.

5. Brower, *Constellations of Intention*, 238.

6. Pearlanna Briggs, *Explicator*, XXI (May 1963), Item 71.

594 Du Côté de Chez Frost

7. Margaret M. Blum, "Robert Frost's 'Directive': A Theological Reading," *Modern Language Notes*, LXXVI (June 1961), 524–25.

8. Roy Harvey Pearce, *The Continuity of American Poetry* (Princeton: Princeton University Press, 1961), 275, 276, 278.

9. Ernest Hemingway, *The Sun Also Rises* (New York: Scribner's, 1926), 225.

10. Emily Dickinson, *The Poems of Emily Dickinson*, ed. Thomas H. Johnson (3 vols.; Cambridge, Mass.: Harvard University Press, 1958), I, 265.

11. Brower, *Constellations of Intention*, 239.

12. Pearce, *The Continuity of American Poetry*, 275.

13. Brower, *Constellations of Intention*, 234.

14. Pearce, *The Continuity of American Poetry*, 275.

15. Reginald L. Cook, *The Dimensions of Robert Frost* (New York: Rinehart & Co., 1958), 138.

16. W. H. Auden, *Collected Shorter Poems: 1927–1957* (New York: Random House, 1957), 142, 143.

17. Ezra Pound, *Make It New* (New Haven: Yale University Press, 1935), 221.

18. Anonymous, "Vorticism" in *Fortnightly Review*, September 1, 1914, as quoted by Emil Stock in *The Life of Ezra Pound* (New York: Pantheon Books, 1970), 166.

19. Pound, *Make It New*, 211.

20. Robert Frost, "Between Prose and Verse," *Atlantic Monthly*, CCIX (January 1962), 54.

21. Sidney Cox, *A Swinger of Birches: A Portrait of Robert Frost* (New York: New York University Press, 1957), 172.

22. Pearce, *The Continuity of American Poetry*, 274.

23. W. H. Auden, *Collected Longer Poems* (New York: Random House, 1965), 125–26.

24. Stevens, *Collected Poems*, 69.

25. *Ibid.*, 28.

Afterword: Frost as Representative of the Eidolons

JAC L. THARPE

Some months before his death at eighty-eight, Robert Frost ended a long public career with a brief career in international diplomacy. Only the Secret that sits in the middle knows what unconscious process developed into that long journey to Russia as cultural ambassador. But the significance of the trip was far greater than the dubious accomplishment in diplomacy suggests. After he had tramped numerous homesteads, climbed various mountains and traveled thousands of miles across the United States as well as Europe, Frost took a last journey that symbolically combined the crossing on Brooklyn Ferry with a real yet unearthly passage to India. Whatever he may have delivered, what he took was a packet of eidolons—the United States stated by its most renowned speaker.

The eidolons, among which was the journey along the open road, were Whitman's idea. Whitman was translating the Greek word that referred to Plato's concept of eternal verities existing in some realm beyond physical nature. Whitman uses the word to suggest that poetry will discover and display the truths that are represented in the colossal panorama of utopian activity associated with the expanse of democratic nationalism. The possibility of human error about the exact nature of an eternal verity allows "eidolons" to refer also to the energizing myths of a society—the ideals, both reasoned and intuited, that guide the society in its development. In a yet more realistic sense, the eidolons are simply the Baconian idols of the cave—established myths by which the society exists, with or without realizing its ideals—nationalistic claims that ideals have been realized. The eidolons, in short, are the major cultural ideas. A humanistic Platonism in the imagination of Whitman, the Great Panavisionist, may of course simply declare that the ideals of the culture are in fact eternal verities.

Frost, somewhat like another innocent abroad, attempted to convey the American eidolons to his nation's most dangerous enemy in a time of crisis. That situation distinguished Frost's trip from those of the few other American literary men who have been in government service abroad. Hawthorne was consul at Liverpool. Lowell was sometime ambassador to both Spain and England. Franklin of course is the prototype of the cultural ambassador. But Frost has the distinction, of which he must have been very much aware, that, as Poet-to-the-Nation, he represented the "flood-tide below me." This idea, also Whitman's, meant that the one speaking contained multitudes from the cultural past.

Frost's trip to Russia was the result of one of the most important American eidolons—striving for success. Frost came from an undistinguished family and grew up in adversity. After an industrious struggle, he had wealth and fame. He then had a distinguished life, climaxed by a series of honors that included appointments to an unofficial laureateship and to unofficial government service.

While the associations may be unpleasant, comparisons with other representatives of the Horatio Alger paradigm show the diversity of the success eidolon as well as Frost's relationship with the cultural past. Frost shares the success story with such diverse figures as Jay Gould and Richard Nixon, both of whom he might have known at some time during his long life. Jay Gould's technological monster may well have been the one with the "goggle glass" eye that invaded Frost's Arcadia. And if Frost had fallen in with the other intellectuals who succumbed to the Communist ideology of the twenties and thirties, Nixon might have gone "breasting like a horse in skirts" in the very American guise of a Red Cross Knight after a dragon in Eden.

Frost's theology resembles that of Billy Graham, another representative of the eidolon of success, except that Frost's theology, in its emphasis on existential self-reliance, is more intellectual and more fundamentally American than Graham's fundamentalism. Frost was in fact so fundamentally American that his theology may have kept him from temptation to Christian as well as Communist sentimentality. The owner of an Arcadian ranch on the Pedernales, with ties to both grass roots and leaves of grass, might have recognized in the poet a similarity of character that combined toughness and compassion. Frost might even have known Horatio Alger himself, whose death in 1899 ended a career with wealth and fame. The success story is quite modern despite its associations with the nineteenth century, and the characteristics of the success vary little, no matter how diverse the successful. These and numerous other figures from both Frost centuries represent the cliches of the culture. Lives of these "great men" remind us that for Americans success means acquisition of wealth as well as fame in a milieu of self-reliant free enterprise of activity.

Of the numerous guises of public man sometimes associated with Frost, that of artist to the republic was the most poetically justified. But official recognition of the arts and the artist had to wait for east coast society to acquire sufficient wealth, leisure and sophistication to afford as well as want an artist in government. The recognition eventually came from a government of the people that, ironically, was established by a descendant of one of the rich merchant princes whose privilege had for so long kept the "beleaguered masses" from privilege. The Kennedy fortune, derived from yet another success, was enough older than Johnson's or Nixon's to seem antique and romantic. America could finally afford, financially if not emotionally, to imagine a Camelot to which to annex Arcadia and briefly support both kingdoms. American imagination has had room aplenty for creating utopias, magic kingdoms and no-man's-lands in the expanse of the virgin land. As if by magic at last, a version of Whitman's humanistic and transcendentalist Eden was taking realistic shape through the realization of the eidolon that was by implication Whitman's most important. The national poet-king emerged to celebrate the greatness of human endeavor and establish a table at which all men could sit in banquet.

What makes Frost unique in his success is that he was the only artist ever to hold a position as national poet. Alger of course rates no comparison. Whittier had the fame, and the hearts of his fellow men. Emerson, famous but never wealthy, represented various eidolons associated with the earlier and much more practical Franklin— independence, self-reliance, puritanism, and peripatetic teaching. Whitman was the greatest poet, as Frost probably knew, but Whitman had neither the fame nor the hearts of his fellow men at a time when the nation could afford to pay for art or wished to buy anything but imports.

What the government and the people eventually bought in Frost were a teacher and a book. Frost was a peripatetic minister coming out of a simple land with a message. The man had gradually become the public man that the nation adored. The book was somewhat shorter than that other single volume of poetry, the one that had codified the eidolons. But they were similar books. *Leaves of Grass* linguistically contained much more of the King James version if less of the Old-Testament theology. Frost's puritanic conservatism issued few invitations to the venerealees walking the strands of all the megalopolises that had grown up on the land. But the *Complete Poems*, operating on a principle of linguistic simplicity resembling Whitman's and the old Puritan "plain style," derived much of its appeal from being a compendium of Old-Testament theology, distrust of modernism, avoidance of cities, attachment to the land, and emphasis on virtue—other eidolons. *Complete Poems* was, precisely, an Old Testament. It even had an Edenic setting; and when the nation's people paid, they paid in great part for the setting—nostalgically buying what might be recollected in tranquillity after apple picking in the age of the dynamo. The eidolon was so unconsciously operative that even those who had no pastoral memories paid for a dream of innocence and remained unaware of the real contents of the volume. The book was in short like a bible that spoke the word about a world that followed the departure from Eden. Nature had fallen with the fall of man. And the topics were man, God and that fallen nature—all of them inscrutable and, taken together, all that was worth discussing in any century. The moralization and later chiding recalled the habits of Old-Testament prophets. The aphorisms were Proverbial. The excoriations were Ecclesiastical. The masques, about justice and mercy, dealt with concepts of God. Frost was, in short, in the fullest sense creating a wisdom literature. We do not only quote his poetry; we also paraphrase a hundred random lines that gradually become so familiar that talking about Frost calls them up unconsciously.

Frost may not have considered himself the epic poet that Whitman conceived of being, but he is bound to have known that what he carried around in his one volume was a statement of the cultural past. Behind the nineteenth century, the first fully American century, lay the currents and streams of idols—puritanism and pragmatism, Hellenism and Hebraism. Frost's poetry was in great part a statement from the past to the twentieth century.

As a statement, the book was very complex, despite what the main outlines reveal. Frost contained all the multitudes that Whitman contained, including Whitman; and the message was not invariably optimistic. Emerson, singularly American as he stood on the pedestal and preached to the people, had the greatest influence on the culture, in great part because he preached, as William James did later, to Frost and to the nation, what people already practiced. Emerson codified the plan for individualistic success that Alger was to popularize and unfortunately seemed to justify the nefarious activities of those many successful men of the Gilded Age whose acquisitions derived from very undemocratic and unedenic principles. And despite his apparent break from the tradition of puritanic severity, Emerson was a puritan as well as a pragmatist. Though hard to see through its association with a Romantic view of nature, transcendentalism recapitulated puritanism in the extreme—precisely in its emphasis on the virtues of Nature. Reducing theology to the point where the fundamental entities—man, nature and deity—form a unity is to strip theology of nearly all its extravagances at last.

This pantheistic reductionism allows the very sensible idea that a cautious Old-Testament approach is the way to deal with either nature or deity. Such a view makes one a conservative, a way of life that both the Greeks and the Hebrews encouraged. Independent self-reliance is the only "way," whether such a road offers hope or not. And self-reliance is a version of the idea that God helps those who help themselves by doing their duties and by producing, a concept that may involve either a stern puritanism or a relaxed deism—the position of either an Edwards or a Franklin. The eidolon of self-reliance, as everyone knows, means that expenditure of energy leads to success. Frost embodies the extremes—both what a Franciscan Emerson preached to the fishes and what the fishes heard, quite American combinations of the practical and the idealistic.

Frost probably thought of himself not as a wandering Christ or a peripatetic Chautauquan with a message, but precisely as Man Thinking. This too was Emerson's idea, an eidolon of the nineteenth century, a period still under the influence of Renaissance humanism and its heritage from the classics. Man Thinking was associated with another Emersonian concept, that of representative man, a concept reflecting the increasing humanism and the diminishing religiosity of the modern world. Representative men were from varied fields of human activity, sharing an inherent sense of the moral law within and the starry heavens above. They were in union with the universe. Each of them was Man Thinking, a concept that for Emerson implied Man Acting and thus producing. The ideal combination of superb characteristics would have produced a natural man resembling Plato's concept of the philosopher-king or Whitman's of the poet. What Emerson had in mind was probably some version of Goethe—poet, thinker, scientist, and diplomat. Some notion of that eidolon is what Frost, consciously or unconsciously, took to Russia both in his own thinking and in the intuitions of the hearts of his fellow men.

As Man Thinking, Frost consciously synthesized the ideas of the major figures of the nineteenth century, with the result that his book contained some dark messages. Whatever Emerson provides of theory is supplemented by what Henry Adams suggests of the possibility of mere complex process, not progress. Earlier, Hawthorne saw both physical nature and human nature through a darker glass than Emerson's transparent eyeball. William James perceived the scientific method of common sense apart from transcendentalist intuitionism. If Whittier may occasionally have been in Frost's cognizance, Melville was as often there.

Among the reasons Frost might have had for disillusionment and unhappiness in 1899 (when Alger died), long before he became successful, was the fact that he was a youthful intellectual at century's end. It was not a pleasant universe even then, and a thinking man was apt to be familiar with the state of things. Frost's own poetic world has concealed the world in which his poetry was produced. Matthew Arnold had already located Western civilization between a world already dead and another powerless to be born. Spengler had already seen a decline of the West. Oscar Wilde was representative man for a legion of intellectuals who invited a new horde of barbarians to refresh the blood lines and make us whole again. In the midst of various activities devoted to outlawing war forever, a gigantic irrational beast was already moving toward birth in 1914, and the beast was of such strength that it would periodically regenerate from its own ash for the rest of Frost's life. Only momentary stay was possible, and everyone recognized the need.

But if Frost had a model as Man Thinking, it was probably Thoreau. Frost may have thought himself a greater man than Thoreau, but Thoreau's transcendentalism allowed, as Whitman's did, for the possibility that physical nature was something more than a mere creation of the mind.

Thoreau viewed nature somewhat more realistically than Emerson did. "Economy" in *Walden* was a chapter on nature's economy—not on the mere idea of saving money by living off the land. "Economy," as Frost, with his education in the classics, would have known, derives from a Greek concept of the household organization with all the practical activity, including financial, that is involved in the operations of a large property. Nature's household included all the aspects of nature. With these varied influences, Frost could envision a poetic world that seemed Arcadian but in which he saw the many ambiguities in man's relationship with nature and with deity. Frost was concerned to see nature as a complex of indifferent forces to which man must respond with such wisdom as he could acquire. This fallen nature had an existence independent of Emerson's Man Dreaming, and Frost was too much of a pragmatist to conceive of an Arcadia in which walls could not fall.

Frost became Man Making, Man Fabricating, Man Doing—speaking the word and performing the deed, with a hint of the Faustian that the allusion suggests. This combination of characteristics led to the production of a body of poetry that created an Arcadian universe much like Prospero's—brave new world with evil in it, ruled by the artistry of the National Poet. But whatever artificial universe Frost invents to enclose or interpret physical Nature, he is no innocent in Eden—either Thoreauvian or Whitmanesque. He may have wished he could be. But Whitman's was the only pastoral world that knew no evil. Activity between man and nature dominated Whitman's world too. The artifact of creativity was the sweetest dream that labor knew.

And Whitman was the greatest influence of all. Frost was like Whitman in making poetry of the facts of the ordinary day and of the usual way of things. What Frost saw with sufficient accuracy to state accurately was remarkable, for he was able to make an image out of a simple fact. He begins early in his work with the observation of the dust that comes off the slow wheel and the calf that stands by its mother. And by some secret method, he takes ordinary objects and turns them into symbols without even looking for symbols. He infuses Platonism and puritanic typology with new meaning simply by assuming that an existent object has a source unknown that accounts for its existence. Only Whitman among American poets saw as much as Frost did. With a similar intuition of mystery and miracle, Whitman speaks of redwood trees, bathers, birds, stars, lilacs and workmen in a hundred activities. The realistic Whitman who perceived them was also the transcendentalist Whitman who created a mythical humanist American Eden in which to locate what he saw. Frost wrote of birches, stars, mowing, wood-chopping, houses. And he placed them in a poetic world of his imagination. Every artist wants his own domain. If Frost's poetic world appears unrealistic, its contents were quite realistic—even ordinary. If Frost sees no wasteland like Eliot's, he finds neither sentimentalized Michaels nor etherealized Uriels. Apparently sentimentalized tales such as that of caring for a bird's nest reveal that a human activity destroyed the bird's natural environment and that the aid given was but a momentary stay for the bird. The temporary human emotion vanished and left the bird to raw nature.

Pastoralism is a characteristic only of Frost's poetry, not of his world-view. Much of what Frost saw is what Whitman saw with a view considerably more visionary than Frost's. Frost poetizes what he sees, but he does not suggest that death and evil and armpits are wondrous elements of some divine plan. Frost in his most sombre moods accepts what is. In his more pleasant moods, he considers that what exists is somehow miraculous enough that miracles are supernumerary. But he chants no songs ecstatic or squares deific. The pauper witch of Grafton and Frost's other poor deranged women are not Millimants or Faerie Queenes or even mothers of the manly and spermatic. Their homesteads are enough like wastelands to show what Frost sometimes found in nature.

If Frost's world is limited, it is limited in great part as the settings of American literature tend to be. American literature has always been regionalistic. When not regionalistic or local colorist, it is ethnic. Exceptions are those works that somehow reveal the author's discoveries of eidolons in local settings. Mark Twain hardly expected Huck Finn to get out of Hannibal. Robinson was best in Tilbury Town. When he went to Camelot, he was a down-east Yankee away from home. Hawthorne wrote the customhouse sketch for *The Scarlet Letter* in part because he wanted to interest local readers. Frost grew up during the local-color movement, and he wrote about what he saw.

Frost critics are as competent as admirers of Frost. But awareness of yet another eidolon may detract from the criticism. The charge is ambiguity. While it is true that Emerson and Whitman sought unity, Melville and Hawthorne found none. Neither could decide about theology and metaphysics. Hawthorne's work is a literal statement of ambiguity—not an ambiguous statement alone but a definite statement that ambiguity obtains as a universal principle. John Barth is currently spending a good deal of energy to clarify paradox as the only rational statement that holds. Between these figures is William James, who provides a rational outline of man's relationship to nature and retains a mystic's will to believe. Among the puritans was the idea that God was an inscrutable omnipotence and the concomitant idea that the strong must perform while they waited to see. Frost is thus in the mainstream of the American literary tradition.

Frost's view is genuinely agnostic—not a theological or even a philosophical position but merely a recognition that one does not know. And if Frost appears to contradict himself, the explanation is quite simple: he tried to tell the truth. In the everyday world, a thing appears at times to be true, and at times its opposite appears to be true. Either is a poetic occasion. Consistency is an ideological hobgoblin, and "truths" are suspect.

Frost has the further distinction that he among modern poets communicated. His contemporaries talked to coteries and still do. Stevens refurbishes the Palace of Art. Eliot dons cassock and lucidly reiterates myths belonging to the world that Arnold had found already dead. But Frost looked around the world. He communicated variously to different men. At one level, he talked of picking apples and being weary. But others saw that apple picking was keeping one of the promises in a fallen world. One of the main secrets of Frost's appeal, what he communicated somewhere in the reaches of the collective unconscious, was a sense of an unsophisticated yet wise and somewhat familiar relationship with hidden things—specifically with nature—a capability that the Romantic poet always claimed to have. Frost makes poetry out of a familiar statement of our ignorance about our relationship with a universe that appears erratic, indifferent, and at times as intelligently hostile as Claggart or Moby Dick. And he does it with a simplicity and a precision of observation that are remarkable. He is representative American man with two souls in his breast.

Not Frost's lack of thought but his tendency to moralize appears his worst fault. And in the later years of his life, when he had had so much experience at teaching in all his various ways and so much experience in adulation, perhaps he began to think himself wiser than he was. And he began to speak out on unpoetic matters. He began to cultivate a satiric form that differed greatly from what we thought of as Frost, though his classical training provided models enough for many forms of poetry. If he ever convinced himself that he was performing Homer's role, perhaps he later considered that Hesiod's role too needed performing when future shock began to cause tremors. He deliberately became a moralist. A man might give advice to the nation without knowing the unknown.

Yet what Frost sought to teach in those years from 1930 on was his own business. And some of what he said was the more intense because it was in reaction to extremes. If he had seen less and read less, he might have been more patient. When he accused the masses and the intellectuals of shifting from extreme to extreme, ideal to ideal, and fad to fad, he was by no means himself extreme. He was far too sensible to feel that men thought themselves brothers or that either legislation or ideals would teach compassionate nobility to anyone, whether Russian peasant or liberal intellectual. He could not have been so innocent as to expect a return to Eden. Perhaps he knew how hard it was to teach himself compassion and nobility. Yet his reservations about legislating happiness did not automatically mean that he preferred that indigents or even lazy men should starve. One may, however, become very impatient with the hired man whose freedom to roam the open road depends on what a working man "provides."

Frost's disapproval of science coincided with a wide movement that persists among poets and even intellectuals, not all of them conservative. But a man so much interested in botanical species and theories of astronomy did not scorn scientific method or the widespread activity of the sciences. What he disliked was the faith in science as a panacea and the narrowminded liberalism of the self-assured materialist. Other figures, from Owen Barfield to Gaston Bachelard, kept up and expanded the tradition of the poet's and the humanist's rejection of science as the one and only source of truth. Scientists themselves were soon to suggest, as Barth says, that knowledge was out and mystery in.

The Secret sits in the middle, and we do not know. That is the situation. All we can conclude is that there are roughly zones and occasionally something that at least appears to present the puzzle clearly. Nowadays, we may have more mercy than justice. We do shift from one extreme to another. We cannot see either out far or in deep because the mind's limitations are in effect the limits of the universe. Science is too much with us, not because of its intellectualization but because of its invalid association with truth when the method itself must of necessity be the Jamesian method of change, revision, and process in the formulation of truth—at best. But we cannot make a truth by insisting upon a truism and break a poet who admits he does not know enough to give a directive. Frost's poetry began to be bad when he thought he ought to take a position. When he talked about what he saw and what he did not know, he wrote his best work.

If Robert Frost was in fact the complex, inconsistent and not invariably admirable man whom Lawrance Thompson characterizes, the characterization is a testimonial to both men. Thompson is admirable for daring to present a view that tarnished the public image, and Frost is admirable for the accomplishment of the artifact, the finished product of the laborer's dream. A man with a great many human shortcomings has performed something admirable if he tries to create a work that embodies his dreams instead of his nightmares. An argument to the man is perhaps not quite fair, to suggest that one respect eighty-eight years of existence against all odds which produced a single volume of words, many of the last ones badly chipped and badly fitted into the artifact. But if we cannot use the man to argue for his performance, we should not use the man to argue against it. Frost is both an Old-Testament Christian and a pragmatic American existentialist. The terms label a lifetime of performance in a world not necessarily made for man.

Contributors

Margaret V. Allen is an independent scholar engaged in American Studies.

David C. Berry is assistant professor of English at the University of Southern Mississippi.

Marice C. Brown is chairman of the English department at the University of Southern Mississippi.

Charles Carmichael is instructor in English at the University of South Carolina.

John Ciardi is Poet-in-Residence at the University of Florida.

Edward Cifelli is assistant professor of English at County College of Morris, New Jersey.

Samuel Coale is assistant professor of English at Wheaton College, Norton, Massachusetts.

John J. Conder is associate professor of English at Vanderbilt University.

Reginald L. Cook is professor emeritus of American literature at Middlebury College.

James M. Cox is Avalon Professor of English at Dartmouth College.

J. Donald Crowley is professor of English at the University of Missouri-Columbia.

Lloyd N. Dendinger is associate professor of English at the University of South Alabama.

James Dickey is Poet-in-Residence at the University of South Carolina.

Margaret Edwards is assistant professor of English at the University of Vermont.

Roger Ekins is director of the Open Community Learning Center at Staten Island Community College.

William R. Evans is assistant professor of English at Kean College of New Jersey.

Alfred R. Ferguson is professor of English and American literature at the University of Massachusetts-Boston.

Sister Mary Jeremy Finnegan is professor of English at Rosary College.

R. F. Fleissner is assistant professor of English at Central State University of the Ohio State Universities.

Albert J. von Frank is a graduate student at the University of Missouri-Columbia.

G. William Gahagan is president and founder of California Friends of Robert

Frost, San Francisco. He was on the faculty with Frost at Dartmouth College in 1949 and was one of Frost's students in 1948.

Joseph M. Garrison, Jr. is professor of English at Mary Baldwin College.

Philip L. Gerber is professor of English at State University of New York, Brockport.

Donald J. Greiner is associate professor of English at the University of South Carolina.

Peter L. Hays is associate professor of English at the University of California-Davis.

Vivian C. Hopkins is professor emeritus of English at State University of New York at Albany.

Frank Lentricchia is associate professor of English at the University of California, Irvine.

John F. Lynen is professor of English at the University of Toronto.

Lewis H. Miller, Jr. is associate professor of English at Indiana University.

George Monteiro is professor of English at Brown University.

George W. Nitchie is chairman of the English department at Simmons College.

Laurence Perrine is Frensley Professor of English at Southern Methodist University.

Peggy W. Prenshaw is associate professor of English at the University of Southern Mississippi.

Robert M. Rechnitz is associate professor of English at Monmouth College.

Victor E. Reichert is lecturer on Biblical Literature at the University of Cincinnati.

Kenneth Rosen is associate professor of English at Dickinson College.

Rexford Stamper is assistant professor of English at the University of Southern Mississippi.

Peter J. Stanlis is professor of English and distinguished professor of humanities at Rockford College.

Edward Stone is distinguished professor of English at Ohio University.

Jac L. Tharpe is professor of English at the University of Southern Mississippi.

Dorothy Tyler is a writer and editor residing in Troy, New York, who was a student of Frost's at the University of Michigan.

Wade Van Dore, who describes himself as Frost's hired man, now lives in Clearwater Beach, Florida.

Nancy Vogel is assistant professor of English at Fort Hayes Kansas State College.

Stephen D. Warner is assistant professor of English at State University of New York at Fredonia.

Gordon Weaver is associate professor of English at the University of Southern Mississippi.

Perry D. Westbrook is professor of English at the State University of New York at Albany.

Index